In the Name

of Elijah

Muhammad

The C. Eric Lincoln Series
on the Black Experience

In the Name of

Elijah Muhammad

Louis Farrakhan

and the

Nation of Islam

Mattias Gardell

DUKE UNIVERSITY PRESS   Durham 1996

Published in the United States under the title
*In the Name of Elijah Muhammad: Louis Farrakhan
and the Nation of Islam*
by Duke University Press
and in the United Kingdom under the title
*Countdown to Armageddon: Louis Farrakhan
and the Nation of Islam*
by C. Hurst & Co. (Publishers) Ltd.
© 1996 Duke University Press
All rights reserved
Printed in the United States of America on acid-free paper ∞
Typeset in Melior by Keystone Typesetting, Inc.
Library of Congress Cataloging-in-Publication Data appear
on the last printed page of this book.

Contents

==

5

The Fall of the Nation *99   Until Death Do Us Part 99   Rapid Islamization Transit 102   To Dismantle an Empire 109   Religion, Perception, and Change 114*

6

The Resurrection of the Nation of Islam *119   From the Nightclub to the Mosque 119   The Fall and Resurrection of the Nation of Islam 122   Kinship, Scripture, and Strategies of Legitimation 125   The Messiah Has Finally Come 127   The Black Path of Redemption 131   Rebuilding the Black House 135*

7

A Nation of Gods: The Creed of Black Islam *144   The Creation of the Heavens and the Earth 144   Demonogony: The Making of a Devil 147   Gods Making Evil: The Problem of Theodicy 149   Death Rides a Pale Horse and Hell Follows with Him 151   The Sleeping Beauty and the Prince of Love 153   The Wheel and Satan, the Challenger 158   Apocalypse Now 160   Religion, Logic, and Configurations of Belief 165   There Are but How Many Gods? 170   Proving the Creed: Religion and Science 174   The Mathematical Code of Islam 176   What is New in New Religions? 181*

8

The Sun of Islam Will Rise in the West *187   Allah's Gradual Approach 187   Follow Bilal into Paradise 194   Qadhdhafi and the Third Universal Theory 197   Islamic Reformer and World Transformer, Qadhdhafi's Twin Role 202   Qadhdhafi and the Nation of Islam 205   The Lost Found Nation of Islam 215   The Five Percent Nation of Islam 224   The Nubian Islaamic Hebrews: The Ansaaru Allah Community 225*

9

Strained Seeds of Abraham: Is the NOI an Anti-Christian, Anti-Semitic Nazi Cult? *232   Christendoom and Crucifiction 233   Black Bridge over Trou-*

10

Preface

For many years I have traveled back and forth between Sweden and the United States, dividing my time between teaching Islamic studies, religion and politics, and the anthropology of religion at the Universities of Stockholm and Uppsala, and observing the Nation of Islam and the rise of a black Islamic urban youth culture in the United States. In a certain sense, the Nation became a window through which the complex American society could be seen. Coming from another culture and not being part of the social phenomena studied, I was afforded a freedom of perspective and a different angle of observation that partly account for the conclusions presented in this volume. Most Americans I have met harbor strong opinions about Minister Louis Farrakhan, the Nation of Islam, and American race dynamics. Though emotionally loaded, these views are not mainly based on actual facts but on the socially constructed and mass-mediated images that are themselves part of the problem. The role of the researcher is related to this web of conflicting images, misrepresentations, and misunderstandings. A social scientist is among other things a cultural translator, whose task it is to contextualize and make sense of the Other. The reader will be the judge of the extent to which I have reached this goal. What also remains is the question of how to solve the social problems of which the Nation of Islam is both a product and a part. My hope is that this study will prove both entertaining and useful in promoting dialogue.

Acknowledgments

A great number of individuals have been of invaluable assistance in making possible this study of the modern history of the Nation of Islam. First and foremost, I want to express my gratitude to Minister Louis Farrakhan for letting me conduct this research and for setting aside so much of his time for interviews and meetings. Besides the Minister, other Muslims have been greatly helpful, and I feel indebted to Minister Don Muhammad of Boston, Minister Khadir Muhammad of Newark, and Brothers Frederick X and Robert 0X of Chicago.

For the parts relating to the American Muslim Mission, I am especially thankful to New York members Imam Ali Rasheed and Brothers Luqman Kareem and Abdullah. To all others in the black community of believers who have been of assistance: respect.

A host of other Americans, academics, colleagues, and friends have been extremely obliging: Dr. C. Eric Lincoln, who introduced me to Minister Farrakhan and shared with me his encyclopedic knowledge of African American religion and culture; Dr. Lawrence H. Mamiya, whose advice pointed me in fruitful directions; eminent Chicago journalist Salim Muwakkil, who introduced me to some essential aspects of the subject; and Dr. Yvonne Yazbeck Haddad, who reviewed the manuscript. The staff at the Anti-Defamation League in New York and Washington have also been of invaluable assistance, especially Edward Suall, Gail Gams, Tomas Harper, and Mira Boland, to whom I am sincerely grateful.

I greatly appreciate all those friends who opened their houses to a visiting Swedish researcher: Mike Hargis, Ingrid Kock, Jacques Wallner, Robert Good, Julia Good, Troy Fiscella, Penny Pixler, Joyce Kornbluh, Hy Kornbluh, Peter Kornbluh, and most of all, Jeff Ditz, who not only showed me wonderful hospitality but also sent me material regularly.

For the Libyan part of the research, the staffs at the World Center for the Studies and Researches of the Green Book, the World Mathaba, and the World Islamic Call Society have been most helpful, and I am especially obliged to Dr. Muhammad Ahmad al-Sharif, Bashir Ali Baesho, Muhammad Galeidi, Dr. Ibrahim Said, Ali Ghadban, and Nasser Amara.

In Sweden, additional individuals, colleagues, and friends have in different ways offered priceless support: Professor Louise Bäckman, Professor Per-Arne Berglie, and Dr. Ulf Drobin have all read different drafts of this study and made intelligent suggestions, as have my colleagues at the Department of Comparative Religion, Stockholm University, and the Department of Theology, Uppsala University. Dr. David Westerlund at Uppsala University not only involved me in stimulating joint projects concerning fundamentalism in a global and inter-religious perspective and the majority's Islam (that is, Islam outside the Arab world), but has in addition regularly read and criticized significant parts of this study.

Without the support of all these wonderful friends, my circle of brothers and sisters, this study would never have been completed. I especially want to express my gratitude to Ulf B. Anderson for his news service, Joan Lindberg for her proofreading, Michael Nord, Anna-Klara Bratt, Conny Lindström, Thomas Hvitfeldt, Börje Bergfeldt, Janne Flyghed, Jonas Fogelquist, Halina Nowicka, Gordon, Dirk Grosjean, and Anna-Karin Larsson for their contributions of various kinds.

Last, but most important of all, my wonderful children, Linus, Emma, Moa, and Ida, have been, as always, lovingly supportive and of extraordinary value.

Introduction

With the fall of the Iron Curtain an era in global politics came to an end, as the Western world no longer could define itself in opposition to communism. During the past few years, we have witnessed a return to a previous pattern in which the Occident seeks its raison d'être by placing itself in opposition to Islam. As it did during the Cold War, the United States still portrays itself as the defender of liberty against totalitarian barbarism, but the symbols of evil are no longer taken from the so-called Evil Empire but from the Muslim world. Saddam Hussein and Mu'ammar al-Qadhdhafi are portrayed as megalomaniac gangsters worthy of an Ian Fleming novel and are made to represent Islam in the dichotomy of them/us, despite the fact that Hussein maintains a secular Pan-Arabian version of nationalist socialism as champion for the Iraqi Ba'ath Party and the Islamic Socialist Mu'ammar al-Qadhdhafi espouses controversial deviations from mainstream Sunni Islam.

As was the case during the Cold War, this dichotomy is reflected in popular culture by the movie industry. In productions such as *Not without My Daughter* and *True Lies,* Muslims replace communists as the scary aliens, the subhuman merciless incarnations of evil bent on destroying what is good and decent. Defenders of the valuable way of life are justified in exterminating this robot-like enemy who is beyond reason and human emotions. The link between Arnold Schwarzenegger's Arab hunt in *True Lies* and the onslaught on Arab civilians in Operation Desert Storm is obvious: the victims were mere stereotypes, impossible to identify with. CNN blurred the distinction between drama and reality in a war enacted as a live-action spectacle in our living rooms.

The reason for returning to the opposition between the West and Islam is due not only to tradition but also to the global ambitions of both parties. When Francis Fukuyama asserted that the defeat of communism signaled an "end of history" and a worldwide ideological consensus in favor of secular liberal democracy, his vision, as Mark Juergensmeyer notes, was belied by the rise of new religious and ethnical nationalism.[1] Not only is the centripetal movement of global integration challenged by the centrifugal movement of ethnical fragmentation, but the West's claim to a rationale for global consensus is also challenged. When President Bush proclaimed victory for the "New World Order," he was offering a pre-dated vision of global hegemony for the American model of society.

Akbar Ahmed suggests that instead of the clumsy global classifications of First, Second, Third World, North-South, East-West, the world map of the 1990s can be divided into two major categories: "civilizations that are exploding, reaching out, expanding, bubbling with scientific ideas, economic plans, political ambitions, cultural expressions and those that are imploding, collapsing on themselves with economic, political and social crises which prevent any serious attempts at major initiatives.[2] Though perhaps overly simplified, Ahmed's perspective is still illuminative for an understanding of the global trends of the 1990s. The imploding nations, for example the few remnants of communist countries such as the Democratic Peoples' Republic of Korea, pose no serious threat to the exploding civilizations. In the present process of shaping a world culture or a global civilization, the "American" impact is set forth with a self-confident arrogance. The term "American" is not used here as a national or geographical but a cultural concept, as its exploding character already transcends nationality and geography. I choose the term "American" because the United States is taking the lead in and English is the lingua franca of a civilization that includes other nations and linguistic groups in the West, East, North, and South. This exploding civilization with global ambitions is characterized by consumerism, and its cultural impact is felt wherever we find McDonald's, Coca-Cola, Pizza Hut, CNN, Madonna, MTV, Mickey Mouse, Levi's, *Dallas,* and other cultural symbols. "It also has a sacred pilgrimage place," Ahmed notes. "Disneyland is like the Vatican for the Catholics, Makkah for the Muslims and Amritsar for the Sikhs. An entire civilization is here defined and many generations, in their millions, visit it."[3] Unlike Mecca, the Vatican, or Amritsar, Disneyland can be duplicated: there are now two in the United States, one in France, and one in Japan, which reveals this civilization's ability to transcend ethnicity and geography as nonwhite societies like Japan can align with "America" through, for example, one of this civilization's most powerful bodies, the G-7.

Beneath the surface of glimmering consumerism is a belief in liberal democracy, capitalist economy, and secular politics. At its best it promotes freedom of speech, intellectual pursuits, scientific endeavors, emancipation of women, and individual liberties. Had the self-presented saga of "American" civilization been the true story and its advantages been, as promised, inclusively intended, its project might have realized the success so arrogantly asserted. Concealed behind ideological ideal images is the backyard of global poverty, racism, sexism, classism, and the totalitarian denial of peoples' right to self-determination. The gulf separating professed ideals and experienced reality provides fertile soil for alternative ideologies.

Islam is the most rapidly expanding religion in the world and is presently the only other exploding civilization with global ambitions. It checks unrestrained materialism with spirituality and points to the aforementioned backyard conditions as evidence of the failure of man's self-sufficiency: If this does not work, why not try the way of God? Far from a proposal based on a rejection of man's capabilities, Islam believes in man's ability as God's vicegerent to establish a benign society. Islam, its advocators claim, provides social justice for all of mankind and is the guarantor against poverty, racism, classism, and sexual degradation of women. As complete a vision of civilization as the "American," Islam provides an alternative model of democracy, economy, and politics, thereby formulating a true challenge to Bush's New World Order.

In the process of polarization, Islamist ideologists launch alternative stereotypes, in which the Westerner represents "the Other." Fundamental to Islam are the dichotomies between *dar al-Islam* (the abode of Islam) and *dar al-kufr* (the abode of unbelievers), between *dar al-salaam* (the abode of peace) and *dar al-harb* (the abode of war). In Arabic, the word for the West is *gharb,* which also signifies the place of darkness and the incomprehensible. *Gharib* is the alien and *gharaba* means "strangeness."[4] In Islamist thought, "American" culture is depraved, immoral, and Godless and represents a compassionless threat to the valuable way of life. An extreme Islamist is justified in killing foreigners in Egypt or Algeria to protect what is good and decent using a logic akin to the Western legitimation for killing Muslims. The victim is subhuman, an image, impossible to identify with.

In the context of a revived juxtaposition between imaginary "America" and "Islam" it may be interesting to observe Islam as an American religion. Immigrants and guest students comprise the large majority of American Muslims, with a variety of individuals from more than sixty nations who represent not only different linguistic, racial, national, and ethnical categories,[5] but also different cultural and religious categories, as Islam is far from the monolithic entity imagined by many of its advocators and opponents. Estimates of the total number of Muslims in the United States vary considerably, but a reasonable figure for 1993 would be approximately eight million, including an estimated three million African American Muslims. There are more than 1,200 mosques of all sizes located throughout the United States, although 70 percent of the Muslim population is concentrated to ten states: California, New York, Illinois, New Jersey, Indiana, Michigan, Virginia, Texas, Ohio, and Maryland.[6]

Islam is thus well on its way to surpassing Judaism as the second largest religion in the United States, dwarfing also classic Protestant denominations such as the influential Episcopal church. Divinely mandated to summon all of mankind, the Muslim *dawa* (mission) in the West is bound to make an imprint on American society, and a far from insignificant number of American converts are found in this western *umma* (community of believers). The greatest impact has been made in the African American community, although the call has not gone unheard among Americans of European or Latin American descent. The overwhelming majority of American Muslims keep a low or apolitical profile, a fact that is perhaps overshadowed by the February 26, 1993, bombing of the World Trade Center and the subsequent arrest of Egyptian Islamist Sheikh Omar Abdel Rahman. A national coordination of American Muslim organizations was first attempted in 1952, and political lobbying has begun only relatively recently.[7] Muslim Political Action Committees (PACs) focus on "Islamic issues," mainly in the field of foreign policy, and in domestic matters strive to secure nondiscriminatory free exercise of religion. Whatever sympathies or antipathies American Muslims feel for the rising surge of Islamism (improperly known as "fundamentalism") in the Muslim world are largely expressed within the confines of their own community and do not reach the outer society.

Vociferous exceptions do exist, however, mainly in the African American community. The present study focuses on the most renowned and controversial of these groups, the Nation of Islam (NOI). This organization was established during the Great Depression in the rapidly expanding inner-city ghettos of the industrial North. The Nation was from the very beginning exclusively black and formulated emphatic political demands. The United States was depicted as the modern Babylon soon to be destroyed by the wrath of God, whereupon the blacks would ascend to their predestined position as world rulers. We see in the NOI a combination of the notion of militant Islam and the legacy of classic black nationalism, and the movement produced some of the leading African American nationalists of the twentieth century: Elijah Muhammad, Malcolm X, and Louis Farrakhan. The controversial positions of the Nation quickly attracted the attention of mainstream media and American domestic security agencies. In 1962, the Federal Bureau of Investigation (FBI) described the NOI as "an organization which is violently anti-white, anti-Christian, anti-integration and anti-United States."[8] Infiltrated and monitored since World War II, when the Nation supported Japan in what was seen as a war against white world supremacy, the movement strengthened its position as the largest black nationalist organization in the United States. The politico-religious influence the Nation undoubtedly enjoys in the African American community, not least among the urban youth, does not cease to dismay the official United States.

The present leader of the NOI, Minister Louis Farrakhan Muhammad, frequently makes headlines. Farrakhan was the strong man behind the 1995 Million Man March, which turned out to be the greatest black manifestation thus far in the history of the United States. He accepts financial aid from Libya, expressed sympathy for Manuel Noriega, and pledged his support for Saddam Hussein in the Gulf War. Speaking out in 1992 during the bloodiest uprising of the twentieth century, in Los Angeles, Farrakhan said that violence was the only resort of the oppressed and stressed that unless justice is created, America will be doomed: "the worst is yet to come."[9] Farrakhan is said to be a "reverse racist," an "anti-Semite," a "black Hitler," a "bigot," a "hate monger," a "demagogue," and an "Islamic fundamentalist." Despite the fact that the Nation's opinions are frequently debated, qualitative research is rare. Studies on the Nation, with some notable exceptions, have been based mainly on secondary sources of information due in part to the unwillingness of the NOI to be an object of academic inquiries.[10] The present study, which is mainly based on field research, recorded interviews, taped lectures, and the writings of the movement's spokespersons, aims to correct this unsatisfactory situation by presenting a comprehensive modern history of the Nation of Islam, with a particular focus on its "Second Resurrection" commenced in 1977.

Chapters 1 and 2 provide a background and summary descriptions of classic black nationalism and black American Islam prior to the "First Resurrection" of the NOI in 1930. Chapter 3 traces the rise and development of the Nation of Islam during the earthly presence of the Messenger of God, the Honorable Elijah Muhammad, between the years 1930 and 1975. The counterintelligence activities that the FBI directed against the Nation are the subject of chapter 4, which includes a discussion of the murder of Malcolm X. Chapter 5 describes the Islamization process initiated by Messenger Muhammad's successor, his son Wallace D. (later Warithuddin) Muhammad, a process that transformed the movement into a nonradical, depoliticized, mainstream Sunni Muslim organization. This process is known as "the fall" by the believers in Farrakhan's NOI. The second resurrection that began when Louis Farrakhan assumed the role of Peter in fulfillment of the Scriptures, is the subject of chapter 6, which also includes a discussion of the Messiology of the NOI. Chapter 7 is a lengthy discussion and analysis of the complex NOI creed, a discourse that hopefully will facilitate an understanding beyond the simplified media reports. The shifting relations between the NOI and the Muslim world are discussed in chapter 8, including the Libyan connection and a presentation of some minor black nationalist Islamic organizations in the United States. The role of the NOI in the predominantly Christian black community is the subject of the first section of chapter 9. That chapter's second section discusses the alleged anti-Semitism of Farrakhan and the NOI. The third section of chapter 9 turns its attention to the relationship between the NOI and white far-right nationalist organizations, or the so-called Nazi connection. Finally, the role and function of the NOI in contemporary American society is examined in chapter 10. Militant Islam as part of black youth culture, with its musical missionaries in the hip-hop movement are discussed, as well as the NOI's positions and practical activities in a wide range of fields, including its struggles to rid the black communities of drugs and crime and to realize African American empowerment and self-determination.

This study adopts a hermeneutically oriented emic perspective, which accounts for its narrative style. When I, for instance, write that "God came in the person of Master Farad Muhammad," or "the naive quest of the white devil to prolong his rule," this does not mean that I necessarily subscribe to what is stated, only that believers do. To prefix each matter of belief with an "according to" would not only take the thrill out of a fascinating and suggestive story, it would also be an implicit way to take exception to the "bizarre beliefs" of the Other. While an "according to" qualification is employed when necessary for the sake of clarity, I prefer when possible to write from the perspective of the believer. This in no way makes me a believer, and I, as a researcher, have the great advantage of not even being able to apply for membership. I am a white devil, which, in this respect, is rather convenient. While my colleagues often run the risk of, at one point or another, being viewed as prospects for conversion, I am not expected to believe or, I suspect, even to understand things properly. When Minister Farrakhan gave me permission to conduct this study at a May 1989 meeting in his Chicago South Side Palace, he told me to investigate everything from every angle. I should go to his backers and enemies alike and shun no effort to be objective. My intention is to present my findings as truthfully as possible, yet objectivity is a misleading honorific label and nonapplicable to humanistic and social research. Any human understanding of an object goes via the subject's mind as medium and is thus transformed into a subjective image of the object observed; it can only be grasped through the filter of perception, structured by the observer's frame of reference. What is presented here is my understanding of the Nation of Islam, its history, ideology, relations, roles, functions, and transformative processes. Although efforts are made to combine an emic perspective with etic analysis, the final result can never be equated with fundamental truth, nor with the image of the Nation from the actor's point of view.

Throughout this study the concepts *black, African American, Blackman,* and *Blackamerican* are used interchangeably for denoting Americans of African descent, the latter two being used in NOI literature and sermons. The word *black* is used in the terminology of the Nation of Islam both as a national/racial concept and as a theological one, signifying the Original People, goodness, and Godliness, and, as such, transcends the color of skin. A Native American, a Native Hawaiian, a Hispanic, and an African American are all "black" at this level of meaning. The contextual usage of the term will clarify on which semantic level it should be understood.

Other concepts of central significance for this thesis are *nation, nationalism,* and *religious nationalism,* terms that require a short discussion due to the fact that their definitions are unclear and ambiguous, differing considerably in meaning from user to user, across time and space. Although nationalists, like Mu'ammar al-Qadhdhafi and others, ascribe *nation* a permanence of existence, as if nations were as old as human history, the modern usage of the word stems from the eighteenth century.[11] It became popularized through political usage meant to produce feelings of loyalty and solidarity between a people and a state. Contrary to the a priori definition of *nation* claimed by nationalists, *nation* is defined a posteriori, that is, nationalism produces the nation and not the other way around.

A *nation* is an imagined community of people founded on selected criteria as language, history, culture, destiny, and religion, to which sentiments of belonging, loyalty, and solidarity are attached, together with a theory, if not a practice, of legitimate political authority. Here I differ from Juergensmeyer, who defines the nation as "a community of people associated with a particular political culture and territory that possesses autonomous political authority."[12] Accomplished independence as a criterion would make the concept too narrow, as it would exclude a great number of self-defined nations, like the Kurd, Basque, and Tibetean. In my usage, the nation names a collectively articulated ambition to achieve political independence, either in a separate state or in a confederation.

Nationalism is an ideology that gives priority to the *nation* over other imagined communities such as class and gender. A nationalist believes that a woman has more in common with men of the same nation than with women of another nation. Explicitly exclusive and easily aligned with chauvinism, racism, and xenophobia, nationalism postulates the unique and corporate character of the nation, to which a defined system of meaning is ascribed. Nationalism produces national awareness and national identity by references to a perceived origin, constructed through a nostalgic projection of the nation back into a legendary time, a shared history, and an envisioned destiny. Nationalism can be political and/or cultural. Politically, national self-determination is said to be the only legitimate form of political administration, either in a sovereign state or as part of a federation. Cultural nationalism seeks to preserve particular features, like handicrafts, language, clothing, festivities, music, and sports, which are considered to be generic to the national identity.

Religious nationalism postulates that nations are divine creations with specific God-given purposes and features. The nation is often believed to stand in a unique relationship with the Creator(s), from which both specific obligations and exclusive rights are derived. Nations are thus ascribed certain roles in the grand divine design known as the history of mankind, the outcome of which frequently is revealed and included as central to the national identity. One's own nation is often regarded as the predestined leader of the nations of the earth. Frequently collateral to this thesis is the belief that members of the "chosen nation" are themselves reflections of the divine. Here we encounter a mystic knowledge, a national gnosis, asserting that world history will conclude in the foundation of a nation of gods. Religious nationalists of this variety usually combine this notion with a vision of an apocalyptic battle, enacted between nations divine and diabolic. The Nation of Islam belongs to this category, and I hereby invite the reader for a fascinating journey into the world of black Islamic nationalism in the United States of America.

1

Restoration of Dignity: The Rise of Black Nationalism

═══

This chapter will discuss the black nationalist tradition that provides a significant ideological background for the Nation of Islam. Wilson J. Moses defined the years 1850 to 1925 as its "golden age," as this period "saw the flourishing of all the major black nationalists, with one exception—Elijah Muhammad."[1] With the addition of Muhammad's successor, Minister Louis Farrakhan, this is a valid statement. It also points out the direction in which the legacy of black nationalism was to be cultivated. After the climax represented by the Universal Negro Improvement Association (UNIA) prior to the imprisonment of its founder, Marcus Garvey, the central tenets of classic black nationalism were developed by religious preachers of various movements, the most successful being the Nation of Islam.

Black to Basics In spite of their disagreements and differences in character and perspective, the different proponents of black nationalism operating during the classic period share some essential basics on a more general and abstract level, as has been convincingly shown by Moses. He argues that classic black nationalism was "absolutist, civilizationist, elitist, and based on Christian humanism."[2] Though radical in its call for black political empowerment, the ideology was predominantly conservative in regard to traditional values articulated in mainstream American culture. The path toward liberation was envisioned as an emulation of European civilization, including its institutions of education and industry. Black nationalism was based on an organic view of races, derived from contemporary Western theories about races as different "personalities." The race was seen as an authoritarian, structured entity with specific features, differentiating it from the other race personalities inter-acting on the global stage of world history. A notion of cyclical time frequently added a mystical dimension to world history, an idea that was to become fundamental in the later religious nationalist creeds.

The concepts of race and nation differed considerably from their defi-nitions in the late twentieth century. In the black nationalist usage, the distinction between race and nation was frequently blurred, due in part to the unique situation of the African Americans. Descendants from a wide variety of African peoples and cultures merged into a "nation" during the centuries of slavery. Over time a pan–African American identity was formed based on a shared social history commenced in the holds of trans-Atlantic and inter-American cargo ships. As race became a factor deter-mining social, economic, and political status, it also became a criterion for the black nation in America.

Black nationalists were influenced by the nineteenth century's scien-tific and romantic European, especially German, discourse on race. Prior to the rediscovery of the work of the biologist Gregor Johann Mendel, founder of the modern theory of genetics,[3] race had a wider meaning. Its definitions were generally in line with the German *Volk* and owed much to the Pan-German *völkisch* tradition.[4] The race transcended biology and acquired national romantic meanings of a spiritual, psychological, and cultural kind. Race solidarity was organic, and by "nature" members of a race were believed to share mental and spiritual qualities, from which shared ambitions and a common destiny were derived. Besides physical features, criteria today applied to define nation, ethnicity, and culture were employed. In his 1897 essay, "The Conservation of Races," promi-nent black nationalist W. E. B. Du Bois identified eight races in the world, using language, religion, geography, and history as criteria: "[The eight races] are the Slavs of Eastern Europe, the Teutons of middle Europe, the English of Great Britain and America, the Romance nations of Southern and Western Europe, the Negroes of Africa and America, the Semitic people of Western Asia and Northern Africa, the Hindoos of Central Asia and the Mongolians of Eastern Asia."[5] Black nationalism offered solu-tions to the problem of identity so crucial for post-Emancipation black discourse. Caught up in the peculiar position of being American but not American, African but not African, black nationalists suggested various concepts for their own national identity, none of which so far has been re-ceived with universal agreement. The heated debate over whether or not they should be called Negroes, Colored or Blacks, Negro-Saxons, Anglo-

Africans, Euro-Africans, Afro-Americans, African-Americans, or, most recently, African Americans, highlights the emotional significance of the dilemma.

Some tendencies of black nationalism have emphasized one side of the bipolar identity at the expense, to a certain degree, of the other. There is one category of nationalist ideologies that underlines the importance of physical and/or cultural repatriation; this move toward separatism has never been exclusive but has always been opposed by advocates that stress the American side of the identity. A back-to-Africa agenda thus cannot be, as sometimes has been suggested, the criterion for black nationalism. Many spokespersons have agitated for equality in a multiracial United States, while at the same time stressing the qualities of their distinct black national identity.

Black religious nationalists advance the race-organism thesis by adding divine intention to the meaning of its existence. Generally, the African American is said to be of the "chosen people," created in His likeness. The aboriginal African culture is seen as the cradle of civilization, where it all began. For various reasons, not infrequently due to past transgressions against God's will, blacks lost their leading position among other races. Colonization and slavery are presented as hard but necessary parts of a greater divine plan in which blacks are predestined to reascend as the guides of mankind. Black religious nationalists have championed alternative concepts for their own people that reflect the perceived divine meaning of existence. In the United States movements can be found that advocate that African Americans properly should be named *Ethiopians* (African Orthodox Church, Rastafarians, and others), *Moors* (the Moorish Science Temple), *Jews* (various black Hebrew organizations), *Nubians* (the Ansaaru Allah Community), and *Bilalians* (the American Muslim Mission). The Nation of Islam, which argues that they are *the original black Asiatic man,* is an early proponent of this tradition.

Classic black nationalism held the concept of civilization as a central tenet. The word had become increasingly popular in the academic discourse since its introduction in the eighteenth century. Even though the concept of civilization acquired different meanings in the Anglo-Saxon, French, and German vocabularies, it quickly became diffused as an honorific label, colored with pride as the hallmark of advanced nations. In popular usage it became equated with European culture and society, and thereby became related to the theory of evolutionism. Beginning with its breakthrough in the late nineteenth century, evolutionism came to dominate the academic understanding of man and society for several decades, which is why it also had a direct bearing on black nationalist theoreticians.

Evolutionism was formulated in a time of unsurpassed European optimism. Mankind was believed to be close to reaching its predestined stage of perfection with the help of omnipotent science. The intelligentsia was heralded as the vanguard of civilization, able to solve the mysteries of the universe and to pave the way for a new world in which the liberated rational man would be established. The theoretical roots of evolutionism received nourishment from Enlightenment thought, the Hegelian view of history, and Comtean positivism. But the history of ideas cannot be isolated or used as the sole explanation for the development of theories. To reach a more complete understanding, we have to move beyond the universe of ideas and examine the world political scene.

Evolutionism originated in the context of European imperialism and colonialism, especially their conquest of Africa. The European superpowers incessantly forced their way into "new" areas with their military and commercial spearheads. During this expansion, a stream of "new" peoples were "discovered," confronted, and, in some manner, subjugated. Colonialism and its slave economies created a need to legitimize this new world order. Two trends related to this process of legitimation are significant for our purposes: the anthropological theory of a hierarchy of races and the racial reinterpretation of Christianity. Evolutionism made its breakthrough with the works of Herbert Spencer and Edward B. Tylor, a development that concluded the previous debate about whether or not the newly subjugated peoples in the outskirts of Europe were at all human. The differences between "them" and "us" were explained by the same process of evolution that Darwin outlined in the field of natural science. Mankind had gone through a series of evolutionary stages, and living proof could be found along the route of European expansion. Technological development was equated with mental evolution: the intellect of the "savage" was as primitive as his tools. The researchers projected their findings back into prehistoric times and made the contemporary cultures an image of their own cultural origin. From this primeval "savage," "primitive," or "natural" (as opposed to cultural) stage man had gone through a mental evolution, reaching ever higher stages and finally resulting in the pinnacle of culture: the European civilization as the crown of creation.[6]

These imperial ambitions were accompanied by an erasure of African influences on Christianity. The Middle Ages had black Madonnas, and artists could use dark tints to depict Jesus. Now, the complexion of God, the angels, Jesus, Mary, and the apostles became increasingly more European. The West Asian Jesus of Nazareth turned into a blond, blue-eyed white man, with a mission to save the peoples of the world. The African fathers of the church—Clement, Origen, Tertullian, Cyprian, Dionysos, Athanasius, Didymus, Augustine, and Cyril—were presented as "Greeks" and the Hellenic civilization was said to owe nothing to African impulses. The importance of the early African churches in Ethiopia and Egypt was diminished, just as the pre-Christian Egyptian civilization was de-Africanized.[7] Troublesome facts, like the existence of African saints, were explained by theological rationalizations. Thus, the black saint, St. Benedict the Moor, was said to have been originally a white man, who prayed to God to make him so ugly that he would be rescued from all temptations by the opposite sex. God granted his sincere wish and made him black.[8]

Light and dark is a basic dichotomy applied in Christianity to symbolize the distinction between the realm of God and Satan. What is good and innocent is "white" and what is evil and cunning is "black." We speak of a "white lie," "innocence as white as a lily," and "white magic." But a "black cat" brings bad luck, an evil soul is "black," and when the stock exchange crashed it was called a "black Monday." This kind of color symbolism acquired new meanings when it was applied to people with white and black complexions. To explain the diversity of races descending from a created single couple, morality was associated with skin color. Black skin was a divine punishment for past transgressions. Blackness as the curse invoked upon Ham and his son Canaan was sometimes said to be a mild form of leprosy with an excess of pigment as the only symptom.[9] Ham and Canaan as the cursed progenitors of the black race are analogous to Cain, who allegedly was marked by God with blackness, which was in turn inherited by his offspring.[10] So pervasive was the merging of moral quality with complexion that a good black man was said to have a white soul.[11] Blacks, unlike whites, required spiritual bodies of a different hue in the Resurrection. They would be cured of their deformity and rise in perfected white.[12]

The precolonial existence of Islam and Christianity in Africa was ignored, as was the content of the various African religions, and so the inhabitants could be presented as living their life in barbarous fear and superstition. The Europeans became deputies of God, obliged to spread the light on the dark African continent. Both trends converged in the legitimation of the European presence in Africa and of slavery as an institution. The colonial power could be presented as the benevolent father, who in his mercifulness engaged in civilizing and developing these savage people, blessing them with his refined culture and religion. A few fortunate individuals were rescued from the dark continent to be raised in Christian surroundings. Slavery and colonialism were thus depicted as the "white man's burden," as it was lyricized by Rudyard Kipling, the great poet of English imperialism:

> Take up the white man's burden
> Send forth the best ye breed
> Go bind your sons to exile
> To serve your captives' need.[13]

These basic arguments of legitimation were absorbed by the thinking of leading black nationalists at the time. European culture was highly valued, and Africa was seen as almost helplessly underdeveloped and barbarous; thus, colonialism was believed to be somewhat justified. "They do not seek to repress the Africans," Booker T. Washington explained in Berlin in 1910, speaking of German colonialism, "but rather to help them that they may be more useful to themselves."[14] The Africans in America had to be civilized, and different programs for racial improvement were envisioned. Bishop Turner argued that God temporarily allowed the enslavement of Africans because they needed to be civilized, but he also condemned the Anglo-Americans for defaulting from their part in God's project: "We gave the white man our labor, yes! In return he should have educated us, taught us to read and write, at least, and seen that Africa was well supplied with missionaries."[15] Booker T. Washington condemned slavery as such, but in underlining its indirect benefits he nevertheless reflected proslavery argumentation: "We must acknowledge that, notwithstanding the cruelty and moral wrong of slavery, the ten million Negroes inhabiting this country, who themselves or whose ancestors went through the school of American slavery, are in a stronger and more hopeful condition, materially, intellectually, morally, and religiously, than is true of any equal number of black people in any other portion of the globe."[16] Racial self-improvement and civilizing were key themes in the program of Booker T. Washington (1856–1915). Freed by the Act of Emancipation in his early childhood, Washington realized that liberation required more than formal freedom. He improved his personal conditions through education and hard work and envisioned such a path of progress as the only one possible for the black community. On July 4, 1881, Washington inaugurated the Tuskegee Institute in Macon County, Alabama. The pedagogy applied at this school stressed the combination of manual labor, industrial training, and intellectual learning. Washington believed that a meaningful education should teach practical skills and civilized manners: "We wanted to teach the students how to bathe; how to care for their teeth and clothing. We wanted to teach them what to eat, and how to eat it properly, and how to care for their rooms. Aside from this we wanted to give them such a practical knowledge of some one industry, together with the spirit of industry, thrift, and economy, that they would be sure of knowing how to make a living after they had left us. We wanted to teach them to study actual things instead of mere books alone."[17] In the subsequent growth of the Tuskegee Institute, the students themselves cleared the ground and constructed the buildings. They founded industries like brick making and wagon production, planted their own crops, and raised their own cattle. In all things Tuskegee strived to be self-sufficient and beneficial to the surrounding community. Acquiring useful knowledge would make blacks wanted and respected in society, and thus automatically lead to an improvement of race relations.[18] An industrious race of morally conservative and well-behaved individuals could accommodate perfectly the prevailing Anglo-American culture. In the eyes of Booker T. Washington, such blacks would make a positive contribution to, rather than endanger, the social fabric of Southern society. "In all things purely social we can be as separate as the fingers, yet one as a hand in all things essential to mutual progress," said Washington, speaking on race relations at the Atlanta Cotton Exposition in 1895. In the same speech he played upon the Americans' xenophobic fears of new immigrant waves and underlined the proven loyalty of the blacks. Advancing his argument, Washington doomed agitation for social equality as "the extremest folly," claiming that progress and equality only could be "the result of severe and constant struggle" for self-improvement, and that "no race that has anything to contribute to the markets of the world is long in any degree ostracized."[19]

Washington's position was challenged by his antagonist, the Pan-African ideologist W. E. B. Du Bois (1869–1963), who argued that Washington represented "the old attitude of adjustment and submission" and that his program "practically accepts the alleged inferiority of the Negro races."[20] The anticapitalist Du Bois suggested that the Tuskegee machine was set up to produce an obedient pool of cheap labor and prevent the spread of socialism and industrial union organizing. The black intelligentsia was launched as a racial advance guard to complement Washington's elite of black industrialists. Du Bois said he "believed in the higher education of the Talented Tenth who through their knowledge of modern culture could guide the American Negro into higher civilization."[21]

As a journalist, editor, and researcher, Du Bois was clearly influenced by the academic discourse of the time. His early writing reflects the thinking of German racial theorists. As a young student who regarded Bismarck as his hero, Du Bois received a two-year grant to study at the University of Berlin. He became fluent in German, studied the works of nationalist theoreticians, and "sat under the voice of the fire-eating Pan-German [Heinrich] von Treitsche."[22] Inspired in part by the German *völkisch* tradition, Du Bois wrote "The Conservation of Races" for the American Negro Academy in 1897. In this address Du Bois presented the race as an organic entity and a mystical force. He believed the "deeper differences" between the races to be "spiritual" and "psychical." Each race strives in its own direction to develop its distinct message and thus contributes to the predestined perfection of human life. Reflecting evolutionist theories, Du Bois argued that blacks were "members of a vast historic race that from the very dawn of creation has slept, but half awakening in the dark forest of its African fatherland." The African Americans had yet to develop their particular message for world civilization, which could be accomplished only by refusing to be absorbed into white culture. The qualities of the black race had to be preserved and, to this end, separate racial institutions of education, economy, and art must be established.[23]

During his long and energetic life, Du Bois gradually evolved toward a Pan-African socialist position, and he became renowned as a fierce agitator for black civil rights. Working through the organizations he cofounded, the Niagara Movement and the National Association for the Advancement of Colored People (NAACP), Du Bois moved from the more separatist camp of the Negro Academy toward a struggle for integration and ethnic pluralism. This does not, however, signify a complete abandonment of his original ideas. Though Du Bois came to "believe in the ultimate triumph of some form of Socialism the world over,"[24] his definition of socialism reflects black nationalist tenets in its Afrocentrism and authoritarian corporate collectivism. In his autobiography Du Bois explained socialism to be "disciplined economy and political organization in which the first duty of the citizen is to serve the state . . . the African tribe, whence you all sprung, was communistic in its very beginnings. No tribesman was free. All were servants of the tribe of whom the chief was father and voice."[25] Authoritarian collectivism was also an important part of the philosophy of Du Bois's mentor, Alexander Crummell (1819–98). As a missionary in Liberia between 1853 and 1873, his goal was to uplift the Africans from "the rudeness of barbarism." His view of Africa was at that time essentially congruent with the general European conception of the continent. Echoing the attitudes of evolutionists and missionaries, Crummel wrote in 1854: "Darkness covers the land, and gross darkness the people. Great evils universally prevail. Confidence and security are destroyed. Licentiousness abounds everywhere. Moloch rules and reigns throughout the whole continent, and by the ordeals of Sassywood, Fetiches, human sacrifices, and devil worship, is devouring men, women and little children."[26] The obligation of the enlightened blacks of the Diaspora was to return to Africa as redeemers and shed the benevolent light of Christianity and Victorian civilization; only then could Africa awaken after centuries of slumber and recapture its divinely ordained place. Returning to the United States after twenty years of service, Crummell tried to adapt his ideas of civilization, evangelization, and separation to the changing American scene. He founded the American Negro Academy in 1897 to accomplish "the civilization of the Negro race in the United States, by the scientific processes of literature, art and philosophy."[27] Crummell had a romantic, idealistic conception of race and was influenced by the works of German theoreticians such as Johann Gottfried von Herder and Friedrich Schleiermacher. Crummell wrote, "Races, like families, are the organisms and the ordinance of God."[28] He was convinced that temporary black inferiority would turn into "that superiority and eminence which is our rightful heritage, and which is evidently the promise of our God."[29]

While in Liberia, Crummell began to collaborate with a repatriated black nationalist, Edward Wilmot Blyden (1832–1912). Born in the Danish West Indies, Blyden went to the United States to become a clergyman. Denied admission to three theological colleges because of his complexion, he came under the influence of the American Colonization Society (ACS). In 1850 Blyden was sent to the new Republic of Liberia, which had come into existence as a result of ACS lobbying,[30] where he completed his theological education. To gain knowledge of his fatherland, Presbyterian pastor Blyden studied Arabic, Greek, and Roman classics and historians. He discovered that Africa had a long and glorious past with great historical civilizations in West Africa, Ethiopia, and Egypt, and he predicted that a corresponding shining future would be realized under the aegis of Christian civilization.

Like Crummell, Blyden was influenced by German nationalist theories, especially the ideas of von Herder. Blyden believed races to be "great organic types of being,"[31] each with a distinct "personality" that should be developed separate from the others in order to serve humanity at large. Blyden argued that by carefully cultivating the distinct quality of the black race—spirituality—the Africans could balance the competitive, materialistic traits of the European race, which would otherwise ruin the creation.[32] This could only be accomplished by repatriation of Christian, educated blacks of unmixed African descent. Blyden envisioned repatriation as a crucial part of God's predestined plan for global development. He interpreted the increasing racial antagonism in the United States as being designed by God: "I think that God who has His hands both upon Africa and America will deepen the prejudice against the Negro in the United States. He will continue to harden Pharaoh's heart, until the oppressed shall be driven from the house of bondage, as Israel was from Egypt, to do his work in the land of his fathers."[33] Blyden was a champion for the back-to-Africa movements that flourished in cycles during the time of classic black nationalism. For blacks, returning to Africa to build a prosperous future on their own terms was a tempting alternative to fighting for respect and self-determination in a society that had used them as slaves. According to Edwin S. Redkey, the back-to-Africa boom of 1890 attracted mainly lower-class Southern blacks for whom the middle-class-oriented plans of Washington and Du Bois seemed unrealistic.[34] The appeal of repatriation was thus often personal and economic. Permanent poverty nursed the dream of a paradise across the sea, but leading black advocates, like Blyden, had a more idealistic and long-term vision about the significance of repatriation.

Bishop Henry McNeal Turner (1834–1915) of the African Methodist Episcopal Church was one of the most prominent voices for repatriation in post-Reconstruction America. Bishop Turner had long been interested in the prospect of his fatherland and the possibilities of repatriation. He became convinced that it was hopelessly naive to seek equality in surroundings so permeated with racism. "By virtue of lynchings, murders and outrages perpetrated upon our people," Turner branded the United States as "the worst, the meanest country" on the earth. The only roles assigned to blacks in America seemed to be as "menials, scullions, servants, subordinates and underlings."[35] In 1883, the democratic experiment of the Reconstruction ended when the Supreme Court overturned as unconstitutional the Civil Rights Act of 1875. Turner concluded that such a Constitution was "a dirty rag, a cheat, a libel and ought to be spit upon by every Negro in the land." He told his audience that "if the Court's decision is right and is accepted by the country, then prepare to return to Africa or get ready for extermination."[36]

In Turner's mind, the blacks' future was in Africa. He did not propose a mass emigration but a continuous flow of dedicated, ambitious, honest, proud Christian blacks who were willing to work hard for African self-determination. He declared that Africa could well do without "all the riffraff white-men worshipers, aimless, objectless, selfish, little-souled and would-be-white Negroes."[37] The returning ex-slaves would evangelize Africa and defend the continent from the Europeans, who at that time had begun the colonization of Africa's interior. It was the repatriates' divine duty to build a strong Christian Africa, a project that when accomplished would benefit all Africans wherever they might reside. "Africa will be the thermometer that will determine the status of the Negro the world over," Turner proclaimed, and the American "Negro will never be anything here while Africa is shrouded in heathen darkness."[38]

In response to Turner's agitation the International Migration Society was formed in 1884 as a vehicle for repatriation. An account of the history of this back-to-Africa group, its successes and setbacks, would stray too far from the scope of this study.[39] It must be emphasized, however, that neither this society, nor the older ACS, received unequivocal support from leading black spokespersons. The black nationalism of the United States always has focused on two geographical entities, Africa and America. Exodus never has been the sole aim, nor the sole solution, proposed by its advocates. Many black nationalists totally rejected the prospect of repatriation in favor of establishing black self-determination and African national consciousness in America. In fact, the motives of the emigration societies have been questioned, and perhaps justly so. The American Colonization Society had the support of a mixed constellation of white individuals and groups. Some were idealistic philanthropists, while others were slaveholders who were eager to export free Africans in order to secure slavery as an institution. On the eve of emancipation, many whites envisioned black repatriation as a convenient way of solving upcoming problems of coexistence, and they could evoke the late President Jefferson in support of the suggested solution, who believed that blacks were improvident, sensual, extravagant, and weak in faculty.[40] Jefferson assumed that they were incapable of fitting into American life and suggested that "when freed he [the black man] is to be removed beyond the reach of [racial] mixture."[41] It is no wonder that an important segment of black spokespersons, such as Frederick Douglass, David Walker, and Booker T. Washington, remained opposed to the project of repatriation.

Another important theme of classic black nationalism was the mystical and mythical view of history called *Ethiopianism*. Ethiopia has long occupied a special position in both European and African thought. In medieval Europe, Ethiopia was a Christian empire south of the feared Islamic hordes. According to legend, it was governed by Prester John, the descendant of Salomo and Sheba, who ruled with the help of a wonderful mirror in which he could see every event in every part of his empire. The legendary country was inhabited by fabulous creatures, such as the salamander, which dwelled in fire, and the warlike Amazons.[42] For Africans, Ethiopia was the strong native civilization that successfully resisted European colonization efforts. When the Italian colonial army was defeated in the 1896 battle of Adowa, the echo resounded all over the black world.

In addition, Ethiopia had a deeper significance. By studying the Bible, the enslaved population in the New World discovered an ancient African civilization that revolutionized their image of Africa. Passages like Psalms 68:31, "Princes shall come out of Egypt, Ethiopia shall soon stretch out her hands unto God," were crucial for the elaboration of a mystical and cyclical historiography. Ethiopia symbolized Africa, which was envisioned as the cradle of mankind and identified with the Promised Land. As a necessary divine lesson, God put the originators of civilization to "sleep" and world hegemony was transferred to other races. God allowed foreigners to conquer Africa and His Chosen People were scattered throughout the Diaspora, but white supremacy was only temporary. Pharaoh would be forced to free the enslaved and God would bring home the exiled. In God's words to his beloved black nation through the prophet Isaiah 43:5–6: "Fear not for I am with thee: I will bring thy seed from the east, and gather thee from the west; I will say to the north, Give up; and to the south, Keep not back: bring my sons from far, and my daughters from the ends of the world." Completing the turn of the cycle, the star of Ethiopia would again shine to the awe of mankind. Ethiopianism as a religious nationalist tradition has long been an underlying theme in the African American community, where it found expression in slave narratives, slave songs, preaching, folklore, art, and literature. Ethiopia embodied the suffering and the hope of salvation, as expressed in the words of Frances Ellen Watkins Harper:

> Yes, Ethiopia yet shall stretch
> Her bleeding hands abroad
> Her cry of agony shall reach
> Up to the throne of God.[43]

A Black Moses in the House of Pharaoh   Ethiopia was a powerful symbol in the teachings of Marcus Mosiah Garvey (1887–1940), who electrified his readers and audience with his soul on fire: "Wake up Ethiopia! Wake up Africa! Let us work towards the one glorious end of a free, redeemed and mighty nation. Let Africa be a bright star among the constellation of nations."[44] "At this moment methinks I see Ethiopia stretching forth her hands unto God, and methinks I see the Angel of God taking up the standard of the Red, the Black and the Green, and saying 'Men of the Negro Race, Men of Ethiopia, follow me.' And tonight we are following. We are following 400,000,000 strong. We are following with a determination that we must be free before the wreck of matter, before the crash of worlds."[45] Marcus Garvey represents the climax of classic black nationalism, forcefully combining all its dominant themes in ideology, but he also transformed it significantly by reaching beyond the elite and catching the attention of urban and rural proletarians with his magnificent populist rhetoric. Black nationalism as a grassroots mass movement, spiced with a militarism derived from World War I, suddenly constituted a center of aspiration in black America. In the aftermath of the Garvey fever is found the genesis of the Nation of Islam, which attracted followers of Garvey and adopted crucial elements of his ideology.

Marcus Garvey was a descendant of the Maroons, the runaway slaves who established freed communes in the central Jamaican highlands. A skilled printer, Garvey moved to Kingston and was, at the age of twenty, a foreman at the P. A. Benjamin Company when the Printers' Union called a strike. Elected strike leader, Garvey lost an uneven fight against the big company, whose imported scabs broke the workers' solidarity. The experience taught Marcus Garvey the need for organized action, but it also imbued him with a lifelong skepticism regarding unionism and class-based struggle.[46]

As a blacklisted labor martyr, he made a few less-than-successful attempts to establish political periodicals, before leaving Jamaica on a two-step journey that would determine his future. Working his way throughout the West Indies, Central America, and northern South America, Garvey came to realize the universal repression his people were suffering. Eager to learn about the conditions of blacks in other parts of the British empire, Garvey sailed to England where he became associated with the militant Pan-African pioneer Duse Mohammed Ali. Dissatisfied with white world supremacy and inspired by nationalist discussions in London's black exile community, Garvey read the autobiography of Booker T. Washington "and then," he later stated, "my doom—if I may so call it—of being a race leader dawned upon me." Garvey continued: "I was determined that the black man would not continue to be kicked about by all the other races and nations of the world. . . . I saw before me then, even as I do now, a new world of black men, not peons, serfs, dogs and slaves, but a nation of sturdy men making their impress upon civilization and causing a new light to dawn upon the human race."[47] In the summer of 1914, Garvey returned to Jamaica to found the Universal Negro Improvement Association and African Communities (Imperial) League (UNIA), with its motto "One God! One Aim! One Destiny!" Through the UNIA Garvey sought to unite "all the Negro peoples of the world into one great body to establish a country and Government absolutely their own."[48] The road toward race redemption and black self-determination was envisioned as a process of cooperative racial improvement. Inspired by the progress of Booker T. Washington, Garvey made an unsuccessful attempt to establish a Jamaican Tuskegee. Writing to Washington for advice and financial support, Garvey was invited to visit the United States. Washington and Garvey were never to meet, as the sage of Tuskegee died before Garvey was able to depart for the United States in 1916.

While touring thirty-eight states to study black reality, Garvey founded the first North American branch of the UNIA in Harlem, New York, in 1917. Factionalism and intrigues that threatened to ruin the Harlem chapter prevented Garvey's return to Jamaica. He decided to settle permanently in the United States and transferred the headquarters and presidency to Harlem. The move was strategically wise as Harlem was a growing center for black consciousness. Garvey claimed an instant success, with an increase in membership from 600 to 12,000 in a few months.[49] These figures must be read with some caution, as is true of all UNIA statements concerning their actual numerical strength. In 1928, Garvey boasted that his then declining organization had eleven million members in three thousand local chapters all over the world.[50] Notwithstanding the uncertainty as regards the exact number of members, it is probably safe to say that UNIA at its strongest constituted the largest black nationalist organization in the world, with local chapters and sympathizers in the Americas as well as Africa.

The rise of the UNIA was related to World War I. The outbreak of the Great War ruined the image of European culture as the highest possible form of civilization. This notion had already been shaken when the Japanese negated the thesis of white invincibility in the 1905–6 war with Russia. With World War I, it received a final blow. Could a people that legitimated their world hegemony in the name of their superior Christian ethic and then engaged in such a vicious war really be that advanced and culturally refined? Garvey remarked, "For the Anglo-Saxon to say that he is superior because he introduced submarines to destroy life, or the Teuton because he compounded liquid gas to outdo in the art of killing and that the Negro is inferior because he is backward in that direction is to leave one's self open to the retort 'Thou shalt not kill,' as being the divine law that sets the moral standard of the real man."[51] Imperial competition was an important factor in the Great War and the European states enrolled thousands of African soldiers. This fact did not fail to impress black Americans. An article in Du Bois's *The Crisis* described the war in the Congo under the headline: "Black soldiers fighting to protect the civilization of Europe from itself." When the United States entered the war in 1917, only a few leading black nationalists resented black participation.[52] Most spokespersons urged the blacks to register for the draft. "Let us," Du Bois wrote, "while the war lasts, forget our special grievances and close ranks shoulder to shoulder with our white fellow citizens . . . fighting for democracy."[53] White politicians expressed similar opinions; for instance, Theodore Roosevelt, while addressing a black assembly, argued that America's fight for international justice also would lead to a "juster and fairer treatment in this country of colored people."[54] African Americans responded en masse: more than two million blacks registered for the draft and 370,000 were called to service.[55] The survivors returned to find a postwar society as unequal as before. Now, even nonradical black spokespersons reacted with anger. Kelly Miller stated that no one could expect "the Negro soldiers of the World War to revert with satisfaction to the status they occupied before the war for the emancipation of mankind."[56] The black soldiers had learned how to use arms, how to battle, and how to win. Out of the wartime aftermath arose a revitalized black radicalism.

Perhaps more than any other contemporary black leader, Garvey embodied this radical change in attitude. He felt that he headed a race on the

move, ready to retake their former position of glory. Garvey was convinced that the races moved in cycles of ascendancy and descendancy.
"Today the Negro seems to be the footstool of the other races and nations
of the world," Garvey wrote. "Tomorrow the Negro may occupy the highest rung of the great human ladder." Racial status is in the hands of God
and history proves that white supremacy is far from determined by nature. Garvey further stated, "When Europe was inhabited by a race of
cannibals, a race of savages, naked men, heathen and pagans, Africa was
peopled with a race of cultured black men, who were masters in art,
science and literature; men who were cultured and refined; men who, it is
said, were like the gods."[57] A mythic historiography flavored with racial chauvinism flourished in Garvey's thinking. Reversing the black-
because-cursed thesis found among white Christians, Garvey claimed
that Adam and Eve were black as were their two sons Cain and Abel. After
Cain had murdered his brother, God showed up asking for Abel. Cain
"was so shocked that he turned white," Garvey wrote. Cursed with "the
affliction of leprosy" Cain "became the progenitor of a new race." The
white offspring of Cain hid in dark caves for centuries, making the skin
permanently white and sensitive to the sun's hot rays.[58] Like Blyden and
Turner, Garvey thought it naive to expect that whites would give blacks
justice and freedom. "The attitude of the white race," he wrote, "is to
subjugate, to exploit, and if necessary exterminate the weaker peoples
with whom they come in contact."[59] Convinced that each race should live
and develop separately, Garvey called for race solidarity, repatriation,
and Pan-African liberation: "As four hundred million men, women and
children . . . we are determined to solve our own problem by redeeming
our Motherland Africa from the hands of alien exploiters and found there
a government, a nation of our own, strong enough to lend protection to
the members of our race scattered all over the world, and to compel the
respect of the nations and races of the earth."[60] The African empire envisioned was a utopian ideal state. Garvey's ideas on the future government
were inspired by Aristotle and Plato[61] and compatible with the authoritarian collectivism of the classic black nationalist tradition. The state
should be headed by a supreme president, "endowed with absolute authority," who should "devote his entire time to the sovereign needs and
desires of the people." He should embody the will of the entire population, thus preventing "fractional party fights" and selfish "interests of
classes." To avoid corruption, the president should be removed from all
personal friends; he should hold his administrators strictly accountable,

and if they were found guilty of any malfeasance, they should be publicly disgraced and stoned to death.[62] In part, this corporate monoracial state resembles the ideal propagated by fascism and nazism. In fact, Garvey once claimed to be the first fascist and the one that Mussolini copied.[63] However, this does not imply any unconditional support for the politics of Mussolini. When Italy attacked Ethiopia in 1935, Garvey called for an armed defense and promised in a militant poem that "we'll march to crush the Italian dog."[64] Garvey's claim, nevertheless, indicates a degree of kinship between black and white extreme nationalism, an issue to be further discussed in chapter 9.

The "African Fundamentalism" of Marcus Garvey can be described as a return to Africa, mentally if not physically. Garvey stressed the need for an Afrocentric re-education, rejecting emulation of white institutions: "Any race that accepts the thoughts of another race, automatically becomes the slave of that other race."[65] The Africans, "at home or abroad," must recreate a world they can, truly and racially, call their own. This pertains to all fields, including religion. In a famous statement, Garvey launched the idea of a black God: "If the white man has the idea of a white God, let him worship his God as he desires. If the yellow man's God is of his race let him worship his God as he sees fit. We, as Negroes, have found a new ideal. Whilst our God has no color, yet it is human to see everything through one's own spectacles, and since the white people have seen their God through white spectacles, we have only now started out (late though it be) to see our God through our own spectacles . . . through the spectacles of Ethiopia."[66] Randall K. Burkett has described the religious ethos pervading the UNIA. Garvey's language was laden with religious symbolism and vocabulary; he spoke of Africa's redemption, and urged his followers to go out as missionaries to save the African Americans. UNIA preached the Gospel and was described as the great ark of safety. Each UNIA chapter elected a chaplain who was an ordained minister. Chaplain-General George Alexander McGuire wrote the *Negro Ritual,* which prescribed the standard order to be followed in UNIA meetings and included a baptism and burial service for UNIA members. For use in the juvenile branches, McGuire wrote the *Universal Negro Catechism.*[67]

To spread his ideas Garvey founded three journals, *The Negro World, The Negro Times,* and *The Black Man.* Garvey proved to be an eminent journalist. Praised as the "best edited colored weekly," *The Negro World* quickly reached a wide circulation, estimated at between 60,000 and 200,000 copies sold during its most prosperous years. Certain sections were printed in Spanish and French for the benefit of readers in the West Indies and Africa. The front page of *The Negro World* was always written by Garvey and began to acquire a semisacred quality. It was always read aloud at the Sunday evening service of the local UNIA chapters.[68]

The UNIA, however, was far more than an organization devoted to mere propaganda. As Garvey wrote, "The race can only be saved through a solid industrial foundation." In 1919, Garvey launched the Black Star Line, a steamship company "owned, controlled, and manned by Negroes, to reach the Negro peoples of the world."[69] Later that same year he announced the foundation of the Negro Factories Corporation in order to "build and operate factories in the big industrial centers of the United States, Central America, the West Indies, and Africa to manufacture every marketable commodity."[70] The formation of the Black Cross Nurses demonstrated the ability of the coming independent nation to aid and assist the needy. The establishment of a uniformed army, the African Legion, was a visible expression of the preparedness to liberate and defend the black nation with force if necessary.

"No one knows when the hour of Africa's redemption cometh," Garvey wrote. "It is in the wind. It is coming. One day, like a storm, it will be here."[71] The expectations ran high in August 1920, when Garvey and the UNIA called a world convention in the newly acquired headquarters, the Liberty Hall, in Harlem. Staged as "The International Convention of the Negro Peoples of the World," the meeting drew delegates from all over the United States, the West Indies, Central and South America, Europe, Asia and Africa.[72] The convention, with an estimated 25,000 participants and listeners, was opened with an impressive parade. The delegates drafted and signed a black Declaration of Rights.[73] A national anthem, "Ethiopia, Thou Land of Our Fathers," was adopted together with a national flag in red, green, and black. Garvey was elected Provisional President of the African Republic and designated a ministry for the government in exile. Influenced by the Freemasons, a set of honorific orders—for example, the Knights of the Nile and Distinguished Service Order of the Nile—was created. "Up you mighty race! You can accomplish what you want!" Garvey thundered and the fever rose high.

For the next few years the UNIA was at its peak, but troubles soon were to become evident. The activities of the militant nationalist organization attracted the attention of the security police from concerned colonial powers, that is Britain and France.[74] In 1919, the Bureau of Investigation of the Department of Justice, the FBI's predecessor, placed Garvey under surveillance.[75] In charge of the operation was a young agent who later would become one of the most powerful men in the United States, J. Edgar Hoover. According to Richard G. Powers, Hoover was determined to destroy Garvey: "Hoover wrote his superiors that while 'unfortunately' Garvey had not yet violated any federal laws that would permit his deportation, perhaps a fraud case involving Garvey's promotion of the steamship line might be a way of getting him out of the country."[76] The opportunity Hoover waited for came in 1922. Garvey was perhaps too much of a visionary idealist to be a successful day-to-day director of a commercial enterprise. Lacking relevant shipping knowledge, the board members of the Black Star Line easily became the victims of confidence men. They paid excessive prices for dilapidated ships and had in general far greater expenses than income in the few trading expeditions that took place at all. While this was going on, the Bureau scrutinized each move. At least once, they threw a wrench into the works of the Black Star Line. When the company made a downpayment for the *S.S. Orion,* in 1921, William J. Burns, director of the Bureau, briefed the board of directors of the company selling the ship. Based on Burns's allegations, the seller concluded that UNIA in reality was "the communist party which is affiliated with the Russian Soviet Government" and the purchase was never concluded.[77]

In January 1922, Garvey was arrested on a charge of using the mails for fraud.[78] The attorney claimed that Garvey and three assistants had knowingly and "with criminal intent used the mails to promote the sale of Black Star stock after they were aware that the financial condition of the line was hopeless."[79] Garvey dismissed his lawyers and rather arrogantly took charge of his own defense. He was sentenced to a maximum of five years in prison and a $1,000 fine. While released on bond and awaiting an appeal, Garvey's hazardous ventures continued with new companies and visionary projects. Perhaps a remark by an UNIA member, stranded in Liberia because of his organization's mismanagement, can summarize the outcome: "This movement is not doing the right thing; their speech is alright, but their business is far from what it should be."[80] In 1925, Garvey's appeal was rejected and he was sent to the Atlanta penitentiary. Two years later Garvey was released and deported to Jamaica. He was hailed as a national hero and tried energetically to revive the UNIA. After another peak at the sixth International Convention held in Kingston in 1929, the UNIA split into United States– and Jamaica-based factions. This marked the final blow; by 1935 Garvey had moved to London, where he died five years later.

The rapid rise and fall of the UNIA represents the climax of classic black nationalism. With the advent of Garvey, the nationalist tradition was popularized and dispersed throughout the African American community. After an intermediary period of diminishing influence, black nationalism made a comeback in the mid-1960s and again in the mid-1980s. Presently, Garvey is back at the forefront of the debate. For the Afrocentric neonationalists, Garvey is one of the founding fathers and his *Philosophy and Opinions* recommended reading. Garvey is frequently invoked in the lyrics of hip-hop, ragga, and reggae, the music of the black nationalist religions that carried on the legacy of the black Moses. Like other great men, he grew even greater beyond death. In the early 1990s, Garvey's prophetic words in his first message from the Atlanta penitentiary seemed close to fulfillment: "When I am dead wrap the mantle of the Red, Black and Green around me, for in the new life I shall rise with God's grace and blessing to lead the millions up the heights of triumph with the colors that you well know. Look for me in the whirlwind or the storm, look for me all around you, for, with God's grace, I shall come and bring with me countless millions of black slaves who have died in America and the West Indies and the millions in Africa to aid you in the fight for Liberty, Freedom and Life."[81]

2

The Crescent of the Occident:
Islam in Black America prior to 1930

===

This chapter will examine African American Islam prior to the birth of the Nation. The first part is dedicated to the African Muslims who were brought as slaves to *dar al-kufr,* the abode of the unbelievers. After a short note on the early Christian black nationalist encounter with Islam, the latter part deals with the Moorish Science Temple (MST). As the first movement to fuse black nationalism with Islam, the MST is an important predecessor to the Nation of Islam.

Black Muslim Slaves and Scholars   Islam has had a long but hidden presence in America. Some researchers trace the first Muslims in the New World to pre-Columbian times. Clyde Winters argues that Muslims from Mali may have been the first to establish colonies in America.[1] Ivan Van Sertima proposes a pre-Islamic African settlement in Central America,[2] and like historian Kofi Wangara finds it likely that Islam made its first contact with the Americas through one or two pre-Columbian expeditions from the Mali Empire. In 1311, the Muslim ruler Abubakari II sent an expedition of two hundred master ships and an equal number of supply ships west over the Atlantic. As only one ship returned and its crew was unable to report the fate of the others, Abubakari II himself led a fleet of two thousand ships sailing westward. Abubakari II never returned, and Van Sertima suggests that he actually reached America.[3] Wangara and Leo Weiner both argue that a pre-Columbian African trade was established with the Americas and discuss possible Africa, particularly Muslim Maningoan, influences on Central American Indian language, religion, and art.[4] In a 1992 speech, Libyan leader Mu'ammar al-Qadhdhafi supported the thesis of a pre-Columbian Muslim arrival to the New

World, adding his suggestion that the continent was "discovered" by the Muslim Amir Ka.[5]

Speculation aside, we find Muslims among the early Spanish explorers. African Muslims, either enslaved or hired, worked as navigators, guides, and sailors for the Christian conquistadores. Some of these Muslim pioneers opened new avenues into the New World. The first non-Indian to enter present-day New Mexico and Arizona was a black Muslim known as Estevanico. He established the first documented contacts with the Hopi and Zuni civilizations and is said to have planted in 1539 the first crop of wheat in America.[6]

The vast majority of African Muslims who arrived in what is the present-day United States were not adventurers but captives, brought to the continent in the holds of slave ships. Allan D. Austin calculates that 10 percent of the slaves exported to the colonies were Muslims. After the War of Independence, the number of Muslims increased to an estimated 15 percent due to the new Americans' preference for slaves from Senegambia, an area with large Islamic populations.[7] Some of the traded Muslims were well-educated *ulama* (Islamic scholars) and *fuqaha* (Islamic jurists), while others were ordinary members of the *umma* (the community of believers). Most of these Muslim slaves remain anonymous, and only a limited number of individuals emerge from the mist of contemporary indifference to become tangible for later historians. These individuals share a dramatic life story with their anonymous coreligionists, but they have managed to attract the attention of some philanthropist, abolitionist, journalist, or slave owner who cared to put their stories on paper. A few outstanding Muslims wrote their own autobiographies, in English or Arabic, for the world to know. Unfortunately, the scope of this study excludes the possibility of animating them all here, but a few exemplary voices from the past will illustrate the early presence of Islam in North America.

Abdul Rahahman, a Fulani military leader and a well-educated Muslim scholar, was ambushed in 1788, brought to the coast, and sold to a British trader. After an extremely long and rough journey from the Gambia to Spanish New Orleans, via the Caribbean Sea and the Mississippi River, he was sold to a farmer who renamed him "Prince," because a Mandingo translator could tell of his royal family. Returning to his masters after a brief period as a runaway slave, he was put in charge of the farmer's cattle and made an overseer. Around 1807 Rahahman met an old acquaintance, John Coates Cox, while in Natchez on an errand. Cox had been given asylum and medical treatment by Rahahman's father, the commander in the great city of Timbo. After having been restored to health, Cox was safely escorted to the Gambia River, where he could embark on a British ship and sail home. Although Cox's efforts to purchase and free Rahahman failed, Prince became a local celebrity when Cox's story became publicly known. Southern papers published his autobiography, and the American Colonization Society (ACS) took an interest in him. Would not this royal scholar be a perfect agent for the society, spreading the gospel in West Africa? Wisely, Rahahman played his part of the game. When asked to write in Arabic, Rahahman wrote, he said, the Lord's Prayer to the amusement of his audience. Under the guise of evangelizing Africans living under the Islamic yoke, Rahahman raised enough money to purchase his family's freedom. To the disappointment of the ACS, Rahahman never abandoned his faith. Upon reaching the shores of Africa, he openly resumed his Islamic identity, and the Lord's Prayer proved upon examination to be the *Fatih,* the opening surah of the Qur'an.[8]

On Selapo Island, Georgia, we find another Muslim slave, Bilali, who was a Fulani from Timbo and an Islamic scholar who must have completed a high level of education in Islamic jurisprudence, judging from the manuscripts he left behind. One document proved not to be the diary the researchers had expected to find but a series of excerpts from the *Risala,* a legal treatise of the Maliki school, the Islamic legal school that is dominant in Western Africa. Furthermore, the subject of the excerpt dealt with the prescribed relations between masters and slaves, which indicates that Bilali compared his experiences with the considerably different Islamic view on the subject in question. In 1813, during the second American war with England, Bilali was entrusted with military leadership over eighty armed slaves. He pledged to defend the island if attacked, and assured his master that he could "answer for every Negro of the true faith, but not for the Christian dogs you own,"[9] a statement indicating a Muslim congregation in the area. When he died many years later, Bilali was buried with his Qur'an and his prayer rug.[10]

Omar Ibn Said was born around the year 1770 in Futa Toro, a town by the Senegal River. He worked as a teacher in Keba, west of the Niger, before he was captured and brought to North Carolina. After his owner treated him with great cruelty, Omar ran away into the woods; he was later captured and held in prison in Fayetteville, North Carolina, where he astonished his jailer by writing a succession of lines in "strange characters" with coal on the prison walls. The news of this remarkable inmate reached the governor's brother, who purchased Omar and gave him a relatively better future. Omar Ibn Said is then believed to have converted to Christianity, but some signs indicate that this was either a fake conversion, as in the case of Rahahman, or a blending of the two faiths. For instance, several of the Christian texts written by Omar, such as the Lord's Prayer or the Twenty-third Psalm, are each preceded by the *Bismillah,* the introduction to the surahs of the Qur'an: "In the name of Allah, the Beneficent, the Merciful."[11]

Another slave, Job Ben Solomon, managed to write at least two complete versions of the Qur'an from memory,[12] which proves that the words of God through his prophet could be kept intact in the *dar al-kufr* (the abode of unbelievers). But did Islam survive beyond the first generation of slaves? Could Muslim slaves establish an Islamic tradition by instructing their children and evangelizing among their fellow slave workers? Was the rise of a black Muslim movement among Southern migrants in the Northern cities the surfacing of a hidden tradition? Is there a connection between this possible Islamic tradition and the later expansion of Islam in the African American community?

Based on the scarce sources available, it seems that the first two questions can be answered in the affirmative. Documents show that Muslim families gave their children Islamic names and education. We know from an observer who visited the Sea Islands in the late 1850s that, for example, the family of the above-mentioned Bilali were practicing Muslims. In 1940, a team of researchers published a series of interviews with ex-slaves from this region. On Sapelo Island they met Shad Hall, one of Belali's descendants. "All ub em sho pray on duh bead," Hall recalled. "Dey weah duh string uh beads on duh wais. Sometime duh string on duh neck. Dey pray at sun-up and face duh sun on duh knees an bow tuh it tree times, kneelin on a lill mat."[13] Another Bilali descendant relates the following memory of Bilali and his wife: "Bilali an he wife Phoebe pray on duh bead. Dey wuz bery puhticluh bout duh time dey pray an dey bery regluh bou duh hour. Wen duh sun come up, wen it straight obuh head an wen it set, das duh time dey pray. Dey bow tuh duh sun an hab a lill mat tuh kneel on. Duh beads is on a long string. Bilali he pull bead an he say, 'Belali, Hakabara, Mahamadu.' Phoebe she say, 'Ameen, Ameen.' "[14] The ethnologists also found some descendants of a small Muslim congregation on nearby St. Simon Island. Ex-slave Ben Sullivan remembered native Africans who were practicing Muslims. Among others, he recalled a man named Israel who "pray a lot wid a book he hab wut he hide, an he take a lill mat an he say he prayuhs on it." Another Muslim friend of the past was Daphnee who "weah loose wite veil on he head . . . [and] he bow two aw tree times in the middle uh duh prayuh."[15]

The memory of Islam thus proved to be alive as late as the 1930s, the decade in which the Nation of Islam was founded. It is, however, obvious that we encounter a memory, not a living faith. While some Muslim slaves were able to pass their faith on to their children, Islam seems to have been transformed into a curiosity in the minds of their grandchildren. The essentials of Islam appear to have been lost over time. This is evident in the case of several descendants who allege that their forefathers used to "bow to the sun," something a Muslim would never do. The Christianization of African Muslims may have passed through a syncretistic stage in certain areas. Reverend Charles Colcock Jones of Georgia wrote in 1842 that slaves in his district "have been known to accommodate Christianity to Mohammedanism. 'God' say they, 'is Allah, and Jesus Christ is Mohammed—the religion is the same, but different countries have different names.' "[16] The ex-slave Rachel Anderson remembers the harvest festivities customary to the Sea Island that show some Muslim influence: "We hab a big feas. All night we shouts ab in duh mawnin right at sunrise we pray an bow low tuh duh sun."[17] Unlike the situation in Brazil and the Caribbean, it is reasonable to conclude that Islam slowly disappeared in the black community during the epoch of slavery. The rise of Islam in twentieth-century black America cannot be attributed to a surfacing of an unbroken underground tradition, although the existence of black Muslim slaves has a given role in the rhetoric of modern black Islamic preachers. An Islamic religious work, written in Arabic by a black slave and Muslim scholar, is for Imam Isa of the Ansaaru Allah Community "evidence that the first language of the Black slaves residing today in America was Arabic and that Al Islaam was their true way of life when in Africa."[18] This notion of Islam as an African religion is a key factor in the Muslim revival in the United States.

When black nationalist intellectuals in the late nineteenth century rediscovered Africa, they also encountered Islam. They found great Islamic civilizations in West Africa and made note of the relatively harmonious integration of Islam into the various local African cultures. Bishop Turner and Edward Wilmot Blyden both launched the vision of a future Christian Africa as the redeemed empire and dedicated much of their lives to this end. Despite their Christian conviction, they were both impressed by the accomplishments of African Islam, which they readily acknowledged. Bishop Turner expressed his admiration of the well-educated black Islamic scholars he found active in West Africa.[19] Through his studies and personal experience, Blyden became aware of the different status blacks assumed in Islam as compared to Christianity. "The Negro came into contact with Christianity as a slave and as a follower at a distance. He came into contact with Mohammedanism as a man, and often as a leader."[20] Blyden frequently lectured on "The Qur'an in Africa," emphasizing the significance of Surah thirty-one, named after the black sage Luqman the Wise. God "gave Luqman wisdom," and the advice Luqman gave his son is extended to all Muslims. Islam thus gives tribute to a black man as the pattern of wisdom for all believers to emulate, which Blyden compared to the intellectual incapacity and mental inferiority ascribed to blacks by the church of his time.[21] Blyden criticized the attitude of contemporary white Christian missionaries in their relations with the African people. The colonial variety of Christianity was designed to perpetuate racial inequality, Blyden argued, contrasting this with the Muslim message of universal brotherhood: "Islam extinguishes all distinctions founded upon race, color or nationality."[22]

Besides Luqman, the single most powerful symbol for the connection between Africa and Islam is Bilal Ibn Rabah. He was a black slave of Abyssinian origin owned by Ibn Khalaf of the mighty Ummayyah clan in Mecca. Bilal was one of the first Muslims recorded in history and was severely brutalized when his master tried in vain to force him to become an apostate. Abu Bakr then ransomed Bilal, who became a close companion of the Prophet Muhammad. Bilal had a melodious voice and became Islam's first *mu'adhdhin,* the reciter of the call to prayer.[23] The fact that a black former slave is the prototype for the Muslim call that five times a day resounds from the minarets of the mosques is given a tremendous symbolic significance: it is the black man who leads humanity to God.

Islam thus could be presented as an African religion, while Christianity became associated with colonialism and slavery. In Islam many blacks found a faith that was on their side, traditionally opposed to European expansionism. Islam thereby could serve as a vehicle for black unity and resistance, as it did in the creed of the Nation of Islam. Elijah Muhammad taught that "Islam is the natural religion of the Black Nation,"[24] while the blacks could expect nothing good from the Christian church: "There is no hope for us in Christianity; it is a religion organized by the enemies (the white race) of the Black Nation to enslave us to the white race's rule. But our unity under the crescent with our Allah's guidance can get us anything we desire and some of this earth we can call our own."[25] The Nation of Islam was not the first faith to claim Islam as the African Americans' "original" and "natural" religion. It was preceded by another urban-based nationalist religion, the Moorish Science Temple, which helped pave the way for the NOI.

Noble Drew Ali and the Moorish Gospel   Noble Drew Ali (1886–1929) presented himself as a prophet, or "an Angel of Allah," sent to bring "the everlasting Gospel of ALLAH."[26] Born Timothy Drew in North Carolina, he migrated to Newark, New Jersey, to work as an expressman. According to legend, he made a pilgrimage to North Africa where he studied with Egyptian Islamic scholars and received permission from the King of Morocco to teach Islam in the African American community. Other legends claim that his father was a Moroccan and his mother a Cherokee, who both were initiated into the Modernist Islamist Salafi movement of the famous Jamal al-Afghani during his later visits to the United States in the early 1880s.[27] In 1913, Ali resumed a Moorish identity and established the first Adept Chamber of the Moorish Science Temple of America (MST) in Newark. Following the slow but steady growth of his following, new temples were founded in Pittsburgh, Detroit, and some sites in the South before 1925, when Noble Drew Ali moved to Chicago and established a headquarters and what later became the largest Moorish chapter.

The Moorish Science Temple combined the legacy of Marcus Garvey with the notion of Islam as the old-time religion of the black man. Its spokespersons rejected all terms previously used for the African nation in America. In act 6 of the *Divine Constitution,* the Prophet instructs his followers that "they are not Negroes, Colored Folks, Black People or Ethiopians, because these names were given to slaves by slave holders."[28] They should now openly declare their true identity as "Moorish Americans," "descendants of the ancient Moabites," later known as Morrocans.[29] The Moabites were part of the divine "Asiatic nation," the original inhabitants of the earth and progenitors of all nonwhite nations.[30]

The physical part of man was created in the Garden of Eden in the Holy City of Mecca in the land of Canaan. Seeking new land, the Moabites migrated into Africa and received permission from Pharaoh to settle in the northwest, where they founded the great Moroccan empire.[31] Before long the Moorish civilization flourished. Prior to the giant earthquake that created the Atlantic Ocean, the dominion of the Moroccan Empire included all of Africa and extended across Atlantis into present-day

North, Central, and South America.[32] As long as the Moors remained faithful to their ancient heritage, Allah blessed them with prosperity. Generations later, the Moors lost their racial consciousness, which ultimately caused their downfall: "Through sin and disobedience every nation has suffered slavery, due to the fact that they honored not the creed and principles of their forefathers. That is why the nationality of the Moors was taken away from them in 1774 and the word negro, black and colored, was given to the Asiatics of America who were of Moorish descent, because they honored not the principle of their mother and father, and strayed after the gods of Europe of whom they knew nothing."[33] But the time of suffering is soon to end. The tribulations experienced are but material reflections of a spiritual battle. The original Asiatic man has throughout history been in constant struggle with the Devil, who resides in man as his lower self.[34] To assist man, the love of God manifested in flesh in the Moorish prophet Jesus.[35] His crucifixion marks the beginning of the end for the Devil. Jesus was then reincarnated in the prophet Muhammad, who in 1453 succeeded in partially fettering and then decapitating Satan.[36] To complete the cycle of racial redemption, God chose "North America to make his headquarters in the West."[37] Noble Drew Ali is Jesus Christ and the prophet Muhammad reincarnated, the third and final carnal manifestation of Allah, sent "to redeem men from their sinful ways; and to warn them of the great wrath which is sure to come upon the earth."[38]

In 1927, the Moorish Science Temple published the *Holy Koran,* which is not to be confused with the Holy Qur'an of the orthodox Muslims. The *Holy Koran* of Noble Drew Ali is a pamphlet of sixty-three pages. The first chapter deals with the "creation and fall of man." Man is a "thought of Allah," infinite, eternal, and uncreated as his Owner. This is the true ontology of "spirit-man." Man is a seed of Allah holding in himself the attributes of Allah, with true divine potential. For a seed to grow and unfold it must be planted in soil. The same applies to the seed of God. The cosmos is divided into three stages of divine emanations with decreasing speeds of vibration: the plane of spirit, the plane of soul, and the plane of things made manifest. Creative Fate gave to spirit-man a soul and a body of flesh, that he may function on all three cosmological planes. Man must learn a multitude of lessons on each plane to realize his divine potential: "Perfected man must pass through all the ways of life, and so a carnal was full manifest, a nature that sprang forth from fleshy things. Without a foe a soldier never knows his strength, and thought must be developed by the exercise of strength. And so his carnal nature soon became a foe that man must fight, that he may be the strength of Allah made manifest. . . . When man has conquered carnal things his garb of flesh will then have served its purpose well and it will fall; will be no more."[39] Emancipated, the soul-man has to struggle on the soul plane to complete his victories. "Unnumbered foes" will seek to destroy him, and these have to be defeated. But now Allah is leading, so there is no doubt of the outcome. The soul coming this far cannot fail: "When man has conquered every foe upon the plane of soul the seed will have full opened out, will have unfold in the Holy Breath. The garb of soul will then have served its purpose well and man will need it never more, and it will pass and be no more and man will then attain unto the blessedness of perfection and one with Allah."[40] The student of esoteric Christianity will perhaps recognize the anthropology described above. The introductory chapter of the *Holy Koran* is taken verbatim from an introductory text of the *Aquarian Gospel of Jesus the Christ,* written by Levi H. Dowling (1844–1911) and published in 1907.[41] The only deviation is that the word "God" has been replaced by "Allah."

According to Ewa S. Dowling, "scribe to the Messenger," Levi studied etheric vibration and meditated for forty years before he received his commission from Visel, the Goddess of Wisdom or the Holy Breath, "to be the message bearer for the coming age."[42] Levi's mind was capable of tuning in "the Akashic Records," which register every thought and deed on an etheric plane. Collecting and translating these Akashic impressions, Levi learned about the redeeming gnosis, the cosmic cycles of ages, and the Christ made manifest in each age. According to the religious philosophy of Levi, our solar system completes a grand cycle in 26,000 years by passing backward through the zodiac. Each sign corresponds to an age of approximately 2,100 years. Man was given his carnal hide in the Taurian age, Abraham lived in the Arian age, Jesus of Nazareth lived in the Piscean age, and the world is now about to enter the Aquarian age. Aquarius is an air sign, and the age to come is preeminently a spiritual age in which the lessons of the gnostic master Jesus the Christ can be fully comprehended by the masses. The Christ of the Piscean age said, "I came to show the possibilities of man; what I have done all men may do, and what I am all men shall be."[43]

By tuning in the thoughts, words, and deeds of Jesus of Nazareth, Levi could tell the complete and true history of his life and career. Jesus was not always the Christ but received his Christship by virtue of an exemplary life of meditation and advanced spiritual studies. Mary and Elizabeth, the chosen mothers of the long promised sons, had been educated by spiritual masters in a sacred grove in Zoan, Egypt. They transmitted this esoteric knowledge to their sons, Jesus and John, who thereafter received educations relating to their different tasks. John was brought to the temple of Sakara in Egypt where he "became a master mind and learned the duties of the harbinger."[44] In the meantime, Jesus traveled through India, Tibet, Persia, Assyria, Greece, and Egypt. He studied with Brahmanic priests, Lamas, Magians, and other religious masters before going to Sakara to complete his studies in the Temple of the Brotherhood. There Jesus passes six Brotherhood tests before he received the highest degree, "the Christ," and left the temple as a redeemer.[45] The work of Jesus the Christ as described by Levi is, as noted, at odds with the version of the New Testament. The Christ is foremost a mastermind, a teacher of Gnosis, showing man how to conquer his lower self, the necessary victory before man can enter the plane of soul. The teachings of the Christ were too advanced to be fully understood by the masses of his age but will come to fruition with the coming Aquarian age.

As noted by Abbie Whyte, a large part of the *Aquarian Gospel of Jesus the Christ* was plagiarized by Noble Drew Ali.[46] Nineteen chapters, close to half of the *Holy Koran,* are copied from the work of Levi. However, this is not acknowledged by Noble Drew Ali, who instead refers to an esoteric Muslim tradition: "The reason these lessons have not been known is because the Moslems of India, Egypt and Palestine had these secrets and kept them back from the outside world, and when the time appointed by Allah they loosened the keys and freed these secrets, and for the first time in ages have these secrets been delivered in the hands of the Moslems in America."[47] With the exception of a few necessary alterations, the lessons are plagiarized verbatim from the *Aquarian Gospel.* Concepts such as "God" or "church" are replaced with the counterparts perceived to be more Islamic: "Allah" and "temple." The Moorish Science Temple taught that Jesus, like all other manifestations of Allah, was black. A passage in the *Aquarian Gospel* indicating another race for the principal actor is consequently altered. Mary and Joseph return to Jerusalem to seek their missing youngster and ask the guards, "Have you seen Jesus, a fair-haired boy, with deep blue eyes, twelve years of age, about these courts?"[48] When this event is related in the *Holy Koran* we are simply told that "Mary asked the guards had they seen Jesus, a little boy about twelve years old."[49] Another feature of the Moorish edition is its selective character.

The *Aquarian Gospel* is composed of 182 chapters, of which only eighteen are included in the *Holy Koran*.[50] I have not been able to detect any deeper logic that would explain the exclusion of the other parts. It appears as though the author of the *Holy Koran* wanted to present a shortened and Moorishized version of the *Aquarian Gospel* and simply included the chapters judged to be most significant for this purpose.

These omissions had negative effects for the *Holy Koran* as literature. Chapter 15 of the *Holy Koran* is chapter 65 of the *Aquarian Gospel*. It relates the story of Jesus' forty days in the desert, where he victoriously wrestled with the Devil. The following chapter of the *Holy Koran* is chapter 168 of the *Aquarian Gospel,* in which the reader is suddenly placed in the middle of another drama. Jesus has already been arrested and Pontius Pilate makes a final effort to release him. Without knowledge of the preceding, omitted events, the reader can only be confused. In the *Holy Koran* as in the *Aquarian Gospel,* we follow Jesus to India. With some minor gaps, the *Holy Koran* relates the religious discussions held between Jesus and Hindu and Buddhist scholars. While the *Aquarian Gospel* continues the unfolding of the secret gnosis by an account of Jesus' meetings with sages from Persia, Assyria, and Greece, the *Holy Koran* takes a shortcut and abruptly returns the principal actor back to Egypt, thereby making inexplicable his later postmortem manifestation among the brethren in Greece.

The Silent Brotherhood of Gnostic sages in the *Aquarian Gospel* and the *Holy Koran* was in the Moorish creed a secret Muslim society, guarding the hidden sacred truths for centuries before passing them on to Noble Drew Ali. This secret fraternity suggests a Masonic influence on the thoughts of Levi and Noble Drew Ali. Chapters 5 and 6 of the *Holy Koran* (chapters 20–21 in the *Aquarian Gospel*) reveal Masonic themes. An Indian Prince had observed the young Jesus disputing with the priests at a Jewish feast and had been duly impressed. Eager to meet with him, the prince went to Nazareth where he saw Jesus climbing up a twelve-step ladder, while carrying a compass, square, and ax.[51] These tools have a symbolic significance in Masonry, as they are the visual expression of the spiritual tools instrumental to the implementation of the aim of the secret society: the mental reconstruction of the destroyed Temple. Jesus gives a similar elaboration on the craft symbolism: "These tools remind me of the one we handle in the workshop of the mind where things were out of thoughts and where we build up character. We use the square to measure all our lines, to straighten out the crooked places of the way, and make the corners of our conduct square. We use the compass to draw circles round our passions and desires to keep them in the bounds of righteousness. We use the axe to cut away the knotty, useless and ungainly parts and make the character symmetrical. . . . And on the twelve-step ladder we ascend until we reach the pinnacle of that which life is spent to build—the Temple of Perfected Man."[52] Moors and Masons share a number of tenets. Organized in temple branches, known respectively as chambers and lodges, they seek to restore a fallen humanity through the esoteric wisdom derived from a secret circle of Eastern sages. Moorish legends claim that Noble Drew Ali himself was taken to Zoan, Egypt, and was initiated into the same secret fraternity as Jesus, while other legends claim that the prophet had been a high-level Shriner. The Moorish Science Temple is not, however, an offshoot of black Masonry. This is obvious, as the *Holy Koran* excludes a key Masonic sequence from the *Aquarian Gospel:* the chapters that describe how Jesus passes through the hierarchy of mental stages by a series of secret initiations and finally reaches the highest degree: Christship.[53]

Besides Masonry and the Gnosticism of Levi, the Moorish creed is influenced by Islam, principally Ismailiyya, Ahmadiyya, and Sufism, as well as the black nationalist tradition. The second half of the *Holy Koran* is devoted to black nationalist themes. By adhering to a strict standard of conduct considered to be their original way of life, the process of racial improvement would commence. A Moorish American abstains from drugs, luxury, gossip, and criminality; he is honest, just, and generous. Traditional family values are central, as is the need for cleanliness, education, and hard work. The Blackman is a thought of Allah, temporarily in a carnal hide in the world of things made manifest. The black aboriginal culture is the cradle of civilization. Following a period of racial greatness, the Moors lost world dominion to the white race, which they had begun to admire. With the advent of Noble Drew Ali, the third and final manifestation of the love of Allah, the black American would unite as a man and regain knowledge of his divine identity. To prepare the black community for the new gospel, Allah sent a harbinger: "In these modern days there came a forerunner, who was divinely prepared by the great God-Allah and his name is Marcus Garvey, who did teach and warn the nations of the earth to prepare to meet the coming Prophet; who was to bring the true and divine Creed of Islam, and his name is Noble Drew Ali."[54] Marcus Garvey thus assumed a pivotal position in the Moorish creed. As did his forerunner, Noble Drew Ali urged the black community to separate from their former slave masters as a road toward racial redemption. The *Holy Koran* 48:6–7 declares: "We, as a pure and clean nation descended from the inhabitants of Africa, do not desire to amalgamate or marry into the families of the pale skin nations of Europe. Neither serve the gods of their religion, because our forefathers are the true and divine founders of the first religious creed, for the redemption and salvation of mankind on earth. Therefore we return the Church and Christianity to the European Nations, as it was prepared by their forefathers for their salvation."[55] To mark their new awareness of their true and divine identity, the Moors dressed in what they perceived as the original Islamic fashion of northwestern Arabs. All men wore long white robes and red fezzes, and all women shielded their heads and bodies. On ceremonial occasions, the men would wear Turkish-styled festive clothing, while the women would wear red turbans and yellow Turkish-inspired dresses. The believers further changed their American names to Moorish names by adding an "El" or a "Bey." Noble Drew Ali issued a "National and Identity card" for all of them to carry, and a Moorish national flag was used as a complement to the Star-Spangled Banner. The Moors adopted the flag of the Kingdom of Morocco, which is red with a green five-pointed star in the middle and is said to represent love, truth, peace, freedom, and justice. According to Moorish legend, the flag is 10,000 years old and was stolen by the United States administration in the eighteenth century, when it deprived the blacks of their identity. Noble Drew Ali is said to have retrieved it from the storeroom of the White House, after which President Woodrow Wilson authorized the prophet to teach Islam and return the African American to his true nationality.[56]

Arthur H. Fauset reported that members were taught that an Islamic sign of the final days, a shining star within a crescent moon, had been seen in the heavens. This was interpreted to mean that the turn of the present cycle was about to close. Soon, the destruction of white supremacy would be enacted as the day of the Moors would be ushered in. A series of racial disturbances involving MST members took place. In Chicago, members confronted whites on the streets singing the praise of their prophet who had freed them from the curse of the Anglo-Americans.[57] Disputes with police authorities followed and Noble Drew Ali ordered his fellow Moors to "cease all radical or agitating speeches" and to "stop flashing your cards before Europeans as this only causes confusion."[58] In an "Additional Law," the prophet cautioned his members not to "use any assertion against the American flag or speak radical against the church or any member of any organized group."[59] Far from preaching rebellion, the Moorish Science Temple kept a low political profile. Members were advised to respect the inequalities of social stratification. The *Holy Koran* instructed "The honor of a servant is his fidelity; his highest virtues are submission and obedience." "Be patient therefore, under the reproofs of thy master; and when he rebuketh thee, answer not again. The silence of thy resignation shall not be forgotten."[60]

The absence of social revolutionary rhetoric, however, did not prevent the Moors from being targeted by American police. The mere existence of organized blacks, no matter how law-abiding, seems to have been sufficient reason to make security agents alert. During the depression, for instance, the Moorish Science Temple began to be monitored by the FBI when an agent came across a flyer judged to be subversive. In the flyer, the Moors interpreted the depression as a sign of the coming wrath of God. Money was "the root of all evil" causing the decay of human civilization: "On account of money, this world has become a Hell to all nations and to all men. . . . Money is the lock, politics is the chain to freedom. The lock and the chain have been broken."[61] The special agent who obtained this flyer reported back to his office that the Bey heading the local Adept Chamber of the MST "was a fanatic on the subject of the equality for all races."[62] The surveillance intensified during World War II when the MST was suspected of being "hostile to the interests of the [U.S.] government."[63] The war was believed by many Moors to be "a war between the white and colored races," and at least one Moorish organizer taught that the Moors would not be "molested" but would benefit from the victory of their Asiatic brethren.[64] Agents infiltrated all Moorish chapters, but the Moors' alleged collaboration with the Japanese could not be confirmed. The average notion was quite the opposite, as stated by the Newark division of the FBI: "Aside from one or two cases, there has been no trouble caused by members regarding compliance with the Selective Service Act, and investigations made here to date failed to disclose any pro-Japanese or un-American teachings."[65] After the war, the FBI's interest in the MST diminished to routine surveillance and was concentrated on other black nationalist organizations such as the Nation of Islam (as I discuss in chapter 4).

Years earlier, an event relating to the police had occurred that would dramatically alter the future of the Moorish Science Temple. Following the example of Marcus Garvey, the Moors established "the Moorish Industrial Group" and founded small businesses in various fields. Besides operating restaurants and barber shops, the sale of religious paraphernalia proved to be a lucrative venture. In 1929, a number of top MST officials made considerable profits, selling relics, charms, magical potions, and Moorish pictures. When the prophet disapproved of further advancement in this area, his leadership was challenged by Sheik Claude Green, a former MST business manager.[66] Green, who was a Tuskegee graduate and a real estate broker, headed a splinter group that took control of the Unity Hall in Chicago, ousting Noble Drew Ali from the MST headquarters. Five days later Green was shot and stabbed to death in his office by a hit squad.[67] Searching for the murderers, the police arrested a number of Moors, the prophet included. The arrest of Noble Drew Ali provoked Moorish unrest, and the police had to release the prophet after failing to obtain any relevant information from him.[68] The freed prophet was ill and never recovered. He died in his home on July 20, 1929. Many Moors blamed his death on the police and violent upheavals followed.[69] In line with the MST teachings, some followers believed that Noble Drew Ali soon would return reincarnated. One Moor said at the funeral that "the prophet's spirit will come back to enter one of the governors."[70]

In the aftermath of the prophet's death, the Moorish Science Temple split over the issue of successorship, and two principal national branches soon crystallized. One fraction claimed that Noble Drew Ali was reincarnated on August 7, 1929, in the person of John Givens El, the prophet's chauffeur. Members of this group strictly observed the dietary laws, avoiding meat, eggs, alcohol, and tobacco. Male members neither shaved nor cut their hair.[71] Givens El died in 1945 and his movement split into seven divisions, with a 1994 total of thirty affiliated temples. The principal branch was taken over by Sheik Richardson Dingle El, who in 1975 declared himself to be Noble Drew Ali III.[72] The Givens El division was opposed by another, reportedly larger principal branch, headed by Charles Kirkman Bey, one of Noble Drew Ali's earliest converts. Bey's faction claimed to follow the spirit of Noble Drew Ali under the earthly leadership of his designated heir. Kirkman Bey reformed his branch, allowing males to shave and cut their hair, and was less strict in the observance of conduct and dietary laws.[73] Kirkman Bey died in 1959 and was succeeded by F. Nelson Bey (1959–67), J. Blakely Bey (1969–71), and the present leader, Robert Love El. The Kirkman division is still the main Moorish branch with more than 130 temples.[74]

In addition to these two principal divisions, a large number of competing smaller factions were established in subsequent years; most of these remained local, with a few claiming national status.[75] According to an estimate by Muhammad Al-Ahari Bektashi, Moorish groups total no more than 40,000 members.[76] The most successful of the new Moorish branches was established in the mid-1970s when the black Chicago street gang Black P Stone Nation acquired a Moorish identity, when its leader, Jeff Fort, converted in prison, taking the name Imam Malik and renaming the gang El Rukn. This development, which added some five thousand Moors to the South Side Chicago street scenery, is further discussed in chapter 8.

3

The Genesis of the Nation of Islam

—

This chapter will provide a brief account of the history of the Nation of Islam (NOI) between the years 1930 and 1975. The formative years of the NOI will be presented in the context of black urbanization. Some theories about the "true" identity of its founder will be accounted for, as will the subsequent evolution of the NOI, its basic tenets, and principal actors.

Behold, I Will Send You Elijah   In a modest shack in Bolds Springs, near Sandersville, Georgia, a quiet town between Atlanta and Macon, a baby boy was born on October 7, 1897. He was named Elijah Poole and was the sixth of Wali and Marie Poole's thirteen children. His father was a poor sharecropper who also served the local black population as a Baptist preacher. Living conditions were hard, as they were for the multitudes of sharecroppers, who at the yearly "settle" often would learn that they had made only a few dollars that year, if they did not end up in debt to the plantation owner.[1]

In the early 1900s, Elijah had a terrifying experience that would haunt him for the rest of his life. Disobeying his father's strict orders one day, he left the dirt road leading to the family cabin for a shortcut through the woods. Elijah hid at the sound of approaching boots and saw three white men leading a captured black man he recognized from town. He watched the white men brutalize and insult their captive before hanging him from the neck by a rope. After the three men strolled away, Elijah crawled out from his hiding place and made his way to the body. Standing beneath the lynched man, Elijah felt something wet dripping down onto his neck: blood. The scene froze in the child's mind and would serve as a constant reminder of the white man's evil nature.[2] As a symbol for white Christian order, a lynched Blackman dangling from a tree would be standard decoration in the NOI Temples Elijah would head as an adult.

When Elijah was six years old, his family moved to Weona, Georgia, where his father again tried to make ends meet as a sharecropper. The young Elijah had to quit school after the fourth grade in order to assist his father in the fields. His lack of formal education would later in his life be interpreted as evidence of his having received a unique guidance: the knowledge he displayed was explained as divine wisdom. Elijah left home at the age of sixteen and met Clara Evans, whom he married in 1917. The newlyweds returned to Weona and moved in with Elijah's brother Sam and his family, who lived in a shack belonging to a white plantation owner. When Clara gave birth in 1921 to Emmanuel, the first of the couple's eight children,[3] Elijah found work in Macon at the Cherokee Brick and Tile Company. Shortly thereafter he got a job at the Southern Railroad Company but was forced to leave after an incident with a white employer. In April 1923, the young couple decided to seek prosperity in the North.

By moving to Detroit, Elijah and Clara Poole became part of the great migration that would transform black America from a rural Southern into an urban, mainly Northern, population. The harsh realities of sharecropping on former slave plantations, combined with Jim Crow legislation, a revived Ku Klux Klan, and new machines that increasingly replaced manual labor drove the migration from the South. Further, blacks were drawn by the North's booming industry, as well as the exhortations of black spokespersons for Southern blacks to move North to "the promised land" and the fabulous stories told by relatives and friends who had migrated.[4] Between 1910 and 1970, six and a half million blacks moved from the South to the North. Although most moved after 1940, the black population in Chicago grew from 44,000 in 1910, to a total of 109,000 in 1920, and 234,000 in 1930.[5] Detroit's black population grew by 611 percent between the years 1910 and 1920.[6] In 1940, the United States' black population was still 77 percent Southern and 49 percent rural. By 1970, black America was only half Southern and less than 25 percent rural. The urbanization would continue, as the 1980 census showed that 85 percent of the African American population lived in urban areas.[7]

The routes north from the deep South were famous. Sons of the Mississippi Delta, such as Howlin' Wolf and Muddy Waters, would capture in music the blues of migration to the big, booming, strange cities. James Thomas's "Highway 61" and Big Joe William's "Highway 49" are but two of the canonical blues songs that lyricize the northern route along which blacks traveled by the thousands.[8] B. B. King, who also moved north from the Delta, captures the black experience, from the slave ships to the Chicago ghettos, in "Why I Sing the Blues":

> When I first got the blues, they brought me over on a ship
> Men were standin' over me and lashed me with a whip
> And everybody wanna know why I sing the blues
> Well I been around a long time, I've really paid my dues
> I've laid in the ghetto flats, cold and numb
> I heard the rats tell the bedbugs to give the roaches some
> Everybody wanna know why I'm singin' the blues
> Yea', I've been around a long time, people, I've paid my dues.[9]

The rural migrants had to find ways to adjust to the unfamiliar urban life. The expanding cities suffered from growing pains. When blacks moved into a neighborhood, whites moved out and certain areas rapidly deteriorated into slums. Racial and ethnic tensions grew. Occasionally, severe race riots exploded, like in the "Red Summer" of 1919. "Detroit is on fire and Chicago is burning down," Pine Top sings in the "East Chicago Blues," a song about a 1917 massacre on blacks.[10] Small-scale incidents of racial violence, such as firebombing or assault, occurred constantly, and the first black gangs were organized to defend the black neighborhoods against the raids of violent white racist gangs.[11] The revived Ku Klux Klan spread to the Midwest, and in 1924, a Klan candidate for mayor received more than one-third of the vote in Detroit.[12] A great number of new religious movements flourished in the African American settlements. Storefront churches were crowded together with the facilities of black Hebrews, Daddy Grace, Father Divine, the Moorish Science Temple, Ethiopian churches, black Masons, Elks, and other fraternities. Sociologically, these organization' appeal could be explained in part by the frame of reference they provided, through which the black experience could be understood. Membership offered, in addition, a fellowship and recommended fixed patterns of adjustive behavior in a new and changing reality.

The young Pooles moved into a neglected house in the originally Jewish area called Paradise Valley, which was rapidly transforming into a black ghetto. Shortly after arriving in Detroit, Elijah Poole was caught up in the Garvey fever and joined the Universal Negro Improvement Association (UNIA), along with numerous other Southern immigrants.[13] Elijah worked in different industrial plants in the 1920s, while four more children were added to his family, Ethel, Nathaniel, Lottie, and Herbert.[14] Trying to support his family, Elijah was forced out of his job in the Great Depression. With Elijah unemployed, the Poole family was compelled to live on welfare in order to supplement the salary Clara could bring home from her work as a maid for white families; occasionally, the Poole family lined up for the soup kitchens. Elijah joined the crowd of thousands of desperate workers that showed up outside manufacturing plants each morning hoping, mostly in vain, to get hired. As conditions worsened, Elijah sought escape in the bottle, which sometimes forced Clara and the children to go out looking for him.[15]

Still unemployed in 1931, Elijah heard of a mysterious prophet with a strange message; known both as W. D. Fard and Master Farad Muhammad, the prophet taught that Islam was the old-time religion of the African Americans.[16] He also claimed that they were not so-called Negroes on the bottom of society, but rather royals of the Original People from the holy city of Mecca. Elijah became intrigued and visited a meeting in a rented hall in Detroit. While sitting in the back, listening to Master Farad deliver a sermon, the Truth dawned upon Elijah. According to the historiography of the Nation of Islam, Elijah then forced his way through the crowd, took the prophet aside, and discreetly whispered: " 'I know who you are, you're God Himself.' The certain man [Master Farad Muhammad] whispered to him, 'that's right, but don't tell it now! It is not yet time for it to be known.' "[17] Thus commenced a unique relationship between God and the man who would become his Messenger in the latter days. Master Farad Muhammad visited his disciple each day for a period of nine months, corresponding to the length of pregnancy, to raise Elijah in divine wisdom. The two men were to collaborate closely for a period of three and a half years. Besides missionary and administrative tasks related to the movement God established, the Nation of Islam, God prepared Elijah for the coming tidings of which only He, at that time, had knowledge.

A Voice of One Crying in the Wilderness   Master Farad Muhammad made his first appearance in Detroit's black ghetto on July 4, 1930. In the trembling heat of a city summer, the prophet of God came disguised as a house-to-house peddler. Knocking on the doors of the newly urbanized Southerners, displaying his artifacts, raincoats, and fabric, he declared his true motive wherever he felt he had found fertile soil: he was an Arab from the holy city of Mecca on a mission from God, who wanted his chosen people back. The African Americans were of the lost, but finally found Nation of Islam, the tribe of Shabazz that had been stolen by the "Caucasian cave man" or the "blond blue-eyed devil" and brought as slaves to "the wilderness of North America." He had been assigned the task of reintroducing them to their original way of life. They must now return to the fold of Islam and relearn Arabic, their mother tongue. They should stop eating unhealthy soul food and return to their original diet, eating only once a day. Upon completing this process of reculturalization, God would redeem them by returning them to Mecca, capital of the promised land. There, they would experience no more suffering but would reunite with their kind and reassume their life as royalty in the most magnificent affluence imaginable.[18]

Numerous theories as to the true identity of this mysterious person have been suggested. Was he a Palestinian exile or a Druze from Syria or Lebanon? Was he a *sayyid,* that is, a descendant from the Prophet Muhammad ibn Abdullah of Arabia? Was he a former member of the Moorish Science Temple or a black Hebrew? Was he an undercover agent, either pro-Japanese or pro-Nazi? Was he simply a confidence man, making a living at the expense of uneducated Southerners who felt alienated in the city? Three theories have proved to be the most enduring: the Moorish theory, the black Hebrew theory, and the fraud theory. A fourth theory circulating among conventional African American Muslims is described in chapter 5.

Arna Bontemps, Jack Conroy, E. U. Essien-Udom, and Clifton E. Marsh suggest that Master Farad Muhammad had been a member of the Moorish Science Temple who tried to take control following the assassination of Noble Drew Ali.[19] "Fard claimed that he was the reincarnation of Noble Drew Ali," Essien-Udom writes. "By 1930 a permanent split developed in the movement. One faction, the Moors, remains faithful to Noble Drew Ali, and the other . . . remains faithful to Prophet Fard."[20] I have not been able to find any substantial evidence in support of this suggestion, neither in the early teachings of the NOI, nor in the FBI files. There are no reincarnation theories in the NOI creed, nor any statements about a Moorish identity for the blacks in America. In addition, Fard is said to have ousted two early converts for preaching the Moorish doctrine.[21] The creeds of the Moorish Science Temple and the Nation of Islam do have tenets in common, but these are better explained by reference to an exchange of ideas and the common roots in the black nationalist tradition, specifically the legacy of Marcus Garvey. The Nation of Islam commenced at the time when the Moorish Science Temple split into a number of warring factions, and many Moors were among the earliest individuals who were attracted by the NOI and who could feel at home in this new black Islamic nationalist movement.[22]

Howard Brotz suggests that W. D. Fard is identical with a black Hebrew rabbi named Arnold Josiah Ford, who disappeared from New York in 1930.[23] Ford was a Barbadian who became a close companion to Marcus Garvey after World War I. He wrote a number of popular UNIA songs, such as "Ethiopia Thou Land of Our Fathers," and also authored the "Universal Ethiopian Hymnal."[24] When Ford failed to persuade Garvey to adopt Judaism as the black man's religion, a conflict between the leaders developed, which resulted in Ford's expulsion from the UNIA in 1923.[25] The following year, Ford established the black Hebrew congregation Beth B'nai Abraham (BBA). Ford taught that the African Americans actually were the people of the covenant. Before the impending fall of Babylon— that is, the destruction of the United States—the African Americans had to turn away from mystifying Christianity and regain their lost knowledge of Self and God through the black path of gnosis, the Kabbalah. After six years of fluctuating membership and financial difficulties, the BBA collapsed. Ford announced that he would move out of Babylon, convert to Islam, and sail to Ethiopia. Brotz believes that Ford was impoverished and unable to take his family to Africa. Instead, Ford allegedly assumed a new identity and founded another and more successful nationalist religion.[26] Explaining Fard's supposed conversion to Islam, Brotz claims that Ford "correctly foresaw that Judaism did not offer any real possibilities as the basis of an anti-white movement."[27]

The Fard-is-Ford thesis may be "attractive," as Albert Ehrman puts it,[28] but it is hardly convincing. Could Ford, a renowned personality in black nationalist circles, have managed to change his identity and establish a nationalist religious movement without being recognized? There is no reason to doubt that Ford made it to Africa. Robert A. Hill and Barbara Bair assert that Ford obtained land from the newly coroneted emperor of Ethiopia, Haile Selassie, and established a small colony of repatriates. Ford convinced more than fifty members of his former congregation to join him, but the experiment failed. The majority returned to the United States, and Ford died in Addis Ababa in 1935, one year after the community's dissolution.[29]

The third theory, the Fard-is-a-fraud thesis, revolves around information obtained by the Federal Bureau of Investigation (FBI). In a 1958 FBI memorandum, a bureau agent states that the Nation of Islam has claimed that Fard is Allah. "In view of this," the agent wrote, "any information developed concerning the actual origins and life of W. D. Fard is extremely important to the investigation of the NOI and should be pursued vigorously and imaginatively."[30] The FBI claimed that Fard's fingerprints were identical with those of a Wallie D. Ford, which were found in the files of the Los Angeles Police Department and San Quentin prison.[31] Wallie D. Ford had a record of arrests and served a three-year term in San Quentin on drug charges.[32] Upon his release in May 1929, he told his former fiancée Hazel that he would start anew as a silk peddler in the Midwest. The FBI files concerning Fard's whereabouts prior to his first arrest in 1918 are contradictory. Ford told the California state parole authorities that he was born in Portland, Oregon, on February 25, 1891, to Hawaiian immigrants.[33] Hazel believed that Ford, the father of her child, was actually Fred or Wallace Dodd, born in New Zealand on February 26, 1891.[34] The contradictions of the FBI files have, however, one common denominator: they all classify Fard/Ford/Dodd as white.

Based on information channeled by the FBI, the *Los Angeles Herald Examiner* journalist Ed Montgomery established the Fard-is-a-fraud school, when he was able to "expose" the NOI founder as a "white dope peddler" who admitted to being a "fake."[35] The Nation of Islam claimed that the San Quentin record had been altered and the fingerprints doctored,[36] and NOI apologist Jabril Muhammad (then Bernard Cushmeer) and his friends visited the editorial office of the "lying devil" and urged him to prove his claim.[37] In the light of the FBI's counterintelligence activities directed against the NOI, the evidence presented above very well could be fabricated. During the 1950s and 1960s, the FBI frequently furnished what they called "derogatory information" to selected reporters in hopes of disrupting the growth of the NOI,[38] as I discuss in chapter 4. The FBI files' picture of Ford/Dodd has, furthermore, only a remote resemblance to the one of Master Farad Muhammad printed in the NOI papers.

All three theories accordingly must be rejected until they are supported by supplementary evidence. For the purpose of this study, all theories about Master Farad being someone other than God in Person are irrelevant. To the believers in the Nation of Islam, he is irrefutably God, Allah, who came to deliver his people of choice from their exile. He was born in Mecca on February 26, 1877, and was half Original, half white, as this would allow him to travel among friends and foe alike. He came alone to the Wilderness of North America on Independence Day, preceded by a sign of his wrath to warn the pale cavemen that their time was up: the New York Stock Exchange crash.[39]

A Nation of Islam   God descended in Detroit incognito and, except for revealing his true identity to Elijah, he posed officially as a prophet from Mecca, saying, "more about myself I will not tell you yet, for the time has not yet come."[40] Master Farad Muhammad renamed Poole, Elijah Karriem, and made him a top Laborer (an NOI official). With his assistance, the prophet preached the gospel of black redemption. Master Farad wrote two manuals for the movement composed of 154 *Lessons,* contained in the *Secret Ritual of the Nation of Islam,* which was transmitted orally, and the *Teaching for the Lost Found Nation of Islam in a Mathematical Way.* Besides these, Farad made use of the Bible and the Qur'an, scriptures that required his interpretation in order to be understood fully, and recommended that the community of believers listen to the radio sermons broadcast by the Watch Tower Society and Baptist fundamentalists.[41]

To become a member, one had to complete a written application declaring one's intention to return to the holy original Nation. Enclosed normally would be a request for the Original name. In general, African Americans had until then the surname of their grandparents' slave owner. The ritual repudiation of this remnant of slavery was a symbol for the new member's mental emancipation. In return, he would be given his holy name printed on a national "Identification Card" that showed him to be a righteous Muslim, registered in the divine roll of Mecca.[42] The Nation's membership quickly skyrocketed. The prophet of God started to rent larger halls as temporary temples to accommodate the seven to eight hundred people that would attend the meetings on Wednesdays, Fridays, and Sundays. Most researchers follow Erdmann D. Benyon who estimated a membership of approximately 8,000 at this early stage in the NOI's development.[43] The Detroit Police Department claimed in 1932 that there were "more than 8,000" members in that city alone.[44] The FBI speculated on an even more impressive growth, stating that no less than 35,000 NOI Identification Cards had been issued prior to 1934.[45]

The prophet of God soon became engulfed in practical matters: he created a bureaucracy in order to handle the practical demands of the new movement; established temples and assigned Laborers, officials in the administration; started schools and examined teachers for the necessary reeducation of the sadly misinformed Original People; and laid the foundation for an organizational structure of disciplined Muslim men and women. A central position in the movement was given to the paramilitary male cadre, named the Fruit of Islam (FOI). They were regarded as the fruit of the new creed, bearing within themselves the seeds of the coming transformation of the world. The FOI had the important function of defending the movement against internal corruption and external enemies. Louis Lomax wrote that it was "fear of trouble from the police—and non-believers—that caused Fard to organize the Fruit of Islam."[46] These worries began when the news spread that a fanatic cult teaching ritual killing had been established in Detroit.[47]

The Image of a Voodoo Cult in an Urban Jungle   There are few sources with information about the Nation of Islam during the period of 1930–34, and contemporary sources are spectacular in character. The movement became publicly known in late 1932 when the Detroit Police Department arrested an NOI member for an alleged human sacrifice. The suspect, Robert Harris, admitted to the police that he had ritually killed a man named James J. Smith on a wooden altar in his home on November 20. He declared upon being arrested that it was predestined 1,500 years ago that a "sacrifice" should be made at the ninth hour of that day.[48] Harris said that he was called upon to commit this act, which would transform his "voluntary" victim into a "Saviour."[49] The subsequent investigation revealed a death list that included among others two social workers, Miss Gladys Smith and Mrs. Margret Adele, who had removed Harris from the welfare list when they discovered that he and his family had not lived long enough in the city to receive aid.[50] Harris's arrest made the Nation of Islam headline news as the "Voodoo Cult," and attempts were made to connect the movement with its alleged "violent" counterpart in Haiti. "There is something deadly in trying to mix old jungle rites with all tall buildings and modern urban fixtures," Dewey Jones wrote in an article that maximized the story's dramatic ingredients.[51] Concerned citizens formed action groups to prevent the further spread of the NOI, pledging to "make a determined house-to-house drive against the jungle fanaticism."[52]

Ten days after the ritual slaughter, the police raided the NOI headquarters at 3408 Hasting Street and arrested the prophet of God "on charges of investigation," along with Ugan Ali, a "teacher of the rites." The reaction in the community of Believers was swift. The following day more than 500 members marched to the police headquarters to protest the arrests and demand the immediate release of Harris, Farad, and Ali. The latter's wife, Lillie Ali, acted as spokeswoman for the demonstration and declared that the march would be repeated every day until the prisoners had been freed.[53] The protesters did not have to wait long. Farad and Ali were released when they "agreed to help dissolve the cult," and Harris was declared insane by a sanity commission and committed to the Ionia Institution on December 14, 1932.[54]

What truth can there be in the statements of Robert Harris, which seem to imply a doctrine of voluntary human sacrifice that, as an imitation of Christ, could produce a saviour for the African Americans? In fact, there is nothing in the scattered fragments of doctrine that have survived from this early period that would indicate such a belief. In one of the 154 lessons that Master Farad delivered, however, there is a part that relates to ritual killing. It is found in *Lesson 1,* which was the second lesson an enrolled reconvert had to memorize perfectly before being allowed to proceed in the teachings.[55] It is composed as a series of questions and answers. The teacher asks his student, "Why does [Farad] Mohammad and any Moslem murder the devil? What is the duty of each Moslem in regard to four devils? What reward does a Moslem receive by presenting the four devils at one time?" The student gives the following answer: "Because he is one hundred percent wicked and will not keep and obey the laws of Islam. His ways and actions are like a snake of the grafted type. So Mohammed learned that he could not reform the devils, so they had to be murdered. All Moslem will murder the devil because they know he is a snake and also if he be allowed to live, he would sting someone else. Each Moslem is required to bring four devils, and by bringing and presenting four at one time his reward is a button to wear on the lapel of his coat, also a free transportation to the Holy City of Mecca."[56] The demonology of the Nation of Islam identifies the white man as the Devil. The obvious interpretation of *Lesson 1* in this context would be that each Muslim is required to take the life of four white men. But how should this teaching be understood? The key to a correct understanding, I believe, is the number four, which is the number of the beasts in the book of Daniel:7 that shall be stripped of power by the forces of God in the initial stage of the final battle. Therefore, this teaching has to be understood in an apocalyptic context. The demystifying and social-realist reading of the Scriptures that characterizes the exoteric exegetic of the Nation of Islam gave a specific role for each believer in the coming battle of Armageddon. Reciting lessons of this kind no doubt was a kind of catharsis, channeling feelings of bitterness and hatred toward the whites who were all too powerful to retaliate against in reality.

But teachings of a bloody revenge, as ordained or predestined by God, can always turn out to be fatal. Ali K. Muslim, who was enrolled as Charles 41X in Temple #25, Newark, New Jersey, in the early 1970s, recalls the following story. One afternoon when he was guarding the temple, a man carrying a sack came and asked to meet a temple official. The man said he had come to be awarded with the star-and-crescent lapel pin and the ticket for the trip to the holy land. To prove his case, the man opened the sack, which contained four severed heads. Muslim says he called the police and the man was arrested.[57] The Newark assassin seemed convinced of having acted according to the will of God by transforming the religious symbolism into action. It is reasonable to assume that Robert Harris had a religious frame of reference that structured his understanding of reality. Dr. Slevin, one of the three psychiatrists who declared Harris insane, noted that Harris "was constantly referring to things that happened 1,500 years ago."[58] Harris may have misinterpreted the metaphorical language of the teachings and, under the influence of a mental disorder, decided to engage in the physical battle of Armageddon on his own. The fact that a death list of four "devils" included two social workers who denied him and his family the means of survival is not too difficult to understand. But what about the slaying of John J. Smith? Could it be that Harris, a dedicated believer of a doctrine that identified the Son of Man with the Blackman of America, and who lived in a mental universe in which prophecy was being fulfilled, concluded that a Son of man had to go through the suffering of Jesus of Nazareth in order to become the redeemer of the race? There is no way to establish beyond any reasonable doubt what caused Harris to perform his deed—but the pattern of death symbolism and murder would be repeated in the coming decades, as would the spectacular media "exposures" of a "bizarre" black supremacist religion.

Muhammad is the Messenger of God   When freed, Farad obviously did not plan to dissolve the movement or play down the agitation, although he entrusted Elijah with increasing responsibilities. Soon, the divinely instructed disciple was elevated to the highest rank in the movement. Master Farad Muhammad had used a system of permitting the student ministers to select their leader from among themselves. Now, he called Elijah before the congregation, put his right hand around his shoulder, and declared Elijah to be his Supreme Minister, from that day on to be known by his original name: Elijah Muhammad.[59] The Supreme Minister proved to be a trustworthy appointee and a skilled organizer. He traveled to Chicago to meet with a small group of believers in August 1933. They decided to establish a temple on the South Side of Chicago, which was located at 3335 S. State Street and ceremonially inaugurated on August 10, 1933.[60]

Master Farad Muhammad was arrested two more times in Detroit because of his "cult activities." Finally, he was forced out of the city on May 26, 1933.[61] Farad sought refuge in Chicago, while Elijah, following the pattern laid forth by Ali Ibn Abu Talib, stayed to settle matters before following his teacher.[62] The last official record of Master Farad Muhammad's whereabouts is found in yet another arrest, this time in Chicago for disorderly conduct on September 26, 1933.[63] According to the historiography of the Nation of Islam, Master Farad Muhammad stayed in Chicago until disappearing in 1934, leaving the seed of the United States's largest and most influential black religious nationalist movement to bear fruit.[64] Before he left, Farad summoned the community of believers and officially left the NOI in the hands of his chosen Messenger. "You don't need me anymore," Farad said, "hear Elijah."[65]

While police, puzzled believers, and doubters discussed possible explanations for Farad's disappearance, Elijah Muhammad revealed the hidden secret: Master Farad Muhammad was not a prophet but God himself, who is a black man.[66] God had returned to the abode from which He supervises the destiny of man,[67] and had chosen Elijah Muhammad as his Messenger to guide the lost-found Nation of Islam through the turbulent days to come. When members of the Nation align with the Pan-Islamic community in the *shahada* (the confession of belief)—"There is no God but God and Muhammad is the Messenger of God"—they accordingly have a different interpretation of the identities of God and Muhammad.

Initially, Muhammad's claim was met with skepticism and outright hostility. His wife, Clara Muhammad, assumed the role of Khadidja and became one of the earliest to believe that Muhammad was the Messenger of Allah.[68] The headquarters was officially established in Chicago, but eruptions of violent internal conflict soon forced the Messenger out of town. Among those who turned against Elijah was his youngest brother, Kallatt Muhammad, who had been Supreme Captain of the NOI.[69] In 1935, God warned his Messenger, saying he should leave Chicago because the "hypocrites" were plotting against his life. Elijah Muhammad escaped to Washington, D.C., and would spend the next seven years on the run, mainly on the East Coast.[70] Moving from city to city, the apostle of God taught the message of black Islam as revealed by Almighty God, Allah, and established modest congregations along the way. In 1942, Elijah

Muhammad was incarcerated for refusing to register for the draft, an episode I discuss further in the next chapter. During his imprisonment, Clara Muhammad served as the channel of communication between the Messenger and the community of believers.

Messenger Muhammad won his release in 1946. The subsequent growth of the Nation of Islam has been described in previous studies, notably the ones by C. Eric Lincoln and E. U. Essien-Udom,[71] and so it will be sufficient to give here a summary description of the history of the Nation during the First Resurrection under the earthly leadership of Elijah Muhammad. Areas in which previous research is complemented, mainly the FBI's efforts to neutralize the NOI and an analysis of the NOI creed and its evolution, are found in chapters 4 and 7, respectively.

The Nation of Islam teaches that God is a black man and not an invisible spirit. The African American is not the inferior, so-called Negro but the original man, god of the universe. The primeval black civilization was a divine culture from which originated all science, wisdom, and institutions for human progress. Due to reasons that will be explained later, the black nation of gods lost world supremacy to the white race. The white man differs from the original species in that he is not a creation of God. His is a man-made race, grafted by the dissatisfied black scientist Mr. Yacub approximately 6,000 years ago. Bent on producing a race evil and powerful enough to transform the original harmony into its opposite, Mr. Yacub set out systematically to drain a number of the original people of divine essence. In intervals, the brown, red, and yellow races appeared before his goal was reached: to create a race absolutely bereft of divinity. This was a race whose members were evil by nature, incapable of acting or thinking decently, or submitting to the law of Islam: the blond, blue-eyed white devils. In his omniscience, God gave the Devil 6,000 years to rule the earth. White world supremacy is equated with the evil era of the Devil and explains the experiences of the darker people in late world history: colonialism, slavery, racist oppression, and poverty. The gospel is that the era of the Devil now has expired. God descended in Detroit to reconnect with his lost-found Nation and raise from among them a Messenger. When the mentally "dead" blacks have united in Knowledge of Self and God, white supremacy will fall. God will himself exterminate the devils from the face of the earth in a global apocalyptic fire. Thereafter—in the hereafter—the world will be transformed into the black paradise it is predestined to become, where freedom, justice, and equality (that is, Islam) will be the conditions for eternal times to come.

This is the time when prophecy is being fulfilled. The Bible and the

Qur'an tell the story of the original people. The blacks are the chosen people brought as slaves to the house of Pharaoh but who will soon be saved through an exodus. The United States is identified with Babylon and will be destroyed by the wrath of God. The Nation opposed the strategy of integration delineated by Martin Luther King Jr. and civil rights organizations like the NAACP and the Urban League. Integration with the foul spirits in the habitation of devils is in this context a dangerous suicidal policy. The only reasonable position is to follow the advice of Revelation 18:4, "Come out of her, my people, that ye be not partakers of her sins, and that ye receive none of her plagues." Consequently, the Nation of Islam strove to separate the divine Blackman from the bastion of evil. Far from being an escapist-oriented movement, the NOI as a religion of practice established an interim program that would attract attention far beyond the community of believers.

The Messenger of God argued that blacks in America should be given independence in a sovereign state, either in North America or Africa. Combined with the NOI mythohistory, this frequently repeated demand helped produce a sentiment of national consciousness along the lines drawn by Marcus Garvey. A national flag, on a red background with a white crescent in which a white star shone forth, was designed to replace the Star-Spangled Banner in the NOI facilities. The Fruit of Islam developed into a uniformed army that with military drill and discipline pledged to defend their nation. The territorial demand was intended as a reminder to the black people that their destiny was not necessarily in the ghettos of America, but that they were as justified to self-determination in a land of their own as any other nation on earth. Instead of begging for justice at the white man's feet or setting their hopes on a mystery God's intervention, they should search and find the solution to their problems from within themselves.

More measurable results were achieved in the efforts to create a corporate national infrastructure. Elijah Muhammad taught the blacks to pool their resources to produce jobs and become self-sufficient.[72] In time, an economic empire had been established. The NOI operated a great number of companies, such as bakeries, restaurants, snack shops, coffee shops, barber shops, supermarkets, groceries, cleaners, clothing factories, a fez factory, clothing stores, retail stores, real estate, residential homes (more than two hundred apartment units in Chicago alone), a newspaper plant, and a bank, the Guaranty Bank and Trust Company. They had a transportation system, including a fleet of tractor-trailers, livestock trailers, refrigerated trailers, in-city trucks, a "fleet of planes" including a jet, and a fixed-base aviation department at the Gary Municipal Airport. The NOI owned tens of thousands of acres of farm land in Michigan, Alabama, and Georgia, operated with modern machine equipment: tractors, cotton pickers, plows, cultivators, combines, hay cutters, balkers, drain drills, and sprayers. They also owned apple orchards, canneries, dairies, dairy herds, poultry farms, cattle farms, grain mills, and warehouses; further, the NOI imported millions of tons of whiting fish from Peru.[73] A doctor's office and a dental suite were operated, and plans for a 300-bed hospital were announced. Finally, the NOI became "the most potent organized economic force in the black community."[74]

Also tangible were the results of the NOI's efforts to establish its own educational system. The public schools were seen as perpetuating white supremacy, and re-education was believed to be the key to national liberation.[75] The first two NOI schools, or Universities of Islam, were founded in Detroit in 1932 and Chicago in 1934, without legal approval. In 1934, Elijah Muhammad was arrested for contributing to the delinquency of minors,[76] and a riot followed when the Detroit Board of Education sought to close down the universities. Finally, the State Department of Public Instruction compromised and collaborated with the NOI delegates in developing a curriculum that made the universities approved as private schools.[77] By 1974, blacks in forty-six cities could send their children to NOI elementary and, in some cities, secondary schools.[78] In an attempt to overcome four hundred years of unequal education, the NOI school year had only a two-week vacation. In single-sex classes, black children received an education with an emphasis on science, mathematics, black history, Arabic, and Islam. Education in all subjects was permeated by the religious doctrines of the Nation in preparation for survival in the latter days.[79]

The NOI stressed a morality said to be original Islamic, but this morality was, in fact, compatible with conservative Christian American standards. Race endogamy within the inclusive black category was strictly practiced.[80] A Muslim man dressed correctly in suit and bow tie, worked hard, and shunned alcohol, narcotics, gambling, and decadent luxuries. A Muslim woman dressed modestly, obeyed her husband, and found pride in taking good care of her family. A Muslim child avoided street culture and senseless play, respected the elderly, and studied hard. All members spent much time with the organization and its activities, from studies and military training, to selling NOI newspapers and other missionary campaigns. Men participated in the FOI classes, women were organized in its female counterpart, the Muslim Girl Training–General Civilization Class (MGT-GCC), and children had their own pioneer organizations.

Through his Messenger, God also taught his nation "how to eat to live." The short life expectancy and the poor standard of health in the black community were seen as a result of soul and junk food. Ideally, an adult Muslim should eat only once a day or once every second day,[81] and regular three-day fasting was recommended.[82] Adherence to the NOI dietary rules, which were more detailed than the ones of Leviticus, would extend one's life by hundreds of years.[83] A vegetarian diet was recommended though not obligatory. "Meat was never intended for man to eat," the Messenger wrote.[84] Meat was divided into two categories: meat that was prohibited, such as flesh and wild game,[85] and meat that was to be avoided, such as beef, lamb, and chicken.[86] Fish of the right kind was seen as healthy food, but scavengers of the sea were forbidden.[87] All fresh fruit could be eaten, while dried fruit, nuts, and some specified vegetables were classified as inedible.[88] All meals should be carefully cooked in the prescribed manner,[89] and every kind of processed, fried, canned, chemically prepared, and fast food should be abhorred.[90]

Fasting was prescribed during the daytime one month a year—not during Ramadan as in mainstream Islam—but in December. While the relationship between the NOI and the Muslim world is discussed in chapter 8, the Messenger's attitude toward conventional Islamic practice will be illustrated here by citing his view on *sawm* (fasting), the fourth pillar of mainstream Islam. Clearly, Elijah Muhammad's unique relationship with God enabled him to correct every Arab misunderstanding of the divine ordinances. Muslims fast in the month of Ramadan because this is the month in which the Qur'an was revealed to Muhammad, as the Messenger noted, but he found this practice odd. Muhammad did not receive the Qur'an overnight, but over a period of more than twenty years. Moreover, as the Qur'an was received without a fasting community of believers, "WHY FAST in that month?": "If you can convince me it is necessary to Fast in the month of Ramadan because of Muhammad receiving the Holy Quran, or the first revelation of the Holy Quran, then I will go along with it. However, since the Quran was received over a period of years, I am very much baffled in trying to understand why we should FAST in the month of Ramadan. . . . OF COURSE, this is the Arab way, in their religious belief, that they should FAST. But I do say that it is not necessary to FAST to get something that you have already received."[91] While Elijah

Muhammad could see no reason for fasting in Ramadan, the practice of fasting in December turned his community away from worshipping the false birthday of a dead prophet.[92] Nonparticipation in the major festivities of a culture is a visible sign of separateness, as practiced by numerous new religious movements. Accordingly, the NOI celebrated holy days of its own. The Saviour's Day, commemorating the birth of Master Farad Muhammad on February 26, was by far the most important holy day. This was also the date of the yearly NOI convention, which attracted tens of thousands of believers who traveled from all over the United States and several foreign countries with NOI chapters.

By 1974, the Nation had established temples or study groups in every state and the District of Columbia. Outside the United States, chapters were found in Bermuda, Barbados, Jamaica, Honduras, Belize, Nassau (Bahamas), St. Thomas, St. Croix, Trinidad, Canada, and England.[93] Elijah Muhammad lived in a grandiose villa, called the Palace, in the integrated Hyde Park area close to the University of Chicago, and spent the winters on a large ranch in Phoenix, Arizona. In 1972, the Nation paid about four million dollars for the St. Constantine Greek Orthodox church on Chicago's South Side, which was to be remodeled into a headquarters temple and a four-year college. Undoubtedly, the Messenger had come a long way since the rented halls of the early days.

Champions for Allah   The Nation of Islam spread its message by using various channels. "Fishing for the dead"—that is, reaching out for non-Muslim blacks—involved holding regular open meetings, mass rallies, and street-corner talks, establishing an effective prison mission, and spreading the Word wherever blacks assembled, from churches and political rallies, to pool halls and bars. The black press began to give the Nation coverage, and Elijah Muhammad became a topic of conversation for hundreds of thousands of blacks all over the United States. Muhammad wrote a column in the *Pittsburgh Courier,* and thousands of letters, applauding or denouncing the Messenger and the paper, poured in to its editorial office.[94] Subsequently, Muhammad's column appeared in the weekly *Los Angeles Herald Dispatch,* which almost evolved into an official NOI organ.[95] In the late 1950s, the mainstream media began an exposure campaign that gave the NOI high visibility. The negative publicity strategy backfired and proved to benefit the Nation (as further discussed in chapter 4).

In 1960, NOI top Laborer Malcolm X founded *Mr. Muhammad Speaks,* which in time became the most widely read paper in black America, with a reported circulation of more than 600,000 copies a week.[96] Besides black Islamic articles by the Messenger of God and others, *Muhammad Speaks* offered high-quality coverage of news relevant to the African American community, both domestic and international. A number of skilled non-Muslim syndicated columnists and journalists contributed regularly or were employed on the editorial staff. When the editorial office was moved to Chicago, veteran journalist Dan Burley succeeded Malcolm X as editor in chief. Author and playwright Richard Durham, a former CIO organizer who wrote Muhammad Ali's autobiography, *The Greatest*, became editor in chief in 1964. In 1969, he was succeeded by John Woodford, former editor/writer of the mainstream black magazine *Ebony*. Woodford stayed until 1972, when he left for the *Chicago Sun-Times* and later the *New York Times*.[97] The frequent allegation linking the wide circulation with the obligation of each FOI soldier to sell a fixed number of copies each week, must be supplemented with another explanation: it was simply one of the very best contemporary black weeklies in the United States.

The NOI ideology was also laid forth by the Honorable Elijah Muhammad in a number of publications: *The Supreme Wisdom: Solution to the So-called NEGROES' Problem* (1957); *The Supreme Wisdom, Volume Two* (undated); *Message to the Blackman* (1965); *How to Eat to Live* (1967); *How to Eat to Live, Book Two* (1972); *The Fall of America* (1973); *Our Saviour Has Arrived* (1974[a]); and *The Flag of Islam* (1974[b]). In addition, the NOI spread its message through audio-recorded speeches and radio broadcasts.

As membership grew, the former practice of routinely replacing a reconvert's slave-name with a holy name was altered. As a rule, a new member was now given an "X" in exchange for the slave name. "X" for ex-slave, "X" for the unknown family-name slavery deprived along with freedom, "X" for the quality inherent in each Blackman that the Devil was still unaware of. If there were several Charles X in a specific temple, they were prefixed with a number according to the order of affiliation. The first Charles became Charles X, the second Charles 2X, and so on. After a period of dedicated service, God could reward a believer by revealing his or her original Islamic name.

This appears to be a smooth success story, but had it not been for the Messenger's ability to raise dedicated champions for the cause, the Nation would probably have remained an obscure organization at the margins of the black community. Among the many outstanding laborers, perhaps none were more effective than a triad recruited in the 1950s and early 1960s: Malcolm X, Muhammad Ali, and Louis Farrakhan. While the latter is focused on later in this volume, the time has come to give attention to the former two who, in their respective fields, would become paramount champions.

When the Messenger of God was released from prison in 1946, membership in the Nation of Islam had decreased considerably. Due to financial difficulties, the NOI ceased paying rent for the temples in 1945 and returned to holding meetings in private homes.[98] Upon his release from prison, Muhammad gathered the scattered followers and had to begin anew, almost from scratch. Thousands of Chicagoans were attracted by his message, and Nicholas Lemann notes that "by the 1940s, Chicago had supplanted Harlem as the center of black nationalism in the United States."[99] In part, the continuous black migration accounts for the expanding membership. During the 1940s the black population of Chicago increased from 278,000 to 492,000, and then to 813,000 in the 1950s.[100] Beyond the industrial sites at the Great Lakes, however, the call of Islam barely resounded, except for one congregation in Cincinnati, one in Washington, D.C., and one in Milwaukee.[101] Previous research confirms the modest growth of the NOI until the 1950s. The subsequent breakthrough was accomplished in part due to the actions of a man released from Norfolk prison in 1952: Malcolm X (1925–65).

Born Malcolm Little the son of UNIA activists Earl and Louise Little,[102] Malcolm's life was to become a symbol for the black version of the American dream. When Malcolm was six years old, his father was murdered, presumably by white racists.[103] Louise was unable to provide for her family and had a nervous breakdown when state welfare workers wanted to place her children in foster homes. She was sent to an asylum, the children were scattered, and Malcolm grew up in different homes in Michigan. A talented student, but discouraged from higher education because of the color of his skin, Malcolm embarked on another career. Leaving for Boston and then Harlem, Malcolm became a street hustler and a burglar, which in 1946 brought him a ten-year prison sentence. While incarcerated, Malcolm was reached by the redeeming message of the NOI, and his life took yet another turn.[104] He used the remaining prison years for dedicated studies and grew intellectually and mentally.

Upon his release, Malcolm rose rapidly in the Muslim hierarchy. In three years, Malcolm X toured the United States and established twenty-seven temples in different cities, a marked increase from the mere seven temples in operation when he left prison.[105] During his successful service as an organizer in Detroit, Los Angeles, Boston, Philadelphia, Atlanta, and other cities, he was also made minister of Temple #7 in Harlem in June 1954. Early in 1963, Malcolm crowned his ascendancy by becoming appointed the first National Representative of the Honorable Elijah Muhammad.

Malcolm X is renowned for his rhetorical skill, representing the epitome of black preacher artistry. Crisscrossing the United States, he appeared on television and radio talk shows and lectured on college campuses and at NOI rallies. In contrast to his leader, Malcolm was electrified by media scrutiny, and the NOI was frequently the talk of the day. In late fall of 1963, a schism surfaced between Malcolm X and his teacher, the Honorable Elijah Muhammad. As the conflict deepened, Malcolm turned against the Messenger, joined the fold of mainstream Sunni Islam, and established an independent Muslim organization. As El Hajj Malik El Shabazz, he seemed to evolve toward a Third World–oriented revolutionary position before he was assassinated in 1965. On the surface, the NOI hierarchy appeared to be guilty, and three FOI soldiers were soon arrested. An account of some less visible events leading up to the murder is given in the following chapter. Here it is sufficient to note that the NOI, branded as Malcolm's killers, suffered a setback that would take years to overcome.

Today, Malcolm X enjoys cult status as a martyr in the struggle for black self-determination. His *Autobiography* is a best-seller and required reading in many high schools. He is hailed by numerous rappers who frequently sample his speeches in hip-hop songs. Malcolm X fever has made a wide range of organizations eager to claim his name, from Trotskyites to black nationalist groups, including the NOI. During Spike Lee's production of the film *Malcolm X,* the script had to be rewritten no less than ten times, in part due to the fervor with which the different camps marketed Malcolm as their champion. Lee received communications from Amiri Baraka, Benjamin Kariem, David DuBois, Malcolm's siblings, Betty Shabazz, Pan-Africanists, and others not to tamper with their image of Malcolm X. Farrakhan and others in the Nation were explicit in their warnings for Lee not to desecrate Elijah Muhammad. Along with the opinions of Warner Brothers and other financiers, Lee was hard pressed in animating the *Autobiography.* Although it is a good film, the end result clearly suffered as a result of too many compromises.[106] Setting aside all speculations on what Malcolm would have evolved into if he were still alive, it should be emphasized that he would not have been the man he was if it had not been for his teacher, Elijah Muhammad. It is equally safe to say that the Nation of Islam would not have been the same without Malcolm X.

Besides Malcolm X, none of Elijah Muhammad's disciples gave the Nation a higher visibility than Muhammad Ali (born Cassius Clay on January 17, 1942), the fabulous heavyweight boxing champion of the world. In March 1961, the young boxer was in Miami training for a fight when he met Captain Sam (today known as Abdul Rahaman), who invited Clay to a NOI meeting that would change his life. Contrary to legend, he was not taught Islam by Malcolm X, but was first educated in the NOI creed by Miami's Minister Ishmael Sabakhan and Jeremiah Shabazz, NOI's coordinator of the Deep South.[107] Clay first met with Malcolm X in 1962, at a NOI rally in Detroit. For three years, Clay's membership in the NOI was kept a secret, in part due to the suspicion that he never would be allowed to fight for the championship if he made his beliefs public. In the buildup to Clay's fight for the world heavyweight title against Sonny Liston, the Messenger advised his members to keep a low profile as he believed Clay would lose. Malcolm X, who at that time was silenced as National Representative, went to Clay's training camp to pray with him.[108] "It's the Cross and the Crescent fighting in the prize ring—for the first time," he reportedly told Clay. There was no way Allah intended for Clay to lose.[109] On February 25, 1964, Clay defeated Liston and announced his NOI membership during the press conference following his victory.[110] That Saviour's Day, Elijah Muhammad told a cheering convention that "Clay whipped a much tougher man and came through the bout unscarred because he has accepted Muhammad as the Messenger of Allah."[111] In a March 6 radio broadcast, the Messenger freed Clay from his slave name, giving him the name Muhammad Ali.

Muhammad Ali's public stand in support of the Nation of Islam made him a target for mainstream American rage.[112] The media refused as a rule to call him Muhammad Ali, and he was denounced by a number of influential columnists. In 1965 he was challenged by former heavyweight champion and Roman Catholic Floyd Patterson, who said that "the Black Muslim influence must be removed from boxing" as it is a "menace to the United States," and he pledged to "reclaim the title for America."[113] Muhammad Ali responded by branding Patterson an "Uncle Tom," and the buildup depicted a clash between Islam and Christianity, separatism and assimilation, a fight that ended in the former's favor when Ali defeated Patterson. In 1966, Herbert Muhammad, son of the Messenger, became Muhammad Ali's manager at a time when Ali was under attack for refusing to serve the United States Army in Vietnam.[114] "Why should they ask me," Ali wondered, "to put on a uniform and go ten thousand miles from home and drop bombs and bullets on brown people in Vietnam while so-called Negro people in Louisiana are treated like dogs?"[115] In 1967, one hour after Ali refused induction, the New York State Athletic Commission suspended his boxing license. All other jurisdictions followed New York's lead, and Muhammad Ali was stripped of his champion title.[116] Muhammad Ali became a symbol for black revolutionary Islam and, as such, was of tremendous importance for the Nation. In the words of Jeremiah Shabazz: "When Elijah Muhammad spoke, his words were confined to whatever city he had spoken in. But Ali was a sports hero, and people wanted to know what he had to say, so his visibility and prominence were of great benefit to the Nation. His voice carried throughout the world, and that was a true blessing for us. There's no doubt, our following increased enormously, maybe a hundred percent, after he joined the Nation."[117] Undefeated in the ring yet bereft of his title, Muhammad Ali began touring the United States, lecturing on college campuses and in temples. He also performed on Broadway, playing the title role in a musical called *Buck White*. Ali became famous as an underdog, fighting alone against an unjust system, and thereby he turned public opinion in his favor. As he began preparing for a comeback, he faced yet another blow: he was suspended from the Nation of Islam. Appearing on television in early 1969, Muhammad Ali had said that he would go back to boxing if the money was right. Elijah Muhammad had tolerated his professional sports career, but when barred by the Devil, Ali should not, the Messenger reasoned, crawl on his knees to get back for the sake of money. When Malcolm X was suspended from the NOI, Ali had sided with the Messenger, but now he found himself suffering a similar punishment. Before long, however, Elijah Muhammad embraced him again after Herbert Muhammad pleaded Ali's cause.[118] On June 28, 1972, the United States Supreme Court reversed Ali's conviction, but the heavyweight title had to be reclaimed with his fists. Through a number of excellent bouts, Muhammad Ali fought his way back. In Kinshasa, Zaire, on October 30, 1974, Ali regained his heavyweight championship by knocking out George Forman in the eighth round. This time, mainstream America, the president included, joined in the chorus cheering the champ in his triumph.[119]

Fighting for Allah in their respective ways, Malcolm X and Muhammad Ali championed the growth of the Nation. In the other corner of the ring, the Devil watched the buildup and prepared to give the divine soldiers a tough bout, a story to which we now turn.

4

Forces of Evil

—

The history of the Nation of Islam is intertwined with the history of American domestic repression. This chapter will examine the attitudes and activities of the Federal Bureau of Investigation (FBI) toward the Nation of Islam. This is necessary due, in part, to the fact that much of the information on the Nation of Islam reaching the American public has been produced or channeled by the FBI. The chapter ends with a discussion concerning the possible reasons why the bureau went to such lengths in their efforts to neutralize a religious movement.

An Asiatic Assault on Babylon   The Nation did not attract the attention of FBI domestic intelligence until during World War II. As noted in chapter 1, the Japanese victory over Russia in 1906 was widely interpreted in racial terms among nations living under the yoke of white hegemony. The sun of the Eastern emperor shone even brighter after the Great War, in which the Christian Western nations slaughtered their image of supreme refinement along with their populations. The interwar period was characterized by economic depression and the rise of populist nationalist ideologies. In the 1930s, before the deadly chauvinism inherent in National Socialism was generally understood, both blacks and whites in the United States expressed sympathy with the ideological sentiments voiced in German politics. The *Chicago Defender,* the city's most widespread black newspaper, decorated the front page for years with two rows of swastikas, signifying only the importance of racial consciousness.

When Japanese nationalists vowed to challenge white world supremacy in a war of propaganda, they sought and found common ground in sections of black America. In Detroit in 1930, an African American city worker named George Grimes founded the Development of Our Own as a political organization for black empowerment. The organization was taken over by a Japanese reserve major, Satochasi Takahashi, who attempted to transform it into "a national group organized to fight the whites of the world." According to the Detroit Police Department, Takahashi developed contacts with a W. D. Feraud, leader of "the Moslem Temple of Islam cult."[1] Whatever collaboration may have existed appears to have ended when Takahashi "sought to lead the Muslims to swear allegiance to the Mikado."[2] Takahashi was deported after a police raid on the organization's headquarters, in which a program for the unification of all nonwhite peoples of the world was found. His wife, an African American militant, Mrs. P. T. Sherrod, continued the work, but in 1935, the Development of Our Own split into three competing factions and declined in importance.

The fact that the Muslims were reluctant to give up their proclaimed independent nationhood to the son of Amaterasu does not signify any support for the official American interpretation of the coming world events. African Americans had participated in World War I "for the emancipation of mankind" without experiencing any liberation. Now, they were urged to engage in a "war for democracy" for a country denying them civil rights. Concerning the Allies' war against Nazi Germany, the Muslims doubted the value of fighting for any of the white supremacist powers. Furthermore, the rays of the ascending Asian sun seemed to burn only the pale-skinned nations.[3] Claiming citizenship in the Nation of Islam, the Messenger's followers refused to register for the draft under the Selective Service Act of 1940. The FBI launched a large-scale investigation of African American Muslim movements in order to disclose possible anti-American teachings. In contrast to what was observed at the Moorish Science Temple of America, the informants reported pro-Japanese attitudes at the NOI meetings. "The white devils desire the colored people to die with them in the Army and Navy" a Minister reportedly stated, "it will not be long before the Japanese will be over here. . . . [t]he time has come when the white devils will be destroyed by dark humankind."[4]

In September 1942, the FBI arrested eighty-five African Americans from three organizations, the Peace Movement of Ethiopia, the Brotherhood of Liberty for Black People of America, and the Nation of Islam. The vast majority, sixty-five defendants, were Muslims. "Sentence me to fifty years if you want," Allah ben Aiken said. "The white man is reaching the end of his rope after 6,000 years and I won't do anything to stop him."[5] Fifty-six defendants received three-year terms for failure to register for the draft.[6] Emmanuel Karriem, son of the Messenger, was sentenced to five years, while his father awaited trial for sedition. Upon being arrested, Elijah Muhammad explained his position: "I realize that failure by me to register constitutes a violation of Federal Law but the reason I did not register is that in 1931 Allah told me I was registered as a Moslem and belonged to him. . . . Allah has told all Moslems that they should remain righteous and not engage in fighting or military service of any kind."[7] The NOI spokespersons undoubtedly interpreted World War II in eschatological terms. They were living in the first stage of Armageddon. The burning world was a divinely directed cataclysm leading toward the prophesized destruction of the race of evil. The Japanese were seen as instruments of God for the extermination of his enemies. The believers had been informed of the war of Armageddon when visited by God a decade earlier; he then assured his Nation that sufficient precautions had been taken to secure military superiority for their Asiatic brethren. When interrogated by the FBI in 1942, Elijah Muhammad said that "Allah has taught that blueprints of a plane which carries bombs, was [sic] given to the Japanese from the Holy City of Mecca, and that these blueprints had been there for thousands of years. These bombs would go into the earth for at least a mile and would throw up earth to a distance of one mile, so that it would make a mountain. I have reminded registered Moslems of this [sic] teachings."[8] The final battle was postponed and things went back to normal. One million blacks had fought in the war and returned to a segregated native country. When released in August 1946,[9] Elijah Muhammad continued to oppose the regime of evil. The Federal Bureau of Investigation matched the subsequent growth of the Nation by an extended program of surveillance.

Exposing the Nation   In recent years there has been an increasing interest in studies of American political intelligence and domestic repression. The FBI counterintelligence aimed at Martin Luther King Jr. and the Southern Christian Leadership Conference, the Black Panther Party, the Student Nonviolent Coordinating Committee, the Republic of New Africa, Malcolm X and black nationalists in general, the American Indian Movement, the New Left and the Socialist Workers Party has been explored by various scholars.[10] No research, however, has focused directly on the federal conspiracy against the Nation of Islam.[11] This is all the more remarkable since the Nation of Islam outnumbered most, if not all, of the organizations mentioned above and was targeted prior to these.

The FBI interest in the NOI is reflected in the Security Index, a listing of prominent dissidents dating from 1939. The largest category listed 673 members of the Nation of Islam, followed by 476 communists.[12] The following account of the FBI's covert actions against the NOI at best can be seen as a rough delineation, which hopefully will inspire further research in this field. Primary sources are the files of W. D. Fard (100-43165, 105-63642), Elijah Muhammad (105-24822), and COINTELPRO–Black Hate Groups (100-448006), all with numerous subfiles. These files have been obtained through the Freedom of Information Act (FOIA). As David J. Garrow points out,[13] the headquarters's files contain only a part of the documentation generated by the bureau. Two-thirds of the paperwork produced in field offices remain in local archives and are hard to obtain through FOIA requests. Furthermore, much of the text in the released files is deleted. The FOIA allows deletions to protect "confidential sources"— that is, highly placed informants—and matters of "national security." The latter exception seems to have an inclusive definition and is frequently used to screen out information. With these limitations in mind, it is still possible to present a shortened story of the federal agents' crusade against the Nation of Islam.

On December 31, 1956, J. Edgar Hoover, director of the FBI, requested authorization from Attorney General Herbert Brownell "to install technical surveillance on the residence of Elijah Mohammed or any address to which he may move in the future." The director explained his motives: "The Muslim Cult of Islam is composed entirely of Negroes. Its leader, Elijah Mohammed, claims to have been sent by Allah, the Supreme Being, to lead the Negroes out of slavery. Members fanatically follow the teachings of Allah, as interpreted by Mohammed; they disavow allegiance to the United States; and they are taught they need not obey the laws of the United States. Allegations have been received that its members may resort to acts of violence in carrying out its avowed purpose of destroying non-Muslims and Christianity."[14] On January 4, 1957, taps were installed at Elijah Muhammad's house at 4847 S. Woodlawn Avenue in Chicago.[15] In subsequent years, additional means of technical and microphone surveillance were employed to cover the alternative residences of the Messenger.[16] Combined with strategically placed informants, these sources provided the bureau with excellent information regarding the activities, membership, policies, business, and programs of the NOI.[17] The data thus obtained became the basis for several phases of counterintelligence activities.

In 1959, the FBI launched a large-scale media campaign. In this first phase, the FBI briefed selected journalists who willingly channeled the view of the bureau to the American public. The special agent in charge (SAC) in Chicago, wrote: "Originally the program was centered around espousing to the public, both white and black, on a nationwide basis the abhorrent aspects of the organization and its racist, hate type teachings. This was done in such leading magazines as *Time, U.S. News and World Report, Saturday Evening Post* etc., as well as through newspapers."[18] The sudden outburst of media interest is commented on by NOI apologist Jabril Muhammad (then Bernard Cushmeer). His view might have seemed overly paranoid to some readers, but Cushmeer was correct: "Back in 1959, the white press, as if on signal, launched a furious attack on Messenger Muhammad and the Nation of Islam. . . . white America spewed forth a flood of articles, both superficial, spurious and poisoness [*sic*] in nature. . . . They conspired to deceive the public. . . . Members of a large orchestra do not accidentally play the same tune."[19] The FBI scheme to disrupt the growth of the Nation of Islam by public exposure proved to be counterproductive.[20] In the early 1950s, there had been fifteen NOI temples. In December 1959, after the launching of the FBI campaign, there were fifty temples in twenty-two states and the District of Columbia.[21] The FBI followed the results closely and concluded that "Muhammad and the NOI thrived on publicity. He did not particularly seem concerned whether this publicity was critical or otherwise . . . any type would attract the Negro . . . to his temples."[22]

In 1962, a new counterintelligence phase was launched as the employed sources disclosed that Muhammad used his "followers to purchase expensive cars and homes for him; to provide him with bodyguards and servants; and to give him other manifestations of affluence. These luxuries have been obtained at the expense of his followers who are, in the main, extremely poor."[23] Using anonymous letters and additional media exposure, the bureau now emphasized the "fraudulent character" of the NOI, alleging that it was established only to enrich the leaders by exploiting gullible blacks. This new angle caused no upheaval in the membership. Disappointed, the SAC in Chicago noted that "the personal extravagance of Muhammad and his family also apparently had little if any effect on the masses of his followers. Apparently they expected him to live lavishly and are willing to make extreme monetary sacrifices in this regard with blind subservience.[24] The agent's astonishment only proves his lack of understanding of the sociology of religion. C. Eric Lincoln explains that lower- and middle-class congregations tend to differ in their attitudes regarding their shepherds' expected standard of living. Black middle-class churches are headed by pastors who are supposed to live simply, rejecting the riches of this world and thereby showing themselves worthy. However, a life in poverty would not prove any religious point for the permanent underclass or the working class, who expect their leaders to live in affluence. This is the only way for the poor to participate in the glamorous way of life. By personal sacrifices they can provide the pastor with a fancy car or a New Year's trip to the holy land. As the shepherd is the symbol of the flock, they can bask in his sunshine and enjoy his experiences vicariously.[25] The bulk of NOI members are from the lower strata of the American socioeconomic hierarchy. The Messenger's Chicago Palace, his beautiful resort in Phoenix, his extravagant cars, and his private jet were the only such things Muslims could point to and proudly call theirs.[26] The FBI exposure of Elijah Muhammad's riches only strengthened the image of him being the true Messenger of Allah.

A third phase of this early FBI campaign to expose Muhammad to his followers focused on his sexual life. Back in 1960, the taps revealed that Elijah Muhammad had "domestic difficulties . . . which could conceivably be used in the future as a counterintelligence move."[27] Two years later, the bureau reported that they continued to receive information "that Elijah Muhammad is engaging in extramarital activities with at least five female members of the NOI. . . . [H]is wife, Clara, has become aware of his infidelity which has resulted in domestic strife."[28] The bureau believed that these "paradoxes in the character of Elijah Muhammad" would make him "extremely vulnerable to criticism by his followers," and since the Honorable Elijah Muhammad held absolute power in the NOI, "any successful attack on his character or reputation" might prove to "be disastrous for the NOI."[29]

By exposing Muhammad's extramarital affairs, the bureau hoped to break up his marriage, ruin his reputation, and "affect the continued growth of this hate organization."[30] The FBI's director wrote that "Chicago and Phoenix should make recommendations concerning the use of information thus obtained [through four strategically placed informants, wiretaps, and bugs] to discredit Elijah Muhammad with his followers. This could be handled through the use of carefully selected informants planting the seeds of dissension through anonymous letters and/or telephone calls and through other selected actions indicated by the available information. Any such plans, of course, must be approved by the Bureau in advance before any action is taken."[31] The bureau's obsession with the sexual activity of dissident leaders is well documented. The sexually phobic attitude prevailing in the top leadership of the FBI was nursed by a puritan, Victorian code of sexual behavior that denied others those pleasures officially forbidden for themselves. Paradoxically, technically advanced voyeurism was the method employed by these guardians of decent morality.

David J. Garrow describes how the bureau spent years exercising surveillance over the nightlife activities of Martin Luther King Jr., breaking into hotel rooms to install microphones in the hopes of documenting damaging information on King's sexual life. The information thus obtained on King's, in Hoover's words, "obsessive degenerate sexual urges"[32] was used in a campaign directed toward King's exposure and neutralization as spokesperson for black civil rights. The campaign culminated with William C. Sullivan, assistant director in charge of the Domestic Intelligence Division, mailing King a tape with "highlights" from the recordings, enclosed with a letter suggesting suicide as the only alternative to public embarrassment: "You better take it before your filthy, abnormal self is bared to the nation."[33] Unfortunately for the bureau, Mrs. Coretta King opened the envelope, believing it to be a recording of some of her husband's public speeches. She listened to it briefly, discovered the true contents, and immediately called her husband, who, accompanied by Andrew Young, Ralph D. Abernathy, and Joseph Lowery, joined her in listening to the entire recording. The plot was disclosed and failed to break either the marriage or the spirit of King.

The FBI interest in the sexual life of Elijah Muhammad was thus normal in the subculture of the bureau. The bedroom scrutinizers discovered that Elijah Muhammad had engaged in a number of extramarital affairs with some of his young female secretaries. At least four girls, Sisters Evelyn, Rosary, Rosella, and Lavita, became pregnant.[34] The FBI director considered this to be excellent material to capitalize on and wrote to the SAC in Chicago: "Chicago is authorized to prepare and mail an anonymous letter to Clara Muhammad. . . . Chicago is also authorized to prepare and mail similar anonymous letters containing substantially the same information as the letter mailed to Clara Muhammad to the selected individuals listed. . . . The letters, which are to be handwritten on commercially purchased stationery without markings, should follow the sample letter

proposed in reairtel. Each letter, however, should contain minor variations so that each will not appear to be an exact copy of the original. These
letters should be mailed at staggered intervals using care to prevent any
possibility of tracing the mailing back to the FBI."[35] To the plotters' disappointment, the plan to discredit Elijah Muhammad in this manner proved
to be unsuccessful. The FBI reports that "the wife did come to hate some of
the secretaries but Muhammad continued his activities."[36] Clara Muhammad remained loyal to her husband up until to her death in 1972, and the
believers closed ranks. The FBI observed, "The results of this exposure left
the feeling that Muhammad's extracurricular escapades were accepted by
his followers, their belief apparently being motivated by the fact Muhammad as the messenger of Allah was divinely inspired and missioned."[37]

The FBI made a series of miscalculations. The Victorian code of sexual
conduct normative in the minds of the FBI leadership was not universally
accepted. Exposure of transgressions might be useful in cases such as the
one concerning Gary Hart, whose followers were mainly from the white
middle class. The NOI rank and file followed other standards. Many were
raised in inner-city ghettos, a culture in which males proved their masculinity by being lady-killers.[38] Furthermore, Islam expresses a positive
attitude toward sex as compared to puritan Christianity. Muhammad ibn
Abdullah had eleven or twelve wives and strongly disapproved of self-
denying sexual abstinence and monastic asceticism.[39] In addition, Elijah
Muhammad was the Messenger of Allah and adhered to standards laid
forth by previous prophets. According to Malcolm X's *Autobiography,*
the Messenger told him, "I'm David. When you read about how David
took another man's wife, I'm that David. You read about Noah, who got
drunk—that's me. You read about Lot, who went and laid up with his own
daughters. I had to fulfill all those things."[40] This conversation took place
a few months before Malcolm X was silenced as the national representative of Elijah Muhammad. If the FBI's effort to expose the Messenger's
personal life attained only modest results, the bureau now used the data
more profitably as part of an escalating conflict culminating in the murder of Malcolm X.

X Terminated   One of the most debated events in the history of the Nation of Islam is the February 21, 1965, assassination of Malcolm X, which
belongs in the same category as the murders of President John F. Kennedy
and the Swedish prime minister, Olof Palme: killings clothed in mystery.
Unsolved questions haunt the public mind and have inspired a number

of freelance private eyes to launch individual investigations, none of which has presented a solution that is universally accepted. In the case of Malcolm X, we know that it was a conspiracy involving more than a lone assassin. Trapped on the scene by a furious crowd at the Audubon Ballroom in Harlem was Talmadge Hayer (alias Thomas Hagan), but four other suspects got away. The police subsequently arrested Norman 3X (Butler) and Thomas 15X (Johnson), who together with Hayer, were convicted of murder in the first degree in 1966.

The verdicts did not put the case to rest. Were these really the guilty parties? If so, did they operate on command of the NOI leadership or alone? Were they a part of a larger conspiracy? Were the defendants, at least Norman 3X and Thomas 15X, themselves victims of a conspiracy? Have they spent decades in prison as innocent men, as they claim? Was the FBI, or possibly the CIA, the real conspirator, orchestrating the assassination? Three major schools of thought have crystallized over the years: the NOI-conspiracy thesis, the intelligence-community-conspiracy thesis, and the combined-conspiracy thesis.

The school suggesting that the assassination was ordered by the NOI leadership initially became the standard theory in the media. Malcolm X had received death threats from the NOI since turning against Elijah Muhammad. Tapped conversations revealed an intense hatred toward Malcolm X for defaming the Messenger. Cartoons and statements published in *Muhammad Speaks* clearly illustrated these fatal feelings of hostility. Some of Malcolm's followers issued an instant verdict. On Monday night, Temple #7 was devastated by an explosion, painting the sky with the flames of retaliation. *Newsweek* editor Peter Goldman provided the best founded arguments for the NOI-did-it thesis. As argued by Goldman, it does not rest its case on the convicted being the actual assassins—that is, Thomas 15X and Norman 3X may be innocent, while the NOI is still guilty.[41]

The intelligence-community-conspiracy thesis appears in several varieties, imparting guilt to the FBI or the CIA, with or without assistance from the Mafia. While the former school of thought contends that the intelligence community lacked sufficient motive to kill Malcolm X, this school asserts that the FBI/CIA really had reason to kill. Trotskyist George Breitman believes that Malcolm was evolving toward "a synthesis of black nationalism and socialism that would be fitting for the American scene and acceptable for the masses in the black ghetto."[42] Karl Evanzz points to the international role Malcolm had begun to assume, which possibly

could have connected the black struggle in the United States with movements, governments, and leaders counted among the enemies of the
United States government.[43] Support for this thesis is found in FBI and CIA
documents released through the FOIA, which expose informants and
agents provocateurs operating in the inner circles of Malcolm X and
Elijah Muhammad, respectively.

The third school holds that either the NOI leadership and the intelligence community collaborated, or that freelancing FOI soldiers were set
up to commit the murder by someone in the NOI hierarchy acting on
behalf of the FBI. Karl Evanzz believes this to be one possible explanation,
while Spike Lee, in yet another version, argues that the FBI knew what
was about to occur through their informants in the Nation and did what
they could to facilitate the murder.[44] While no school has been able to
prove its case beyond any reasonable doubt, enough facts have surfaced
to shed some light on hidden parts of the fatal course of events.

Through technical surveillance and top informants, the FBI discovered
tensions between Malcolm X and other high-ranking Laborers in the NOI
hierarchy. Malcolm crisscrossed the country, giving lectures and appearing on talk shows, at a time when the Messenger's health was deterior-
ating. The National Representative was a press favorite and although
Malcolm always emphasized that he was only a student of Elijah Muhammad's, he overshadowed his teacher in some respects. Malcolm's
fame caused envy among the Laborers, a jealousy that the bureau cap-
italized on.

Released files show that a number of FBI informants infiltrated the NOI,
including at least one close enough to the Messenger to be given the
private number to his secret hideout and to be able to discuss domestic
questions with him and his wife.[45] The federal informants were used to
"plant the seed of dissension," thereby increasing the internal hostilities.
By 1961, Malcolm was troubled by rumors that he sought to "take over the
Nation." He was said to be "taking credit" for the Messenger's teachings
and trying to "build an empire" for himself.[46] Malcolm began to suspect
that the root of the envy was the Messenger himself. The FBI followed the
development and was ready to make its next move.

In 1962, the bureau decided to add some tension. The information obtained about Elijah Muhammad's extramarital affairs was again used "to
expose Muhammad to his followers,"[47] by mailing a series of anonymous
letters to "selected individuals" in the NOI hierarchy.[48] Although the
names of the addressees are deleted, it is apparent that Wallace D. Mu-

hammad and Malcolm X received the information. Malcolm described in his *Autobiography* how truly shocked he was upon learning that Elijah Muhammad was a "betrayer," an "adulterer," and a "dupe."[49] There are reasons to doubt this self-described reaction. Malcolm was streetwise and knew the realities of black city culture by heart. As he also notes in his memoirs, hints about the Messenger's sexual life had been circulating since 1955 and had not caused this mental turmoil.[50] What actually hurt him was learning that two former girlfriends, whom he had recommended as secretaries to the Messenger, Sisters Evylyn and Lucille, had become pregnant. Malcolm once planned to marry Evylyn, and he now felt that Elijah Muhammad had treated her disrespectfully.[51] Malcolm had the courage to confront the Messenger, and the FBI was pleased to learn about their argument. When Malcolm passed on the word to colleagues in the Nation, Elijah Muhammad interpreted his actions as a buildup of a personal power base, a notion reinforced by FBI informants and others. In May 1963, for instance, a bugged conversation in the Messenger's Phoenix residence revealed one minister stating to Elijah Muhammad that "too much power has gone into his [Malcolm's] head."[52] When Malcolm made his famous comment about the assassination of President Kennedy as "a case of chickens coming home to roost," Elijah Muhammad was presented a golden opportunity to suspend his National Representative.[53]

The fact that Malcolm's remark was not the real reason for his removal is evident, for Elijah Muhammad felt threatened by Malcolm X. He sought to neutralize him, either by forcing him into obedience or by removing him completely. Malcolm was at first suspended only from public speaking; he continued as minister of Temple #7, but was never to regain the trust of Elijah Muhammad. The Messenger spoke to an unknown minister on a tapped phone in December 1963, saying that Malcolm X "is turning out just the way I thought he would." He continued, "I did not think he would ever be able to take a spanking," and "everywhere [Malcolm] went he wanted to be idolized as the boss."[54]

Listening to the increasing hostility within the Nation, the FBI decided to fuel the flames. In a memo dated February 7, 1964, the FBI suggested a move that "could possibly widen the rift between Muhammad and Little and possibly result in Little's expulsion from the NOI."[55] Whatever specific action took place is deleted from the files, but the desired development, whether due to the activities of the FBI or not, became reality. In March 1964, the Messenger decided to extend the suspension indefinitely, and Malcolm announced his establishment of Muslim Mosque, Inc.[56] Promptly, the FBI decided to recruit black informants to infiltrate the new splinter group. When learning about Malcolm's plans to visit Africa and West Asia, the CIA initiated a separate program designed to monitor his foreign contacts and activities.[57] A few weeks later, Malcolm went on *hajj,* the pilgrimage to Mecca. In a famous letter, Malcolm wrote that sharing bread and belief with white Muslims made him realize that they are not incurably evil. "We were *truly* all the same [brothers]," he wrote, "because their belief in one God had removed the 'white' from their *minds,* the 'white' from their *behavior* and the 'white' from their *attitude.*"[58] This hardly impressed the NOI cadre. Raymond Sharieff, supreme captain of the FOI, later wrote in *Muhammad Speaks:* "Malcolm goes to MECCA. He makes a pilgrimage and for the first time Malcolm gets a chance to eat out of the same dish with the devil. This excited Malcolm, lover of the devil. Malcolm, came back from Mecca worshipping the devil because this was the closest that he had ever gotten to be in the society of the devil. . . . Judas Iscariot ate out of the same dish with Jesus, but Judas was not a Jesus. Judas was a betrayer."[59] Renamed El Hajj Malik El Shabazz, Malcolm made contact with influential Islamic leaders and organizations. The Muslim World League hoped Malcolm would "correct the image" of Islam in black America, and he was therefore provided with credentials from al-Ahzar, the respected Islamic university. These moves suggest that Malcolm was preparing for a *dawa* (mission) competition with the Messenger. Prominent Mecca-based Sudanese *ulama* (Islamic scholar), Sheikh Ahmed Hassoun, returned with Malcolm to work as a spiritual guide, and the Saudis allegedly made a financial contribution.[60] A convert to mainstream Sunni Islam, Malcolm maintained a black nationalist orientation. Whites were excluded from the Muslim Mosque, Inc., as well as from the secular political movement founded in June 1964, the Organization of Afro-American Unity (OAAU).[61]

As part of the process of building a new profile, Malcolm began hurling verbal assaults against Elijah Muhammad and the Nation. In June 1964, Malcolm appeared on different radio programs, publicly denouncing Elijah Muhammad for his extramarital affairs and reassuring his listeners that he could never again represent such an immoral man.[62] Returning from a second African tour of meetings with prominent African and Muslim leaders in November 1964, Malcolm stressed the link between African American liberation and Third World revolutionary movements and states. Previously, Malcolm had urged Blackamericans to form rifle clubs for self-defense.[63] Now, violence was legitimate if it were used to overthrow the racist power structure in America. Black liberation was to be achieved "by any means necessary."[64]

In this context, Malcolm began to accuse the Nation of Islam for deliberately holding back the revolution. Malcolm divulged an alleged "conspiracy between the Muslims and the right wing of this country."[65] By using radical rhetoric, Elijah Muhammad lured the most dissatisfied African Americans to the Nation, where he kept them passive.[66] "What Elijah Muhammad is teaching is an insult to the entire Muslim world,"[67] Malcolm claimed, portraying the Messenger as a corrupted man, more interested in money, wealth, and sex than black progress.[68] Six days later, Malcolm was shot to death.

At the subsequent trial in 1966, Talmadge Hayer, a twenty-two year old from Paterson, New Jersey, testified that Norman 3X and Thomas 15X were innocent strangers and that he was not a follower of Elijah Muhammad. The Messenger confirmed that Hayer was a perfect stranger. In 1977, Hayer (now known as Mujahid Halim) admitted that he actually had been in the Nation at the time of the assassination.[69] He maintained that Norman 3X and Thomas 15X were innocent, but he now revealed the names of four co-conspirators, all members of the Newark Temple #25. In the winter of 1977–78, attorney William Kunstler tried to no avail to reopen the case. The district attorney and the courts refused, arguing that the testimony did not constitute new evidence.[70] The fact that Norman 3X (renamed Muhammad Abd al-Aziz) and Thomas 15X (renamed Khalil Islam) are innocent seems reasonable. Norman 3X was a karate expert and FOI lieutenant, Thomas 15X a former bodyguard of Muhammad Ali and an NOI enforcer. Both were well-known New York Muslims and would have been easily recognized by Malcolm's security staff had they appeared at the Audubon Ballroom that day.[71] Abd al-Aziz and Islam were released on parole after first serving twenty and twenty-two years in prison, respectively.[72]

Mujahid Halim (Hayer) testified that the murder was committed in retaliation for Malcolm's attacks on Elijah Muhammad. Many Muslims recall a tight internal climate at that time. Subcultural values such as obedience, discipline, and commitment enhanced the notion of the brotherhood as a mighty body of divine soldiers. No one was allowed to defame the Messenger of God or harass the chosen Nation.[73] Offenders disrespecting the Messenger were roughed up and, in a few cases, killed. Malcolm's public blasphemy was an intolerable offense. On a bugged phone in March 1964, Elijah Muhammad told a top Laborer that it was time "to make an example" out of Malcolm. "With these hypocrites," the Messenger maintained, "when you find them cut their heads off."[74] During the remainder of 1964, *Muhammad Speaks* published a series of attacks on Malcolm. Minister Farrakhan wrote, "Only those who wish to be led to hell, or to their doom, will follow Malcolm. The die is set, and Malcolm shall not escape, especially after such evil, foolish talk about his benefactor. . . . Such a man as Malcolm is worthy of death and would have been met with death if it had not been for Muhammad's confidence in Allah for victory over his enemies."[75] As Malcolm continued to attack the Messenger, Raymond Sharieff sent Malcolm a telegram on December 7, 1964, officially warning him that "the NOI shall no longer tolerate to [*sic*] scandalizing the name of our leader and teacher the Honorable Elijah Muhammad."[76] A *Muhammad Speaks* cartoon appearing in January 1965, showed the severed head of Malcolm X bumping down the road to a graveyard for traitors.[77] An editorial branded Malcolm a Judas, whose tongue should be cut off and delivered to the doorstep of the Messenger.[78]

Malcolm stayed at a house that legally belonged to the Temple #7 as a minister's residence. The Messenger demanded that Malcolm evacuate the property of the Nation.[79] Malcolm refused, however, arguing that he had more than earned it through years of dedicated service. On February 14, 1964, Molotov cocktails set the house on fire.[80] Malcolm and the NOI blamed each other. Yusuf Shah (then known as Captain Joseph) was commander of the Temple #7 FOI at that time. When interviewed by Spike Lee in 1991, Yusuf Shah said that the firebombing "was done by [Muslim] zealots."[81] Temple #25 in Newark had a reputation of being number-one enforcers, zealots that would punish anyone defaming the Messenger of God. According to former NOI members, the vengeance squad operated without direct orders and read between the lines for what should be done. Was the murder of Malcolm X an act of freelance assassins? In a sworn 1979 affidavit, Halim (Hayer) revealed the names of four FOI soldiers as his co-conspirators.[82] Speaking with Yusuf Shah, Spike Lee named these Newark Muslims as having been connected to the assassination. "That's about all of them," Yusuf Shah replied.[83] Mujahid Halim said in his statement that the ring of zealots had begun planning in June 1964. But were they acting with or without orders?

We know from the FBI files that the bureau had at least one, possibly two, informants in the NOI's top leadership. One informant was close enough to Elijah Muhammad to share in very private, delicate matters.

The other informant (assuming they are not one and the same) was placed in Temple #7. The top informant is described by the bureau as "a highly sensitive source," whose protection demanded that "information furnished by this source that is disseminated must be paraphrased."[84] The actual identity of this top informant has not been definitively determined. Louis Lomax wrote that John X Ali was a former FBI agent.[85] Ali was made national secretary under Malcolm X in 1958 and transferred to Chicago headquarters in the early 1960s. Karl Evanzz notes that Ali abstained from taking legal action against Lomax for his statement and suggests that John X Ali was in fact the FBI's top informant in the NOI. As national secretary, he had access to the excellent data found in the FBI files and was perfectly suited to act as an agent provocateur.[86] Moreover, John X Ali was the only Laborer at the very top who was not related to the Messenger either by blood or marriage.[87] John X Ali was among the NOI hawks who sharply condemned Malcolm and called for retaliation. On February 19, 1965, John X Ali reportedly checked into the American Hotel in New York. The following day he was seen with Talmadge Hayer, the would-be assassin.[88]

The FBI placed or recruited informants within the inner circle of Malcolm's companions as noted above. One of these was an undercover agent named Gene (X) Roberts, who worked as Malcolm's bodyguard on the day of the murder. Roberts later infiltrated the New York chapter of the Black Panther Party and surfaced as the state's star witness in the 1970–71 "Panther 21" case.[89] Although he was not the only informant present at the Audubon, Roberts is the only known informant who had a top position. As part of the security, Roberts had a position suited for covert action. When Malcolm began speaking a few minutes before the assassins opened fire, Gene Roberts signaled that he wished to be relieved from his position close to Malcolm. Another guard filled his post and Roberts took a position at the near entrance.[90] It cannot at this point be determined if this was merely coincidence, or if Roberts was Malcolm's O'Neal, the undercover agent inside the Chicago Panthers' security force who instigated the murders of prominent Panthers Fred Hampton and Mark Clark.[91]

To summarize: the FBI learned from its sources about growing tensions between Malcolm X and Elijah Muhammad and decided to use the opportunity. With the help of strategically placed informants, the wheel of animosity was pushed into motion. The FBI may have known of Malcolm's affection for Sister Evelyn Williams, and therefore mailed him selected highlights from the tapes of the Messenger's private life. As the conflict escalated, the FBI took steps to widen the rift between Elijah and Malcolm with the aim of causing Malcolm's expulsion. Malcolm then established the MMI and OAAU, which were infiltrated by the bureau. From there, the informants had only to encourage the increasing hostility and the conflict would become self-generating, moving toward the desired culmination. All parties made their contribution to the setting: Malcolm with his defamatory attacks, the NOI staff with their call for violent retaliation, and the FBI with its encouragement of the escalating feud. The dye was in fact cast and Malcolm did not escape.

Whether the Newark zealots operated with or without orders cannot be positively determined. Most likely, the assassins believed that they had a divine obligation to remove the traitor and possibly received an initial signal from the uncompromising John X Ali or another top Laborer, possibly on the FBI pay roll.[92] Clearly, the fatal outcome pleased the bureau. In retrospect, the SAC in Chicago bragged that the scheme was "the most notable" of all the "factional disputes" that the FBI's personnel "have developed."[93] Later, Minister Farrakhan realized that he had been predictable enough to be used as a pawn in the federal conspiracy, much like the folktale in which the boy tricks two giants into fighting each other by throwing stones on them from a hiding place. "The FBI was working to create the division," Farrakhan acknowledged, "and then of course they wanted to feed into this division, so that we could fight and kill each other, and they would get rid of two birds with one stone."[94]

Did the FBI have a role beyond manipulating the two camps so that they were at each other's throats? Did Gene Roberts or some other undercover agent in Malcolm's group furnish the hit squad with relevant information? Though the murder fits into the pattern of covert FBI actions to remove black dissidents in the 1960s, theories to this end rest mainly on indications and speculation. The complete role of the federal agents cannot be determined until all files are declassified and the concerned special agents in charge are allowed to speak out. Two additional files do indicate that facts remains to be unmasked. In March 1969, the SAC in Chicago wished to recontact the loyal *Chicago Sun-Times* reporter William Jones to furnish him with a sample of critical NOI remarks against Malcolm X. Such articles usually produce unfavorable reactions toward the NOI, the agent reflected, "particularly since the NOI in many quarters is still regarded as guilty for the death of Malcolm X."[95] This remark indicates that at least this agent no longer considered the NOI to be guilty. In

August 1969, the SAC in Miami was prepared to expose the NOI and requested material about the conflict between Malcolm X and Elijah Muhammad. The SAC in Chicago strongly disapproved, stating that "at the present time, Chicago does not desire to rehash some of the exposures that occurred around the time of the defection of MALCOLM X LITTLE as top level sources could be endangered and future activities thereof curtailed."[96] This suggests that top-level FBI informants had been crucially involved, informants that still held key positions in the NOI hierarchy in 1969.

A Federal Conspiracy to Neutralize the Nation of Islam   During the 1960s, the unrest in black America was growing intense. The year 1964 not only marked the famous "Freedom Summer," but also great racial rebellions in the North. On July 18, 1964, riots began in Brooklyn; within weeks, rioting swept through cities in New York, New Jersey, Illinois, and Pennsylvania. The great 1965 Watts uprising in Los Angeles was followed by a hot summer in 1966, and then 150 reported riots in 1967, notably the violent upheavals in Detroit and Newark.[97]

J. Edgar Hoover saw no economic or social causes behind these outbursts. Asked by President Lyndon B. Johnson to explain the reasons, he presented a report saying that "Black Power advocates" and "criminal, subversive and extremist elements" were fanning the flames of "spontaneous outbursts of mob violence," and concluded that "certain individuals who have been prominent in the civil rights field must bear a major burden of the guilt and responsibility for the turmoil created by these riots." Furthermore, the report traced contacts between black dissidents and the antiwar movement, and the FBI saw the Communist Party, United States of America (CPUSA) behind the upheavals, exploiting racial issues to create "the chaos upon which communism flourishes."[98]

The outcome of the report was an extensive program providing the FBI with more money and more agents. In December 1967, Attorney General Ramsey Clark created an interdivisional intelligence unit to use FBI reports to compile a master index, organized on a city-by-city basis. This was to be a form of extensive community surveillance of dissident individuals and organizations. In the fall of 1967, the FBI used their experience in developing informants (an estimated one-third of 3,198 members were informants in the CPUSA) to create a TOPLEV (top level) informant program, later known as BLACPRO, in order to infiltrate militant black nationalist organizations. In October 1967, an even more pervasive and grassroots-oriented program was initiated, the "Ghetto Listening Post," in which 3,248 informants were enlisted by the summer of 1968.[99] This number was deemed insufficient by Hoover, who developed a quota system, in which all field agents were obliged to enlist a certain number of ghetto informants. To structure the intelligence data, the security index was supplemented with a computerized rabble rouser Index, later renamed the agitator index, with subfiles on important organizations, such as the Nation of Islam.[100] All these organizational developments were, or would become, part of a new counterintelligence program created to subdue black wrath: COINTELPRO—Black Nationalist Hate Groups.

The idea behind this program was not to assemble intelligence in a passive manner, but to use it in an active effort to neutralize domestic dissidents. It was officially initiated in a memo from the director on August 25, 1967, and the directives gave no room for misinterpretations: "The purpose of this new counterintelligence endeavor is to expose, disrupt, misdirect, discredit, or otherwise neutralize the activities of black nationalist, hate type organizations and groupings, their leadership, spokesmen, membership and supporters."[101] On March 4, 1968, the program was expanded from twenty-three to forty local FBI offices, adding five long-range goals: (1) "prevent the coalition of militant black nationalist groups" that "might be the first step toward a real 'Mau Mau' in America, the beginning of a true black revolution"; (2) "prevent the rise of a 'messiah' who could unify and electrify the militant black nationalist movement"; (3) "prevent violence" by identifying "potential troublemakers and neutraliz[ing] them"; (4) "prevent militant black nationalist groups and leaders from gaining respectability, by discrediting them"; and (5) "prevent the long range growth of black nationalist organizations, especially among youth."[102] Among the listed targets were the Nation of Islam and the Honorable Elijah Muhammad. The offices were ordered to submit the name of the responsible officer and a summary of black nationalist organizations in their field, including a list of dangerous individuals, within thirty days. They were furthermore instructed to suggest counterintelligence actions by separate letter.[103]

Before we look into the specific actions taken by the bureau, it should be emphasized that in several cases the local FBI offices advised that no counterintelligence action be taken at all. Ten offices reported no black nationalist organization in their field except for the Nation of Islam. Most of these offices understood the NOI to be a nonviolent religious organization, and they could see no point in initiating a counterintelligence action. The report from SAC in Richmond is representative: "The only Black

Nationalist Movement to exist in the Richmond territory is the Nation of Islam. . . . The Richmond office has informant coverage of this organization and through its informants and other sources has determined that the NOI in Richmond is a non-militant black nationalist group. Richmond NOI members are constantly taught to avoid all forms of violence and to use force only to defend oneself and then only when absolute necessary. Any infraction of this rule results in the guilty members being suspended. . . . Richmond knows of no organizations and individuals within its territory that should be considered for current counterintelligence action."[104] The SAC in Milwaukee underlined the fact that "the NOI in Wisconsin has abstained from participation in civil disorders" and advised that action from the FBI might be counterproductive: "It is felt that a counterintelligence program instituted against the NOI may change the present situation."[105] Other offices suggested counterintelligence action against the Nation of Islam despite the fact that NOI members were known to abstain from racial violence or rioting.[106]

In order to present the FBI's counterintelligence activities against the Nation of Islam, it is perhaps wise to return to the original orders as set forth in the memo from August 25, 1967. The director specifies four avenues for counterintelligence action to be implemented by the special agents in charge. Each method will be illustrated with a few representative examples of counterintelligence activities put into practice.

> 1. Efforts of the various groups to consolidate their forces or recruit new or youthful adherents must be frustrated. No opportunity should be missed to exploit through counterintelligence techniques the organizational and personal conflicts of the leaderships of the groups. . . .

The New York office (NYO) reported that they had been "unable to make a penetration into the top leadership of the NOI in NY, as far as informant development is concerned," but they believed that some leader could turn informant "when their economic security is jeopardized." To "shake the confidence of the membership in their leaders" and to create factional splits and a general loss in membership and recruiting abilities, the NYO prepared a "large comic-book type publication made up to ridicule the leaders. This book depicts [FBI deletion] living the good life, having good homes, big cars, and wearing fine suits. It is felt this type publication would be an effective method of securing initial unrest and would appeal to a wide, generally uneducated audience."[107] NYO advised that the publication should be sent in unmarked envelopes to thirty-six NOI members on the security list and 237 other selected members. The NYO assumed that when disseminated, the publication would cause members to "become disenchanted in the organization, cause others to be disillusioned and perhaps future membership also be reduced." In addition, it "could cause these above three individuals to feel that the literature was made up by some other NOI leaders of the NY area," which is why it was hoped that the distribution "will result in internal strife, distrust, and disorder within the NOI itself."[108]

The director authorized the NYO to mail the booklets, thus paving the way for more action.[109] New York FBI agents phoned the leaders depicted in the booklet they had produced, pretending to be infuriated members of the NOI. The agents "clearly conveyed the impression to them that several NOI brothers were going to 'take care of them' for stealing the dues of the membership."[110] The booklet also created distrust between the NOI headquarters and the leaders of the New York mosque. From Chicago, New York members were urged to get a receipt for the money they contributed, and the supreme captain of the FOI flew in to investigate "the possibility that some high officials of the New York NOI were not turning in all money to Elijah Muhammad."[111]

Like many other dissident organizations in the United States, the Nation was aware of FBI methods such as surveillance and paid informants. Security consciousness contributed to the creation of a culture of suspicion, easy to capitalize on by the federal agents through bad-jacketing targeted individuals. The SAC in Miami initiated an interview program with local NOI officials and members, providing opportunities to discreetly indicate to some of the persons interviewed "that other specific individuals previously interviewed had cooperated with the FBI."[112] Rumors spread accordingly. The Miami minister officially threatened members with drastic actions if they cooperated with the bureau, and pleased agents continued to fuel the drift toward intracongregational dissension with more interviews and bad-jacketing. This created an atmosphere of brotherly distrust, thus setting the stage for subsequent counterintelligence actions, such as sending anonymous letters to NOI headquarters with slander against the Miami minister.[113]

2. Be alert to determine evidence of misappropriation of funds or other types of personal misconduct on the part of militant nationalist leaders so any practical or warranted counterintelligence may be instituted.

One common counterintelligence move was to mail Elijah Muhammad bogus letters from anonymous local members pretending concern over their ministers' alleged misbehavior. This was done by, among others, agents in Tampa,[114] Birmingham,[115] Norfolk,[116] San Antonio,[117] Chicago,[118] and Miami.[119] The reported effectiveness of such actions varied from no tangible results (Birmingham) to the removal of the targeted minister and subsequent destabilization of the local congregation (in Miami).[120]

Another method used was to use planted informants to spread false rumors and accusations within the local mosque, as was the case in Houston. The Dallas mosque lacked a minister, which is why the minister in Houston regularly visited the neighbor congregation to conduct meetings. The SAC in Houston found a golden opportunity to "arrange through appropriate communication and informants to accuse [FBI deletion] of taking the Dallas money and bringing it to Houston . . . and planting the idea with Houston NOI that [FBI deletion] has another woman in Dallas."[121] The results of the counterintelligence actions pleased the Houston office, which reported to headquarters that "several top officers" had been "demoted" and "chaos" ruled among members, causing "considerable consternation within the entire NOI organization." The SAC in Houston hoped "to continue to capitalize on the chaos," feeling that the problems would easily increase through "appropriate informant handling."[122]

3. Where possible, efforts should be made to capitalize upon existing conflicts between competing black nationalist organizations.

As with the implementation of the COINTELPRO methods described above, the implicit order was to create conditions for counterintelligence action. If there were no internal intrigues, personal conflicts within the targeted organization were "developed." If the NOI leadership proved to have moral integrity, informants planted seeds of mistrust concerning targeted leaders. If the NOI had good working relations with other black nationalist organizations, conflicts to capitalize on were created. Orchestrating mutual distrust set the wheel of animosity in motion, sometimes accelerating toward violent vendettas, letting the bureau reap a harvest of permanently silenced militants at a low federal cost. The notorious and repeatedly deadly clashes between the Black Panther Party and the California-based United Slaves organization of Ron Karenga provide but one example of successful FBI-produced conflicts.[123]

In comparison, the FBI-directed interorganizational conflicts involving the Nation of Islam had less serious results. When the militant separatist Republic of New Africa (RNA) was founded in 1968, the Detroit division proposed that "a turmoil" be created between them and the NOI. An initial move would be a letter on the stationery of the RNA directed to a "substantial number of rank and file [NOI] members," inviting them to shift membership from the NOI to the RNA, while pointing out that "Elijah Muhammad had been deceiving them" for the enhancement of his "own financial self-interest."[124] The eventual role of the FBI in the escalating conflict between the two organizations cannot be clarified as the relevant files are heavily deleted, but mutual suspicion between the Nation and the Republic of New Africa was still evident, at least in the Midwest, in the late 1980s and early 1990s.

Federal agents were involved in provoking conflicts between the Black Panthers and the Nation of Islam in New York, Chicago, San Francisco, Richmond, Atlanta, and Buffalo.[125] It was hoped that by "carefully planning, an open dispute" would develop "between the two organizations."[126] Bogus letters should "direct their hatred toward one another."[127] The tension created was then used to further counterintelligence actions. In Atlanta, Panthers attacked NOI members selling newspapers, and the local FBI agents were ordered by headquarters to "consider this incident in submitting a counterintelligence proposal directed toward causing further animosity between these two extremist groups."[128] In other instances, however, the bureau stopped suggested moves directed toward the instigation of violence, such as when the director turned down the New York division's idea of addressing a letter from the Harlem mosque to Huey Newton, threatening to "discipline" the Panthers.[129]

As noted above, some offices reported that no militant black nationalist organization was present in their territory. Such a situation did not necessarily hinder the creativity of ambitious agents. In Mobile, Alabama, the special agent noted the nonexistence of any militant group qualified for counterintelligence measures and thus suggested "that the Bureau might consider the creation of a paper Negro nationalist group for the purpose of drawing together militant leaders and militant groups in order to plant seeds of dissension among such leaders."[130] Whether any such organization came into existence or not cannot be clarified until more files are released by the bureau. Several black nationalist organizations still suspect one another of being FBI creations, a suspicion that severely contributed to an atmosphere of mutual distrust among groups who otherwise might have cooperated.

4. When an opportunity is apparent to disrupt or neutralize black nationalist, hate-type organizations through the cooperation of established local news media contacts . . . careful attention must be given to the proposal to insure the targeted group is disrupted, ridiculed, or discredited through the publicity and not merely publicized.

The use of cooperative journalists to channel derogatory information about targeted groups and individuals is an old FBI method that lends an aura of objectivity to the bureau's subjective understanding of a specific matter. Despite the FBI's precautions, this method can still prove to be counterproductive, and two examples will show its double-edged nature. In December 1968, the SAC in Chicago asked the bureau for authorization to provide *Chicago Tribune* journalist William Jones, "who has been utilized in the past," with data to enable him to "expose some possible fraudulent aspects of the NOI and the so-called economic program to the membership of the organization and also to the general public."[131] Authorization was granted, resulting in the article "Black Muslims Set Their Sights on the Supremacy of Capitalism" being published in the Sunday edition of the *Chicago Tribune* on January 26, 1969.[132] Instead of creating the desired damage, the exposure had the opposite effect. Elijah Muhammad was so pleased with the publicity that he wrote an open letter thanking William Jones and "the great *Chicago Tribune* newspaper for mentioning us in its mighty fine paper."[133]

The goal came closer to being fulfilled in Miami. In January 1969, the Miami division wanted to provide Richard Whitcomb from Channel 7 of WCKT-TV with material for a documentary film that would "hamp[er] future activities of the local NOI group."[134] Authorization was granted because WCKT had been "extremely cooperative with the Bureau in the past." The local agents were told to "stress the importance of exposing and ridiculing NOI money-making schemes which milk members in order to fill the coffers of Elijah Muhammad."[135] The program, "Fear of the Secret Dark," aired in October 1969, with "highly successful results" in the eyes of the FBI. Whitcomb underscored "the extreme nature of NOI teachings" and showed "that NOI leaders are of questionable character and live in luxury through the large amount of money taken from their members." Attendance by visitors at weekly NOI meetings in the area dropped by 50 percent, proving "the value of carefully planned counterintelligence action."[136] In fact, the film was so successful that Elijah Muhammad, who frequently let unfavorable media items pass without comment, criticized Whitcomb vehemently in a *Muhammad Speaks* rebuttal.[137]

Knights of Americanism and the Threat of Black Islam   On March 8, 1971, members of an antiwar group called the Citizens' Commission to Investigate the FBI broke into the FBI agency in Media, Pennsylvania, and got away with some one thousand pieces of bureau documents.[138] When they began to send a steady flow of embarrassing samples to the press, Hoover decided to terminate the counterintelligence programs: "Although successful over the years, it is felt they should now be discontinued for security reasons."[139] The FBI later added an "except in exceptional instances" clause to the order of termination.[140] Hoover died on May 2, 1972, and thus was spared the experience of a temporary collapse of the bureau's surveillance machinery. When the Watergate scandal unraveled in 1974, amendments to the Freedom of Information Act were passed over President Nixon's veto. This opened up FBI files an unusual degree and lead to an unprecedented public exposure of domestic intelligence.[141] When information about FBI repression against domestic dissidents reached the American public, questions began to be raised about the reasons for bureau activities that seemed to be out of place in the officially open and democratic United States. Some commentators blamed J. Edgar Hoover personally, reducing the discussion on the necessary reform of the FBI to a question of how to avoid another Hoover.[142] Others believed the FBI to be an instrument for the ruling powers, used to crush radical revolutionaries.[143] While both arguments contain some degree of truth, the FBI phenomenon cannot be reduced to one or the other.

Concerning the first argument, it must be noted that Hoover was not alone. Every president during the relevant period not only approved the work of the bureau, but himself initiated new efforts to combat the perceived threat.[144] Although Hoover had tremendous personal power, the FBI was a team, composed of individuals adhering to the norms of the bureau subculture. They took individual initiatives and rearranged counterintelligence activities that continued after the death of Hoover.[145]

The second argument overlooks the considerable autonomy of the bureau, making the "mere-tool" thesis absurd. Even if reworked in a less conspiracy-minded fashion, the second line of argument fails to explain the sum of bureau undertakings. What made the Nation of Islam—perhaps a rhetorically radical, but in any practical sense, a nonrevolutionary religion—qualify as a target for the bureau? Why did the FBI waste so much energy documenting the sexual habits of a nonviolent reformist such as Martin Luther King Jr.?

David J. Garrow argues for the broader "cultural-threat" thesis, suggesting that the bureau was more a reflection of mainstream American cultural values and society than the product of certain individuals or organizational structures. The argument holds "that the essence of the Bureau's social role has been not to attack critics, Communists, blacks or leftists per se, but to repress all perceived threats to the dominant, status-quo oriented political culture. . . . [T]he Bureau was not a deviant institution in American society, but actually a most representative and faithful one."[146] Garrow is, I believe, on the right track. The cultural-threat argument explains the seemingly irrational xenophobic, sex phobic, and ethnocentric attitude of the FBI, which chose the same enemies that many mainstream Anglo-Americans would regard as their own foes. The Nation of Islam hardly represented a communist threat. The FOI soldiers could not be seriously judged as capable of overthrowing the contemporary power structure in the United States. Whatever threat they represented must be understood at another level. I propose that the growth and development of the NOI, as well as the FBI reaction to the perceived threat they represented, has to be seen in the context of "Americanity" or the "American civil religion."

The religion of the Republic, alternatively known as "Americanity" or the "civil religion" of the United States,[147] is the semireligious dimension of the notion of America as a melting pot. Immigrants from various European countries, adhering to different religions and denominations, were supposed to substitute their particular identities for their new identities as Americans. A child of the Enlightenment and the Hegelian notion of progressive evolution, the creation of the United States of America was depicted as a fulfillment of mankind's ambitions to create a better world. Multicultural tolerance was achieved through transcending the specific, by projecting unifying fundamentals on a higher level of abstraction. The separation of church and state was supplemented by introducing a religious dimension as a central rationale for the American project, making Americanity a creed and the United States an instrument of God's work in the world.

As discussed by Robert N. Bellah in his classic essay on the American civil religion, Biblical themes and symbols are used in the historiography of the United States.[148] The Americans are identified as the "chosen people," who through an "exodus" from Europe reached the "promised land"

and there founded the "New Jerusalem." American civil religion has its own prophets (Benjamin Franklin, Thomas Jefferson, George Washington), its own martyrs (Abraham Lincoln, the Kennedys, all soldiers killed in war), its own sacred events (the Declaration of Independence, the Boston Tea Party), its own sacred places to which pilgrimage is made (Gettysburg, the Tomb of the Unknown Soldier, Lincoln Memorial), its solemn rituals of commemoration (Independence Day, Memorial Day, Thanksgiving Day, Veterans Day), and its sacred symbols (the Stars and Stripes, the White House, the Statue of Liberty).

As the sacred expression of the American dream, Americanity preaches all the values, norms, and ideals associated with the American way of life. The United States is the defender of freedom, democracy, and moral decency against every form of totalitarianism, which during the Cold War was principally defined as communism but is now increasingly being replaced by Islam. In this fortress of individual liberty with equal opportunities for all, each man can reach success. The legend of Horatio Alger is described by Sherry B. Ortner as a key scenario from American culture, formulating both the American conception of success—wealth and power—and suggesting a strategy for its achievement. The exemplary scenario, well known from an endless series of Hollywood productions, runs thus: "poor boy of low status, but with total faith in the American system, works very hard and ultimately becomes rich and powerful."[149] The ideology of Americanism pays homage to the lonely individual with a trust in God and denies the existence of collective injustices.

Civil religion is by definition unifying and ecumenical. It formulates one community, as opposed to the church, which only constitutes one community among others.[150] Initially, inter-Protestant divisions were transcended. During the late nineteenth century the concept of Christianity was broadened to include Roman Catholicism. After the end of World War II, Judaism was assimilated into mainstream American culture and the Judeo-Christian tradition became the foundation for the project of Americanity.[151] Islam, however, was never incorporated. Muslim immigration began in 1860 with immigrants from Greater Syria. Well aware of the traditional Christian antagonism against Islam, they chose to keep a low profile, unwilling to put the constitutional freedom of belief to the test. As described in chapter 2, the bulk of early American Muslims did not arrive as voluntary migrants but as slaves. Neither of these roots of the nineteenth-century Islamic presence in America was to nurture the tree of Americanism. On the contrary, Islam and communism were together depicted as cultures of evil, as negations to be defined against in the creation of the American understanding of self. As a result, the descendants of Africa and Islam found themselves placed in a parallel relation of opposition to the American dream. Islam was never assimilated into the unifying Judeo-Christian tradition that would constitute the fundament of Americanity, and African Americans were not included in the liberty preached but were taken there as slaves.

Black Islam questions the project of Americanity and points to the discrepancy between professed ideal and experienced reality. Its doctrinal presentation of the past and present theologies of the NOI skillfully uses the key symbols of Americanity, which are given a renewed and reversed meaning in order to expose its evil nature. Contrary to being the achievement of God in the world, the United States is presented as the creation of the Devil. The fervent iconoclastic assaults are designed to awaken the mentally sleeping blacks from the nightmare of the American dream. The United States is the "land of the free, home of the slaves."[152] In an often printed NOI cartoon, the Statue of Liberty is standing with her lamp lifted. The caption below is a travesty of the original poem: "Give me your rich, your famous, your anti-black, yearning for white supremacy. . . . We'll leave the light on for you."[153] Louis Farrakhan argues that what for Europeans was a golden door, was an anteroom to prison for "the masses of black people who still huddle and yearn to breathe free."[154] The "Statue of Liberty," Khallid Abdul Muhammad exclaimed, is "nothin' but a whore in the harbor. Standing there with her torch, ready to pull her dress up and shine the light and let the ships come rollin' in."[155] Elijah Muhammad saw the Star-Spangled Banner not as a symbol of liberty but as signifying slavery, suffering, and death.[156] The Messenger dubbed Independence Day a festival of hypocrisy, as the Founding Fathers denied African Americans their independence.[157] "Fourth of July / A Fuckin' lie / When did we ever / get a piece of the pie," Public Enemy rhymes in a song about the holy days of the American civil religion, days "crazy as Hitler Day."[158] Another recurrent NOI cartoon depicts Uncle Sam as Satan, the dragon serpent of Revelation 12:9, "which deceiveth the whole world," Uncle Tom included, but which will be defeated by the Lamb, that is Elijah Muhammad. The African American should reject the White House as a center of legitimate authority and instead is to pledge loyalty to the NOI headquarters, "the Black House," which is "the seat of divine government for the black nation."[159]

The real threat presented by the Nation is to be found on this cognitive level. It represents a fundamental ideological attack on the civil religion, reversing the value of Americanity to its opposite in the dichotomy of good and evil. The iconoclastic rhetoric of the NOI spokespersons ruin the public image of American identity. This rhetoric constitutes a blasphemous assault on the ideological foundation of American society, questioning its very raison d'être. Americanity is supposed to transcend ethnicity and religion. The NOI spokespersons expose this as untrue, saying that neither blacks nor Muslims participated on an equal basis in the shaping of American culture. Moreover, the NOI position is a rejection of the very project of Americanity, giving priority to a separate national identity.

If Garrow is right in regarding the FBI as a reflection of American society and culture, the FBI reaction to the apostasy of the Nation can be explained. For most of its history, the bureau was largely a homogeneous community, with carefully recruited agents from conservative, mainstream, white, male culture,[160] established to defend good old America. As knights of the American dream, their crusade against a community of ideological fifth columns was an obligation and not a deviation from what the agents understood their mission to be.[161]

In practice the members of the Nation were denied their constitutional rights, which guarantee all American citizens the freedom of speech, the freedom of assembly, and the freedom of belief. The rationale for disregarding the very Constitution the agents were employed to protect, I believe, can be explained by the apparent NOI transgression of the unwritten code of Americanity.[162] By publicly reversing the fundamental values of American civil religion and desecrating its prime symbols, the Nation of Islam became "un-American" and thus was targeted for counterintelligence actions.

The bureau's scheme to neutralize the Nation of Islam proved to be a disappointment. Counterintelligence operations thwarted the Republic of New Africa, the Black Panther Party, the American Indian Movement, and other targets but failed to ruin the NOI. Summarizing more than a decade of orchestrated covert actions, the SAC in Chicago complained, "For years the Bureau has operated a counterintelligence program against the NOI and Muhammad . . . despite these efforts, he continues unchallenged in the leadership of the NOI and the organization itself, in terms of membership and finances, has been unaffected."[163] Farrakhan commented in 1973 that the United States government had destroyed every black organization and leader fighting for justice. There is only one man and one organization that remain: the Nation of Islam under the divine guidance of the Messenger of Allah.[164] The FBI never did realize that their actions were perfectly suited to the eschatology of the Nation. When Elijah Muhammad was imprisoned, it was interpreted as fulfillment of the suffering a Messenger of God must suffer. When local police forces assaulted the NOI Temples, as in Los Angeles in 1962, New York in 1972, and Sacramento in 1974,[165] the police not only assumed the role of the Roman, Babylonian, Egyptian, and Meccan armies attacking the righteous, but defined who was who in the final battle. When the FBI launched media campaigns and when other covert actions were exposed by double agents,[166] the Nation of Islam reacted with no surprise. The bureau was but one part of the forces of evil who in the latter days are supposed to behave in this manner.[167]

Exposed to the American public, the FBI COINTELPRO turned into a powerful argument confirming the NOI creed.[168] "The Holy Quran warns the Muslims that the devils see you," Farrakhan said in 1974. "The United States Government has paid enemies and informers in every temple, among every society of Muslims. Whenever you meet, the devil meets with us. Whenever you pick up the phone to talk, the devil is listening." By their actions, the federal agents were playing right into the hands of the people of God. The demons in the government of America "shall pay for every evil done against the righteous, for there is a God on the scene in the Person of Master Fard Muhammad," Farrakhan exclaimed.[169] Resorting to repression, the agents initiate the apocalypse. Elijah Muhammad explained that "America wishes to oppose Allah (God) in this work of bringing justice and freedom to her once slaves, but this is just what Allah (God) wants. He (Allah) wants America to attack Him, to get the fight started and to bring His judgment against her with the fullness of His strength and power."[170] The COINTELPRO era has been since then part of a general street knowledge, popularized through speeches, movies, and music. Public Enemy rapped in 1988:

> Power Equality
> And we're out to get it
> I know some of you ain't wit'it
> This party started right in '66
> With a pro-Black radical mix
> Then at the hour of twelve
> Some force cut the power

> And emerged from hell
> It was your so called government
> That made this occur
> Like the grafted devils they were.[171]

Assisted in this manner by the bureau, the Nation of Islam became established as the largest black nationalist organization in the United States and retained the structure roughly delineated in earlier chapters until 1975. That year, events of ultimate importance took place that forever would affect the Nation, events to which we now turn.

5

The Fall of the Nation

═══

This chapter will examine the rapid transformation of the NOI, which commenced when Wallace D. Muhammad assumed leadership, a process known as "the Fall" among the followers of Minister Farrakhan. After an account of the religious, organizational, and political recasting of the movement, the chapter ends with a discussion about the possible reasons for the smooth transition.

Until Death Do Us Part   The first Christians eagerly anticipated the return of Christ during their own lifetimes, when they personally would experience the establishment of the kingdom of God on earth. In a similar manner, members of the Nation expected the imminent destruction of Babylon and the unveiling of God, the black man. Elijah Muhammad was the last Messenger of God, sent to the lost-found at the end of time. The era of the Devil had expired, and the dawn of the seventh millennium was at hand. Modern research shows the extent to which a charismatic leader of a new religious movement is identified with the movement; he or she embodies the sect in a symbiotic relationship. In the case of the NOI, the identification is strengthened by the organic understanding of race. The Nation composed one body, governed by Elijah Muhammad as the head governs the human body. It is no wonder that the membership were as ill prepared for the ailing of the Messenger as the first Islamic community had been when Muhammad ibn Abdullah fell sick in Medinah.

In December 1973, the *New York Times* reported that the seventy-five-year-old Messenger was close to death, and the newspaper predicted that a violent struggle for power would be triggered in the Nation. Minister Yusuf Shah of Temple #2 reacted strongly in a *Muhammad Speaks* rebuttal. He compared the Messenger's age with that of his past colleagues: Noah lived for 950 years, Abraham for 175 years, and Moses for 120 years, which made the Honorable Elijah Muhammad, "whom God taught face to face," still a youngster.[1] In a second article, Minister Shah declared that it is the *New York Times* journalist who is sick and assured the believers, "Let no one deceive you. The Messenger is in good health, feeling fine and teaching strong."[2] National Representative Louis Farrakhan denied in a similar vein that the Messenger was ailing: "I cannot conceive of a God who would raise up a Messenger to do a job and take that Messenger away before the job was done."[3] In an editorial of September 1974, Charles 67X rallied against the disbelievers' attitude when frequently raising the question of the Messenger's closeness to death. This time, the NOI spokesperson confirmed the rumors, only to transform Elijah Muhammad's condition into a mighty sign. "Messenger Muhammad's illness is serious. He has been at death's door many times," but each time he was brought back as proof of the power of God. "As He teaches us of . . . the great ability of His God to deliver Him from affliction—Messenger Muhammad also tests us and our belief in Him and our belief in the God He represents to us."[4]

As the Messenger's condition worsened, the need for a proper interpretation grew. In November 1974, Minister Karriem wrote, "We see the Messenger ailing not because of any failure to take care of Himself; not because of any transgressions, but only to fulfill the history of the Scriptures as it is written of him in the Bible, Isaiah, Chapter 53: 'He was wounded for our transgressions . . . and with His stripes are we healed.'"[5] If the members of the Nation only reluctantly began to mentally prepare for the Messenger's death, another organization eagerly looked forward to it. Back in 1969, FBI headquarters wrote to the special agent in charge (SAC) in Chicago: "The NOI appears to be the personal fiefdom of Elijah Muhammad. When he dies a power struggle can be expected and the NOI could change direction. We should be prepared for this eventuality. We should plan how to change the philosophy of the NOI. . . . The alternative to changing the philosophy of the NOI is the destruction of the organization. This might be accomplished through generating factionalism among the contenders for Elijah Muhammad's leadership or through legal action in probate court on his death."[6] The FBI scrutinized the potential heirs of the Messenger, giving special attention to the members of his royal family. One strong contender, who was very close to his father, was Herbert Muhammad, also Muhammad Ali's manager. As early as 1968, the bureau concluded: "If Herbert Mohammed could be removed as successor to the leadership of the NOI, it would place our top level NOI informants in a better position to neutralize the extremist cult."[7] In addition, the FBI considered Herbert Muhammad to be "the key person . . . in keeping Wallace Muhammad . . . to regain close rapport with his father." This required that measures be taken, because the FBI hailed Wallace D. Muhammad as "the only son of Elijah Muhammad who would have the necessary qualities to guide the NOI in such a manner as would eliminate racist teachings."[8] Whatever actual support the FBI managed to give Wallace D. Muhammad cannot be determined from the nondeleted sections of the released files. We are thus left to give an account of the visible history, making no claims of having determined the FBI's role in the coming events.

According to official medical documents, the Messenger of God died of congestive heart failure on February 25, 1975.[9] The anticipated struggle for the position as his *khalifa* ("successor" of Muhammad) never took place. The matter was resolved as a family matter in the closed inner circle of the NOI leadership.[10] In his opening remarks on Saviour's Day, February 26, National Secretary Abass Rassoull "announced that the mantle of leadership has fallen to Minister Wallace D. Muhammad."[11] The new leader received the unanimous acclamation of 20,000 believers who had gathered in Chicago to commemorate the birth of Master Farad Muhammad.

Wallace D. Muhammad was born on October 30, 1933, as the seventh child of Clara and Elijah Muhammad. In the NOI historiography, his birth was surrounded with legends pointing toward the divine purpose of his existence. The number seven has paramount importance, as it symbolizes the reestablishment of black world leadership and stands for perfection, masculinity, the coming of God, and the divine judgment over the unjust.[12] God, in the person of Master Farad Muhammad, had determined the sex of the child before its birth. He then wrote "Wallace" in chalk on the back of a door in the home of His Messenger-to-be, and foretold that the coming child would succeed his father as spiritual head of the Nation of Islam.[13] Wallace D. Muhammad argues that his coronation was predestined: "It was God's plan . . . by me being born at the time when (my Father) was in contact with His Savior, the God in Person, helped to form me, not only as a child of His loins, but a child for the Mission."[14] Upon completing high school at the University of Islam, Wallace D. Muhammad was put to service in different positions in the NOI hierarchy, from soldier in the Fruit of Islam (FOI) to minister at the Philadelphia temple. In

October 1961, he was sentenced to a three-year jail term for violation of the draft laws.[15] He spent his time in prison reading Islamic studies and began to realize the dissonance between mainstream Islamic doctrines and his father's teachings. Since that time, he nursed the vision of a reformed community of believers, fully in line with the Sunni Islamic world.[16]

Elijah Muhammad could not tolerate the fact that Wallace did "not believe that Allah has visit me in person [nor] that I am the Messenger of Allah,"[17] and so Elijah put a ban on his son. The ideological rift with his father resulted in Wallace's defection from the Nation in 1963 and the formation of the Afro-Descendant Upliftment Society.[18] In mid-December 1964, he closed down this rival group and, after the assassination of Malcolm X, returned to the fold of his father. On two future occasions, in 1969 and 1971, Wallace D. Muhammad was suspended due to his dissident views. He was readmitted from the last suspension as late as 1974.[19]

When installed as supreme minister of the Nation of Islam, Wallace D. Muhammad hinted at the changes to come. He swiftly declared his mission to be of another character than his father's had been: "My role is not that of a Messenger of God, but that of a Mujeddid. M-U-J-E-D-D-I-D, meaning 'One to watch over the new Islam' and see that it is constantly and continually being renewed."[20] With astonishing speed, Wallace Muhammad initiated a process of Islamization that would transform the Nation religiously, organizationally, and politically.

Rapid Islamization Transit   Religiously, the supreme minister intended to introduce complete congruency with mainstream Sunni Islam. To achieve this goal without causing an upheaval among the rank and file, Minister Muhammad presented each change of direction as being a fulfillment of his father's will. Wallace Muhammad argued that the specific message presented in the era of the Honorable Elijah Muhammad was necessary for a time when the Blackamerican was slumbering at the bottom of society. When the doctrine had filled its purpose, it should be substituted with more advanced teachings to pave the way for further progress. In terms of scripture, the Messenger raised the mentally dead up from the graves by a message that had to come in a concealed form. This was "the first resurrection," which is now followed by the second, in which the veil is gradually removed. In the words of Minister Muhammad: "The First Resurrection brought great fruits and great manifestations of Divine Being. The Second Resurrection brought in complete light."[21]

One of the prime features of the old Nation was its concrete exegetical orientation in matters of exoteria. The NOI's interpretation of scripture produced a doctrine that held that God was no mystery spirit but a black man. The blacks were the original people, the cream of creation, gods of the universe. The Devil was not an angel of evil but the white man. Armageddon was a very physical battle in which the white race would be exterminated and the earth thereby cleansed of evil. The hereafter signified the establishment of paradise on earth, in which the community of believers should live in the actual city of the New Jerusalem, which had been prepared by God as a dwelling for his people for thousands of years. This material delineation became the focus of the initial phase of Wallace D. Muhammad's reinterpretative process.

"The road to God is a physical road," wrote Minister Muhammad, but "physical things are only signs of a higher knowledge."[22] Elijah Muhammad had told the believers that they were members of a "baby-Nation." In Wallace's mind, this did not signify a recently awakened community of gods that would grow in wisdom and regain world hegemony. Instead it legitimized his strategy of reinterpretation, beginning with a transition in exegetical orientation: "We must read the Holy Quran with an adult mind and come away from the baby mind, because we are no more a baby Nation."[23]

Minister Muhammad moved the apocalypse from the physical to the spiritual level and at the same time brought it closer to fulfillment. The Nation of Islam was identified with the promised return of the Messiah. The biblical Jesus was presented as a sign for a people with essentially the same experiences as his. Like Jesus, the blacks had been rejected, humiliated, and nailed on a cross (hung from trees).[24] With the Nation of Islam as "the Body-Christ," the dawn of the new world had finally arrived—with the key role still reserved for the chosen ones: "It is time that the Black man and woman of America stand up and take on their Divine Appointment as the Resurrected Christ, the World Saviour," the Minister wrote.[25]

Facing the end, it proved less dramatic than previously expected. "If you think physical blood has to be shed to kill the devil, you are very mistaken," Wallace Muhammad stated.[26] "The Bible never told you that the devil was going to be killed by any kind of physical destruction."[27] In Revelation 19:15, the weapon of the Christ who came to destroy the regime of evil was a sharp sword, representing, according to the Minister, the tongue with the power of truth. The fire of Armageddon turned into moral teachings, in a spiritual remaking of the world.[28] The Apocalypse slowed down to an evolutionary process, in which humanity grows from dust to a divine community, called the New Jerusalem.[29] The prophecy of doom was thus replaced with a philosophical conclusion, close to the Hegelian notion of the perfection of man as the predestined purpose of history.

The process of reinterpretation, with its shift in orientation, seems to have been rejected by sections within the community of the believers. This is reflected in a *Muhammad Speaks* article by Raymond Sharieff, NOI minister of justice, who wrote that some "Muslims have grown to be seriously attached to the Lessons and old language." Intent on advancing the NOI reformation, the supreme minister therefore wished to update God's 154 lessons "to eliminate the confusion that was created by those who did not have the secret knowledge." To comfort those who perhaps would hesitate to accept alterations in the divine message, Sharieff presented this modernization as something Wallace Muhammad "promised His Honorable Father He would do."[30]

The hallmark of the old Nation was the ever-repeated statement that the white man was the Devil. The meaning of this central pillar of belief must now, according to the supreme minister, be "taught in higher language."[31] "White" was equated with "colored," which was explained as a filter of perception. The "Jinn mentality" or the "Caucasian mentality" had been colored by the false notion of supremacy, negatively affecting the different races' perception of each other and self.[32] "I'm not calling [white folks] 'devil,'" the Minister wrote, "I'm calling the mind that has ruled these people and you 'devil.'"[33] Transferring the color symbolism from the biological to the psychological level, black and white became attitudes and different ways of behavior. Again, the shift in orientation was presented as progression and not alteration. Supreme Minister Muhammad explained, "In the Lessons we said that the white man had to be destroyed because he couldn't be changed. Because many of us did not understand the wise teachings of the Master, we thought that He meant that physical white flesh had to be destroyed. The 'white' man is not flesh, he is a lie. 'Whiteness' is a mental falsehood that has been formed in the minds of not only physical white people, but people all over the world."[34] Each fight needs appropriate weaponry. Annihilation of a specific race is ineffective in dealing with a mentality. The Minister wrote, "Even if we were to select a physical group of people as 'the devil' and destroy them physically tomorrow, you would have the same problems as you have today."[35] The victorious party would automatically become victims of the supremacist mentality in their moment of triumph. Again, proper divine knowledge was seen as the only means capable of cleansing the mind from the mentality produced by the archdeceiver. The transition of color symbolism enabled the Muslims to deal with the enemy within. Na'im Akbar wrote, "Most importantly, we are now better equipped to identify the devils among us who have been masquerading under a costume of blackness and executing diabolical deeds among us."[36]

The de-demonization of the white man was accompanied by a de-deification of the black man. "The Honorable Elijah Muhammad said you are the god," wrote Wallace Muhammad, "He did not mean that you are God the Creator with a capital 'G'—He meant that you are a god on your own plane of activity."[37] Minister Muhammad thus reinterpreted the meaning of this central tenet of the Nation of Islam to signify no more than the mainstream Islamic vision of mankind's ability. When the prophet Muhammad died in the year 632 (or, 11 in the Islamic calendar), an epoch closed. From the days of Adam onward, God raised prophets when it was necessary to correct the direction of his creation. Muhammad ibn Abdullah was the last prophet, delivering the final message to mankind. After his death, humanity had reached the age of majority. She was for the first time in history capable of creating a benign society by using the blueprint received with the Holy Qur'an. Minister Muhammad related the teachings of his father to this idea. The Blackamericans are capable of mastering their own destiny and creating a good life by submitting to the will of God and using His revelations as a divine charter.[38]

Associated with the previous perception of the inherent divinity in the black race was the concept of original man. In the *Lessons* studied in the old Nation, one question asked, "Who is the Original Man?" The students should answer properly, "The Original Man is the Asiatic Black Man, the Master, the Owner, the Cream of the planet earth, the Father of Civilization, and the God of the Universe."[39] Redefined by Wallace Muhammad, the original man signified a state of consciousness derived from the original closeness to God. Black referred "to the man who was born in darkness and out of darkness and whose mind developed so strong that it was able to bring light out of darkness."[40] While this statement seems close to the teachings of Elijah Muhammad,[41] Minister Muhammad emphasized that he was not speaking about physical but mental darkness and light. In the teachings of Minister Muhammad, black and white signified two essentially different categories of minds. The former is defined by its close rapport with God and the latter by separation from the Creator. The black mind rests in the divine by submitting to his will, while the white mind is lost in the confusion caused by its rebellion against divine will.[42]

The reorientation described above moved the Nation of Islam considerably closer to mainstream Sunni Islam. Far from being a uniform religion, Islam is heterogeneous. Theologically and organizationally, Islam harbors a rich spectra of doctrinal varieties, as I discuss further in chapter 8. Here it is sufficient to state that the NOI's identification of Master Farad Muhammad as God in person and Elijah Muhammad as his last Messenger is heretic from a mainstream Islamic perspective. Therefore, the reinterpretation of this cornerstone of the NOI creed was decisive for the Islamization project of Wallace Muhammad.

Minister Muhammad approached this very delicate matter by quietly substituting the title "Messenger" with "Master," when mentioning his father in sermons and articles.[43] After a period of subtle preparation, the time had come to address the matter more directly. In early 1976, "Master Fard Muhammad and the Honorable Master Elijah Muhammad" were heralded as "two great and masterful teachers."[44] In March 1976, Wallace Muhammad revealed the "true identity" of Master Farad Muhammad, who was said to be an ordinary Muslim who, upon a visit to the United States in 1930, was truly moved to find the blacks in such a poor condition. Observing the failure of the church and immigrant Muslims to address the problems of the African American in a constructive manner, "he designed a skillful plan" to uplift the black community and bring them into the Islamic fold. By studying the Creation, Master Fard discovered that physical birth or existence precedes spiritual birth. Finding the Blackamerican "completely dead," he understood that he could not teach them the spirit of Islam directly. First, they had to be given a material existence; they would go for the bait of satisfied needs and wants. According to Minister Muhammad, Master Farad said, "Tell them Elijah, that if they follow you and me, they will get good homes, money, and friendship in all walks of life. Tell them that the streets of the holy land where their ancestors came from are paved with solid gold."[45] Master Farad Muhammad told Elijah Muhammad to attract the African Americans "at any cost. Once they were gotten into the temple, they would gradually come into knowledge."[46] Then he left Elijah Muhammad, leaving only a picture of himself reading the Holy Qur'an. This picture would direct the future course of the Nation, when it was ready to appreciate true Islam. Members would study the Holy Qur'an, thereby finding the real God and thereby turning into mainstream Muslims. Wallace Muhammad indicated that the source of this astonishing new information was none other than direct communication with the man involved. The Minister stated that Master Farad never went anywhere: "Master Farad Muhammad is not dead, brothers and sisters, he is physically alive and I talk to him whenever I get ready. I don't talk to him in any spooky way, I go to the telephone and dial his number."[47] In the community of mainstream African American Muslims, this is part of the basis for a widespread thesis as to the identity of Master Farad Muhammad, which is contrasted with the three other enduring theories described in chapter 3, as well as the belief in Farad's divinity. The author has frequently met with Muslims who testify that they know someone who has actually met with this mysterious Muslim, named Abdullah, who reportedly died in 1992 or 1993. Descriptions and valuations of this Abdullah vary considerably, ranging from those who condemn the man as an Ismaili or Sufi heretic, to those who state that he honestly tried to teach Islam and left when he found himself misunderstood, and to those who assure that he was in fact a noble *sayyid* who designed as skillful *dawa* strategy of the sort described above. As is the case with the other three theories, however, the factuality of this thesis has yet to be verified with more substantial evidence.

Minister Muhammad argued that his father abdicated in his testimony and vacated the position of Messenger of God to Muhammad ibn Abdullah, the Seal of the Prophets in mainstream Islam. God was deanthropomorphized and merged with the general perception of him in the Islamic world community. Eventually, the appreciation of Master Farad Muhammad deteriorated. Imam Sidney R. Sharif wrote in 1985 that the old Nation had been under the spell of a witch doctor: "That 'witch doctor' was Master Fard Muhammad. The Muslims consequently viewed themselves as 'black gods,' while they viewed the Caucasians as 'racist devils.' The old Nation of Islam was populated by people who had moved from the position of being the victims of racism to the position of racist themselves."[48] Imam Sharif viewed Master Farad as "a pretender." Farad displayed a false concern for the plight of the African American and told them that he was sent by God to save them. "But his plan was not to deliver [them] from bondage. His plan was simply to use them to destroy America," Imam Sharif wrote. "Yes, the truth is that Master Fard Muhammad was or is . . . a friend and a close associate of the Devil himself."[49] The demonization of Master Farad Muhammad did not, however, make Elijah a messenger of Iblis. Elijah Muhammad was still held in honor as the founder of a black pride that, by the help of the true God and Minister Muhammad, now could grow out of race chauvinism and evolve into a mature Islamic consciousness.

Besides matters of orthodoxy, the Islamic call for orthopraxy must also be taken into consideration. Any movement that calls itself Islamic and at the same time disregards the remaining four pillars, will be questioned by other Muslim groups and individuals. The praxis of *salat* (prayer), *sawm* (fasting, observed in Ramadan), *zakat* (taxation to finance social welfare), and *hajj* (pilgrimage to Mecca), with minor variations according to the four different legal schools of Sunni Islam, unifies the Sunni Islamic family. Steering toward the mainstream, the NOI's deviations in this respect were corrected. Here, the transition was less delicate and apparently went smoothly.

The fast had previously been observed in December by the NOI members, as I described in chapter 3. In August 1975, Wallace Muhammad declared that the NOI henceforth "will be observing the month of Ramadan fast in the proper month and will be celebrating the completion of this fast with our Muslim brothers and sisters the world over."[50] In order to avoid upsetting the feelings of elder members, the minister simply added a bridge to the old norm, by asking the membership to fast on Christmas Eve and the last day of December this last time. "We will do this fast commemorating the great service to Islam all over the world given by the Honorable Master Elijah Muhammad."[51]

Muhammad Speaks was increasingly used to inform the readers of mainstream Islamic practices, including the proper way of prayers (which was formally instituted in October 1975),[52] charity, and pilgrimage.[53] Quotations from the Holy Qur'an in Arabic and English appeared regularly. The success of Wallace Muhammad's Islamization process was acknowledged by mainstream Muslim leaders in the United States and abroad. Muhammad Abdul-Rauf, a prominent spokesman for the conventional Muslims in the United States, applauded the accomplishments of the minister. Previously, the Nation was giving Islam "a bad and confusing image." Now, he said, there was "very little difference" between the NOI and mainstream Islam, which is why Abdul-Rauf urged the believers to accept NOI members as fellow Muslims.[54] Sheikh Muhammad Ali al-Harakhan, secretary-general for the Saudi-based Muslim World League, was equally pleased, hailing the minister for his teachings of true Islam.[55] In 1978, Wallace D. Muhammad was chosen by a number of rich Persian Gulf states to be the sole consultant and trustee for the recommendation and distribution of their economic support to Muslim movements in the United States.[56] As a further sign of his status, Wallace D. Muhammad was elected in 1986 to the prestigious Supreme Council of Masajid of the

Muslim World League, with responsibility for the American mosques.[57] Further, religious Islamization was paralleled by organizational reforms and political reorientation.

To Dismantle an Empire Organizationally, the de-demonization of the Caucasian was followed up in June 1975, by the lifting of the color ban on the NOI membership: "Those whites who identify with our thinking can come in and join us and take a lead in giving moral direction to the world," the Minister declared.[58] Not surprisingly, this innovation was met with opposition from within the ranks of the NOI. Jamillah Muhammad rebutted the members who "out of ignorance viewed this change as a contradiction to the principles established by the Honorable Elijah Muhammad," when it should actually be understood as a natural evolution of these principles.[59] Minister Muhammad made similar assurances: "We are making more efforts now than ever to keep out 'white' people. Not white-skinned people, but white-minded people."[60]

To prevent organized opposition and eliminate the risk for a coup d'état, the military cadre, the Fruit of Islam (FOI), was dissolved. C. Eric Lincoln, writing on the old Nation, points out that the increasingly powerful FOI had become a state within a state, a development reducing rank-and-file members to "second-class citizens again, even in the Black Nation of Islam." Lincoln believes that the FOI, which was responsible for internal discipline, was a decisive component in the anticipated struggle for power in the Nation of Islam. Lincoln continues: "And if the FOI is recognized as a key weapon in that struggle, will there not be increasingly tense intrigues among the leadership for control of the secret army?"[61] Clearly, Wallace D. Muhammad was of a similar opinion: "The morals had gone out of the [FOI] leadership. It became a political order. And it was hooligans; it became nothing more than just a hooligan outfit, a hoodlum outfit, of men who were just playing politics and playing revolution. Not a revolution that carried its attack outside; a revolution that kept its attack inside. Directed at leaders that showed a future."[62] With this elite of the status quo neutralized, organizational reforms were pushed forward. The Nation of Islam was an extremely hierarchical organization, with the semidivine Messenger as the single authority in religious as well as worldly affairs. In an NOI "State of the Nation Report" of 1976, Minister Muhammad summarized planned and effectuated reforms. All official staff members in the NOI would henceforth be subject to election by the membership. A National Decision Making Board would serve as a governing body for the general affairs. New national bodies were instituted for the financing of the movement, mosque administration, interorganizational relations, social programs, and business operations.[63]

During the leadership of Elijah Muhammad, the Nation had developed into a strong economic force. As with the other sectors of the NOI body, the financial empire was tied tightly to the Messenger personally. Wallace Muhammad now claimed that "no one knew the condition of the business because no accounting systems were in effect to monitor national income and expenditures." Scrutinizing the financial situation, Minister Muhammad noted that "the economic health of the Nation of Islam is not what it was projected to be."[64] Long-term debt commitments had financed large-scale projects, putting strains on obligatory donations and draining other financial enterprises from their profit. Wallace Muhammad systematically separated business activities from the mosque structure, advising that, "With the exception of a few Mosque related businesses (such as the Muslim press) most of the business now owned by the Nation of Islam will be turned over into the hands of management teams selected from the general body."[65] The privatization of the NOI companies, which were by many rank-and-file members viewed as their common property and an important source of pride, led to considerable internal criticism. Wallace Muhammad later defended his dismantling of the financial corporate body by stating that "the building of a material empire is not now, and has never been, the main object of religion."[66] The quota system previously used for selling copies of the Muslim newspaper was abolished, which partially accounts for the 28 percent drop in circulation between 1974 and 1975, reaching a low point of 400,000 copies a week.[67]

The Islamization process is further reflected in a continuous change in names: of the organization itself, its press, its facilities, and its members. In November 1976, the Nation of Islam became the World Community of al-Islam in the West (WCIW), only to be renamed the American Muslim Mission less than two years later, in April 1978.[68] *Muhammad Speaks* became *Bilalian News* in November 1975, reflecting Minister Muhammad's wish to connect the Blackamerican to Bilal Ibn Rabah, the black companion to the prophet Muhammad. From 1981 to 1985, the newspaper was renamed no less than four times and is presently called *Muslim Journal.*[69] The universities were renamed Sister Clara Muhammad Elementary and Secondary Schools. In January 1976, the "temples" were renamed "mosques" and in March 1977, "masjids." At the same time many mosques substituted their number with a meaningful name. The former Temple #7 in Harlem, New York, for instance, became Malcolm Shabazz Masjid, in honor of its former minister as a form of symbolic restitution. The "ministers" became "imams," and Wallace Muhammad "chief imam," reflecting the title's Sunni meaning.[70] In February 1976, Imam Muhammad encouraged all members, as well as the entire African American community, to drop their previous names "and take on the divine names of the Holy Qur'an."[71] Wallace Muhammad finally let the name of the false God go and renamed himself Warith Deen, and later, Warithuddin Muhammad.

Politically, Imam Warithuddin Muhammad steered the movement away from its former radical criticism of America. The previous staunchly black nationalist position was remodeled along more genuinely Islamic lines. Initially, the call for Blackamericans to identify themselves as Bilalians was fully in line with the Ethiopianist theme of black religious nationalism as described in chapter 1. In his first speeches, Imam Muhammad sounded much like his father, communicating the classical sectarian understanding of self, complete with an overestimation of his own organization's role in world history, as well as the idea that everyone else intensely follows the group's undertakings: "The people of the world are expecting much from us because they see us now just coming into our Divine role. They know that our light is just dawning on the globe and that, pretty soon, it will rise to light the world."[72] The agenda would eventually alter. Gradually, Imam Muhammad transformed the political appeal of the movement, as some traits of the old Nation were recast and only temporarily remained central tenets. Racism in Christianity was still condemned but in a more Islamic manner. Proceeding from the mainstream Muslim ban on portraying God, the wciw launched a campaign to picket each church displaying a Caucasian image of Jesus.[73] In June 1977, a committee was formed to urge all congregations in the United States to remove all racial images of the divine.[74] Not confining the drive to Christianity, Imam Muhammad cleared all remnant notions of black nationalism from his own doctrine. He stated that "there are no radical teachings in the Holy Qur'an on race,"[75] and concluded: "Al-Islam is not a religion for any one race, it is a religion for all people."[76]

Elijah Muhammad's vision of a separate black state in America was transformed into a wish for realizing Muslim independence *within* the United States, similar to that of the Amish position: self-supporting, autonomous in religious matters, and politically quietist.[77] Though the Amish community provides its members with a living example of the project's possibility, the commune envisioned by the American Muslim Mission is less introverted. Imam Muhammad does not wish his followers to withdraw from the outer world, but states that "God obligates us to seek acquaintance with all people because this earth was not made to separate man."[78] Believing that "God has not called us to be nationalist,"[79] Islam and not black nationalism is the source of the project's legitimacy: "Just as Prophet Muhammad (PBUH) was divinely missioned to establish an independent Islamic Community in Medinah, Imam Muhammad is duty-bound to establish an independent Islamic Community in America."[80] During the leadership of Elijah Muhammad, the Nation of Islam had purchased 4,600 acres of farm land in southern Georgia. Imam Muhammad declared his intention to establish an independent Islamic community there, named Elijahville.[81] In 1983, the American Muslim Mission held its first national convention in Elijahville, but the project eventually failed.[82] In 1987, revived expectations focused on another farm bought in Mississippi. The farm is only 630 acres but sufficient for a modest beginning and enough to enthuse the believers: "In a few years from now, Allah willing, we will have established the first independent self-governed Muslim community in North America."[83]

Remnants of previous themes notwithstanding, the general picture shows that, step by step, the old nationalism was dismantled. In March 1976, Wallace D. Muhammad abandoned the old national banner, introducing a new flag with the Holy Qur'an, transcending nationality, as a symbol.[84] In 1977, Imam Muhammad abolished the very cardinal point of his father's legacy: the notion of the African Americans as a separate nation striving toward political autonomy.[85] Waving the Stars and Stripes, he talked about American patriotism and integration, stating that he did not think that his father "ever truly envisioned seeing a physical nation with a different flag than this [Star-Spangled Banner]."[86]

The next dramatic innovation was the 1977 call for African American Muslim participation in mainstream America's Independence Day celebrations.[87] In his 4th of July address, Imam Muhammad declared his sincere wish that everyone "come together in the spirit of genuine patriotism, not having any old emotional hang-ups with the American flag or the American government." What formerly was known as the scriptural Babylon suddenly emerged as "the greatest land on the face of the earth."[88]

In some political respects, Imam Muhammad began to sound more like a conservative Christian than a black theologian of liberation. He not only opposed the 1984 candidacy of Jesse Jackson,[89] but said that "on the whole, the Reagan administration has been good for the country."[90] Imam Muhammad began talking about Muslim support of the society's institutions as a religious obligation, and the former conscientious objector promised that, if needed, he himself would enlist and "go to war in defense of this country."[91] Imam Muhammad tried to convince the black nationalist followers of Elijah Muhammad that the United States deserved respect as a country fully in accord with the will of God. He also sought to convince United States authorities that his followers no longer should be perceived as enemies but loyal citizens, assuring that the "Muslim is no threat to American society or civilization."[92] In December 1977, Imam Muhammad was invited to visit President Jimmy Carter at the White House.[93] In February 1992, his efforts were given a further sign of success when Warithuddin Muhammad became the first imam to offer morning prayers in the United States Senate.[94]

Most significantly, Imam Muhammad tried to persuade his previous iconoclastic followers to reevaluate and embrace the American civil religion. He argued that "although America mistreated her slaves and denied them equal opportunities, Allah blessed America because she had the right disposition."[95] Imam Muhammad thus made a serious attempt to link essential Islamic elements with Americanity, aligning Prophet Muhammad ibn Abdullah with the Founding Fathers. Imam Muhammad "pointed out that the Constitution of the United States is basically a 'Qur'anic document.' Its principles were presented to the world over 1,400 years ago by Prophet Muhammad (PBUH)."[96]

Completing the process of transformation, it should come as no surprise that Imam Muhammad dropped the name American Muslim Mission, thereafter (in late 1987) dissolving the entire organization, urging the former membership to affiliate with any local mosque. He then resigned as imam for the Chicago Masjid.[97] Concerning the latter move, Imam Muhammad said that he felt more comfortable with not being responsible for any particular Muslims but free to serve all as an independent Muslim scholar.[98] Asked why he felt the name American Muslim Mission should be dropped, Imam Muhammad made the following statement, which the author believes also explains its subsequent dissolution: "It's just the final step in the process of bringing our membership into the international Muslim community and to conform to where there's a normal Islamic life—just normal, practical Islamic life. The hangover from yesterday of 'Black Nationalist' influence is something that we have to get rid of, because it was in conflict with the open society and democratic order of an Islamic community."[99]

Religion, Perception, and Change   From the perspective of a historian of religion, the (r)evolution described is remarkable indeed. When Elijah Muhammad assumed the role of Messenger of God, the Nation of Islam developed a staunch black religious nationalist ideology and a hierarchical corporate organizational body, which after a process of institutionalization remained largely intact until February 26, 1975. Upon accepting the mantle of his father, Wallace Muhammad went straight to the tailor and remade his clothing according to modern Islamic fashion. In a few years, Imam Muhammad almost completely managed to change the character of the movement before its final dissolution. The great change appears as sudden as it was far-reaching. How is this sweeping development to be understood?

James E. Whitehurst finds it to be "an exciting contemporary example of Ernst Troeltsch's analysis of the way a 'sect' grows up and becomes a 'church'; it initially deviates from orthodoxy, gradually gains respectability, and finally returns to the establishment."[100] This application of Troeltsch's sect/church model is, I believe, far from relevant. "Church" is too much a Christcentric concept to be projected onto other religions without distortion. "Orthodoxy" is an imprecise concept when applied to Islam. It must be either far too generally or far too specifically defined to be analytically meaningful. Moreover, one might ask what "orthodoxy" could possibly be referred to in this context. Besides a possible initial influence from Ismailiyya, to be discussed later, the Nation of Islam grew out from, not Islam as such, but the tradition of black religious nationalism. As a religious movement, it can be seen as having developed into mainstream Sunni Islam but not returning to its fold. The official "church" (following Whitehurst and Troeltsch) it defined itself in opposition to was a combination of American civil religion and the black church before the era of black theology—not the values and doctrines held by the world Islamic community.

More fruitful is the approach suggested by Lawrence H. Mamiya.[101] He applies, in his own words, "a quasi-Weberian" analysis and argues that the changes can be explained in part by the dialectical relationship between religious ideas and socioeconomic conditions. To some extent I will follow the direction suggested by Mamiya when giving attention to the internal class composition of the movement. The Nation of Islam, which originated as a lower class–based movement, became over the years increasingly middle class. This in turn effected the worldview of the members who experienced the class transition, making them ready to welcome the changes introduced by Imam Muhammad. The analytical perspective suggested should not be understood as an attempt to reduce religion to an appendage of ideas tied to the economic engine of social life. Individuals of a certain class do not share identical political or religious ideas, automatically or mechanically produced by common experiences. The relationship between the realms of ideas and socioeconomic conditions is far more complex and dialectical. Avoiding that kind of determinism, it is equally important not to fall into idealistic reductionism and explain the evolution of ideas without reference to social and political factors. Any reasonable approach has, I believe, to be holistic in orientation if we are to advance our understanding of religion and change.

Weber argued that repressed or subordinated religious and ethnic minorities, through their exclusion from positions of political influence, tend to concentrate on the economic sphere of activity. He further suggested that "the Protestant ethic," "the inner-worldly asceticism" rationally expressed in work as a calling, unintentionally lead to the creation of "the spirit of capitalism." Puritan morality with its ideals of decency, honesty, and assiduity as means of honoring God produced a disciplined labor force and modern capitalist entrepreneurs. With the religious ban on wastefulness and extravagant pleasures, investment of accumulated capital was regularized and modern "rational" capitalism became a reality.[102]

A similar process can be discerned in the Nation of Islam. In the first decades of the movement's existence, African Americans largely lacked influence in state or federal politics. The black community was equally weak in terms of economic power. The NOI's economic approach to empowerment was combined with a Puritan morality. The Protestant ethic of the Nation of Islam, with its ban on lavish pleasures and demands for hard work channeled into continuous enterprise, resulted in the formation of an economic empire with assets estimated to be as much as $80,000,000.[103] The attempt to create a black infrastructure was no end in itself but a method to achieve the interim aim: national self-determination. Separatism was an early phase leading toward the apocalyptic extermination of evil and the transformation of the world into a black paradise. The combination of rigid morals, education, and rational enterprise with an end that never materialized altered the class composition of the Nation. An increasingly greater part of the membership became skilled white- or blue-collar workers, shop owners, lawyers, doctors, and the like. As the need for skilled administrators grew in the Nation, greater efforts were made to attract converts from higher social strata in the African American community. The new inroad added to the middle-class segment in the Nation of Islam. In the meantime, the general conditions of the African American community changed. From the New Deal to Reaganomics, blacks experienced relative progress. The differences in infant mortality, average family income, and education between whites and blacks decreased gradually. The African American community became more stratified, with the percentage of middle-class blacks increasing. Desegregation was officially implemented and blacks made inroads into the political scene, as elected officials in state and city administrations.

In its intellectual aspect, religion is a theory about the world, how and why it was created, and how man relates to and should act in the world. Religion constructs an order and provides the adherent with a frame of reference that governs his or her interpretation of experiences in and of the world. New religious movements must put a special emphasis on doctrine to win converts to the new creed. A convert adopts a new frame of reference that restructures his or her perception, emically explained as "a new light" or as having been "born again." Describing his conversion, Malcolm X testifies how profoundly the central NOI thesis, "the white man is the devil," revolutionized his perception of past experiences. The whites he had known passed before his mind's eye: the unidentified whites who killed his father, the whites who took his mother off to an asylum, the white man who discouraged his further education, the whites in the white-only dances where he shined their shoes, the whites he steered to black prostitutes, the white cops, the white judge who sentenced him, and the white prison guards.[104] Suddenly, it all made perfect sense. During the following years, Malcolm studied black history and society with the adopted frame of reference structuring his perception. As no theory is identical to reality, the latter will always be a source of instances that contradict the theory. The cognitive mapping of the world is a subconscious selective process: we see what we expect to see and suppress or negate what does not fit in. Accepting religious dogma requires a mental compartmentalization, separating what is allowed to reach consciousness and what is stored in the subconscious. When Malcolm went through the traumatic conflict with the Messenger, his belief in the dogma of the Nation weakened and previous contradictions stored in the subconscious reappeared. Whites whom he had met on his tours and who shared similar criticisms of the American sociopolitical system were reevaluated from cunning devils to sincere humans. Without the former filter of perception, Malcolm was able to meet whites on hajj and embrace them as brothers.

I suggest that the great change accomplished by Imam Warithuddin Muhammad was less abrupt than it appeared to be. The Nation directed its message to the black underclass, where it found blacks whose life experiences made the NOI creed reasonable. Membership in the Nation brought about changed experiences. Addicts, prostitutes, convicts, unskilled workers, and unemployed blacks assumed a stable lifestyle. Quitting drugs, they married, studied, and worked hard, perhaps starting their own enterprises. Members became increasingly healthier and wealthier. Experiences of satisfied wants and the general progress of the African American community contradicted the dogma that identified society as intrinsically evil. The Nation was an authoritarian movement led by the Messenger whose direct channel of communication with God was the source for matters of belief. Many members felt, in addition, personally indebted to Elijah Muhammad for the progress in their lives. The firm belief in the Messenger maintained the NOI creed as a frame of reference, by which the changes in personal life and society were interpreted. The internal discipline was tight enough to make members conceal eventual doubts. Perhaps only a member of the royal family could have transformed the dogma of the Nation and weakened the belief in Muhammad as the last Messenger of God. When Imam Muhammad presented each innovation as a deeper understanding of the established divine truths that he had promised his father to convey, he provided the members with a mental tool with which to bring the religious creed in greater harmony with experienced reality. He gave them a bridge to a new context, in which Elijah Muhammad and his message (and thereby the years in the NOI for each individual member) still could be highly valued as necessary. Now, "higher knowledge" should accompany the higher standard of living in a society blessed and not doomed by God. This could possibly be a reasonable explanation for the relatively smooth implementation of the sweeping changes of the NOI *perestroika*. Had the internal NOI class composition remained intact and the black community's position in American society not improved, the mainstreaming project of Imam Muhammad would either never have been initiated or would have been doomed to failure.

This argument also provides a perspective with which to understand the quick success of the schismatic groups appearing in the wake of Imam Muhammad's Islamization reforms. A large part of the African American community considered their underdog position to be permanent. Many NOI members still belonged to the lower class, thus bringing the reform ideas of Imam Muhammad in contradiction with their perceived experiences in and of society. When Minister Farrakhan called for a restoration of the Nation, he directed his message to fit the conditions of the black underclass, to once again base the Nation in its origins.

6

The Resurrection of the Nation of Islam

—

This chapter will describe what is known as the second resurrection of the Nation of Islam. The first part provides a biographical sketch of Minister Louis Farrakhan Muhammad. Then I account for Minister Farrakhan's accentuation of eschatological teachings and rebuilding efforts.

From the Nightclub to the Mosque   Minister Louis Farrakhan Muhammad was born with the slave name Louis Eugene Walcott in the Bronx, New York, on May 11, 1933. He is the son of West Indian immigrants; his mother was from Saint Kitts in the eastern Caribbean, his father, whom Louis says he never met, was Jamaican, and his stepfather was from Barbados. Farrakhan describes his childhood warmly, expressing his deep affection for his mother Mae (née Clark) Farrakhan.[1] She was at the periphery of the movement of Marcus Garvey and gave her son racial pride and identity, along with a musical education. Louis Walcott was given a violin at the age of five and soon proved to be a talented musician. He moved with his mother and brother Alvan (1931–94) to Boston, and at the age of twelve he began touring with the Boston College Orchestra. As a young violinist he won the competition in the popular Ted Mack Original Amateur Hour, played on national radio shows, and was one of the first blacks to appear on national television. The Walcott family attended St. Cyprian Episcopal Church, where Louis came under the influence of the black nationalist champion, Rev. Nathan Wright. Leaving Boston, Louis Walcott studied at the Winston-Salem Teachers College in North Carolina. After two years, Louis returned to Boston and married his high school sweetheart, Betsy (now known as Khadidja), in 1953, with Wright presiding.

Louis Walcott by then had discovered that he had a very good singing voice. He had begun singing calypso, the folk music of the Caribbean. As Calypso Gene, also known as the Charmer, Louis was able to make a good living by entertaining at various night clubs. At this point in his musical career, he was for the first time told of the message of Elijah Muhammad. Louis ran into a friend who informed him of a prophet visiting Boston, preaching that the white man is the devil. Though Walcott as a child already had been bitterly opposed to racial prejudice in American society, he felt this radical teaching to be quite bizarre and paid no further attention to it. That same year he was introduced to Malcolm X at a nightclub. He describes his own reaction as somewhat nervous, thinking that he did not want to have any contact with a man with such a strange name, who preached hatred of the white man. Louis Walcott kept his feelings to himself, gave Malcolm a big showbiz smile, and shook him off.

A few years later, in 1955, Walcott was playing in a Chicago nightclub called the Blue Angel. There he met the same friend again, who told him that the Muslims were having their annual Saviour's Day convention in the city, and he was asked to come. Louis Walcott went to hear the Honorable Elijah Muhammad and said the truth dawned on him. Shortly thereafter, he became Louis X, a dedicated follower of the Messenger, and enrolled in Temple #7, New York, under the ministry of Malcolm X.

Initially, Louis X continued in his old profession, working in a nightclub in Greenwich Village. The Nation of Islam at that time held an explicitly negative view about this source of income. Athletics and entertainment were almost the only avenues available for African Americans aspiring to a personal career and acceptance in the official United States. Elijah Muhammad felt that too much time already had been spent singing and dancing for the Devil, when the energy more properly could be used in the service of racial upliftment. Consequently, Malcolm X ordered Louis X to either give up music or his place in the mosque within thirty days. Farrakhan says he made up his mind immediately but used the time for consideration to give a last series of shows. On the very last night, Louis X showed his audience the full range of his talent in a splendid crescendo, not knowing that a top manager was present. The manager found Louis X in his dressing room and offered him a lucrative contract to be signed the day after. Tempted, Louis went to bed and was given a vision: "And in that vision I saw two doors. Over one door was written 'success.' I could look into that door and I saw an amount of gold and diamonds which represented, of course, riches that would accrue. But there was another door, and over that door was the word 'Islam.' And it had a black veil over that door. And in the vision I chose the door of Islam."[2] Walking through the door behind the black veil, Farrakhan put his life in the service of the Nation. Malcolm X immediately discovered Louis X's ability as a public speaker and placed Louis X in the temple's ministry as an assistant to him. While he served under Malcolm X, he was also enrolled as lieutenant in the Fruit of Islam (FOI) and felt very much at home in the disciplined military organization. Unable to find a permanent job in New York, Louis X willingly accepted the offer to return to the city of his childhood as assistant minister and captain of the FOI in the Boston Mosque. Pleased by the work of Louis X and the visible growth of the local membership, the Messenger then let him ascend to the position of minister.

Continuing to be artistically creative, Louis X wrote and directed two stage productions, *Orgena, A Negro Spelled Backwards* and *The Trial.* The former dramatized the enslavement of the Africans and their transformation to so-called Negroes at the bottom of American society. In the latter play, the Devil is finally charged for his evil deeds and receives his death penalty. Minister Louis X also composed a number of popular NOI songs, including two major hits, "White Man's Heaven Is Black Man's Hell" and "Look at My Chains."

In 1964, Louis X replaced Malcolm X as minister of the Harlem Temple, where he was put to the test by a black community who generally loved Malcolm X. When Malcolm was assassinated in 1965, the major newspapers put the blame on the Muslims. In an act of revenge, followers of Malcolm X firebombed the Temple #7 and tensions in black Harlem grew intense. Louis X managed to ride out the storm and rebuild the mosque, making it the largest congregation thus far in the history of the Nation. Reflecting his success, Louis Farrakhan was in 1967 elevated to the position of national representative of the Honorable Elijah Muhammad.

In 1972, New York police attacked the Harlem Mosque. As adherents to the right of self-defense, the Muslims fought back. One patrolman was shot and another severely beaten by infuriated Muslims. The news spread like fire and thousands of Harlem residents gathered to defend the mosque. As rioting began and police cars burned like torches, Louis Farrakhan heightened his fame by his competent handling of the situation. On top of a sedan in the middle of the chaos, he managed to control the unrest without giving way to the police force.[3]

Emerging as a major spokesman for the racially radical section of the black community, Farrakhan's reputation steadily increased. In June 1974, he was able to attract one of the largest gatherings of any black leader thus far in the United States, when 70,000 listeners showed up at his Black Family (Memorial) Day lecture at Randall's Island, New York.[4] The Nation of Islam seemed to move toward the forefront of black aspiration. Farrakhan and his fellow believers thought that Lazarus was finally emerging from the tomb to reclaim his true position. The end was approaching—but in a different way than members were expecting.

The Fall and Resurrection of the Nation of Islam   The ascendancy of Louis Farrakhan made him a chief contender for the position of the Messenger's *khalifa,* or successor, during the speculation surrounding the ailing leader. As mentioned previously, the NOI disappointed those who were eager to see the Nation torn apart by displaying a unified front to outsiders. Farrakhan submitted to the leadership of Wallace D. Muhammad, declaring his appointment to be "the will of God."[5] Officially, no hints of internal disunity over the reformation process were seen. Interviewed by reporter Randy Daniels for CBS-TV after lifting the NOI ban on whites, Wallace Muhammad denied being criticized by Louis Farrakhan who, he said, was one of his "strongest supporters."[6]

Internally, the story reads differently. According to Louis Farrakhan, Wallace Muhammad transferred him from Harlem to "a dirty little place" on the West Side of Chicago, with his former New York assistant, Kareem Abdelaziz (formerly known as Larry 4X), as his new boss.[7] The West Side had up until the 1950s been mostly white, populated by immigrants from Eastern Europe. In a few years it turned predominantly black and became overcrowded. While the South Side had its ghettos, like Harlem it was associated with black consciousness and aspirations. The West Side was by contrast weak in institutions and connoted utter despair.[8] The transfer thus was designed to remove Farrakhan from a base in the midst of large militant black nationalist circles.

Abass Rassoull, who in 1970 was appointed national secretary by the Messenger and continued in this position during the initial period of Wallace Muhammad's leadership, was the architect behind the plan. Rassoull was convinced that National Representative Louis Farrakhan would challenge Wallace's bid for power. It was Rassoull who scheduled the speakers at the 1975 Saviour's Day convention in a manner that resulted in Farrakhan's being squeezed in between known loyalists who would pledge allegiance to Wallace as the Messenger's successor. Shortly thereafter, Rassoull advised Wallace Muhammad that it would be wise to dismantle the New York power base and transfer Farrakhan to Chicago where he could be kept under close supervision. According to Rassoull, he had no idea that Wallace would disrespect Farrakhan and place him at the West Side instead of at the main temple. Rassoull saw to it that Farrakhan's moves and speeches in the United States and abroad were closely monitored, so as to diminish the risk of a schism forming. Before long, Rassoull was himself suspended as national secretary, a removal he has never accepted as legitimate.[9] Increasingly aware of the new regime's intricate efforts to neutralize him, Farrakhan was finally convinced of its intentions when he met with an old female seer in California, who told him that the new leadership was out to crush him.[10]

Farrakhan then accepted invitations from Africa and the Caribbean.[11] Touring the globe, Farrakhan says he noticed that in every multiracial society, irrespective of its official ideology, the black man was to be found at the bottom of society. Discovering ghettos, racism, and prejudice as realities even in Muslim countries convinced him to oppose the Islamization plans of Wallace Muhammad as the African American path of salvation.[12] Returning to the United States, Farrakhan discreetly made his discontent with Wallace Muhammad known within the Nation. He met with Jabril Muhammad in Los Angeles in September 1977,[13] and convened with members in Florida and Las Vegas.[14] As word spread, a close circle of like-minded dissidents was formed, including his old associate, Jabril Muhammad, and the leading female theologian, Sister Tynetta Muhammad. Finally, on November 8, 1977, Farrakhan felt strong enough to officially declare his intention to reestablish the Nation of Islam "on the platform of the Honorable Elijah Muhammad."[15]

Minister Louis Farrakhan is considered to be predestined for the mission, in that his elevation "was a conscious [decision] made by God thousands of years ago."[16] Farrakhan argues that Elijah Muhammad knew of the coming events, including the necessity for him to depart from his Nation. Knowing that he and his mission would be betrayed in his absence, the Messenger prepared by seeking a successor strong enough to save his legacy in the future turmoil.

Farrakhan interprets the Messenger's conflict with Malcolm X in this context. Elijah Muhammad initially thought Malcolm was the man he had been told by God to seek, the man who would rebuild his work when he was gone. Testing Malcolm's character, Elijah Muhammad encouraged jealousy and animosity directed against him. Malcolm could not handle it and turned against his leader. Elijah Muhammad then realized that Farrakhan was the successor he wanted and had him endure a similar treatment, strengthening him to meet the opposition of internal and external foes. Troubled by this experience, Farrakhan went to a top leadership meeting. When he began speaking about the atmosphere of envy within the Nation, Elijah Muhammad abruptly intervened by hitting the table saying, "Brother, seek refuge in Allah from the envier when he envies." The Messenger walked out of the room, came back five minutes later and said, with what Farrakhan later understood as a reference to Malcolm X and himself, "Brother Farrakhan, when you gonna put a piece of board in the corner of a building, to uphold the weight of the building, you gotta put a lot of stress on it. And if it cracks under the weight, that's not the board you were looking for. You throw it away and get you another one."[17] In the early 1970s, Elijah Muhammad held a series of lectures called the "Theology of Time," in which he unraveled the NOI creed in a systematic manner. Later, this series was to be interpreted as part of the Messenger's preparation for the time when he was no longer present. At one of these lectures, Elijah Muhammad told the audience that one of his "greatest teachers" was present. Turning toward Louis Farrakhan, who was seated among the other ministers, the Messenger told him to come out of hiding so everyone could see him. With Minister Farrakhan at his side, Elijah Muhammad then said, "I want you to pay good attention to his [Farrakhan's] preaching. His preaching is a bearing of witness to me and to what God revealed to me. . . . Everywhere you hear him, listen to him; everywhere you see him, look at him; everywhere he advises you to stay from, stay from."[18] Though it was a sign of great honor, the statement was given further weight when interpreted in the light of the Fall, as would another prediction of Elijah Muhammad. In September 1974, the Nation attracted a second huge crowd at Randall's Island that year, this time with some 40,000 in the audience. Enthused, Minister Farrakhan exclaimed to the Messenger "that it looked like soon we were gonna capture New York City for Islam." Elijah Muhammad, relates Farrakhan, "put his head down, and he looked so sad, and he said 'Brother, the time is soon coming when you may go to the Mosque, and you will not find a Believer there other than yourself.' "[19] This was difficult to understand at the time, but in less than a year and a half Farrakhan was persona non grata in the mosque he had headed and the rostrum was occupied by unbelievers.[20] Farrakhan now understood why the Messenger had assigned him the difficult task of rebuilding the mosques in Boston and Harlem and what was presently expected of him: "The building of the Mosque in Boston, the rebuilding of the Mosque in New York, was preparation. Now Elijah is gone. His son is in power. The Nation takes a totally different turn. People are disillusioned, angry, bitter, because everything that they suffered and sacrificed for is gone. And it is into that backdrop that I again came to rebuild his work. Not a Mosque but his work. And here we are, all praise is due to Allah."[21]

Kinship, Scripture, and Strategies of Legitimation   The royal family was held in great esteem in the Nation of Islam. God's elevation of Elijah Muhammad as his Messenger distinguished his kin as a chosen family. As discussed earlier, the Messenger kept the power within the family, and most top laborers were related either by blood or marriage. Imam Warithuddin Muhammad had the great advantage of being the seventh son of the Messenger, a fact that greatly contributed to the legitimation of his successorship. Farrakhan himself confirms the validity of the principle of kinship by recalling his thoughts as the news of the Messenger's death rocked the Nation. He considered his own abilities to lead the community but hesitated. Wallace Muhammad said he knew the next step, and as he was the son of Elijah, Farrakhan submitted and felt his duty was to obey him.[22]

The families of Elijah Muhammad and Louis Farrakhan are related by marriage, a fact integral to the latter's claim to power. In 1975, two of Minister Farrakhan and his wife Khadidja's nine children,[23] daughters Donna and Maria, married Elijah Muhammad's grandson Alif Muhammad and his nephew Wali Muhammad, respectively.[24] In 1990, a third daughter, Hanan (Iris) Farrakhan, married Kamal Muhammad, son of Elijah.[25] The importance of kinship is demonstrated by Farrakhan's conscious efforts to place his position and mission in that context. In recent years he is often flanked by Rasool and Ishmael Muhammad, sons of Elijah Muhammad, when making public appearances. At the top in the present NOI hierarchy is Sister Tynetta Muhammad, who is presented as the wife of the Messenger. As Elijah Muhammad was never officially remarried following the death of Clara Muhammad, this could possibly mean that Tynetta Muhammad (formerly Denear) was one of the "Islamic" wives, or the so-called secretaries of the Messenger. Moreover, Farrakhan himself claims to be the spiritual son of Elijah Muhammad. Farrakhan stresses the fact that he never knew his biological father, who died when Farrakhan was quite young, and thus describes himself as fatherless before meeting the Messenger. Farrakhan said, "I am the child of my father, the Honorable Elijah Muhammad. I know of no other father but him. . . . He fathered me in wisdom, knowledge and understanding. . . . So if I am anything of value today, it's because I had a good father, a good example and a good teacher."[26] In the historiography of the resurrected Nation of Islam, Farrakhan's claim to be the rightful heir of the Messenger is further supported by Elijah Muhammad's alleged designation of him as successor, by scriptural analysis, and by references to prophecies by Elijah Muhammad. Nation of Islam theologian Jabril Muhammad repeatedly argues that Elijah Muhammad appointed Minister Farrakhan as his heir. He notes that on one occasion, Elijah Muhammad, at a 1972 seminar for NOI laborers at the Palace, told Farrakhan "to sit in his seat in his absence."[27] Jabril Muhammad recalls that in 1969, when Farrakhan had the flu, a Sister told him that the Messenger had said that Farrakhan should be mindful of his health "for Aaron was given a hard time by the people after Moses had left."[28] To fully understand the meaning of the last utterance, which is strongly emphasized in the Nation, one must consider the NOI's reading of the Scriptures and religious historiography.

The Nation stresses the old proverb, history repeats itself. Studying history, the NOI spokespersons say that whenever a people deviate so far from the path of God that their destruction is warranted, God raises from among them a "warner." Should the people heed his teachings, they are saved from destruction and made successful. Should they reject the warner, they are punished and ultimately doomed. There are profound similarities connecting these repeated instances throughout history. The context, the conditions, the warner, those who recognize him, and those who reject him all share a striking sameness. "If we truly grasp it," Jabril Muhammad writes, "we will be in the position to grasp the reason history repeats itself, and deeper, why there must come an end to this world—and end to the repetition of certain types of history."[29] Adopting an established method from Christian theology, Jabril Muhammad argues that a preordained representative relation connects certain persons and events (types) of the Scriptures with persons and events of today (antitypes). A mere similarity is not enough, the type and the antitype must be a preordained and predesigned part of a divine scheme. The type has its own place and meaning, that is, an existence independent of the antitype that it prefigures. The antitype transcends the type and fulfills that of which the type was a sign. It follows that the antitype is greater than the type, being the inner meaning of the type that at the historical time of the type could not possibly have been properly understood.

When the Sister said that Elijah Muhammad had referred to himself as Moses and Farrakhan as Aaron, Jabril Muhammad argues, it should be understood in the context of types and antitypes, signs and fulfillment. Moses found his people enslaved and ignorant. He righted them as a nation and led them out of Egypt. Before reaching the promised land, Moses departed to meet with God. In his absence, the chosen nation fell into disbelief through the worship of the golden calf. While the Bible charged Aaron with making the calf, the Holy Qur'an identifies Samiri (or Korah) as the betrayer. In the Qur'an, Aaron is raised by God to meet Moses' request for a helper when he was chosen as His Messenger: "And give me a Minister from my family; Aaron my brother; Add to my strength through him, and make him share my task."[30] When Moses prepared to leave, he put Aaron in charge of the nation: "Act for me amongst my people: Do right, and follow not the way of those who do mischief."[31] Defending Moses' legacy, Aaron was the single voice of opposition when Samiri led the nation astray. The people, however, insisted on following Samiri until the return of Moses, and Aaron temporarily gave in. When Moses returned, he asked what kept his appointed from acting when the people followed a wrongdoer. Aaron replied that he did not want to cause a division among the people. The Qur'an emphasizes the necessity for maintaining the people's unity. Samiri is best dealt with by Moses, who punished him.[32]

The antitypes are easily identified. Moses is Elijah Muhammad, who prepared to go and meet with God and assigned Farrakhan to be his Aaron, leaving the Nation and his legacy in his charge. When Wallace D. Muhammad fulfilled the role of Samiri and led the believers astray, Farrakhan was the only one remaining faithful. Knowing the paramount importance of the chosen nation's unity, Farrakhan wisely preferred to temper his anger with the mischiefmonger. The one crucial element missing in this correspondence between the scriptural types and their modern-day antitypes is that Aaron preserved unity by leaving Samiri to be dealt with by Moses upon his return. In this case, this would mean that Elijah Muhammad is not gone forever, that he is in fact alive. This notion is at the very center of the new NOI creed and became a principal argument proving the legitimacy of Minister Farrakhan's mission.

The Messiah Has Finally Come   An element of skepticism was already present at the first announcement of the Messenger's death. "We who believe and know him, won't accept anything until we see his body," said a relative when confronted with the news.[33] Sister Tynetta Muhammad, the leading theologian in the Nation, describes a vision she was given the evening of February 25, 1975: "I dreamed that the Honorable Elijah Muhammad sat upright on the funeral bench where he had been lain with the sheet wrapped across his body in the style of the Ihram garments worn by the Pilgrims during Hajj. When I saw him sitting in this position, I exclaimed several times, he is not dead!"[34] Abass Rassoull, who is not a member of Farrakhan's Nation, attests that he has been visited by the Messenger on a few occasions after his alleged death. Rassoull describes how deeply affected he was when he heard the news of the Messenger's death. Elijah Muhammad had told him that there would be no such thing as a leader after him, because he was the fulfillment of all prophecies, and he promised Rassoull to be present at the time of Armageddon. When the Messenger was gone, the mental universe of Rassoull was shattered. He was so depressed that he could not stand to look at himself in the mirror. In that downhill mental condition, he saw Elijah Muhammad for the first time since his departure: "I was lying on my back, wide awake and His head and shoulders appeared in a circle in front of me, about four feet above the bed. He did not have his fez and He did not speak; He only smiled. He was there for two or three minutes. After He left, I got up, washed for prayer and said prayer. I have not missed a day of prayer since then, nor have I ever doubted again."[35] With the Messenger of God alive, other prophecies of his can be properly understood. The Honorable Elijah Muhammad, writes Jabril Muhammad, once said to Minister Louis Farrakhan, "I am going away to study. I will be gone for approximately three years. What I have given you is just a wake-up message. Don't change the teachings while I'm gone. If you are faithful, I will reveal the new teachings through you on my return."[36] Another alleged forecast was made by the Messenger upon the death of his wife, Clara Muhammad, in 1972. Shortly afterward, Elijah Muhammad gave a lecture and, Farrakhan recalls, said, "There was a great prophet whose wife died. And three years after his wife died, the End came."[37] The congregation, not knowing exactly what prophet Elijah Muhammad had in mind, believed the Judgment to be coming in three years and there was great rejoicing. Today, the believers conclude that the prophet that Elijah had referred to was Muhammad ibn Abdullah. The end of the Meccan period arrived three years after the death of the Prophet's first wife, Khadidja. The Prophet Muhammad learned of a death plot and escaped to Yathrib. The Medinah period, when an independent Islamic nation came into existence, began then. Farrakhan declares that the modern course of events should be understood by reference to this historical résumé: "We believe that Elijah Muhammad is not dead physically. We believe he is alive. We believe that during that time in the hospital he went through what they call death, and we believe that he was made to appear as though dead. [But] I believe that he escaped."[38] The Messenger of God is believed to have learned of a fatal conspiracy involving the intelligence community of the United States. Elijah Muhammad had been warned by God that they plotted against his life, and God sent angels to his rescue. The NOI "do not mean anything spooky" by angels, but it refers to black helpers of God, sent from His abode above. In this case, the divine soldiers miraculously concealed the Messenger from the assassins and transferred him to God.[39] Minister Farrakhan first blazed the news of Elijah Muhammad having escaped a death plot at his 1981 Saviour's Day speech. Two years later, the full status of Elijah Muhammad "as a man who today sits on the right hand side of God the Almighty, soon to return and deal with the living and the dead," was officially proclaimed.[40]

The theologians of the Nation of Islam argue that the Holy Scriptures of Islam, Judaism, and Christianity should be properly understood not as historical narratives but as signs and descriptions of events to be fulfilled in the latter days. In the Holy Qur'an 23:50, Allah says, "And We made the son of Mary and his mother as a Sign."[41] According to Louis Farrakhan, this clarifies the fact that Jesus of Nazareth was not the Messiah but that his life pointed toward the coming of a Messiah. A Messiah that was to be a black man, with, as the Bible puts it, hair like lamb's wool and feet looking like they had been burned in an oven. The Christian clergy tries to convince humanity that Jesus the prophet was the Messiah and that we can postpone our demands for justice until the day of his return. This is extremely foolish talk, Farrakhan says: "There is no man sitting out in space with a wounded side and blood pouring out his side for 2,000 years, waiting to come back and take you to the Kingdom. Stop it, Reverend! We got to understand it better than that. Jesus was not our first astronaut."[42] Jesus of Nazareth is dead; he was not the Messiah. It is obvious, Farrakhan said, "by checking out his deeds. He didn't save the world. It's still a misery out there. But he pointed towards the coming of a Saviour who was to raise the dead."[43] According to the Nation of Islam, that man is the Honorable Elijah Muhammad, who raised the so-called mentally dead Negroes up from their grave in the mud of American society. He made the blind man see, the deaf man hear, and he gave the dumb man voice. Observers of the Nation could have expected this development, as the Messenger was already hailed in messianic terms prior to his departure. He was a fragile little man and frequently portrayed as "the Lamb," with power to defeat the beasts in the approaching apocalypse, and Farrakhan did at least once depict him as Jesus.[44] The long awaited Messiah is finally here and he is black. This, Farrakhan says, puts the religious man who eagerly expects the coming of the Lord to a severe test: "What would you do if [the Messiah] came? And he was Black? Would you let him in or would you call 911 and say 'its a nigger at my door?' To the extent you cannot hear wisdom coming from a Black man's mouth, it is to that extent you are condemned to destruction."[45] Realizing that he was the antitype of the biblical Christ, Elijah Muhammad knew from Scriptures about the forthcoming events and prepared for them. After a much-appreciated speech by Minister Farrakhan, the Messenger reportedly sent him a letter, stating that he prayed to Allah, asking that if the minister ever turned into a hypocrite, Allah would go after him to bring him back. Minister Farrakhan was disturbed. How could the Messenger think he would betray him? A similar incident took place a few years later. Some sisters were praising Farrakhan, telling the Messenger how famous he was becoming. Elijah Muhammad interrupted, shouting, "Yes, so the whole world will see him when he betrays me!" Minister Farrakhan felt hurt and confused. Later, Elijah Muhammad reportedly made his first direct reference to the minister as Peter: "I tell you like Jesus told Peter, 'The devil desires you that he might sift you like wheat.' " Later still, he stated his antipathy for Peter, telling Farrakhan to be like Paul.[46]

Like Peter, his antitype Farrakhan at a certain point betrayed his Messiah and denied him.[47] He then ascended and proved to be the rock on which to build the foundation for the new Nation. The Nation was preordained to fall and to rise and never to fall again. Minister Louis Farrakhan then proceeded to fulfill the role of the type preferred by the Messenger. Crisscrossing the United States, covering nearly fifty cities, Farrakhan preached the new gospel at the core of which was "the identification of the Hon. Elijah Muhammad as the Christ."[48] Farrakhan's tour was, according to Jabril Muhammad, the equivalent of Paul's travels, making Farrakhan the antitype of Paul: "As Paul was to Jesus, according to Christian theology, so is Min. Louis Farrakhan to the real Christ."[49] The modern Paul is clear about his obligation: "My work is to make his great commission known. To say to the Jews who are looking for the Messiah, to say to the Muslims who await the Mahdi, that Elijah Muhammad is not Messenger of God. That he is the Messiah that the whole world is looking for. And that I and my work in America is the witness that the Messianic age has in fact begun."[50] Followers of Imam Wallace Muhammad accused Farrakhan of preaching what he knew was a lie, when he spoke of Elijah Muhammad as being alive. They asked him for proof. Had he met him? Had he spoken to him? Farrakhan says he countered by suggesting a postmortem. "Let us exam the body. Let us exam the body and the teeth of this man. Since he had a dentist in Mexico, let us bring him as witness, and if that is in fact him I won't say anything more."[51] Not surprisingly, Imam Muhammad declined the offer, and Farrakhan continued his preaching. For seven years, Farrakhan relied solely on scriptural exegesis and argumentation. But, as Jabril Muhammad observes, "If, in fact, Aaron in your Bible is a sign of Min. Louis Farrakhan Muhammad, then it follows that a modern Moses—the Hon. Elijah Muhammad—must at some point make contact with Min. Louis Farrakhan."[52] In 1985, Moses did call for Aaron to meet with him and confirmed the truth of the new gospel.

The Black Path of Redemption   On September 17, 1985, Minister Farrakhan was in the quiet Mexican hamlet of Tepotzlan and received a vision in which his divine power was further reinforced.[53] In the vision, Farrakhan walked up a mountain to an Aztec temple together with some companions. When he got to the top of the mountain, a UFO appeared. Farrakhan immediately realized the importance of the moment. In the cosmology of the Nation, God supervises humanity from a great manmade planet circling Tellus. This planet, which is discussed in the following chapter, is known in the NOI as "the Mother Ship" or "the Mother Wheel." In the Bible, it is known both as Ezekiel's Wheel and as the New Jerusalem. In this heavenly abode is a magnificent city, prepared as a residence for the new civilization that is to replace the present world order after the battle of Armageddon. On the Mother Wheel too, are small spacecraft carriers, called "baby planes," piloted by helpers of God. Frequently, the smaller crafts visit earth on various expeditions ordered by God, such as when Elijah Muhammad was rescued from hired assassins in 1975.

The circular space ship did not come directly over the mountain but stayed off the side, and a voice called Farrakhan to come closer. Farrakhan, feeling a bit afraid, asked his companions to go with him but was corrected from the spacecraft: "Just you, brother Farrakhan." He obeyed, and as he walked closer, a beam of light, resembling the sunlight piercing through a window, came out of the wheel. Farrakhan was told to relax and was brought up into the plane on this beam of light. He was placed next to the pilot. Farrakhan could feel his presence but could not see him. The spacecraft took off with Farrakhan, who knew that the pilot was sent by God and was to take him to the Mother Wheel. Approaching the man-made planet, the pilot turned the spaceship around and with great speed backed into a tunnel in the main wheel. This tunnel was made of something brownish in color, which looked like fabric but was stronger.

After docking, the door opened and Farrakhan was escorted by the pilot to a door and admitted into a room, which was totally empty except for a speaker in the ceiling. From that speaker Farrakhan heard the well-known voice of the Honorable Elijah Muhammad, which confirmed his being alive. Farrakhan was authorized to lead his God-fearing people through the latter days. Elijah the Messiah spoke in short, cryptic words. Farrakhan, anxious to do the work he was obliged to do, tried to ask him for advice concerning some of the perplexing problems he faced down on earth. Elijah Muhammad gave only short answers, as a man who does not waste time by long discussions anymore. His words had a new weight, each word being loaded with a world of meaning. As the Messiah was speaking, a scroll full of divine cursive writing was rolled down inside Farrakhan's head. Farrakhan for a moment saw a reflection of this scroll, containing the full message from God to humanity, before it was gone, placed in the back of his brain. Then Elijah Muhammad said, "I will not allow you to see me now. You have one more thing to do, then you can come and be with me, and I will show myself to you face to face." The Messiah did not say exactly what this last thing Farrakhan had to do was, but left it to Farrakhan to find out. Farrakhan believes the relevant information has been put into him already and will appear when the time has come.

Elijah Muhammad then started telling Farrakhan about a war that President Reagan was planning and ordered him to hold a press conference to expose Reagan's evil schemes and tell him and the rest of the world from where he got his information (this plan and related events is discussed in chapter 8). Elijah Muhammad then dismissed Farrakhan with these few words in a stern voice: "You may go now." Farrakhan was escorted back to the little wheel by the same pilot, whom he still could not see but only could feel his presence. The spacecraft shot out of the tunnel and then stopped abruptly. The pilot then took the plane up to a terrific height and maneuvered the vehicle to allow Farrakhan to look down on the wheel. Farrakhan saw a city, a magnificent city, the New Jerusalem, in the sky. Instead of going back to Mexico, the craft carried Farrakhan with tremendous speed to Washington, D.C., and dropped him off outside the city. He walked into the capital and delivered his announcement, the final warning to the United States government.[54]

After Farrakhan awakened from the vision, his memory of the experience temporarily vanished. Two days later, on the morning of September 19, 1985, a great earthquake rocked Mexico City. This divine act brought the vision forcibly back into Farrakhan's mind, and he related it to his wife Khadidja—just as the prophet Muhammad ibn Abdullah told his wife, Khadidja, of his vision. Sister Tynetta Muhammad was also present the first time Farrakhan told anyone of his experience. Later on, the authenticity of his vision was confirmed. Farrakhan was leaving Arizona for a speaking engagement in New York City. As he traveled, he was followed by a fleet of divine space carriers. According to Farrakhan, the news reported that fifteen squadrons of four little wheels, going at the speed of 150 miles per hour, were seen moving from the Southwest to the Northeast. Farrakhan claims that everywhere he went the wheel followed to remind him of his mission and to assure him that he is backed by God: "The Messiah is alive. He is in the world. The power of God is present in America with me."[55]

To Farrakhan and the believers, the significance of this vision cannot be overestimated. It proves not only that Elijah Muhammad is alive but that he is, in fact, the Christ who will return with power to slay his enemies in the final battle. The vision further authorized Farrakhan's position as Elijah Muhammad's national representative and rejects the claim of Imam Warithuddin Muhammad to be the true heir of his father. As the observant reader undoubtedly has noticed, the vision completes a development that has an interesting historical parallel: the deification of Master Farad Muhammad following his departure and the elevation of his closest associate, Elijah Muhammad, to the position as Messenger of God.

From the observer's perspective it is tempting to limit the interpretation of this development to its significance for the struggle for power in the movement. While this context, of course, is important, such a "profane" reading runs the risk of glossing over the deeper religious meaning of the events. Reflecting on how this development was at all possible, a highly interesting feature of the NOI teachings emerge, which opens up an avenue for deepening our understanding of the NOI creed. While this is discussed in more detail in the next chapter, some initial remarks here could perhaps be of service to the reader.

In mainstream Islam, as well as in Judaism and Christianity, the Creator is, ontologically speaking, essentially different from his creation. Between the Creator and his creation is an unbridgeable gulf; consequently, mystics who seek ways to transcend the gap seem suspect in the eyes of mainstream theologians. Should the mystic sage strive to trespass the ontological border—that is, search not only for immediate closeness to God, but Oneness with God—he is likely to be charged with heresy. The NOI's doctrinal development I describe above violates the mainstream Islamic theology, in which the possibility for man to grow into divinity does not exist.

The Nation of Islam does not share this mainstream view of the basic divide between the nature of God and the nature of man. According to the blackosophic NOI teaching, the black race in its natural state is divine. There is a seed of God a priori at the root of existence in the nature of each black man and woman. Man has the potential to ennoble the divine within and reach his apex of existence: to become God. In Gnostic Christianity, Jesus is a spiritual master who shows the potential of man to evolve into divinity. As Jesus was the son of his Father, we are all children of God: "Ye are all gods, children of the Most High God."[56] Herein lies the secret mystery: the Son of Man is identical with the Son of God. In the Nation, this notion is articulated by the belief in the black path to divinity, which enables each black man and woman to become Saviour and Lord. The deification of Master Farad Muhammad and Elijah Muhammad is thus connected to the core of the NOI creed—and is not as odd as it may seem at first glimpse.

When Master Farad Muhammad left the earth and ascended to the Mother Wheel, he entrusted his Nation in the hands of his Messenger. When Elijah Muhammad departed, he left Minister Farrakhan in charge as his national representative. A scroll containing God's message to his people was placed inside Farrakhan, making him a divine mouthpiece. In a certain sense, this indicates that Farrakhan replaces Muhammad as the Messenger of God. Being fully aware of the mainstream Islamic belief in Muhammad ibn Abdullah as the Seal of the Prophets, the theologians of the Nation avoid using this term when describing the role assumed by Farrakhan. Sister Tynetta Muhammad compares Farrakhan's vision with John's vision at Patmos.[57] Jabril Muhammad, discussing the type-antitype correspondence of Elijah Muhammad—Moses and Louis Farrakhan—Aaron, notes that in Exodus 7:1, God said, "See I have made thee [Moses] a God to Pharaoh; and Aaron thy brother shall be thy prophet." Elijah Muhammad is thus exalted into godhood—but does this not make Farrakhan a prophet? Jabril writes, "I should say not! He is more than that!"[58]

Who, then, is he? Transcending the role of Aaron, Farrakhan is on the black path of deification. Master Farad Muhammad raised Elijah Muhammad, who raised Louis Farrakhan, who is now raising the black Nation to its predestined glory.[59] This means that "Minister Louis Farrakhan is going through the same renewal process the Honorable Elijah Muhammad went through."[60] Farrakhan is the one standing at the tomb of Lazarus, the black man, calling him back to life.[61] At a 1989 dinner at the Palace, Farrakhan said, "I am the man everybody is looking for. I am a Messiah. Elijah Muhammad was raised by Master Farad Muhammad to become the Messiah and he raised me to become the little Messiah. Read the scriptures, there are two Messiahs coming in the Latter Days."[62] Farrakhan is thus a black redeemer, sometimes referred to as a "little Jesus,"[63] who "has grown sufficiently into the mind of Christ."[64]

Although Farrakhan himself denies being a prophet,[65] he partly fulfills the function of a prophet. The divine scroll placed inside Farrakhan enables him to communicate the will and thoughts of God to His chosen people in this precarious era, which is close to the end of time. Farrakhan is surrounded by a staff that records his speeches and makes notes of his utterances. Every word coming from Farrakhan is not from God. The Nation carefully distinguishes revealed divine sayings from the human words that pass through the same lips, as did the Muslim congregation in Mecca and Medinah when listening to Muhammad ibn Abdullah. Farrakhan has no knowledge of the scroll's full contents, but says that the scroll "is there, and I know it is inside, and under the right circumstances things will come out of me that I have never thought of before. But if you give me questions, I give you answers. If you come back with light, what you think is light, God will bless me to shed light on anything that you already know. Because something has been put in me, not just for my immediate community, but for . . . the entire world."[66]

Rebuilding the Black House   The first years of Minister Farrakhan's efforts to resurrect the Nation of Islam were characterized by conflicts with Imam Warithuddin Muhammad and a slow but steady consolidation of the new organization. Initially, Imam Muhammad dismissed Farrakhan's mission as reactionary and contrary to the intentions of Elijah Muhammad. In 1978, Imam Muhammad argued that Farrakhan's reestablishment of the NOI on the former platform meant that the minister "has broken from the program, the plan, the scheme of the Nation of Islam . . . and has not understood and accepted the psychology and gradualism for the total religious transformation of the Lost Found Nation of Islam in America."[67] Imam Muhammad reassured his followers that he, and not Farrakhan, walked the path of God and challenged Farrakhan to prove his position by paralleling the success of the World Community of al-Islam in the West. He ended his appeal to Minister Farrakhan by emphasizing that the challenge should not be seen as one of enmity. On the contrary, he gave his word to those eager to see a black Islamic civil war: "You bastard! You'll never pull me out in the street to do one ounce of harm to Minister Farrakhan! You go to hell, you bastard!"[68] Despite the fact that Imam Muhammad was seen as a new Absalom (who destroyed his father David's kingdom), Farrakhan urged his followers to cool down the animosity.[69] Interviewed by Spike Lee, Farrakhan said the low profile was a wise tactic. Learning his lesson from the assassination of Malcolm X, Farrakhan restrained from publicly rebuking Imam Muhammad. "I knew that if I had stood up to attack him, there were those in his camp poised to kill me," Farrakhan explained. "I'm lucky to be alive. But I'm strong now. I have soldiers now, everywhere."[70]

Farrakhan denies that he sought to recruit followers from the old membership of the Nation of Islam, and spokespersons from both camps emphasize that there never has been a large migration between the groups. Martha F. Lee believes this to be a contributing factor to the factions' peaceful coexistence.[71] While it is true that Farrakhan has attracted most of his current membership outside the former NOI membership—not least among those too young to have been adult followers of Elijah Muhammad—there is reason to doubt this description. Yet both parties share an interest in retaining this viewpoint. Imam Warithuddin cannot undermine his authority as the true interpreter of his father's intentions or the validity of his Islamization project by acknowledging a flow of members to Farrakhan's Nation. Minister Farrakhan wants to avoid being accused of causing division and much less *fitna* (an Islamic civil war), something that the Prophet Muhammad had described as the worst possible consequence for Islam. The call of Minister Louis Farrakhan was in fact intensely debated in the black Muslim community. Was Elijah Muhammad only a great teacher of Islam as Imam Muhammad holds, or was he in fact

the Messenger of God as Farrakhan argues? Had Elijah Muhammad intended a gradual religious transition to mainstream Sunni Islam, or did
he actually bring a distinct message, specific for the African Americans?
Was Elijah Muhammad dead or elevated into a living Messiah? These
central theological questions divided the WCIW/AMM and led to several
schisms in local congregations—for example, in Boston where at least
half of the membership is said to have broken with Imam Muhammad and
sided with Farrakhan.[72]

In 1981, the resurrected Nation called its first national convention.
Following the deification of Elijah Muhammad, the Nation now cele-
brates two Saviour's Days, commemorating the October 7 birth of the
Messiah in addition to honoring the birth of God in the person of Master
Farad Muhammad on February 26. As Farrakhan seemed to be success-
fully meeting the challenge of Imam Muhammad, their relationship dete-
riorated. Imam Muhammad warned every African American Islamic convert "to be especially aware of the impostor who stands up in the name of
Al-Islam."[73] When Farrakhan came to national attention during Jesse
Jackson's primary race in 1984 (which is described in chapter 9), Imam
Muhammad assured concerned Americans that Farrakhan "misrepresented" Islam and does not speak for the Muslim community.[74] A true
Muslim, Imam Muhammad wrote, knows that Muslims are not all black,
but of all races, which means that "you cannot be a racist and call yourself
a Muslim."[75] Mustafa El-Amin wrote a book describing the differences
between conventional Islam and Farrakhan's teachings.[76] Less diplomatically, Imam Sidney Rahim Sharif condemned Farrakhan for "promoting himself . . . in an effort to line his pockets and amass an army of
slaves."[77]

From their perspective, NOI members felt that Wallace Muhammad literally had sold his soul to the Devil. As the beast of the Revelation,
who emerged in an evil quest to prevent the victory of God's forces, he
had to be slain in the fulfillment of predestined eschatology. "It would be
best," wrote Jabril Muhammad, "for the haters of Allah . . . and Bro.
Farrakhan to cool off, back off and rethink things before the fullness of
Divine wrath falls."[78] Rumors started circulating in the African American community that both groups prepared for a holy war against the
hypocrites. The wheel of animosity was finally tempered as Minister
Farrakhan and Imam Muhammad met in a series of secret negotiations
in 1983. Reportedly, they made a peace treaty, stipulating that neither
party should engage in character assassination–type language. The par-

ties were to endeavor to ignore each other, as ideological reconciliation proved impossible.[79] The truce was put to test when a statement by Imam Muhammad in late 1989 was interpreted as a threat against Farrakhan's life.[80] The tension cooled off in January 1990, when Minister Farrakhan and Imam Muhammad met during a conference of forty-one Islamic governments in Jeddah, Saudi Arabia.[81] This was followed up at an Islamic convention in Chicago in September 1990, where the two Muslim leaders publicly embraced each other.[82]

In 1986, Imam Muhammad's organization lost a case in the probate court. In 1979, three of Elijah Muhammad's illegitimate children filed suit to recover assets transferred to Imam Muhammad's organization. After seven years of litigation, the Cook County Circuit Court ruled in favor of the estate.[83] A legal mess still drags on concerning other assets, including some 20,000 acres of farmland in Michigan, Alabama, and Georgia. The court's decision made Imam Muhammad declare his organization bankrupt, and he sold the limestone-and-marble Chicago Palace to the Nation.[84] On July 31, 1988, Farrakhan proudly announced the purchase of the Stoney Island mosque and school at a price of $2,175,000. This was presented as "the Victory": the NOI was finally to return "home."[85] Farrakhan's headquarters were situated in an old funeral parlor on the South Side's 79th Street, but now plans for a renovation of the former NOI flagship into a "national center" were announced.[86] On Saviour's Day, October 7, 1988, Farrakhan attracted a crowd of twelve thousand people assembled under tents on the grounds at the Stoney Island Mosque.[87] Farrakhan later described the symbolic significance of this event: "It is not a coincidence that we were driven from that house in 1977 like Muhammad was driven from Mecca and ten years later he marched back at the head of an army of 10,000. It is not accidental that ten years later we had a contract on the building, and it is not an accident that the number of persons who camped on the grounds of that sacred place were a little over 10,000."[88] On Saviour's Day, February 26, 1989, Farrakhan inaugurated the national center, which was named Mosque Maryam in the honor of black womanhood.[89] The renovated mosque is impressive; it is an entire complex, including a library, a masjid, a huge main mosque with an auditorium large enough for thousands of people, a gym, a twelve-classroom elementary school, and facilities for secondary education. Skilled Turkish artisans have made the mosque a "jewel" with Qur'anic verses in twenty-three-carat gold leaf decorating the nineteen arches inside the mosque and the seven-story dome. A giant gold-leafed eight-pointed star with "Allah" in its center circled by twenty-four windows complete the dome.[90] In front of the seats in the main auditorium is a restricted area called the Holy of Holies, covered by a solid blue drape. Here is an Egyptian marble sarcophagus that according to the inscriptions was intended for Elijah Muhammad, but which of course is empty. Outside, on top of the white dome, a glowing star and crescent rotates against the Chicago skyline.

Numerous factors explain the success of Farrakhan's rebuilding efforts. While most of these are described later in this study, a few remarks on the personal qualities of Louis Farrakhan should be noted. He is still musically active and, in 1984, put out a record with his songs, *Let Us Unite*.[91] Above all, he is an eloquent speaker in the great oral tradition of African American preachers, in which great emphasis is put on the speaker's personal charisma and oratorical ability. When at the rostrum, Farrakhan is a preacher-artist who fully uses his gifts as an entertainer to deliver a splendid performance. His long lectures are composed much like orchestral numbers. He starts by displaying a theme, then varies the expressions, moving his audience to tears and laughter, serious consideration and explosive anger, before reaching the grand finale in which he dramatically drives his points through. Farrakhan combines a number of diverse roles during each sermon, such as the strong warrior, the trickster, the stern father, the heartwarmer, the stand-up comedian, the encyclopedic scholar, and the Doomsday prophet. As is common in the black church, a kind of dialogue is established as the preaching evokes responses from the audience, with the worshipers shouting cries of approval such as "That's right," "Tell it like it is," "Go on, Minister, go on," and "Teach, Brother, teach."

There is no doubt that Farrakhan's oratorical brilliance contributes heavily to his rising popularity and explains in part the crowds that jam auditoriums when he speaks. Farrakhan is able to attract a larger audience than any other black spokesperson: 35,000 people showed up at Madison Square Garden, New York, 17,000 in Los Angeles, 26,000 in Detroit, 19,000 and then 15,000 in Atlanta, 15,000 in Chicago, 21,000 at Jacob Javits Center in New York, and 10,000 in Baltimore. The high visibility Farrakhan has had since 1984 contributes to this popularity. He frequently makes headlines and appears at the center of several current controversies, thereby making him a spectacular celebrity whom people desire to see in person.

Besides the sermons delivered by Farrakhan and his top Laborers, the

Nation of Islam spreads the black Islamic nationalist message through hip-hop music,[92] radio and television broadcasts, audio and videotaped lectures, literature, and its own organ, the *Final Call.* As of September 1995, Minister Farrakhan could be heard on forty-eight different radio stations and seen on at least ninety-nine different television channels across the United States.[93] Books, tapes, and videos are sold by mail and in the various mosques and Afrocentric bookstores dotting the country.

In 1979, Farrakhan took out a mortgage on his house to finance the establishment of the *Final Call.*[94] The title is derived from Qur'an 74:8 and connotes a certain sense of eschatological urgency: "The Final Call will not be issued forever."[95] Initially it was produced in the basement of Minister Farrakhan's home and appeared only irregularly. In 1983, the *Final Call* was made a monthly and became a biweekly by the late 1980s, produced in modern facilities at the Final Call Building on Chicago's South Side. Under the direction of Abdul Wali Muhammad (1954–92) as editor in chief, the *Final Call* reached a wide circulation, which is said to be the largest in Blackamerica.[96] The new editor in chief is James Muhammad, a veteran NOI journalist. The circulation reached 500,000 copies of each edition in 1994, at which point Farrakhan set the goal to one million.[97] The reader should be aware that the *Final Call* is not comparable with the average sectarian paper. As was the case with *Muhammad Speaks,* the wide circulation is explained not only by mandatory selling drives but also by the paper's professional quality. The *Final Call* publishes well-written and researched articles relevant to the African American community; further, it is connected with the major news agencies and has an above-average international section. Ali Baghdadi covers the Muslim world, along with contributions from syndicated columnists and skilled freelance writers. The *Final Call* runs interesting articles on black music, art, and culture as well. Besides items of general interest, the paper publishes religious articles and interpretations of events from a black Islamic nationalist perspective. The *Final Call* also publishes excerpts from Farrakhan's speeches and reprints speeches and articles by Elijah Muhammad. Theologians Jabril Muhammad, Tynetta Muhammad, and Abdul Allah Muhammad are regular contributors to the *Final Call.* Undoubtedly, this technique of mixing NOI material with articles by professional nonmembers is effective and allows the paper to attract readers far beyond the NOI membership.

Organizationally, the second resurrection began with study circles in the homes of followers or rented halls. Following the steady growth of the

Nation, with a boom in the mid-1980s and continued expansion since then, mosques and study groups were established in every state and the District of Columbia. To be chartered as an affiliate mosque, a group of active believers, numbering no less than forty, must submit a signed letter of application to the NOI headquarters, declaring their intention to live by the rules and regulations specified by Minister Farrakhan and his chiefs of staff. The NOI administration is consciously modeled as a sovereign state, with its own ratified constitution, which is said to be "provisional" since actual black sovereignty has yet to come. The governing body of the NOI consists of the national representative of the Honorable Elijah Muhammad—that is, Minister Louis Farrakhan as the head of state—and his cabinet called the National Council of Laborers. The administration is then subdivided into ministries, each of which is headed by a minister who is directly appointed by the national representative: The chiefs of staff assist the national representative in the general direction of all operations of the state. The minister of finance is responsible for the state budget and the fiscal program. The minister of commerce is responsible for business development, nationally and internationally. The minister of defense, presently Abdul Sharieff Muhammad, has authority over the training of the military male cadre in the Fruit of Islam (FOI) and advises the national representative with respect to the "integration of domestic, international and foreign military policies relating to the national security."[98] Following the principle of gender separatism, the National M. G. T. Captain or national instructress of women is responsible for the training and teaching of the female members. The minister of education administrates all adult education programs and the Universities of Islam. The minister of youth, presently rapper Prince Akeem, is responsible for propagating Islam among African American youth and tasks related to younger members. The minister of health, presently Dr. Abdul Alim Muhammad, is responsible for all programs related to national health and human service. In addition to these ministers, the national council also includes representatives from the six regions, into which the various mosques are grouped geographically. Minister Don Muhammad heads the eastern region, Minister Ishmael Muhammad (son of Elijah) heads the central region, Minister Ahvay Muhammad heads the western region, Minister Robert Muhammad heads the southwest region, Minister Vann Muhammad heads the southern region, and Minister Abdul Arif Muhammad heads the mid-Atlantic region.[99]

A key role in the NOI project to redeem the black nation is given to the divine army, the Fruit of Islam. Farrakhan takes exception to the old military training wherein the soldiers often looked on themselves "as an army of killers." While they should not be soft, they should hide their power and look on themselves as an army of saviours.[100] The presence of disciplined soldiers gives the NOI events a special atmosphere and the Nation an appearance of a mighty body. Underscoring the meaning of an army under the command of the exalted Messiah, Farrakhan told his soldiers: "Military training implies tactics. Military training implies maneuvers. Military training implies going behind the lines in enemy territory. Military training implies establishing a beachhead in enemy territory and then proceeding to take control. Military training implies WAR."[101] While asserting that the FOI will not be the aggressor, Farrakhan assures that "we will whip the hell out of any that comes against us, short or tall, armed or unarmed."[102] One such incident occurred on January 9, 1994, when four white police officers tried to force their way into the Harlem mosque in response to a bogus robbery-in-progress call. After the aforementioned 1972 attack against the Temple #7, the New York Police Department established a policy to let a police supervisor personally handle matters involving NOI mosques. Violating this official rule, the four officers refused to leave their guns with the FOI security men and dashed up the stairs. They were hurled out by Muslim soldiers and the fighting spilled onto the sidewalk as police backup arrived at the scene. All four police officers were beaten up and hospitalized, one officer had his gun taken away, and another lost her radio. Soon, the mosque was under siege with the police blocking the area with squad cars and SWAT snipers placed on adjacent rooftops. Four hundred Muslims were inside, with other soldiers joined by angry Harlem residents taking to the streets ready to defend the mosque. Police borough commanders, black politicians, and Minister Conrad Muhammad finally negotiated an end to the standoff after five tense hours.[103]

During Farrakhan's ministry, the Nation further began to rebuild and expand its international network. NOI emissaries travel all over the globe, from the Caribbean to New Zealand, to propagate black religious nationalism.[104] Besides reestablishing chapters across the West Indies, in Canada, and in Great Britain, the NOI opened an African mission in 1990, headed by NOI African representative Abdul Akbar Muhammad, with headquarters in Accra. Farrakhan has a long-standing close relationship with President Jerry Rawlins of Ghana, a country receptive to black nationalism since its independence under President Kwame Nkrumah.[105]

During October 5–9, 1994, the Nation of Islam held its first International Saviour's Day conference in Ghana, attracting a crowd of 30,000 including some 2,000 African Americans. President Rawlins opened the event, declaring that the "fulfillment of the destiny of the African continent . . . will come when the descendants of the slaves who built other nations . . . refashion their links to the Motherland."[106]

7

A Nation of Gods: The Creed of Black Islam

==

The Creation of the Heavens and the Earth   In the Beginning there was blackness, a triple blackness of space, water, and divinity. The One Supreme God came into existence at the origin of the universe, seventy-six trillion years ago. He willed himself into being in the form of a black man, cell by cell, in a process that took him six trillion years. The Supreme God created himself out of the blackness of space and the blackness of water, which composes three quarters of the body.[1]

Before the creation of the world, the black man was in existence: "Before there was a sun or stars, we were. He [the First One] created us out of this black material in the darkness of space, and we took our color from the darkness out of which we emerged."[2] The First Supreme One was a warrior who, in order to combat darkness and shed light, created the sun, which represents freedom and creativity, out of his fire, which is Truth. He imbued the planets with life and had them submit to the sun, and called it the solar system.[3]

All that exists in the universe is created by the Black Intellect, or Divine Wisdom.[4] There is no higher intellect than that of man, because the spirit of divine wisdom, love, freedom, justice, and equality can only manifest itself through human flesh: "Man is God and God is man."[5] The black man thus has no birth record: he has always existed, making the black race a nation of gods, originating in the Originator, descending from the base of his wisdom.[6]

As helpers of the Supreme God, a council of twenty-four imams—gods or black scientists—was established. It is composed of twelve greater imams,[7] the first God and the next eleven ones, and twelve lesser imams, referred to in Revelation as the "four and twenty elders" and called the "exalted assembly" in the Holy Qur'an.[8] Their number will always remain intact, but their seats will be filled by a succession of Gods, as no God lives forever.[9] At any one time there is but one God in charge because "two Gods cannot serve at one time."[10]

The last thing to be created in the present solar system was the moon; thus the order of creation is man, earth, sun, stars, and moon. The moon was created sixty-six trillion years ago by a black scientist who sought to destroy the black race—a cosmic suicide wish, because, if it were successful, the destruction would have returned everything to the state before the Beginning. That imam—who, of course, was not identical with the Supreme God—first tried to force his rule upon the original people but failed. Jealous as a God can be, he therefore decided to destroy it all. He drilled a tube into the Earth's surface, all the way down to the center, and filled the shaft with the same powerful explosives other scientists use to raise mountains and lower valleys. The dynamite blasted a piece of the Earth 12,000 miles into space. This piece of the Earth became the moon, which turned over and poured out her water, thereby depriving herself of life and becoming a dead body rotating around Earth.[11]

The making of the moon altered the time frame in which the great cycles of history move. Originally each greater cycle lasted 35,000 years, which represented the circumference of the planet Earth at that time and also the time it took for a complete rotation of the poles to occur. After blasting away the part we now call the moon, the circumference became approximately 25,000 miles, and it took 10,000 years fewer to complete a rotation. The great cycles of world history were from then on 25,000 years each. For each cycle, a Supreme God from the divine council is in charge, taking his turn in contributing to the evolutionary process that shaped the present world.[12] After completion of a cycle, "another God would be given a chance to show forth his Wisdom to the people."[13]

After the moon came into existence, the Supreme One ascended to his throne, concealing his true identity until the end of time. Only a closed secret society composed of a number of elected men, the divine circle of twelve greater and twelve lesser Imams, had the true knowledge of God.[14] They guarded the secret, passing it on from son to son, and were not allowed to reveal it until the end of time.[15] Why would God hide himself from his creation? The underlying reason is related to God's plan for humanity: the perfection of man.[16] The fact that a frustrated scientist tried to destroy the Creation, when he could not force his will upon the people, made manifest the negative side of the original life and highlighted a problem that had to be mastered if perfection was to be realized. God concealed his true identity in order to allow mankind's individuation process to begin gradually, a maturity process that presently is reaching its climax after making real progress during the two latest cosmic time cycles. "50,000 years ago," Elijah Muhammad claimed, "God taught me, a [divine] black man disagreed with the eleven scientists." He propagated a new teaching, arguing that the original people must prepare, because there will be a time when evil will be manifest and rule the world.[17] The embodiments of evil will possess such enormous power that the Blackman, if not strengthened and hardened, will not be able to regain global hegemony. Confronted with this God's appeal for a period of training, the eleven decided to let him go and prove the value of his new wisdom somewhere else. The God, named Imam Shabazz, traveled deep into Africa. Through an intensive program the Blackman developed into a person, strong, powerful, and, in the long run, undefeatable.[18]

"Fifteen thousand and sixty-eight years ago," Jabril Muhammad wrote in 1985, "the Supreme Being, Who is a man, called the other 23 Scientists into a secret conference to get up the future of the nation."[19] These divine scientists, the descendants of the original Ones, are the above-mentioned guardians of the sacred knowledge of God concealed for sixty-six trillion years and the holy architects of modern world history.[20]

Foremost among this assembly of gods was a Supreme Being, Master Farad Muhammad. He is not identical with the First One who laid down the foundation for the creation of the heavens and the earth and "the base for that which other wise Gods later come and did."[21] Master Farad Muhammad is the first God to have the same power and wisdom as the First One had in the Beginning. In fact, as Master Farad Muhammad has the power to return everything to nothing and then bring forth a new and better creation from himself, he is "superior of even that First One."[22]

The secret brotherhood of gods, which is the "we" and "us" of the Holy Scriptures, "saw down the corridors of time" all the way to the hereafter, and wrote it down in the Mother Book.[23] They recorded everything that was to take place, but in a codified language, and decided to "seal the book," which was not to be opened until the latter days.[24] Portions of the Mother Book were later to be revealed—still codified—to various prophets raised by God. The Torah, the *Injil* (the Gospel), and the Holy Qur'an are thus parts of, but not identical with, this Mother Book.

Among all the things foreseen by these scientists was a time when evil would be fully manifest and rule the nations. This era, hard but necessary in the divine scheme for the perfection of mankind, was to expire at the end of time. In the latter days, the seal is to be broken and the prophecy fulfilled and properly understood—after which time the hereafter will be realized and true knowledge of God will bring profound happiness in a perfected world.

Demonogony: The Making of a Devil   The wise imams foretold that 8,400 years later, the original people would be divided among themselves, whereby 70 percent would be happy and 30 percent would be dissatisfied. Out of the dissatisfaction, an evil scientist would be produced. He would be obsessed with a desire to create a force terrible enough to destroy the original harmony. This man would be born twenty miles from the holy city of Mecca, and his name would be Mr. Yacub.[25] In the year 8,400, according to the Original calendar, an unusual boy was born to parents belonging to the dissatisfied section of the original people. His head was abnormally large and contained an enormous capacity for bizarre intellect and science.[26] At the age of six, this boy was playing in the sand with two pieces of steel. He discovered their magnetic power and the law behind it: "like repels and unalike attracts." He then looked up at his uncle and said, " 'When I grow up, I'm gonna make a people to rule you.' And the uncle said, 'What would you make but what causes mischief and the shedding of blood?' And the little boy said, 'I know what you know not.' "[27] Bent on his evil quest, Yacub went to school, specializing in medical science, biology, and chemistry. While in the laboratory studying genetic engineering, he discovered that in the germ of the Blackman there are two operating principles, a positive and a negative. There is one dominant, black germ and one recessive, brown germ. Enthusiastically, the young Yacub exclaimed, "If I could separate this brown germ from the black germ, and graft it with its final state, I could produce a people unalike. And because they are unalike, they could be attractive, and if I teach them how to master their own original people then I would make a Master."[28] Graduating from the best university at the age of eighteen, Mr. Yacub became a voice for the dissatisfied. He preached rebellion and made promises of riches for those who followed him, saying that he would turn the rest of mankind into the servants of these affluent rulers-to-be. As he made converts in the holy city of Mecca, the authorities became alarmed. They arrested him along with his circle of dissidents and threw them all in jail.[29]

When the king of Mecca heard the news, he realized who this man must be. He went to see Mr. Yacub in his cell, calling him by his real name, saying he knew all about him and his mission from the Mother Book. The king and Mr. Yacub made a deal, allowing the latter to take off with his followers. The Original government rounded up all of the 59,999 dissatisfied people, brought them to ships at the harbor, and sent them into exile on an island called Pelan (in the Bible named Patmos) in the Aegean Sea.

On Pelan, Mr. Yacub immediately began to work with a staff of medical doctors, priests, and cremators. By practicing a strict code of birth control, killing all the darker babies and saving the lighter ones and letting them breed, he produced the brown race. By successive gene manipulation, Mr. Yacub grafted new races in intervals of 200 years, each lighter than the one before, possessing less and less divine substance. After 600 years, a race of weak-blooded, weak-boned, weak-minded, pale-faced people was finally grafted: the blond, blue-eyed white devil.[30] The white man is thus neither truly human nor created by God. He is a "snake of the grafted type,"[31] a "skunk of the planet earth,"[32] and totally deprived of divine substance, which makes him intrinsically evil by nature. Any objection the white man may have against being identified as the evil arch-deceiver is brushed aside with the argument that it is not the spokespersons of the NOI who are calling white people devils. "God say you're the real devil. And you damn sure are. Ain't another devil nowhere else. Ain't no use you get mad with me, white people. You are the devil. The only hell-raiser on the earth. I'm not sayin' that you are responsible, 'cause you are made devil. But I'm not goin' make a mistake in thinkin' that you can be made better through love. . . . You are nothing but a devil in the plainest language. The arch-deceivers of the people of the planet earth. The number one hater, murderer, killer, liar, drunkard, home-monger, hog-eater. Yeah, you're number one."[33] White Christian fundamentalists claim that the Creation took place 6,000 years ago. However, their intellects are limited, for they were grafted 6,000 years ago; life existed before their birth and will exist long after they are gone. God in his omniscience gave the Devil six thousand years to rule the earth, a time of evil that is now approaching its preordained end.

Not all devils are fully aware of their evil nature. In fact, the vast majority is about as indoctrinated and misinformed about their true identity as are the original people. There is, however, a closed secret society of white supremacists who have complete knowledge of their devilness and who conspire to rule the world: the Freemasons. While the ignorant white people represent the stone that blocks the Blackman's re-ascendancy, "on top of the stone were the wise shriners, those of 32 and 33 degrees masonry, who are the keepers of their ignorant brothers, the wise white people who run the show."[34]

Freemasonry does have an impact on American society. Fifteen of the Founding Fathers who signed the Declaration of Independence, including Benjamin Franklin, were Freemasons, and Masonry had a discernible influence on the drafting of the Constitution. George Washington was a Mason, as were at least thirteen other presidents and at least fourteen vice presidents. In 1978, thirty-six senators and one hundred representatives were Masons.[35] The pyramid with the all-seeing eye depicted on the dollar bill is a Masonic symbol for the unfinished Temple of Salomo, and the Great Seal of the United States also contains a number of Masonic symbols.[36]

Farrakhan argues that Masonry is built on the truth of Islam, although the highest level is only thirty-three degrees, whereas the complete wisdom of Islam is 360 degrees of power. The secret society is based on wisdom derived from Islam through spying on the black scholars of Mecca and through studying the knowledge of the now sleeping black gods. This explains why the Masonic lodges and temples carry names from the Muslim world—Aleppo, Syria, Medinah, and Mecca—and why Masons wear fezes. Further, when Masons reach the thirty-second degree of the mental ladder of wisdom, they are said to get out of the Bible and into the Qur'an, and greet each other with *as-Salaam Alaikum*.[37] These white rulers fully control the world but will not tell mankind that their power is based on Islam. "So, George Washington, your first President, did not want Islam to be taught ever among the slaves, but he was a Muslim shriner, a 33 degree Mason," Farrakhan explained. "33 degrees of the circle of Islam were studied by the Founding Fathers. . . . But they wanted no Islam among the slaves."[38] The Nation of Islam considers the Masons to be chief devils, masterminding the evils inflicted on the original people and the institutions of indoctrination that prevent the full knowledge of God, man, and devil to be known.

Gods Making Evil: The Problem of Theodicy   As in all religions that postulate the existence of a benevolent, omnipotent, and omniscient creator, the existence of evil and of the creation's defects must be given a reasonable explanation. The Nation of Islam has had to struggle with the problem of doctrinal theodicy. If God is good and black and has a covenant with his people, the black original nation, why did he allow the grafting of the Devil? Why did the Blackman have to go through the cataclysm of slavery? What possibly could be God's meaning in letting his people experience the burden of white supremacy? Pondering these questions, the Nation finally arrived at the following understanding.[39]

In the cosmological creation, God created the positive and the negative, a duality that inheres in all things created, from the finest particle of matter to the largest planet. The dialectic of good and evil was present within the original people. They were created out of God's substance, but metaphorically, like the planet they emerged on, they were not made perfect. There is a wobble in the planet's motion. God compensated for this wobble by making the planet obedient to a natural law that lessens the effects of the friction produced by the motion. Should the planet disobey, she would cause her own destruction. The wobble in the black man's nature is the possibility for doing evil, which God compensated for by offering the original people the law of Islam, through which evil is controlled. All things created obey Islam, the natural law, but mankind differs in that it has a free will. The harmony in the original civilization was not perfect, as evidenced by the abortive attempt to blow up the planet Earth. There existed a tendency to underestimate the power of evil, which reduced the understanding for the necessity of Islam. As man deviated from the straight path of Islam, there arose a hazardous friction in the evolutionary process of humanity. God, whose plan, as noted above, is the perfection of mankind, decided in his omniscience to conduct an experiment, to teach the original people their innate potential for good and evil. With self-knowledge, blacks can realize their divine capacity and become like gods, but first they must learn how to defeat evil and master the Qur'anic device: "enjoining what is right and forbidding what is wrong."[40]

Mr. Yacub, who thought he was rebelling against God when he grafted the Devil, was in fact used as a tool to perform the will of God. He extracted the negative from the black man, and grafted a manlike creature out of the pure concentrate of evil. The white man "is the negative side of the original nature."[41]

While in the anthropology of the early Nation there was an unsurmountable chasm between the nonwhite and the white, today they have an element in common. The whites originated in the blacks who originated in God, which indirectly makes the white man created and leaves him a road of salvation. As Farrakhan emphasizes, "You cannot reform a devil. All the prophets tried and failed. You have to kill the devil. It is not the color of the white man that is the problem, it is the mind of the white man that is the problem. The mind of white supremacy has to be destroyed."[42] The past six thousand years of white world hegemony has been a pedagogical experiment that effectively taught the original people about themselves. They have been ruled by their own potential for evil, visibly manifested as the white devil. The era of evil created a dreadful dead end for mankind's motion, destructive enough to return the original people to Islam, crying for God's intervention.

The pale-skinned pedagogical tools thereby have served their purpose and can be removed as historical waste from the face of the earth. Once saved, the blacks will never again underestimate their innate potential for evil and let the Devil within loose. They will follow the path of Islam and ultimately arrive at their raison d'être: to become a nation of gods, making the hereafter a true paradise. "We are not here just to be here," Farrakhan explains, "we are all here to make a contribution to the onward march and evolutionary development of man in his pathway to God."[43] The imminent extermination of evil should not necessarily be understood in its physical sense. Should the present world rulers willingly abdicate and commit mental suicide, that is, erase the mentality of white supremacy, "Armageddon can be avoided."[44] Jabril Muhammad emphasizes that there is a possibility for the devils to save their lives.[45] Farrakhan, however, is not especially optimistic about that possibility. "Unfortunately," he argues, "the world rulers are so upset over their loss of power that they really don't give a dog about a new world reality. If they're gonna lose power they'll take the whole world down with them."[46]

Death Rides a Pale Horse and Hell Follows with Him   When the race of white devils finally came into existence, they were shipped back to the original people to cause the mischief for which they were grafted. Instantly, an unpleasant atmosphere poisoned life in the first civilization. Children started disobeying their parents, man and wife began to quarrel, arguments between best friends suddenly broke out. Wise as they were, the aboriginal inhabitants promptly understood that this sudden disharmony resulted from the slimy pale stranger clinging about their feet.

Decisively, the strong black warriors caught the devils, tied them up, and forced them to cross the burning sand of the Arabian desert to the hills and caves of Caucasus. Here, the Caucasian caveman was left alone. To prevent him from reentering the realm of the righteous, God placed a flaming sword at the eastern gate and ordered the Muslims living in the adjacent area to set up armed guards to patrol the border.[47] These events are dramatized in the Masonic initiation ceremonies in which the initiates are stripped of their clothing, clad in fur, bound with a rope, blindfolded, and literally forced to cross burning sand. The very name Europe is derived from this part of the devils' history, as "Eu" means "hillside and caves" and "rope" means "to bind in."[48]

The Devil was preordained to rule the world but could neither manage to get up on his feet nor communicate in an intelligible language. While the original people built pyramids and advanced in the disciplines of art, philosophy, and Mathematics, the white devil crawled on all fours and made love to other animals. The present-day status of the white man's pets is a remnant from this period. "Who is the [white] man's best friend?" Farrakhan once asked his audience, "You? No—the dog. He and the dog had a love affair."[49] The rulers-to-be coped so poorly that a process of de-evolution began. The devils became increasingly more savage and animal-like. Hairy fur soon grew to cover their faces and bodies. Darwin's theory thus must be reversed, because apes and monkeys came from the Caucasian caveman. When the white devil shouts his favorite cry of surprise, "Damn, I'll be a monkey's uncle," he *really* knows what he is talking about.[50]

After a passage of two thousand years without the Devil making any moves to reach beyond his savage condition, God sent Moses to teach the basics of humanity. The Devil gave the prophet a hard time, and Moses had to sleep in a ring of fire to keep the brute from consuming him. He invented the girdle to straighten the devils up, and finally had a small band walking on their feet. Moses did a tremendous job in trying to civilize the savages: teaching them how to wear clothes, what to eat, and how to cook.[51] And God said, "Be fruitful and multiply, and replenish the earth, and subdue it: and have dominion over the fish of the sea, and over the fowl of the air, and over every living thing that moveth upon the earth."[52] And the Devil went out, conquering and subduing the world, exploiting the creation and forcing his dominion over every nation.

Everywhere the imperialistic Devil went he found the original people. The white man is not native anywhere—he is not native Asian, native Australian, native African, native American, not even native European.[53] When Columbus set sail, he had to travel westward to reach India, because the flaming sword and the Muslim patrols blocked the eastern gate to Asia.[54] When the Devil "discovered" Mexico, he found the Blackman there—"the Olmec civilization is an African civilization, brought to the

Western hemisphere long before Columbus was around."[55] When he conquered North America, he found red Indians who had been living there in exile for 16,000 years as punishment for breaking the laws of Islam.[56]

When the Devil traveled around the globe, establishing white world supremacy, Revelation 6:8 was fulfilled: "And behold a pale horse; and his name that sat on him was Death, and Hell followed with him." A pale horse rode into Africa, America, Asia, and Australia; Farrakhan exclaims, "wherever you Caucasians went you brought Death to the people. Wherever you went you brought Hell to the people."[57] The fulfillment of Revelation, of course, anticipates the end.

The countdown to Armageddon started when the devil John Hawkins, piloting the slave ship *Jesus,* arrived at the shores of West Africa.[58] He captured the specially toughened and well-prepared twelfth tribe of the original people, headed by Imam Shabazz, known in the Scriptures as Abraham, and brought them to a life of slavery in the wilderness of North America. This eschatological milestone made God's dramatic words to Imam Shabazz in Genesis 15:13–14 come true: "Thy seed shall be a stranger in a land that is not theirs, and they shall serve them; and they shall afflict them for four hundred years; And also that nation, whom they will serve, will I judge: and afterward shall they come out with great substance." The fulfillment is stressed by the NOI as undisputable evidence that identifies the principal actors of the Bible as the blacks, evidence that reduces the Jews to a nation of impostors. The importance of this for the NOI relationship with the Jewish community and the alleged anti-Semitism of Minister Farrakhan is discussed in chapter 9. In effect, slavery brought the original people like a Trojan horse into the fortress of evil, giving the African American a key role in the approaching apocalypse.

The Sleeping Beauty and the Prince of Love   In order to let the Devil embark on his evil quest to institute a global regime of oppression and injustice, the original people were put to "sleep." They "died" mentally, morally, and intellectually, and so temporarily lost world hegemony. These key concepts signify the common NOI metaphors for black unawareness of their true, divine nature.[59] Before a collective cultural amnesia settled on the divine nation, God left signs of its true position as the crown of creation. These signs will be helpful in the present process, when the Blackman is to awaken from his coma. The most significant of these signs of superiority are the pyramids and Kaba's black stone.

In the sandy desert of present-day Egypt, remnants of a grandiose civilization long past stand for the world to admire. When archaeologists try to solve the riddle of the pyramids they will, Farrakhan argues, discover the ancient cradle of civilization: "They are now unearthing civilizations under the sands of Africa that are more sophisticated and more developed, that show more signs of higher mathematics and law and science than the present world in which we live. The first wonder of this world are the pyramids and the sphinx. And the whole history of the world is written in the stones of the pyramids. . . . White folks have yet to figure the pyramids out—the black man put it there, left it there . . . and went to sleep. So that when the white folks built their world, they would still have to go back to Egypt to find out where it all began and they would see this sphinx, majestically sitting there, a black face on the body of a lion, saying, 'I am the ruler. I am the lion. I am the King. I am asleep, but I've left a sign that before you were—I am, and after you go—I shall be. For I am the Alpha and the Omega, the Beginning and the Ending of it all.'"[60] In the holy city of Mecca stands a house anointed for worship and covered with a black veil: Kaba. In the corner there is a black stone. In the *hajj* rituals, Muslims counterclockwise circle (*tawaf*) the Kaba seven times and preferably reach the black stone to kiss it. According to the NOI, it is not a coincidence that a *black* veil covers Kaba, in which is found a *black* stone.

The stone in the corner was given to Abraham by the angel Gabriel to symbolize the covenant between God and his people. This position, common throughout the Muslim world,[61] is qualified by the Nation of Islam on the basis of color. "If color don't make a difference, why isn't it a white veil and a white stone?" Farrakhan asks rhetorically.[62] Addressing the world Islamic community, Farrakhan observes, "Muhammad kissed the stone . . . Umar kissed the stone. So, all Muslims that go to Mecca kiss the stone. What will you do when the black man comes that the stone represents, will you kiss him?"[63]

Kaba has more to tell the world. The veil symbolizes the fact that a mental veil of ignorance temporarily would cover the people that the house represents and hamper true knowledge of God. "*Beitu'llah* [the house of God]," Farrakhan says, represents human beings who "in the remotest antiquity were the house of God. God's spirit dwelled in them. God's guidance emitted from them. At one time the whole earth moved around the Original People, the original house, who were in fact the very personification of a divine being."[64] The four hundred years of bondage in a foreign land have now passed. The sleeping beauty will awaken when the divine prince of love gives her the kiss of life. She will resume her true identity and will stand before God as a bride adorned for her husband, worthy to rule for eternity.

When Mr. Yacub grafted the blond, blue-eyed white devil, he said, "when six meets seven, when the sixth thousand years are up, in the seventh thousand year, God will come Himself" and judge you. Six and seven add up to thirteen, a number defamed by the devils as unlucky, for it represents their demise. This decoded citation means that God will be fathered by "a seven" brought forth from the womb of "a six." Seven stands for perfection and judgment, and a man called by that number is the standard-bearer of the black nation, from the tribe of Shabazz,[65] or Shebah in the Qur'anic and biblical spelling.[66] The white man or woman is a six and the child produced by a male seven and a female six carries the divine genetic message derived from his father.[67]

On February 26, 1877, a fairly light-skinned boy was born in the holy city of Mecca. "His father was one of the twelve major scientists,"[68] a jet-black man, named Alphonse Shabazz, whom the boy would refer to as "God," and his mother was a white Muslim, sometimes said to be a descendant of the few white Muslims who were left behind when the devils were brought to Caucasus, at other times said to be taken from "the hills" or "the Caucasus mountains."[69] The young boy first realized who he was at the age of six when in a vision "he saw himself pushing the Fords, the Du Ponts and the Rockefellers into a lake of fire."[70] He was the foretold Son of man, born for a specific mission described in Matthew 24:27–28: "For as the lightning cometh out of the east, and shineth even unto the west; so shall also the coming of the Son of man be. For wheresoever the carcase is there will the eagles be gathered together." The boy was destined to go west to deliver his people and bring down the American eagles who, as noted in Isaiah 14:13–15, have ascended over the clouds, thinking they were like God, and yet they "shalt be brought down to hell." As told in Romans 8:3, "God sent His son in sinful flesh," meaning he would assume the appearance of the enemy. In His divine wisdom, he chose a semiwhite garment to sneak into the midst of the devils "as a thief in the night."[71]

In the year 1930, whose digits add up to 13 (1+9+3+0), the ninth planet of our solar system was discovered. Nine, being the last numeral, signifies completion or finality, and this was God's way of letting the devils see both the end of the solar system and their rule.[72] God in Person "came to the people who walked in darkness,"[73] that is during the depression, and chose the fourth of July as the day for his manifestation. The coming of God on the day when Americans celebrated Independence Day was significant. Elijah Muhammad wrote, "[I]t is their day of great rejoicing. As with former people and their governments, their destruction took place when they were at the height of their rejoicing."[74]

God came in the person of Master Farad Muhammad and found a deprived black community. They had been without a relationship with God for centuries, thus making them unable to conceive divine life. "The Black man and woman of America are styled scripturally as a virgin," Farrakhan said, and Master Farad Muhammad "came for one purpose: to make you pregnant with divine life."[75]

The Lord of Retribution raised a Messenger "produced by the suffering and longing of generation upon generations of black people, whose blood cried out for justice, and not only justice—but for revenge."[76] God anointed a poor black man who only had finished the fourth grade in school and turned the unlearned one into a teacher. Only God's intervention can make the virgin conceive: the barren black nation produced a saviour who resurrected the dead.

Logically speaking, the coming of God implies that he was once gone. According to the Holy Qur'an 15:36–38, God and the Devil made a temporary deal. The archdeceiver said to Allah, "Oh my Lord! Give me then respite till the Day the [Dead] are raised." To which God responded, "Respite is granted thee—till the Day of the Time Appointed."[77] This signifies a period in world history when God would be absent—how else could the Devil perform his evil task? Because of the Devil's evil teachings and wicked behavior, God would return at a time when mankind surely is at loss, that is, the present-day time of confusion, sick mentality, and amorality.[78]

The present state of the world proves God's temporal absence. As he had the power of righteousness, mercy, and blessing, he could also withdraw it, leaving his children on their own. But why would he do such a thing? Farrakhan compared this scenario with the human family.[79] The children are initially dependent on their parents for food, clothing, and training. Then comes a time when the children start challenging the authority of their parents, despite the gratitude they should feel. They disobey and finally compete for the position as head of the household. At this point the parents decide that it is time for the children to establish a house of their own. The Supreme God made a similar decision when the original people began disobeying Islam and challenging his authority. His children now have to live on their own, make their mistakes, and find their way to a decent living.

When youngsters establish their independence, they are generally tired of their parents' warnings and so are apt to misjudge reality and perhaps fall for different kinds of temptations. Watching them go alone is the tempter, the archdeceiver who prepares to move in on them, snaring them as prey. Iblis said in Qur'an 7:16–17, "I will lie in wait for them on Thy Straight Way, Then will I assault them from before them and behind them, from their right and from their left." Before they know it, the youngsters find themselves in trouble so deep that they cry for their parents: Help me, father! I will never mistrust you again!

Satan will stubbornly resist God, increasing his tricks to rival God as he reappears to claim what is his. Initially, the Devil tried to obstruct the divine Messenger by repudiating and ridiculing him. The Honorable Elijah Muhammad brushed the offenses aside as he was divinely empowered to voice his lonely cry in the desert, declaring his intention to persist in teaching "to the End of the World, putting to death every infidel that I find."[80]

Frustrated by the success of the Messenger, the archdeceiver resolved to rely on outright repression, enrolling all of his trained foot soldiers in the police and military departments, as described in chapter 4. Despite all the accumulated efforts of these agencies, the NOI refused to crumble, which explains why the by-now desperate Devil orchestrated a lethal conspiracy against Elijah Muhammad's life. In 1975, the hit squad went into action, only to find another body in the Messenger's place. God had rescued Elijah Muhammad's life, as he promised when giving his holy apostle his difficult mission. Disappointed but not entirely puzzled, the Devil switched to an alternate plan b, designed to eliminate or at least disseminate the Nation. The Devil has always managed to seduce some strategically placed individuals in the camp of God, using them for shrewd plots. Now, he went for the Messenger's son, making him an Absalom. Bursting with perverted satisfaction, the Devil observed the fall of the Nation, naively hoping for a prolonged respite.

After the resurrection of the Nation, members wrestled with the meaning of the mass desertion during the fall. Apostasy is a capital crime in Islam and brings severe consequences even in the afterlife. As stated in the Holy Qur'an 2:217, "If any of you turn back from their faith and die in unbelief, their works will bear no fruit in this life and in the Hereafter; they will be the companions of the Fire and abide therein." The members of the old Nation were seriously in danger when they rejected the one they formerly declared their belief in, for "how shall God guide a people who disbelieved after their belief and [after] they bore witness that the messenger is true and after clear proofs [of Allah's sovereignty] had come unto them. And God guideth not wrong-doing folk."[81]

In an effort to bring release to possibly guilt-ridden apostates, Jabril Muhammad focuses on "how" as the key word in this Qur'anic statement, arguing that it refers to a method used by God to bring his will about. When Elijah Muhammad departed, he ascended to God "and was exalted over everybody except Master Farad Muhammad."[82] Elijah Muhammad proved himself to be the foretold lamb of Revelation 5:12–14, "that was slain to receive power" after which "every creature" in the heavens and on the earth realized his true identity, "and the four and twenty elders fell down and worshipped him." The fall of the Nation was a divinely ordained transition to the next stage in the apocalyptic scheme. With Elijah Muhammad back on stage as the Christ, the table has turned to the deadly surprise of the once jubilant devils.

When Peter drew his sword to defend Jesus, according to Matthew 26:51–52, he was told to put it back in the sheath because all who "take the sword shall perish with the sword." These were the words of Jesus before his departure. The devils were given respite until the day when the Blackman is raised from the dead. Then God is to come and destroy the devil and kill all his followers.[83] In charge of the extermination of evil, Jesus will have another attitude. "When you see him coming in the clouds of heaven, what does Jesus have in his hand?" Farrakhan asked; he answered, "He has got a sword, and it's dripping with blood. No come back to teach nobody. He comes back to judge the wicked."[84]

The Wheel and Satan, the Challenger Central to the NOI teachings of the end is the man-made planet Farrakhan is said to have visited, as described in chapter 6. This planet is variously referred to as the Wheel, the Mother Plane, or the Mother Ship. In the Bible it is known as Ezekiel's wheel or the New Jerusalem.

Ezekiel saw the Mother Plane in a vision, and he called it a wheel because of its shape. He saw four creatures appearing in the wheel and heard the voice of one telling another to take coals of fire and scatter them over the cities.[85] What he saw was, according to Elijah Muhammad, "the wheel-shaped plane known as the Mother of Planes, [which] is one half-mile by a half mile and is the largest mechanical manmade object in the sky. It is a small human planet made for the purpose of destroying the present world of the enemies of Allah."[86] The man-made planet is a scientific masterpiece and a "display of the power of the mightiest God, Master Fard Muhammad, to Whom praises are due for ever." It is capable of staying in outer space for up to one year without coming into the reach of earth's gravity and can produce its own sphere of oxygen and hydrogen "as any other planet is able to do."[87] In this heavenly abode, God and some of the divine scientists dwell in a magnificent city, the New Jerusalem, prepared as a residence of refuge for the faithful brethren who are to survive the final battle and form the nucleus of the new civilization.[88]

The four creatures in Ezekiel's vision represent the four colors of the original people, the black, brown, red, and yellow. The coals of fire refer to the bombs that are to be dropped on the cities in the battle of Armageddon.[89] These bombs contain the same type of dynamite once used to raise Mount Everest and the other mountains on earth. Each bomb is timed and has a motor, taking the bomb one mile down into the earth before exploding, killing people fifty miles around, pushing up mountains on each side.[90] These dreadful weapons are carried by "baby planes," frequently said to be 1,500 in number,[91] piloted by divine soldiers of retribution created solely for this purpose. Each smaller spaceship is armed with three bombs and will be assigned a specific area to destroy.[92]

According to the NOI, the Devil tries to prepare against the threat from outer space. In the 1960s, as the United States and the Soviet Union competed to be the first nation to land people on the moon, Elijah Muhammad asked for the reason behind spending all this money to reach out in the sky to planets on which they cannot live: "Do they think these planets serve as great fortifications of God and they could cast their bombs on these planets and destroy them? Or, do they fear attacks upon themselves coming from these planets?"[93] Yes, the Devil is fully aware of the divine scheme to end his wicked rule. This is why NASA classifies all reports of UFOs as strictly secret. This is the reason for spending billions of dollars on military space technology. The Strategic Defense Initiative continues to burden the already strained American budget, despite the fall of the Soviet Union and overall global nuclear disarmament. The only explanation is that Star Wars was never really intended to protect American citizens against the profane missiles of the Soviet Union, but was and is regarded by the devils as a shield against the holy missiles of divine retribution.

When the space shuttle *Challenger* was to be sent out into space in

1986, it had a hidden mission, as can easily be guessed from its given name. It was a spy ship, built for intelligence purposes in a naive attempt by the Devil to prevent the destruction of Babylon. But, as God states in the Holy Qur'an 86:15–16: "they are but plotting a scheme, and I am planning a scheme." The spy ship that sought to challenge God exploded seventy-two seconds after takeoff. For the NOI this is no coincidence, but refers to the seventy-second Surah of the Qur'an where the incident is prerecorded.[94] The devils in Surah 72, "The Jinn," verses 8–9 lament: "And we pried into the Secrets of Heaven; But we found it filled with stern guards and flaming fires. We used, indeed, to sit there in (hidden) stations, to (steal) a hearing; but any who listens now will find a flaming fire watching him in ambush." The devils' pathetic endeavor to survive by means of a massive military mobilization is doomed to failure. The world as we know it is coming to an end. With the arrival of al-Mahdi (Master Farad Muhammad) and the Messiah (Elijah Muhammad), the final battle has already begun.

Apocalypse Now   The Nation of Islam lives at the end of time. According to the eschatology revealed by Master Farad Muhammad, the era of the Devil expired in the year 1914. Since then "man has been preparing for the final showdown."[95] The blacks, depicted as Lazarus, are in a resurrectional process, accentuated by the coming of God in the Person of Master Farad Muhammad in 1930. When the blacks are restored mentally and united racially, the stage will be set. Besides the military mobilization mentioned above and the politics of genocide designed by the government in Washington, D.C.,[96] the Devil tries to counteract this process with nonracist liberal arguments, luring the blacks to stay put in Babylon, thus prolonging the respite. As the original people expect the onslaught any time now, world events are interpreted in this context. World War II was identified as Armageddon and the Japanese were believed to be the helpers of God, backed by his space force as indicated in chapter 4.

Wars, earthquakes, floods, droughts, famines, criminality, widespread amorality, and dollar crises are all seen as the birth pangs of the real New World Order.[97] The Messenger temporarily increased the fever of anticipation with certain statements, such as his declaration that the 400 years of bondage expired in 1955 or that "the years 1965 and 1966 are going to be fateful for America, bringing in the 'Fall of America.' "[98] The members thus lived in constant tension, with occasional moments of peaked expectations and disappointments.[99] How does this influence the minds of the believers? What happens to a congregation when set dates pass without the divine forecast coming true? In their now classic study *When Prophecy Fails,* Festinger, Riecken, and Schachter disclosed a pattern that may be relevant also for the Nation of Islam: "the increase of proselyting followed unequivocal disconfirmation of a belief."[100]

Festinger and his associates studied an American sect led by a Mrs. Keech, who said that she had been contacted by intergalactic "guardians" informing her of a coming calamity. A great flood was to engulf the northern hemisphere at dawn on December 21, 1956, but her faithful congregation would be rescued from the cataclysm by being evacuated in flying saucers to a safe planet designated by the guardians.[101] When nothing happened, Mrs. Keech first broke down and cried bitterly. The atmosphere of disillusion did not, however, remain long, as Mrs. Keech pulled herself together, summoned the group, and convincingly announced a new message she had been given: God had been so pleased by the little congregation's dedication that he decided to call off the cataclysm. Mrs. Keech and her followers had saved the world! With the failure turned into a victory, the members were strengthened in their belief and spurred to declare their triumph to the world.[102]

Members of a sect are strongly bound together by their common conviction that they are a part of an elite privy to the ultimate hidden truth. Nonmembers' reactions of skepticism, scorn, and mockery further strengthen their internal bonds and feelings of separateness. Sect members survive by clinging to the shared truth, thus making them psychologically inclined to interpret the world in congruence with their beliefs. A sudden dissonance between belief and experienced reality constitutes a blow to the basic sectarian notions of identity and world. The psychological reaction tends to favor rationalizations, restoring consonance between belief and experienced reality. With the acute threat removed, accumulated emotional tensions can be released in a feeling of relief at having been "saved." This, in turn, gives the members renewed energy to joyfully bear witness to what, on a psychological level, is true: the world has been saved![103]

A similar pattern can be found in the development of, among others, the Seventh Day Adventists,[104] the Jehovah's Witnesses,[105] and the Nation of Islam. This pattern becomes discernible in the Nation as expectations waxed and waned without prophecies being fulfilled, and it could be a part of the explanation for the increased proselytizing following the Nation's rationalization of the death of the Messenger as the Messiah's tactical "departure."

After apocalyptic significance had been read into the American wars in

Korea and Vietnam, the Cuban missile crisis, the bombing of Tripoli, and the invasions of Panama and Grenada, the next eschatological peak was the outbreak of the Persian Gulf War. According to the eschatological scheme revealed by God to his original people, Armageddon would start as a war in West Asia between Muslims and non-Muslims.

When Saddam Hussein occupied Kuwait—or to Hussein's mind, re-united the nineteenth province with its fatherland—he skillfully played the Muslim card. The anti-Islamic policy that for such a long time had characterized the secular Arab-nationalist Iraqi Ba'ath leader was offi-cially forgotten. Hussein suddenly depicted himself as the guardian of all Muslims in a quest for liberating the holy shrines of Mecca, Medinah, and Jerusalem from the non-Muslim tyrants. When his Christian foreign min-ister, Tariq Aziz, flew to Egypt to negotiate in August 1990, his airplane was named *Salah al-Din,* which was a clear signal to the Muslim world. Salah al-Din, or Saladin, the Kurd, is the all-Muslim hero who in 1187 liberated Jerusalem from the crusaders. Hussein happens to have been born in Takrit, Salah al-Din's native town. The message was that Saddam Hussein is the modern-day Salah al-Din who will defeat Israel, the cru-sader state, and its Western backers in a jihad.[106] Even though some Mus-lim states sided against Saddam Hussein, many Muslims, not least the rank and file, saw the mother of all wars in these terms.

Minister Farrakhan Muhammad's interpretation placed the conflict in an apocalyptical context. Farrakhan was part of a group of about 400 Islamic leaders invited to Baghdad in January 1991.[107] Upon his return on January 14, 1991, two days before Operation Desert Storm was launched as the Allied attacked the Iraqi forces, Farrakhan proclaimed, "This war, should it start in a few days, will be that which the scriptures refer to as the War of Armageddon which is the final war . . . it will engulf the entire planet."[108]

When the apocalyptical expectations seemed to be frustrated as the United States–lead United Nation forces routed the Iraqi army, rational-ization began. Under the caption "So, you think the war is over?" an edi-torial in the *Final Call* warns the reader from "questioning whether this 'really' is the final war." The reader is asked if he realizes "the tremen-dous impact, the ripple affect [*sic*] against America that the devastation of Iraq is causing throughout the so-called Third World?" Then, the reader is reminded that "the War of Armageddon is not between Bush and Hussein but . . . between the rightful owner of this earth and the abusive tenant who has overstayed his lease . . . between Black and white." The Gulf War

turned into a prelude to the final battle and the editorial closed trium-
phantly: "Now that the American public have endorsed the wicked actions of their government, nothing can hold back God's war on America.
The drought has already come to California. Let's see if Mr. Bush can rout
out God."[109] Further elaborating on the theme of the Gulf War as "a prelude to the Great Battle," Tynetta Muhammad focused on another aspect
of the Gulf conflict, relating it to prophecy. According to the NOI, a sign of
Armageddon is the darkening of the sun and the falling of a black rain.[110]
When Saddam Hussein set some 600 oil wells on fire in the Persian Gulf,
a black cloud was formed, blotting out the sun, lowering the temperature,
and causing black rain showers. These clearly were, writes Tynetta Muhammad, "physical signs of Armageddon," part of "a progression of intense Divine destructions coming to pass on man and mankind at the end
of the world."[111]

The Nation of Islam holds no doubts about the coming events that have
been described in detail by God. Armageddon is a racial war, following a
period of increasingly acute interracial hostilities, "as nation shall rise
against nation."[112] Racist attacks and ethnic chauvinism will foster racial
solidarity and force the nations to separate from each other, after which
they will be dealt with by God, as described by Jesus: "And before [the
Son of Man] shall be gathered all nations; and he shall separate them one
from another, as a shepherd divideth *his* sheep from the goats. And he
shall set the sheep on his right hand, but the goats on the left."[113] God's
nation is then well provided for, while the wicked nations meet their just
fate: "Then shall he say also unto them on the left hand, Depart from me,
ye cursed, into everlasting fire, prepared for the devil and his angels."[114]
Al-Mahdi and the Messiah will be in the world, overthrowing wicked
governments, a prophecy that, according to the NOI, was fulfilled with the
downfall of the communist regimes in Romania, Poland, Czechoslovakia,
and the other countries of the former Eastern Bloc.[115]

After the actual outbreak of war in West Asia, where the fire most likely
will be sparked off in Palestine, a civil war will begin in Eastern Europe
and spill out over the Caucasus region. In this context, it is of course
interesting to note that the war in former Yugoslavia broke out shortly
after the Gulf War, as did the civil wars in the Caucasus region in the
former Soviet Union. The race antagonism will also have other centers, in
Southern Africa, North America and Western Europe. From all those focal points, the race war will spread out and in the end culminate in a giant
clash between the forces of good and evil.

Eight to ten days before the end, a trumpet of doom will issue the final call. Spacecrafts will spread leaflets in Arabic and English, urging the original people to get together. Guides will be strategically stationed, showing the faithful where to gather for the subsequent rescue operation.[116] This is the very last chance for the original people. Even those who until then were unbelievers will, under certain circumstances, have an opportunity to "get a late pass," as lyricized by the rappers Public Enemy.[117] Then, baby planes will undertake an operation space-bridge, carrying the faithful to the Mother Wheel, where they will be lodged in New Jerusalem.

Now the real calamity can begin. Nature will rise up against its evil exploiters. Petrified devils who try to escape by ships will be hurled back on the coasts by violent waves. The Messiah will be manifest with his soldiers, "coming in the clouds of heaven, coming in [space warplanes], with power to deal with his enemies."[118] The dreadful bombs mentioned above will be dropped, erasing every atom of the Devil from the face of the earth. The extermination will be absolutely complete, destroying all stock markets, skyscrapers, transportation nets, harbors, cities, and hamlets. Every trace and deed, including the languages, knowledge, and thoughts of the devil, will be eradicated in the global atomic-chemical fire, as described in 2 Peter 3:10: "the heavens shall pass away with great noise, and the elements shall melt with fervent heat, the earth also and the works that are therein shall be burned up." The earth and atmosphere will be burning for a period of 390 years and then cooled down for a period of 610 years.[119] The idea of the millennium, central to most apocalypse-oriented Christian sects and movements, reappears in the NOI eschatology, but will be experienced on the Mother Ship and not on earth. The postmillennial world will be transformed into a paradise, created on the burned out earth by the Supreme Being as soon as the temperature is back to normal. Life will then return on earth. New vegetation will grow, new varieties of animals will be created and new waters will fill lakes and rivers.[120] "This is the way of the Gods," wrote Elijah Muhammad, "One God is not allowed to pattern after another God when it comes to universal change."[121]

To this earthly black paradise, the original people will return as the New Jerusalem is gently brought down from space: "And I saw a new heaven and a new earth; for the first heaven and the first earth were passed away. . . . And I saw the holy city, New Jerusalem, coming down from God out of heaven, prepared as a bride adorned for her husband. And I heard a great voice out of heaven saying: . . . God himself shall be with them, and be their God. And God shall wipe away all tears from their eyes; and there shall be no more death, neither sorrow, nor crying, neither shall there be any more pain: for the former things are passed away. And he that sat upon the throne said, Behold, I make all things new."[122] They will be a new people, a nation of gods, young, beautiful gods, who will look sixteen years old forever and never grow old or sick. The blacks will regain world supremacy, never to lose it again. They will have learned their lesson well and will definitely keep their negative side under perfect control, which is why the Devil will never materialize again. To God's satisfaction, mankind will be truly perfected and freedom, justice, and equality, that is, Islam, will characterize the life of the divine nation.

With history's aim thereby attained, the cyclic changes of the universe will cease. "The Present God's (Master Fard Muhammad's) Wisdom is infinite," wrote Elijah Muhammad, "No Scientist can see an end to This Man's Wisdom coming in the future. That is why the Bible and the Holy Quran refer to Him as the Wisest of Them All and say that He will set up a Kingdom (Civilization) that will live forever."[123]

Religion, Logic, and Configurations of Belief   If studied carefully, large parts of the elaborated NOI creed appear to be highly illogical. Different statements contradict each other, they are inconsistent and arrive at different, mutually exclusive conclusions. Adam is on the one hand identified as Yacub, the evil scientist who fathered the Devil, and on the other hand he is a black man and progenitor of the black race. Moses is on the one hand "a God" for the devils, their teacher and leader in Caucasus,[124] and on the other hand he is the black hero, delivering his black nation from the evil pharaoh in Egypt. God is on the one hand the One, without associates, eternal and infinite, and on the other hand we learn of a plurality of Gods, none of whom live forever. These apparently contradictory theses are all matters of belief; they are all regarded as true. How can this be possible? In order to discuss this central question—central not only for understanding the Nation of Islam, but all religions—let me first present in more detail the two conflicting theses involving Adam, the creation of the black man, and the making of the Devil, before suggesting an approach to formulate answers to the questions raised.

All central doctrines preached by the Nation are supported by an elaborate scriptural exegesis, proving the irresistible logic of the creed. When contradictory themes are at hand, we find the same or similar verses used to support both, different ends. Mr. Yacub, for instance, is sometimes presented as Adam. He "and his wife" are the parents of the white people, who could be defined as "the Adamic race."[125] In this context "the pre-Adamites represent the Black man."[126] When Genesis 1:27 is referred to— "God created them in his image"—it means that Adam made them in his own form or appearance: "They are in the image and likeness of a human being (black man), but are all together different."[127] Adam and his home-made devils are then expelled from Eden, that is, forced to leave the pre-Adamites' residence and taken to the caves of Caucasus, and God placed Cherubims—decoded by the NOI as Muslim patrols—and a flaming sword of Islam to prevent him from returning.[128] A verse from the Holy Qur'an 2:30 is frequently used to support this line of reasoning. Sometimes, the original people appear as the angels, abhorring the idea of an evil vice-gerent on earth and questioning the Supreme God, "Wilt Thou place therein one who will make mischief therein and shed blood?" God re-plies, "I know what ye know not." The secret reason God has in mind is the necessary manifestation of the negative side of the pre-Adamic origi-nal people as a pedagogical lesson.[129] In other instances, as noted earlier in this chapter, it is Mr. Yacub's uncle who questions him. In this case, Mr. Yacub switches roles and speaks the lines of God. In both instances, the white man is created, who becomes the temporary vicegerent, or ruler, of the earth and enslaves the abdicated genuine owner, the pre-Adamite black man, who dozes off.

A diametrically opposed argument holds Adam to be the progenitor of the original people. "Adam is our common father," Farrakhan said, "The Holy Quran says Allah created Adam from black mud fashioned into shape."[130] Here, Genesis 1:27 is cited to prove the argument: "God created man in His own image," that is, because he is black, we are black, and vice versa, because we are black, he has to be black.[131] In this case, the black man is presented as Adamic, created to be vicegerent on earth.[132] The one to oppose the creation of Adam is, following this argument, not an angel on the side of God, but the fallen angel, Iblis or Satan. Here, the NOI theologians chose another set of verses from the Holy Qur'an, 2:31–36 and 7:11–18, commenting on God's creation of Adam. After he created Adam, it says he breathed into Adam of his inspiration, which proves that "the nature of God and the nature of the Black man is one and the same nature."[133] Then God taught Adam the names and the natures of all the angels and he commanded the angels to bow down to the man that he made. Angels are the obedient servants of God, but one of them, Iblis, refused to bow down, saying, "I am better than he: Thou didst create me from fire, and him from [black] mud."[134] Farrakhan comments, "that's the mind of Satan," thinking he is better because he is different, alluding to the presumption that white skin would make a man superior.[135]

In this context, the Devil reappears in Genesis 3:1–15 as the serpent who caused the fall of Adam and Eve in the Garden of Paradise, which in this case is a euphemism for the original people's loss of world supremacy and the subsequent transformation of the world from the original paradise into a wrecked abode during the era of evil. God cursed the Devil and fixed the length of his rule, as well as creating a relation of eternal enmity between the offspring of the white and black progenitors.[136]

What we have here, then, are two mutually exclusive arguments, both of which are matters of belief. How can this be? For a nonbeliever this appears to be highly illogical. Adam cannot be the progenitor of the Devil and the progenitor of the divine nation at the same time. The problem posed is central for understanding religion as it points to a feature I believe most creeds have in common: *at a certain level of systematization religion tends to be illogical.*

Any historian or anthropologist of religion who studies a society's or a group's religion from the perspective of a nonbeliever will eventually face the same problem. He or she records the myths and legends of the people, gathers different conceptions or articulations of faith, and observes ritual performances. Then, the researcher begins the work of systematization, sorting and arranging the material to make it comprehensible and ready for analysis. Frequently, he or she will find different myths founded on contradictory terms. Mythological sections may diverge, resurfacing in dissimilar versions, overlapping each other but striving in different directions, refusing to harmonize. Articulations of faith, recorded from the same group of adherents or even from the very same individuals, may deviate essentially.

Troubled by the coexisting, logically incompatible statements, a temptation may arise to reconstruct a coherent system without illogical relations. The researcher bends his material, cuts short a section of a myth here, omits another there. He or she may stress some articles of faith and neglect another set, adding one part of a ritual where it seems to fit, temporarily or even permanently leaving misfit aspects of the ritual aside. In the end, he or she may have managed to construct an intelligible religion, logically congruent and ready to present in a monograph or essay. What the researcher actually has been doing is constructing a coherent system without correspondence to reality. He or she has created an artificial faith, a religion without one single adherent, a one-dimensional on-paper-only-religion that goes to print and ends up on the shelf of a university bookstore.

In everyday religious life, such a coherent system will not be found. Religion is always, though not exclusively, irrational; it is never totally congruent, but always multidimensional, alive, and vibrant. We cannot judge a religion with the alien set of logical standards of the nonbeliever, for the religion has a logic of its own.

Still, it is not impossible for a nonbeliever to make sense of a religion if the demands for logic and coherence are not pushed too far. A conceptual tool for understanding coexisting inconsistencies in religion was developed by Åke Hultkrantz. Studying the religion of the Shoshoni Nation in Wyoming, he ran into a perplexing problem. In the fall and winter, the Shoshoni narrate sacred cosmological myths, where the world is created by the mythological wolf and his associate, the coyote. In the summer, the Shoshoni perform the sun dance ritual, in which homage is paid to Tam Apö, the Supreme Being and Creator, and his associate, Mother Earth. Yet the Shoshonis are Christians, who on Sundays go to church and pray to God and his associate, Jesus Christ. We are thus faced with no less than three different sets of mutually exclusive supreme beings and associates, coexisting in the religion of the same people and the same individuals. If systematized from the outsider's perspective this tends to violate our sense of logic. The crux, or finesse, is that from the believer's perspective, *it is not systematized.* Each set of supreme being and associate has its place in alternative configurations of belief. Each configuration of belief constitutes a logically coherent system. The contradiction is an illusion originating in the etic perspective, as the configurations of belief are *alternative,* making mutual exclusiveness and coexistence logically possible. In everyday religion the different sets of supreme beings and associates never meet, they are summoned at different times, and so the paradox is emically nonexistent.[137]

A religion is never one system, but several configurations, combined on a certain level of abstraction (that is, not on the level of reality) as they appear among the same people. A living religion emerges as a series of emotional, intellectual, and behavioral processes, relating to different dimensions of everyday or special-day life. For one to properly understand the meaning of religion, the religion should be accepted as such and not transformed to satisfy an observer's need for order and logical coherence. Adam, father of the Devil, and Adam, father of the black man, have their logical place and role in two alternative configurations of belief. Elijah Muhammad, Louis Farrakhan, and other preachers, elaborating on different themes of the NOI creed, never evoke the alternative images simultaneously. The inconsistency is illusory, for it only exists in the mind of the outside observer, leaving the believer untroubled.

Another aspect of mythological truth emerges from pondering the colorful NOI demonology and eschatology. Fascinating narratives appear in several variations, which differ in details depending on the personality and mood of the orator, the response from the audience, and the context of the event. Farrakhan adjusts his speeches depending on the audience: the same theme is presented in different ways according to whether it is a university lecture, a sermon for the believers, or a political gathering. Still, the diverse versions are all equally regarded as true. The NOI has so far not produced a sacred scripture of its own, which is why no specific version of, for example, the making of the Devil has been fixed as orthodoxy. Progressing from the same basic notions, the dialogue between the leading characters varies, new details and deviations may be woven into the drama, and others will be omitted, downplayed, or altered. When speaking of "belief" here, though, it should thus not be understood as literal belief. Mythology as a genre has certain requirements. Generally it should communicate key existentialist elements and profound knowledge, but it should also be entertaining, dramatic, thrilling, and fun. Humor is a vital ingredient in most mythology. Greek and Scandinavian religious narratives include many burlesque elements, as do Chinese, Javanese, Yoruba, Tupi-Guarani, Shoshoni, and Australian sacred tales, as well as the lore of the Nation of Islam. Though certain religious individuals may disagree, humor does not desecrate sacred wisdom; rather, it makes it attractive. The comedic elements may not be matters of belief, nor the precise lines of the mythological actors, nor every detail of the story. What is a matter of belief is the kernel, the inner meaning of the narrative, and the consequences of the drama portrayed.

NOI members need not necessarily believe that Mr. Yacub had an enormous head and was nicknamed "Big Head" by his original contemporaries.[138] Further, they do not necessarily believe in the reverse Darwinism or that the pets of the present-day white man are remnants of ancient love affairs. What they do believe in are certain central points and their consequences. For instance, they believe that the black man is God's creation, making them his people. They believe that the black aboriginal culture is the cradle of civilization. They believe that white supremacy is against the long-term will of God and that he will reorder the global power structure, by force if necessary. They believe in a glorious post-retribution future for the black man in a world reflecting the true intentions of God.

Alternative configurations of belief and the requirements of mythology as a genre help to explain other inconsistencies, such as the different roles of Moses. A popular theme in Blackamerican religion, the suggestive symbolism of the Exodus is far too rewarding to leave aside in order to focus on Moses' less-renowned work as the devils' cultural hero. Typically, the NOI sermons evoking the rescue from Egyptian bondage greatly exceed the ones presenting Moses' remarkable efforts to civilize the white devils. In this case, though, the contradiction posed by the two Moseses has turned up in the NOI, and Farrakhan presents a rationalization: "[Moses] had two missions. He had one in Europe among the whites and one in Egypt among the Blacks. He dealt with the white first."[139] As such a remark focuses on the inconsistency of the creed, evoking more questions than it solves, these two roles of Moses are rarely mentioned in the same speech.[140] Though perhaps an unrepresentative example, Farrakhan's suggestion of Moses' double missions points to another interesting aspect related to the inherently illogical component of religion. Not infrequently, a text-oriented religion's theological elite, well versed in the sacred scriptures, may be bothered to find contradictory statements. A different kind of systematization may be undertaken, rationalizing conflicting elements and publishing philosophical treatises expounding explanations and solutions to the religious riddles. This kind of over-systematization has the comparable benefit of constructing a religion with at least *one* believer, the philosopher, and perhaps a circle of disciples. Still, a clear distinction must be made between this elite religion and the folk religion of the majority, who may neither be able to nor interested in reading the tracts of the philosopher of religion. So far, the NOI has only begun to develop defined strata along these lines. Should an elite religious segment materialize in the future, a conceivable puzzle to wrestle with would be the existence of a plurality of gods in such a staunchly monotheistic religion as Islam.

There Are but How Many Gods?   A difficult problem posed in the NOI creed is the abundance of conflicting statements concerning the oneness and plurality of God(s). On the one hand, the Nation of Islam accepts the Islamic principle of monotheism, as presented by the Messenger of Allah:

"A Muslim is one who believes in the One God. It is forbidden by Allah (God) for us to believe in or serve other than Himself as a god. He warns us not to set up an equal with Him, as He was the One in the beginning from whom everything had its beginning and will be the One God from which everything will end. He is independent, having no need for anyone's help."[41] On the other hand, as described at length above, there exists an abundance of statements involving a large quantity of gods. The First Supreme God has associates and helpers, such as the divine council of twenty-four Imams or "Gods," Master Farad who is "God in person," his father, Alphonse, who is "God," Adam, Moses, Imam Shabazz, and other principal actors who are "gods," and the black race which constitutes a "Nation of Gods."

Following this argument, none of these Gods are congruent with the description of the Eternal One God of mainstream Islam. Nothing lasts in eternity, and the Creator is no longer present. "There is no God Living Who was here in the Creation of the Universe, but They produce Gods from Them and Their Wisdom lives in us."[142] The Gods of the Nation of Islam are accordingly *mortals,* who are born, live, and die in a manner unfamiliar to mainstream Islam.[143] The multiple Gods are not equals, but have different characters and possess varying degrees of power. The First One, the self-created Supreme Being who brought the Universe into existence seventy-six trillion years ago, was one of the wisest and potent of all Gods, surpassed only by Master Farad Muhammad, who is the God foretold to come in the Holy Scriptures, who would be "Wiser than Them all."[144]

Another feature of God that is in sharp conflict with mainstream Islamic theology is the anthropomorphism stressed by the Nation. The God of the Nation of Islam is no "mystery God," not invisible formless, or "a spook," but "a material Being."[145] All scriptural references to God's hands and feet, his coming, going, talking, walking, hearing, flying, riding, and the like are understood in an absolutely literal sense by the NOI theologians. God is not "a spirit"—"Spirits do not have feet and hands."[146] If he created man in his image, it follows that "if He were a spirit and not a man, we would all be spirits and not human beings."[147] Spirits are subject to man and not man to spirits,[148] as there exists "no higher intelligence than that of man,"[149] which is why "we cannot make Him other than man, lest we make Him an inferior one."[150] In fact, says the Messenger of Allah, "If I would say that God is not a man, I would be a liar before Him and stand to be condemned. Remember! You look forward to seeing God or the coming of the 'Son of Man' (a man from a man) and not the coming of a 'spirit.' Let that one among you who believes God is other than man prove it!"[151] Statements like this contradict common Islamic theology, as actually confirmed by the Messenger in the same book from which most of the above "God is a man" arguments are cited: "The number one principle of Islam is a belief in Allah (God); *the belief in a power higher than man.*"[152]

Paradoxical indeed, but how is this to be understood? As an avenue of illumination, I would suggest a Gnostic Christianity–oriented explanation. As Gnosticism is a religious tendency pervading parts of several religions of West Asian origin, such as Judaism, Islam—especially in its Shiite and Sufi varieties—Christianity, Manichaeism, and the Druze religion, elements from all these traditions can be discerned in the NOI creed. Although, as will later be suggested, Ismailiyya Shiism and/or Druze traditions probably contributed a number of significant basic notions in the first formulation of the creed, it seems that influences from Christianity, the dominant religious tradition of American society, subsequently remodeled the black Gnosis.

Despite ironic statements making fun of the Trinity and Christianity,[153] the Gnostic interpretation of this part of the creed is, I believe, applicable. The Gnostic allegory should not be taken too far, however, as many essential differences obviously do exist. The suggestion is certainly not that the esoteria of the Nation of Islam is Gnosticism, only that this part of the NOI teachings embraces a rationale similar to selected parts of the Gnostic creed, making the Nation profess a specific black Gnosis, which could be termed *blackosophy.* As in Gnosticism, the NOI doctrines revolve around a hidden, esoteric kernel, never explicitly delineated but hinted at in mystic words and euphemisms understood only by the initiated. God is spirit after all, *but spirit manifested in man and only in man,* whereby it is, on a certain level of truth, correct to say that "man is God and God is man."[154] There is an element of divinity a priori in each black man and woman, who "are born genetically to manifest the characteristics of God."[155] The human brain is a transmitter, a receiver of electrical energy or the power of God.[156] If man submits to God, the power of God will begin to manifest in man,[157] as "all Muslims are Allahs."[158] In much the same, but reversed, manner, the Devil is also spirit, traveling in human bodies, manifesting in white flesh, using the brain as a transmitter of evil. [159] As in Gnosticism, this is not understood as reincarnation but as *representation* of the divine or the diabolic, as realization of embedded true nature and *actualization* of dormant potentials.

As in Gnosticism, the NOI teaches that in original time, during the first giant time cycle, there was a unity of God and man. God created himself in the form of man, and the community of the aboriginal man was a Nation of gods. What is described in Scripture as "the fall of Adam" is a reflection of a most significant event on a higher level in the first cycle: the separation of God and Man, "God in His fallen state is man."[160] Farrakhan teaches that "Adam's fall is only a picture of man's fall from his divine position with God."[161] God concealed his identity and Man lost knowledge of Self, which equals true knowledge of God. Bridging the cycles and natures is "the divine being on the inside of Self," leading "the Self to the Source of Self,"[162] embarking on the path toward self-realization: "man in his exalted state is God."[163]

The Supreme God manifest in the Beginning and the twenty-three scientists are black men, fully grown into divinity, displaying all the creative power of God and therefore termed "Gods." They are still men, which makes the description of them accurately anthropomorphous, and they are still morals, which explains the paradox of dying Gods. When they die, the divine wisdom will still exist, but be manifest in another physical body from the same lineage,[164] making the power and wisdom of God, through this human brain chain, extend from before to beyond the creation. Adam, Moses, and the rest of the Gods are accordingly humans mastering the esoteric secrets, allowing the divine will and wisdom to fully manifest in their bodies. The difference in power and wisdom between the various Gods is a result of the different degrees of divinity reached by respective individuals. Master Farad Muhammad was, according to my understanding of the hidden creed, born to a man belonging to the closed circle of blackosophic or Gnostic sages and destined to reveal the secret knowledge to the lost-found in the Western hemisphere.[165] He had developed the divine capacity to its maximal degree, making him uniquely a manifested "God in Person," as is argued by Elijah Muhammad: "'Fard' is a Name meaning an independent One and One Who is not on the level with the average Gods (Allahs)."[166] Farrakhan asserts that a man possessing divine guidance has power and "that power, is of Allah and is Allah."[167] Such a man produced by a people, suffering and oppressed, encapsulating power that will bring about a change for the dissatisfied, is not what the NOI would term a national leader, but "a God." Not *the* God, but a God.[168] Man is thus God only to a certain extent; God is manifest through him, comes in his body, making him what perhaps could be called a *partial representation,* as God is not confined to the material person in question.

As discussed in the previous chapter, the role of Master Farad Muhammad and later of Elijah the Messiah is similar to the role of Jesus in Gnostic Christianity: they represent the fullness of God in man, and by their powerful example they demonstrate the exalted state that every human being can evolve into: "Ye are all Gods, children of the most High God." The key concept of the Nation of Islam is, as in Gnosticism, *knowledge of self*. The code that like a mantra produces the mentality necessary for the divine to evolve is "I-Self-Lord-Am-Master," that is I.S.L.A.M.[169] To know oneself is to know God, to unveil the hidden, as *true anthropology is theology*.[170] Farrakhan has already followed the lead of Elijah Muhammad along the path to attain divinity,[171] and he is therefore "a saviour" or "a [little] messiah" today. The black nation is in a similar vein "a virgin people" destined to produce a generation of saviours as the hidden knowledge of God becomes revealed throughout the Nation.[172] "Everyone of you," the believers are taught, "will be Gods."[173]

This could possibly be the explanation for the plurality of Gods in a monotheistic religion. The riddle is derived from the unusual terminology of the NOI. Whereas the Gnostic creeds speak of "angels," making anthropology equal to angelology, the Nation insists on terming each man who is an actualization of the dormant divinity "God." Still, there is but One God, eternal but hidden except in his manifestation or realization through man, in man. When Christians speak of the Trinity, the NOI has to multiply the number of divine manifestations that still add up to One.

A final word of caution must again be added. This analysis or exposition of the esoteria of the Nation is based on implicit elements and surfaced hints and allusions. So far, I have not come across a comprehensive emic description of the esoteric teachings, and additional aspects may remain to be uncovered. Esoteria is esoteria, and the Nation of Islam therefore makes no outright attempts to publicly prove their arguments, while they in other matters of belief make considerable efforts to demonstrate evidence for their doctrines as discussed below.

Proving the Creed: Religion and Science   The creed of the Nation of Islam was established by God himself, which is why the believers are certain as to its infallibility. Elijah Muhammad was fond of making bold statements, offering rewards of $10,000 to anyone who could prove him wrong in any detail.[174] Not confined to this "burden of proof" manner of argument, the NOI selectively uses the findings of Western scholarship to prove its creed. This underscores an interesting double standard in regard to science and the established intelligentsia. The NOI strongly denounces the

American educational system as a product of the Devil's society. Populist oriented, they stress their leaders' lack of formal education,[175] repeatedly pointing out that the Messenger "only went to the fourth grade of school."[176] The knowledge preached by the Nation is absolute, derived directly from God; it is divine wisdom in contrast to the relative wisdom of academic graduates.[177]

Paul Boyer shows how this anti-intellectual tendency of the NOI is shared by other American millenarian advocates of the late twentieth century. Many lay-oriented Christian fundamentalist prophecy popularizers emphasize their lack of theological training, academic education, and institutional ties, proclaiming that they aim to be understood by the people rather than praised by the learned.[178] "Despite the popularizers' strident populism and suspicion of authority," notes Boyer, "they exhibited a touching eagerness for intellectual respectability. The visible anxiety of the fundamentalists to have learning on their side pervaded this genre."[179] Prophecy writers invoked the name of learned scientists, cited secular scholars, added terms from the vocabulary of science, and not infrequently styled themselves as "doctors."

A similar ambivalence is clearly discernible in the Nation of Islam. Sermons and books are interspersed with "facts" and findings of natural science. The NOI draw selectively on chemistry, biology, genetics, mathematics, and astronomy and often apply a pseudoscientific line of reasoning to prove their creed. They quote genuine and self-styled Ph.D.'s from universities or sectarian circles as authorities on an equal footing.

Archaeologists and anthropologists who adhere to the theory that man originated in Africa receive considerable attention and are repeatedly mentioned in sermons. Farrakhan's favorite anthropologist is "Dr. Leakey [who] discovered that the root and the origin of man was in Africa." Farrakhan then makes a broad generalization, in one sentence concealing the academic debate on the subject, "and all scholars admit today that Africa is not only the cradle of civilization, Africa is the birth place of the human family."[180] Because of the revealed doctrine of the divine self-creation occurring seventy-six trillion years ago, the NOI rejects the evolutionism advocated by these scholars. It is likewise necessary to disavow the existence of a time when dinosaurs ruled the earth. The NOI asserts that dinosaurs never existed except in the imagination of white scientists. They point to the fact that "scientists at the Smithsonian acknowledge that their displays are based on artists' conceptions and limited fossil findings."[181] Ava Muhammad claims these fossils to be manufactured to promote the hoax and views Steven Spielberg's 1993 hit movie *Jurassic Park* as yet another "manifestation of the power of the Caucasian people to deceive."[182]

The findings of Gregor Johann Mendel at the turn of the century give rise to another theme frequently used by Farrakhan to prove the creed's compatibility with modern science. Mendel, Farrakhan explains, came up with a theory while studying genetics that "light skin is recessive, and dark skin is dominant, light eyes are recessive and dark eyes are dominant, and you can get the recessive from the dominant, but you can not get the dominant from the recessive."[183] This proves that the black people had to be the original people: otherwise black people would not be in the world at all; "if [white people] were the first people, we could never have been, because it is a genetic, biological, mathematical impossibility for two white people to produce black offspring."[184] As physical anthropology and racial biology gave way to medical genetics, the Nation of Islam found new evidence for their revealed truths. "By studying the DNA of every human being on the earth, [the scientists] traced the origin of all human beings back to the black woman," Farrakhan insisted during a speech at Michigan State University.[185] The Nation of Islam is encouraging their young members to enroll at American universities and has established a "Historical Research Department."[186] Among other pressing tasks for the emerging community of black Muslim social scientists, plans are being made for a group of archaeologists to excavate at Patmos in the Greek archipelago to prove the origin of the white devil.[187]

One of the most prominent sciences in the service of the NOI is, however, not a mainstream discipline taught at the American universities, but numerology, the esoteric use of mathematics in scriptural exegetics.

The Mathematical Code of Islam   When the authors of the Mother Book had recorded everything that was to take place, they sealed the book, deciding that it should not be opened until the latter days. In 1975, the year of Elijah Muhammad's departure and subsequent exaltation as the Messiah, the moment finally came when the seal was broken and the secrets of the Holy Scriptures were unraveled.[188]

The leading female theologian, Sister Tynetta Muhammad, was in Libya in 1975 producing a tune called "The Muslim Song and March for Victory," based on Surah 110, *al Nasr,* or "Help." At the same time in the same country, she claimed that the computer Sufi, Rashad Khalifa, discovered the "underlying Mathematical Code of the Holy Qur'an's Revelation based on the number 19."[189] This is not a coincidence but proves that the NOI was meant to adopt the use of the code to transcribe the hidden message from God to humanity, even though it would take five more years before Tynetta Muhammad would meet Rashad Khalifa and be given her "introduction to the study of the number 19."[190]

Surah 110, which is the surah revealed to the Prophet Muhammad on his farewell pilgrimage to Mecca, contains exactly 19 words, with the first verse composed of exactly 19 letters in addition to the opening *Bismillah* which contains exactly 19 letters. This gives three separate occurrences of the number 19. Three multiplied with 19 gives 57, a figure conveying the birth date of the Prophet in A.D. 570. A new message from God to humanity was about to be revealed.[191]

Rashad Khalifa was born in 1935 in Tanta, Egypt, the son of a sheikh of the Sufi order Shadhili. In 1959, he went as a student to the United States and received his doctorate in biochemistry in the early 1960s. Following a period as a United Nations agricultural adviser to Libya, Khalifa settled in Tuscon, Arizona, where he later established a mosque and propaganda center for the United Submitters International.[192] Khalifa represents a minority tendency in Islamic modernism, which has been described as Islamic Protestantism on the grounds that it disavows the *sunnah* (exemplary behavior of the Prophet Muhammad) and *hadith* (narrative of the Prophet's sayings and actions) as post-Muhammad invented distortions, which are held accountable for the decline of Islam. Khalifa argues that those who advocate the sunnah and the hadith are "idolaters," while the "true believers uphold the Qur'an, the whole Qur'an and nothing but the Qur'an."[193]

As had many Muslim Sufis before him, Khalifa pondered over the inner meaning believed to be embedded in the fourteen letters, known as the "Qur'anic Initials," that in different sets are prefixed to twenty-nine surahs. By using computer analysis, the secret was "unveiled,"[194] and Khalifa was led to the discovery of the number 19 as the code of the Holy Qur'an.[195] In 1981 he presented his findings in *The Computer Speaks: God's Message to the World*[196] and published the first of three translations of the Holy Qur'an based on his computer analysis.[197] The following year he produced a Qur'an commentary with mathematical proof of the miracle.[198]

The existence of some secret proof in the Qur'an is, according to Khalifa, indicated several times in the Holy Scripture. In Qur'an 25:4–6, the unbelievers ask for evidence to prove that the verses were not fables and lies invented by men. God tells the faithful to respond, "Say, He Who knoweth the secret of the heavens and the earth hath revealed it."[199] Explains Khalifa, "It was the will of God, the author of Quran, that the secret Quranic proof shall await an era of mathematical sophistication, when the people can both understand and appreciate the miraculous intricacy of this proof."[200]

Khalifa further claims that he was predestined to be "the messenger of the covenant" with his name "mathematically coded into the Quran."[201] In 1971/1391 his soul was taken to the abode of the past prophets and introduced to them, in a journey that recalls Muhammad ibn Abdullah's souls ascension to the heavens.[202] The messenger of the covenant is ordained to confirm and clarify the previous revelations with "the Final Testament," that is, a purged and decoded Qur'an. In 1985, Khalifa found nine violations of the mathematical code in the Qur'an. All violations are in the last two verses of Surah 9, and Khalifa concluded that the verses were fabrications inserted by scribes.[203] The messenger was in addition obliged to reinstate true Islam by rejecting unwarranted innovations, such as the corpus of traditions. Mislead by Satan, man-made texts were confused with the divine revelations, resulting in the corruption of Judaism, Christianity, Islam, Hinduism, and Buddhism. Khalifa envisioned that when purged of unwarranted traditions, it was possible to consolidate "all the messages delivered by all of God's messengers into one global message."[204] To this end, Khalifa established the United Islamic Nation (UIN) in 1985, proclaimed as "the richest and most powerful nation on earth."[205]

Like most radical reformers challenging established religious hierarchies and creeds, Khalifa's mission was not appreciated but considered blasphemous. Khalifa saw the attacks from mainstream Islamic scholars as confirmation of his mission, reflecting the Qur'anic assertion that all messengers had been rejected and ridiculed. Khalifa self-confidently predicted that all Muslim regimes that remained outside the UIN would fall at the hands of God. In December 1987, a pleased Khalifa observed that three stubborn Muslim presidents had fallen.[206] Muslim hostility further increased when Khalifa, in September 1989, declared that he was commanded by God, through Gabriel, to announce that he was the Expected One, the Messiah, Christ, and Mahdi. Anticipating reactions of scorn and doubt, Khalifa predicted that his mission would be universally acknowledged only after his death.[207] A few months later, on January 31, 1990, Khalifa was found stabbed to death in the kitchen of Masjid Tucson.[208]

Rashad Khalifa had calculated that the end of the world would occur exactly 309 lunar years or 300 solar years from the year of his calculation, which was 1980. Khalifa concluded that the "world will end in the year 2280 A.D."[209] For the Nation of Islam, which adopted the number 19 as a decoder for the Holy Scriptures, the latter calculation was unbefitting, specifying the end in too distant a future. By combining forecasts by Elijah Muhammad with the code, Tynetta Muhammad suggested that the 1990s were to be "the final decade," with the end to be expected in the year 2001.[210]

The code was used by Khalifa to analyze the Qur'an in its original, Arabic language. Tynetta Muhammad expanded the code's instrumentality, arguing that God spoke in all languages of the world community at once, by using "an underlying linguistic code common to all."[211] This code is in the universal language of mathematics, "which is the true definition of Islam."[212] Tynetta Muhammad wrote, "Hidden in language are the mathematical keys to deciphering God's hidden messages to the world. So by examining individual letters, syllables, words and numbers, carried over into the English language, we are using the mathematical language in its proper terms in learning to speak well in our communication with God."[213] By using the code, the Nation of Islam amasses great quantities of evidence for its creed's infallibility. A few examples will be sufficient to demonstrate its use. The code was, as noted above, based on the 14 mysterious "initial letters" of the Qur'an. These 14 letters appear in 14 different sets over 29 Surahs. The result is 14+14+29=57; 57 is 19 × 3 and half of the total number of surahs, which is 114 and a multiple of 19 × 6. Add a zero to 57 and the year 570 is given, which is the date of the Prophet Muhammad's birth and a multiple of 19 (19 × 30). This points to another year, 1930, when God in Person came to his lost-found Nation. Return to 57, reverse the number and add the prefix 19 and you will be given yet another important year, 1975, when the Messenger departed and the code was discovered. Remove the prefix and you get 75, which means you should go to Surah 75 in the Holy Qur'an, which is called "the Resurrection," for proof of Elijah Muhammad being alive and united with God.

The year 1975 could also be read as 97:1–5, which points to the surah *Al-Qadr*, "the Majesty," where we learn about the revelation given to the Prophet Muhammad on the Night of Majesty, said to be "better than a thousand months." "Thousand" is here given a dual interpretation. First, the number points to the year 1975, as it was exactly 1000 years since another major scientific breakthrough occurred in Islam: the establishment of the Al-Ahzar University in the very same country where the code was discovered. Second, "thousand" draws attention to the predesignated time for the burning and cooling of the earth after the onslaught of Armageddon. Victoriously concluding this war are, as earlier observed, a divine fleet of spacecrafts, and reports of UFOs have bearing on all this.

On October 7, 1985, Sister Muhammad reports, fifteen sets of UFOs in formations of four were observed for ninety minutes and clocked flying at three hundred miles per hour.[214] The first two sets of numbers, 15 and 4 gives the number 154, which is the exact number of lessons delivered to the Nation by Master Farad Muhammad. The number 154 can, of course, be resolved to 19 (15+4=19). The next two sets are 300+90=390, which represent the exact number of years the earth will burn with fire. After the fire, the earth will cool off for the rest of the millennium, 610 years, before it again becomes inhabitable. The number 610 is the year of the Prophet Muhammad's appointment as Messenger of Allah, and resolved individually, the two sets, 390 and 610, equal 19 (6+1+0+3+9+0). Reversing 39 to 93 and adding it to 61 equals 154, the number of lessons and a connection to the number 19, as we have seen.

The number of letters in the names of persons is also highly significant. The name Ronald Wilson Reagan reveals his true identity as it carries the mark of the Beast, 666. The name Elijah Muhammad equals 14 letters, the same number as the mysterious Qur'anic initials. In spelling the name of his Khalifa, Louis Farrakhan, we count exactly 14 letters, which, of course, is not a coincidence.[215] In the spelling of Master Fard Muhammad there are exactly 19 letters, the number of the code. Adding all three sets of letters, we arrive at the number 47. Surah 47 is entitled "Muhammad" and contains all three sets of initials designated in the code, which is why "the name Muhammad most surely is certainly Minister Farakkhan's name as Well."[216] The number 47 reversed is 74, which refers to Surah 74, "The Hidden One," in which the code was found hidden in verse 30. Add the prefix and you again get the year of the Son of Man's appearance, 1930. From the year 1930 to the year 1986, when Tynetta Muhammad wrote her book on the code, we count 56 years, which is the exact number of verses in Surah 74.

The Nation of Islam has in addition adopted the Abjad scheme for the numerical value of Arabic letters also used by Rashad Khalifa. The Arabic word for "one" or "unit" is *Wahid,* which has the numerical value 19,[217] making the code, when transcribed in spelling, mean "one," which is the central theme of the Qur'an: the oneness and unity of God. Tynetta Muhammad notes that the numerical value of "one" and the spelling of "Master Fard Muhammad" both resolve to the number 19, and so displaying the identity of the Mahdi as the One.[218]

The number 19 communicates a symbolic image of the universe and the ultimate destiny of mankind. "One" represents the masculine aspect of the self-created First Supreme Being and "nine" his feminine presence, illustrated by the sun and the nine planets. The unity of the masculine and feminine represent not only the power of reproduction but of creation, making the code equal to the key that unlocks the divine force inherent in man, the full expression of which is the Gnostic aim of oneness of God and man, the closing of the cycles: as it was in the Beginning so shall it be in the End; God is Man and Man is God.[219]

What is New in New Religions?   In closing this chapter's outline and analysis of the NOI creed, one might be justified in raising the question posed in the subheading above. Any reader familiar with comparative religion will have noticed the composite character of the creed, with elements from a considerable number of other religions incorporated in the belief system of the Nation.

The Islamic and Christian foundation for the Nation of Islam will by now be obvious to the reader. The holy scriptures used are the same, although the interpretation may deviate. They share a number of central features, including principal actors such as the Son of Man, al-Mahdi, and the Messiah, although their specific identities and conceptual interpretations differ. Besides these general Islamic and Christian roots, other movements have a discernible bearing on the NOI. The process when God creates himself resembles the doctrines of Druze, Ismailiyya, and, to some extent, Jewish kabbalah. The first divine emanation in the next stage of the Creation is the Divine Wisdom or the Cosmic Intellect, in the NOI described as the Black Intellect. In the kabbalah of Isaac Luria, the first to be created out of this divine light is in the form of the primordial man, Adam Qadmon, a theory represented also in the NOI.[220] Next in the Creation, the NOI declares a divine council of scientists, or imams. This recalls the doctrines of Ismailiyya and Imamiyya branches of Shiite Islam. According to a *hadith* in the collections of Imamiyya, Ali Ibn Abu Talib, the first imam after the prophet Muhammad, is reported to have said, "God is one; He was alone in His singleness and so He spoke a word and it became a light and He created from that light Muhammad and He created me and my descendants [the other imams]."[221] The imams were accordingly created by the first emanation of divine light, an act predating the subsequent creation of the material universe.[222] The idea of imams as embodiments of divine light is emphasized in Ismailiyya Islam and could be taken to extremes, as in the Druze doctrines of al-Hakim as God in Person—an idea akin to the NOI notion of Master Farad Muhammad. The notion of a divine lineage of imams, with the transfer of manifested divinity from father to son upon the former's death, is a component of both Imamiyya and Ismailiyya and, furthermore, is expressed by the NOI's idea of divine lineages of scientists, or imams.

Basic themes of Ismailiyya and Druze doctrines resurface in the NOI creed to such an extent that the suggestion that Master Farad Muhammad was an immigrant Druze stands out as rather appealing, especially as the early Druze immigrants frequently established themselves as peddlers,[223] as did Master Farad. Based on comparison, an argument could be made for an Ismaili or Druze foundation for a creed recast on black nationalist and Christian grounds either by Master Farad or others upon his disappearance.

In addition to the elements mentioned above, further corresponding themes can be identified. Ismailiyya has developed a notion of cyclical time. In its early formulation, time moved in a great cycle, divided into seven millennia. Each millennium was inaugurated by a *natiq,* an enunciator of a new revelation and law, accompanied by a *wasi,* a spiritual legate who lays the foundation for the Imamate, or Shii doctrine of a righteously established state administration, and transfers the esoteric secrets to the seven imams of the period, who are all his descendants. Later, astronomical speculation conceived a great cycle of 360,000 years, divided into lesser cycles, each guided by a planet and divided into seven millennia, with it all ending in the great Resurrection.[224]

According to Ismaili doctrine, in the beatific cycle prior to the present cycle of confusion there was a race of humans superior to ours. They lived in a time ushered in by the universal Adam, who appeared in the first cycle's sixth millennium on the island of Sri Lanka. The true knowledge of time was openly preached, and man lived an "angelic" life until the cycle of epiphany closed and the cycle of occultation began, in which the true Gnosis is concealed and only taught to a closed circle of earthly angelic descendants.[225]

One of them, Adam, who is not identical with the universal Adam we met above, but a "partial" or "episodic" Adam, manifesting to initiate each cycle, is invested as the enunciator of the new law. Adam is accordingly not the first man but one of the last survivors from the previous cycle. In the Ismaili exegesis of Qur'an 2:30, it is the angels of the cycle of unveilment (the original people in NOI terminology) who abhor the introduction of the new era and question the imam who gravely responds, "I know what ye know not." The hardship experienced in the present cycle is a necessary phase, the completion of which leads to a perfected state, the aim of Creation.[226]

Central in Ismaili Gnostic speculation is the divine potential a priori embedded in man as a focus for man's ambitions. Ismailiyya holds the aim of mankind to be a resurrectional process, in which by knowledge of Self, man undergoes an "angelomorphosis."[227] The NOI's division of mankind into two opposing categories, "gods" and "devils," black and white, is similar to the Ismaili classification of those who have an angelic potential, those who, on this plane in this time cycle, reflect angelic archetypes from higher planes at times past and times to come, and those who are reflections or manifestations of Iblis, of the diabolic.[228]

The Ismaili Gnosis identification of true anthropology as angelology is, phenomenologically speaking, not unique, but central for the Gnostic speculation found in its Judaic, Christian, and Druze varieties. It is similarly discernible in Sufism, especially in the speculations of Ibn Arabi followers, where this notion is expressed in the doctrine of the "Perfected Man," *al-Insan al-Kamil*. The mystic sage, following Muhammad's example, strives to achieve this stage, where the Suf encompasses all divine attributes and rises into "the Muhammadan reality," or "the universal intelligence," the creative principle and the cause of the perfected man.[229]

Like the Nation, Madame Blavatsky and the Theosophists held a racial theory on human evolution combined with a notion of cyclical time. As does the NOI, Blavatsky believed that history moved in cycles of 25,000 years, stressed the value of elitism and hierarchy, and believed that divine energy and creativity were made manifest through human races, although she believed the Aryans and not the blacks were the crown of human evolution.[230]

Turning to African American religion, the blackosophic speculation concerning the divine within the black race is found, among others, in the Rastafarian religion, originating in Jamaica in the same year that Master Farad began his mission in Detroit. Comparing the NOI with Rastafarianism, we find a wide range of tenets in common: the black race as a community of gods; the black aboriginal culture as the cradle of civilization; blacks as the principal actors of the Bible, including being the people of the covenant and the descendants of the tribe of Shebah; the white man as evil by nature; the Western world as Babylon; separatism; apocalyptic orientation, and so on. Both religions, furthermore, derive a great deal of inspiration from Marcus Garvey, whose thoughts and ideology to a large extent are adopted by these black nationalistic religions.[231]

The notion of the Devil as the negative side of the black man could be found in the Moorish Science Temple, although the MST does not believe that he manifests carnally as the white devil. Other black nationalist religions, such as the Ansaaru Allah Community, the Temple of Love, and others do hold the white man to be the Devil, but these were founded after the NOI. The making of the races as a successive process of degeneration by the pouring out of divine substance is found in the Native American group known as the Dreamers, founded by the prophet Smohalla, who taught that only the red Indians were "of original God-created stock."[232]

The similarities between the Moorish Science Temple and the Nation of Islam should by now be obvious to the reader. Rooted in the tradition of classic black nationalism, Noble Drew Ali formulated some basic notions that were later adopted by the NOI, including a blackosophic rationale; the black race as the original Asiatic man; the aboriginal American culture as originally black Islamic; the covenant between the black Creator and his people; the idea of a "Silent Brotherhood" (in the Moorish terminology) as guardians of the secret knowledge of God; and the importance of recreating racial solidarity as a prelude to the predetermined black liberation.

The similarities between Moorish and Masonic speculation have already been noted, and the Masons have a bearing on the NOI. Freemasons, like the NOI, believe that man is a fallen god and that humanity is rising into divine perfection.[233] Black Masonic speculation on the nature of the African American, the possibility of reaching different degrees of ennobled divinity, and the future destiny of the race have elements in common, as does their hierarchical organizational structure.[234] Black Masons and the NOI, moreover, both interpret certain kinds of disasters, such as fires and natural calamities, as divine acts of retribution against the whites.[235] However, it is in an essentially inverted fashion that the Masons figure prominently in the NOI creed. The NOI maintains that the white Masons are a secret society of devils perfectly aware of their evil origin and in control of the white man's world.

Armageddon as a racial war is a favorite motive for a number of white religious extremist groups and preachers in the United States and is also a common theme in various black religious nationalist movements and sects. A comparison between black and white religious nationalism is provided in chapter 9.

The apocalyptic orientation of the NOI is shared by millions of Christian Americans who believe in prophecy. A number of beliefs are held in common by the NOI and Christian millenarians: the eschatological interpretation of events in the world such as wars, natural calamities, AIDS, and increasing drug and crime rates; the special attention given to Israel/Palestine as a trigger for the final battle; the rapture, in which the faithful brethren are to be miraculously saved from destruction by being evacuated from earth by God Almighty; the idea that America will be destroyed. One prophecy writer even identified the Beast as Ronald Reagan and many gave a leading role to Saddam Hussein.[236]

The Nation of Islam belongs to the broad category termed new religious movements (NRM). In the United States alone there are, according to a conservative 1989 estimate, some 2,000 NRMs.[237] Many of these have some traits in common with the NOI, not least in incorporating exciting elements, such as UFOs; Pyramidism; Armageddon implemented by nuclear weapons; genetics; the brain as a transmitter for the divine; the possibility to "tune in" into other people's thoughts; true self is God, and the like.[238] Upon investigating and analyzing the creeds of these NRMs, one will probably find that they are largely composed of elements previously found in old religious movements, as is the case with the NOI doctrines. The black gospel of Master Farad Muhammad, Elijah the Messiah, and his representative Louis Farrakhan clearly demonstrates external influences and borrowings. Does the composite character of this gospel invalidate its message? Most certainly not; if it were not irresistible, the gospel would not have survived history. Neither does its composite character rule out the label "new," for it is a new rearrangement of selected sentiments and elements adopted as meaningful; that is an undoubtedly appealing reformulation of a black worldview. The dependence on the legacy of the past upon reflection should come as no surprise. A creed entirely composed of unique elements not found in other ideologies or traditions would suggest a totally alien origin, disconnected from the world to which it belongs. Any new religion has this composite character, reflecting an almost truistic argument as to how the human mind comprehends this world and its transformations. We are born into a world in which we communicate with words that were created before we arrived, think in terms and concepts already present, and use knowledge accumulated over generations: that is, *we think in terms of the past.* Irrespective of how innovative a person may be, his mind will almost exclusively be filled with concepts and ideas not originally his, but of others, from the past. Change will accordingly always be understood in terms of the past. We apply our old conceptual tools to make sense of what is new in a process that is simultaneously, but slowly, transforming our thinking. The same rule applies to the emergence of new religions: they will always be created in terms of old religions and constructions of belief. Notwithstanding the relative amount of innovative elements that are incorporated, the creed mainly will be filled with elements of the past. Yet the religion is defined as new and actually constitutes a vehicle for renewal and transformation, to different degrees and extents affecting and changing the world as it contributes to the legacy of "the old," the category imposed on us all.

The old established creeds may not favorably view the new formulation presented by a new religious movement, which places the old and the new in opposition, as the new would not have appeared if its ideologues and followers had been satisfied with the old. This tension characterizes the relation between the Nation and the older versions of Islam, to which I now direct our attention.

8

The Sun of Islam Will Rise in the West

—

This chapter will examine the Nation of Islam in relation to mainstream Islam. The Nation's understanding of its role in the global Islamic community will be described and special attention will be given to the NOI's association with Mu'ammar al-Qadhdhafi and the Libyan *Jamahiriya*. At the end of the chapter, three minor black nationalist Muslim organizations in the United States will be presented.

Allah's Gradual Approach   In matters of doctrine, Islam stands forth as a liberal and tolerant religion, a fact at times overshadowed by the publicity given to intolerant Muslims. Within Islam there coexist a rich spectra of divergent views and interpretations of the creed. Orthodoxy as a concept was developed within Christianity and is less relevant a concept when applied to an understanding of Islam. As noted by John L. Esposito, this has made some observers distinguish between a Christian emphasis on correct doctrine (orthodoxy) and an Islamic emphasis on correct behavior (orthopraxy). This distinction is not unproblematic and it should not be understood as opposing mutually exclusive concepts; as it does not rule out faith as such, it may be regarded as a call for the actualization of faith.[1] The God of Islam demands not only words but deeds, making Islam a religion of practice in which each believer has a responsibility to realize God's will. In Qur'an 4:136 the basic creed of Islam is established: "O ye who believe! Believe in God and His Apostle, and the scripture which He hath sent to His Apostle and the scripture which He sent to those before. Any who denieth God, His angels, His Books, His Apostles, and the Day of Judgement, hath gone far, far astray." To accept the beliefs thus set forth is to be a believer, and to act accordingly is to be a Muslim. The one dominant doctrine of Islam is the sovereignty (*rabb*) and unity of God (*tawhid*). The fact that "theology" (*ilm al-kalam*) also is known as or referred to as *ilm al-tawhid*, "the science of (divine) unity,"[2] is but one illustration of monotheism as the paramount profession of Islamic belief. Another nonnegotiable doctrine is the position of Muhammad ibn Abdullah as the seal of the prophets: after him God will not call another messenger (*rasul*).

The combination of these two unconditional matters of belief constitutes the first pillar of Islam, the *Shahada:* "There is no God but God and Muhammad is the Messenger of God." Adherence to this confession of faith is a minimum standard for a group or movement to qualify as Islamic. Any deviation from it will push its members out to the margins at best and make them heretics or apostates at worst, as is shown by the recurrent controversies concerning the relative legitimacy of movements such as the Ahmadiyya or the Alawiyya.[3]

The alternative NOI understanding of the *Shahada*, identifying Master Farad Muhammad as God and Elijah Muhammad as the Messenger of God, is undoubtedly blasphemous in mainstream Islamic eyes. Given the low political profile chosen by the majority of Muslim immigrants in the United States at the time of the media's discovery of the Nation of Islam, the vociferously militant attitude of the black nationalist Islamic movement further added to the animosity felt by many mainstream American Muslims, and some of their spokespersons officially denounced the NOI. The Federation of Islamic Associations of the United States and Canada did not recognize the Nation of Islam as truly Islamic and felt uneasy with its existence.[4] Sunni Muslim Shaykh Dau'd of Brooklyn declared in 1967 that all African Americans attending his State Street Mosque should carry Sunni Muslim identification cards. Those who refused were suspected NOI sympathizers and were denied admission.[5]

In the 1950s, one group that publicly attacked Messenger Muhammad was the Muslim fringe movement Ahmadiyya. Since the 1921 establishment of their American headquarters in Chicago, the Ahmadiyya endeavored to obtain converts in the black community. Their condemnation of the NOI was perhaps part of a twofold strategy to establish a profile as a genuine Islamic alternative among the African Americans and to enhance a mainstream Islamic status in the Muslim community. In a public statement, Abid Nurrid of the Chicago chapter denounced the NOI as "a most dangerous cult . . . using hatred to amass money and power" and claimed that the "corrupted and mutilated teachings" constituted a danger to Islam and the national security.[6]

The recurring conflicts between the Nation and other Islamic groups with a predominantly black membership occasionally ended violently,[7] as did the theological dispute with a group of black Hanafi Muslims, headed by Hamaas Abdul Khaalis. As Ernest 2X McGhee, he held the position of secretary under Minister Malcolm X in Temple #7, but was replaced by John X Ali in 1958. Shortly thereafter, Ernest 2X and a few fellow dissidents left the NOI and established a Hanafi Muslim group in Washington, D.C. As Hanafi leader Hamaas Abdul Khaalis, he turned against the NOI and criticized Elijah Muhammad fiercely.[8] In the wake of the police attack on the NOI mosque in Harlem in 1972, and the division among immigrant Muslims over that issue,[9] Khaalis took action. He circulated an open letter, defaming the Messenger as "a lying deceiver" who lured "former dope addicts and prostitutes to monklike lives of sacrifice" that would "lead them to hell,"[10] a charge he would later repeat on television.

Rebuking their opponents among Muslim immigrants as "paid agents of the CIA,"[11] the NOI denounced Khaalis, whom they described as a "modern-day 'Uncle Tom'" who "filled his pockets with the devil's money."[12] Condemned as "the white man's tool," Khaalis was warned with a reminder of God's Qur'anic promise about how to deal with his enemies: "Surely those who forge a lie against Allah will not prosper."[13] Khaalis did not prosper. In January 1973, seven fellow Hanafis were murdered in their 116th Street residence in Washington, D.C. Five of the victims were children, including babies who were drowned in a bathtub.[14]

The murderers were all soldiers of the FOI, but the subsequent trial failed to impart direct guilt to the NOI leadership, who denied ordering the defamers' death.[15] Salim Muwakkil, former Black Panther and NOI member and today one of America's most distinguished black journalists, is convinced that the hit squad was comprised of unauthorized freelancers who looked on themselves as modern-day assassins who would go after whoever defamed the Messenger.[16] The Hanafis, however, held the NOI responsible and Khaalis, who escaped the fatal attack, was determined to exact revenge. One of the assassins was slain in prison, and in March 1977, an armed group of Hanafis seized hostages and killed one reporter when they occupied the B'nai B'rith headquarters, the Islamic Center, and the City Council chambers in Washington, D.C., in an unsuccessful attempt to press demands for retribution.[17]

Despite assurances to the contrary, the Nation of Islam was not untroubled by the criticism issuing from the Muslim world and an accommodating process commenced. Elijah Muhammad made his hajj to Mecca on three separate occasions, in 1959, 1967, and 1971, where he conferred with scholars from the Muslim world.[18] Through studies of the Qur'an and an increasing dialogue with Muslim *ulama* (Islamic scholars), the Messenger of God gradually sought an accord with and brought his movement closer to mainstream Islam, or at least to a "proto-Islamic" position,[19] which earned him respect from former critics of his work.[20]

When Elijah Muhammad departed, his son Warithuddin (then Wallace) Muhammad greatly accelerated the Islamization process, consistently purging the movement of what he thought of as heterodox remnants from an immature past, as described in chapter 5. Upholding the divergent features of the Messenger's teachings as unconditional divine truth, Louis Farrakhan reestablished the Nation on what he believed to be the platform of Elijah Muhammad and thereby inherited the somewhat problematic relationship to a Muslim world community that he was forced to come to terms with.

Farrakhan, who claims to be guided continually by the Honorable Elijah Muhammad, was advised by him to establish friendly relations with the "orthodox" Muslims. Elijah Muhammad warned Farrakhan not to repeat Hitler's decisive mistake of waging war on two fronts simultaneously. The Muslim world could make a strategic ally in the war against the enemies of God in the government of America, "and when that number one enemy is removed," Elijah advised Farrakhan, "then we can settle our differences."[21]

The present top leadership of the Nation, being widely traveled in Muslim countries, have fully mastered the Islamic rituals and behavioral patterns and, in addition, are increasingly well read in Islamic religious literature. This knowledge enables them to be accommodating of Islamic orthopraxy. The process of outward Islamization has not been carried as far as it has been by the followers of Imam Warithuddin Muhammad, whose imitation of Muslim Arab style is ridiculed. Emphasizing blackness and separateness as religious values, Farrakhan denounces the lack of originality and the inferiority implied in fully adopting Islamic-Arabian customs. What is the use in shifting the focus of an unreserved admiration, from imitating white Christians to white Muslims? For an African American, in this context what would be the principal difference between laying on a conk of burning congolene to straighten the hair and wearing long garments, twisting a new-grown beard, and mumbling *al-hamdulillah, al-hamdulillah* (All praise is due to Allah alone)? The African Americans have no need to be anyone else but their true selves, stresses Farrakhan: "We, the black people of America, who are now accepting Islam, are not converting to a religious faith, nor are we adopting an Arab faith, but we are returning to the nature of God which is our own nature. So in reality when we are accepting Islam, we are accepting what belongs to us. And when we strive to become true Muslims, we are actually only ourselves."[22] With a certainty derived from being the original people, any self-denying conduct is denounced as unworthy and unredeeming, which explains why the NOI Islamization is of a Black-americanized version. Adjustment to mainstream Muslim behavior does not require adoption of cultural features, such as an Arabic dress code. While male followers of AMM or other Islamic movements with a predominantly black membership generally wear white robes and crocheted hoods, NOI men keep their suit and bow tie outfit, arguing that the robed fashion is an alienating exoticism.

While exoticism may appeal to a limited number of searching black individuals, as the presence of a few African American converts to the Hare Krishna movement might suggest, Farrakhan is convinced that most black Americans would be repelled. NOI mosques, which have a mission to call every dead in the streets back to life, are placed in the heart of the black community and great care is taken to make a new visitor feel at home. This is the underlying reason for the double arrangement in the houses of worship. In the beautifully decorated Mosque Maryam, new visitors to the open Sunday sermons will be shown a seat in a churchlike grand hall. Though the sexes are separated, with the women on the right side and the men on the left, instead of the common Muslim practice of placing men in front and women in back, the service would in most other respects follow a procedure well known to most blacks with a Christian background: sitting on rows of benches, they would listening to introductory and keynote preachers, and giving an offering. Perhaps they would miss bursting out into gospel tunes, but would enjoy other music, for example the NOI "National Anthem." Should the first-time visitor respond affirmatively to the obligatory questions raised at the end of each service—if he believed that what he heard preached is the truth and good for his people and would he "return home," that is join the Nation—he would gradually be introduced to the more Islamized parts of the NOI worshipping schedules and facilities. In the basement of the Mosque Maryam, he would see a hall equipped and decorated as a traditional mosque and after a period of learning be invited to participate in *Salat al-Juma*, the obligatory Friday prayer of mainstream Islam, and listen to an *al-Juma* address, possibly delivered by an African guest imam. Farrakhan stresses the wisdom of this gradual approach. Had the unknowing first-time visitor been confronted with a fully Islamic ritual, complete with the congregation sitting on the floor, listening to Arabic preaching, and prostrating itself, he would have felt alienated and perhaps reacted disrespectfully, mocking that which he did not understand.[23]

Compared to the Nation prior to Elijah Muhammad's departure, the NOI has to a larger extent adopted the outward forms of Islamic orthopraxy. All members are given a prayer book dealing with *salat* as performed in the Muslim world and are urged to conform to its standard.[24] The NOI has its version of *zakat*, even though the almsgiving still shares elements of their Christian surrounding, borrowing strategies from both the black and the electronic churches of America. Additionally, NOI members hold their prescribed fast in Ramadan,[25] following the Islamic lunar calendar, and hajj is recommended.

Even the opening words of the services, alluding to the first pillar of Islam, the confession of belief, have been reformed or Islamized. Prior to 1975, the NOI's deviation from the universal Islamic understanding of the *Shahada* was explicit. In his 1973 Saviour's Day introduction of the Honorable Elijah Muhammad, Farrakhan said, "We bear witness that there is no God but Allah, Who came in the Person of Master Farad Muhammad, and that Elijah Muhammad surely is the Last and Greatest of the Messengers of Allah."[26] After the NOI's "second resurrection," the opening words were gradually revised in a Sunni direction. Still outside mainstream lines, Farrakhan opened a service in 1980 with the following introduction: "In the name Allah the Beneficent, the Merciful, the One God who came in the Person of Master Farad Muhammad, to whom praise is due for ever. We thank Allah for blessing us, the black man and woman of America, with a divine leader, a divine teacher and a divine guide in the personage of the Most Honorable Elijah Muhammad, the Messenger of Allah."[27] Ten years later, the explicit identification of Master Farad as God in person and Elijah Muhammad as Messenger of God was often carefully removed, accommodating the words to mainstream Sunni Islam.[28] Farrakhan said, "In the name of Allah, the Beneficent, the Merciful. I bear witness that there is but one God, Creator of all things, Revealer of all truths, Sender of all prophets. To him alone do I submit and seek refuge. We thank Allah for sending Moses and the Torah, or the Old Testament. We thank Allah for sending Jesus and the Gospel, the good news, or the New Testament. We thank Allah for sending Muhammad and the Holy Quran. I personally give praise and thanks to Allah for raising up in our midst a divine leader, teacher and guide. A man who has made the Torah, the Gospel and the Quran relevant to our struggle for liberation, and relevant to the struggle of all oppressed people, wherever they may be found on earth. I greet all of you, brothers and sisters, with the greeting words of peace, thanking Allah for the Honorable Elijah Muhammad: As-Salaam Alaikum."[29] The concept of gradual evolution toward conventional Islamic praxis is applied to explain the differences in the level of mainstream adherence between the old and the new Nation. In agreement with the reasoning of Imam Warithuddin, Farrakhan presents the Islamization as being in line with the true intentions of Elijah Muhammad, even though the imam is said to have exceeded the limits and gone too far, as the Messenger "never intended for us to follow completely what is called orthodox Islam."[30]

Aware of mainstream Islamic denunciations of Elijah Muhammad as "an impostor," occupying Muhammad ibn Abdullah's position as Messenger of God, and the Muslim scholars' appreciation of Imam Warithuddin for finally giving the NOI members "true Islam,"[31] Farrakhan sought reconciliation with the *ulama*, asserting the necessity and ultimate success of the strategy of gradualism. Reaching out for his black people in the West, God in his omniscience applied a well-tried method, Farrakhan argued, proving his claim by the means of comparison.[32]

When God in the year 610 called Muhammad ibn Abdullah to be his Messenger, the Arabs were living under the conditions of *jahiliyya*, "the period of ignorance," ruling out the possibility of presenting the complete will of God at once. The Messenger worked for twenty-two years transforming the life of his people. Including the period of the "rightly guided khalifs," it took fifty-one years to bring the Arabs into the Islamic civilization. The African Americans were found lost in a period of ignorance, the depth of which was even worse than that experienced by the Arabs. The Arabs had at least lived in their own country and spoken their native language, while the blacks were deprived of their freedom and their original culture during slavery. Given these conditions, Farrakhan told a group of *ulama* at a Mecca meeting in 1989, it would be impossible to present "the perfection of the Quran . . . without a serious time of preparation."[33] Elijah Muhammad was divinely guided to adopt a gradual approach, based on a knowledge of the African American reality, which explains his success where the mainstream Muslim *dawa* activities so obviously have failed. Now, with Blackamericans returning to Islam "in millions," a firm foundation is laid from which they can evolve.[34] Gradualism has the diplomatic advantage of communicating a promise of steady progress acceptable in multiple camps while its actual content is left implicit and thus open for alternative interpretations. In espousing gradualism Farrakhan can establish links with and gain support from different Islamic institutions, based on their respective assumptions of where such gradualism will lead, without compromising the NOI's ideals.

Follow Bilal into Paradise New fortification lines defending the deviating features of the NOI creed run parallel with the adjustment to outward Islamization. In the old Nation, the criticism coming from Arab Muslims was easily declared irrelevant with reference to their status as white Muslims, believers "by faith and not by nature."[35] According to the revealed historiography, these white coreligionists were descendants from the few female devils who were left behind when the king of Mecca forced the white devils into Caucasian exile 6,000 years ago. White Muslims are "not true believers,"[36] but pale copies who will escape the destruction but not enter the postapocalyptic world.[37] In time, this dismissal-oriented line of reasoning decreased as contacts with the Muslim world improved. Arab Muslim delegations were received with great esteem by the Messenger, as for instance when the foreign minister of the United Arab Emirates, Ahmed K. Sowaidi, visited the NOI in 1972.[38] Elijah Muhammad invited white Muslims to eat dinner at the Palace and to participate as guests in the Saviour's Day festivities.[39]

This attitude of reconciliation and collaboration necessitated a refurbished mode of explaining the differences of opinion between the two camps. Farrakhan proceeds from a perspective familiar from the intra-Islamic debate between various conservative, modernist, and Islamist tendencies concerning which path God has ordained as traversable in the twentieth century. As will be obvious, white Muslims still cannot count on having a valid ticket reserved for the NOI hereafter, but the arguments are now refined and Islamized, and a road to redemption is cleared by offering orthodox Muslims an opportunity to respond as Bilal calls humanity back to God.

In matters of doctrine, the orthodox Muslims and the NOI follow routes running in directions disparate enough to rule out the possibility that both travel the same road. One of them must have left the straight path and must therefore change or die. Farrakhan asserts that the Nation has "a superior guidance" through "the hidden Ones," or "the hidden Imams,"

Master Farad Muhammad and Elijah the Messiah.[40] "We see ourselves as being directly guided by Allah," Farrakhan said. "This is why we do not accept the guidance of the scholars of the old world of Islam. They must be reformed. They must be guided back to the right path."[41] As do many Muslim modernist and Islamist ideologues,[42] Farrakhan argues that the traditional Islamic position of favoring the implementation of Islam in state and society through a blind and unconditional imitation (taqlid) of the past, obviously has led to internal stagnation and decline. If religion does not evolve in step with the evolution of society, it ceases being a useful guide and becomes hampering and oppressive instead. "The Islamic world has degenerated," Farrakhan argues. Who are they, trying to teach the NOI true Islam? They should better take a closer look at themselves.[43] The very condition of the Muslim world proves that its authorities have drifted far astray. In addition to the poverty, exploitation, and racism poisoning life in the traditional Islamic heartland, the Muslim world is divided into a large number of warring states and sects. Today, Farrakhan charges, you find internal Muslim strife with "Sunni, Shia, Hanafi, Sufi, killing each other," a situation that stands in sharp contrast to what was preached and realized by the Prophet: the believers' unity as a reflection of God's unity.[44]

The traditional Islamic reliance on the hadith is taken as another example of contemporary Muslim deviation from the straight path: "Muslims have raised the hadith and made it equal to the Qur'an. Wrong brothers, that's why we deviated. We've taken our doctors of law for lords besides Allah."[45] Muslim scholars may denounce the NOI teaching that Master Muhammad is God in person as shirk (polytheism, idolatry), but in reality it is they who deserve to be criticized, Farrakhan exclaimed in anger: "The Muslim world bows to America, and you know she is an infidel—and go charge me with shirk! Religious hypocrisy! You bow to America!"[46] The criticism voiced within the ranks of the ulama should come as no surprise, Farrakhan argues, as "some of the scholars are devils" who "study the faith to cause people to deviate."[47] Their kind have caused "the human family to fall into a state of spiritual darkness, yet claiming God." "Come on Muslims," Farrakhan said, "I don't care how many prayers you make, you are as far away from the life of God as the sun is from the earth."[48] Final Call Middle East correspondent Ali Baghdadi takes a similar position, writing that "the majority of so-called Ulema . . . violate the principles of Islam that they espouse. . . . They are motivated by personal gains and interests and not religious and moral convictions."[49]

God's foreknowledge of the internal decline and corruption that were to appear within the Eastern community of believers made him reveal to the Prophet Muhammad that a necessary future renewal was ordained to come from a faraway land. In the latter days, Muhammad ibn Abdullah said in a hadith, "the Sun of Islam will rise in the West." Another tradition specifies the identity of those given the honor of realizing the divine scheme. The prophet Muhammad said, "I heard the footsteps of Bilal going into Paradise ahead of my own." The interpretation of this hadith is unambiguous, Farrakhan says, as Muhammad ibn Abdullah "didn't mean his own personal footsteps. He was white. He was an Arab. And he was saying that it is the Blacks who are going to lead the Arab world back to the faith that they had forsaken, and lead them into the Paradise their God promised to them by the prophet Muhammad (Peace Be Upon Him) and the Quran."[50] The scholars of the Muslim world know that renewal is an unavoidable necessity but have, Farrakhan asserts, difficulties in accepting leadership from the African American. "They want Islam to come from white people and not from black people, and then if it comes from black people those black people must be under their control."[51] The Prophet Muhammad, knowing that a racist element would block clear sight in the latter days, advised those future white Muslims in a hadith: "You should accept wisdom and leadership even if it comes from one whose skin is black as soot and whose hair is like dried raisins."

Some mainstream Arab Muslims, uncomfortable with facing a situation in which racial prejudice was reversed and would negatively affect them, fiercely condemn Farrakhan for being "a black racist" and introducing color into Islam. Acknowledging the criticism, Farrakhan agrees that Islam does not teach color, but says that Muslims do.[52] Given the racism prevalent in Muslim society for centuries,[53] the sudden assurance of the multiracial brotherhood of Islam is brushed aside as hypocritical lies, impressing no one.[54] Farrakhan claims that the time has come for a test in which mere lip service will not do: "You Muslims who have problems with Black people, what would you do if the Mahdi was in fact Black? Would you handle it? Would your latent or dominant racism stop you from accepting your salvation? That is the greatest trial of all for the whole world. Can you accept Mahdi and Messiah as Black people? If you can't, then you go out with this world as it goes out."[55] Black world hegemony as a future possibility has been envisioned by at least one white Muslim. This Muslim revolutionary, who himself has chosen a direction leading to confrontation with the mainstream scholars of Islam, is Libya's Mu'ammar al-Qadhdhafi, who for a long time has given the NOI both financial and moral support.

Qadhdhafi and the Third Universal Theory   Few contemporary Muslims have as dubious a reputation in America as "the brother-leader" of the Green Jamahiriya Revolution. Branded the "mad dog of the Middle East" by President Reagan, Qadhdhafi is made out to be the evil of Islam personified. The media's misrepresentation of Qadhdhafi necessitates a short background delineation of his religio-political thoughts and deeds before an account for the Libyan cooperation with the NOI is given.[56]

When Libya attained independence on Christmas Eve, 1951, a new state without historical precedent came into existence. Libya is geographically a United Nations General Assembly–directed agglomeration of three fringe areas, or in Bearman's words a "by-product" left over from "the European encirclement of surrounding African territories."[57] Tripolitania in the west historically and culturally belongs with Maghreb, Cyrenaica in the east with Egypt, and Fezzan in the south with southern Algeria and Sahel. This huge, residual, 94 percent desert territory, measures roughly one-fifth the size of the United States but has a low density of population, with approximately one million citizens in 1951 and 4.3 million in 1992. The concept of citizenship in a unified state administered by a legitimate government was unfamiliar and scarcely comprehensible to the new Libyans. On the contrary, a tradition of opposition and resistance against whichever rulers claimed dominion over the area and its population was deep rooted. None of the imperial powers—the Romans, the Ummayyads, the Abbassids, the Fatimids, the Mamluks, the Ottomans, or the Italians—exercised control over the vast desert interior, but were mainly confined to the coastal citadels. The Italians came the closest to forming a unified jurisdiction over the three territories after their 1911 invasion. During their southbound penetration of the desert they were opposed by experienced Bedouin warriors led by the legendary guerrilla leader Umar Mukthar, whose execution in 1932 marked the end of effective resistance. Full control was, however, still beyond the reach of the Italian colonial regime.

States must sign treaties with other states and the Italian invaders desperately sought after any head of state from whom they could seize sovereignty. They found Idris al-Sanusi, grandson of Muhammad Ali ibn al-Sanusi (Evans Pritchard's "Grand Sanusi," the legendary founder of a revivalist militant Sufi brotherhood, the Sanusiyya),[58] gave him the title of amir, and made a peace agreement.[59] Idris al-Sanusi's collaborationist move jeopardized his influence over the Cyrenaica tribesmen, a development that partly explains why he went into Egyptian exile and, using Egypt as a base, provided support to the desert guerrillas. At the outbreak of the Second World War, al-Sanusi sided with the Allies and formed a battalion mainly composed of warriors from a mighty Bedouin tribe, the Libya. When peace came in 1943, the Sanusiyya exercised influence over Cyrenaica but never achieved a similar status in Tripolitania or Fezzan. Still, as leadership over the latter territories continued to be fragmented, al-Sanusi was the closest figure of indigenous authority to be found, and he became King Idris I in a federal constitutional monarchy established upon independence.

When petroleum was discovered in 1961, one of the world's poorest countries found a route out of misery.[60] Two years later, King Idris I abandoned the federal constitution in favor of a unified monarchical autocracy. The regime of King Idris was marked by social unrest and tribal opposition fueled by the nepotistic, highly unequal redistribution of oil revenues and the monarch's dependence on his Western backers, chiefly England and the United States.

Among those opposed to King Idris I was a young officer, Mu'ammar al-Qadhdhafi, born in 1942 in the Bedouin Berber tribe Qadhidhafa, which lived in the Sirte Desert. Qadhdhafi's family still reside there, and he frequently returns to resume his Bedouin lifestyle.[61] Qadhdhafi's political thoughts must be understood in this context, further, in light of the events of his youth: the creation of Israel in Palestine, Gamal Abd al-Nasser's Arab Nationalist revolution in Egypt in 1952, the FLN liberation struggle in Algeria, and the French nuclear bomb testing in Sahara. In 1963, Qadhdhafi followed the strategy of Nasser, by enrolling in the Benghazi Military Academy, where he one year later formed a secret cell of revolutionaries, the Unionist Free Officers. Ousting King Idris on September 1, 1969, Colonel Qadhdhafi was confident that his action was in the best interests of "the Arab nation," but he had only vague ideas of what to do with the power. The Revolutionary Command Council announced the leitmotiv in the Nasserite slogan, "Liberty, Unity, Socialism."[62]

"Liberty" chiefly meant freedom from foreign domination. The Italian nationals were repatriated and their property confiscated. British Petroleum was nationalized, the other petroleum companies gradually taken over, and the Western military bases, the British base at al-Adem and the American base at Wheelus Field, were closed down.

"Unity" was a call for the creation of a single Pan-Arabian government. As early as September 2, 1969, Nasser's emissary Mohamed Heikal was told that Libya wanted union with Egypt: "Tell President Nasser we made this revolution for him. He can take everything of ours and add it to the rest of the Arab world's resources to be used for the battle."[63] Nasser, Sudanese president Jafaar Numieri, and Qadhdhafi signed the Tripoli Pact, which aimed at a merger of Egypt, Sudan, and Libya, but Nasser's subsequent death in September 1970, thwarted the plans.[64] Still dedicated to Pan-Arabism, Qadhdhafi made a series of agreements aimed at a union, none of which resulted in actual merger: Libya, Egypt, and Syria in 1971 and 1972; Libya and Tunisia in 1974; Libya and Syria in 1980; Libya and Chad in 1981; Libya and Morocco in 1984; Libya and Algeria in 1987; and finally, Libya and Tunisia in 1988.

"Socialism" was not modeled on any of the different Marxist branches. Qadhdhafi is said to have read Castro only "for what he said about how to make a coup, not for guidance on the content or purpose."[65] "By socialism," Qadhdhafi declared on the first day of the revolution, "we mean above all an Islamic socialism. We are a Muslim nation. We shall therefore respect, as commanded in the Quran, the principle of private property, even of hereditary property."[66]

The history of the Libyan revolution has been that of a quest for the implementation of a number of fundamental principles believed to be deeply rooted in Bedouin Arab and Berber tradition. First, the state is considered an alien, utterly repressive institution that ought to be abolished. Second, power must be decentralized and local autonomy guaranteed. Third, Islam is the natural law, and a return to the pristine principles established by God through the Prophet Muhammad is sufficient for realizing social harmony.[67] By the mid-1970s, Qadhdhafi had developed an ideology that clearly departed from his original pro-Nasserite policy in respect to both economics and politics.[68] He formulated his ideology in *The Green Book* or the *Third Universal Theory*,[69] which is believed to be the solution for a humanity suffering under the yoke of the other two competing global systems, capitalism and communism. The *Jamahiriya,* "(populist) society of the masses," envisioned is utopian, describing an ideal future, and should not be confused with present Libyan reality.

The first of three parts in the *Green Book* is entitled "The Solution of the Problem of Democracy: 'The Authority of the People.'" Here, Qadhdhafi intends to prove the fallacy of every existing mode of government and to present his model for true people's power. Parliaments are seen as an undemocratic fraud, as "democracy means the authority of the people and not an authority acting on their behalf."[70] The political party, representing a section of the population with common interests, is "the modern dictatorial instrument" striving for power with which to rule nonmembers.[71] The party is always a minority, relative to the community as a whole, and given the division of power between leaders, members, and voters, the fraudulent principle of representation is multiplied. Proletarian dictatorship is by definition undemocratic and will never reach its alleged aim of creating a classless society as, with the passage of time, characteristics of the defeated classes will reemerge within the victorious working class. Not even plebiscites provide a solution as they deny true participation, reducing the voice of the people to a "yes" or a "no."[72]

The solution, according to Mu'ammar al-Qadhdhafi, is a radical decentralization: "Direct democracy . . . is indisputably the ideal method of government."[73] Implementation of direct democracy necessitates an elaborate, coalitional organization based on small autonomous local units cooperating with other autonomous units in matters of mutual concern. All units combined on a national level form the society's highest authority, "The General Popular Congress," composed of delegates chosen by the local assemblies, women's organizations, trade unions, and student associations. Representation is thus reintroduced but differs from parliamentary democracy in that the delegates only have a mandate to communicate the agreed-on position of the base unit, thereby steering clear reintroducing an institution empowered to make decisions in the name of the people.

In the second part, "The Solution of the Economic Problem," Qadhdhafi argues for the abolishment of "wage-slavery," which would thereby end exploitation without terminating free enterprise. Workers should be partners in self-administered companies and the profit divided into three shares to provide for the coproducers' needs, reinvestment, and community projects.[74] Land cannot be owned as it belongs to the community, including future generations. While "land is no one's property," "everyone has the right to use it, to benefit from it by working, farming or pasturing."[75] Housing is a need and if someone else exercises control over your need, your freedom is denied. The solution to this problem is granting everyone the right to own his home and simultaneously declaring illegal the holding of real estate for the purpose of renting.[76]

In the third part, "The Social Basis of the Third Universal Theory," Qadhdhafi elaborates on a number of themes relating to man as a social being: family and tribal life, nation and nationalism, women, minorities, art, and sports. Qadhdhafi's thoughts on nationalism, minorities, and blacks have a direct bearing on the NOI's relationship with Libya. Nations, Qadhdhafi believes, are by "nature" and historically, a large family passing through the tribal stage toward evolving into a nation, unified through a web of social bonds between its members. This stands in contrast to states, which are political entities formed for various reasons, all fundamentally nonessential in respect to "nature"; hence, states rest on a shallow foundation compared to the compelling social solidarity of a nation.[77]

Multinational states will rarely survive, as the "natural" aspiration for national independence inevitably will escalate into conflict.[78] Nationalism is for mankind a compelling "law of nature" and is presented by Qadhdhafi as "the genuine and permanent driving force of history."[79] Nationalism as a primary, natural force of man and the struggle for national independence as an expression of nature constitute important elements in the common ground found between Qadhdhafi and Farrakhan. The priority given to the social factor, the bond uniting a family, a tribe, and a nation, is taken to such an extreme for a Muslim ideologist that it exceeds religion. Religions can unite nations under one government, but only temporarily until the social/national factor reasserts itself, tearing apart the monoreligious but multinational society. Equally damaging is a plurality of religions within a nation, making one religion per nation the proper rule, a notion compatible with the NOI thesis that Islam is the religion of the original people, not whites.[80]

Minorities have indispensable "social rights,"[81] and any repressive governmental measure violating these human rights is an act of injustice. The minority's "political and economic problems can only be solved," Qadhdhafi writes, "by the masses in whose hands power, wealth and arms should be placed."[82] Blacks are given a key role in future world history. The consequences of slavery did not end with the Emancipation but have resulted in a mixture of feelings that "constitutes a psychological motivation in the movement of the black race to vengeance and domination."[83] An interesting notion of cyclical time resurfaces in this context when Qadhdhafi proves his case by reference to the "inevitability" of "social historical cycles." The "yellow" dominion was replaced by white hegemony, which will unavoidably give way to black supremacy. The expected empowerment has been temporarily hampered by the blacks' low standard of living and "backward social traditions" but ultimately "the blacks will prevail in the world."[84]

Islamic Reformer and World Transformer, Qadhdhafi's Twin Role   Qadhdhafi avoids explicit references to Islam in the *Green Book,* as the ideology is "universal," transcending religious divisions to embrace all of humanity. Still, the Third Universal Theory is based on Qadhdhafi's vision
of a pristine Islam. In fact, the *Green Book* is presented to Muslims as the
result of *ijtihad,* representing "a secular interpretation of the basic Islamic
principles."[85] Qadhdhafi is said to have been "guided by divine inspiration to formulate the eternal Truths" of the *Green Book.*[86] Qadhdhafi
maintains it to be strategically wise to leave religious references out of the
Green Book "until they [the non-Muslim part of the world's population]
adopt this theory and then we will tell them that this is what Quran ruled
and this is Islam. We will find that they will become Muslims, saying if
this is Islam, then we are Muslims."[87] Mu'ammar al-Qadhdhafi asserts his
policy to be the genuine representation of divine intention in a setting
that is scarcely better than the Arabic epoch of *jahiliyya.* Internal factors
such as the conservative *ulama*'s blind emulation of the past and corrupt
Muslim regimes, combined with external factors such as "the Western
Crusader-Zionist conspiracy," have caused a process of degeneration.

The Libyan revolution of September 1, 1969, marks the dawn of a hopeful new beginning as is indicated by the official term for the takeover: *al-
Fath,* "victory or opening." *Al-Fath* is a key concept bursting with meaning; the first surah of the Qur'an, or opening chapter of the miracle, is
al-Fath; the first transtribal wars of conquest that victoriously opened up
the way for Islam are known as *al-Fath.* Used by Qadhdhafi, the concept
signals a repetition of the Prophet Muhammad's undertakings, a reopening to the way of the golden age.

Qadhdhafi assumes the role of a *mujeddid,* a reformer or reviver destined to guide the Muslim world back to the straight path. Renewal implies a return to the roots, and Qadhdhafi's approach is radical indeed, removing a number of central Islamic traditions as alien, post-Muhammad
innovations. Repudiating all governmental systems in Muslim history,
from the khalifates and sultanates to monarchies and republics, Qadhdhafi upholds the ideal model established through the Prophet Muhammad, which is said to have been reinstated with the Libyan *Jamahiriya.* In
Qur'an 42:38, God decrees "mutual consultation" (*shura*), interpreted as
equal rights of decision, to be the primary principle of Islamic government. In a modern society, Qadhdhafi says, the one viable "application of
the Shura Principle" is the system of direct democracy set forth in the
Green Book.[88] As the implementation of an Islamic government is or-

dained by God, all Muslims are duty bound to transform their societies in accordance with Libya's political system of federated popular congresses.

When the *Jamahiriya* phase was announced on the 1977 anniversary of the birth of the Prophet Muhammad, Qadhdhafi declared the *Sharia* to be Libya's law and the Qur'an its constitution, boldly asserting that Libya is the first country to implement a true Islamic legal system in the modern era.[89] Previous attempts, such as the one made by Saudi Arabia, are disqualified not in the least because of the legal status ascribed to the hadith. In mainstream Sunni Islam, the corpus of traditions is the second source for *Sharia,* and quantitatively the largest. This has historically been a means of manipulation and could very likely be misused by unjust rulers again, Qadhdhafi argues: "The problem is that we have before us hundreds of thousands of Ahadith that were modified . . . by the rulers. Now it is possible that the Saudi Arabians may make up a hadith in order to justify their dissolute life, gold, silver and wealth."[90] Due to the fact that the authenticity of the traditions can be questioned, Qadhdhafi takes a "Protestant" position, insisting that Muslims go back to the Qur'an alone.[91] Disregarding the hadith and advocating a return to the divine revelation is actually following the sunna of the prophet who never relied on the traditions as a source for guidance besides God: "We want to go back to the Original Islam," Qadhdhafi said, as it was before the post-prophetic "struggle for power . . . which produced the forged *Hadith* and split up the religion into various sects."[92] Far from taking a literalist approach to the Qur'an as the *Sharia* of the country, Qadhdhafi stresses the need for *ijtihad* if its eternal principles are to be properly applied in a modern society.[93] Two examples will be sufficient for illustrating the approach taken by Qadhdhafi: his view on the traditions of polygamy and *zakat.*

Qur'an 4:3 states that if a believer fears that (female) orphans will be unprovided for, then he should marry two, three, or four women, on the condition that they will be treated equally. This does not, Qadhdhafi argues, establish polygamy as the norm. It was a strategy for securing financial and social security in a kinship-based tribal society. Today, orphans and widows will be provided for by the welfare state, thus making polygamy outdated and establishing monogamy as the norm. This common modernist approach is taken one step further by Qadhdhafi, who argues that "if man is allowed more than one wife, then the woman must also have the right of more than one husband."[94]

Zakat proves social justice to be an Islamic imperative. The editorial board of the *Islamic Call* monthly declares that Islam "does not accept that wealth be monopolized by a few while the majority suffers from poverty and deprivation."[95] *Zakat* is a call for the expropriation of capitalist fortunes and equal redistribution of wealth, constituting the divinely ordained base for the Islamic socialism delineated in the second part of the *Green Book.* "The Quran," Qadhdhafi asserts, "advocated socialism long before Marx and Lenin," and is far better qualified to establish freedom, justice, and equality than a godless communism.[96]

The open-minded attitude toward conventional Islamic traditions is taken to such an extreme by Qadhdhafi as to disqualify the *hijra* as the beginning of the Muslim calendar. The actual *hijra* of the Prophet did not take place on 1 Muharram, Qadhdhafi correctly notes, but two and a half months later. Instead, the Muslim calendar should properly start with June 8, 632, the date of the Prophet's death, as this marks a new era, in which mankind is mature enough not to require that additional prophets be sent by God. In 1978, Qadhdhafi announced the introduction of a new calendar dating from the death of the Prophet (D.P.), thereby placing Libya ten solar years behind the rest of the Muslim world.[97]

The frequent breaks with tradition have elicited opposition from both the traditionalist *ulama* and Islamist movements. Challenging the scholars in 1978, Qadhdhafi called for an "Islamic revolution" and urged his followers to "seize the Mosques," arguing that the people were more qualified to interpret Islam than the reactionary *ulama.*[98] This Islamist camp represents the single most potent opponent against the regime of Qadhdhafi, who advocates an alternative vision of political Islam and underground activism. Islamist movements such as the Muslim Brotherhood are consequently sharply condemned by Mu'ammar al-Qadhdhafi as "traitors of Muslims" and "nothing but a colonial and Zionist tool" that must be routed "before it destroys Islam."[99] This militant attitude is a hallmark of Qadhdhafi, integral to his vision of obedience to God. A Muslim submits to no one but God, and as Islam is a religion of practice this is a call for "freedom and liberation and for revolting against any form of oppression and dependence to any force," making global revolutionary activism a religious duty.[100]

For the promotion of Qadhdhafi's Islamic vision, the World Islamic Call Society was established in 1970 with headquarters located in Tripoli. The society supports missionary activities (*dawa*) and establishes Islamic society centers all over the world. It publishes magazines, such as the monthly *Risalat Al-Jihad,* finances mosque construction, organizes

Muslim world meetings and interfaith seminars, and encourages Islamic self-determination wherever Muslims face hardship.[101] Qadhdhafi denounced Muslim dependence on either of the two superpowers of the Cold War and has supported Islamic liberation movements operating against regimes backed by the United States, as well as the Soviet Union, such as the Muslim guerrillas of Burma, Thailand, the Philippines, and Afghanistan.

Giving precedence to orthopraxy over orthodoxy, Qadhdhafi is convinced that revolutionaries the world over, despite ideological and/or religious differences, need to cooperate. In 1981, the World Mathaba was established as a new International of revolutionary forces.[102] Aiming at, on a pragmatic and practical level, coordination of all movements fighting against "imperialism, zionism, racism, reaction and fascism," two world congresses have been held in Libya, in August 1981 and March 1986.[103] In addition, a Pan-Indian conference gathering a large number of representatives from the native communities in the Americas, was organized in 1988 in Tripoli by the World Mathaba.[104] At the second Mathaba conference, delegates were sent from states (among them Cuba, Vietnam, Nicaragua, Uganda, Ghana, and North Korea), liberation movements (such as Farabundo Marti para la Liberación Nacional-Frente Democratico de Revolucionario FMNL-FDR/El Salvador, M 19/Colombia, Irish Republican Army/Northern Ireland, Moro National Liberation Front/the Philippines, African National Congress and Pan-African Congress/South Africa), representatives from the so-called Fourth (or First) World (such as Aborigines/Australia, Maoris/New Zealand, Native Americans/United States and Canada), and minorities (such as African Americans and Hispanics/U.S.A.).

Qadhdhafi calls for "the creation of a liberation force for joint combat" against "the common enemy of liberty, peace and progress," which is "led by the USA."[105] The idea of having the United States fighting on a hundred fronts explains the key role assigned to the American dissidents. African Americans are considered to be among the most potentially explosive groups, whose most important spokesperson is held to be Minister Louis Farrakhan.

Qadhdhafi and the Nation of Islam The flexible modernist view on Islamic doctrines contributes in part to Qadhdhafi's tolerant attitude regarding the deviating features of the NOI creed. Qadhdhafi has for many years been the Nation's most prominent supporters in the Islamic heartland and has regularly assisted the NOI whenever the need has arisen. Farrakhan has reciprocated with a steadfast defense of the Libyan revolutionary when he comes under attack from the United States government, and the *Final Call* frequently carries pro-Libyan articles. Although Farrakhan's and Qadhdhafi's visions deviate, there are tenets in common between the NOI policy and the Third Universal Theory, politically, economically, socially, and religiously.[106]

The mutual sympathy and appreciation between the NOI and the Libyan leadership began as a continuation of the friendly relationship that, to the annoyance of the CIA, was established between Elijah Muhammad and Qadhdhafi's first mentor, Gamal abd al-Nasser. Elijah Muhammad had met with Nasser on his first tour in North Africa in 1959. According to the Messenger, Nasser gave him a royal welcome and suggested that he teach in Africa, especially French West Africa, where he could expect to gain a following in the millions. Supplementing his persuasion, Nasser allegedly offered Muhammad a palace, should he agree to establish headquarters on the mother continent.[107] When Nasser died in 1970, the Messenger personally wrote an obituary in *Muhammad Speaks,* declaring that "the Nation of Islam has lost a great friend." He praised Nasser's efforts to industrialize Egypt and his attempts "to help the poor in that area and throughout Africa to do something for themselves, in a modern way."[108]

In 1972, on his second tour in the Muslim world, Elijah Muhammad and a NOI delegation, which included Muhammad Ali, visited Libya as honored guests of state and the Messenger personally met with Qadhdhafi.[109] The NOI participated in the World Islamic Call conference of the same year, represented by Raymond Sharieff, Herbert Muhammad, and John X Ali. According to the Federal Bureau of Investigation, the major Libyan papers carried detailed descriptions of the NOI's progress and called for support of the African American coreligionists by the global Muslim community.[110]

When the New York police force attacked the Harlem Mosque in 1972, Libya was alone among the Muslim countries to officially express its concern. The Libyan consulate sent a letter of support and in Tripoli, the United States chargé d'affaires was called in to receive an official protest from the Libyan government.[111] The "Black brethren of Libya" did not confine themselves to verbal support but also contributed with substantial financial aid. NOI national secretary Abass Rassoull, for instance, received $2,300,000 from the Libyan embassy in Washington, D.C.,[112] and

Libya provided an interest-free loan of $3,000,000 when the NOI later in 1972 purchased what became their national center on Chicago's South Side.[113] "Pleased by the efforts of the Honorable Elijah Muhammad," the Libyan government thereafter reduced the loan and promised further "assistance . . . both financial and educational," including "teachers and books."[114]

Following the reformation at the hands of Imam Warithuddin Muhammad and the subsequent split of the NOI, Libya officially tried to stay neutral. Muhammad Ahmed al-Sharif, director of the World Islamic Call Society, has received Imam Muhammad twice, but in a 1989 interview indicated a far better relationship with Minister Farrakhan and the NOI. Farrakhan by then had been received on three separate occasions and his national representative, Abdul Akbar Muhammad, had been a frequent guest of Libya. The World Islamic Call Society provides the NOI with Qur'ans and other reading materials, as well as financial support for specific NOI programs, such as the prison mission.[115] Less diplomatically, Bahir Ali Baesho of the World Mathaba denounced the policy shift initiated by Imam Muhammad. The new regime turned the AMM into "a mainstream movement, more interested in preserving the United States than uplifting the African American Nation."[116] In a similar vein, other Libyan officials expressed more unequivocal support for the work of Minister Farrakhan as compared to the policy of Imam Muhammad,[117] and from the 1980s onward, links of mutual solidarity and cooperation were forged. These links are of two kinds, financial and religio-political, with the former being motivated by the latter. Besides the World Islamic Call Society's support mentioned above, Libya has occasionally tapped its flow of black gold revenues in support of Farrakhan's efforts to rebuild the Nation of Islam. "We've came back," Farrakhan stated, "by the grace of God and the help of Brother Mu'ammar Qadhdhafi. This is why we will always love him, admire and respect him and stand up and speak on his behalf."[118]

Compared with the United States's foreign aid to friendly African organizations or governments, American churches' financial support of Christian missions in Africa, or U.S. companies' joint ventures with Libya, the Libyan aid to their black Muslim compatriots in America has been a drop in the ocean. Yet, when "news" of any Libyan assistance has been "exposed" by the media—as for example in May 1985, when the NOI accepted a $5 million interest-free loan for investment in its black enterprising program[119]—it has been presented as a scandal. Less public attention has been focused on the other, and in the author's opinion more interesting, field of solidarity, the religio-political.

The *Final Call* frequently carries articles on Libya, describing the comparative benefits of a Muslim revolutionary society. Libyan advancements in the fields of economics, human rights, and education are highlighted, and the Libyan perspective on the various issues of conflict with the United States is presented to counterbalance the negative image portrayed by mainstream American media.

Besides media coverage, the NOI participates in different religious, political, and academic conferences organized by Libyan institutions. In his contribution to the 1983 "First International Symposium on the Thought of Muammar Al Qathafi," held in Benghazi, Libya, Maleek Rashadeen (formerly known as Harold X) of the NOI praised Qadhdhafi for reaching the same "prophetic" conclusion as Elijah Muhammad and Louis Farrakhan, describing the future role of blacks as "the cornerstone of God for his new social, economic, political and divine order." Rashadeen then advanced his thesis by identifying a possible internal agent for the downfall of the United States: "Imagine 70% of America's army made up by well-trained, dissatisfied, angry black men and women. . . . America is definitely going to fight a major world war outside, with a rebelling black and white army and revolution inside her borders."[120] Qadhdhafi latched on to this idea, which reappeared in a direct appeal aired by satellite to the NOI Saviour's Day convention, held in Chicago in February 1985, and relayed to NOI mosques all over the United States. The participation of the Libyan revolutionary enhanced the prestige of Minister Farrakhan as the agent for radical change in black America. Presenting Qadhdhafi as "a freedom struggler who makes his resources available to the cause of armed [revolutionary] struggle all over the world," Farrakhan stressed what a unique opportunity this was, to meet with and listen to a man who is otherwise deliberately presented with a deformed image by the media of the common enemy.[121]

In his address, Qadhdhafi claimed that black America was an "extension" of their common homeland, "our mighty continent Africa," present in America long before the whites arrived and with a just claim to priority and power. Qadhdhafi urged the African Americans to form an alliance with the Native Americans and fight for independence. Focusing on the estimated 400,000 black soldiers enrolled in the United States Army, Qadhdhafi drew attention to the possibility of directing a decisive blow against the American government: "this number is enough to create a strong army for you . . . to defeat your enemy." Hailing Farrakhan as "a gift from God" raised "to lead this battle to the final emancipation," Qadh-dhafi promised assistance from the Libyan government: "We support you to create [an] independent state, to create [an] independent black army. We are ready to train you [and] to give you arms, because your cause is [a] just cause."[122] Qadhdhafi's call for a black military insurrection made headlines in American media[123] and was denounced as "outrageous" by White House spokesman Larry Speaks.[124]

Farrakhan said he was perfectly aware of the anger he provoked by inviting Qadhdhafi to speak, but added that he did not care: "You were angry with me before I brought him." And to those who accuse Qadhdhafi of terrorism, Farrakhan said, "Terrorism like beauty is in the eyes of the beholder. When Jesus comes here, he's gonna terrorize you too."[125] This does not, however, signify that Farrakhan complies with Qadhdhafi's call to arms. Although Qadhdhafi's plea for an armed black mutiny was inspired by NOI spokesman Maleek Rashadeen, Farrakhan dismissed the idea as unrealistic. Qadhdhafi lacks a full understanding of the American scene, Farrakhan said, and emphasized that the Nation is "not bereft of ideas and strategies" for its "own liberation": "We don't need nobody outside of us to tell us how to win the fight. . . . Qadhdhafi can't guide us. We know this terrain, and we know the enemy and we know the time. . . . My Brother [Qadhdhafi] is a revolutionary and I told him that I am one too, but my revolution has to be brought about by this book, the Quran, and not by buying weapons. Because I can't out-weapon the weaponman, see, and if I start arming the Brothers the government will come down on us instantaneously."[126] There are neither any positive indications that arms have been supplied, nor evidence that Libyan-organized military training of the NOI soldiers actually has taken place. Still, the NOI's link with Libya was the focus of "the most ambitious of the CIA's domestic intelligence gathering projects," called CHAOS,[127] and the FBI allegedly tried to ensnare Farrakhan on charges of a terrorist connection between him and Qadhdhafi. In 1987, Imam Malik and four soldiers in his notorious Chicago black Muslim street gang, the El Rukn (formerly the Black Stone Rangers), were arrested for plans to commit terrorist acts in the United States on behalf of Qadhdhafi.[128] Branded by the Chicago police and media as a drug-trafficking gang of black street fighters, the El Rukn view themselves as a militant black nationalist Muslim advance guard. Though primarily based on the teachings of Noble Drew Ali and the Moorish Science Temple, the El Rukn has a working relationship with the

NOI. The name El Rukn was believed to be Arabic for "black stone," alluding both to the Kaaban symbol for the covenant between God and his people and to the rejected stone becoming the head of the corner, mentioned in Acts 4:11. Since the 1960s, the El Rukn (then the Black Stone Rangers) has had the double reputation of being the most ferocious, violence-prone gang in Chicago and also a black nationalist youth movement working for community improvement.[129] Among other things, the El Rukn imposed a ban on crack cocaine in Chicago, thereby making the city relatively free from the crystal plague until their leaders were imprisoned, after which Chicago experienced the same kind of crack epidemic as other cities.[130]

On July 31, 1987, the police raided the El Rukn's mosque on the South Side of Chicago and confiscated an entire arsenal including an antitank rocket.[131] The prosecution argued that two of the defendants had traveled to Libya in 1986 and arranged a deal with Qadhdhafi to supply the El Rukn with arms and $2.5 million in return for terrorist acts.[132] While in federal correctional facilities in downtown Chicago awaiting sentencing, the El Rukn brethren were, according to Minister Farrakhan, approached by federal agent Joe Louis. He allegedly offered them lighter sentences in return for testifying that Farrakhan was part of the 1986 El Rukn–Libyan deal and that they were to report back to the minister and be paid through him upon completing any terrorist acts.[133] The El Rukns, who reportedly refused the offer,[134] argued in vain that the case should be dismissed as it was built on COINTELPRO-style FBI-fabricated evidence,[135] and Imam Malik was convicted on all forty-nine counts of conspiracy and weapon possession.[136]

Minister Farrakhan actually did travel to Libya in 1986, defying President Reagan's executive order forbidding United States citizens to visit the Libyan *Jamahiriya*. Farrakhan participated in the second Mathaba Congress, held in Tripoli between March 15 and 18. The fact that Farrakhan was given the honor of introducing Qadhdhafi before the assembly on the opening day is a clear indication of the importance ascribed to the Nation and its leader for Libya's foreign policy.[137] In his address to the Mathaba Congress, assembled to "create a United Front against the U.S.," Qadhdhafi reiterated the key role of "the 400,000 Blacks who are mobilized in the American Army." He related his 1985 satellite exhortation "to an immediate rebellion" and his hope for a successful approach to the brethren in arms: "American Blacks must, overtly and covertly, appeal constantly to their brothers recruited to the military institution and to the

American police and make them promise to desert these institutions [bringing their arms] and to sabotage them from the interior."[138] In Libya addressing the Mathaba delegates "on behalf of the oppressed Blacks, Indians and Chicanos," Farrakhan stressed the revolutionary potential of the more than fifty million blacks, Native, and Latin Americans "strategically placed in the belly of the beast." If they unite "and link with the struggle of Third World peoples," a decisive blow could decapitate "the head of imperialism" and "bring into existence a new social, political and economic order."[139]

Farrakhan then told the Mathaba Congress of the vision he was given in September 1985, which I partly described in chapter 6. In the vision, he received information of a secret war-planning meeting between President Reagan and his Joint Chiefs of Staff.[140] As events unfolded, Farrakhan began to understand that Libya was the target of the conspiracy and, with the Sixth Fleet in the Gulf of Sirte, he disclosed the revealed plans for a U.S. war on Libya, including a list of bomb targets. Farrakhan added a warning for President Reagan to leave the *Jamahiriya* alone.[141] At a press conference held shortly before his departure, Farrakhan had already warned President Reagan that the NOI would not be silent should the president actually provoke a war. "We will appeal to those oppressed members of the armed forces . . . not to fire a shot against any African country, against any fighter for justice," Farrakhan said, indicating that the black soldiers would be receptive. "Our people refuse today to be the pawn in the hands of military, multinational corporate interests."[142] President Reagan was actually planning for a war on Libya, making detailed plans the very month Farrakhan was given his vision.[143] The Reagan administration's general pretext for aggression against Libya was that Qadhdhafi was a "menace to U.S. interests," not least in his support of militant organizations opposed to U.S.-backed regimes.[144]

The hijacking of TWA Flight 847 to Beirut by Shiite militants, which included the taking of twenty-nine American hostages for seventeen days in June 1985, brought terrorism to the forefront of the American agenda. Although unconnected to Libya, it provoked a presidential speech denouncing five "terrorist states": Iran, Libya, North Korea, Cuba, and Nicaragua.[145] Libya, a country mentioned in Ezekiel, occupied a crucial place in the eschatological drama envisioned by Reagan, who saw the September 1 revolution as "a sign that the day of Armageddon isn't far off. . . . Everything is falling into place. It can't be long now. Ezekiel says that fire and brimstone will be rained upon the enemies of God's people. That must mean that they'll be destroyed by nuclear weapons."[146] Moreover, the North African country was undoubtedly the most easily attacked of Reagan's "terrorist states." In a State Department study published in January 1986, Qadhdhafi was said to use terrorism "as one of the primary instruments of his foreign policy," despite the fact that no factual evidence for this grave accusation was provided.[147] The specific pretext for the American attack on Libya came with the April 5, 1986, bombing of a Berlin discotheque in which one American soldier was killed and sixty persons injured. The Reagan administration blamed the Libyan secret service for the bombing and, claiming self-defense against terrorism, decided to retaliate.[148]

On April 15, 1986, U.S. aircraft hit six main targets in Tripoli and Benghazi, killing thirty-six people according to United States's official figures, or roughly 100 according to journalists based in Tripoli. Officially striking against "terrorist facilities," the actual targets did not correspond to this description but rather to key points in Libya's system of communications and command, including Qadhdhafi's home in Tripoli.[149] The operation, which evidently attempted to kill Qadhdhafi, was in this respect a major intelligence failure, as the Libyan leader was in his Bedouin tent in the Sirte Desert. In the bombing of Qadhdhafi's Tripoli residence, the bedrooms of his family were devastated. His wife, Safia, and three of the couple's children were rushed to the hospital for intensive care. Qadhdhafi's sixteen-month-old adopted baby daughter, Hana, was beyond help and died hours later from brain damage.[150]

This incident focuses on power as a determinant of political concepts. If a relatively powerless state engages in this type of activity, it is termed "terrorism." If a relatively powerful state does the same, it is termed "self-defense" or "a clinical operation." Imagine what would have been said, had the Libyan air force attacked the White House, missing President Reagan but severely injuring his wife, Nancy, leaving one daughter dead and two sons hospitalized. Denouncing the act as "the most expensive assassination attempt in the history of the world," Farrakhan questioned the government's true intentions: "When would white racist Reagan go to war over the killing of a black soldier in Germany? Lying devil!"[151] The Nation of Islam argues the existence of a higher power than the United States administration. Tynetta Muhammad of the NOI assures her readers that the events of April 15, 1986, were properly documented by God and thereby added to the list of crimes committed by the Devil: "Unknowing [sic] to the vast majority of the world's population, there appeared on the day of the battle, in the sky over Libya, the curious sighting of a bluish-green object which was both photographed and fired upon in the aftermath of the United States' terrorist raid on Tripoli. . . . In the secret files of the United States government, such objects are listed as UFOs, or Unidentified Flying Objects. According to the Divine Teachings of the Honorable Elijah Muhammad these spacecrafts are identified and are not coming from outer space. They are the Baby Wheels flying out from a larger Wheel called the Mother's Wheel described in Ezekiel's vision and can be seen at least twice a week."[152] When Farrakhan returned from his eleven-nation tour in June 1986,[153] United States attorney general Edwin Meese called for his arrest for traveling to Libya in violation of President Reagan's executive order.[154] The threat of prosecution was motivated by Farrakhan's outspoken support for and collaboration with Qadhdhafi in a time of escalating conflict between the United States and Libya, making the defiant minister a matter of national security.

The Nation of Islam moved in turn to prevent an arrest by filing suit against President Reagan, Edwin Meese, James Baker, and George Schultz for violation of Minister Farrakhan's rights under the First Amendment to freedom of religion, freedom of speech, and the right to travel.[155] In his welcome home address, Farrakhan denied being defiant, because defiance is an act of rebellion by someone inferior against his superior. Farrakhan said, "I do not recognize Mr. Reagan as my superior. I do not recognize his moral or his legal rights to tell me, a son of Africa, where I can go and where I cannot go. I'm not defying the President. I'm saying to the President, I am a free Black man and I go where I please and I say what I please when I please as I please."[156] The American government never proceeded to put Farrakhan on trial but NOI fears of being victims of a FBI conspiracy soon resurfaced. In 1988, Lewis Meyer argued that Louis Farrakhan was the target of a covert operation, COINTELPRO-style, initiated by the newly established Joint Terrorist Task Force. Meyer acted as defense attorney for black activist Bob Brown, who was imprisoned in connection with the arrest of "the Libyan eight," a ring of alleged agents accused of plotting against the lives of Oliver North and other government officials in retaliation for the murder of Hana Bint Qadhdhafi.[157] "Using a so-called Libyan and/or foreign connection theory," Meyer wrote, "the bureau launched a full scale investigation, surveillance and counter intelligence operation against Minister Louis Farrakhan and the Nation of Islam." Meyer claimed that Arab-looking and -speaking FBI agents were involved in the surveillance, and further held the FBI responsible for orchestrating the Jesse Jackson–Louis Farrakhan controversy that disrupted the primary race in 1984.[158]

In light of earlier FBI activities to disrupt and discredit the Nation of Islam and other black nationalist organizations, as described at length in chapter 4, this is hardly inconceivable. During the Reagan years, a number of spectacular terrorist acts were struck against American or American-allied interests,[159] moving "terrorism" to the forefront of the agenda for the U.S. government and media. Reagan declared "war on terrorism" and focused the confrontation-oriented side of his foreign policy on "terrorist states" as the archenemies of mankind. Islam seemed suddenly at the vanguard of terror; consequently, the link between a vociferous black Islamic dissident who depicted Reagan as the Beast of Revelation and Muammar al Qadhdhafi, who appealed for armed rebellion, could hardly avoid arousing the attention of the Joint Terrorist Task Force.

A series of mirror relationships in which both sides in a bipolar relation of opposition view the other as *the* expression and/or cause of evil was created during this time: Reagan versus Farrakhan, Reagan versus Qadhdhafi, Reagan versus Khomeini, all symbolizing a fundamental opposition between the American and the Islamic way of life. This bipolar opposition was to escalate after the fall of the Berlin Wall and the dismantling of the Soviet Union, and has continued to be a prominent feature of the postmodern era.

During the Reagan years, the number of black converts to Islam rose rapidly in the United States. This process already had begun in the aftermath of the hippie and New Left era, when religion emerged as a trend in alternative America. A great number of black political activists converted, or "returned," to Islam, notably individuals such as LeRoi Jones, who became Amiri Baraka,[160] H. Rap Brown, who became Imam Jamil Abdullah Al-Amin,[161] and Dhoruba Moore, who became Dhoruba Al Mujahid Bin Wahad.[162] As of 1993, African Americans constituted about 42 percent of the Islamic community in the United States, and Islam's appeal as the black man's old-time religion seems to be continually increasing. A number of reasons explain the Islamic upsurge in the black community. Unlike Christianity, Islam is not tainted by the history of Western expansionism and imperialism and is often presented as an "African" religion. In uncertain times, Islam provides stability, fixed norms, family values, and the solidarity of a brotherhood, in addition to being politically correct in growing numbers of African American circles. Most blacks who join the fold of Islam affiliate with mainstream organizations, like the less-politicized Tablighi Jamaat. A few prominent mainstream Islamic organizations with a predominantly African American membership have been established apart from the former American Muslim Mission, notably the Dar ul-Islam movement and its militant offshoot Jama'at al-Fuqra.[163] A significant minority, however, enroll in Islamic black nationalist organizations. The religious differences between the two strains of African American Islam in the past led to mutual denunciations. In January 1985, a confederation of African American Muslim organizations called the National Islamic Assembly (NIA) was established with the intention of bridging the gap between the various black Islamic branches. The diplomacy of the NIA has succeeded beyond expectations to bring black believers together, according to a 1989 interview with Farid Muhammad.[164] "As long as Islam is being taught, there's a unifyin' basis," Minister Khadir Muhammad of the NOI commented. "There is no trouble amongst us as groups, there's no difference amongst us as groups."[165]

The black Islamic nationalist branch is composed of a number of more or less schismatic movements. Besides the Nation of Islam and the Moorish Science Temple(s), three of these organizations deserve attention in this study: the Lost Found Nation of Islam, the Five Percent Nation of Islam, and the Ansaaru Allah Community.

The Lost Found Nation of Islam   Louis Farrakhan was not the sole opponent to the Islamization process initiated by Imam Warithuddin Muhammad. Predating Farrakhan by a few months was a former NOI Laborer named Silis X Muhammad. Alarmed by the rapid dismantling of the Nation and the reevaluation of the former doctrines, including the identities of Master Farad and Elijah Muhammad, Silis came forward on August 21, 1977, declaring a "spiritual war" against the regime of Imam Muhammad.[166] Silis Muhammad personally delivered a letter to Imam Muhammad, offering him a "release" from his mental "prison," caused by the Imam's "insane desire for leadership." In the letter, Silis wrote that he had been ordained to restore the Nation and charged Imam Muhammad for purposefully misinterpreting the doctrine of the second resurrection to legitimize his change of direction. Imam Muhammad was said to be unknowingly used by Allah to cause the fall of the Nation, thereby paving the way for the true agent of prophecy fulfillment: "I have arisen from the grave," Silis declared, "and am thereby living proof of the second resurrection."[167]

Silis Muhammad then moved to Atlanta, Georgia, where he established the headquarters for his splinter organization, The Lost Found Nation of Islam (LFNOI). Despite Silis Muhammad's advantage of being the first to announce the reestablishment of the Nation, his effort was overshadowed when Farrakhan officially broke off relations with Imam Muhammad and refounded the NOI with Chicago headquarters in November 1977. An overwhelming majority of the faithful followers of Elijah Muhammad's original teachings joined up with Farrakhan, although a number of former NOI dignitaries closed ranks with Silis, notably John X Ali, Jeremiah Shabazz, Wali Bahar, and John Muhammad.[168] In the subsequent development of the two competing Nations, Farrakhan's NOI grew rapidly and dwarfed the LFNOI. While the NOI opened mosques and, to a lesser extent, schools all over the United States and began to expand abroad, the LFNOI had only established twenty-one mosques and not one single school by 1992.[169] The NOI points to these facts to demonstrate the relative shortcomings of the LFNOI. NOI Minister-in-training Eddie X wrote to Silis Muhammad, "If you [and not Farrakhan] are the Chosen One, as you obviously contend, then where are your works of comparable worth?"[170]

The leaders of the two Nations both claim to be *the* genuine heir of the legacy of Elijah Muhammad, blaming the other for deviations and unwarranted innovations. Departing from a shared pool of basic ideas, the two Nations developed along disparate tracks, adding religious differences to the initial personal contest for leadership. Silis Muhammad sharply criticized Farrakhan for misrepresenting both Elijah Muhammad and his message on a number of crucial points: the Messiology,[171] the eschatology, the anthropotheology, the interim program, and the relationship with mainstream Islam. As these points of departure all are interrelated, they will be discussed concurrently with an examination of the LFNOI alternative creed.

Silis Muhammad, who claims that Elijah Muhammad died in 1975, advocates an alternative eschatology in tandem with Messiology. According to the LFNOI, the end of the old world has already come, dividing humanity into dual categories of "out-worlders" and "New Worlders,"[172] which consequently makes the hereafter an essentially realized "here now."[173] Only the coming of God in person "held back the destruction of this devil playground in order that every willing Black Son and Daughter might see the Promised Land."[174] Silis Muhammad preaches an alternative version of the Holy Trinity, in which Master Farad Muhammad is identified as "Our Spiritual Father." Master Farad Muhammad met with Elijah Muhammad upon descending from Mecca, situated in "Heaven," in a quest for finding his Nation lost in "Hell." Elijah is said to be the antitype of Mary, mother of the Saviour Jesus.[175] Malik Al-Akram, LFNOI minister in Atlanta, wrote, "Our real Spiritual Father is Master Farad Muhammad who spiritually impregnated our Spiritual Mother, the Honorable Elijah Muhammad, who gave birth to the Body Christ in the person of the Muslim believers and in particular to a special Son, Silis Muhammad."[176] In 1991, the Lost Found Nation of Islam introduced Elijah Muhammad's birthday, October 7, as Mother's Day for the African American community.[177] The Body Christ concept was taken over from the WCIW stage of Imam Muhammad's reformation process (see chapter 5), but was then reinterpreted. Though a Gnostic rationale similar to the NOI's is discernible in the teaching that "God is the Divine Truth in Black People perfected,"[178] the LFNOI creed represents a simplified, somewhat vulgarized version of the Gnostic theme. As is the case in the NOI creed, the LFNOI believes that all blacks have by nature a divine disposition, but whereas Farrakhan argues that the full expression of divinity is a remote possibility under the present conditions, Silis Muhammad claims a fait accompli for himself and his followers. "The reality of God being Man is today accepted," Silis said, referring to himself and the LFNOI as "living proof: GOD IS MAN."[179]

Interesting testimony in this regard comes from a white female, Mrs. Ida Hakim, who is married to a God and has witnessed both in the LFNOI paper *Muhammad Speaks* (not to be confused with the old NOI paper *Mr. Muhammad Speaks*) and before the congregation. "I know that I am the devil by examining myself," Ida Hakim told a Saviour's Day audience in 1991. "I am not a member of the Nation of Islam, nor can I ever qualify to be a member" as the NOI "is for those who have the nature of Islam." She recalled how she "came into Islam through the mercy of a God named Khalid Hakim" who gave her two sons. Silis Muhammad in his mercy has accepted her as "a Muslim by faith," and "to be accepted by God is certainly a great blessing." She says that she looks to her husband "for further knowledge of God" and can therefore "testify that the Black Man is God, Allah, the Victorious, the Beneficent, the Merciful."[180] If all believers are Gods, representing Jesus, one among them is the paramount expression of black divinity. Mustafa Nasir Saleem recalls his first meeting with Silis Muhammad: "It was on this day that I heard the voice of the Lord. It was on this day that I laid my eyes upon the Most Honorable Silis Muhammad. . . . I knew that He was the Lord, the Christ, that Saviour that my mother had prayed for."[181]

The LFNOI teaches that the blessed day when God would dwell on the earth among his people has finally come: the moment that all the previous prophets prayed for is living reality. The community of believers share the unique experience of walking with God, talking with him, and receiving his divine counsel. The gratitude felt for this blessing is captured in the following prayer to Silis Muhammad: "O'Lord! Silis Muhammad! Praised be Thy Holy Name. O'Lord! Great art Thee. Worthy art Thee to be called Praised. Worthy art Thee to be called God, Allah, The Son of a Man. To Thee is due honor, power and glory, and riches untold. Upon Thy head do I place a spiritual crown, as a symbol of Thy wisdom, knowledge and understanding. In Thy right hand a scepter, as a symbol of Thy might, authority and majesty. In Thy left hand a bow, a symbol of Thy strength and courage. Upon a throne shall Thou sit, raised upon the earth at the House of God, in Mecca, Arabia. Worthy art Thou to rule and govern . . . O'Muhammad! O'Silis Muhammad! My Lord, my God, my Saviour, my Redeemer."[182] Infidels, such as Atlanta journalists Larry Copeland and David Goldberg,[183] have accused the saviour and his queen, Harriet Abu Bakr (also known as Misshaki Muhammad)[184] for living a life in luxury at the expense of gullible poor blacks contributing to their upkeep. Yet their present standard of living is but a token of what shall come in the near future. They deserve better accommodation than the Taj Mahal,[185] and their fellow Gods in the LFNOI are also entitled to escape the ghetto, like a collective Cinderella, to a fundamentally different life. Under the direction of Silis Muhammad, a kingdom of gods shall soon be established, where they will wear "amulets of gold and green robes of the finest silk and gold embroidery while reclining upon their thrones."[186]

The Lost Found Nation of Islam teaches that this kingdom will be established by an exodus to the promised land that is rightfully theirs: "Allah has promised you plenty of good food, big beautiful homes that are already built in the East, enough money to share with all 35 million of our people, plenty of oil and solid gold. You have a homeland to return to that you can call home."[187] As for the NOI, this implies the escape from an imminent destruction of the Devil's empire, but the vision is elaborated differently. Only America is to be destroyed, and the Old World, Europe included, will be saved.[188] The believers will not escape the calamity by evacuation on spaceships, but will migrate by airplanes and ships to present-day Saudi Arabia and Egypt, where they will resume power and establish a government of gods.[189]

Silis Muhammad assures his followers that they are gods, and while they may still lack full knowledge of their creative power—how they once created the rivers, the trees, and the animals—they will soon grow into divine wisdom. He claims that one day, they "will be taken to a particular place in Egypt and there taught for about twenty years the knowledge of our entire solar system." They will learn "how we hung the planets out there, how we created the earth," as well as the "difficult" task of "do[ing] the Milky Way."[190] This school, "The Sacred College of Elders," was responsible for the deifying education of Master Farad Muhammad[191] and is roughly the equivalent of the Gnostic esoteric studies offered to the select by the Silent Brotherhood in secret Egyptian temples and caves, according to the teachings of the Moorish Science Temple.

If all blacks are Gods by nature and if the believers already are manifest Gods, why do they need Silis Muhammad? This question, once raised by a skeptic, was answered by the saviour Muhammad with reference to the special, supreme gifts given to him: "You need me for guidance. You need me for a point to rally around and you need me to give you the divine solutions to your salvation. You need me to call upon the Scientists to send the earthquakes, to send the hurricanes, to send the floods. That's why you need me and that's what I can do."[192] The LFNOI shares the NOI's belief in the Mother Ship and the divine circle of scientists but ascribes a less-refined role to the sages, closer to the first NOI teachings of the 1930s than to Minister Farrakhan's present elaboration. Silis Muhammad teaches that all calamities the Devil attributes to natural causes are in fact man-made, produced by the scientists upon demand.[193]

When Elijah Muhammad died, the white devil was relieved, mistaking his death for an "all clear" signal. But, Silis Muhammad exclaimed in triumph, Elijah was "only a forerunner"—the one they should fear is Silis Muhammad himself. Elijah Muhammad was not given the power to ask the scientists for an earthquake or a hurricane to devastate parts of America. That power was given to Silis Muhammad alone, because he has "enough hate" in him to fulfill such a role. Silis Muhammad pledged to prove his destructive capacity to the audience, saying that they can already read in the papers of calamities perpetrated in "California and Texas and when I leave Georgia, you can read about what's taken place here."[194]

The unique power infused in his divine body enables the saviour to make detailed demands with which the devils must comply. Silis "humbly" has asked "the President" and "the Georgia Police Chief," for "all of our followers to be given free passages to Africa from port to port." In addition, he wants "land, sufficient enough for us, a Nation 35 million strong" as well as "farm equipment." Making his demands before a jubilant Atlanta audience, Silis exclaimed, "This is what I would like for you to do, Mr. President, Mr. Georgia police-chief. . . . Now, Mr. Chief, if you don't do it, I am gonna ask the Scientists to flush California, I'm gonna ask the Scientists to let the earthquake come on and split California in half, in two. I'm gonna ask for that! I'm asking for polio to strike your little white babies!"[195] The idea of a partial Armageddon—not engulfing the entire planet and certainly not being ushered in without Silis the Saviour's order and before the community of believers has escaped and safely established themselves in their homeland—ruled out the Gulf War as an initial apocalyptic spark. There is still time for organizing the exodus and it is within this context that the Gulf conflict should be considered. Why are Israel, Saudi Arabia, and the United States allied at the end of the devils' era? It is because all three deceitful nations share an interest in keeping the black gods from what is rightfully theirs: the promised land.[196]

Neither the Jews nor the Arabs have been chosen by God. Both Moses and the Prophet Muhammad of Arabia fatally mistook the people they found for the people they were looking for. In addition, they were in error with regard to timing: no prophet was supposed to come to the chosen people before the coming of God.[197] The Jews have perpetrated the greatest lie in modern times, claiming descent from Abraham through Isaac and Jacob and fabricating evidence to support their false claim of having been in Egyptian bondage.[198] "The true history of the Jewish people confirms that they were never in Egypt as slaves,"[199] Silis wrote. The Jews are not from Abraham's seed, but from Lithuania. Due to Moses' error in teaching these devils, they migrated east to find the land he mistakenly promised them. After World War II, the Jews, fully aware that they were impostors, went to the United Nations, which allowed itself to be fooled by this shameless hoax and gave them a homeland that is not theirs.[200]

The Arabs, in a similarly fraudulent claim, trace their genealogy back to Ismael, while in fact "the Arab nation was born through Isaac's offspring, not Ishmael's offspring."[201] Ismael, builder of Kaaba and holy king of Mecca, is of the original people, thus making the Blackman in America Ismael's seed. Some Arabs from the seed of Easau, the lineage from which Master Farad Muhammad was to come, went to Mecca, but only as guests of Ismael, and are therefore not entitled to the land.[202] The Saudi Arabians know this, and their desperate, greedy clinging to riches that do not belong to them is the reason for the Saudi ruling family's efforts to "keep us [the Blackman] from the knowledge of ourselves and pour millions of dollars into Black neighborhoods in America to promote [ungodly] orthodox Islam."[203] The wealth of Egypt and Saudi Arabia is the property of the African American: "Since our People are God's Chosen People we are entitled to the land, gold, oil, diamonds and big beautiful homes in our Original Homeland that Allah promised us."[204]

Calling for "reparations," the LFNOI has established a "war chest" to finance a petition before the International Court of Justice of the United Nations.[205] A National Commission for Reparations composed of lawyers has been set up, with the express goal of having the United Nations force the United States government into giving the African Americans "gold, land, equipment and machinery and other forms of compensation."[206] The call for reparations has support within the black community and is voiced in different ways by a wide range of black leaders, from Farrakhan to congressman John Conyers. They generally point to the compensation paid by Germany to the Jews and the land given them by the United Nations, as well as the reparations paid by the U.S. government to the Native Americans and Japanese Americans.

The LFNOI, while awaiting the result of these demands, moved to recreate an independent black community. Compared to the NOI, the accomplishments in this field are modest, but are ascribed great importance. In 1991, the LFNOI bought a twenty-acre "prime residential" lot in Fulton County, Atlanta, with money collected or earned by the sale of LFNOI-produced bean pies and *Muhammad Speaks.* This land acquisition is viewed as a first step in "Project Exodus," the creation of a separate all-black Muslim community, called the New Mecca. In February 1992, the pioneer settlers held an open house "to celebrate this historical event," a "milestone in the Nation's history," and plans for further housing, industry, and business developments in New Mecca were disclosed.[207]

Project Exodus and the demand for tax exemptions until reparations have been paid are but provisional measures taken while the LFNOI awaits the return to the black Muslim homeland. The real exodus will take place any day now, as the prophecies of Revelation have been fulfilled. The Book of Revelation describes the rise, fall, and resurrection of the Nation, a history in which all the principal black Muslim actors have played their prescribed role. Master Farad Muhammad is God, the Father, and the Woman with the Child is Elijah Muhammad bearing Silis the Saviour. Threatening the woman and child are two dreadful beasts. The first Beast, or the Anti-Christ, is identified as Imam Warithuddin Muhammad, "who ordered the books and writings of the Last Messenger of Allah brought to the Temple where they may be destroyed and that the Truth would be forgotten."[208] Imam Muhammad rejected "the idea that the Black Man is God"; denied Elijah's role as Messenger; refuted Master Farad as God and conspired "with Saudi Arabia which wishes to keep you blind to the Truth."[209]

Following the first Beast is a second, which would, according to Revelation 13, have the appearance of a lamb, speak like a dragon, and deceive them all with his power and miracles and create a great following before being destroyed by the real Lamb. According to Silis Muhammad, this description fits Minister Louis Farrakhan Muhammad perfectly: Farrakhan appeared after the first Beast, is "looked upon by a number of his followers as being the Messiah,"[210] and speaks a draconian mixture of truth and falsehood, not totally rejecting but neither completely accepting the idea that God is man, while weaving in the false teachings of orthodox Islam in true Islam as taught by the Woman. He performs miracles and displays great power, causing tens of thousands to flock when he appears to lecture, and has temporarily managed to deceive the majority of black Muslims.[211] Silis Muhammad circulated his charge against Farrakhan, identifying him as the second Beast as well as Aaron, here interpreted as a false prophet, a cunning disbeliever, who denied Moses (Elijah Muhammad) and his God (Master Farad Muhammad), in numerous letters sent to the cadre of NOI ministers.[212]

Besides attempts from Farrakhan and several of his ministers to refute this theological theory by an exchange of correspondence with Silis Muhammad, this caused an outcry, not surprisingly, for revenge against the slanderer. Several FOI soldiers in Chicago indicated to the author that Silis Muhammad's blasphemous defamation was unforgivable and that his days were numbered. On their side, the LFNOI spoke of a "spiritual cold war" and believed that Farrakhan feared for his life.[213] As rumors of an internal black jihad escalated, a sudden change in direction took place in 1992. Abdul Allah Muhammad (formerly known as John Shabazz), a columnist at the *Final Call,* denounced David Goldberg, the journalist mentioned above, and proposed that the attack against Silis Muhammad was indirectly aimed at Farrakhan. Silis Muhammad, who during his first period in the old NOI was enrolled under the ministry of John Shabazz, thanked his "first teacher" at length. He called for a joint defense in the future and assured the NOI that "we are all one Nation of Islam."[214] The truce bid was appreciated by Minister Farrakhan, who in an open letter of

February 7, 1994, invited Silis Muhammad to the NOI Saviour's Day convention, assuring that he would be "treated with the courtesy and love that is demonstrative of our brotherhood," and expressing his hope that the wounds would heal so "that we may become once again a united Nation of Islam."[215] Though Silis himself declined the offer, the LFNOI was represented by his wife Harriet Abu Bakr, who in her address said that her husband wanted Minister Farrakhan to be the voice to speak before the United Nations on the behalf of black people demanding reparations.[216] The outcome of this sudden switch toward a reconciliation will have to await future judgment. Secret talks of an eventual merger or at least a truce between the two Nations have reportedly been undertaken. This has been done before to no avail. Silis states that he met with Farrakhan in the fall of 1977 and in January 1989, the latter occasion predating the "Farrakhan is a false prophet" charge related above.

Unification implies a number of harmonizing measures that are difficult to accomplish: the excesses of character assassination will have to be forgiven, the religious differences will either have to be bridged or a hitherto unprecedented pluralism allowed, and, above all, either Silis Muhammad or Louis Farrakhan will have to submit to the leadership of the other. Most likely, the result will be a tactical cease-fire similar to the agreement reached between Imam Warithuddin and Minister Farrakhan.

In contrast to Louis Farrakhan and the Nation of Islam, the LFNOI has not even partly engaged in an accommodating process toward mainstream Islam.[217] They "are too intelligent to accept the untruths" of the "orthodox teaching about Muhammad of 1400 years ago being the last or final messenger." Conventional Islam belongs to the realm of falsehood that disappears with the New World: "Elijah Muhammad closed the door to the old world and the old ways of Islam."[218] Point three of the new declaration of faith adopted by the LFNOI states: "we believe both the Bible and the Holy Quran only take us up to the general Resurrection. We believe this is the day of the general Resurrection and a new Book is being revealed."[219] Unfortunately, the author does not have access to this new holy book that supersedes the Qur'an. Parts of this have been disclosed in *Muhammad Speaks,* and the new Revelation seems to replace the central message of the Qur'an, saying, "The Son of Man is God and besides Him, there is no God."[220] The core of the LFNOI creed is thus emphasized as the belief in *Theos Antropos* (or, "the Divinity of Man"), a theme that also pervades the teachings of the NOI and that reappears in the creed of the next schismatic black Muslim movement to be described.

The Five Percent Nation of Islam   The Five Percenters were established by Father Allah (born Clarence Smith on February 21, 1928) in 1963 after a schism with the leaders of NOI Temple #7.[221] He had enrolled as Clarence 13X upon his return from two years of service in the United States Army in the Korean War.[222] A gifted philosopher, Clarence 13X began questioning the divinity of Master Farad Muhammad, as he was not a black man. Reprimanded for distortional teachings, Clarence 13X left the Nation of Islam and set up his own group. The name, Five Percenters, is derived from the NOI lesson that teaches that 85 percent of the African Americans are still asleep. Ten percent have gained knowledge but sold out to the white devils, that is, the "talented tenth" of W. E. B. Du Bois reevaluated. Five percent are the poor righteous teachers, missioned to preach the redeeming black Gnosis through which Lazarus will awake. Another feature of the Five Percenters is an absence of formal leadership and a direct democratic system of decision-making. If all black men are gods, how can a hierarchical structure such as the NOI's be justified? Instead, the Five Percenters convene at boroughwide meetings, called parliaments, which provide a democratic forum for the loosely knit network of members.

In June 1969, Father Allah was shot to death by unknown assassins. His earliest followers, a group of nine called the First Nine Born, carried on the teachings in which a leading role was assumed by Justice. In the years to follow, the Five Percenters were feared by the police to be an unruly group of black teenagers renowned for direct actions, such as muggings and bank robberies. In an FBI memo, the Five Percent Nation was said to constitute a "mysterious armed group of Negro youth" who were "prepared to die" fighting white supremacy.[223] Eventually, they obtained recognition as a youth organization and municipal authorities paid for their headquarters, "Allah School in Mecca" in Harlem, until 1988. Initially a New York–based youth group, the Five Percenters had a boom in the late 1980s, with its principal missionaries in the hip-hop movement, and can now be found all over the East Coast, parts of the Midwest, and the greater cities on the West Coast. As rap is discussed in chapter 10, here it will be sufficient to emphasize that the Five Percenters mainly are strong among the urban youth, musicians, artists, teachers, and gang members.

Doctrinally, the difference between the Nation and the Five Percenters is more a matter of degree than principle. Plunging deeper into the black Gnosis than the average NOI member, the male Five Percenter is a "God" and the female an "Earth." Typically, a Five Percenter adopts a name reflecting his or her divinity, like "Supreme Allah," "Born Islam," "Divine Justice," or "Universal God." Influenced by Sufism, Father Allah developed a "divine science" based on the "Supreme Alphabet" and the "Supreme Mathematics," teachings that in turn influenced the evolution of the NOI creed. During Minister Farrakhan's leadership, the former animosity between the two groups has been long since bridged. NOI members view the Five Percenters as philosophy-oriented (although some would say premature) youths, and Five Percenters fully respect Farrakhan, although the NOI's strict rules of conduct and its dress code prevent full-time membership. Five Percenters show up at NOI rallies and Sincere of the Brand Nubian says that Farrakhan is "definitely representing the masses of the people."[224] The *Final Call* reciprocates by carrying sympathetic articles on Five Percenter rap artists, and Farrakhan has frequently stressed the two groups' brotherly unity.

The Nubian Islaamic Hebrews: The Ansaaru Allah Community   For a New York resident or visitor unfamiliar with the black scene, the Ansaaru Allah Community (AAC) stands out as the most eye-catching black Muslim group, due to their dress code and their street-peddling ventures. Since 1978, Ansaaru men have worn long white garments (*jallabiyya*), white loose-fitting pants, a white shawl, and a white turban or crocheted hood, and have carried a staff.[225] Ansaaru women wear a white waist-long cape covering the head and shoulders over a white dress, a long white shirt, and a white face veil. Male members are supposed to quit any job outside the community and most start walking the streets, peddling perfume, oil, and Ansaaru literature and thereby contributing to the everyday street scene.

The Ansaaru Allah Community's headquarters is located in Brooklyn, where their beautiful Ansaar Masjid is situated.[226] Motivated by the example of the prophets, the Ansaars have separated from the unfaithful outer society and live communally, practicing collective ownership of property and goods.[227] Although circles of believers can be found in major cities all over the United States, the Ansaaru Allah Community is mainly an East Coast movement, despite the worldwide following, numbering in millions, claimed by its founder As Sayyid Isa al Haadi al Mahdi.[228]

Data concerning the history of the cult and the biography of its founder differ considerably, depending on whether it is culled from outside critics and scholars or from the cult's own historiography.[229] The following account is based mainly on the group's self-description; conflicting accounts are given in the endnotes.

As Sayyid Isa al Haadi al Mahdi claims to have been born in the Sudan on June 26, 1945, as the son of Al Haadi Abdur Rahman al Mahdi, the grandson of the Mahdi Muhammad Ahmad of Sudan (1845–85). He thereby traces a direct descendancy from the Prophet Muhammad through Ali Ibn Abu Talib and Fatima. Isa's American mother, Faatimah Maryam, was allegedly not accepted by the royal family but was escorted back to the United States where a Massachusetts birth certificate was drawn up. The boy was named Dwight York; the surname is said to come from his mother's previous husband.[230] At the age of seven, Isa was allegedly taken back to live with his family in the Sudan where he mastered his native tongue, Arabic, and was "foretold to possess the light." He returned to the United States, spent his adolescent years in New Jersey, enrolled in Sheikh Daoud's State Street Mosque in Brooklyn, and then returned to Africa to attend universities in the Sudan and Egypt before settling permanently in the United States.[231]

The Ansaaru Allah Community was officially founded on June 26, 1970,[232] an event presented as "the victorious opening of the seventh seal,"[233] whereby "the Aquarian Age" was ushered in.[234] The reason for choosing this date rather than 1967, which is the year Isa established his first Islamic commune, named Ansaar Pure Sufi, or 1969, when they were transformed into the Nubian Islaamic Hebrews,[235] is related to prophecy and the Muslim *mujeddid* tradition, as it was exactly one hundred years after Muhammad Ahmed (whom the AAC regard as the Mahdi) founded his commune in Jazir Abba in the Sudan.[236] As the seventh stamp was unsealed, the Last Day dawned, bringing in the Judgment between the years 2000 and 2030.[237] Isa claims to be the Lamb of Revelation, a *khalifa* of the Sudanese Mahdi,[238] the *Qutb* (axis) of the Universal Order of Love, Sufi Order of the Sons of the Green Light,[239] a divine Supreme Being,[240] an Angel and the Holy Ghost,[241] a Saviour,[242] a *mujeddid* and a Messiah, anointed to be the head of the Body Christ, that is, the Ansaars.[243] His power to heal and perform miracles as well as unravel the hidden divine truth is said to have been given by Allah through al Khidr, the highest of all the angelic beings, known in Christianity as Michael and in Judaism as Melchizedek. Isa traveled to the Sudan in 1973 and met As Sayyid Mahmuwd, who initiated him into the Order of Al Khidr and the Sufi Order of *Khalwatiyya* as preparation for his role as *mujeddid,* and anointed him into Messiahship.[244] The initiation took place at the junction of the two Niles, where he met the archangel al Khidr, the head of the twenty-four Elders of the Revelation and teacher of all the prophets,[245] who became the most important of all the masters who guide the pen and thought of Isa al Mahdi.[246]

As may already be obvious to the reader, the Ansaaru Allah Community differs intrinsically from the black Muslim organizations described above. While the AMM, the LFNOI, and the Five Percenters all have departed from the fold of Elijah Muhammad, the AAC creed is nourished from four principal sources: previous black Muslim doctrines (the Nation of Islam, the Five Percenters, and the Moorish Science Temple), Sufism, the Sudanese Mahdiyya, and Judaism. Isa studied the NOI Lessons, read *Muhammad Speaks,* and discussed with followers of Elijah Muhammad and Clarence 13X during the 1960s and early 1970s.[247] Elijah Muhammad is held in high esteem as "the greatest black man ever to be born in America," but Isa rejects Elijah's position as a prophet, arguing that his true function was to be the herald of Isa al Mahdi.[248] Isa's alternative perspective on Elijah's mission, his objection to the NOI's identifying Master Farad Muhammad as the Mahdi, as well as other less central points of disagreement, added to the tension between the two parties contending for the position as the advance guard for the African American "resurrection." The wheel of animosity accelerated in the 1980s, but stopped short of the holy war that was said to be impending. In 1988, Isa al Mahdi and Minister Farrakhan began a dialogue and decided to focus on their common ground rather than their differences. Isa recalled and destroyed pamphlets attacking the Nation and the heat on the street cooled off. Taken as a whole, Isa argues, the AAC and the NOI combine to make a Nation that will be mightier than ever, religiously, militarily, and economically.[249]

As does the Nation of Islam, the Ansaar teach a specific black Gnosis, combined with white demonology and the necessity for racial solidarity and separation from evil. The doctrinal foundation for these central features of the AAC creed differs, however, from that of the Nation, as it is derived from esoteric Sufi speculation. Isa al Mahdi teaches that the Creation is divided into seven planes or moods of vibrations. The more the speed or rhythm decreases, the more material the reality. Man was created *Ruhw,* a "soul" when he was in *Malakuwt,* the realm of angelic beings. As his vibrations slowed down, he was given an etheric form, or spirit, and as the speed further decreased, he was finally given his physical body.[250] Women were created on the physical plane and given souls from men, placing them one degree below men.[251] The soul in the black man and woman is a spark of Allah, and by praising Allah, he and she will be given a divine light that illuminates the inner heart and helps him and her to communicate with the inner senses.[252] Correlated to the seven planes are the seven seats or chakras of man, whereby man can tune into the spiritual world, or begin ascending back to his origin. He will ultimately rise into "the Bosom of Allah," the "perfected state," where he reaches the union with Allah.[253]

The white devil is the physical offspring of the fallen angels and houses the unholy spirit of the cursed Jinn, but has neither soul nor spark of Allah. As the soul is the source of emotions and controls laws and morals, the white man has neither emotions nor morals and cannot submit to the law of Allah. Like a soulless animal, the evil Canaanite sometimes appears to show emotions and affection but is actually only working on instinct. The cursed race of evil can, like cold-blooded animals, feel no sympathy or love, nor act with consideration to others. As reptiles shed skin, the pale creature has a sensitive skin that peels easily under the rays of the sun.[254] Isa al Mahdi proudly affirms his teachings to be racist, but says that it is not his interpretation: "it is the [explicit] law of the Bible and the Qur'an."[255] Allah himself is a racist and "the Messiah Jesus was also a racist."[256] The prophets were all sent to a specific people: the blacks, who properly should be called "Nubians," as they are the descendants of Noah, through Cush, the father of Nubia. His offspring inhabit the present-day Sudan and became "Hebrews" after the work of the prophet Abraham, whose legacy they were to cultivate.[257] Allah's message is restricted to his people because the cursed race of physical devils is beyond redemption: "There is no such thing as 'good Devils' (CT [Curse Them]) nor will there be anyone to aid this race of Evil beings (the Canaanite—pale man, CH [Curse Him]). They have already been judged as guilty."[258] This conviction runs contrary to the mainstream Islamic doctrine of the global community of believers, transcending all ethnic and racial divisions. Isa al Mahdi is vehemently opposed to orthodox Sunni Islam, especially the version taught by the Saudis. This aversion is due to Saudi Arabia's financial support for a select number of American Muslim organizations that they consider as rightly guided, as well as their claim to lead the Muslim World at the expense of Isa's champion, the Mahdiyya of the Sudan. Isa asserts that the Wahhabi Muslims "are nothing more than communist desert Arab Marxists,"[259] engaged in a "worldwide plot to kill all potential Nubian leaders," as shown by the murder of Malcolm X.[260]

Mainstream Muslims are condemned for hiding the fact that Muhammad and all other prophets were Nubians[261] and for elevating untrustwor-
thy man-made stories, the hadith, to a level on par with the Qur'an.[262]
They are also condemned for placing Muhammad ibn Abdullah above all
other prophets, when they all properly should be held in equal regard[263]
and for preventing the believers from reading all the Scriptures that were
revealed before the Qur'an.[264] The mainstream Muslim argument that the
Torah and the Injil have been tampered with, and therefore reduced in
value, is dismissed by Isa who claims that all Scriptures, the Qur'an
included, have been changed but only to the degree allowed by Allah and
should still be used for guidance.[265] Along with the holy books recognized by mainstream Muslims—the Torah, *Zabor* (Psalms), *Injil,* and the
Qur'an—Isa adds two more, both said to be mentioned by Allah in the
Qur'an: *As Suhuf* (the Pure Pages) consisting of four books, revealed to
the prophets Adam, Seth, Enoch, and Abraham, respectively, and *Al Hikmah* (Wisdom) revealed to the prophet Luqman.[266]

The Pure Pages have been passed down secretly through the generations. Abraham gave them to Ismael, who took them to Egypt where
they were guarded by the ancient esoteric brotherhood. The Pure Pages
were later handed over to Ali Ibn Abu Talib, who brought them to the
Sudan, where they remained until 1973, when they were entrusted to Isa
al Mahdi by his teacher, As Sayyid Mahmuwd. Isa was given the *As Suhuf*
in 1973 and the *Al Hikmah* in 1970, which he has published parts of in his
pamphlets.[267] Isa denounces all previous translations of the Holy Scriptures and poses as the nineteenth translator of the Qur'an. Since the Ansaaru Allah Community, like the NOI, believes the number 19 to be the supreme code of the Qur'an (Isa alleges that Rashid Khalifa adopted Isa's
teachings of the number 19), the claim to be the nineteenth translator implies that his work is as flawless as the code.[268] The translation by Isa is
published with a large number of explanatory remarks added in parentheses, which lends an aura of divine authenticity to what are, in fact, Isa's
interpretations. One example, the translation of Qur'an 6:112, will be sufficient: "And thus have we made for all Prophets an open enemy, human
devils (Satan in human forms), and the Jinn (the evil demons which is
their spirits) who inspire some of them (to devil worship) over others (the
normal Canaanites, pale race of devils) to adorn (make them wealthy) to
say deceptive things (to lie to the whole world and make people believe
they are not the devil in physical form). And if it be the will of your
(Muhammad) sustainer they (the physical devils) would not be able to do

so. (Allah lets the pale race of devil test you) so leave them (don't mix with them) in their fabrication (lies)."[269] The Ansaaru Allah Community, although not being *Shia,* argues that Ali Ibn Abu Talib was the true successor to the Prophet Muhammad, which reduces the three first khalifs recognized by Sunni Muslims to usurpators. Isa al Mahdi follows the line of imams acknowledged by Imamiyya Shiites down to the eleventh imam, Hasan al-Askari, who, according to the AAC, closed the "first cycle" of imams.[270] The second cycle closed with the Seal of Imams, Muhammad Ahmad al Mahdi of the Sudan, who is believed to be "the only true Mahdi" and "the guide for the world."[271] The code confirms his position, as al Mahdi is the nineteenth imam after Ali, and the *Raatib,* the theological work by al Mahdi, is arranged in 4×19 sections.[272]

In the AAC version of the *Shahada* (the first pillar of Islam, or, confession of faith), the Mahdiyya addition is adopted, closing the second part with ". . . the Mahdi Muhammad Ahmad is the Successor to the one sent (Muhammad)."[273] Adherence to Mahdiyya practice, in some instances combined with elements from Judaism, partly explains further deviations from Sunni orthopraxy. The Mahdiyya model of *salat* is adhered to and Isa holds it to be meritorious to read the *Raatib* after the early morning prayer.[274] Although the communal Friday Prayer, *Salat al-Juma,* is not canceled, it is transformed into a preparatory gathering for the observance of the Sabbath, which is regarded as the true and original Islamic day of communal worship.[275]

Zakat is interpreted by the AAC to legitimate the practice of street peddling for adding to the cult's collective assets, allegedly used for propagation of true Islam and the realization of a separate Islamic community in the West.[276] Hajj is recommended, but only for members who "are spiritually ready," and should preferably take place during *Umrah,* the lesser pilgrimage, and not at the greater pilgrimage when the rites are controlled by the ungodly Wahhabis. During hajj, the Ansaars further avoid a number of rites, such as the kissing of the black stone and the stoning of the Devil, which are said to be unwarrantable innovations.[277]

Other practices are derived from the Hebrew part of the AAC identity and rest on Judaist ground, such as the AAC adherence to the dietary laws of Leviticus, the prohibition for male members to trim their hair or shave their beard, and the abolishment of the Muslim ban on alcohol.[278] In addition, Isa has disclosed the secret 100th attribute of Allah to be Yahweh, and holds that its recitation will open the way to paradise.[279]

Besides the claim to being the one Elijah Muhammad came to herald, the single most important source of Isa's legitimacy is his kinship with the royal family of al-Mahdi of the Sudan. Isa frequently displays his genealogical chart, publishes numerous photos from his travels in the Sudan showing himself "reunited" with his true family, and presents colored pictures of himself and al Mahdi, both with a shining aureole.[280]

When the news of Isa's teachings and claims of kinship reached the al-Mahdi family in the Sudan, they were, according to Gutbi M. Ahmed, "furious" and initially "decided to file a legal suite against Isa."[281] The family never pressed charges, however, and in 1978 Sadiq al-Mahdi, prime minister of the Sudan at that time, made his first visit to the Brooklyn Mosque.[282] To the disappointment of Isa's critics, Sadiq expressed delight over finding a vibrant Mahdist following in the West and thus gave the AAC a needed aura of legitimacy.[283] The Ansaars of East and West are still separate entities and even though Isa has shown some readiness to reform his organization after Sudanese suggestions,[284] the AAC is unlikely to be transformed into Mahdiyya proper.

9

Strained Seeds of Abraham:
Is the NOI an Anti-Christian, Anti-Semitic Nazi Cult?

—

Islam shares its theological roots with Judaism and Christianity. All three religions trace their origin to the One True God and his Covenant with Abraham. While Jews and Christians trace their religious tradition through Isaac, the son of Abraham and Sarah, Muslims trace their tradition through Ismael, the son of Abraham and Hagar. Thus, they are all children of Abraham, and Muslims argue that they together form a Judeo-Christian-Islamic tradition, a claim with special political implications in the United States. Jews, Christians, and Muslims pray to the same God, whose will is revealed in Revelation through mainly those same prophets, who preached a similar moral founded on similar divine sanctions against the threat of an approaching apocalypse. The common Abrahamic ground is, however, recurrently obscured by relations of opposition and conflict, and traditional tolerance and coexistence seem far less powerful an image than traditional enmity and exclusive claims.[1] Mutual mistrust is intrinsic to the relations between the Nation of Islam and its Christian and Jewish detractors and contributes to a number of popular NOI as well as anti-NOI themes and related controversies.

The multifaceted and transforming relations between the Nation of Islam and Christianity are the subject of the first part of this chapter. Although the NOI bases a large portion of its teachings on the Bible, it initially viewed Christianity as a slave philosophy, designed to keep the Blackman an ignorant "Negro" on the bottom of society. The NOI thus earned its reputation as an anti-Christian and thereby alien and dangerous body, an opinion that still is heard, despite the changes within both black Islam and Christianity that have transformed the relations between these two sons of Abraham. The Nation of Islam is commonly criticized for propagating a vicious anti-Semitism. Minister Louis Farrakhan is frequently portrayed as a black Hitler, a bigot and hatemonger, thriving on popular prejudice against Jews and Judaism. Related to this constantly repeated accusation is a notion of the NOI as a black Nazi-styled organization, allegedly part of a semisecret, right-wing extremist network. The latter part of this chapter aims at a balanced presentation of the NOI's positions in this regard by piercing through the mist of misunderstanding and incrimination that clouds a better understanding of the NOI.

Christendoom and Crucifiction   As noted in chapter 3, the original teachings delivered by God in the person of Master Farad Muhammad through his last Messenger, Elijah Muhammad, were vehemently opposed to most of the Christianity then taught by mainstream denominations in the United States, not least the black Church. Christianity was portrayed as the leading ideological weapon of white world supremacy, designed to keep humanity from the true knowledge of God and thereby under the rule of the Devil. To a certain extent, the early NOI constructed its doctrinal identity within the black community through a series of negations of Christian elements and conceptions of faith. Christianity, instead of offering salvation and eternal life, "is a curse" to the African American, "full of slavery teaching,"[2] whose sign is death.[3] The Bible was denounced as "The Poison Book," a tainted collection of God's revelations, distorted by the white devils "to make it suit themselves and blind the black man."[4] Operating in a predominantly Christian culture, the Nation still made frequent use of the Bible, which in the early days often was more referred to than the Holy Qur'an, but taught that the Holy Spirit could not be understood without the divine interpretation and proper knowledge of history given by God through his Messenger.

The church, said Messenger Muhammad, fooled the African American into turning the other cheek when attacked, advocating patience in a world of injustice while promised a reward in the afterlife. But there are no gardens of paradise beyond the grave as compensation for the suffering of this world; that is just another of the Devil's hoaxes. Elijah Muhammad declared, "There is no such thing as dying and coming up out of the earth and meeting those who died before you. I say get out of such slavery teachings. It keeps you blind, deaf and dumb to reality. . . . When you are dead, you are DEAD."[5] Heaven and hell are not postmortem destinations but conditions on earth. Hell is when you are enslaved, poor, and deprived of true knowledge of Self and God. Hell is when someone else controls you and your life. The white man enjoys a heavenly affluence in the same world in which the black man endures hell, a situation bound to continue until the curse is lifted. Contrary to the otherworldly interpretation given by the church, the Resurrection and the hereafter also signify what is to be realized here on earth: the awakening of the blacks from their mental death and the transformed world after the approaching battle of Armageddon.[6]

The pagan origin of Christian holidays, such as Christmas, was another theme elaborated by the NOI to create, or recreate, a separate identity. "The Christian holidays," Elijah Muhammad wrote, "are holidays for white people and not for Black People."[7] December 25 is not the birthday of Jesus but of Nimrod, the evil white demon who opposed Moses, which explains why the devils celebrate this day by drinking alcohol and eating swine. The commercially oriented Christmas patron, Santa, hides his true identity in his name. He is Satan, teaching blacks to lie for their children and tricking them into spending their money buying gifts in the white man's stores.[8]

The basic Christian principle of the Trinity is also a falsehood. God is a black man and not a spirit, the Holy Ghost is not an independent entity equal to God, and Jesus is not the biological son of God, but his prophet. Jesus did not die for our sins to save the world, a fact clearly demonstrated by the present conditions on earth. Jesus of Nazareth was not the Saviour, but a sign of one to come. In the sermons of the old NOI, the alternative biography of Jesus was used to reject central Christian doctrines such as the virgin birth, the Crucifixion, and the Resurrection. The following is "the true history of Jesus," as revealed by God in the Person of Master Farad Muhammad to his Last Messenger.[9]

Joseph and Mary went to the same school and fell in love as children, but Mary's father disapproved of them getting married because Joseph was poor and had no future. Joseph married another girl and soon was the father of six. One day, Mary's father went on a three-day business trip, leaving his daughter to care for the family farm. Mary took advantage of this opportunity and called for Joseph to help her out, which he did in more than one respect. After a few months, Mary's father noticed that she was pregnant and was told who was responsible. Joseph, who initially denied being the father, learned from a seer that the child Mary was carrying was a great prophet whose name was included in the Qur'an. Unfortunately, the medium also gave notice of the coming prophet to the authorities, who promptly set up a committee to track down the parents.

As the time for Jesus' birth approached, the committee ordered that all male babies born in that week be killed. Joseph built a hideout for Mary in one of her father's stalls, and the baby was delivered but was only temporarily safe. Joseph decided to send Mary and Jesus to Egypt, and under the cover of a dark cloud, he sneaked them past the patrolling deputies to the camel station. He helped Mary and the child mount a mail camel familiar with the route and told the camel to take the family to Cairo.[10]

In Egypt, Jesus began school at the age of five, and proved to be a talented student. At twelve years of age, Jesus was approached by an old sage who came to teach him how to use the "radio in the head," that is, to receive divine messages and practice mind reading. This knowledge proved useful as Jesus was ordained by God two years later to teach among the devils in southern Europe. The foundations of his divine teaching were freedom, justice, and equality, and he was to warn the devils that their evil behavior would cause their own destruction if they did not change their ways. Though Jesus taught modest audiences of no more than thirty-five, and not the exaggerated multitudes mentioned in the Bible, he still caused alarm among the authorities. They announced a reward, not thirty pieces of silver but 2,500 pieces of gold for his head or $1,500 if captured alive.

Jesus taught for twenty-two years on the run, using "the radio in the head" to tune in and avoid the patrols. The frustrated law enforcement agencies nicknamed him "Christ," meaning "troublemaker," as he constantly slipped through their net. Jesus' mission came to an abrupt halt when he tuned in to a divine message that told him he was too ahead of his time for his teachings to be understood: Jesus was 2,000 years too early. Shortly thereafter, in a rainy Jerusalem, Jesus was preaching under the awning of a Jew's store. The owner became annoyed by the crowd blocking his showcase and dashed out, yelling at those assembled to disperse or he would call the authorities. Recognizing the preacher as the wanted troublemaker, the greedy Jew contacted the authorities. Two deputy sheriffs responded to the call, rushed to the scene, and arrested Jesus. The first sheriff to arrive suggested that Jesus agree to being killed by him, for this would give him the greater reward, and, in any case, Jesus faced capital punishment. Jesus was standing with his arms and hands stretched forth in the position routinely demanded by policemen at arrests. The deputy sheriff stabbed Jesus with his sword, piercing him through the heart, all the way into the wooden board he was leaning against. Jesus' death was so sudden, God revealed to Elijah Muhammad, that the blood stopped circulating immediately, freezing the dead body in the outstretched position: Jesus thus died in the form of a cross, not on a cross.

This alternative Jesus biography is creatively ahistorical, placing him in a familiar Blackamerican context: he is the illegitimate offspring of a poor father who disappears early in his life. He is raised in a matrifocal family and cultivates short memories of a male adult who paid him attention. He leaves home in his early teens and adopts a lifestyle disliked by the authorities. Restlessly on the move, making the streets his home and gangs on the streetcorner his audience, he is constantly in trouble with the law but has the capacity of an outlaw hero to outsmart the police. Betrayed by another black urban stereotype, the Jewish store owner, he is finally caught and killed by the police.

The biblical and NOI biographies of Jesus have a direct bearing on the African American context, and the theme is frequently elaborated upon by Minister Louis Farrakhan when preaching the Gospel of the messianic age: "I don't waste time giving you historical escapades, puttin' you in a time machine that you can run back 2,000 years ago or 4,000 years ago," Farrakhan told his audience. "If 2,000 years ago and 4,000 years ago has no relevance to the time period we live in, we don't need to talk about it at all."[11] The NOI teaches that 75 percent of what is stated about Jesus in the Bible refers to a future messiah, which explains why Jesus said "you *shall* know the truth and the truth *shall* make you free."[12] The Jesus of the Bible is thus a sign of a coming saviour—first said to be Master Farad Muhammad and now identified as Elijah the Messiah—but also represents the divine potential at the root of each African American's nature.

The fact that the Nation denies that Jesus of Nazareth died on a cross does not make the dramatic death scene of the gospel less real. "Crucifixion ain't no fiction," as Public Enemy rhymes.[13] The crucifixion described in the New Testament is, Minister Farrakhan explains, "a symbol of a people who have been killed mentally, morally, socially, spiritually, economically and politically." A people who have been crucified, lynched, mocked, yet are feared because the Devil sees them as potential rulers; "if he can just shake loose from the force of death and come up [out] of his shallow grave, he would ascend to the heights," and so "they put a stone in front of his tomb."[14] The slain Saviour is thus identified as the African American, the grave represents America, and the stone signifies a stone-hearted people—that is, the white devils—that block the way for the Blackman's resurrection.[15] The alternative NOI history of Jesus also contains some of the Gnostic elements that were elaborated later and pushed to the forefront, at the expense of other aspects of the entertaining alternative biography. The radio in the head is a euphemism for the telepathic connection between a realized Self and the source of existence, as well as the wonderful abilities of a liberated mind. Jesus is Man Perfected, and as "the perfect example of human potential" he shows the way to exalted godhood, the divinity each of God's children is designed to evolve into.[16]

The NOI theologians argue that mainstream Christianity's blasphemous understanding of Jesus as the unique result of a spirit God's adulterous intercourse with a married woman and as a divine being from outer space, as a mysterious being of an essentially different and therefore unattainable nature, was designed to avert the oppressed from the true meaning of the "children of God" concept: the divinity of man.[17] Combined with the bizarre idea of blacks praying for deliverance before the body of a dead white man, and putting all their hopes in his suddenly jumping down from the cross to settle the scores with his enemies, Christianity was made the Devil's tool to maintain his rule.

The Messenger made repeated remarks on the evil conditions prevailing under "Christen*doom*" and the dreadful consequences awaiting those who remain under the spell of Satan when the final call sounds. "The worship called Christianity," Elijah warned, "dooms Black Americans to an eternal death in the fire of hell" soon to be kindled over America.[18] The Honorable Elijah Muhammad taught that Christianity was intended for the white man, while Islam was the religion of the original people. Christianity and Islam were depicted as polar opposites: division/unity, slavery/freedom, poverty/wealth, and hatred/love. This series of fundamental oppositions was symbolized on a board that was standard decoration in the NOI temples prior to the Messenger's ascension into messiahship. Placed behind the pulpit, the two-part picture displayed the words "Christianity" on the one side and "Islam" on the other. Beneath "Christianity" was placed the Star-Spangled Banner, the words "Slavery—Suffering—Death," the Christian cross, and a picture of a lynched Blackman hanging with a rope around his neck. Beneath "Islam" was the red NOI flag with the star and crescent and the words "Freedom—Justice—Equality." In between the two, a question of crucial future importance was printed: "Which One Will Survive Armageddon?"

Black Bridge over Troubled Waters   One major reason for the NOI's criticism of Christianity is related to the role of the black church in American society. As C. Eric Lincoln and Lawrence Mamiya have pointed out,[19] past research has largely seen the black church as a monolithic entity, a perspective that has led to its rigid classification in terms such as other-worldly, compensatory, assimilationist, conservative, and the like. This mode of characterization misses the historical dynamism of an evolving institution and fails to explain the socio-political roles of a church, which, in the words of Gayraud Wilmore "is at once the most reactionary and the most radical of black institutions."[20] The "dialectical model" proposed by Lincoln and Mamiya is methodologically more fruitful, as it allows the multifaceted church to be seen in all its complexity and historical transformation. They identify six main pairs of dialectically related polar opposites held in constant tension, with the church moving through history in the continuum between the poles: priestly versus prophetic functions, otherworldly versus "this-worldly," universalism versus particularism, communal versus privatistic, charismatic versus bureaucratic, and resistance versus accommodation.[21] It is the last set of polar opposites that primarily is of interest here.

The first independent black churches to be established in the eighteenth century were part of and developed in "the liberation tradition" of black Christianity.[22] Established by freedmen in black communities in Northern and Southern cities, these churches took the survival tradition of "the invisible institution," the semisecret black congregations of the slave communities, a step further. To counter white control and prejudiced oppression, the first independent churches created institutions for racial elevation in the areas of economy, education, and politics. The black church established societies for mutual aid, banks, insurance companies, and schools: it also emphasized the need for land as crucial for self-determination. The clergy were engaged in the back-to-Africa movement, Pan-Africanism, and in the abolitionist movement. Black Christians dominated the scene of classic black nationalism, as described in chapter 1, and contributed to making the black church a radical force in American society, a vehicle for black consciousness, racial justice, and reparations.[23]

The deradicalization of the black church began in the first part of the twentieth century. The deterioration of race relations—with Jim Crow legislation in the South and race riots in the North—combined with the effects of the Great Migration and the black churches' newly established status as respectable institutions to move the church toward the pole of accommodation. The black clergy largely adopted the conservative evangelical and revivalist Christian understanding of a nonviolent, patiently suffering, and otherworldly white Jesus, which became the authoritative model for Christianity. Modeling itself on its white counterparts, the black church rejected the black nationalist position of Henry McNeal Turner, Marcus Garvey, and Alexander Crummell, and assumed an increasingly more conservative or collaborationist position in American society.[24]

With the advent of the Great Depression, the move toward the accommodationist pole was almost complete, thereby leaving vacant the position of resistance, which was to be filled by the rise of numerous urban radical sects and cults, one of which was the Nation of Islam. It was the deradicalized black church that was targeted by the Messenger of God and his ministers. Minister Malcolm X charged, "The greatest miracle Christianity has ever achieved in America is that the black man in white Christian hands has not grown violent. It is a miracle that 22 million black people have not *risen up* against their oppressor. . . . It is a miracle that a nation of black people has so fervently continued to believe in a turn-the-other-cheek and heaven-after-you-die philosophy! It *is a miracle* that the American black people have remained a peaceful people, while catching all the centuries of hell that they have caught, here in the white man's heaven! The *miracle* is that the white man's Negro puppet 'leaders,' his preachers and the educated Negroes laden with degrees, and others who have been allowed to wax fat off their black poor brothers, have been able to hold the black masses quiet until now."[25] The Montgomery bus boycott in 1955 and the civil rights movement of Martin Luther King Jr., described by Lincoln and Mamiya "as a major watershed in the annals of Black Church history,"[26] were the first post–World War II black Christian reactions to tensions created by a continuously unjust Christian society and the anti-Christian challenge voiced by Malcolm X and the NOI. The campaign for desegregation and civil rights was, however, reformist and not radical in orientation. The political and religious reformism of King's early period was to be seriously questioned by the Black Power movement, which led to the rise of black consciousness in all aspects of black life, the church included.

The development of a Christian black theology of liberation came some three decades after the foundation of the NOI, from which it undoubtedly received initial sparks of inspiration. As black Christianity, especially in its classic black nationalist variety, helped shape black Islam, the NOI as a religion of resistance in its turn contributed to the formation of the black liberation theology of the black church. Black theologian Gayraud Wilmore acknowledges that "the only *distinctively* Black theological reflection in written form that anyone was aware of prior to 1964 was produced by the religious leaders and teachers in the Nation of Islam."[27] In the late 1960s, ghetto priests laid the first foundation for the new understanding of the Christian message. One of these preachers was Albert B. Cleage Jr., who, inspired by Malcolm X, began preaching the gospel of the Black Messiah, "a revolutionary black leader, a Zealot, seeking to lead a Black Nation to freedom."[28]

In 1969, James H. Cone published *Black Theology and Black Power* as a first outline for the content of a black theology. It was followed the next year by *A Black Theology of Liberation,* said to be the first comprehensive black Christian theology ever written. Here, liberation is not only seen as consistent with the gospel but *as* the gospel. Cone's definition of the task of black theology is "to analyze the nature of the gospel of Jesus Christ in the light of oppressed black people so they will see the gospel as inseparable from their humiliated condition, bestowing on them the necessary power to break the chains of oppression."[29] Cone also acknowledges the influence from black Muslim theologians Elijah Muhammad and Malcolm X and asserts the thesis that black religion is authentic only when identified with the struggle for black freedom.[30] Cone believes that to be a genuine Christian, Malcolm's race critique has to be incorporated. He argues that Malcolm's black theology was not a replacement for Christian theology but an "indispensable corrective."[31] "Black Theology," Cone writes, "arose as an attempt to stem the tide of the irrelevance of Christianity by combining both Christianity and Blackness, Martin and Malcolm, Black Church and Black Power, even though neither side thought it was possible." King stood as a symbol for a Christian civil rights movement that remained Christian and nonviolent and called for integration. With the advent of the new black nationalist surge, the struggle was de-Christianized, emphasizing the NOI's call for self-defense and separatism. The advocates of Black Power were "hostile to Christianity, viewing it as a white religion," and most Christians saw Black Power as "the opposite of everything their faith represented."[32]

Following James H. Cone, a number of influential black theologians and scholars, such as Gayraud Wilmore, William Jones, Major Jones, Cornel West, Charles Long, DeOtis Roberts, and others, have contributed to a rich and varied theoretical construction of black liberation theology and established numerous organizations for converting theory into practice. Demands for reparations, black self-determination, the construction of an

independent black economy and education—demands that had characterized the classic black nationalists of the older liberation tradition and
were adopted by movements such as the Nation of Islam—were again
voiced from the rostrums of the black churches.

Lincoln and Mamiya examined the influence of black liberation theology on the urban clergy nationwide and found that it had only a limited
impact, with 34.9 percent of the respondents acknowledging the influence of the above-mentioned theologians. Age, education, and denomi-
nation were found to be the most significant variables. Clergy under forty
with a high level of education were the most strongly influenced. Black
Methodists of the African Methodist Episcopal branch were the most positive (66.2 percent) and Black Pentecostals of the Church of God in Christ
the least influenced (17.9 percent).[33] Compared with the grassroots-based
liberation theology of Latin America, Lincoln and Mamiya conclude that
black theology has failed to move beyond the intellectual elite in the
black middle classes.[34] The older and less theologically coherent liberation tradition is, on the other hand, pervasive in the black church. The
black congregations in general expect their pastors to address political,
social, and economic problems, and 91 percent of the clergy supported
participation in civil rights protests.[35]

The political comeback of the black church was manifested in Jesse
Jackson's 1984 primary race. Over 90 percent of the black clergy declared
their support for Jackson within two months of his announcement that he
intended to run for the presidency.[36] Reverend Jackson, who stood firmly
in the traditions of Booker T. Washington and Martin Luther King Jr.,
rewrote the liberation theology into a leftist political agenda and gave
speeches more akin to sermons than mainstream political addresses.[37]
Minister Farrakhan also endorsed Jackson's candidacy and the Nation of
Islam became involved in a mainstream political campaign for the first
time in its history.

The black church in America now has a serious competitor in Islam, in
both its mainstream and black nationalist varieties. As black Islam became an agent for resistance, the church is being challenged by an Islam
operating in segments of black America either neglected by the church or
in which the church has failed to make itself relevant: the prisons, the
permanent poor, the urban youth, and—a category conspicuously absent
in the church—black urban males.[38] The Nation of Islam has its very
strongholds among these segments, a phenomenon that is further described in chapter 10. Even more than becoming a competitor to the

church, Farrakhan believes Islam's real challenge to be the re-creation of a racial unity in which blackness as a theological concept transcends religious barriers. Farrakhan adheres to the mainstream Muslim understanding of Islam, Christianity, and Judaism as the more or less correct expressions of the One True Faith. "God did not send men with all of these different labels for His religion," Farrakhan asserts. "He has one faith, one religion. We call it Islam; He calls it Islam, obedience to His will. Moses called it obedience to God. Jesus called it obedience to God's Will." The three religions that uphold the legacy of Abraham thus comprise "one faith, one religion."[39]

As sections of the black church moved closer to the NOI's black liberationist position, a process of cooperation began. Initiated during the latter part of Messenger Muhammad's regime, the call for black Muslim/Christian unity has advanced in the NOI agenda and is now given top priority. Minister Farrakhan has said, "We must find the common bond in all of the prophet's teachings so that we can bring people of faith together rather than splintering humanity in the name of faith, causing them to fight and kill together."[40] In the NOI theology, black unity is the ideal, a natural reflection of *tawhid,* God's unity. The present intra- and interreligious divisions are a result of the regime of evil, and reunification is a prelude to liberation: "I don't like to see Christians divided against each other. I don't like to see Muslims divided against each other, and I don't like to see Muslims and Christians divided against each other. I hate to see all of this that has separated us one from another, these artificial barriers that have been imposed upon us by an enemy. . . . We wanna remove all of these artificial barriers, that we understand that We are One, that God is One, and His faith is One."[41] The overture to the black Christian community is essential, for African Americans are one of the world's most church-oriented populations, with 78 percent claiming church membership in 1978.[42] Farrakhan says he preaches in as many churches as he does mosques,[43] and Christian pastors and preachers are frequent guests at NOI services. Akbar Muhammad claims that Farrakhan has a larger Christian than Muslim following,[44] which, if speaking in terms of influence rather than membership, probably is correct. African Americans thus can remain Christian but still unite with Farrakhan, as blackness transcends man-made divisions. Black is in this respect a theological concept representing divine essence, the nature of creation. To be black is to be back on the track to divinity, making competition for souls irrelevant: black *is* soul, is God, is liberation. Consequently, Farrakhan, like the

Prophet Muhammad ibn Abdullah, has "chosen not to try to convert a human being to a faith that he was given in the very nature in which he was created." [45]

Black Christians have responded favorably to the call for black reunification. Reverend Cecil Murray of the First African Methodist Episcopal Church said before 17,000 listeners at an NOI rally in Los Angeles that there are no divisions between black Christians and black Muslims.[46] Maxine Walker, editor of the Christian magazine *The Platform,* hails Farrakhan in almost messianic terms, saying he is on a mission from God to liberate his people, with a role similar to Moses' in Egypt, Daniel's in Babylon, and Jesus' in the Roman Empire.[47] On June 13, 1993, a Christian pastor delivered a keynote address at Mosque Maryam for the first time. Given the honor was Rev. Hycel B. Taylor, former president of Operation PUSH and pastor of the Second Baptist Church of Evanston, Illinois. Introduced by Farrakhan, Rev. Taylor recited in English the Muslim prayer *Al Fatih* and spoke about the need for black Muslim-Christian unity.[48] Another sign of the materialization of interreligious black unity came on October 24, 1993, when Rev. Ben Chavis, executive director of the NAACP, mounted the rostrum at Mosque Maryam with the Bible and the Qur'an in his hands. Reading from both Holy Scriptures, Rev. Chavis spoke of the necessity to build bridges and described the event as a holy moment in black history, a final reunification of God's people.[49]

The call for religious unity does not lessen Farrakhan's critique of "white" or "white-oriented" Christianity. Delivering a sermon in a church, Farrakhan argued that he is "a better Christian than practically all the preachers of Christianity," because he is in the world, but not of the (Devil's) world. He is a true Christian with personal knowledge of and friendship with Christ, that is, Elijah the Messiah, the divine warrior, who has come to judge the wicked. As Christ's herald, Farrakhan "is on the battle field for my Lord," intending to spread the truth no matter what resistance the Devil can mobilize. Backed by God, Farrakhan says he "don't care nothing about what they say," he keeps on walking "in the Hell with a gasoline jacket on."[50] It is thus Farrakhan and not the pope who represents Christ, who himself finally will distinguish who is genuine and who is an anti-Christ.[51] Says Farrakhan, "Very humbly, in the sight of God, I [Farrakhan] am much more important than the Pope. . . . You can't compare the leader of a false religion with God's servant who comes to condemn it. Whether you are Catholic or not, the Pope is not Jesus' vice-regent on earth. He's an imposter, and today God is gonna lift up the shirts of his garment and show you what is underneath it."[52] The pope cannot be a true Christian as he represents the old evil world that is on its way out and that has a long-standing record of racism and collaboration with the Devil. "When our fathers were in slavery," Farrakhan charges, "the church was here, the Pope was here, but nobody healed the wounds of the slaves. The church walked by on the other side."[53] It is only "if we understand the true Christ doctrine" that nationalism, racism, and sexism will come to an end and "humanity will then have a new beginning."[54]

In concluding this section it should be pointed out that according to Farrakhan, the deterioration of true religion is not confined to Christianity. As discussed before, the era of evil caused the Muslim world to deviate and has had a devastating effect on all religions globally. Farrakhan writes, "The hidden force of Satan has come into the mosque, the synagogue, the church, and has overpowered the preachers, teachers, sheiks, mullahs, cardinals, popes, and the common religious worshipper. Sadly enough most religious people do not even realize that they . . . are off the path of God. The [takeover] has been so subtle and skillful that Satan has made these religious institutions a part of his plan while the religious leaders think they are planning salvation for the people."[55] The solution is unification across all religious barriers, which could be realized, Farrakhan believes, if the focus moves beyond what divides different faiths to consider instead the common ground they share. Speaking in Chicago on September 2, 1993, at the centennial convocation of the Parliament of the World's Religions that gathered 6,000 representatives from 125 religious groups,[56] Farrakhan proposed the formation of "a world community of human beings committed to transcendent values and principles."[57] All spiritual men and women should rise to challenge racism, sexism, and extremist nationalism and unite by putting aside the differences between their faiths and looking for the common principles that undergird them. As his message unfolds, the reader should note that what is defined as the common ground is basically identical to (black) Islam, which to Farrakhan is not so much the name of a religion but rather the nature of Creation. Farrakhan argues that practically every religion represented at the convocation believes in a transcendent Being, but gives him different names to represent his various attributes. All religions believe that he reveals knowledge of the truth, the power of good and evil, and the imminent justice that will one day prevail.

Farrakhan has stated that although he calls himself a Muslim, a submitter to the will of God, he considers himself "also a Christian" or "crystallized into Oneness with God following the example of Jesus Christ," and he is "also a Hebrew," and believes in all the scriptures the prophets brought. As did Buddha, Farrakhan seeks enlightenment, which is why he thinks he "could be considered a Buddhist." Buddha, Tao, Zoroaster, Shinto, Confucius, and Christ "taught principles that we all attempt to practice."[58] Although practiced in different manners, Farrakhan specifies these common principles as prayer, love and brotherhood, fasting, struggle against internal and external evil, and pilgrimage, the meeting of the devotee with the One God. Despite all those messengers preaching similar principles, the world has sunk into darkness to such a degree, Farrakhan holds, "that it looks like Jesus never walked among us, Moses never walked among us, Muhammad never walked among us, Buddha and Confucius never walked among us. It looks like no Holy Man never walked among us." All religions have proven their failure, which is why they all are looking for someone to come and straighten out the confusion and initiate a change in direction. And today, if humanity could look beyond color and listen to Farrakhan, salvation can come. Farrakhan concludes, "We have all been trained to listen to those who are white, but we have never been trained to listen to wisdom coming from those who are of the rejected and despised of the earth. But today, coming from the despised and rejected, God will grant us light [that we could unite] and save our planet."[59] While Farrakhan spoke about unity, his very participation caused division in the Parliament of the World's Religions. Several days after it convened, four Jewish organizations withdrew their sponsorship upon learning that Farrakhan was allowed to participate and walked out. The national office of the Anti-Defamation League declared it impossible to participate at the event as Farrakhan "continues to espouse and promote classical anti-Semitic notions of Jewish domination and control."[60]

Blacks, Jews, and the Nation of Islam   A 1987 "Special Edition" on Louis Farrakhan, widely circulated to American media and politicians by the Anti-Defamation League (ADL) of B'nai B'rith as a periodic update, illustrates the image of Minister Farrakhan prevalent in mainstream American society, as "the anti-Semitic and racist leader of the Black Muslim sect known as the Nation of Islam."[61] As this "Special Edition" also illustrates the tendency to deliberately quote Farrakhan out of context, three citations chosen and published by the ADL will provide a point of departure for discussing the alleged anti-Semitism of the NOI. As stated in the "Special Edition":

> Speaking in Madison Square Garden on October 7, 1985, Farrakhan said, "The Jews talk about 'Never again.' . . . Listen, Jews, this little black boy is your last chance because the Scriptures charge you with killing the prophets of God. . . . You cannot say 'Never again' to God, because when he puts you in the oven, 'Never again' don't mean a thing."
>
> Addressing an audience in Los Angeles in 1985, he referred to Judaism as a "dirty religion" and Israel as "a wicked hypocrisy."
>
> Broadcasting over Chicago radio station WBEE on March 11, 1984, Farrakhan stated: "Here come [*sic*] the Jews don't like Farrakhan, so they call me Hitler. Well, that's a good name. Hitler was a very great man. What have I done? Who have I killed? I warn you, be careful, be careful. You're putting yourself in dangerous, dangerous shoes. You have been the killer of all the prophets. Now, if you seek my life, you only show that you are no better than your fathers."

These citations of statements made by Minister Farrakhan seem to irrefutably prove his anti-Semitism. The issue, however, is far more complicated and requires a contextualization to be genuinely understood.

When Jesse Jackson declared his intention to run in the 1984 primary race for the Democratic Party's presidential nomination, long-standing tensions between the African American and Jewish communities came to the fore. While Jackson had the support of an overwhelming majority of blacks and would secure close to 90 percent of the black vote, less than 10 percent of Jews supported him, and Jackson was vehemently accused of anti-Semitism by Jewish organizations and spokespersons. With most of the Jewish community not only outside of but hostile to the Rainbow Coalition, the black-Jewish alliance from the civil rights era was effectively dissolved. What had happened? A brief historical overview of the black-Jewish relationship in the United States will facilitate an understanding of Farrakhan's present role.

The first Jews to arrive in the New World in the seventeenth, eighteenth, and early nineteenth centuries adhered to a conservative line of thinking and kept a low or apolitical profile. Most were German Jews from business-oriented middle-class families seeking prosperity in a land free from anti-Semitism, and they did not differ from other whites in their attitudes toward slavery: those in the North tended to oppose the institution, while those in the South tended to favor and benefit from it. There were Jewish slaveholders and slave dealers, as well as Jewish abolitionists.[62] Starting in the 1880s, this pattern began to change with the influx of working-class socialist Jews from Russia and Eastern Europe, who jammed the poor sections of New York and Chicago. Within forty years, the new and progressive Jewish immigrants outnumbered their conservative brethren by eight to one, and the newcomers changed the political profile of American Jewry with their call for union organizing and social revolution.[63] Meanwhile, anti-Semitism found its way to the United States, with the passing of an increasing number of discriminatory acts barring Jews from "better" neighborhoods and universities, thereby necessitating Jewish mobilization for civil rights.[64] Blacks, Jews, and Catholics—"Koons, Kikes, and Katholics"—were targeted by the revived Ku Klux Klan, and in 1913 a Jewish factory owner became one of the very few whites lynched in the South.[65]

The anti-Semitic sentiments of the Western world, which culminated in the horror of the Holocaust, made Jews inclined to identify with another oppressed community, also the victims of racist injustice: African Americans. From the 1909 establishment of the first major civil rights organization in the United States, the National Association for the Advancement of Colored People (NAACP), to the desegregation campaign in the South and the 1963 March on Washington, Jews were there to form a coalition with blacks in a fight for common causes. Jews were major financial contributors to the NAACP, the Congress of Racial Equality, the Student Nonviolent Coordinating Committee, and the Southern Christian Leadership Conference; also, Jews often held leadership positions or functioned as advisers and speechwriters in these organizations. Almost two-thirds of the white Freedom Riders were Jews, and along with black churches and homes, synagogues became targets for Ku Klux Klan terror bombings.[66]

An image of Jews as a somewhat different and benign group of whites emerged for a large section of black America. The picture is, however, far from unambiguous. While Southern blacks generally could acknowledge the progressive role of Jews, the migrant to the urban North not only met Jewish radicals, but was confronted by another, conflicting, image, the Jewish slumlord and ghetto store-owner, that is, the Jew as an ordinary white racist exploiter. Jews moved into slum shopkeeping, a niche others found unprofitable, and many Jews kept their shops or real estate in the ghettos when the composition changed from Jewish to black. This gave

Jews high visibility, and tensions, akin to the black-Korean tensions of the late 1980s, began to arise.[67] Nicholas Lemann recounts an example from the West Side of Chicago. Lawndale had been 13 percent black in 1950 and was 91 percent black by 1960. "A sociologist seeking to understand the roots of black-Jewish tension in America could find no better case study than Lawndale in the 1950s," Lemann writes. "Many of the panic-peddlers, landlords, usurious furniture renters, and purveyors of inferior produce in the area were Jewish. Blacks who moved in usually found that their Jewish neighbors looked at them with contempt, and then quickly moved out, to more affluent neighborhoods and suburbs to the north of Lawndale. Jews who had left Lawndale saw how quickly it became a slum in its black incarnation and wondered what was wrong with those people, who couldn't possibly have had it any harder than their own pogrom-fleeing parents and grandparents from Poland and Russia."[68] The conflicting images of the white Jew began to shift increasingly toward the negative as the African American struggle moved beyond the nonviolent, assimilationist agenda of King to the cry for Black Power in the late 1960s. While the existence of anti-Semitism dropped dramatically in the United States in the post–World War II period, racism prevailed. While American Jews could use university degrees and successful enterprising to make an inroad into the American elite,[69] blacks found themselves stuck at the bottom of society. A coalition is an alliance of equals and socio-political developments had increasingly eroded the common ground that once existed between the Jewish and African American communities.

A web of conflicting interests, misrepresentations, and misunderstandings clouded the black-Jewish relationship. Jews, who felt themselves to be a victimized minority in the United States, saw blacks as akin to Jews in the fight for a society with equal opportunities regardless of race or religion. When blacks voiced the ideas of self-determination and Black Power, and as a consequence ousted whites (most of whom were Jews) from leadership positions in the black organizations, Jews felt betrayed and were alert to possible anti-Semitism. Blacks saw the Jews as an example to emulate and black nationalism as a form of Zionism: Black Power as an equivalent of Jewish power—surely Jews had to understand that. When blacks in the late 1960s and 1970s called for affirmative action to gain access to universities and corporate offices, the Jews who would lose positions if quotas were employed aggressively fought against affirmative action, and blacks felt betrayed by their former allies.[70]

If Jews continued to view themselves as a threatened minority, blacks increasingly came to see them as a part of the white supremacist majority. Black criticism of the wealthy Jewish elite, from the slumlords to university cadres to media and financial corporate executives, was perceived by Jews as a revival of the old anti-Semitic thesis of the secretly conspiring, powerful Jew. This is a sensitive issue, but still part of American reality. As Robert S. Wistrich notes, "The American Jewish community . . . is the largest, wealthiest, most influential and politically powerful that has ever existed in Diaspora history."[71] Jewish influence in American society is illustrated, for example, by the fact that they made up 25 to 30 percent of the media elite in 1982, and the fact that by 1975 they comprised 20 percent of the faculties at top-rated universities.[72]

Many blacks confused Jewish money with Jewish power and failed to understand that Jews could view themselves as outsiders in American society. Black rage over Jews denouncing justified demands as black anti-Semitism—how could anyone that wealthy feel that threatened by such a powerless body as the African American community?—misses two important components. First, the class component: not all Jews are wealthy, because the majority, as with all other peoples, does not belong to the elite. Second, history proves that wealth is an insufficient guarantee against genocide. For instance, Jews in Spain had been very influential just before the Inquisition, and Jews in Germany financially prospered before the Holocaust.[73]

Jews, on the other hand, could not understand the African American reality and greatly underestimated the extent to which racism was still prevalent in the United States. The end of segregation legislation, the goal for Jewish activists, did little to improve the socioeconomic conditions in the urban ghettos and nothing to empower the African American community in their continuing struggle for affirmative action, black economics, and black power. The conflict in Palestine and Israel, in which blacks increasingly came to identify with the Palestinians as another minority without rights or a homeland, further added to the animosity, as did Israel's role as one of South Africa's largest arms suppliers and trade partner.[74]

The twentieth anniversary of the March on Washington illustrates this breakdown in relations, as most of the Jewish organizations that had been part of the 1963 march withdrew their support when the coalition was expanded to embrace the Nation of Islam and Arab-Americans. At this stage, Jesse Jackson appeared and declared his intention to run in the 1984 presidential primary. The Anti-Defamation League had already prepared a memorandum, depicting Jackson as an anti-Semite and a proterrorist, an opinion held by the ADL due in part to his 1979 meeting with Yassir Arafat. The fact that Jackson had challenged Arafat to adopt a mutual recognition policy with Israel did little to change the ADL's opinion. The ADL memo, described by Sheila D. Collins as a "vicious personal attack on Jackson," was widely circulated throughout the Jewish community and among American journalists and policy makers and ultimately set the tone for the future campaign.[75]

When Jackson in late October 1983, made his announcement to seek the Democratic Party's nomination, the militant Jewish Defense League (JDL), founded by ultrarightist Meir Kahane, took action. Under the name of Jews against Jackson, threats against the life of Jackson and his family were issued and pickets set up around his home and his Boston headquarters, carrying signs that read "Ruin, Jesse, Ruin." Soon hundreds of threats on Jackson's life poured in and Jackson felt it necessary to ask the Secret Service for protection, a request they initially denied.[76] At this moment, Minister Farrakhan mounted the Rainbow Coalition wagon, offering Jackson soldiers from the FOI as security personnel. Farrakhan declared that he did not intend to passively watch Jackson being attacked when walking down into the valley of the shadow of death, but that he would go along with him.[77] "When you [Jewish people who dislike Jackson] attack him," Farrakhan told a cheering 1984 Saviour's Day audience, "you are attacking one million that are lined up behind him. You are attacking all of us. If you harm this brother, I warn you in the name of Allah, this will be the last one you harm."[78]

Farrakhan clearly saw the candidacy of Jackson in messianic terms, saying that Jackson had "transcended himself and is on a higher mission from a higher power . . . he's on a mission from God."[79] Jesse, Farrakhan elaborated, speaks like the Christ, sounds like the Mahdi,[80] and, like Jesus, had chosen to ride a donkey (the mascot of the Democratic Party).[81] Jackson was described as America's last chance, and Farrakhan warned that "if anything happens to that Brother, death and destruction will follow as swiftly as 1984 came in on the heels of '83."[82] Initially everything went smoothly, with Farrakhan as an asset to the Rainbow Coalition, reaching sections in the black nationalist and American Muslim communities traditionally aloof from mainstream party politics. Farrakhan took part in the Jackson delegation to Syria, where meetings with Syrian religious leaders and with the Alawi president Hafiz al-Assad resulted in the release of captured U.S. Navy pilot Lt. Robert O. Goodman.[83] Yet storm clouds would soon cover the Rainbow.

Bad feelings arose from a seemingly trivial incident. Jackson was annoyed by Jews narrowing down his political agenda to his position on Israel and his meeting with Arafat, and in an off-the-record "black talk" conversation with *Washington Post* reporter Milton Coleman on January 25, 1984, he referred to Jews as "Hymies" and to New York as "Hymietown," saying "all Hymie wants to talk about is Israel; when you go to Hymietown, that's all they want to talk about." Coleman passed the jive on to *Post* reporter Rick Atkinson, who three weeks later, shortly before the New Hampshire primary, published the story.[84] Jackson first denied making the slur,[85] postponing his confession until he spoke at Temple Abath Yushurun in Manchester, New Hampshire, on February 26, saying it was "not in a spirit of meanness, an off-color remark having no bearing on religion or politics . . . [but] however innocent and unintended, it was wrong."[86] Jewish leaders refused to accept the apology and black campaign laborers, angered by Jewish hostility to the Rainbow, felt that Jackson should not have apologized at all.[87] These reactions, in combination with Jackson's failure to be honest and apologize immediately, created an atmosphere that could have done without Farrakhan's interjection.

Farrakhan, exasperated by the undependability of black journalists, Jewish unfairness against Jackson, and Jewish accusations against himself, worsened the atmosphere. In a radio speech on March 11, 1984, Farrakhan branded Coleman a "Judas," stating that "we're going to make an example of Milton Coleman," and saying that while he "at this point" will suffer "no physical harm," he would be declared persona non grata in every black church and home, including his own. Farrakhan continued, "One day soon we will punish you with death. You're sayin', 'when is that?' In sufficient time. We will come to power right inside this country one day soon. And the white man is not going to stop us from executing the law of God on all of you who fall under our jurisdiction."[88] Although aired on March 11, the media did not publicize the "threat" made by "Jackson's backer" until April 3, the very day of the New York primary.[89] Jackson denounced the threat and called for a meeting between Farrakhan and Coleman in a NBC news interview the same night, a position he was frequently forced to repeat.[90] Although Farrakhan called Coleman to deny threatening his life,[91] most media representatives preferred the lethal conspiracy story that kept circulating.[92]

After the remark had been thoroughly exposed by the media, another part of the same March 11 broadcast surfaced on April 11, only two days before the Arizona primary.[93] Angered by Jewish detractors calling him "Hitler" (Jews supporting Jackson were by the same token called "Nazi lovers"),[94] Farrakhan responded, "Here come [sic] the Jews don't like Farrakhan, so they call me Hitler. Well, that's a good name. Hitler was a very great man. He wasn't great for me as a black person, but he was a great German. Now, I'm not proud of Hitler's evils against Jewish people, but that's a matter of record. He raised Germany up from nothing. Well, in a sense you could say there's a similarity in that we are raising our people up from nothing. But don't compare me with your wicked killers." The press ignored Farrakhan's not too successful attempt to refute the charges, focusing on the word "great." The *New York Post* headline "Jesse's pal says 'Hitler was a very great man'" set the tone, with reporters forcing Jackson to address his views on Nazi Germany and the plight of Jews, instead of his views on Arizona and the plight of Hispanics and Native Americans.[95] A comparison between this quotation and that given in the ADL memo, gives rise to the observation that the ADL excerpt omits Farrakhan's angry refusal to be compared to a murderous devil.

To understand Farrakhan's statement, it is important to grasp his religious frame of reference, his rhetorical style, and his logic of argumentation. The statement is typical of Farrakhan's dispute technique. Electrified at the center of a conflict, Farrakhan catches the verbal punch, holds it up for display, and returns the attack with the playful skill characteristic of an enthusiastic debater. He reinterprets the slur to his advantage: "So, you call me Hitler. Well that's a good name. He raised his people up and I intend to raise my people up." At the same time, Farrakhan is aware of the comparison's many discrepancies: Hitler was a wicked killer, a matter of record that Farrakhan at that moment, speaking for a black audience, took for granted that nobody really could accuse him of being. "What man would I be to praise Hitler," Farrakhan later wondered, "a man that hated black people?"[96]

In Farrakhan's worldview, Hitler was a devil. His evil is taken for granted as a part of his nature. Only historical circumstances gave Hitler the position to fully express his nature and outdo other contemporary devils. Hitler was unique only in that he consistently, and with the employment of all modern techniques then at hand, exterminated other European devils: the Jews. Previously, other devils had implemented similar genocidal drives in Africa, America, and Australia,[97] and with the original people as victims. Thus, for Farrakhan, Hitler's policy is a well-known devil's policy. Farrakhan understands himself as a messianic figure in the front lines against white world supremacy. A resurrected soldier enrolled in the army of God, he believes, can not be compared with an archdevil, for it is ontologically impossible: should this not be evident to everyone? "I wonder," Farrakhan questioned, "why you compare me with Hitler and not Jesus Christ?"[98]

The Farrakhan controversy continued to haunt the Rainbow campaign, with hundreds of editorials denouncing Jackson, linking his opinions with those of the NOI minister.[99] Vice President George Bush even tried to link all three major Democratic candidates, Jackson, Walter Mondale, and Gary Hart, with "the intrusion of anti-Semitism into the American political process."[100] Reagan aides demanded that Jackson disavow Farrakhan's support, while the same staff failed to denounce the support pledged to Reagan by Imperial Wizard Bill Wilkinson of the Ku Klux Klan.[101]

Speaking at the National Conference of Black Mayors in St. Louis on April 19, Farrakhan said that former CIA chief, Vice President Bush, lacked the "moral position" to tell blacks anything about justice and violence, with his "hands dripping with blood of rulers and nations." If mainstream America tried to lock out Jesse and continued to treat him disrespectfully, Farrakhan vowed to lead "an army of black men and women" to Washington, D.C., to "negotiate for a separate territory,"[102] a promise later repeated in kind.[103]

Despite increasing pressure to disavow Farrakhan, Jackson refused "to negotiate away" his "integrity trying to impress somebody," saying he still had "respect" for the minister.[104] The conflict escalated when Kahane's Jewish Defense League announced a march to the NOI Final Call building in Chicago. The Muslims vowed to defend themselves and the JDL canceled the march after learning that several hundred FOI soldiers were prepared to meet them.[105] In late June 1984, after Farrakhan referred to the creation of Israel as an outlaw act and called Judaism a "dirty" or "gutter" religion, Jackson finally gave in and declared that Farrakhan was no longer a part of the Rainbow Coalition campaign.[106] Farrakhan, insisting he had said "dirty" religion, then sued all the papers that reported that he said "gutter" religion.[107] Jackson's repudiation of Farrakhan actually changed little, and what it did change was for the worse. Many blacks felt that he had capitulated, and most Jews thought that it came too late and did not go far enough. According to a survey of 3,609 of the 3,944 delegates to the Democratic Convention, 93 percent of the Jewish delegates had an unfavorable impression of Farrakhan and 78 percent saw Jackson as an anti-Semite. Farrakhan was still viewed favorably by 65 percent of Jackson's delegates (85 percent of whom were black) while 47 percent of all black delegates, regardless of which candidate they were committed to, supported Farrakhan.[108]

For years the media continued to vilify Jackson for anti-Semitism and his relations with Farrakhan, and the controversy colored the 1988 presidential race, despite the fact that the minister never participated.[109] The popular image of an anti-Semitic bond linking Jackson and Farrakhan was lyricized by Lou Reed, who expresses the common white fear of a racist President—if he is black:

> And here comes Jesse Jackson
> He speaks of Common Ground
> Does the Common Ground include me
> Or is it just a sound?
>
> The words that flow so freely
> Falling dancing from your lips
> I hope that you don't cheapen them
> With a racist slip
>
> If I ran for President
> and once was a member of the Klan
> Wouldn't you call me on it
> the way I call you on Farrakhan?[110]

From Dirty Religion Blues to Mendelssohn Violin Concerto   If Jesse Jackson experienced difficulties in shaking off the accusation of anti-Semitism, Farrakhan seems to live at the center of such controversies. When he feels attacked, Farrakhan returns charges in a manner that supports his detractors' picture of him as the anti-Semitic demagogue, which consequently hampers his repeated overtures for reconciliation. His efforts to reach out in dialogue are frustrated by a mutual opposition voiced from sections in the Jewish community and among his own followers, thus forcing him back to confrontation. Since the 1984 campaign, the Jewish focus on Farrakhan has been reflected in an increased NOI focus on Jews. In Farrakhan's speeches, a number of themes are repeatedly elaborated: the gutter religion theme, the Holocaust theme, the Zionist theme, the Jewish impostor theme, and the mighty Jew theme.

Irrespective of whether Farrakhan said that Judaism was a "gutter" or a "dirty" religion in the 1984 radio sermon, the Jewish outrage would, probably, be equally strong and equally misfounded. In numerous later speeches, Farrakhan returned to the theme, using both concepts as synonyms, describing the misuse of religion to cover ungodly human behavior. What was never mentioned in the ADL memorandums and therefore not discussed in the American media (as journalists seldom, if ever, bother to base their reports on Farrakhan's actual speeches, accepting secondary information as a primary source) is the fact that Farrakhan does not speak only of Judaism, but also of Christianity and Islam, and never about the religions as such but the perversion of faith.

In a 1989 speech at the University of Maryland, Farrakhan stated that Israel has not had any peace in forty years, because "there can be no peace structured on lying, stealing and using God's Holy name to shield your dirty religion." If taken out of context, this clearly sounds genuinely anti-Semitic. But let us continue listening to his message as it unfolds. Qualifying his statement in order not to be misinterpreted, Farrakhan emphasized his Islamic faith, saying, "I'm a Muslim. I respect Moses. I respect the revelation Moses was sent with to the children of Israel. How can I dare condemn what God send [sic] down as unclean?" It is thus not Judaism as such, but the practice of certain Jews that stands condemned. Farrakhan continues, "The unclean is our action hiding behind God's name, Jesus' name, Muhammad's name, but we're killing and destroying each other in the name of God."[111] Moreover, in the same speech Farrakhan moved away from Israel to other geographical areas in which religious corruption is especially discernible. Christians slaughter one another in Northern Ireland and Muslims from Iran and Iraq kill each other in the name of Allah, Farrakhan charged, hammering away at his main point: "Killing, cheating, stealing, deceiving in the name of God— that's dirty religion."[112]

As always, Farrakhan does not spare African Americans his rage. Castigating a black audience, Farrakhan said that unless they make religion meaningful in everyday life, then "all religion ain't worth a damn thing, whether it is Islam, Christianity, Buddhism, it ain't serving you at all because you're the same old nigger wrapped up in a Bible, wrapped up in a Quran, wrapped up in a role." Religion is not a surface thing, but must reach the core, create a change in direction, and evolve the believer toward God. Challenging hypocrisy in black Islam, Farrakhan continued with a stand-up act of imitation: "So I'll go to Jumah prayer this week and stay in the congregation, and Friday night after Jumah prayer is over I'll snort some coke and smoke some more reefer and I'll wake up in the morning for my five o'clock salat, and I'll read the Quran and go back out and do evil some more—What kind of religion is that?"[113]

The Holocaust theme touches a raw nerve in the Jewish community, but what many Jews fail to realize is the depth of the open wound in the black community, which hurts all the more as it is felt to be neglected in favor of the Jewish Holocaust. Jewish anger toward Farrakhan's indifference to the Holocaust, highlighted for example in the "Hitler is great" controversy, reflects black anger over a perceived Jewish indifference to the African American counterpart. The Holocaust occupies a given place in the public space, with numerous popular novels and movies focusing on the horror of the crimes against humanity perpetrated by Nazi Germany and their allies. These novels and movies by far outnumber those highlighting the horror of slavery. Farrakhan speaks for a section of black America that has begun to tire of listening to Jewish pain when no one, they feel, wants to listen to theirs. "Jews are sensitive because of their suffering," Farrakhan said, "but we are all sensitive and we have also suffered.... We as Black people, look at our loss. Conservative estimators suggest 100 million in the middle passage. Who will weep for us?"[114] As Jews need to remember, blacks too "need to remember our Holocaust."[115]

As previously discussed, Farrakhan religiously interprets "the black Holocaust" as a necessary lesson because of manifest transgressions and as a baptism of fire before the Blackman could evolve into the predestined divinity of man. Farrakhan argues that if the Devil does not loosen his grip on the present world, God will remove the stone blocking the Blackman's tomb and set the world on fire. It is within this context, with Farrakhan as a doomsday prophet warning of the approaching all-consuming holocaust, that his infamous statement cited earlier should be seen. Describing himself as "the last chance" to avoid a global cataclysm, Farrakhan said, "You cannot say 'Never again' to God, because when he puts you in the oven, 'Never again' don't mean a thing."[116] Farrakhan claims that his warning springs not out of hatred but out of concern, so that Jews do not end up being destroyed by God.[117] Farrakhan, moreover, is not only warning the Jews but also the black community. Upon hearing the reaction of a cheering audience after a similar statement, Farrakhan punched, "Hey! Don't laugh, 'cause 90 percent of you are headin' into that same oven."[118] Here, Farrakhan clearly uses the Holocaust as a metaphor, as an image of Armageddon, with the oven representing the fire of the approaching apocalypse.[119]

Though this metaphor is frequently used, it is bound to be interpreted differently in the Jewish and in the African American communities. For Farrakhan, the coming cataclysm is as real as the Holocaust that Jews (or blacks) experienced, and will affect us all. Again, a better understanding will be reached if we listen to Farrakhan's entire statement: "If I were Jewish I would say 'never again.' I wouldn't like to see a Hitler coming up again. What I say to Jewish people is you can never say to God never again. Because we don't control His power. We may be able to stop another Hitler. But if God decrees an oven for us all no one can stop it. And if you read the Torah as I read it, or read the Gospel as I read it, or read the Quran as I read it, God promised water in the destruction in the days of Noah, but He promised a baptism of fire in the destruction of the present world 'cause this world is totally out of order. You cannot say to God 'never again,' he's gonna put us all in an oven if we're not gettin' this damn thing straightened out, and quick."[120] Connected to the Jewish Holocaust is the Zionist theme, elaborated along two different paths. The first is the common practice of leftist or Muslim critics of Israel to differentiate between anti-Zionism and anti-Semitism,[121] a distinction not always accepted in the Jewish community, where analysts may argue that the former is the latter in a different guise. Farrakhan takes part in the Pan-Islamic front that supports Palestinian rights to their homeland and regards the creation of Israel as the establishment of a modern-day Crusader state. In religious terms, Israel is a wicked hypocrisy, and "Zionists are the outgrowth of Jewish transgressions."[122] Here, Farrakhan cites with approval the orthodox Jews who believe the creation of Israel to be contrary to God's plan, as it only should be established as a consequence of the Messiah's coming. As do many other African Americans, Farrakhan identifies with the plight of the Palestinians, deprived of their homeland at the hands of European power,[123] but also believes "that the Jews deserve, not only deserve but need a homeland."[124]

The second path of elaboration derives from the ideological parallels between the NOI and Zionism. The Nation points to Israel as an example to emulate. The post–World War II creation of an independent Jewish state and the reparations paid to Jews by Germany are seen here as giving a legal precedent to the NOI's demands for a separate state and reparations for all the centuries of unpaid slave labor.[125] Summing up the suffering of the African American, Farrakhan holds America in debt well beyond her assets: "Add it up, white man. The whole world belongs to the oppressed, if you add it up. But we're not asking for the whole thing . . . just give us some of it and let us go to build a nation for ourselves."[126] America came and took Palestine and gave it to the Jews, Farrakhan said, suggesting that blacks ask their African brethren for land as compensation for African involvement in the slave trade: "You helped get us into this hell of a condition. You got land over there that is fertile and mineral rich, outlets to the sea, nobody workin' it. Why should we have 600,000, or so, black men in prison spendin' their time in jail? We got black people that got no jobs but plenty of skills . . . let them go, and let them build a new reality on the African continent, work off their time, building a new nation backed by the money that the government owes us. . . . Don't think that's far fetched, but give us dual citizenship like you did to the Jews."[127] At the very least, the United States should do as the Germans did and recognize the evils they have perpetrated on an innocent people. When East Germany officially apologized to the Jews, Farrakhan argued that America should have "the courage to just use these words, same words, just change it, look, this is how it should read, an official document from the government": "We ask the blacks of the world to forgive us. We ask the black people of America to forgive us for the hypocrisy and hostility of official U.S. government politics towards them, and for the persecution and the degradation of black so-called citizens also after their so-called emancipation in 1863 in our country. We declare our willingness to contribute as much as possible to the healing of mental and physical suffering of survivors, and to provide just compensation for material loss."[128] The black Zionist orientation of the NOI is closely connected to the "Jew as an impostor" theme, frequently recycled in black Muslim sermons. The main point is that the blacks are the original people of the covenant and the principal actors of the Holy Scriptures: "I [Farrakhan] declare to the world that the people of God are not those who call themselves Jews, but the people of God who are chosen in this critical time in history are you, the black people of America, the lost, the despised, the rejected."[129] The white Jew is a European devil, "a Johnny-come-lately Jew," a bold impostor. Twisting the argument turns around the anti-Semitic charge: "Did you know that those Jews are not Semitic people? They're Indo-Europeans. The real Semitic Jews, the Falashas, the dark-skinned Jews of Africa and the Middle East, they're second class citizens and Israel is run by European Jews who are the real anti-Semitic people of the world."[130] The stress placed on blacks as the true people of God makes Farrakhan frequently repudiate similar Jewish claims. He declares as a fact that Israel never was in Egyptian bondage for four hundred years.[131] This fulfills God's prophecy to Abraham/Imam Shabazz in Genesis 15:13–14, with the advent of black slavery in America, and proclaims the Exodus as an imminent reality. The competition for the status as the people of the covenant is the real reason, Farrakhan believes, for the Jewish rage against him and the NOI: "The Jews don't like me 'cause I'm saying they're not the chosen people of God."[132] While religious, as well as many secular, Jews dismiss the NOI's claim to be the chosen people as "ridiculous," a dismissal regarded as a grave offense in the Nation, another attitude holds religion to be irrelevant. As Gail Gams said at the ADL, "You wanna be chosen? Be chosen. Look what it has done for us throughout the centuries to get chosen, I mean, if that's what it's all about—you can have it. Be chosen, go ahead!"[133]

Jewish opposition against Farrakhan has taken different forms over the past years. The ADL has engaged in surveillance, distribution of fact-sheet memorandums to journalists,[134] political anti-NOI lobbying, including pressure put on African American leaders to repudiate Farrakhan, and attempts to block NOI enterprising. Jewish student organizations have tried to prevent NOI spokespersons from speaking on campuses and have frequently staged picket lines to protest eventual appearances. Combined with more militant Jewish activities, such as bombings and death threats, this has strengthened the NOI's notion of the powerful Jew, a notion first based on the black urban ghetto experience of Jewish slumlords and entrepreneurs. As noted above, Jews as a group do wield power in the United States, a question that is difficult to address without being accused of anti-Semitism. Discussing this topic, Farrakhan's statements do resemble classic anti-Semitic positions.

As with the Zionist theme, the "mighty Jew" theme is elaborated in two disparate lines of reasoning, one of condemnation and the other of emulation. Since the Honorable Elijah Muhammad, Jews have been held up as an example for the African American community. Jews teach their children Jewish history and pass on Jewish culture and traditions.[135] Jews have established an exemplary solidarity, building a strong economy,[136] and politically organizing themselves effectively.[137] "Jews are only nearly six million in America," Farrakhan said in 1990. "The Jews have seven Senators and thirty something . . . in the House of Representatives. . . . Here we are, nearly forty million, only have twenty-three people in the House of Representatives [and] no Senator."[138] The lesson is "not to blame the Jews" but to copy their networking and solidarity.[139]

For Erwin Suall at the ADL, Farrakhan's praise of Jews as an example worthy of emulation is not comforting. "From this kind of admiration, you could be killed," he commented. "This is not at all unique . . . for Farrakhan. It is quite common for Jews to be described [by white anti-Semites] in ways that appear to be admirable, almost as if these were qualities that they envy. . . . But, it's precisely those qualities, somehow, that feed this . . . anti-Semitic obsession."[140]

It is along the other line of reasoning that Farrakhan jumps to anti-Semitic conclusions. To question the fact that a number of American politicians are honorary members in the Israeli Knesset is hardly anti-Semitic. It is one thing, however, to point to a powerful pro-Israeli political lobby and another to conclude that "the Jews, a small handful, control the movement of this great nation, like a radar controls the movement of a great ship in the waters . . . the Jews got a stranglehold on the Congress."[141]

The white Jews, who according to the NOI demonology are as naturally evil as all other whites, are denounced as "masters" of the Devil's world. Although less powerful than the secret society of chief devils, the Masons, the white Jews control the American Medical Association, the universities, Hollywood, and the government.[142] Jews are especially dangerous as they represent the foxy type of devils, masquerading as friends of the African American. "When you get the Jew out of hiding," Farrakhan said, "he's the last barrier you got to get by."[143]

The former coalition between Jews and African Americans was a snare designed to keep the civil rights movement within the confines of the present system of white supremacy, a manipulation that still is a reality and has caused the present crisis in black leadership.[144] Farrakhan makes no secret of his intentions to "break up the relationship" between blacks and Jews, a relation he describes as one between exploited and exploiter, oppressed and oppressor, with roots in the slave trade: "They never tell you that . . . some of the biggest slave merchants were Jews. The owners of the slave ships were Jews. They were then masters of the channels of distribution. From that day we had a relationship. You and they. They own the house, you clean it. They buy the food, you cook it. They own the property, you rent it. They got the store, you buy from them. You got the talent, they're the agent and the manager. . . . It's been a master-slave relationship. We don't want that kind of relationship. We want a relationship equatable and on just terms."[145] To prove his claim, Farrakhan had the Historical Research Department of the NOI initiate a study of Jewish involvement in the slave business, which was published in 1991 as *The Secret Relationship between Blacks and Jews.* Judged by the strict standards of historical scholarship, the study is absolutely unreliable. Based primarily on Jewish historical literature, it may seem to be revealing and accurate for a nonacademically trained reader, but the study contains numerous fundamental methodological flaws. For instance, it lists the number of Jewish soldiers who upheld slavocracy in the Caribbean or enlisted in the Confederate Army but does not mention the total size of the armed forces or the number of Jews in the Union Army. Moreover, it lists the number of Jewish slave dealers and the number of slaves they owned, state by state, but not the total number of slave dealers and their stock of human chattel.[146] By using this technique, generalizing the particular and providing lists of involved Jews but not figures of comparison, an image of Jews masterminding the slave trade is constructed. Eugene D. Genovese, one of America's most prominent slave historians, claims that the study "rivals *The Protocols of the Learned Elders of Zion* in fantasy and gross distortion. The absurdity of its pretensions to scholarship are outweighed only by its sheer viciousness."[147]

The NOI's use of the study as "irrefutable evidence" for claims of disproportionately high Jewish involvement in the slave trade or frequent Jewish sexual abuse of black female slaves,[148] will undoubtedly fuel the flames of black-Jewish animosity and hamper the efforts made by Louis Farrakhan to reach a constructive dialogue with the Jewish community.[149] In *The Secret Relationship,* the NOI authors build their case by using the very method they accuse the ADL of: decontextualization and highly selective reading. Dialogue depends on mutual recognition and respect, and neither will be possible if the characterization of the other is based on this type of distorted and futile evidence.

Farrakhan, who aspires to a greater role in mainstream American politics and in the African American community, has to reach a reconciliation with the Jewish community. The struggle he finds himself locked in is not the real jihad he mobilizes for and anti-Semitism has no place at the top of his agenda. As noted by C. Eric Lincoln, "it is unfortunate that those old echoes of anti-Semitism have not been put to rest. He [Farrakhan] has too much to say about the urgent problems facing . . . America to be alienated by racial rhetoric."[150] In an attempt to reach reconciliation with the Jewish community, Farrakhan gave a musical performance in Winston-Salem, North Carolina, on April 18, 1993, and played a Felix Mendelssohn violin concerto as a symbolic message.[151] Shortly after his sixtieth birthday, Farrakhan repeated his euphonious peace gesture before a Chicago audience of 3,000 on May 17, 1993, hoping "to undo with music what words had done."[152] Although appreciated in sections of mainstream America, Farrakhan's overture, including his frequently repeated offer to sit down with any responsible Jewish leader in a constructive dialogue,[153] was met by the Jewish community with skepticism at best and disdain at worst. While Michael Kotzin of the Jewish Relations Community Council doubted Farrakhan's sincerity,[154] Erwin Suall of the Anti-Defamation League said that "one has to be a fool to take seriously that [Farrakhan playing Mendelssohn] represents a gesture to the Jewish community. The fact that he plays the music of a dead [Jewish] convert to Christianity is no gesture at all."[155]

Within parts of the black community and the more hardcore anti-Semitic fraction of the NOI, Farrakhan's move was criticized for going too far.[156] He should not repeat Jackson's mistake of bowing down and humiliating himself to be accepted by his enemies. Farrakhan, faced with Jewish dismissal and black disparagement, gave a speech entitled "Has Farrakhan changed direction?" in which he rebutted charges of having compromised: "Brother Farrakhan has not changed his direction one atom's weight. If I change my direction, I will have deviated from the path laid down for me by God and His Apostle, the Honorable Elijah Muhammad. . . . God will punish you if you turn from me as long as I don't turn from truth. Truth is one thing but strategy, tactic is another. . . . It's not for me to tell you at every turn what stratagem or tactic I am applying to get us safely to the goal and objective. It's not for me as a general to tell you that. The generals are not to tell tactics, the generals give orders. And that's my job to give orders and your job is to obey the orders."[157] When preparations for the 1993 March on Washington began, Farrakhan, who had given the shortest speech in his life at the 1983 march, was again scheduled to speak. During the 1980s, Farrakhan had become much more influential in the African American community but was also targeted as a leading anti-Semite. Reacting against the NOI's participation, Reform Rabbi David Saperstein wrote to the organizers. He referred to a 1988 agreement to not invite Farrakhan and said that if he was to speak "obviously, all of the Jewish groups will be forced to withdraw."[158]

In the face of losing Jewish participation and financial support, the organizers banned Farrakhan from the march,[159] but he managed to turn the incident to his favor. Soldiers in the FOI distributed copies of the Saperstein letter to the crowd,[160] and Farrakhan lashed out at cowardly black leaders who "bow down and compromise a principle of ours for the sake of a few dollars." No Jew would tolerate any black or white person telling them whom they could invite to their events, Farrakhan wrote, threatening to "expose Jewish influence over Black leaders." He stated he would "never again ask for a dialogue with the Jewish community" and ended with a warning to "the so-called leaders" that the day has come that "you will either feel the wrath of angry Jews for doing what is right or the wrath of Allah and our people for betraying what is in the best interest of the liberation of our people."[161] The crisis manifested in the black leadership was resolved at a September 16 meeting arranged by the Congressional Black Caucus (CBC). CBC chairman Kwesi Mfume announced a formal CBC-NOI alliance and pledged that "no longer will we allow people to divide us."[162] At the meeting, Farrakhan was also embraced by NAACP chairman Rev. Ben Chavis and Jesse Jackson, who entered the sacred covenant with the NOI to work for real change.[163]

Media reports on the long sought "peace pact toward true black power" and an unprecedented "black united front"[164] alarmed the Anti-Defamation League, which historically was part of the civil rights movement, and which still "values the friendship" with the NAACP and CBC. "When we see them developing a coalition with Farrakhan, it's obviously very painful for us," Erwin Suall commented, adding that he personally thinks the ADL must "be quite forceful with them" and eventually "sever the relationship that we've had with these organizations and causes for decades."[165]

At this critical point, NOI national assistant, Khallid Abdul Muhammad (born Harold Moore Vann) entered the debate. Defending his leader from critics who implied that Farrakhan had turned soft by playing the violin, Khallid remarked, "David played on the harp, but when it was time to take Goliath out, he pulled his slingshot out, struck Goliath in the head, took Goliath's sword and chopped his head off and went back and played a tune on his harp."[166] This parable was related in a speech at Kean College, New Jersey, on November 29, 1993, in which Khallid lavishly attacked Jews, Catholics, whites, and blacks. As the media followed their now familiar pattern of publishing articles based on ADL reports instead of actual NOI speeches, Khallid's outrageous statements are only partly known. Most articles followed the ADL full-page ad in the *New York Times,* on January 16, 1994, with excerpts from Khallid's New Jersey performance.[167] When, for example, Khallid asked the audience who the slumlords of the black community are, the ad correctly states "the so-called Jew," but omits the context of "the white slumlords, the white so-called Jew slumlords, and other white slumlords."[168]

This is not pointed out to diminish the anti-Semitic flavor of Khallid Abdul Muhammad's remarks, but only to let the full context be known. Khallid, who is a less sophisticated speaker than Louis Farrakhan, represents the more hard-core youth segment of the Nation. He is a rapper who has performed with Public Enemy on their album *It Will Take a Nation of Millions to Hold Us Back* and with Ice Cube on the *Death Certificate* and *Lethal Injection* albums, a fact that probably accounts in part for his popularity among black urban youth. Understanding black rap talk is a requirement for understanding Khallid's speeches, in which macho rap and stand-up color his views. Khallid said to the mixed audience of blacks and whites, "It's gonna be a rough ride, buddy. It's gonna be a rough ride. You better buckle in, buckle up, guys, buckle your seat belts. If for any reason this auditorium becomes depressurized, automatically, oxygen masks will fall from the ceiling. Please make sure to fix the elastic band around your head firmly, and put the mask over your mouth and nose first. And then help the white person next to you. I didn't come to Kean College to tiptoe through the tulips. I didn't come to Kean College to pussyfoot. I didn't come to Kean College to dillydally or beat around the bush. I didn't come to pin the tail on the donkey. I came to pin the tail on the honkey. . . . Good evening, this is truth hour, and don't you touch that dial, stay tuned in."[169] Even taking black rap into consideration, however, Khallid is undoubtedly, if not in NOI terms anti-Semitic, anti-whatever-Jews-are-called.[170] He has the audience participate by answering his questions, working up a frenzy. "A Jew states that Jews 'were among the most important slave dealers'," Khallid began, "What did he say? They were among the most important what?" "Slave dealers," shouts the audience. Khallid then goes on with Jesus' words to the Jews, "You are of your father the devil. What did Jesus say?" and gets the loud return, "The Devil!"[171]

Jews are of the synagogue of Satan, chief liars and master devils who run the "Jew-nited Nations" in "Jew York City," and who deserved Hitler,[172] but Khallid does not confine his rage to them, as he also attacks homosexuals, the pope,[173] whites, and black "race traitors." His hate became most explicitly manifest when discussing what South African blacks ought to do with white folks. Whites, Khallid maintained, should be given twenty-four hours to get out, and those remaining should be exterminated: "We will kill the women, we will kill the children, we will kill the babies. We will kill the crippled, we will kill 'em all. We will kill the faggot, we will kill the lesbian, we will kill them all. . . . Kill the old ones too. Goddamit, if they in a wheelchair, push 'em off a cliff in Cape Town. . . . I said kill the blind, kill the crippled, kill the crazy. Goddamit, and when you get through killing 'em all, go to the goddam graveyard and dig up the grave and kill 'em, goddam, again. 'Cause they didn't die hard enough."[174] Next to whites, Jews included, Khallid Abdul Muhammad unleashes his wrath on blacks who dissent against his and the Nation's positions. Spike Lee is portrayed as a Judas paid $30 million for his *Malcolm X* movie, "a bubble-eyed, pigeon-toed, Jiminy Cricket, grasshopper-lookin' Spook Lee [who] is trying to turn you away from your salvation." An "X" fever that does not turn blacks to the "X-perts who can X-plain who you are . . . who can set an X-ample" is counterproductive, with blacks "X-citingly" bearing X-caps and X-signs "X-ternally" instead of internally, Khallid argued. Worse than confused blacks are used blacks, running errands for the Devil, "When white folks can't defeat you, they'll always find some negro, some boot-lickin', butt-lickin', butt-dancing, bamboozled, half-baked, half-fried sissiefied, punkified, pasteurized, homogenized nigger that they trod in front of you."[175]

Within a few days after the aforementioned ADL ad in the *New York Times,* more than 400 editorials and articles condemned the NOI, as did the entire United States Senate in a resolution passed by 97 to 0.[176] The speech by Khallid Abdul Muhammad was denounced not only by Jewish and white spokespersons and organizations, but also by a wide range of influential blacks, such as Jesse Jackson, Kwesi Mfume, Wyatt Tee Walker, and Rev. Al Sharpton.[177] For Farrakhan, the Kean College speech was devastating, surfacing shortly after the sought-after black unity between the NOI and black mainstream organizations had become reality.

On February 3, 1994, the day after the CBC had declared the covenant with the NOI nullified, Farrakhan called a press conference and announced that Khallid Abdul Muhammad was dismissed as minister and national assistant. Farrakhan stated that he had warned Khallid several times earlier that his language was inappropriate and ultimately would backfire. This time, because the speech had reached nationwide attention, Farrakhan said he had to publicly rebuke Khallid Muhammad: "I found the speech, after listening to it in context, vile in manner, repugnant, malicious, mean-spirited and spoken in mockery of individuals and people, which is against the spirit of Islam. While I stand by the truths that he spoke, I must condemn in the strongest terms the manner in which those truths were represented."[178] What these "truths" were supposed to be was not specified by Minister Farrakhan, except the point regarding Jewish slaveholders. "Jewish scholars have said that 75 percent of the slaves owned in the South was owned by Jewish slaveholders," Farrakhan argued. "They said it, we didn't say it, they said it, and if Brother Khallid had just quoted the book, nobody would have been able to condemn him or call him anti-Semitic."[179] Farrakhan's words and actions failed to impress Abraham Foxman, national director of the ADL, who termed it "double talk." Farrakhan only "rejects the manner of the message—not the message. He says the message is the truth. And it's the manner of the delivery that he does not like, so he doesn't reject the message, doesn't reject the messenger, just doesn't like the way he delivered it."[180]

By dismissing Khallid Abdul Muhammad as national assistant, Farrakhan runs the risk of repeating the mistake made by Elijah Muhammad when he silenced Malcolm X. Khallid Muhammad has a growing reputation as "a new Malcolm" and is held in esteem as a strong freedom fighter.[181] Maneuvering to avoid a schism in the NOI, Farrakhan spoke approvingly of Khallid as a "warrior" and a "beautiful black stallion," saying he remained a member of the Nation and could regain Farrakhan's trust after demonstrating willingness to adhere to the true teachings of Elijah Muhammad.[182] It seems that Farrakhan's mixed message draws criticism not only from the ADL but also from his followers. According to *Chicago Sun-Times* reporter Mary A. Johnson, the suspension of Khallid Abdul Muhammad "stunned many supporters," who were "upset" over the ADL's successful effort to force Farrakhan to repudiate and fire his national assistant.[183] At a February 5, 1994, speech at Baltimore Community College, his first public appearance since his dismissal, Khallid confessed that "this is the most difficult and trying time" of his life. He declared full loyalty to Minister Farrakhan and the NOI, saying to those who would "love to see a split" that they would not "hear one paragraph, not one sentence, not one word against Louis Farrakhan."[184]

When Khallid Muhammad was shot on May 29, 1994, the parallel with Malcolm X ran closer. Khallid had given a speech at the University of California at Riverside and went to his car. In the parking lot, James X Bess appeared with a gun, wounding Khallid Abdul Muhammad, four of his bodyguards, and a bystander. An aggravated crowd of some seventy people jumped on the assailant before police came to his rescue. James X had been expelled by Khallid and/or his close aide, Wazir Muhammad, as minister of the Seattle Mosque three years earlier. Claiming loyalty to Farrakhan, James X established a splinter group representing the "true" philosophy of the NOI and he seemed to be out for revenge.[185] Khallid Muhammad and the others survived, James X included. The latter's time may be short, however, as Khallid called for a people's court to exact justice, meaning that the prisons hardly will be safe for him. Concerning the assault, the central question awaits its answer: Was James X Bess a lonely lunatic or was he used by any of those forces that would benefit from a repetition of the Malcolm X murder story? An indication of a third-party involvement surfaced in the later speculations of a power struggle in the Nation between Conrad Muhammad of New York and Khallid Muhammad, comparable with the "two birds with one rock" concept of the 1960s. Made wise by past events, a unity meeting between Khallid and Conrad Muhammad was called in an effort to counter further escalation of the internal differences.[186] In the wake of other developments, Farrakhan could then quietly reinstall Khallid Abdul Muhammad as minister on July 1, 1995.

Anti-Semites or Anti-Satanites?   The early NOI position reflects that period's black notion of Jews as a somewhat different and more benign sort of whites. For the Honorable Elijah Muhammad, the Jews were primarily an example to emulate. Jewish solidarity, economic advancement, and the struggle for self-determination in a land of their own were all depicted as successfully realized parallels to the NOI path of black liberation. The Holocaust was used as an argument for the necessity of separation: Jews thought they were integrated in German society, and look what happened! The present hard-core faction of the Nation that at times charges Farrakhan for deviating from the teachings of Elijah Muhammad when searching for reconciliation with the Jews has a meager case insofar as the Messenger's speeches and writings are concerned. Although scattered unfavorable statements can be found, especially concerning Israel and Jewish business in black ghettos, it is generally the case that if Jews are considered separate from their fellow devils, it is as a body to emulate or as a theological analogy.[187] In addition, the NOI at that time cooperated willingly with Jewish businessmen, lawyers, and entrepreneurs.[188] Apart from the NOI's belief that the blacks are the chosen people of God, which implies a repudiation of any other group that claims that identity, Jews as such had no given position in the Messenger's agenda, and their place today is primarily a result of the sociopolitical developments that changed the pattern of black-Jewish relationships.[189]

As opponents to black power, Jewish organizations will attract fire from advocates of black self-determination, Louis Farrakhan included. As an opponent to perceived Jewish power in America and West Asia, Farrakhan similarly invites Jewish animosity. Confronted with attacks from well-connected Jewish organizations, an image of the Jew as a well-organized and mighty enemy emerged, an image that not only was identified as anti-Semitic by Jewish observers but that also facilitated the introduction of anti-Semitic sentiments into the mental universe of the Nation. Facing a situation in which Jews appeared in the enemies' front line, the past was reconsidered in the light of the present, and *The Secret Relationship between Blacks and Jews* unraveled: they are not only against our liberation but were responsible for our enslavement.

To the extent that the study is based more on poor scholarship than bad will, it can be reexamined and its conclusions corrected. As it stands, it adds to the emerging anti-Semitism in the African American community and obscures the true historical dynamic of the slave system. Harold Brackman has easily refuted the main arguments of *The Secret Relationship*,[190] and the historical distortions put forward by the NOI turn into a boomerang that might ruin the legitimate black demands for reparations. To change an unsatisfying reality, each component has to be identified and clearly understood in order to appropriately address it. Jews, as do all people who were involved, have to reflect on their part in the old slavocracy as well as on the current social codes of racism, both institutionalized and unarticulated. The tendencies to think that a black cannot be a racist and to dismiss justified criticism against black misbehavior as racism, have their counterparts in the idea that a Jew cannot be a racist and the dismissal of justified criticism against Jewish misbehavior as anti-Semitism. If reparations are a legitimate demand from white America, Jews cannot be excluded. As Farrakhan has said, "Do you mean to tell me that Jews have never done any evil to Black people? And if I point it out, does that mean that I hate Jews? Is there no pain on our side? Were they not involved in the slave trade? Yes, they were. . . . And to the extent that they were involved, somebody has to bring them to account. And I believe that has fallen on me."[191] Is Farrakhan basically an anti-Semite? From a mainstream Jewish perspective there might be no question about it, but Farrakhan denies the charge,[192] repeatedly defending his statements by emphasizing that he only speaks of certain Jews and their particular behavior. "Why can't I be critical of certain aspects of Jewish misbehavior, manipulation, exploitation of the black experience?" Farrakhan asked. "And if I do that, why paint me as an anti-Semite?"[193] This might generally be true, but equally obvious are the instances when the particular is generalized and the Jews as a people are genetically ascribed malicious characteristics.

According to Farrakhan, white Jews are devils, a matter of belief that could be taken as anti-Semitic if considered out of context. While it is understandable that Jews focus on this part of the NOI's demonology and find similarities between subsequent derivations and the propositions of classic white anti-Semitism, it would nonetheless be a misrepresentation, a case of substituting the whole for the part. For Farrakhan and the NOI, the focus is not on the Jews but on white world supremacy, the Devil's global hegemony. Jews are devils not because of their Jewishness but because of their whiteness. The NOI ideology is in this respect a racist theory about genetic qualities. Black Jews are by the same logic of the original people and not devils. The NOI has had a good relationship with a variety of black Hebrews, like Prince Asiel Ben Israel and Rabhee Ben Ammi of the Original Hebrew Israelite Nation, and the NOI uses the Torah with other Holy Scriptures.[194] The Nation of Islam spokespersons are basically anti-Satanites, and the primary reason for them being termed anti-Semites instead of racists is that Jews only seem to be sensitive enough to pay serious attention to what is said in the black community.

This does not exclude anti-Semitic traits in Farrakhan's speeches or the present NOI ideology, traits that are growing in importance and that probably will be further reinforced by the escalating conflict between the NOI and Jewish organizations.[195] Farrakhan's present obsession with Jews mirrors the Jewish obsession with Farrakhan. The Anti-Defamation League of B'nai B'rith identifies Farrakhan as the number one anti-Semitic propagator in America, surpassing by far white extremists in regard to the number of people reached.[196] Their activities to expose Farrakhan, to pressure black leaders to denounce him, to stop the use of university funds to pay NOI speakers' honorariums, or to block NOI enterprising,[197] conspire to create an image of Jews as a better-organized body of devils, dedicated to frustrating the Blackman's resurrection. "You're not gonna to be free," Farrakhan told his audience, "before you get past the Jew."[198]

While the ADL works exclusively by peaceful means, other organizations target Farrakhan more militantly. When Farrakhan or any of his top ministers are scheduled to speak at colleges or universities, Jewish militants frequently try to disturb or disrupt the meeting. Pickets with Jews shouting "Who do we want?—Farrakhan! How do we want him?—Dead!" are far from unusual and the Jewish Defense Organization had Farrakhan on top of the death list found by police investigating a bombing of Arab-American facilities. The Jewish Defense League has staged at least one "Death to Farrakhan" march, on Saviour's Day, October 7, 1985.[199] On several occasions, direct confrontation between militants of the FOI and the JDL have been only narrowly averted,[200] and the question remains how long a serious clash between the two camps' more venturesome activists can be avoided.

Farrakhan carefully cultivates a macho image, which is connected to the black counterpart of the Jewish battle cry "Never Again!" For blacks, this means never again slavery, never again being reduced to a subhuman chattel, never again returning offenses with a "yessir" or "nomassa." When Jewish student groups voice criticism against Farrakhan coming to their campuses, or when the ADL tries to make black people denounce Farrakhan, the standard black reaction becomes an angry cry: "the Jews are not going to tell us who our leaders are going to be!" Farrakhan's popularity to a large extent depends on the notion of him as a bold, proud, strong, free black person, not a "boy" but a man, who will never bow down to any white person, Jews included. The more visible the pressure, the greater the prestige, as long as he does not crack under it. "We're not going to tell our people to turn the other cheek—that's how we lost all our cheeks," Farrakhan argued, encouraging his people to "stand up like men and women! And if you're gonna die, then damn it, die fighting for your liberation!"[201]

In addition to his "not a slave" image, Farrakhan places the Jewish opposition to his mission in a religious context. The Devil's world is built on falsehood and deceit, which is why "the most dangerous man or women is one in whom God has placed the truth," Farrakhan stated. "When such a man appears, that kind of man will be lied upon by the arch-deceiver and liar. They must paint the bearer of truth as a wicked man, so that you will close your ears to the truth that will mean your salvation and their damnation."[202] Living in the messianic age, experiencing the biblical narratives as they materialize, gives the scriptural context for Farrakhan's understanding of experienced Jewish aggression. "You didn't like Jesus and you don't like Farrakhan, and Farrakhan is doing the same work among my people as Jesus did among his people. And I have the same enemies, only that my enemies are much more sophisticated, much more powerful."[203] Farrakhan asks, Who disliked Jesus? The Roman authorities (the American government), the scribes (the media), the Pharisee (the mainstream religious clergy of all faiths) and the Jews (the white Jews).[204] Farrakhan does not believe that it is a coincidence that he repeatedly has been termed "a black Hitler": "Look at the seed that is planted. If you tell young Jews that here's a new Hitler coming, if you were Jewish—how would you take that? Do you think young Jews want to repeat the horrors of the Holocaust? No. So, in the heart of young Jews, the seed of murder is planted for Farrakhan."[205] The classic foundation of Christian anti-Semitism, popularized throughout the centuries with or without the authorization of church and government, is the image of Jews as Christ killers. The obvious reply to anyone who brands such a remark as anti-Semitic is also a classic, seemingly innocent but viciously false, reference: "They killed Jesus. I didn't write the Bible. I didn't write the Quran. Both the Bible and the Quran say the Jews did it. I didn't say it. If the book is anti-Semitic, then burn the Bible—don't burn me. If the Bible accuses the Jews of murdering the prophets, and the Quran does the same, then you take that up with God. I didn't write any of the books, I'm just quoting the books."[206] Jewish opposition strengthens Farrakhan's self-esteem as a messianic liberator, and his angry counterattacks are hailed with standing ovations. "This is not 2,000 years ago. You're not gonna harm me without serious consequences," Farrakhan warns, "I'm very special in God's eyes . . . if you attempt to harm me, He will kill you all."[207]

In concluding this section, it should be emphasized that anti-Semitism has not, thus far, been a dominant, constant feature of Farrakhan's ideology, regardless of what is being said in the American media. Neither is anti-Semitism what attracts the multitudes that jam the halls and stadiums where Farrakhan speaks. A 1994 Time/CNN poll showed that only a fifth of the blacks familiar with Farrakhan thought him anti-Semitic, while two-thirds viewed him favorably.[208] What does appeal, it seems, is Farrakhan's boldness and his stand on and proposed solutions to a wide range of serious problems presently affecting African Americans, Hispanics, Native Americans, and poor whites, which are discussed in the following chapter. African Americans are generally not anti-Semites, they are problack and increasingly Afrocentric. They are used to seeing their heroes denounced by the white (Jewish or non-Jewish) American press and are capable of forming their own opinions. The inflexible refusal of Jewish organizations to engage in a dialogue with Farrakhan and the NOI is hazardous, as it might widen the rift between the African American and Jewish communities and give the tainted seed of anti-Semitism an opportunity to grow.

The Nazi Connection   Anti-Semitism is thought by some scholars to be the link between the Nation of Islam and white right-wing extremist nationalists, such as the Ku Klux Klan (KKK), the White Aryan Resistance (WAR), and some of their fellow racists at home and abroad. The British

based antifascist journal *Searchlight* revealed increasing contacts between England's National Front (NF) and the Nation of Islam in the
1980s,[209] and positions Farrakhan and the NOI on their map showing Britain's right-wing extremist network.[210] Reports of WAR leader Tom Metzger
pledging support for the NOI,[211] of Farrakhan convening with German
Nazis and LaRouchies in support of Saddam Hussein,[212] or of a "New
Axis" linking "Islamic fundamentalists"—a label erroneously applied to
Farrakhan and Qadhdhafi as well as Khomeini—with neo-Nazis,[213] seem
to support the thesis that the NOI is a sort of black Nazism headed by Louis
"black Hitler" Farrakhan.

Paradoxical as it might seem, there does exist a kind of relationship or
mutual understanding between black and white radical racialists that
extends back in history to the era of classic black nationalism, before the
first resurrection of the NOI. The common ground is laid out by Marcus
Garvey, who said that he believed "in a pure black race just as how all self-
respecting whites believe in a pure white race, as far as that can be."[214]
Garvey argued that all whites shared the perspective of white supremacy
and the intention to make permanent its hegemony. White unionists and
communists might theorize on interracial class solidarity and use the
African American as front-line soldiers to overthrow the American capitalist society, but will, if successful, create a communist version of white
power with their former allies still on the bottom. White liberals and
"psuedophilanthropists" fool the blacks into viewing some whites as
their friends and disarm their anger by redirecting them from the race
struggle toward the "impossible dream of equality that shall never materialize." The "greatest enemies" of the African American are thus those
whites who "hypocritically profess love and fellowship for him" when in
truth they "despise and hate him."[215] Garvey wrote, "I regard the Klan, the
Anglo-Saxon Clubs and White American Societies, as far as the Negro is
concerned, as better friends of the race than all other groups of hypocritical whites put together. I like honesty and fair play. . . . potentially, every
whiteman is a Klansman, as far as the Negro in competition with whites
socially, economically and politically is concerned, and there is no use
lying about it."[216] This reasoning was adopted and accentuated by the
Nation of Islam in the theory of the genetic evilness of all whites, reducing the difference between white racists and professed antiracists to a
distinction of the devils' strategies to get their prey, the people of color.
Malcolm X termed the dual categories of devils "wolves" and "foxes," of
which he, like Garvey, undoubtedly preferred the former: "The white

conservatives aren't friends of the Negro . . . but they at least don't try to hide it. They are like wolves; they show their teeth in a snarl that keeps the Negro always aware of where he stands with them. But the white liberals are foxes, who also show their teeth to the Negro but pretend that they are smiling. The white liberals are more dangerous than the conservatives; they lure the Negro, and as the Negro runs from the growling wolf, he flees into the open jaws of the 'smiling' fox."[217]

When Malcolm X turned against the Messenger as the rift between them widened, he accused the NOI of having entered into a secret agreement with the American Nazi Party and the Ku Klux Klan. "I know for a fact," Malcolm X told the press a week before his assassination, "that there is a conspiracy between . . . the Muslims and the Lincoln Rockwell Nazis and also the Ku Klux Klan."[218] Concerning the latter, Malcolm referred to a series of negotiations between the Klan and the NOI, which had been conducted at the home of Atlanta NOI minister Jeremiah X in 1960. Malcolm said that they were trying to make a county-sized tract of land in Georgia or South Carolina available for the Muslims, thereby making the program for a separate state feasible. He said that he himself had taken part in one of those meetings, in December 1960, and had reported back to Elijah Muhammad. Malcolm continued to deny any further knowledge of the outcome, but alleged that the Nation could from then on operate without hindrance in Klan territory in the South and that the whole direction of the NOI changed. While it formerly had been militant, the NOI became oriented to the accumulation of wealth, in effect disarming the black struggle.[219] In addition, Klan historian David Chalmers reports that in 1964, the said Jeremiah X attended a daylight Klan rally in Hurd Park, Atlanta, and was praised by Imperial Wizard Robert M. Shelton.[220] FBI files confirm Malcolm's testimony regarding a meeting between Klan officials and NOI leaders, and report that it took place in Atlanta on January 28, 1961. Malcolm was to have stated that he had 175,000 separatist followers and that they "were soliciting the aid of the Klan to obtain land."[221] Karl Evanzz, who views John X Ali as the FBI's man in the top leadership of the NOI, notes that Texas multimillionaire and far-rightist Haroldson Lafayette Hunt began funding the NOI shortly after John X Ali's ascension to the post of national secretary early in 1960.[222] Evanzz claims, in addition, that it was John X Ali who proposed the NOI-KKK land deal that he says was worked out by Malcolm X, with real estate agent Slater Hunter King arranging the actual purchase.[223]

Apart from other reasons, one motive for an agreement with the KKK can have been to avoid negative experiences, such as those from Alabama. The NOI had bought farmland near Pell City, Alabama, and the local Klan took an active part in the white popular front against the Muslim farmers. One-tenth of the population in St. Clair County assembled at a meeting and vowed to oust the NOI from their land. Sixty-three prized dairy cattle were either shot or poisoned, the Klan leased adjacent farmland to encircle the Muslims, and local blacks were jailed on suspicion of being "unregistered Muslims" in violation of an Alabama law forcing NOI members to report to the police if staying in the state for more than five days.[224]

Whether operating on directions from the FBI or not, it was John X Ali (who today is a follower of Silis Muhammad) who arranged for American Nazi Party leader George Lincoln Rockwell to speak at the 1962 Saviour's Day celebration in Chicago.[225] When people booed and started leaving as the Nazi leader approached the rostrum flanked by ten of his storm troopers, John X Ali urged them to let Rockwell use his freedom of speech. In his short address, the Nazi commander said the Messenger was to his people what Adolf Hitler was to the Germans, and ended with a "Heil Hitler."[226] Although this was the first and last event to which Rockwell was invited as a speaker, he did attend at least one other Muslim meeting, an NOI rally on June 25, 1961, at Uling Arena in Washington D.C., where he donated twenty dollars and pledged support for their policy of racial endogamy.[27] These kinds of occasional contacts between white racists and/or neo-Nazis and the Nation of Islam continued through the shift of NOI leadership to Louis Farrakhan. It appears as though the white Nazi-styled organizations are more impressed by Farrakhan than he is by them; these organizations proclaim their support for black separatists as a strategy generic to the development of a post–World War II version of the Third Position, which claims to be an alternative to both capitalism and communism.

The story of the British National Front (NF) is instructive here. The Third Position traces its roots to Italian leftist fascism and the leftist Nazism of the German brothers Greger and Otto Strasser. The Strasser brothers advocated a kind of national bolshevism, founded on class struggle, national romanticism, and back-to-nature ideals, in opposition to Hitler's increasingly more far-right position. Third Positionists usually condemn Hitler for betraying the true National Socialism when he purged the Strasser brothers from the German NSDAP.[228] In the early 1980s, the Third Position, which had existed as a more or less suppressed faction of John Tyndall's National Front, was elaborated by a new generation of neo-

Strasserite theoreticians and gained power in the party by a skillfully planned coup.[229]

With a new package espousing anticapitalism, anticommunism, environmentalism, and racial separatism, an interest in historical and contemporary black radical nationalists followed. The two NF publications *Nationalism Today* and *National Front News* carried positive articles on African revolutionaries such as Burkina Faso's Thomas Sankara,[230] Ghana's Jerry Rawlins,[231] and Libya's Mu'ammar al-Qadhdhafi,[232] but also on Islamists, such as Iran's Ayatollah Khomeini.[233] Essays applauding the works and ideas of Marcus Garvey, Malcolm X, Elijah Muhammad, and Louis Farrakhan also appeared in these publications. National Front ideologists argued that Marcus Garvey was instrumental for the creation of a "broad front of racialists of all colours," for which his meetings with "the reactionaries of the KKK" were seen as setting a "historical precedent." Garveyism was hailed as the "mirror reflection of the White Pride movement," on the grounds that he advocated an African Africa and a European Europe, and "espoused a sincere racialism, but condemned mindless racism."[234] The new NF leadership thus made a distinction between racism and racialism, a philosophical reasoning not always appreciated, if at all understood, by NF grassroots members. This confusion would eventually lead to an internal revolt, as I discuss below.

During the 1984 American presidential primary, when the NF hailed Jesse Jackson's candidacy,[235] the British Third Positionists discovered Louis Farrakhan and began covering his activities.[236] The National Front press wrote about the history of the NOI, supported Farrakhan's call for a separate black state and his disdain for interracial marriages, and urged white nationalists to connect with the Nation.[237] "Louis Farrakhan is a God-send to all races and cultures," the NF staff declared,[238] and to let the readers judge for themselves, *Final Call* editor Abdul Wali Muhammad was invited to contribute to *Nationalism Today* a full five-page article, including a photo-essay and the NOI program.[239] The next stage in this development was for the British white nationalists to make direct contact with the NOI as the "common cause must be turned into practical cooperation."[240] In May 1988, a senior official of the National Front leadership traveled to the United States and was greeted by the leading American "Friends of the Movement" Mat Unger, alias Mat Malone, and Robert Hoy, who since their 1987 visit in Britain had sought to establish an NF-related Third Positionist movement in the United States and had made contacts with different American separatists.[241] During his U.S. tour, the NF representative was invited to visit NOI Mosque #4 in Washington D.C., headed by Minister Alim Muhammad, to study their antidrug program.[242]

On British soil, the National Front distributed leaflets in support of the Nation of Islam,[243] and declared in an *Nationalism Today* editorial that "Black Power and White Power are not enemies. They are allies in the struggle to resist and defeat the race and nation destroying Capitalism that is engulfing the globe. Unity in diversity is not a slogan, it is a Way of Life."[244] The new direction envisaged by the Third Positionist NF leadership was not easily swallowed by the rank-and-file white extreme nationalists. The *Nationalism Today* editorial board admitted to being "under intense pressure" from "a tiny, reactionary element *within* the Movement,"[245] reflected in letters to the editor that accused the leadership of "Bolshevik jargon." "I prefer Hitler as 'comrade' to any Black Power hottentot who wants to take my hand," one letter stated, "because Hitler is of my people, my race, my culture and my idealistic kindred," going on to ask what weird sort of racialism and National Socialism they profess in calling Farrakhan a comrade.[246] The National Front ideologists, however, continued to espouse their ideas, declaring that they had "little or nothing" in common with their Nazi predecessors. They viewed "negative racism" as a condemnable product of Britain's imperialist past and argued that their racialist position was basically antiracist, dedicated to the preservation of "all the wonderful variety of races and cultures of the world." "We do not see Blacks or Asians as enemies, but as potential allies," the staff declared and assured the readers that they were "not interested in alleged [white] superiority."[247] They argued that nationalism will never advance if trapped by racism and warned that although "telling jokes about 'stupid niggers' might win a bit of cheap popularity" it also "perpetuates the division between people that should be working together to defeat ... multi-racialism."[248]

It seems that this logic was beyond the grasp of the general NF membership. Not being allowed to be a racist even in the National Front was simply too much.[249] After the humiliating local elections in June 1989, in which NF candidate Patrick Harrington campaigned with backing from black separatists in Vauxhall (a southern London area with many immigrant residents),[250] many NF members revolted. A majority deserted the NF for the National Front Support Group, a splinter group led by former NF youth leader Joe Pearce, or Tyndall's new organization, the violence-prone British National Party, a more classic National Socialist organization. The "official" National Front dissolved in 1990 and the former leaders moved to France under new identities.[251]

Although the British National Front during its Third Positionist phase between 1983 and 1990 seems to have been the neo-Nazi party that most wholeheartedly pledged support for Farrakhan and the NOI, occasional overtures from American anti-Semites and/or neo-Nazis have been made. Farrakhan does not endorse the revisionist position, but it should be noted that the list of speakers invited to address the infamous 1985 Saviour's Day convention—in which Qadhdhafi participated by satellite—featured Arthur Butz of Northwestern University. Butz used the opportunity to present his Holocaust-denial thesis published in the revisionist best-seller, *The Hoax of the 20th Century.*[252] Further, Tom Metzger, former Grand Dragon of the Knights of the Ku Klux Klan and founder of the California-based White Aryan Resistance,[253] symbolically donated one hundred dollars at a NOI Los Angeles P.O.W.E.R. rally in 1985.[254] Metzger also took the opportunity at a 1985 Michigan meeting of Klansmen and other white supremacists to declare approvingly that Farrakhan has understood that America is like a rotting carcass, with the Jews living off the carcass like parasites.[255] In a 1989 interview with James Ridgeway, Metzger expressed a Third Position—oriented ideology and confirmed his interest in the NOI's policies, alleging that for a time he had had meetings with Farrakhan about splitting up the United States into different mono-ethnic states.[256]

Until 1990, the neo-Nazis' admiration for Farrakhan and the NOI was one-sided. The *Final Call* did not run corresponding supportive articles on the white nationalists and suppressed information regarding the contacts that did exist. This general rule was temporarily revised in 1990–91, starting with the March 21, 1990, issue of *Final Call,* which featured an essay by Gary Gallo, head of the small U.S. Third Positionist National Democratic Front (NDF). Gallo, who had stayed with the British National Front for a year in the mid-1980s, delineated the NDF program of racial pride, anticapitalism, and anticommunism and offered a solution to America's race problems. "The NDF will divide the U.S. into completely independent nations based on race," Gallo wrote. "The Blacks will get 13 percent of the soil of America as they make up 13 percent of the population," he explained, adding generously that there "will also be multiracial states for those who want to live as a multiracialist," before dictating that "the bulk of the country will be a pure White nation."[257] In July 1990, Farrakhan granted an exclusive interview to *Spotlight,* the Liberty Lobby weekly that in the early 1980s was the United States's most widely circulated far-right periodical. "If we want to be honest, America was not founded by White people for Black people or Hispanic people or for Native Americans or for Asians or for Jews," Farrakhan said. "It was founded by White people for White people." Applauding prowhite whites and problack blacks, Farrakhan elaborated on the need for a separate racial development. "You're not going to integrate with the Blacks in the ghettos of Washington," Farrakhan stated. "But when we [the NOI] get finished with these people, we produce dignified, intelligent people. The American system can't produce that. We can. Give us a chance to make our people worth something."[258]

As the U.S. government became increasingly more involved in the escalating conflict in the Persian Gulf, Farrakhan and the NOI took part in the disparately composed antiwar movement. In the course of events, the NOI made contact with LaRouchies operating, as is their strategy, under various fronts. Lyndon H. LaRouche is the founder of a far-right political cult that over the years has crisscrossed ideologically from the far left to the far right, seeking alliances, advocating conspiracy theories, and bizarre agendas—such as using soldier-citizens to colonialize Mars. LaRouche ran for president in 1976, 1980, 1984, and 1988, and his parties abroad, such as the Swedish *Europeiska Arbetarpartiet* (the European Labor Party), repeatedly try to make inroads in national elections outside the United States. In 1988 LaRouche was convicted on fraud and conspiracy charges, and was released in 1994.[259]

The LaRouche organization for years has been in contact with the Iraqi Baath Party and different fronts, such as the Schiller Institute and Food for Peace, cosponsored antiwar demonstrations and conferences, and become part of various antiwar coalitions.[260] Nation of Islam Minister Alim Muhammad appeared on the podium together with Helga Zepp-LaRouche, wife of Lyndon and head of the Schiller Institute, at a Paris conference on November 23–24, 1990, which was assembled to demand Lyndon LaRouche's immediate release from prison.[261] Alim Muhammad again addressed a LaRouche conference held in Chicago on December 15–16, 1990.[262] The NOI's involvement with LaRouche continued with *Final Call* editor in chief Abdul Wali Muhammad writing an article based on documentation provided by the *Executive Intelligence Review,* a LaRouche front promoting his conspiratorial views. Abdul Wali Muhammad alleged that President Bush was moving "very close to total, unfettered dictatorial power" in a plan to "suspend the Constitution," a scheme that "also advocated the roundup and transfer to 'assembly centers or relocation camps' of at least 21 million Black Americans." In the article, Muhammad argued that "LaRouche, a world-renowned economist, is in prison for his outspokenness against the world power brokers" following a character-assassination campaign launched by the media machine, which is controlled by international drug traders, and further attested that "Mr. Bush has similar, although much more malicious, intentions toward the Honorable Louis Farrakhan."[263] A further instance of a LaRouche-NOI connection was the presence of LaRouchie Sheila A. Jones at the Saviour's Day celebrations in February 1994.[264]

What could possibly be the underlying reason for this unholy relationship between the Nation of Islam and the various white neo-Nazi leaders and organizations? The alliance theory proposed by Lisbeth Lindeborg,[265] Anna-Lena Lodenius and Stieg Larsen,[266] and *Searchlight,* that with slight variations prospects that a white-black extremist coalition has been established, gives too much credence to the small white Third Positionist groups' own fantasies of "a New Axis." While a connection undoubtedly does exist, the nature of the relationship has not been analyzed. The alliance theory is based on an incomplete understanding of the religious motives underlying the Nation of Islam's position. The relationship between the Nation and white extreme nationalism has to be seen in the context of the former's apocalyptic perspective.

Answering a direct question about the relationship between the Nation and the white extremist nationalists mentioned above, Farrakhan denied any direct contact: "I have never met with any of them and their leaders. I have never written to them, nor have I received any correspondence from them."[267] This might literally be true, taking into account three possible circumstances: the National Front representative visiting the United States in 1988 only met with Minister Alim Muhammad of Washington, D.C.; Tom Metzger could be exaggerating and might have met with one or more top laborers and not with Farrakhan in person; and the interview was made in May 1989, the year before Farrakhan used *Spotlight* as a forum through which to address the white far-right nationalists. On the other hand, Farrakhan confirmed a level of mutual understanding: "[The white racialists] see integration as the destruction of their race and their people. And since I represent the Honorable Elijah Muhammad and his plan not of integration but of separation, they feel that they have common cause with me, though there is no linkage of myself with the KKK or any of these groups that you name. But I must tell you that I have got respect for any white man who wants to keep his race white, 'cause I certainly wanna keep mine black."[268] When questioned about the fact that these same organizations and groups are brutally attacking black people in the United

States and Europe, Farrakhan vowed to "always defend the black community" but asserted that whites offending and murdering blacks is simply an expression of normal behavior, of the predisposition "in the nature of white men."[269]

The increase in racial antagonism is only a sign of the setting sun. In the transitional period of time leading to the final battle, the nations are supposed to separate and polarize in an escalating race war. God says in the Holy Qur'an, "And the day when the Hour comes, that day they will be separated one from the other."[270] The Ku Klux Klan, Nazi skinhead, and WAR violence is thus "part of the drama, the worldwide drama the prophets foretold." The original people have to wake up from their mental slumber, realize the evil nature of the white man, and move out of Babylon in order for the final phase of divine retribution to begin. White hate groups unknowingly dig their own graves as their overtly aggressive racism "fulfills prophecy" and hastens the onslaught of Armageddon as they "make it uncomfortable for black people to stay here." The Ku Klux Klan, the Aryan Nations, and their kinsmen are to be exterminated in due time, but they are temporarily useful and pedagogically suited to their role as the obvious devils.[271]

The mutual understanding is thus a mutual recognition of enmity and partition. The Nation of Islam spokesmen reject every comparison between the NOI and the KKK, "a proven group of murderers, rapists, lynchers and cowards,"[272] and make use of each instance of white extremist violence against the black community.[273] NOI London minister Wayne X, reacting to the tidal wave of racist attacks against blacks in Britain, said, "As the power of the Caucasian rule continues its decline, the forces behind white world supremacy will stop at nothing to prevent the rise of Black people. Many more of us will be attacked and many more of us will be murdered. Our only salvation is our unity and the program established by the Honorable Elijah Muhammad that is being exercised today by the Honorable Louis Farrakhan."[274] For the white extreme nationalists, the relation with the NOI is also only temporary and expedient. No matter how much respect white nationalists might claim to have for Farrakhan and his followers, they are still niggers with an intolerable attitude. Tom Metzger, who attested his support for Farrakhan, is a principal director behind the West Coast violence-prone bonehead gangs[275] and is most likely an inspiration for the eight Fourth Reich Skinheads (FRS) who were arrested on July 15, 1993. The FRS, who claim to be the armed wing of Metzger's WAR, planned to instigate a race war by bombing the Los Angeles First AME Church and spraying the congregation with machine-gun fire, but the plot was exposed by undercover FBI agents. Besides arms and explosives, the Feds discovered plans to assassinate a number of black activists, among them Louis Farrakhan.[276]

If the relationship between the NOI and white extremist groups is not that of allies, another kind of relationship is discernible. In chess, the white and black men exist to defeat each other, but share a mutual understanding of the game's nature and make some similar moves. The white and black men engaged in the fateful game of Armageddon also share the basic perception of the contest's nature. A comparison between the NOI and white religious racist creeds show a number of interesting ideological parallels. For instance, the Christian Identity movement believes that the people the world know as Jews in reality are Euroasian Khazars and not the principal actors of the Holy Bible. The Lost Tribes of Israel are identified with the modern day British, German, Nordic, and, by extension, white American populace. A large number of Identity preachers adhere to the "two-seed" theory, in which Eve not only carried Adam's breed, Abel, but was seduced by Satan, the snake, and gave birth to his son Cain. After Cain had slain Abel, Adam, the first white man, passed his seed over to Seth, who became the father of the white race. Cain's seed became the Jews, who literally are the breed of the devil. The other races are the descendants of other cursed progenitors, and constitute the evil stock of subhuman lowlifes, "mud people," who have no souls and are on the same spiritual level as animals.[277] In its different varieties, the Ariosophic Christian Identity movement is the religious rationale behind a large number of white racist organizations,[278] such as the Posse Comitatus,[279] the Aryan Nations,[280] the Covenant, Sword and Arm of the Lord,[281] the Christian Defense League,[282] the Order,[283] WAR, and parts of the Ku Klux Klans.[284] These white religious racists teach separation from evil in all walks of life, and some groups seek to establish an independent Aryan Nation, often, though not exclusively, placed in the Northwest. They advocate an independent economy, establish separate schools, impose their own jurisdiction and set up their own armies, which differ from the FOI in that they are heavily armed and often professionally drilled in various camps located around the country.

Another religious racist creed is preached by Ben Klassen,[285] who founded the Church of the Creator in 1973. Creativity opposes the Identity doctrine, questioning why any sane white man would "break [his] neck to distort history" only to pose as "a descendant of such trash." Klassen states that there is no historical evidence that the Ten Tribes of Israel ever existed and got lost, and if they did—good riddance.[286] Opposed to all "spook believers," that is Christians, Muslims, Hindus, and others, Creativity is a kind of socioreligious Darwinism, dividing mankind into nature's finest (the white master race) and the unfittest (the Jews and the mud races). The latter are nonhumans and not created in the likeness of God, who is an athletic, vibrant man with blond hair and blue eyes, the epitome of an ideal Nordic man, as Klassen discovered after God descended in 1986 to confer with him in person about the Earth's problems. At that meeting, God also made a binding covenant with the white race, promising their deification should they only prove themselves worthy by exterminating all mud races.[287]

Christian Identity and Creativity adopt an underdog position, believing that the divine white race is victimized under a regime of evil, presently known as the Zionist Occupation Government (ZOG), composed of Jews and their masochistic white marionettes. Holding poor whites under the grip of Jewish bankers, ZOG has imposed unconstitutional evils, such as busing and affirmative action. They spread their position through Jewish-controlled media and movies and ultimately intend to exterminate the Aryans through the combined effects of crime, drugs, immorality, race mixing, homosexuality, and abortions. As is the case with the NOI, the Christian Identity and Creativity Churches are extremely apocalyptically oriented, interpreting everyday events as parts of an ongoing global race war that ultimately will escalate to the final showdown and the total extermination of the inferior evil races. The Church of the Creator and some Identity groups further understand this race war in the context of a higher divine agenda: the deification of the Aryan man, truly in God's likeness.

These parallels between black and white religious nationalism should not be understood as resulting from a direct borrowing, although a conceptual influence is discernible.[288] Their affinity is rather a derivative of their common roots in the late-nineteenth-century discourse on race and nation. As discussed in chapter 1, each race was seen as an organism with specific genetic, inner as well as outer, characteristics that together constituted a set of distinct race personalities. The race organism was believed to be corporate and hierarchical, ideally led by an elite of individuals that personified or perfected the racial features. University disciplines dedicated to the study, classification, and purification of the races were established. Through physical anthropology, race biology, and later, medical genetics, a pure, healthy breed, and thereby a bright racial future, would be secured. In its different elaborations, the race-organism theory affected Pan-German, Pan-Arabian, Pan-African, and other nationalist movements and blended with totalitarian political ideologies, that is, National Socialism and fascism. The scientific speculation was also combined with a religious reading of racial history and was adopted by various churches, especially in the Protestant and Mormon traditions, as well as in numerous marginal religious movements, such as Theosophy, Anthroposophy, Ariosophy, and British Israelism.[289]

To conclude this discussion of the NOI-Nazi connection, it can be established that it is difficult to determine where on a political scale Farrakhan and the NOI should be placed. As a religio-political ideologist, Farrakhan moves in a different universe than secular politicians, making the left-right scale an inadequate tool of classification. Walking the straight path revealed by God as the road to liberation makes Farrakhan adopt political positions both to the right and to the left, as I discuss further in the following chapter. In his support of the left, Farrakhan holds Fidel Castro of Cuba in great esteem and has repeatedly hailed progressive parts of the Cuban society. Malcolm X admired Lenin and Stalin,[290] and Red China received favorable coverage in *Muhammad Speaks.* Farrakhan's involvement in one of the most leftist presidential campaigns in the United States, his support of liberation movements in Latin America, Africa, and Asia, and his fight to end the exploitation of the poor, are all part of a traditionally leftist agenda.

In support of the right, Farrakhan voices traditional conservative and extremist nationalist themes. The NOI hails God, nation, and the nuclear family. They oppose the prochoice stand on abortion, denounce homosexuality, subscribe to a conservative view on gender relations, preach conservative religious morals, and envision a future corporate economic structure in the coming independent, authoritarian state where law and order will rule. As in the theories of fascism and nazism, the individual is always subordinate to the abstract greater body, the nation or the race.

To a certain extent, it is possible to propose that the NOI represents a Blackamerican Third Positionist ideology. To the extent that it does, it is a homemade brand and not inspired by white Third Positionist organizations and ideologists. Politically, Farrakhan is inspired by the great African American nationalists, chiefly Elijah Muhammad but also Malcolm X, Marcus Garvey, Booker T. Washington, W. E. B. Du Bois, Alexander Crummell, Bishop Turner, Gabriel Prosser, Nat Turner, Noble Drew Ali, and others. The black nationalist ideology merges with Islam, a religion that also claims to be the third alternative between and beyond capitalism and communism, to form the Third Position of the NOI, the practical implications of which are considered in the following chapter.

10

A Divine Nation in a Decaying World

—

This chapter will examine the rising appeal of the Nation of Islam in the contemporary United States by discussing Minister Farrakhan's proposals and the practical actions undertaken by the NOI in different fields of black life, ending with its call for black reunification and civilizing efforts.

Gangland Gangstas Turning Gods Black Islamic nationalism has become widely popular among black urban youth, and Farrakhan exerts an influence with these youths that far exceeds the actual membership of his organization. This is truly significant, given the fact that 84 percent of black Americans live in metropolitan areas and the fact that the African American urban population is a young population, with a median age of 24.9 years old for blacks compared to 34.6 years for other city dwellers.[1] The vitality of black Islam as an integral part of contemporary black youth culture is visible in the new black independent movies, in the hip-hop movement, in artifacts and clothing, in literature and comics, in college life, in graffiti and other arts, and in gang symbolism. While black Christian clergy ponder over why the new generation is absent from the church, black youths gather by the thousands to listen to the sermons delivered by Minister Farrakhan. He has a rather unique capability to reach deeply into the souls of black youths. Farrakhan seems to be able to talk to them in a way that really makes them listen, even when he puts them down.

This rapport enables Farrakhan to criticize and redirect destructive behavioral patterns. "Look around you in the society. Sodom and Gomorrah is lightweight," Farrakhan thundered to a predominantly black student audience. "Your heads are full of reefers, your veins so full of heroin and your noses so full of cocaine or you're so busy at the party chasing one another sexually that you become a modern Rome."[2] Emphasizing that such behavior is unworthy for a member of the original nation, Farrakhan infuses them with pride in their black heritage, a new self-esteem and a mission to accomplish: "You're dealing with death today, brothers and sisters, and you don't have time to play and party. You better put down your little drugs, the little silly reefer. You don't need to be high. You need to be more sober than the judge to get out of this condition. You need to wake up and see that your life is threatened."[3] Gangs, or "nations" as members call them, have become one of the most prominent and deadly components of black and Hispanic youth culture.[4] In Los Angeles alone, the police department recorded at least 771 gang-related homicides in 1991.[5] Los Angeles County district attorney Ira Reiner, in a controversial study published in May 1992, concluded that 47 percent of all black men in Los Angeles between the ages of twenty-one and twenty-four showed up in police gang databases. Reiner estimated a total Los Angeles gang population of 150,000 members in 1,000 different gangs.[6] The study caused an uproar among black activists, and critics discovered at least 5,000 duplications and names of dead people among those counted.[7] Even if the actual figure decreases by a few more thousand, however, no one can deny that "gang-banging"[8] poses an extremely serious problem, and the Los Angeles Police Department (LAPD) claimed that it has identified at least seventy cities nationwide where affiliates of the Los Angeles–based Crips and Bloods federations have been established.[9]

The situation is similar in Chicago, with some 50,000 gang members belonging to different nations with a growing network of affiliates or chapters in other cities, such as Milwaukee, Minneapolis, Kansas City, Des Moines, and Tulsa. For reasons yet to be explained, gangs are more prolific in the Midwest and on the West Coast than in New York, Philadelphia, and other big Eastern cities. Malcolm Klein, a leading gang expert for the past thirty years, says that if the problem is not curtailed in the gang heartland, it is only a matter of time before the nations will expand eastward. In 1961, there were only twenty-three cities with known street gangs. After a decline in the 1970s, gang membership rose again in the 1980s and by 1992 gangs had become established in no less than 187 cities.[10]

By gang-banging, Farrakhan tells the black youth, you are playing right into the hands of the Devil, who plans for your destruction and floods your communities with imported narcotics and guns. African Americans do not produce Chinese Mac-10s or Israeli Uzis, and blacks do not operate arms import/export businesses. "We are not the gun runners," Farrakhan charged. "White folks [are] bringing guns in, feeding them to black gangs, inspiring the black gangs to kill each other."[11] Promoting crime, gang wars, and illicit drug use are all part of a grand design, a pretext for an impending lethal attack: "A climate is being created in America to kill all black people. The press is part of the conspiracy . . . to paint black people as though we were all criminals, we are all animals, we are all drug-users, we are all gang-bangers, so that it justifies white police, white sheriff departments, coming into our community, treating us in any way they see fit—they got a license to kill."[12] This is not paranoia, Farrakhan believes: "After you live in America and see evils that are going down, no black people are paranoid. We *know* that there is a plan being made ready to be used against our rise."[13] Compare this with American foreign policy and a congruent pattern emerges, Farrakhan argues. Before the bombing of Libya, Qadhdhafi was hounded throughout the American media as "the mad dog of the Middle East," which created an atmosphere in which military action could be justified. Prior to the invasion of Panama, the press turned against former United States ally Manuel Noriega, depicting him as a top drug lord responsible for providing cocaine to the American youth. Now the administration has turned against the black youth, and, Farrakhan told his audience, "when they move on you, they've already created the climate. Like they did for Qadhdhafi, like they did for Noriega, the climate has been created for you." They are justified in exterminating all blacks, because "you're savage, cruel, you're wild, uncivilized, you're destroying our beautiful country, see?"[14]

In January 1992, FBI director William Sessions announced that three hundred FBI agents, whose foreign counterintelligence assignments were rendered obsolete by the fall of the Soviet Union and its Eastern Europen allies, were to be reassigned to assist the police in their assault on the street gangs "in the largest reallocation of resources in agent history."[15] The true underlying reason for this decision is, according to Farrakhan, the fear of a black messiah, an obsession that since the days of J. Edgar Hoover has grown all the more acute. Standing at the tomb of Lazarus, the call of God through Minister Farrakhan has reconnected the African American with the divine within. Back on the path, the black Muslim woman "can produce mental giants. [She] can produce Gods . . . [and] that's why the white man is afraid today."[16] The government, which panicked when it realized that a generation of black saviours is about to be delivered, now targets black youths in a "plan to kill off the black male, spare the female and leave you, the Black woman, as the booty, the prize for white men to enjoy your beauty as they kill your men."[17] The government's scheme, Farrakhan holds, fulfills yet another part of the Scripture: "When you read your Bible about Herod, when you read about Pharaoh, you are reading about the mind of the administration in Washington, D.C."[18] Farrakhan claims he realized how far the government's plot really had advanced as a result of two seemingly disconnected events in 1989. The first was the military massacre of Chinese youths protesting against their government in Tienneman Square, Beijing. The second occurrence was a call from Minister Don Muhammad, the eastern regional representative of Minister Farrakhan, who told him that members of Boston Roxbury gangs came to seek refuge at the mosque, asking for advice on how to effect a truce. The truth dawned on Farrakhan while pondering over why President Bush had not spoken out against Deng Xiaoping: Bush and his chiefs of staff were planning a similar onslaught against black youths under the pretext of curtailing rampant gang life.[19]

From the fall of 1989 to the present, Farrakhan has toured the inner cities of America in a "Stop the Killing" campaign, aiming to create a truce between the gangs and to put an end to black-on-black crime. "The Bloods and Crips are not natural enemies," Farrakhan said in 1990, addressing a crowd of some 17,000 that jammed a Los Angeles stadium. They have been made enemies as the Devil "intervened and turned brother against brother." The time has come to reunite the people of God and redirect the frustrated anger of the black warriors against their real enemy: "With the teachings of the Honorable Elijah Muhammad, by the grace of Allah, we will have this [black] Nation up and strong. We'll have the Crips and the Bloods, we'll have them as one family, as an Army of God movin' for the liberation of our people."[20] The first cease-fire between the Bloods and Crips was declared on April 28, 1992, only one day before the black-Hispanic ghetto of South Central Los Angeles exploded. Hundreds of buildings were set on fire, shops and malls were looted, thousands of people were beaten, and many were murdered in a fierce collective outburst of anger. The rebellion lasted for five days and moved out from the ghetto into Hollywood, Beverly Hills, and Santa Monica. President Bush and General Colin Powell declared a state of emergency, imposed a curfew, and banned the sale of gasoline to prevent the use of Molotov cocktails and other poor-man's weapons. They sent in 2,500 soldiers from the army, 1,500 marines, 10,000 soldiers from the National

Guard, 3,720 sheriffs and police officers, 2,300 California highway patrol-men, and 2,700 firemen to end the uprising. In the aftermath, statistics showed the Los Angeles rebellion to be this century's greatest, numbering 58 dead, 2,328 injured, 16,291 arrested, and an estimated damage of one billion dollars.[21]

The rebellion was triggered by a rather commonplace event. On March 3, 1991, the unemployed black construction worker Rodney King was forced out of his car by four white police officers. Under the supervision of Sergeant Stacey Koon, officers Laurence Powell, Timothy Wind, and Theodore Briseno assaulted the defenseless King by kicking him and hitting him with a stun gun and steel batons. Koon and Powell filed a report stating that they intervened against a berserk individual on angel dust and then went home after yet another day of routine police work. Police brutality with racist undertones is far from unusual and nothing would have singled out this event had not an onlooker videotaped the assault. The video was aired again and again, and a stunned American nation could in slow motion watch how King was blasted with a stun gun and received fifty-six crushing blows and several random kicks which resulted in a broken leg, nine skull fractures, a broken cheek bone, a shattered eye socket, a split inner lip, and a partially paralyzed face.[22]

The trial was moved to Simi Valley, a small almost all-white town, so that the LAPD officers, in the judge's estimation, "would not be unfairly treated due to adverse publicity,"[23] and a jury composed of ten whites, one Asian, and one Hispanic was selected. When the trial began, the jury fore-man declared that "I believe it's the responsibility of the court to punish [criminals], not the police officers."[24] After studying the video, the jury acquitted the four officers on all charges of assault with a deadly weapon, excessive force, and filing false police reports.[25] That night the battle cry "No justice—no peace" was sounded and the rebellion was on. As it spread to Atlanta, Seattle, Oakland, Philadelphia, Madison, and a dozen other cities in the United States and Canada, King pleaded in vain for an end to the violence.[26] "King could not stop what he did not start," Far-rakhan stated. "Injustice started the fire and only justice can put it out."[27]

Mainstream commentators frequently denied that political motives had brought people into the streets, describing those involved as criminal "rioters" and "looters." This was also the position of President Bush, who said in a televised speech on May 1, "What we saw last night and the night before in Los Angeles is not about civil rights. It's not about the great cause of equality that all Americans must uphold. It's not a message of protest. It's been the brutality of a mob, pure and simple."[28] The rebellion, although socially complex with numerous motives underlying it, was clearly a political act, determined by the frustrating reality of its under-privileged participants, which suggests that such an event is bound to happen again, if social conditions are not fundamentally changed. The blatant injustice manifested in the verdict was far from the single cause of the rebellion; "King was just the last straw" that broke the camel's back.[29] In a postindustrial, commercially and materially oriented society, with the South Central Los Angeles black unemployment rate hovering around 50 percent, with a black high school dropout rate of 63 to 79 percent, and with more than 40 percent of the black/Hispanic population living well below the poverty limit, traditional political avenues of protest such as strikes are not available. Considering the composite socioeconomic con-ditions at hand, a general loot is the late-twentieth-century equivalent of the early-twentieth-century's General Strike, a collective expression of the powerless's power, hitting the system where it hurts most.[30]

For years, black and Hispanic activists have sought in vain to use peaceful means to draw attention to the plight of the inner cities' under-class. "Now America is interested," Farrakhan commented. "What made the elite interested? VIOLENCE. If the people of Los Angeles had gone home and sulked and marched peacefully, who would have heard their cry?" Relating the events to the theme of his community-organizing tour, Min-ister Farrakhan repeated his warning of a federal conspiracy to extermi-nate the enemies of the Devil: "The National Guard, federal troops, tanks and heavy artillery seen in Los Angeles is a sign that the worst is yet to come."[31]

In the aftermath of the Los Angeles rebellion, the Bloods and Crips announced a truce on May 5, 1992, citing as their motives the staggering unemployment figures, rampant police brutality, the escalating body count, and the negative media publicity against gang activities. Their action was followed by a number of more or less affiliated gangs, such as the Pirus, Hoovers, Fuzz Town Mafia, Home Street, Hack Gang Watts, and Rolling 60s. The morning of the truce, a flyer was circulated claiming that the real reason for the truce was to "merge both gangs into an anti-police army," further stating that "for every black man that's shot, the Crips/ Bloods will shoot two policemen."[32] A security intelligence report issued by police authorities claims that the gangs are planning an armed insur-rection under "the direction and leadership of Muslims," and Mike Davis believes that the flyer is a COINTELPRO-style hoax aimed at disrupting the gang unity process.[33]

Minister Farrakhan and the NOI clearly have been instrumental in bringing the gangs together and redirecting their activities toward community improvement and political empowerment.[34] "From here it's like the human rights movement," gang coordinator Daude Sherrill told *Final Call* reporter Rosalyn X Moore. "It's about taking our voice to the United Nations and getting this country brought to trial for masterminding a whole situation that caused millions to lose their lives and [for us] to demand reparations for the descendants of slaves."[35] The united gangs of Los Angeles released a set of demands for rebuilding and improving the city with new hospitals, recreation centers, trees, and schools. They further insisted that state-financed work should replace welfare. In return, the Bloods and Crips declared their intention to stop drug trafficking and get the drug lords to finance community improvement. The united gangs promised to match funds for each building constructed and also to match funds for an AIDS research and awareness center, all under the motto, "Give us the hammer and the nails, we will rebuild the city."[36] When the gang treaty seemed to hold, the example spread to other cities like Minneapolis, Boston, and Chicago, in which gangs and community activists formed Unity for Peace coalitions.[37] In May 1993, a three-day National Summit for Urban Peace and Justice was held in Kansas City, gathering some 150 members from gangs in two dozen cities. At a news conference, organizers pleaded to broaden the truce nationwide and presented a list of recommendations for improving downtrodden neighborhoods and ending police brutality, signed by eighty gangs and other organizations.[38] Additional national peace summits followed in 1993 with an increasing number of participating gangs, in Cleveland on June 4–6,[39] in St. Paul, Minnesota, on July 14–18,[40] and in Chicago on October 21–25.[41]

Farrakhan was invited by the organizers to address the gang summit in St. Paul, despite the fact that promises of support from white liberal corporations and individuals evaporated when the news came out.[42] Before some 900 participants gathered at Mt. Olivet Baptist Church, Farrakhan said that though the new generation is the most powerful ever produced, it is also greatly misunderstood by its elders and parents, because these black youths are different, representing not hope but fulfillment. They are the first generation strong enough not to bow down to Baal, but they were brought up without guidance from the lost generations. Dropping out of an intentionally destructive educational system, lacking faith in corrupt politicians, and feeling indifferent toward pastors and parents, they turn to the gangs, where "they find what they can't find in church, in the home or at school. They find a brotherhood, they find a camaraderie, they find a security, but they don't find guidance." These black youths become fearless, without respect for a law that does not respect them, and engage in self-destruction. "I'm not here as an entertainer," Farrakhan continued, "I love you and I am willing to give my life for you because I see you as greater than myself." The present situation of gang warfare without any results other than a decimated new generation, a booming funeral business, and babies killed in drive-by shootings, is intolerable. Farrakhan warned the gang members to stop the killing, lest God let them die at the hands of the number one killer, the blood shedder, who kills animals and humans without a reason. Referring to the street-gang movie *Menace II Society,* Farrakhan said, "If you are Menace II, who is menace number one? White folks have gone all over the world as a menace number one to all societies. The Native Americans met menace number one. Our fathers met menace number one. Africa met menace number one. Africa, the Isles of the Pacific, and the Caribbean and South America, they have met the violence of menace number one. You grew up under a cold, heartless killer and you have become like your former slave masters. You are menace number two, but you are not a menace to him. You are a menace to yourself, your people, and to your own family. So what do you need? You need guidance and a new direction."[43] Farrakhan also addressed the Chicago summit that drew gang leaders from sixty-seven cities in twenty-seven states,[44] from gangs with an estimated total membership of several hundred thousand, emphasizing that peace is serious and that nobody should try to use it for personal gain by furthering drug trading and crime.[45] The peace movement's detractors focus in part on the latter theme and warn of the possibility that the truce might be a cover for a tactical restructuring of black organized crime. Mira Boland of the Anti-Defamation League believes that "the most notable result of reaching out to gang-members could be decades of heightened violence and criminality."[46] She compares the present truce bid with the afore-mentioned efforts in the 1960s to reform the Chicago gangs and predicts a similar failure.[47] Conrad Worrill of the National Black United Front and columnist of the *Final Call* rejects the comparison, saying that unlike the 1960s, today's peace and unity efforts were initiated by the gang leaders themselves.[48] Earl King of No Dope Express, cosponsor of the Chicago summit, claims that during the past year crime had dropped by 27 percent in the city, due in part to the truce proclaimed by gang leaders.[49]

In Chicago, where gangs are more tightly structured than in Los Angeles, a truce between the city's twelve major gangs was declared in October

1992. Wallace "Gator" Bradley, former enforcer of Gangster Disciples—
Chicago's largest gang with an estimated membership of 30,000—echoes
Farrakhan when describing the principal reason behind the truce worked
out with the assistance of jailed gang leaders: "The brothers in the penitentiary as well as many of the younger brothers on the street have all
come to realize that we as a people have become part of a genocidal plan
to annihilate black males. We understood that we could no longer be part
of that plan. We had to be 'United in Peace.' "[50] Farrakhan's influence is
also a main reason why the ADL's questions the real motive behind the
street-gang truce. In this regard, Boland points to Farrakhan's view that
the young have been born to settle the score, and further, quotes Crip
member Diamond's statement after a NOI laborer's postrebellion visit to a
Los Angeles housing project, that "the enemy is not red or blue [i.e., the
colors of Bloods and Crips]. The enemy is white."[51] Fear of the consequences of a united black politicized front of combative gang members is
probably part of the reason for the active opposition to the peace movement waged by the police departments in the cities where the truces have
taken effect.[52] Farrakhan himself says that the brothers did not come
together at his urging or the appeal of any other of those working with the
gangs. The one to be honored is Allah: "God is present among those young
people. They are the future leaders. . . . In these young brothers, I see the
Genesis, I see the birth, the beginning and rise, of a new nation."[53]

The Hip-Hop Mission   Farrakhan, of course, has not been alone in his
efforts to reach out to the gangs. Besides numerous community activists
and black leaders like Ben Chavis, Dick Gregory, and Prince Asiel Ben
Israel, rap artists have been the single most important source of inspiration. As most of these "nation conscious" hip-hoppers are influenced by
Minister Farrakhan, Elijah Muhammad, and Malcolm X, the NOI ideology
has had a pervasive impact on contemporary black youth culture.

Hip-hop/rap music is a translation of the young black urban experience. Compared to blues music, which originated among the sharecroppers and cotton pickers of the agrarian South and moved North to
the expanding industrial sites of the Midwest in the Great Migration,
rap music has a significantly different mental orientation. Blues music
in general has a somewhat resigned, slow, almost fatalistic attitude, expressing patience and acceptance of a suffering that is presented as a
natural, almost unavoidable part of life: "I am broke, I lost my job, my
landlord kicked me out, my baby left me, but I still got my bourbon and

my guitar and I am singing the blues." Rap is by contrast chaotic, fast, energetic, and aggressive. Rap has a militant revolutionary attitude in its rhythmic call for justice or destruction. Rap is the patience that finally has expired.

Rap music as such originated in Harlem and the South Bronx in the 1970s, but it traces its roots to earlier musical styles like African jive, soul rap, and bebop, as well as to the radio jive DJs and older branches of the great African American oral tradition.[54] In the 1970s, rap was a genuine street beat, performed on the street corners or in the urban parks, with the loudspeakers plugged into lamp posts. In the 1980s, the popularity of hip-hop accelerated like a rocket, and the genre is presently a multibillion-dollar industry, filling the pockets of producers and record company executives, while still retaining its base in the black/Hispanic youth culture of the urban poor.

The hip-hop songs, in general, are rhythmically moving postmodern collages, with samplings from various sound sources, from older hits to political speeches and TV news, often overlaid with explicit rap/toast lyrics. This very explicitness frequently has been denounced as destructively amoral and obscene, and certainly, many male chauvinist rap artists who confine their lyrical content to ego-boosting descriptions of sex, violence, drugs, and easy money. Farrakhan belongs to the category of black activists and religious leaders that condemns this specific hip-hop trend.[55] The real significance of hip-hop is not, however, related to those rappers but rather to the religio-politically oriented "message rap" artists, who have steadily found success since the mid-1980s. At the first annual Hip-Hop Conference at Howard University in 1991, the Defiant Giants declared, "In the Chinese Revolution, when Mao Tse Tung led the Chinese Revolution, all cultural art forms, all poetry, all plays that were not totally intertwined and geared towards the revolution of the Chinese people were wiped out, and the people who produced them were wiped out. In the Mau Mau Revolution in Kenya, if your drum wasn't playing to the revolution, if your dance wasn't dancing to the revolution, they busted up your drum, they busted up your dance, and they busted you up too. This is the direction that hip hop music is going. Making the artists accountable, and these rappers are rapping what should be rapped, and what will be rapped here at the crossroads."[56] Message rap is today's most influential political musical genre, addressing issues like police brutality, injustice, exploitation, poverty, drugs, gang violence, racism, and ethnic conflicts. Although some "raptivists" belong to the radical left, like 2

Black 2 Strong and the Disposable Heroes of Hiphoprisy, the large major-
ity of the more popular North American rappers adhere to the broad black
nationalist Islamic tradition. Even though some bands support Imam
Warithuddin Muhammad, such as Divine Styler, or adhere to the Five
Percent Nation of Islam, such as Queen Latifah, Lakim Shabazz, Poor
Righteous Teachers, and Brand Nubian, they are also influenced by the
teachings of Minister Louis Farrakhan and the Nation of Islam, as are
Public Enemy, Ice Cube, KAM, Professor Griff, MC Ren, Big Daddy Kane,
Paris, Mister Cee, K-Solo, Skinny Boys, Defiant Giants, Sister Souljah,
and Prince Akeem. These are but a few of the more renowned rappers
who agree with Afrika Bambaataa, when he shouts in the song "Say It
Loud (I'm Black, I'm Proud)," that Farrakhan is "my leader, my teacher,
my guide."[57] The raptivists intend to raise the level of black consciousness through, as KRS-One terms it, "edutainment,"[58] in order to advance
the cause of united black action and to get ready for the imminent revolution. In the words of Public Enemy:

> Let's get this party started right
> Right on, c'mon
> What we got to say
> Power to the people, no delay
> To make everybody see
> In order to fight the powers that be.[59]

The hip-hop movement's role in popularizing the message of black militant Islam cannot be overestimated. What reggae was to the expansion of
the Rastafarian movement in the 1970s, so hip-hop is to the spread of
black Islam in the 1980s and 1990s. Teenagers dance into black consciousness and internalize the NOI creed through hip-hop albums. The
Defiant Giants emphasize that hip-hop is "God's music," based on the
teachings of Elijah Muhammad and the inspiration of Louis Farrakhan,[60]
saying that they "rap strictly for the revolution and resurrection of our
people."[61] K-Solo raps that he is "a messenger from a Muslim Empire /
here to let you know what Allah requires," urging blacks to "listen to Big
Brother Farrakhan."[62] Shockin' Shawn of the Skinny Boys says that they
"want to conquer [the black youth] by the thousands, by the millions. We
want our music to have so much of an impact that the youth will run to
the Nation."[63]

Rap lyrics frequently, though not always explicitly, allude to NOI teachings and use code words or metaphors unintelligible to those unfamiliar

with black Islamic beliefs, like "dead niggaz" (non-Muslim blacks), "Yacub's crew" (whites), or "cave bitch" (white female). Expressing thanks and support for the Nation of Islam and Louis Farrakhan has become almost standard practice on the rap albums, and long quotations from NOI literature are often included in the lyrics or in the background shout-outs. Brand Nubian, for example, rapped the following from one of the NOI's study lessons:

> Need Him Allah, God, Islam,
> as I proceed to
> civilize the uncivilized
> word of wisdom to the group from the wise . . .
> The Asiatic Blackman
> is the Maker, the Owner,
> the Cream of the Planet Earth,
> Father of Civilization,
> Gods of the Universe.[64]

Further, Farrakhan himself appears with Professor Griff, KAM, and the Underground Soldier,[65] and prominent NOI officials, such as Khallid Abdul Muhammad, occasionally perform with rap groups at concerts or on albums. Many black rapping youths, like Kool-Aid and Rapp-Operaman, both soldiers in the FOI, acknowledge Khallid Muhammad as "the stepping stone to get into the Nation of Islam."[66] In addition, a number of rising hip-hop stars are coming up from within the Nation. Perhaps most renowned is Prince Akeem from Chicago, who was born into the Nation and attended their elementary school. Following a period of time spent with the El Rukns in his early teens, Akeem returned to the fold after he was told by Allah in a vision that Farrakhan needed a youth official and that he was the one. Farrakhan eventually appointed him the minister of the youth, but he is often referred to as minister of rap. Akeem, who believes Allah is raising him to succeed Minister Farrakhan when the time comes, views his musical career as a mission to reeducate the Blackman and therefore takes many of his lyrics directly from the teachings of Elijah Muhammad, which is evident on the album *Coming Down like Babylon*.[67]

Other raptivists evolved into the philosophy of the NOI, such as Ice Cube, who apart from Ice-T is the high priest of West Coast gangsta rap. Born O'Shea Jackson near Watts in Los Angeles, Ice Cube made his first hits with Niggaz with Attitude (NWA) and recorded songs that anticipated the rage of the Los Angeles rebellion. The NWA hit *"F*** tha Police"* echoes anger and retribution:

> F*** the police, coming straight for the underground
> A young nigger got it bad 'cause I'm brown
> And not the other color
> Some police think they have the authority
> to kill the minority . . .
> Pullin' out a silly club so you stand
> With a fake-ass badge and a gun in your hand
> Take off the gun so you can see what's up
> And we'll go at it, punk, and f*** you up.[68]

When NWA broke up, Ice Cube went East and put out *Guerillas in tha Mist* with Da Lench Mob, featuring militant songs such as "Buck tha Devil" and "Freedom Got an A.K."[69] Ex-convict Shorty of the Lenchmob crew joined the NOI and changed his life in a "whole damn 360 degree turnaround: I don't drink no more, I don't smoke, I'm married now."[70] Ice Cube landed in Greenwich Village to produce *Amerikkka's Most Wanted* and started hanging out with Public Enemy's Chuck D and Brother Drew, who introduced him to the teachings of Minister Farrakhan and the Nation of Islam. While retaining a good portion of his gangsta aura, Ice Cube's album *Death Certificate* shows more of a black Islamic nationalist perspective and his *Lethal Injection* is heavily influenced by NOI philosophy.[71] Ice Cube now says he stands "hand-in-hand with the Nation,"[72] but will continue his mission from his special raptivist platform, outside the official NOI ranks: "When you got an X, brother, you fall under the spiritual laws of Islam and some of the language I use, I can't use it. Some of it is getting to dead people, so I got to try to get a hold of them the best way I can. The Minister [Farrakhan] told me in exact words that I do more for him being outside the Nation than I do with an X."[73] Perhaps more than any other hip-hop group, Public Enemy has been pivotal in spreading the NOI creed to Blackamerican youths. Beginning with their second album, *It Takes a Nation of Millions to Hold Us Back,* their lyrics have the sound of pumped-up black Islamic lectures.[74] Chuck D, the ideologist of Public Enemy, says he puts rhythm to the essential teachings of Minister Farrakhan and turns them into rap music.[75] On the album covers of *Fear of a Black Planet* and *Apocalypse 91 . . . The Enemy Strikes Black,* Public Enemy is flanked by FOI soldiers, and their live performances feature dancers dressed as armed-combat soldiers. The paramilitary uniforms symbolize the coming autonomy of the black nation, Chuck D explains. Every independent nation in the world has an army and the African Americans, who form an independent nation, have the same right as other nations to defend their independence. White America might feel threatened, but Chuck D finds this perfectly natural. They *should* feel threatened because they *are* threatened.[76] In their lyrics, Public Enemy spreads the news from the black underground, as a "CNN of black culture,"[77] and addresses issues of central significance for the black and Hispanic population, such as the need for reeducation, the need for ridding communities of crime and drugs, and the need for creating respect for women. They also criticize police brutality, economic oppression, and racial inequality, and call for black solidarity, black unity, and black Islam.[78]

Moreover, Nation of Islam fund-raising rallies and Saviour's Day festivities frequently feature rap artists,[79] Donald Muhammad runs a permanent column in the *Final Call*, "Muhammad Inside Music," with news from the hip-hop and black music world, and Muslim raptivists engage in "Stop the Violence," antidrug, antiracist, and community improvement rallies. Rappers were instrumental in propagating for the October 16 Million Man March and put out an album named *One Million Strong*, featuring among others hip-hop stars Ice Cube, Brand Nubian, KAM, Ice-T, and Snoop Doggy Dogg.[80] In addition, raptivists drop messages in the new tide of black movies, such as *Do the Right Thing, Boyz in the Hood, New Jack City, Menace II Society*, and *Juice*, or even in action movies such as *Trespass*. Through rap music, the NOI creed becomes a part of the everyday life of black youths. Farrakhan stresses that this is crucial: "You don't wanna come here sit'n' listn' to Farrakhan for two hours, that's a little bit too much. But turn on the box and the [Public Enemy] are getting to you with the Word, and whities sayin' 'Oh, my God, we gotta stop this!' But it's too late now, baby! When you got it—it's over. When the youth got it— it's over . . . the white world is coming to an end."[81] The official United States has not been unaffected by the rising tide of black Islamic and/or Afrocentric raptivists. The FBI has reacted against lyrics that "encourage violence against and disrespect for the law enforcement officer."[82] Controversy raged over Ice-T's "Cop Killer," a police organization called for a boycott of Warner Brothers, and his album was eventually withdrawn from the market.[83] Jewish organizations tried to persuade CBS to stop the distribution of Public Enemy's single "Welcome to the Terrordome," and although CBS did not comply, the lobby succeeded in getting the video banned from the Canadian video channel MuchMusic.[84] The Anti-Defamation League listed Public Enemy, Professor Griff, and Ice Cube on their widely circulated report on *Black Demagogues and Extremists,*[85] the Simon Wiesenthal Center called for a boycott of Ice Cube's *Death Certificate,*[86] and presidential candidate Bill Clinton denounced Sister Souljah as a black racist at the 1992 Rainbow Coalition Leadership Summit.[87]

The Defiant Giants note that mainstream, or "whitestream," America has been slow to react to the violent, nonmessage tendency of gangsta rap, arguing that the white man "loves it when we say how we're going to uzi up our own brothers and sisters." The Defiant Giants contrast this with the attitude toward the serious raptivists, alleging that "the white man is afraid when we expose him for what he really is. When we call him a Zionist, a capitalist, a fascist, an imperialist. When we call him a murderer, a liar, a lyncher, a raper, a robber. When we expose him as a punk, a criminal, a faggot, a gangster. When we call him Lucifer, the Jinn, a snake, a devil. That's when he gets afraid. He's a beast in human form. He's afraid when we rap like this."[88] Sister Souljah's comments point to the gulf dividing the raptivists' audience from government officials and the mainstream media: "When the white press tries to attack black leaders, we wind up loving those leaders even more. We know that they must have done something right. You cannot tell kids in this country anything about a rapper. Rappers are the most powerful entity anywhere for young people."[89] The culture clashes manifested in the media during the past few years depend to a certain extent on the fact that the actors live in separate worlds. When Sister Souljah states that "we're livin' in a war zone" and "if black people kill black people every day, why not take a week and kill white people?" Bill Clinton might interpret this as a declaration of war, as if Sister Souljah was a warmonger who encourages black people to attack white people. For Sister Souljah, who lives in a different world, there already is war. The black urban communities she refers to are war zones, with body counts such as these: between twenty-five and forty blacks are murdered each day in America, and in the early 1990s, violence was the highest cause of death for black males between fifteen and forty-four years of age. Statistics show that a black male between fourteen and twenty-four living in ghetto areas would have been safer as an American soldier in Vietnam.[90] Sister Souljah cannot be a warmonger if she mobilizes for defense, sending out a wake-up call to her own community as well as to white America, which seems indifferent to the plight of the black communities. "I was just telling the writer," Sister Souljah explained, that "if a person would kill their own brother, or a baby in a drive-by, or a grandmother, what would make white people believe [he] would not kill them too?"[91]

Hip-hop, even in its most militant forms, reaches an audience that far exceeds the black and Hispanic youth it primarily addresses. In this context, an interesting shift of attitude is discernible. Until the 1960s, black youths generally regarded whites as role models and sought to bend nature to comply with their wishes, as, for example, when they used congolene to straighten their hair. One now can observe a reverse tendency, in which white youths look to blacks for role models. Today you might find white people wearing African medallions, X-marked clothing, and dreadlocks. Even President Clinton can be seen jogging around the White House with an X-cap on his head. Though this does not indicate any presidential support for the agenda of Malcolm X, as was made obvious by his outlash against Sister Souljah, it does underscore the new fashionability of African American culture.

This new trend means that black Muslim raptivists are selling tens of thousands of albums to white fans who dance to their own destruction. Ice Cube says that this will not make him compromise his message; on the contrary, he will continue selling truth. When asked if he still agrees with the NOI belief that all white people are devils, Ice Cube replied that he does: "All snakes ain't poisonous, but they all snakes. You got some whites out there that are strictly devils and you got some that . . . are harmless." As Cheo H. Choker notes, *Lethal Injection* opens with "the shot." A generic white man waits impatiently in a hospital for "Dr. Cube" to give him an injection, "much like the way eager white fans line up at the cash register to purchase their annual hit of Ice Cube's funk-laden Black anger." Dr. Cube approaches the white man with a loaded pistol, saying, "You want me to blow your head off you gullible muthaphukka? And you're actually gonna pay me for it? Brace yo' self!" and then gives him his shot in the neck. Ice Cube explains that it is "really about killing off the white way of thinking," calling it "bullshit" to actually put a bullet in someone's brain; he "wanna put the truth into their kids."[92]

Pumping up the dried bones in the valley of death, black Islamic hip-hop has become an avenue for the prophesized resurrection. Musically animated, the original man rises from the tomb to perform the break dance that will mark the end of the present cycle and bend the wheel of history "to the East, Blackwards."[93] Resounding from the black loudspeakers in the belly of the beast is the primordial rap of the divine, for I am the Alpha and the Omega, the Beginning and the End:

You never thought it would come but
you was wrong see
Now ya on the floor beggin' for mercy
Please brother it's too late
In Dayz 2 Come is your Prophesized Fate
The name of the game is RAPTURE.[94]

When Somethin's Wrong in tha Hood, Who Are You Gonna Call?   Narcotics, especially the epidemic usage of crack cocaine and heroin, constitute a major stumbling block to be overcome, should Lazarus not get a quick return ticket. According to Farrakhan, the deadly crystal flood is a key element in the Devil's scheme to whitewash his backyard: "[Imitates white devil speaking] 'Feed them cocaine. Then make it a pure form that they can smoke and call it crack, and feed it to the young warriors among them so that they now will turn the power of their youth and their anger and hostility on themselves. Let us destroy this people!' The plan is evident, isn't it?"[95] Prince Akeem emphasizes that as the African Americans do not own ships or planes, "how in the hell can we bring dope into this country?"[96] Charges that the intelligence community involved in drug trafficking to the black community are not confined to the NOI, but are part of a general street knowledge that makes black youths refer to the CIA as the "Cocaine Importing Agency."[97] A 1990 poll showed that 60 percent of the black respondents believe it to be true or possibly true that "the government deliberately makes sure that drugs are easily available in poor black neighborhoods in order to harm black people."[98]

This may seem like far-flung paranoia, but the suspicions are not totally unfounded conspiracy theories. The administration in Washington, D.C., has a long record of involvement in the drug racket. After World War II, the CIA reconstructed the heroin-trafficking Mafia and the Corsican crime syndicate as part of a campaign to break the radical European labor movement.[99] In the late 1960s, a heroin epidemic followed a decade and a half of CIA collaboration with opium dealers and corrupted regimes in the golden triangle of Burma, Laos, and Thailand. In return for fighting communists, the CIA even assisted the drug czars by shipping opium in American military airplanes,[100] and heroin was smuggled into the United States inside the returning corpses of Americans who died in Vietnam.[101] In the course of the Afghan war, the Southwest Asian heroin trade boomed. The golden crescent's share in the U.S. heroin market increased from a minor portion before the Soviet Union's invasion of Afghanistan to about 50 percent by 1984. Again, this was made possible by U.S. intelligence protection. "Heroin was shipped out in the same trucks that brought in covert U.S. aid to the Afghan guerrillas."[102] The pattern is comparable to that of the inter-American cocaine trade. The CIA's complicity with organizations responsible for flooding cocaine from South and Central America into the United States in the 1980s was of such crucial significance for the drug traffic that Peter D. Scott and Jonathan Marshall conclude in their well-documented study *Cocaine Politics:* "The history of official toleration for or complicity with drug traffickers in Central America in the 1980's suggests the inadequacy of traditional 'supply-side' or 'demand-side' drug strategies whose targets are remote from Washington. Chief among these targets have been the ethnic ghettos of America's inner cities (the demand side) and foreign peasants who grow coca plants or opium poppies (the supply side). Experience suggests instead that one of the first targets for an effective drug strategy should be Washington itself, and specifically its own support for corrupt, drug-linked forces in the name of anticommunism."[103] In communities with high unemployment rates and limited job opportunities to low-income sectors, drug dealing has become a tempting road to individual fortune. For many ghetto youths, the successful dealer is the role model of the American dream. "Dope has become a major employer in urban communities," Farrakhan writes. "The dope industry is greater than a $300 billion industry, three times the size of General Motors."[104] With drugs as a chief cause of black-on-black street violence and other crimes, combating dope has been singled out by the NOI as a prime target for direct action.[105] Responding to a perceived call from victimized residents of drug-infested black neighborhoods, Muslim soldiers intervened as "dopebusters" rushing to their rescue.

The "Islamic patrols" began after Glen French, resident manager of the Mayfair Mansions low-income housing project in Washington, D.C., noticed that the drug market shut down when FOI soldiers visited to pass out flyers and sell the *Final Call.* French made a call to Mosque #4 and asked if that could become a regular activity. After reaching an agreement, the FOI set up headquarters in a three-story apartment and began patrolling the grounds. On April 18, 1988, the FOI patrols—named "dopebusters" by a local black paper—came to national attention after a skirmish in which a gunman was disarmed and a media crew filming the incident was roughed up. Due in part to a lack of communication, relations between the Muslim patrols and local police authorities were tense, but a temporary working agreement was eventually set up.[106] The subsequent media coverage of the dopebusters ranged from negative remarks about vigilantes to articles of praise, which claimed that the FOI men did what the police failed to do: rid the area of drug dealers.[107] "It was a living hell," said Betty Adams, mother of three and head of the tenants' association. "There were daily gun shots, there were nightly gun shots. The whole complex . . . was jammed packed with dealers and pushers." Adams expressed her satisfaction with the Muslim patrols: "Children, who once couldn't go outside to play, are now playing. . . . As far as the Nation of Islam being here, I think everyone is happy. I know I am."[108] As the dopebusters' reputation grew, a stream of emergency calls were placed to Mosque #4 from other drug-infested neighborhoods in the Capitol area,[109] and the dopebusters could bask in the sunshine of supportive opinions from residents, elected officials, and police chiefs.

Spurred on by their initial success, the Washington FOI extended their patrolling area to 14th Street, a busy downtown drug and prostitution corridor. When twenty-five Muslim soldiers arrived on the scene, they were approached by a white police officer who declared their doings illegal and said that he would put a stop to it. According to Richard 3X, the officer threw FOI soldier Napoleon Muhammad up against a car and tried to grab him by the neck when other Muslims intervened. "Everyone knows that the Muslims are trained to defend ourselves," said Abdul Alim Muhammad, minister of Mosque #4. "This is our God-given right to defend ourselves . . . against the vicious, malicious police brutality." The policeman put out an officer-in-distress call and soon a force of some one hundred police officers clashed with the "Allahu Akbar"–shouting FOI soldiers. The street battle waged for half an hour, and seven Muslims were arrested before calm was restored.[110]

Though the downtown move failed, the pilot project at Mayfair Mansions succeeded and was extended to the neighboring Paradise Manor housing project.[111] Now almost free from drug dealers, the projects could undergo a multimillion dollar renovation and landscaping effort. At a second anniversary celebration of the dopebusters' arrival, attended by Minister Farrakhan, Public Enemy, police representatives, and city councilmen, the Muslims were praised by the District's antidrug czar, Sterling Tucker: "You have reclaimed this community . . . and we're going to take back the city with your help and everybody's help."[112] In his address, Minister Farrakhan spoke of the cooperation between the Muslims, housing residents, owners, and management as a model for the future: "What we have done, with the help of God, at Mayfair Mansions in that alliance for progress, we can do it for the city of Washington. We can do it for the District, for Prince George's County, for Virginia. We can do it for a sick nation that is crying out for proper leadership."[113] In 1988, the Nation of Islam established an affiliated business venture, the NOI's Security Agency Incorporated, with the parental body located in Washington, D.C., under the auspices of the dopebusters. By 1993, the NOI Security Agency operated in five states, as different chapters of the NOI Security Agency won bids to patrol crime- and drug-infested housing projects in Washington, D.C., New York City, Los Angeles, Baltimore, Philadelphia, Pittsburgh, and Chicago.[114] Muslim guards provide security for Federal Express, a hotel, and a construction site in Washington, D.C.,[115] and, in addition, were called to rid various black and Hispanic communities of drug dealers and prostitutes, to protect black politicians and celebrities, and to guard rallies, concerts, and sports events. Mary Tabor concludes that the unarmed Islamic patrols generally enjoyed what eludes police officers: respect. "In this community, the only ones people listen to are from the Nation of Islam," a man explained to the *New York Times*. The Muslims' prestige within the black community even has spurred other private enterprises in the security sector to copy the suit-and-bow-tie look, such as the New York–based X-men firm (not to be confused with the official FOI or NOI Security Agency, Inc.).[116]

Controversy raged when the Anti-Defamation League began protesting against the contracting of Islamic patrols. Impressed by the dopebusting NOI Security Agency success in patrolling a 1,200 unit complex in Washington, D.C., residents of fifteen federally subsidized housing projects in Venice's Oakwood section on Los Angeles's West Side "concluded that only the Nation of Islam can rid the buildings of the gang activity and drug dealing that have plagued them for years."[117] When the NOI Security Agency made their bid for the several-hundred-thousand-dollar contract with the federal Department of Housing and Urban Development (HUD), the Anti-Defamation League and the Jewish Defense League protested in a letter, stating that hiring the Nation of Islam would be as inappropriate as hiring the Ku Klux Klan.[118] When HUD took the ADL-JDL objection into consideration and reopened the bidding, a resident association launched a petition drive to collect signatures, in order to prove that a majority of residents wanted NOI Security to patrol their crime-ridden area.[119]

As the fight over the contract moved to the Los Angeles Board of Police Commissioners for a final decision, both sides engaged in heavy lobbying. When police officials stated that they probably would recommend that the commission grant the NOI proposal,[120] the ADL reacted swiftly. Prior to congressional deliberations over the HUD appropriations bill, Abraham Foxman and Mira Boland of the ADL recommended that the congressmen consider "whether HUD rules should permit a HUD contractor to spend $644,000 to hire Louis Farrakhan's Nation of Islam to provide security for a federally subsidized housing project." Listing highlights from the NOI's "record of confrontation with the police and others," the ADL officials questioned the use of taxpayers' money to turn "neighborhoods over to their most violent elements."[121] The ADL furthermore sent a letter to the police commission, stating that the NOI "is known for its discriminatory and hateful rhetoric directed against Caucasians in general and Jews in particular." In response, backers of the NOI showed up with petitions signed by about 100 residents and claimed that the NOI, with its record of black pride and self-reliance, would be more effective than the police in stemming gang violence and drug business.[122]

The NOI Security Agency eventually won the contract and began patrolling the Holiday Venice complex in November 1992. Following an impressive start, with crime rates down by nearly 75 percent according to statistics released by the city attorney's office,[123] law officials charged that drug dealing was on the rise again, and the management chose to terminate the contract. While some residents maintained that the increase in crime occurred outside the project, and was therefore beyond Muslim jurisdiction, owner-representative David Itkin charged that the NOI Security Agency had shown a complete failure and replaced them with an armed security firm in October 1993. Company spokesman Abdul Arif Muhammad claimed in his rebuttal that the management was in direct complicity with the LAPD to remove the Muslims and undermine their efforts.[124]

While the capability of the Islamic patrols in Los Angeles's Oakwood section might be questioned, their work in Baltimore was applauded. After a period during which FOI patrols successfully guarded senior citizens from robbers on Social Security check day,[125] the NOI Security Agency won a $2.8 million contract in crime-ridden Flaghouse Courts in June 1993. When the crime rate plummeted by 50 percent, the area of operation was extended to several other public housing complexes, and Baltimore Mayor Kurt Schmoke publicly endorsed the NOI for "bringing stability and peace" to the area, saying that he would "continue to work with that group."[126]

In February 1994, another Muslim security company, New Life, Inc., headed by NOI top laborer Leonard Muhammad, won a contract to provide security for the 1,124 Rockwell Gardens units on Chicago's West Side. New Life had previously won contracts for the Maplewood Court, Harrison Court, and Ogden Court developments, but now wished for a greater challenge. The Rockwell housing development is one of Chicago's most crime-ridden areas and was the first to undergo the controversial "Clean Sweep" operation, a door-to-door, building-to-building search for contraband, criminals, and illegal tenants. After a four-year period of repeated sweeps, the area is still "under gang control, gunfire is routine, drugs are sold openly, and small children can't walk to school safely," the Chicago Housing Authority reported, explaining why the NOI won the bid despite fierce objections from the ADL. "We got one response. And I don't see any reason to reject it. Nobody wants Rockwell because it is a dangerous place. It's more than a notion of ducking and dodging bullets. This isn't a cakewalk."[127] "Police treat you like garbage," Rockwell resident Anthony Thomas said in his endorsement of the new security firm. "The Muslims . . . treat you with respect, and the way they come to us is the way we come back to them."[128]

The NOI Prison Reform Ministry: Let My People Go   In addition to combating drugs and crime on the street, the Nation of Islam reaches out to incarcerated criminals and addicts in a combined rehabilitation and recruiting drive. Social workers and observers have frequently noted the NOI's record of success,[129] NOI officials have received numerous awards for their rehabilitation programs,[130] and a considerable part of the movement's cadre is composed of reformed convicts. The significance of the NOI prison ministry is underscored by the fact that a disproportional percent of the American prison population is composed of blacks. While African Americans constitute about 13 percent of the U.S. population, close to one-half of its prison population is black. In 1991 and 1992, the U.S. courts incarcerated blacks at a rate four times higher than courts in South Africa, and including those on parole or probation, about 25 percent of black males in their 20s were under the control of the criminal justice system.[131] Putting aside the different socioeconomic conditions as a causal variable, blacks, Hispanics, and whites tend to be unequally treated before the law, as blacks and Hispanics almost always tend to receive longer sentences than whites for similar crimes.[132]

With the goal of transforming the convicts into law-abiding, disciplined, and productive men, the Nation of Islam established a "self-improvement program" in the mid-1980s. Based on the teachings of Elijah Muhammad, the inmates are taught Knowledge of Self in a process of replacing a criminal identity with a divine identity. They attempt to "form a perfect union with Almighty God Allah"—that is, *Theos Antropos,* "so that when you see the person, you are actually looking at God."[133] Rekindling divinity turns self-hatred into self-respect, which is said to be the basis for correct and respectful behavior toward other fellow human beings. Upon being released from prison, the new member is given a position in the mosque and in the army, a new sense of belonging, and a set of obligations, ranging from educational classes to military drill, which occupy much of his spare time. The uncompromising and highly elaborate NOI norms for proper conduct, together with a new mission to accomplish, give the ex-convict's life a new direction and the Nation a dedicated soldier.

The Nation is said to have a very strong presence within the prisons and adherents often constitute the most cohesive body of black convicts. Inside the prison walls, the NOI forms a black brotherhood with a structure close to the basically ethnic gangs that form in response to the conditions of jail culture. Belonging to a prison "car" is a road to survival, and strong pressure can be put on individuals without gang affiliation. Membership involves a set of obligations to the collective, and in many prisons a balance of terror is said to exist between the NOI brotherhood and, for example, the Aryan brotherhood and/or other cars.

Prison officials tend to view the NOI convict with some hostility, as a potentially dangerous man beyond effective control who preaches racial hatred. Inmates can be beaten, harassed, punished, and humiliated by prison guards for adhering to the Nation of Islam doctrines.[134] The NOI convicts and other incarcerated Muslims raise demands for a special diet, days of worship and time for prayer, and religious guidance from someone other than the prison chaplain. These demands are often rejected by prison authorities, who claim that they undermine fundamental interests of the state, such as prison security and administrative efficiency. In a study of Muslims in prisons, Kathleen Moore notes that African Americans have been instrumental in bringing the issue of Islam as a religion worthy of constitutional protection before the courts, with a view to ending discriminatory rules.[135] Although Islam has been recognized as a religion deserving First Amendment protection, the NOI and other black militant Muslim organizations have been treated as dangerous cults that should be suppressed in the interest of society, rather than protected. In a series of cases, the courts have more often than not ruled in favor of the Muslims' constitutional rights, but the picture is far from unambiguous.

Islamic commandments have often been prohibited while the practices of other faiths in the same prison have not. In most cases, the courts have ordered the prison administration to make religious facilities available in a nondiscriminatory manner.[136] In a few cases, however, the court took the position that Muslim practices may be prohibited. In *In Re Ferguson,* NOI convicts in Folsom prison contended that their constitutional rights had been violated as they, unlike adherents of all other religious faiths in Folsom, were denied a place to worship. The Supreme Court of California referred to the subversive NOI doctrine of black supremacy when rejecting the complaints: "In the light of the potentially serious dangers to the established prison society presented by the Muslim beliefs and actions, it cannot be said that the present, suppressive approach by the Director of Corrections is an abuse of his discretionary power to manage our prison system."[137] Moore further notes that "analogous claims made by Muslim and Jewish inmates have resulted in dissimilar rulings," not in the least in cases involving a religiously prescribed pork-free diet. In *Kahane v. Carlson,* the Court of Appeals for the Second Circuit, in its 1975 term, stated that "prison authorities must accommodate the rights of prisoners to receive diets consistent with their religious scruples." The following year, in *Jihaad v. Carlson,* the Muslim inmate complained before the same appellate court that he was fed only pork sandwiches, but his request for a religiously proper diet was denied: "The prisoners are not entitled to a special dietary program."[138] Similarly, Christian and Muslim prisoners may be treated unequally. While not denying Catholic inmates the right to attend Sunday Mass, a New Jersey prison prevented Muslim convicts from attending Friday prayer in a case brought before the U.S. Supreme Court, which found that "prison officials had acted in a reasonable manner."[139] While the courts' treatment of Islam has not been uniform, the general trend has been to recognize the Muslim inmates' demands for the right of free exercise of religion when it is framed in the context of anti-discrimination and is not found incompatible with security arrangements. Moore notes, however, that a few cases in the 1980s indicate a possible reversal of this trend. She cites as an example the 1983 ruling in *Thompson v. Kentucky:* "The Free Exercise Clause guarantees a liberty interest, a substantive right; that clause does not insure that all sects will be treated alike in all respects."[140]

The struggle to be allowed free exercise of the freedom of religion when incarcerated is but a small part of the NOI prison program. In a wider context, the prison is seen as a prison within a prison, the greater Babylonian trap with its red and white bars. The Nation of Islam's approach is multifaceted, aiming at physical as well as mental release from the prison or the enslavement under drugs, as well as from the United States and the enslavement under the Devil. In "The Muslim Program," established by the Honorable Elijah Muhammad and still published in each issue of the *Final Call,* point five of the "What the Muslim Wants" section reads as follows: "We want freedom for all Believers of Islam now held in federal prisons. We want freedom for all black men and women now under death sentence in innumerable prisons in the North, as well as in the South. We want every black man and woman to have the freedom to accept or reject being separated from the slavemaster's children and establish a land of their own." In *A Torchlight for America,* Minister Farrakhan elaborates a vision for this program for the 1990s. Farrakhan argues that the rate of recidivism indicates that "the prison system is not set up to reform" the convict. Why spend $18,000 per year per inmate to keep him incarcerated when the Muslims have a successful record of rehabilitation? "Why not let us handle the inmate and lessen the taxpayer's burden?" Farrakhan asks. "We can reform our people and make them productive members of society."[141] This, Farrakhan says, is the most feasible solution for the crime- and drug-ridden American society. Let the NOI handle the "black problem": "We can reform the convict, you can't. We reform the drug addict, you don't. We reform the alcoholic and the prostitute. You don't. We take the poor and give them hope by making them do something for themselves. You don't. We are your solution."[142] Addressing the President and the Congress, Farrakhan urged, "Let our Black brothers out of prison, give us your poor, give them to me—let my people go."[143] Farrakhan believes that since the Africans were involved in the slave trade, they should provide compensation by donating a territory for blacks from the diaspora to start again. Besides citing the creation of Israel as a historical precedent, Farrakhan points to the history of America, Australia, and New Zealand, colonies that were populated by prisoners from Europe: "The work done by former criminals of Europe in establishing America, New Zealand and Australia, has redeemed them in the eye of history. Let the work of the so-called under-class and so-called criminal element among black people be allowed to redeem them in the eye of history by their being permitted and supported in building a new reality on the African continent."[144] According to Farrakhan, besides ridding America of part of its unwanted desolates, the strategic geopolitical advantages of this undertaking are apparent: if the United States improved its treatment of blacks, it would "foster favorable relations with Africa." A nation of repatriated blacks would also "gain for America a strong foothold on that strategically important continent."[145] Clearly, Farrakhan attempts to pose as a rational and reasonable individual. "We are ready to sit down and talk with the American leaders," Farrakhan emphasizes. "Is America ready for us?"[146]

40 Acres and a Mule   The NOI's demand for a separate state as compensation for centuries of unpaid slave labor is in effect a call for the fulfillment of the land reform promised by Union officials during and shortly after the Civil War. The Order No. 15, issued by General William T. Sherman in January 1865, seemed to promise land to the freed African Americans, and blacks in general held the assumption that the government would allocate them forty-acre lots carved out from abandoned Southern farmlands. The establishment of the Freedman's Bureau in 1864–5, and its enlarged jurisdiction granted by the Congress over President Andrew Johnson's veto in 1866, further encouraged the belief in just compensation. Although the bureau did lease out land to black tenants and open up public land for settlement to those freedmen who had capital and tools, no full-scale land redistribution ever materialized before the white backlash that ended the Reconstruction Era.[147]

Farrakhan voices the black sentiment that the issue of justice still has to be resolved. Though the present generation of whites are innocent of what their fathers did, the present black-white inequality is a product of historical injustice. "America, you owe us something," Farrakhan stated, and "we don't want you to dole it out in welfare checks." Just as Germany paid compensation to Israel and the United States compensated the Japanese Americans, the government should now pay their debt to its black citizens. "Now, let's add up what they owe us," Farrakhan urged. "If a hundred million of us lost our lives in the middle-passage, add it up! . . . Three hundred years working millions of slaves for nothing. Add it up!" Continuing to list the evil inflicted on the African American, Farrakhan reminded America of the crimes of slavery that deprived blacks of their freedom, their religion, their culture, and their identity. He recalled the assassinated black leaders and all black soldiers killed in wars, asking how much a black life is worth. "Now, what does justice look like?" Farrakhan asked and gave the answer himself: "Add it up, white folks, you gonna have to give us the whole country. Add it up, white man. The whole thing belongs to the oppressed if you add it up. . . . When I ask for reparations, I'm asking you to save your life, but if you don't want to save

your life, then leave it to God. He'll settle it. Let me tell you how He'll
settle it: an eye for an eye, a tooth for a tooth and a life for a life. Add it up.
Add it up. Add it up. One hundred million in the middle passage and you
have 150 million white people in America today. Add it up. If it's a life for
a life, then God is justified in killing everything that refuses to submit. . . .
You better add it up!"[148] Reparations is a recurring theme in Farrakhan's
speeches. The issue was, for example, put high on the *Black Agenda*
presented to the 1988 Democratic and Republican Conventions.[149] Reparations were given a key status in Farrakhan's address before the African
American summit in New Orleans in April 1989,[150] and again when Farrakhan met with the Congressional Black Caucus in Washington, D.C., in
1990.[151] Farrakhan is, of course, not alone among black leaders in pressing the demand for reparations. In 1987, an umbrella organization called
the National Coalition of Blacks for Reparations in America (N'COBRA)
was established in an effort to make the demand a national priority.[152]
The NOI participates in the N'COBRA meetings, which so far mainly have
attracted radical nationalist organizations, such as the Republic of New
Africa and the New African Peoples' Organization, rather than mainstream groups. Other organizations, such as the National Commission for
Reparations and the International Human Rights Association of American Minorities, opt to advance the question through United Nations
petitions.

Black politicians have introduced the issue in local assemblies, and
resolutions calling for reparations through financing the rebuilding of a
black infrastructure have passed the Michigan State Legislature and the
City Councils of Boston and Detroit.[153] In 1989, 1991, and 1993, Congressman John Conyers introduced a bill in the House of Representatives,
calling for a congressional study of the issue of reparations.[154] While the
N'COBRA discussed the prospect of a general black strike to enforce the
demand for reparations,[155] Farrakhan lent his support to Conyers's 1993
effort to get a reparations bill through Congress, urging the congressman
to call for a march on Washington to put the question at the steps of the
White House and before the world.[156]

"We never received our forty acres and a mule," Farrakhan wrote, linking the government's debt to the heirs of the slave population with the NOI
demand for a separate state: "There are millions of acres of federal and
municipal land and property currently abandoned or not in use. We can
make use of that land by developing agribusiness . . . and by building low-
income housing for the urban homeless, for the poor and for the working

class. . . . The government should consider selling or leasing us the land and property at a price that is mindful that America owes us reparations for the holocaust of slavery."[157] Farrakhan repeatedly argues that reparations, combined with the sum total of savings that the United States would make if it were to release its black prison population into the custody of the Nation, would suffice as an initial economic foundation for an independent black state. "We know it can be done," the minister asserted to an NOI student audience. "We're going in to lay the infrastructure and build us up cities and towns and set up our own flag. Feel it! Just feel it! Feel it, feel it! God—that feel good!"[158]

Vote Black Muslim for Congress   Basically, the Nation of Islam argues that the Devil's society cannot be reformed. Moses provides the recommended strategy that is soon to be fulfilled under the leadership of Minister Farrakhan: a full-scale Exodus. Traditionally, this belief accounts for the refusal of the NOI to participate in the parliamentary democracy of the Devil. But what can be done while awaiting departure time? Here, another biblical type provides a rationale for an alternative strategy occasionally employed by the NOI leadership: Joseph became a master in the very land in which he was sold as a slave. Translated into American realpolitik, this means that although the Nation rejects the legitimacy of the present political system of the United States, political involvement can at times be justified given the right circumstances. "It is difficult for me to advise my followers on taking part in the corrupt politics of our enemies," Elijah Muhammad wrote in the mid-1960s. To serve the Blackman, a politician must have no fear of the Devil, and Congressman Adam Clayton Powell, "though he is not a Muslim," was singled out as a worthy example. "A Muslim politician is what you need," the Messenger continued, and emphasized that "we must give good black politicians the total backing of our people."[159]

Two decades later, the Nation of Islam as an organization got involved in the Jesse Jackson presidential campaign of 1984, as described earlier. Minister Farrakhan registered to vote for the first time in his life and was followed by several hundred black Islamic nationalists and reported gang members in a PR show.[160] Farrakhan vowed to comb every ghetto, barrio and Indian reservation in search of unregistered voters in support of the Jackson candidacy,"[161] and the NOI cadre assisted the Rainbow Coalition in reaching out. Later, when Jackson was forced to rebuke Farrakhan, the minister left the scene in disgust. "My brother and friend Reverend Jackson says he will not accept my support, he will not accept not even kind words of praise," Farrakhan said. "He don't want me, but he will go down to Alabama and sit down with Wallace and call Governor Wallace his friend—a man that lynched black people; a man that castrated black people; a man that denied black people justice . . . but [Jackson] won't walk with me because it's political suicide."[162]

In the course of the 1980s, a stream of black politicians, such as David Dinkins, Douglass Wilder, Norman Rice, Ron Brown, and Michael White, were elected mayors and governors. While Farrakhan says he is happy to see African Americans rise to prominence, he warns of a false sense of euphoria that ultimately will lead to disillusionment and despair. The accepted black leaders have sold out to the Devil, Farrakhan charges: "Our poor people are not aware that this rotten political leadership has made a covenant with death and an agreement with hell."[163] Black politicians that seek to curry the favor of the establishment are mere puppets that will be thrown away as waste after doing their part; it does not matter who is elected, as long as they play by the rules of the Devil. The African American community should thus place no trust in politicians for their salvation: "No politician can save nobody. Politicians are in no saviour business. Politicians are hoodlums. No whore can save you!"[164]

Addressing the need to make black leaders accountable to the community, Farrakhan warned them "to be instructed by the violence" in South Africa, where the black poor "are killing the blacks in privileged positions who have become apologists for white oppressors. . . . Don't say Farrakhan is preaching violence. I'm only telling you what selling out is going to bring you."[165] Vowing to watch these politicians like a hawk, if necessary replacing them with candidates of his own, Farrakhan stresses that "before we become a free people, we are going to have to take care of that kind of business."[166] Tired of watching corrupt black leadership, Farrakhan announced the candidacy of three Nation of Islam members in an unprecedented move in May 1990. "It is time now for us to come out of the mosque," Farrakhan said. "We have something to offer to Black America and we have something to offer to white America. The Scripture says, 'What man having a light would hide it under a bushel basket?' No, take your light out from the bushel basket and you place it on a hill. What hill? Capitol Hill!"[167]

The NOI candidates were Dr. Abdul Alim Muhammad, minister of Mosque #4 and national spokesman for Minister Farrakhan, who ran in the Fifth Congressional District in Prince George's County; George X

Cure, who ran for a vacated nonvoting delegate seat in the District of Columbia; and Shawn X Brackeen, who ran for the D. C. Board of Education.[168] The results were modest for George X and Shawn X,[169] but Abdul Alim Muhammad, who had earned a reputation as leader of the aforementioned dopebusters, fared better in his race against incumbent Democrat Steny H. Hoyer. To face off the Muslim challenge, Hoyer was forced to increase his number of speaking engagements and had to buy television advertisements for the first time since becoming elected to Congress nine years earlier.[170] Abdul Alim Muhammad eventually received 21 percent of the vote in the 60 percent black district. The high expectations were unfulfilled and the disappointed candidate voiced charges of vote tampering. Nevertheless, the fact that one out of five voters supported an NOI candidate for the U.S. House of Representatives must be considered noteworthy.[171] The setback for these pilot candidates does not seem to have discouraged Farrakhan from seeking a larger role in American politics. Asked whether the country will see more NOI candidates running for political office, Farrakhan responded affirmatively. "I believe that we should have representation in legislative bodies, nationally and locally, from aldermanic seats to state representative seats to Congressional seats." Until an independent black state has been established, the minister assured his readers that the Nation will try to influence federal decision making and "move America towards a just agenda in solving the problems of black and white. So politics would not be an end for us. It would be a means to an end."[172]

Aware of his ability to attract a larger audience than any other contemporary black spokesperson, Farrakhan has geared toward national attention. A *Newsweek* poll from 1992 showed that 34 percent of African Americans believed that blacks would benefit if Farrakhan took a larger leadership role on the political scene.[173] In *A Torchlight for America,* Farrakhan presents his political ideology and his vision to rid America of classism, racism, and sexism, the three evils that threaten to destroy the country.[174] Presenting statistics and hard facts to show that America is on her deathbed and in dire need of a new direction, Farrakhan discusses the budget deficit, the federal debt, the unequal distribution of wealth, and the scapegoating of the poor, who "got nothing but the burden and the blame"[175] and "are voiceless in society as it is presently structured."[176] Farrakhan then proposes solutions for rebuilding the economy, improving the public school system, and ending the health-care crisis, and further, stresses the need for developing a sound moral fabric in society. His proposals are largely based on the practical experience of the NOI in those fields, topics that will be presented in more detail later in this chapter. The holistic approach taken by Minister Farrakhan is designed to transcend religious and ethnical divisions. If the Nation of Islam traditionally spoke exclusively for blacks, Farrakhan now seeks a broader appeal: "Let us sit down and talk about bringing real solutions before the American people, as civilized people should and are obliged to do. The Kingdom of God is an egalitarian kingdom structured on truth, where each of us will be treated with fairness and justice. America . . . has within her borders every nation, kindred and tongue. If they could be made peaceful, productive and mutually respecting, you would have the basis for the Kingdom of God right here on earth. . . . This can be achieved by establishing the truth that frees white people from the sickness of white supremacy and frees black people from the sickness of black inferiority."[177] With his torchlight, Farrakhan intends to attract the attention of Americans well beyond the traditional seedbeds of NOI recruitment. "I have to stand and speak for the voiceless, whose leadership has often been quiet or weak in the face of an open enemy," he writes. "Although I have been misrepresented by the media, here is a new opportunity to receive my message and judge it against the criterion of truth."[178] Although not compromising his earlier stands, Farrakhan's manner of expression is more diplomatic in order to fit the tone of public discourse. Blunt declarations of the past, such as "The white man is the Devil," are reformulated into more sophisticated statements, such as "If whites patterned themselves after God then we could follow them. But they have done quite the contrary,"[179] an implicitly restated sentiment that is less likely to be labeled as reverse racism.

An indication of the fact that Farrakhan has been successful in reaching beyond his former insular position in American society was found in the poll published in *Time* magazine in February 1994. The *Time*/CNN poll found that 73 percent of the respondents were familiar with Farrakhan (more than any black politician except Jesse Jackson and Supreme Court Justice Clarence Thomas) and two-thirds of those viewed him favorably. Further, 70 percent of those polled believed Farrakhan says things the country should listen to; 67 percent viewed Farrakhan as an effective leader; no less than 63 percent believed that Farrakhan speaks the truth; 62 percent held the opinion that Farrakhan was good for the black community; and 53 percent considered Farrakhan to be a role model for black youth and somebody they would like their children to emulate. When asked to name "the most important black leader today," Farrakhan ranked second after Jesse Jackson, with 9 percent volunteering his name, three times as many as for Nelson Mandela.[180]

The above-mentioned poll is but one indication that the Nation of Islam presently has a wider popularity than during its former heydays of the 1960s, a fact made obvious by the enormous turnout at the 1995 Million Man March. There are several reasons for this situation. First, the 1960s held a modernist Hegelian view of social history as an ever-progressive development toward a better future. Everything seemed possible, including the dream of the moderate black leadership for a color-blind and just society. The late 1980s and early 1990s, in contrast, are marked by a postmodern questioning of man's rationality and of social history's progressive nature. What if there is no plan, no control, no direction? Doubting rational man reasserts the need of God and favors those religious leaders who claim to know where God wants man to go. Second, the 1990s returned in many ways to the agenda of the 1930s. A tendency toward global integration met an opposing tendency toward fragmentation and a revival of ethnic and national sentiments, ambitions, and conflicts in a time of economic uncertainty, staggering unemployment, and social unrest. Third, Reaganomics made few blacks inclined to identify with the administration as a governmental body on their side and signaled a political shift of attitude advanced by the Republican "Contract with America," aiming to reverse politics such as affirmative action from which the black community has benefited. With widening political, economic, and social gaps separating the white and the black communities, the separatism of the Nation suddenly appears less extremist and more a description of an emerging reality, as symbolized by the O. J. Simpson trial. Fourth, Farrakhan's ability to reach young people, combined with the raptivist tendency of the hip-hop movement, has made black Islam a vital part of an urban youth culture and rendered the NOI and its leader a sort of cult status for a new generation of black youth that lacks confidence in the old political leadership. Fifth, action speaks louder than words, and the NOI's record of practical deeds in successfully confronting some of the worst problems facing American society, such as gang violence, crime, drugs, and poverty, accounts for the respect shown to the minister and his organization. Finally, an increasing segment of the American population has seemingly lost faith in the capacity of mainstream politicians to solve the nation's problems, as was manifested by the interest aroused by Ross Perot's populist, antipolitician, deeds-not-words approach.

If President Clinton should prove to be a disappointment, additional people might be attracted by a message spoken in clear-cut American language, untainted by the past failures of the two traditional political parties. While that message might come from the ranks of successful technocrats or entrepreneurs, there is a possibility that it will come from the ranks of preachers, voicing what seems to be a global trend: Now that we have seen the failure of secular politics, why not try the way of God? Farrakhan, who seemed inspired by the frankness of the United We Stand campaign, might very well make a bid for the position of a black Perot, who with a different brand of populism will challenge the established parties in the future. The nationwide NOI-led campaign in 1995 to get the eight million unregistered black citizens to register to vote was a logical step in this direction.[181]

That is not to say that Farrakhan plans to become a politician proper. Islam and politics are inseparable, as man has the mandate of God to build a perfect society for all. To hand over politics to the politicians is to decline that responsibility, something a man of God cannot do. The American preachers "ought to be ashamed of themselves, bowing down to politicians," Farrakhan exclaimed. "God has never sent a prophet to be the subject of a king, but the prophets make kings, and rebuke kings and set kings down. So we as men of God, who don't have political aspirations, we as men of God will sit down in every city of America and work out the agenda for our people. Certainly, we give the politician the agenda. The spiritual men of God have to get back up on the high position that God has given us."[182]

Farewell to Welfare: The Black POWER of the Nation of Islam   In 1987, four of the most important cities in the United States had black mayors: Chicago (Harold Washington), Atlanta (Andrew Young), Washington, D.C. (Marion Barry), and Los Angeles (Thomas Bradley). "Certainly it makes us feel good," Farrakhan said. "But feeling good can't feed the babies when they're hungry. Feeling good can't pay the rent when the rent is due." Farrakhan urges African Americans to ponder over why they are not any better off in those cities that have black mayors: is it not like voting for a black manager to run a white-owned store? "If political power alone is the answer then we can tell it has failed, but politics cannot in and of itself be an answer. . . . If politics does not open the way for economic development of the people then it is a symbol without substance and has no value for us."[183] Reaganomics signified a backlash from the upper class. The only people who really benefitted economically were those with an annual income exceeding $200,000. In 1989, 4 percent of the population owned more than 50 percent of the country's assets. African Americans constitute about 13 percent of the population, but account for only about 3 percent of the accumulated wealth. African Americans' net worth, the ratio of household assets to liabilities, is nearly ten times less than for all Americans. The median net worth of a black family in 1988 was $4,169 compared to a white median of $43,279. Close to one-third, or 29.1 percent, of black households scored zero or negative net worth. [184] In 1992, the percentage of African Americans living below the poverty level was 33.3, and approximately every second Blackamerican child is raised in poverty.[185] African American unemployment is increasing in central cities, while declining slightly in the suburbs and substantially for the few blacks living and working in edge cities.[186] In certain urban areas, more than every second young black male is unemployed. A comparison between those fortunate enough to have a job reveals continuing racial inequality: a black makes only 60 percent of a white salary. The percentage of African Americans with low-income jobs increased dramatically during Reaganomics. In 1973, 27.7 percent of employed black men were low-wage earners, and by 1987, this figure had jumped to 44 percent.[187]

It is within this context that the economic politics of the Nation of Islam should be seen. True to the teachings of Elijah Muhammad and the legacy of Booker T. Washington, Marcus Garvey, and Noble Drew Ali, Farrakhan gives priority to the construction of a black infrastructure as a means to empower the African American communities and as a step toward desired independence. As the economic empire of the old Nation was dismantled in the course of events following the Messenger's departure, Farrakhan's NOI had to start all over again.

A number of business ventures have been established in different sectors: a chain of Salaam restaurants, Shabazz bakeries, Fashahnn Islamic clothings (featuring for instance the Dress 19 Collection designed by Tynetta Muhammad), clothing stores, food markets, the NOI Security Agency, New Life, the *Final Call*, Books & Tapes, Clean 'N Fresh skin and hair care products, Abundant Life Clinics, real estate in a number of states, fish markets, farmland (which produced its first harvest in 1995), and a Chicago mall of supermarkets and restaurants. Further, ten trailer trucks have been bought as a first step to reestablish a NOI transportation fleet, and a Chicago business center has been bought to house management and media operations as the NOI expands into television. Plans for reopening the NOI supermarkets, reinstituting a Muslim bank, expanding its printing plants, and regaining its farmland have been announced.

To promote black manufacturing, distribution, and resale business, the Nation of Islam inaugurated the POWER (People Organized and Working for Economical Rebirth) program in 1985. That same year the African American community had a purchasing power of $204 billion that mainly poured out of the community into the hands of nonblack, American or foreign, corporations. Black purchasing power, Farrakhan argues, can and must be redirected to support black business and institutions. "You live in the cities and the cities are decaying beneath your feet, but we have the resources to own them, to take them over, but you sitting around here looking for sympathy," Farrakhan charged, "crying and wailing and begging at the feet of white people like a lazy beggar when you can get up and do these things for yourself!"[188]

True to its ideology of "do for self," the Nation of Islam rejects the American welfare system. Though not condemning the individuals who live on welfare, Farrakhan warns of the system's consequences: "Welfare if you turn it around means farewell. It means bye to the spirit of self-determination. It means so long to the spirit that God gives to every human being and the duty that God gives to every human being to do something for self. It makes you a slave. Welfare, farewell."[189] This does not imply that blacks should accept substandard living conditions, only that blacks should stop waiting for the government to improve their situation. Had those in power been genuinely interested in solving the problems for the poor, they would already have done so. Blacks should put all naive expectations aside and get to work, rebuilding their communities and reshaping the future by gradually restoring national independence. To achieve these ends, black economic development is of crucial importance.

The POWER program is "organized for the absolute purpose of restoring Black people in America to their original industrial and commercial greatness" and is committed to the goal that African Americans shall become "self-sufficient in the production of food, clothing, shelter, health care, education, employment and banking."[190] POWER seeks to strengthen black economic cooperation by a system in which producers and consumers both benefit from keeping their capital within the black community. Individuals pay a membership fee of $10 and get a card that allows them to buy products from POWER-affiliated manufacturers at a reduced price. Producers, in turn, benefit from having access to a body of steady buyers.[191] In support of Farrakhan's industrial intentions, the Libyan regime in 1985 granted the NOI a $5 million interest-free loan to be used in the first investments. One year later, a proud Farrakhan could introduce the first line of POWER products, the Clean 'N' Fresh *halal* (legal or permitted) skin and hair care set.[192]

On Saviour's Day, October 7, 1991, Farrakhan launched an additional drive, the Three Year Economic Savings Plan. Admitting that the NOI's economic accomplishments thus far were "nice" but insignificant in relation to the severe economic problems of the African American community, Farrakhan returned to the economic writings of Elijah Muhammad.[193] The Messenger initiated a Three Year Savings Plan, based on the idea that if each Blackman saved five cents a day, twenty-five cents a week, one dollar a month, the black community would in one year have accumulated $260 million.[194] Farrakhan asked his people to send $10 a month. If ten million blacks would save $10 a month, in one year a sum of $1,200,000,000 would accumulated. When Joseph became a master in the land in which he was once a slave, he was given the key to the grain house, an episode now on its way to fulfillment, as the NOI plans to buy farmland in Iowa, Nebraska, and parts of Illinois for the collected wealth. In addition, Farrakhan revealed plans for the establishment of a national black reserve bank as a sign of the coming independence and as an Islamic instrument to advance black enterprising and industrialization, as loans in this bank would be interest free.[195]

The Three Year plan does not seem to have attracted very many black contributors, despite Farrakhan's efforts to get other prominent leaders to support the plan. An update of March 1994, only six months prior to the expiration of the three-year period, noted that the treasury balance was merely $637,000 and the program had an administrative cost of $80,000, computer systems included. "It is imperative that we become consistent in our contributions in order to reach the goals," the officials wrote. "Our economic salvation is at hand, so this program must continue indefinitely. . . . We pray that this year we will reach the ONE MILLION DOLLAR mark to purchase farmland."[196]

Farrakhan suggests that the government should support the Three Year plan by allowing blacks to direct 15 percent of their taxes to the NOI savings program. If the plan works out, the money will be invested to rebuild the inner cities, starting with Los Angeles and Chicago, where the United in Peace gangs have pledged to help. Establishing factories in remodeled and landscaped ghettos will give the cities a last-minute turn-around from the direction in which they now are heading, which is why the government should realize that they and everyone else would benefit from the NOI plan.[197]

The Nation of Islam has been criticized from the African American left for advocating a kind of black capitalism as a solution to the problems of the black community. Farrakhan only recently has begun to address the problem of class, and in general the NOI seems to believe that all social tensions, inequalities, and conflicts can be reduced to race. The black community over the past few decades has become increasingly stratified, with a growing middle class. Traditionally, the NOI has explained black internal class-conflicts in terms of the irreformability of the 10 percent of the population (preachers, business leaders, politicians) who have gained some divine knowledge but have chosen to sell out to the Devil. These 10 percent will be exterminated in the battle of Armageddon, and a class-free corporate society with few, if any, social tensions, will be established. As the black community develops and as lessons from Africa and other black areas are discussed, class divisions will probably be given a more serious consideration. In the 1990s, Farrakhan began addressing problems of relevance to the white underclass. Any real inclusion of whites in the category of the oppressed depends on whether the teachings about the genetic mental differences between the races will receive a more metaphorical interpretation than is presently at hand. Although indications pointing in that direction are found, this is a process that is far from certain to succeed.

The concept of black unity is at the very core of the NOI ideology and is not allowed to be blurred by artificial divisions of the Devil's era. As economic power easily translates into political power, black capitalism is a means to an end, not an end in itself. Questioned by an African American leftist after a speech at Northwestern University, Farrakhan vehemently denied being a capitalist as he is "pro-people," but said he respects capitalism as the only one feasible road of empowerment in American society. Still, Farrakhan maintained that "socialism is more appealing to me than any other form of economical system," but warned against romanticizing communism. Farrakhan combines black enterprising with the notion of race as an organic unity and ideas from the *Green Book*. Resources and means of production "should be collectively owned since all of us share the earth," Farrakhan said, upholding the NOI as an ideal model with "collective ownership based on individual effort."[198]

In this respect, the Nation parallels the Third Position of white radical nationalism and the Third Way of Islam. Rejecting both capitalism and communism, the Nation prefers a third separate path. In a manner similar to the third way of Islamists and the white Third Positionists, the NOI envisions a corporate community administered by a strong state with totalitarian features. The NOI is a highly hierarchical organization in which the different strata are expected to cooperate harmoniously for the good of the common body. In the coming postapocalyptic black state, all members of the reunified race, regardless of class, gender, or family will, as if by natural law, subscribe to basically the same ideology, sentiments, and ambitions.

In the Islamist version, the ideal unity of the *umma* is a reflection of God's unity, *tawhid.* The Islamist revolution will abolish class conflicts and establish a corporate state. In white Third Positionist ideology, class divisions are bridged by the common nationality. An authoritarian monocultural corporate state will solve the problems of contemporary society. In all three varieties, any postrevolutionary remnant of class identity has lost its significance, as extreme poverty and extreme affluence belong to the realm of history. Also in common is the notion of a centralized administration of the collectively owned wealth. The theocratic ideal state advocated by the Nation as the unavoidable future is authoritarian (God rules) and totalitarian (deviations not tolerated) but will secure freedom, justice, and equality for all fortunate enough to pass the gate to the hereafter.

Exit by Reeducation: Road to Freedom   Black children are gods, sons and daughters of the Most High God. The problem is that they are not placed in the right environment and not fed the right food to nourish them so that they can evolve into the god that is their potential, Farrakhan explains, while elaborating on the need for a black educational system. Black children in America grow up admiring what others have built and build nothing themselves. They sit around and admire stars and planets that their fathers created and the germ of that power to create is locked up in them. In the first year of a black child's life, the drive for learning, mastering, and creativity is unhampered; it overcomes its own inabilities, gains motor control, and learns to communicate. Just as the black child is pulled up physically, so should it stand upright spiritually. Here they are, born into the universe, with the book of wisdom all around them—but the white man's education interferes with their learning from the universal book. It becomes a cloud, blocking out the natural light of the natural laws of the natural order of the natural man. "And that is why we need our own school system," Farrakhan said. "The education that we must give these children is an education to make them Gods. Listen now, you don't want them being just a doctor, a lawyer, teacher or a chemist. Their nature is to master the law that governs these disciplines. So, you and I must put'em in a position to become masters of their discipline by making them masters of themselves."[199] The Nation of Islam is highly critical of the American school system, which is seen as a principal means of perpetuating white supremacy by systematic miseducation.[200] A conservative school designed to preserve the status quo is in itself oppressive. Any system, religious or educational, "that is not constantly evolving becomes an opponent to the will of God," as man is not static but ever evolving.[201] Even worse is a school designed to imprint the false doctrine of white superiority and black inferiority in its pupils. The white-centered curriculum is designed to make invisible the history and achievements of the nonwhite peoples, and alienated students consequently drop out of "the killing fields" of public schools. "What happened to the best in the class?" Farrakhan asked. "They're gone. They're dead. They're in jail. They're on drugs. They're destroyed."[202]

African Americans must therefore either gain control over the public schools in their communities or take their children out of these schools. "We need an education that will make us like God Himself," Minister Khadir Muhammad explained, something the public schools cannot offer.[203] Blacks ideally should operate their own educational institutions, as does the Nation of Islam. True and proper education serves two principal purposes: first, it cultivates the gifts and talents of the individual through the acquisition of knowledge and thereby feeds the development toward man's purpose of being, to become one with God and master of existence; second, it teaches how best to be of service to self, family, nation, and the world.[204]

In 1989, the NOI reopened the first Muhammad University of Islam (MUI) since the departure of Messenger Muhammad.[205] Since then, a number of MUIs have been established under the auspices of the NOI Board of Education, on which Tynetta Muhammad and Abdul Alim Muhammad serve as officials. As was the case in the old Nation, most of the MUIs are elementary schools, with a few offering secondary education. Chicago's MUI can provide classes up through high school, and four of its graduates were listed in the 1992 edition of *Who's Who among High School Students*.[206] Successful Muslim students receive awards from the NOI leadership and are praised as role models for the future.[207] In the Muslim schools, classes are held year round, as there is no time for idleness or play. As God is the source of all knowledge, the children should have a "God-centered education,"[208] starting with knowledge of God and knowledge of self.[209] The Muhammad University of Islam focuses on black history, language, mathematics, and science, and attempts also to cultivate moral conduct and discipline. Boys and girls are taught in separate classes, which, according to Farrakhan, enables the young minds to mature in the nature God gave them without distraction. With assurances that separate classes will not lead to inequality between the sexes and that females should not be deprived of any knowledge, Farrakhan speaks of the natural differences God has given men and women and of the need for the female to learn proper homemaking, which is her primary responsibility.[210]

Prince Akeem gives an interesting glimpse of the Muslim education when he relates how he felt when he entered a public high school after studying in a Muslim elementary school. The other children were wearing Afros, and he still had his hair cut short and had on his suit and bowtie. When they were talking about American history and Akeem was asked about George Washington, he did not know who that man was or what he had done, and everyone laughed at him. "We learned that the Original Man was the Asiatic Black Man, the Maker, the Owner, the Cream of the Planet Earth and the God of the Universe. We didn't learn anything about George Washington never telling a lie and Abraham Lincoln." Later that year, Akeem was asked about the moon and responded "that the moon represented equality, because it equalized 139,685,000 square miles of water." Everyone looked at him. He went on to explain that the moon kept "the water from overflowing 57,255,000 square miles of land" and told them the diameter of the sun and the exact weight of the planet Earth, "because these are the things that we were being taught at the [University]. If you are the Original Man then you have to know how much Earth you really own. From then on everybody looked at me differently."[211]

Farrakhan argues that the American educational system should use the MUI as a model instead of putting obstacles in its way. It is not enough to bask in the glory of their own school when the totality of education in America needs to be reformed, because "if our children can't change the environment, then the environment will ultimately change our children."[212]

Artificial Disease and Natural Health Care   AIDS, more than any other lethal disease in modern times, is laden with a pseudoreligious fear of the unknown. Religious moralists of different faiths have been swift to declare AIDS a divine punishment for sexual promiscuity or forbidden sexual relations. Such dramatizations ascribed an apocalyptic significance to the rapid global impact of AIDS. The Nation of Islam has given AIDS a place on their agenda, but not primarily as a sign of the divine wrath that is to be fully unleashed at the approaching final hour. While the NOI spokespersons are explicitly homophobic, AIDS has not been presented as a disease of retribution for sexual transgressions but rather as a product of the devils' desperate desire to survive. By 1992, African Americans accounted for 28.8 percent of all U.S. AIDS cases and 52 percent of all American females and 53 percent of all children with AIDS were black.[213] In 1994, AIDS replaced homicide as the number one killer of black men between the ages of twenty-four and forty-four.[214] "Now, AIDS is runnin' rampart in our community," Farrakhan stated. "AIDS, according to many medical doctors, is not a natural virus. They say it's a man-made virus."[215] The NOI expert on AIDS, the aforementioned medical doctor, Minister Abdul Alim Muhammad, is convinced that AIDS is part of a genocidal plot designed to wipe out the blacks of the world.[216]

The NOI's position is perhaps easy to dismiss as the absurdities of paranoid sectarians, but it is actually not disconnected from reality. In the course of the Cold War, the CIA and other intelligence agencies invested a great deal of energy and money to develop new chemical weapons. In the CIA-financed experimentation with LSD, the Nurnberg Code for medical ethics was violated, as the drug was extensively tested on unwitting subjects. A network of doctors and scientists gave LSD to prisoners and mental patients (in some cases, nearly all were black males) in their search for potential new agents for unconventional warfare.[217] Another superhallucinogen, BZ, was later found to be superior to LSD for chemical warfare and became the army's standard incapacitating agent, deployed in bombs and missiles.[218] Besides LSD and BZ, the CIA had numerous other drugs tested on black prisoners in the search for a superagent. The military dreamed of finding a new chemical weapon that could knock out the enemy or dissolve their will to resist, an agent with obvious advantages: no bloody mess to clean up, no destroyed cities, the whole infrastructure intact, leaving the military free to move in and take over.[219]

By the end of World War II, some 135,000 tons of chemical weapons had been produced in the United States, and the production of novel biological and toxic weapons began at that time. By 1973, $1,500,000 had been spent on chemical and biological research and development, with a peak between the years of 1963 and 1969. During that time the

United States Army examined about 100,000 different potential chemical weapon agents.[220] Although the focus was placed on incapacitating chemicals, like BZ, the new possibilities of genetic engineering to produce a novel type of disease aroused military interest. In a congressional protocol of March 1962, the ongoing research of the microbiologists was described. In the field of viral-genetic experiments, the scientists sought to develop "methods for bringing about mutations and the isolation of mutants," and study "genetic changes in those viruses causing 'chronic illness,'" that is viruses against which immunities are ineffective or eliminated. In addition, the scientists made "attempts to isolate and recombine germ plasms from different viruses to produce a 'new' virus."[221] Salvador Luria, who in 1969 won the Nobel Prize in medicine, urged his colleagues to suspend cooperation with the army research center in Fort Dedrick. Luria was alarmed over the interest shown in exploiting the possibility to create new viruses for military purposes.[222] Moreover, in 1969, a United States Department of Defense spokesman gave the following information on the research aimed at producing a synthetic pathogen suitable for biological warfare to a congressional committee: "Within the next 5 to 10 years, it would probably be possible to make a new infective microorganism which would differ in certain important aspects from any known disease-causing organisms. Most important of these is that it might be refractory to the immunological and therapeutic processes upon which we depend to maintain our relative freedom from infectious disease."[223] Although this cannot be taken as evidence that the U.S. military actually has produced the HIV virus, it does show that research was conducted along the lines of finding a new synthetic superagent with capacities similar to that of the HIV virus. The developments in the fields of genetic manipulation on the molecular level continue to interest military biologists, and researchers at the Stockholm International Peace Research Institute concluded, "the goal might conceivably be an ethnic weapon exploiting biochemical differences between the races."[224]

According to Robert Strecker, between the years 1959 and 1970 more than 300 biological experiments were conducted on U.S. citizens without their knowledge, exploring new agents for biological, chemical, and germ warfare.[225] Unwitting blacks functioned as guinea pigs in the Tuskegee study, a syphilis project initiated in 1932 by the United States Public Health Service that did not end until the truth was exposed by an Associated Press reporter in 1972. Four hundred black males with the fatal disease were studied by doctors who did not treat them, nor tell them of the nature of the disease, but observed how it spread and its effect on those infected.[226]

Farrakhan uses indications such as those above as evidence for the existence of a large-scale genocidal plot. As a resurrected soldier in the divine advance guard, he shakes the sleeping body of potential gods, shouting "If you don't wake up and come together as One you may not live to see the 21st Century": "They're using chemical warfare, biological warfare, germ warfare already on black people. AIDS is not an accident any more than small pox was an accident with the Indians. Sending them blankets and killing them with disease. Remember the Tuskegee experiment, when they infected . . . black men with . . . syphilis and made them think they had something else, and allowed them to cohabit to spread syphilis in and among our people. . . . You need to wake up and see that your life is threatened."[227] The Nation of Islam is far from alone in their belief that the AIDS epidemic is the result of a genocidal conspiracy. In a 1990 *New York Times*/WCBS poll, 29 percent of the black respondents said that it was true or possibly true that the HIV virus was "deliberately created in the laboratory in order to infect black people."[228] Not confining itself to conspiracy charges against the American government, the NOI has taken some practical measures intended to counter the alleged genocidal plan. Besides running informative and advisory articles on AIDS in the *Final Call*,[229] in 1991 the Nation of Islam sent Abdul Wali Muhammad and Abdul Alim Muhammad to Kenya on a fact-finding tour regarding Kemron, a nontoxic AIDS treatment. While there, the team learned about Immunex, which like Kemron contains human alpha interferon. Both drugs reportedly showed miraculous results, including alleged cases with nearly complete reversal of the symptoms.[230]

Abdul Alim Muhammad, executive director at the Abundant Life Clinic (ALC) in Washington, D.C., found out in collaboration with New York doctor and AIDS activist Barbara Justice that AIDS victims were allowed to import nonapproved treatments for personal use. Under the auspices of the ALC, an alternative HIV group was established and after four months of treatment "remarkable progress" was reported for the thirty ALC patients.[231] In February 1992, the NOI acquired exclusive distribution rights for Immunex and made the fight against AIDS a top priority. "We would like [federal] approval," Farrakhan said, "however, we can't wait. We will take any risk, bear any burden to free our people of a man-made disease designed to kill us all." Abdul Alim Muhammad was appointed NOI minister of health and human service and declared that the war against AIDS is being won, but that total victory would not come "until we deal with those responsible for making the AIDS virus."[232]

The ALC received a federal grant of $211,0000 and could expand its service to provide treatment for more than three hundred AIDS victims. In the fall of 1993, twelve black and Hispanic AIDS organizations formed the Sankofa coalition, headed by Abdul Alim Muhammad, to combat AIDS and compete for greater federal funding of AIDS services in the Washington area. Some gay and lesbian coalition members soon expressed concern over Abdul Alim Muhammad's stand on homosexuality and, outside the coalition, arguments were voiced against federal support for the Nation of Islam.[233] Abdul Alim Muhammad said that the coalition was an attempt to be as inclusive as possible and assured that the NOI intended to help all, irrespective of color or sexual preferences.[234] Regarding the actual efficiency of Immunex and Kemron, the National Institute of Health–AIDS Division announced plans for a study on the use of low-dose alpha interferon in the treatment of HIV/AIDS in 1992, but had not begun the study by the summer of 1994 due to delays.[235]

Besides AIDS treatment, the NOI focuses on the health crisis in the black community. In a 1990 report by the U.S. Department of Health and Human Service, a disheartening picture emerges from the statistics revealed. The life expectancy rate for black males is *declining* and is down to 64.9 years as compared to 72.3 years for white males.[236] For black and white females the rate is 73.4 and 78.9 years, respectively. Blacks are more likely than whites to die from cancer, diabetes, stroke, pneumonia, cirrhosis, septicemia, and heart disease.[237] They are more overweight, and they have a higher rate of infant mortality. Poverty and cuts in federal health budgets during the Reagan era are factors in blacks' declining health status, but, the NOI leadership argues, so is the destructive lifestyle of the Blackamerican.

"Most of our sickness can be traced to our rebellion against Divine Law," Farrakhan writes. The biblical patriarchs lived for hundreds of years, and if blacks follow the advice put forth by Elijah Muhammad in *How to Eat to Live,* in three to four generations blacks "would learn how to live 500 to 1,000 years of age."[238] Farrakhan denounces junk food, produced by "merchants of death, masters of chemistry, who color food to make it look better, inject hormones into meat to make it grow bigger and faster, use pesticides to kill insects, poisoning the earth." Declaring "war on obesity," Farrakhan announced in 1991 that he would not accept overweight NOI officials: "I will not have an obese (fat) Laborer standing as a representative of the Teachings of the Honorable Elijah Muhammad to an obese (fat) Nation of people. Every Laborer has 6 months to correct that condition. If, after 6 months, there is no significant progress, you will have to find a position elsewhere. I repeat, I will not have an obese (fat) Laborer in front of obese (fat) people."[239] For twenty years, Farrakhan says he followed the dietary recommendations of Messenger Muhammad, eating only once a day, fasting three days a month, and exercising regularly. When Elijah departed, he lost his discipline and his condition deteriorated. When he realized that he had put on a little extra weight, he discovered that he was far from alone. He had met religious leaders all over the United States and hosted dinners for thousands of pastors, and concluded that the clergy class is entirely too fat. "Every pastor should be an example of Christ-like living," Farrakhan writes. "What would you think about Jesus if you saw him in his holy robes, overweight, with a stomach that made him look eight months pregnant, fat jowls and a fat neck?"[240]

To avoid an early death in a greasy body of garbage, it is mandatory to follow the eight NOI guidelines to a healthy divine life: first, prayer to receive strength and discipline; second, proper knowledge through reading *How to Eat to Live, The Muslim Cookbook,* health magazines, et cetera; third, eat correct food (vegetables, fruit, fish, no flesh, and no chemicals); fourth, exercise; fifth, get rid of all addictions; sixth, get proper rest; seventh, spend time regularly in nature; eighth, get regular dental and physical checkups. With this clean-living agenda, the NOI offers its membership improved health and a prolonged life. To follow the guidelines will definitely promote an above-average standard of health and physical well-being. As is generally true in Islam, however, one should not exaggerate one's commitment in blind obedience. Fasting and hard exercise can be fatal for certain individuals, and the early death of *Final Call* editor in chief Abdul Wali Muhammad, who accidentally died while exercising in the war against obesity in December 1991, made Farrakhan qualify his call by recommending that each soldier consult with a physician to develop an individual fitness and dietary program. By the same token, Farrakhan takes great care to qualify his criticism against the big business of medical care. Though Farrakhan believes in prayer's healing power, which he says cured him from prostate cancer in 1991,[241] secular medicine is not disdained. While pointing out the disadvantages of taking pills as a standard remedy, Farrakhan emphasizes that he is not suggesting that his followers not take the treatments prescribed by their doctors.[242] In the NOI's ideology, the focus on physical well-being is a correlative to the mental awakening. "The Eye of Allah seeks Symmetry in His Creation," Minister Ava Muhammad writes. "He uses His Power of Restoration to destroy the excess fat that has robbed us of our Beautiful Divine Form." Allah is thus making his people an offer they cannot refuse should they want to stay alive and see the hereafter.[243]

"It's a God in the House": Black Islamic Family Ideals   The Nation of Islam holds a patriarchal conservative position on gender relations. This gender separatism prevented my collecting sufficient data and information from the NOI's female members, which is the main shortcoming of the present study. Hopefully, a female researcher will fill the perspective I have left vacant and thus contribute to a fuller analysis of the NOI's ideology and practice.

Like many Islamic movements, the NOI puts great stress on the family as the cornerstone of society. The ideal image is a nuclear family with the man as the self-reliant head of high moral standard, a benevolent provider, and protector of his family. The woman is an affectionate mother and a modestly dressed, obedient, and devoted caretaker of her husband, children, and home. The boys loyally accept their responsibilities and duties; they protect and respect the female and are clean in body and mind. The girls are clean, charming, and graceful, dress decently, and avoid the shameful, and learn how to cook and sew and care for their future family.[244]

What makes the NOI different from mainstream Islamic family ideals derives from its specific religious doctrine of *Theos Antropos*. "When you see a real man you are looking at God," Farrakhan said, assuring his listeners that "there's no woman on earth who would not be happy with a man who is a reflection of God."[245] The black man—God is as naturally jealous and protective as the God of the Scriptures. He does not want his woman to pay any attention to another man, Farrakhan explained. "God says: Thy Lord, Thy God, is a jealous God. I don't want you to have another God besides me. That's the way a man is when he loves a woman. He don't want that woman looking at nobody."[246]

This does not mean that a man is allowed to beat his wife out of jealousy; on the contrary, it is absolutely forbidden. If an NOI man strikes his wife, he is expelled from the Nation for ninety days for the first offense and six months for the second.[247] While NOI law is further discussed below, in this context it should be mentioned that Farrakhan considers the death penalty for adultery to be theoretically justified: "Marriage is the cornerstone of family. Family is the cornerstone of nation. Adultery breaks up marriage, buzz up family, therefore adultery brings about the death of a nation. So, if we love the nation, then we put the individual to death, because the individual is not bigger than the nation. Our problem is that we exalt the individual over the nation. God is not injust. He kills the individual to preserve the integrity of the nation."[248] This quotation should not be interpreted as though Farrakhan views all black men as gods, ipso facto, to whom their wives' attitudes should be one of reverence and obedience. All black men have the potential to evolve into gods. They are made to govern the physical creation, to master the sun, the moon, the stars, the earth, and every living creature, but most men are sadly locked in their fallen beastlike state. Farrakhan accuses the black men of being contrary to their nature. They do not deserve respect because they are not building anything and have no divine ambitions. A woman wants a real man, a man with goals, with discipline, with visions. She wants a man who sees a new world and is willing to go and make it for his wife and children.[249] "God did not give woman to man for man to enjoy her and sit down and do nothin'," Farrakhan exclaimed, "God gave woman to man, according to the Bible, as help mate, to meet your wants, your aspirations. Whatever you want, the woman will help you get there, but if you don't have any aim, any aspiration, any goal in life, you don't need a woman. How could a man need a woman to help him do nothing? And then want her to give him pleasure? For what? You ain't worthy of no pleasure. Pleasure comes after work!"[250] Here, Farrakhan touches a raw nerve in the Blackamerican male community. They live in a society that stresses the male role as a working man who is able to pay for his family's rent, food, and clothing. However, they also live in a society in which black men have a harder time finding a job than white men or black women, a situation that produces feelings of impotence, anger, and frustration. "Women are working more then men, so the women are providing for their children and even for the men," Farrakhan has observed.[251] You see black women in positions, "bringing home the money. Black men sittin' at home, lookin' at soap operas, [and] she's talkin' with the man's voice."[252] This is, according to Farrakhan, contrary to the natural roles of the sexes. "God's order has been turned around. Whenever the natural order of God is violated, there are serious consequences."[253] Some men compensate for this challenge to their perceived masculinity by indulging in domestic violence, by being lady-killers or by moving into crime or dope dealing to obtain riches, often exaggeratedly displayed in symbols of wealth, such as expensive clothing, cars, and jewelry. This in turn might lead to divorce, incarceration, or death, leaving the black woman by herself to take care of the family. Farrakhan said, "And if there is no man, sister, if you gotta be like Hagar, running in the wilderness by yourself with your child, if you gotta be like Mary, with your little baby running from Palestine under death threats from those who are planning against you into Egypt where you can be safe—then the burden will be upon you to start the process of building a new man and a new woman to create a new reality."[254] The Blackamerican family is increasingly matrifocal. In 1992, 46.4 percent of black families were headed by females. For families in which the head of the family was between the ages of twenty and twenty-nine, 60.4 percent were headed by females.[255] The proportion of black children living with two parents declined from 58 percent in 1970 to 38 percent in 1990, and is estimated to decline to 24 percent by the year 2000. In 1988, statistics showed that 64 percent of all black babies were born out of wedlock, compared with 18 percent of white babies. The same year, unmarried black teenagers between the ages of fifteen to seventeen bore seventy-four babies per 1,000 girls, while white unmarried teenagers bore seventeen babies per 1,000 girls. Lenneal J. Henderson concludes, "The traditional nuclear family is an endangered species. Younger parents with less life experience, education or employment are raising larger proportions of urban African American children."[256]

According to the NOI's spokespersons, the Devil knows that his power depends on keeping the oppressed black nation divided. He knows that the family is the cornerstone of the nation, which is why he has systematically scattered the black families since the days of slavery. Today, he seeks the death of the black male by letting them go unemployed, feeding them drugs and guns, throwing them away in jail, or moving in on them as armed gangs wearing blue. At the same time he subsidizes single black women's childbearing, by doling out welfare checks. Farrakhan's call of black Islam is a remedy, a new knowledge of liberation, and "anybody that will come to re-unify the black family is a threat to the oppressive forces."[257]

To counter the situation described above, the NOI calls for a return to the original way of life, which proves to be remarkably similar to that of conservative, middle-class, patriarchal culture. All male NOI members are enrolled in the Fruit of Islam. While renowned for its military and martial arts training, the FOI soldiers serving during the regime of Messenger

Muhammad spent "a lot more time in lectures and discussions on men learning to be men."[258] Farrakhan too emphasizes this aspect in the training of the NOI's military wing. In a December 1993 speech in New York before an audience of 21,000, Farrakhan called on the black men to clean up and to accept discipline and reform. He then pledged to recruit 10,000 volunteers, "real men," willing to reclaim their communities and make them safe for women, children, and the elderly.[259] On January 24, 1994, 12,000 men jammed the Armatory in Harlem and thousands had to be turned away when Farrakhan called a "men only" meeting. "It is not white women or Black women who are filling the morgues of the cities across the United States," Farrakhan reportedly explained. "It is young Black men being killed by young Black men. Our purpose is to discuss with the men how God intends for a man to act."[260] As the black man is God, or has the potential to evolve into the exalted state of divinity, to disrespect a black man is to disrespect God, to hate a black man is to hate God, and to fight a black man is to fight God.

If the black man in his natural state is God, the black woman is Goddess by nature. Here, a shift in language usage is notable. Although the Honorable Elijah Muhammad emphasized that no nation could rise higher than its women, females were clearly reduced to a secondary status. "Islam will not only elevate your women but will also give you the power to protect and control them," the Messenger wrote in 1965. The ideal attitude of a Muslim woman toward her divine husband was eloquently expressed by Sister Denise 2X in 1970: [A Muslim woman] is to her Husband as the Moon is to the Sun. . . . The Muslim Man is the head of the household. He is the maintainer of his family, and as the warm and life-giving power of the Sun keeps all planets rotating in orbit around it, so does the warmth, security and love of the Muslim Husband keep his wife rotating in submissiveness around him."[261] If the woman here does not have power in and by herself, and can come close to power only by submission to a man, the NOI woman of today is said to be as much a reflection of the creative divinity as is a man. The anthropogony of Genesis 1:27 states that "God created man in his own image . . . male and female created he them." "Men want to think that God only created them in His image, but here it says, 'male and female,' " Farrakhan commented. "See, God's power is there in the female along with the male. And any time you have a social order that denies the power of the female, you have a social order that is doomed to failure and an early death."[262] It seems that Farrakhan has not been unaffected by the women's liberation movement, and he makes attempts to sound genuinely antisexist: "The women of the world say: 'No more are we being left out. No more can you take our sons and daughters and leave us at home, cooking and baking and making babies thinking that this is all that we are born into the world for.' I say to the Islamic world, I say to the Christian world: Any nation that puts down its women puts down itself. Any nation that suppresses its women suppresses its future. Any nation that doesn't allow their women to rise up to their true position is a nation doomed to fall."[263] Condemning religious sexism, Farrakhan asserts that "God is not a sexist. Religion needs to be understood in a light that frees women from the oppression of the misunderstanding of scriptural teachers."[264] Farrakhan referred to the fact that Elijah Muhammad "envisioned women flying planes, navigating ships and serving as ambassadors. He wanted to see women in every field of endeavor, except fields that degrade them." Men should "be made to respect women for their brains," instead of reducing them to "objects for sexual gratification."[265] Women do occupy positions of importance in the Nation's organizational structure. The gender separatism has necessitated a double hierarchy with female laborers, and the Nation stresses "the need for military women in the liberation of Black people."[266] The NOI holds "women only" meetings, and two of the most influential theologians and spokespersons in Farrakhan's NOI are women: Minister Ava Muhammad and Minister Tynetta Muhammad.

All this notwithstanding, the reason for the elevation of woman is due to her procreative power. "The woman when true to her feminine nature is really advanced over the man," Farrakhan said. "Not because of her beauty, not because of her accomplishments . . . but because she possesses the womb."[267] Though updated and modernized, the basic view has not really changed since the days of Elijah Muhammad. Female power is in the regeneration of divine life, and to release her own power, a woman must find God in a man.[268] A woman is "God's assistant" and "co-creator" and, given the right circumstances, she "can produce Gods." To disrespect a man was, as we have seen, to disrespect God and "to abuse a woman is to abuse the womb of God."[269]

The woman has the ability to write on the brain of the fetus, as if it were a blank piece of paper. The prenatal engraving can determine whether the offspring is born god or beast, which is why the pregnant woman must be properly protected and guided. Farrakhan recommends the following: first, she should not be deserted, as is too often the case in Blackamerica; second, she should be exposed to love and comfort, guarded from worries

and pain, kept from funerals (where she might think of death and grievances), and protected from bars, gambling parties, and dance halls; third,
the woman should not be allowed to smoke, drink, take drugs, or eat junk
food of any kind; and fourth, she should talk to the baby in the womb by
praying, reciting the Qur'an, and teaching the coming God(-dess) the
truths of the heavens and the Earth as laid forth by the Nation of Islam.[270]

As the Devil fears nothing more than what the divine black womb has
the ability to produce, he established a demonic program of birth control
to kill off future generations of saviours. Under the cloak of prochoice, the
Devil promotes a vicious murder technique called abortion. "You condemn the murder on the streets," Farrakhan said, "but you don't condemn the quiet murder that goes on . . . in abortion clinics throughout
America."[271] The genocidal plan designed by the Devil is a combination
of allowing severe economic conditions to prevail in the black community, while offering poor pregnant blacks the latest wonders of medical
treatment. Still, the choice is made by the woman: "killing mothers in the
killing fields, rejecting your babies while they are in your wombs, killing
your future."[272] Farrakhan is convinced that the prenatal influence makes
the fetus feel if the mother wants an abortion, which is why even unsuccessful attempts will produce children of wrath with murder in their
minds. Although it is possible to compensate with love from a caring
mother, a wish for abortion leaves a wound in the child's mind, a subconscious feeling of being rejected that might account for mistakes made
as an adult. Farrakhan's own mother tried to have an abortion. "She re-
grets that to this day," Farrakhan told his audience. "She begs the pardon
of God for trying to kill this which was in her womb, but she marked me
with her own thinking. And this is what led to my fall from the Honorable
Elijah Muhammad" (after his 1975 departure).[273] Although Farrakhan asserts that he is both prolife and prochoice, he believes that "no one should
be free to kill the fruit of the womb," and reinterprets the prochoice stand
to that of letting the woman choose with whom she wants to commit
herself in marriage.[274] While thus aligning himself with the prolife camp
of the Christian fundamentalists, Farrakhan distances himself from the
most extreme position, making abortion permissible in cases of rape,
incest, and risk to the mother's health.[275]

The black woman's right to determine which man she should devote
her life to is restricted racially to original people only, and NOI spokespersons issue warnings against "that deadly disease called 'jungle fever,'" a
term for interracial relations popularized by Spike Lee's movie of the

same name.[276] Farrakhan regards black-white relationships as remnants of the epoch of slavery, based on inequality, racism, and oppression. It is a sick product of a society that lets the appearance of Caucasians set the standards for beauty, making black men chase white women as trophies and not for true love. White men who prefer black women are simply upholding the tradition of their slave-owning fathers, who came through the back door and picked a slave toy for pleasure.[277] The thrill of interracial sex, fed by the stories of excessive black promiscuity, explains the attraction, and it amounts to sexual exploitation. Farrakhan admits that true love transcends color and race but believes that those who today live in interracial relations merely are acting out a corrupted fantasy held by whites and blacks alike. Before the end of white supremacy and black inferiority, biracial love is impossible.[278]

The Nation of Islam envisions a God-given order of the sexes' different roles, attempting to shield the order from critique with reference to "nature" rather than "culture." Whatever is contrary to the perceived order is then logically termed "unnatural" and thereby dismissed. Homosexuality threatens the perfect order laid forth by the Nation and is as such abominable, a perverse product of a sick society. When white society denies the black man the possibilities of being a real man, he runs the risk of degrading into a homosexual.[279] The understanding minister attacks the cause rather than the symptom: "There are some who are homosexuals, and Brother, this is painful . . . and I know what you say, I hear all your arguments: 'I'm a woman trapped in a man's body, tryin' to get out.' I understand. But even that can be retrieved. God is not saying to the homosexual, 'I don't want you.' He's saying, 'I just don't want that conduct.' And if that conduct prevails my Lord! Where would the human family be? Our women are falling down on each other. It's all because we have so lost our own nature, that the woman finds no comfort in the man, so she finds more comfort in her own sex. But when you meet a real man, Sister, you don't want no play thing when the real things comes along, you understand. And there is something in the man, the real man, that God put in that no woman can give you—ain't it sweet?"[280] Farrakhan, who knows the above sentiment to be certain, as he has "been among lesbians,"[281] appeals to his followers not to cast stones against the manifestations of sin, as none is without sin. The constructive approach is rather to "change homosexual behavior and get rid of the circumstances that bring it about," in accord with the NOI's commission to "change all behavior that offends the standard of moral behavior set by God through his laws and prophets."[282]

Justicia Niger   To establish an independent black Islamic state on American or African soil is, as noted, a chief objective for the interim program of the Nation. Minister Farrakhan heads a theocratic shadow ministry, modeled as the administration of a sovereign state. The Nation has its own judicial system, including sanctions and police, which forms a nucleus of the future government of the United Blacks of America. The aforementioned activities by the Islamic patrols can be seen as an extension of the NOI's area of jurisdiction, a first move to exercise influence and power among the broader black community outside the official membership. In the name of God, Farrakhan "reclaims" jurisdiction over the Blackamerican and is confident of the realization of black independence under his rule in the near future.

In this context, it might be interesting to examine briefly the judicial ideas of Minister Farrakhan. The NOI's sanctions against wife beating and Farrakhan's arguments for the death penalty for adultery already have been mentioned. The death penalty will also be implemented in the future for incest, rape, and interracial sex. By the logic of Moses' law, the incestuous father and the rapist should be put to death, as what they did is equal to death. The law is hard but just, Farrakhan argues, emphasizing again that "the nation is more important than the individual." He claims that "by killing that person in an exemplary way," the other potential sex offenders get the message and restrain their behavior so that they will live.[283] Although not yet in power, Farrakhan assured his listeners that it will not take long before the Nation can issue the death penalty for such crimes against black women: "I can promise you sisters, that as we get stronger and stronger, and Islam becomes more and more powerful in America, I promise you we will put to death every violator of our women. And we really don't give a damn what the white man says. Even if it's your father, we will kill him because he has killed you."[284] In an interesting passage, Farrakhan relates how he handled a Los Angeles case involving rape and attempted murder. A female teenager had been raped by a black man but did not talk about it until she fell in love with another man who was a Muslim. Acting in anger, the man got a gun and with partner went to the offender's house. As the door opened, they recognized the offender from the mosque and hesitated. Should they hit a fellow believer? Making up their minds during a walk around the block, the men returned and shot the offender, who survived. As the word spread throughout the mosque that a Muslim had been shot by fellow believers, the agitated congregation decided to bring the case to Minister Farrakhan, who was in town at that time. Summoning the conflicting parties, Farrakhan became the prosecuting attorney, trapping the rapist with lies. He then assumed the jury's and judge's roles, found the man guilty, and sentenced him to stay out of the Nation until the girl's wounds had healed, which might take the rest of her life. When someone is suspended from the NOI, the members are not allowed to meet, speak, or socialize with that person. In this case, the offender's parents and siblings were all members, which meant that he was cut off from his family, perhaps for life. On another level, to be an outcast equals death, as the offender is deprived of the escape ticket to the hereafter.[285]

According to Farrakhan, when Moses liberated his people from Egyptian bondage, he wanted to make them into a great nation. His people were destroyed by the years in slavery and they felt inferior and lacked self-respect. Although God loved his people, he did not approach them in this situation with love—rather, he gave them a law. "You don't make great nations without a law," Farrakhan explains. "When you have a people that are destroyed, you can only build them up by means of a law" to correct their behavior.[286] The same is true for the African American. The church preaches its message of love, but hate grows because love is a product of righteousness, and the present society produces a wicked behavior pattern. The true message of modern America is hate, not love. This gives rise to the need for a new strategy: "The reason we do not have love among us, is because we who lead and teach are not loving enough to impose a law on our people, that would allow our people to discipline themselves or be disciplined by those who take the responsibility of leadership."[287] Though *Sharia* is the ideal law, Minister Don Muhammad argues that the Nation has "an understanding that we feel supersedes" the mainstream Muslim interpretation, as Elijah Muhammad brought in a "higher understanding" of the perfect law. "There is no difference in the elevation of the law," he maintains, "its degrees in the higher dispensation of it" as "Elijah Muhammad is writing law on the pages of our hearts and our minds."[288] Nevertheless, Farrakhan is impressed by the judicial system practiced in Saudi Arabia. He believes that the relatively low Saudi crime rate is due to the version of *Sharia* in effect and describes approvingly the Saudi penalties of dismemberment in cases of theft and rape. To introduce that kind of Islamic law in the present American society would, however, be oppressive. Before the implementation of God's law, Islamic conditions must prevail. Here, Farrakhan sides with Islamist ideologists, such as Muhammad Ghazzali and Rashad Rida of the Egyptian Muslim Brotherhood, *Ikhwan al-Muslimun,* who argue that the implementation of Islamic law has to await the realization of an Islamic political, economical, and social revolution. As the present society is based on injustice and miseducation, *Sharia* could not yet be applied. Only after an Islamic state based on freedom, justice, and equality has been established could the people raised under those conditions be judged by the strict standard put forth by God.[289]

The Quest for Black Reunification   Over the past years, the African American community has become accustomed to observing Minister Farrakhan on the public battleground, defending the "black" side in a great number of race-centered controversies, be it black versus Jew, black versus Korean, black versus white, or black versus the establishment. Widely publicized, these focal points of conflict have been disparately interpreted in the American communities, not least according to race. Some of these conflicts have come to symbolize the breakdown of American society in a process of ethnic and racial fragmentation. This process undermines the fundament of Americanity and is used by Farrakhan to support the notion of a separate national identity from which sentiments of a separate God-given destiny are logically derived.

When Tawana Brawley told of being kidnapped, raped, and humiliated by six white men, one of whom she believed was a police officer, the white media was quick to question her and her mother's credibility. She fought a legal battle for two years to little avail, but Farrakhan and many blacks believed her and accused the police of a cover-up. Tawana appeared at the 1988 Saviour's Day convention and has since become an NOI member, known as Maryam Muhammad.[290] Farrakhan focuses on race, saying that white men are never accused of raping black women, as black women are considered subhumans: "You're not charged with raping animals! You're an animal! That's why they can raise so much hell about a white woman [raped] in Central Park and then work night and day to say that Tawana Brawley was not raped."[291] When black construction worker Michael Griffith was murdered lynch-style in Howard Beach, Queens, Farrakhan shared the black wrath. When Yusuf Hawkins was chased and slain by thirty to forty white youths from predominantly Italian Bensonhurst, Brooklyn, Farrakhan joined the angry black cry for justice. Al Sharpton led protesters through the area, and they were met by angry white residents who cursed the marchers in a manner that made them readily interpretable as a mob of white devils unmasked.[292] Farrakhan the warrior rushes to the defense of blacks who are perceived as victimized, even if the person in question previously had been opposed to or by the Nation of Islam. Michael Jackson was long condemned as the opposite of an ideal black male, until he was charged with child molestation, after which the NOI defended him as a victimized black. Washington, D.C., mayor, Marion Barry, publicly repudiated Farrakhan as an anti-Semite, but still found the latter at his side when he was framed by the FBI, who had given him crack as part of a drug bust, for which he received six months in prison for cocaine possession. When Qubilah Shabazz was accused of attempting to contract Michael Fitzpatrick, a Jewish government informant, to assassinate Minister Farrakhan as retaliation for the latter's alleged involvement in the murder of her father, Malcolm X, Farrakhan was quick to rush to her side, vigorously defending her as an innocent victim of a federal conspiracy. "If someone is hurt Farrakhan takes on that same hurt," Minister Khadir Muhammad explains. "Its more or less a reaction, if you step on a toe in New York, then the head is liable to say 'ouch' in Chicago."[293]

Minister Khadir's comment makes clear the perception of Farrakhan. Generic in the NOI ideology is the aforementioned organic race concept, derived in part from the German *völkish* tradition and merged with the Islamic ideal of the believers' unity as a reflection of God's unity. Envisioned as an authoritarian corporate entity, Farrakhan personifies an imagined reunified black nation. By focusing on events such as those discussed above, in addition to all the aforementioned facts about racial inequalities in American society, Farrakhan constructs an image of himself as a black freedom fighter. Assisted by the media, he gains high visibility and thereby a platform to expand his reach. As an increasing number of blacks give credibility to Farrakhan's interpretations, a charismatic personality is constructed. Though not as explicit as in the case of Silis the Saviour, to whom prayers can be addressed, Farrakhan is a divine liberator, ascending into messiahship. In the eyes of his followers, Farrakhan is an example of the divinity each black can aspire to realize.

It seems as though the steadfastness of Farrakhan's position has been rewarded by a growing popularity. There was a time when no black politician could publicly stand by Farrakhan's side. When Jesse Jackson was forced to renounce the Muslim leader in 1984, a period of public, and oftentimes opportune, denouncements began. Any black leader who intended to run for public office or establish a political base had to defame Farrakhan, almost as a rite of passage, to get a stamp of official approval. Organizers of African American summits hesitated to invite Farrakhan as a speaker, and if they did, other speakers would inevitably withdraw publicly, thereby stealing attention from the summit's agenda.[294]

Farrakhan benefited from this period in which he was branded an official pariah. All these controversies increased his name recognition, and widespread distrust in politicians and the media made the criticism backfire in part. As Farrakhan's influence grew, it became all the more impossible to isolate him. The same process saw Farrakhan outgrow the uncompromising sectarian dress and put on the clothes of a respected elderly statesman. Previous conflicts were downplayed as "immature," Malcolm X and Martin Luther King Jr. are long since forgiven, and Farrakhan reaches out to organizations that were formerly denounced.[295] Black as a theological concept transcends man-made divisions, and, in 1993, Farrakhan addressed black leaders of all political and religious parties in a call for a broad black united front: "Each black organization and every black leader has a role in the upliftment of our people. We must recognize and respect each other's role and learn to work with those with whom we may be at variance ideologically. We should consider establishing a united front for the purpose of converging our efforts to meet common objectives."[296] The year 1993 was marked by considerable success for Minister Farrakhan's efforts to bridge black divisions and to be accepted in the circle of respected black leaders. He met with Nelson Mandela, something he had been prevented from doing during Mandela's previous United States visit. Farrakhan participated in the African–African American summit in Gabon and was invited to speak at the Parliament of the World's Religions. He addressed the World Conference of Mayors,[297] and he was on the panel of a September 1993 Congressional Black Caucus meeting on race in America. Kweisi Mfume pledged that the CBC "will enter into a [sacred] covenant with the Nation of Islam,"[298] and Reverend Ben Chavis, chairperson of NAACP, embraced the Muslim leader in a public gesture of unity described by Chavis as "the most earthshaking event in [black] America this century."[299]

The traditional isolate-and-condemn strategy of the Nation's detractors backfired. The pressure to ban Farrakhan from the 1993 March on Washington resulted in apologies from black leaders for falling out. When the Anti-Defamation League went public with highlights from Khallid Abdul Muhammad's Kean College speech, the uproar proved relatively easy to overcome, and Khallid could resume office as minister of the Nation of Islam on July 1, 1995. The coalition between CBC, the NAACP, the Rainbow Coalition, and the Nation of Islam was an unprecedented move toward black unification, but it has nothing to do with the ADL's fear of a mainstreaming of anti-Semitism. In Chavis's mind, it was a much-needed response to the grave crisis facing the African Americans, a last-minute realization that only joint efforts could remedy the problems facing the black community.[300]

On Rev. Chavis's initiative, the NAACP hosted a black summit in Baltimore, on June 12–14, 1994, drawing together most of the influential black nationalist and civil rights organizations and leaders.[301] While the mainstream media spoke of a NAACP betrayal of its historic mission, the summit ended with a declaration of unity, pledging future cooperation across previous dividing lines.[302] "The burden of change is on us," Farrakhan declared, calling for joint efforts by black religious and secular nationalists, socialists, and civil rights organizations.[303] In the meantime, Chavis's detractors planned to remove him from his position. On August 20, 1994, one day before a second black leadership summit, Chavis was dismissed for using NAACP funds to cover an out-of-court settlement for a sexual harassment charge. Michael Meyers, who led the "rescue movement," is explicit in saying that the inappropriate use of funds was not the real reason for dismissing Chavis. "I want him ousted on ideological grounds," Meyers said. "Reaching out to Farrakhan was a betrayal."[304]

In the eyes of Minister Farrakhan, the reunification of the black nation is an inevitable phase in the salvation process. Any leader, organization, or institution who disrupts the process of black reunification is therefore "an open enemy" and should be "treated as such."[305] The leaders of the black community, Meyers and his kind included, have to make up their minds about how they would act at the dawn of a new world: "The Hand of God is saying that black folks gotta rise and either we are in the way and will be swept over or we are ridin' the tide, but you gotta be in tune with the movement of the people or you get washed away in the rising tide of the black man and women all over the world: our time has come."[306] With the advent of the October 16, 1995, Million Man March, Farrakhan's words suddenly seemed acutely realistic. Facing a reality of deepening social and economical problems affecting a growing part of the African American community and at the same time listening to the political hardliners of the "Contract with America" opting for "turning back the hands of time, depriving the Black community of many of the gains" made during the past few decades, Farrakhan made what proved to be an extraordinarily successful call for a unified black manifestation.[307] It was to be a "day of atonement," a concept designed to fit also conventional black Christians, and which is to be understood on two levels of meaning. The first relates to the black community and the second to the government of the United States. The blacks, including the leadership, should atone for their failure to accept the divine call for freedom, for having allowed the community to embark on the path of self-destruction, for the failure of the black men to be responsible heads of their families and their community, for neglecting to take control over their destiny, and for not having reconciled their internal differences.[308] If the black community rises up to accept the responsibility that Farrakhan claims God has given them, the government can no longer escape its part of the healing process. This second way in which to understand atonement, Farrakhan reiterated during this Million Man March address. President Bill Clinton had chosen to leave the White House the very day one million citizens had announced that they were coming to see him. From Texas, Clinton spoke about the need to heal the wounds and bridge the black-white divide, but was criticized by Farrakhan for not going far enough. White America must face the truth, acknowledge its burden of guilt, and atone for the era of slavery and for not having evolved out of the mind-set of white supremacy, "which has to die in order for humanity to live."[309]

The preparations for the march went on in the black community under the cover of an almost complete media shadow, as few in official America believed that Farrakhan would succeed and as the reporters were occupied by another expression of the racial divide, the live soap opera called the O. J. Simpson trial. Less than a week before the march, editorial staffs suddenly realized that Farrakhan was about to make history. Thousands of drowsy journalists descended on march headquarters to get last-minute press credentials, causing this part of the organization to collapse. The standardized media image of Farrakhan as a demagogic hatemonger at the bizarre margins of the black community, moreover, turned problematic when checked by the possibility of Farrakhan's making the march a reality. If he managed to reach the goal of a million men, it would imply either that the media image of him needed modification or that one out of forty black Americans were insane. Besides recycling controversial, especially "anti-Semitic," statements by Farrakhan or quoting unidentified "authorities," who claimed that the march would fail to attract more than a 100,000 participants, a common media strategy was the effort to separate the march from its chief organizer.[310] Following the event, a Million Man March poll was used to this end. Only 5 percent said showing support for Farrakhan was the single most important reason for participating, instead identifying "to show support for the black family" (29 percent), "to show support for black men taking more responsibility for their families and community" (25 percent), and "to demonstrate black unity" (25 percent) as the one main reason for their attending, and thereby identifying the three major reasons Farrakhan called for the march in the first place. Less attention was paid to the fact that 87 percent of the respondents had a favorable impression of Minister Louis Farrakhan, a higher level of support than was given to any other leader listed in the poll, including Jesse Jackson and Colin Powell.[311] No one who witnessed the march's show of love, pride, and strength could avoid sensing the enormous support given to the Minister and the quest for black unity. Electrified by the massive turnout at the march, Farrakhan told President Clinton, and others who seek to present the minister as being isolated, to wake up: "You're out of touch with reality. A few of you in few smoke-filled rooms, calling that the mainstream, while the masses of people, white and black, red, yellow and brown, poor and vulnerable, are suffering in this nation."[312]

The Million Man March proved to be the largest black demonstration in the history of black America, dwarfing the famous 1963 march. Police authorities estimated 400,000 participants, while organizers claimed more than one and a half million marchers. The Nation of Islam claims having registered more than one million official participants, who paid $10 for a march package, and added to that number more than half a million unregistered black men and women and nonblack participants. Boston University, in its estimation based on aerial photographs, concluded that the number of participants exceeded one million. Unmentioned in most media reports was the level of solidarity shown by representatives of nonblack communities, such as the Native American and the Latino, who arrived with banners of support. Especially heartening was the scene in which a body of traditionally dressed Koreans showed up carrying slogans of solidarity with the marchers. A roar of surprised joy saluted the delegation, which was embraced by the marchers in a fraternal dance.

The Million Man March could prove to be a watershed in the history of the Nation of Islam. Traditionally marginalized in the black community, whose leaders, as previously noted, almost routinely condemned them, a possible reversal might be the reality of the mid-1990s, in turn marginalizing those who condemn the Muslims. With a few notable exceptions, the march was endorsed by most black leaders and organizations in yet another unprecedented move toward black unity. Coorganizer Rev. Chavis had a sweet revenge as the new national NAACP leadership distanced itself from the march and was bypassed by a large number of local NAACP chapters and perhaps by the bulk of its membership, who in large part seemed to endorse the march. The black unification process seems to imply a radicalization of the black mainstream, which should be appropriately understood as a reflection of the increasing deterioration of the social conditions of the black community. Fundamental social problems favor radical solutions. At the same time, though, another implication should be highlighted: Farrakhan's move toward the mainstream means a mainstreaming of Farrakhan. In the course of that process, Farrakhan has softened his message and sought reconciliation with former foes. The dress of an elderly statesman requires a moderate voice, which is more inclusive and open to dialogue and reason than it is exclusive, uncompromising, and unreasonable. This was clearly the tone of Farrakhan's Million Man March address. While it was necessary for blacks to organize the march, it was emphasized that this did not necessarily mean that they had to become Muslims and members of the NOI. They could perfectly well stay Christian or Jewish and be active in any organization working for black empowerment, be it the Urban League, the NAACP, the All-African Peoples' Revolutionary Party, Operation Push, the Congress of Racial Equality (CORE), the Southern Christian Leadership Conference (SCLC), or the Nation of Islam. The traditionally unequivocal demand for a separate state was substituted with an offer to President Clinton and the administration to join the unified black movement in an effort to move the United States toward a more perfect union, assuring that the Nation and all black participants did not come to Washington "to tear down America. America is tearing down herself. We are here to rebuild" the society.[313]

Children of Armageddon, or, To Civilize the Uncivilized   The NOI acts in a decaying world soon to be destroyed by the wrath of God, appearing in front of the supreme military space fleet. The apocalyptic consciousness pervades the NOI's strategies for guiding the original people safely through the impending cataclysm. The escapist orientation is far from otherworldly, but rather is expressed in practical measures of separation, as the God of Islam demands action and not lip service. Farrakhan is impatient with the tendency of the black church to confine its action to prayer for justice and hopes of an award beyond death. "The Communists say that religion is the opiate of the people. The communists are correct,"

Farrakhan argues. "God did not intend for religion to drug man. God intends for his revealed word to quicken man spiritually, mentally, morally, that man might go out into a material world and make progress."[314]

The NOI's position leads to a paradoxical situation in which preachers of cataclysmic destruction ultimately become constructive. This has always been the central paradox of the Nation of Islam. While vociferously and with inflammatory rhetorical skill appearing as prophets of doom and fundamental devastation of a society dismissed as irreformably evil, all practical measures taken revolve around building for the future. This remarkable optimism articulated at the brink of disaster is derived from the teachings of *Theos Antropos.* "You can accomplish what you will," Farrakhan emphasizes. "Man and woman is God, the force and power to make things happen on earth."[315] Blacks may feel helpless and deprived of the means to transform their reality but should realize that "the complete truth is we have the same powers that He [God] has all the way."[316]

The NOI's philosophy has led to an oscillation between the poles of optimism and pessimism, of constructive action and promised destruction. Any obstruction experienced at the former pole has pushed them to the latter. Exacting reality prevents the Nation from remaining at the pole of doom and engagement revolving around what needs to be done returns the focus to the pole of constructive action. Should observers focus less on the rhetoric of doom and study what actually is being done, a sober dedramatization might replace the excited cries of condemnation. I would argue that if left alone, the Nation of Islam will be of no danger to the present American society, and many of its detractors will most probably end up acknowledging the results as valuable.

Observed from a perspective of civilizing theory, the Nation of Islam is a movement of *autocivilization* that ultimately will adjust a segment of the African American community to the norms of the dominant culture of American society. Central to this argument is the notion that the Nation, un-American or even anti-American as it might seem, is fundamentally a far more genuine American movement than is generally recognized. The call for a return to the original way of life proves on examination to be rather identical with the American way of life. The ideals preached are generally compatible with those of conservative, white, Protestant, middle-class Americans: the NOI hails traditional family values, loyalty to the nation, and obedience to God. They applaud the decent, hardworking, honest, God-fearing heterosexual, who should be neatly dressed, polite, modest, law-abiding, and respectful of authorities. They encourage self-help and mistrust social welfare, value a God-centered education with emphasis on discipline and learning, and are epistemologically convinced of nonrelative universal truths that form the basis for knowledge. They are nonsmoking, nondrinking, clean-living moralists who shun sexual promiscuity, excessive partying, and decadent behavior.

To a large extent, the Nation has kept the agenda of the classic black nationalists and, as such, shares the conservative citizen's abhorrence of "uncivilized" life in the black ghettos. "We are the ones that are living a criminal life, a very wicked and savage life here in America," Farrakhan declares. "Though we have the potentials to be wonderful Muslims our condition is such that no civilized society wants us to be a member."[317] In a sermon at Mosque Maryam, Farrakhan reproached his black audience Booker T. Washington–style: "Our people don't have good manners. We don't respect each others' homes, each others' property. We don't know how to sit down at a table and eat properly. When you deal with black people, we need to be civilized, and taught everything, even how to go to the toilet, how to wipe ourselves properly, how to clean yourself up and make yourself respecting."[318] In his speeches, Farrakhan weaves advisory and edifying comments into the web of religio-political criticism of the present society. The central task for the poor righteous teachers in the Nation of Islam is, as rapped by Brand Nubian, to "civilize the uncivilized." Messenger Muhammad is presented as "the father of a whole new civilization,"[319] a "Master Civilizer" whose divine guidelines "are making civilized people of those who listen and obey."[320] The apocalyptic teachings of an escalating race war thus run parallel with a civilizing project. The NOI advocates revolution but believes that it begins with self-improvement.[321] Should the prophesied destruction of Babylon be delayed, the self-improved community of believers will still remain. The new civilization envisioned will then prove to be the good old American civilization, reshaped as a new body of people make its way into its fellowship. In order to be accepted and respected as a people, the self-degrading and unproductive wailing has to go. Heaven is an earthly condition and membership application requires productivity, as "the very base of heaven is hard work."[322] Blacks should stop waiting for the white man to rebuild the African American areas. "You say the buildings are all run down. Yeah, but they weren't always," Farrakhan emphasizes. "Whatever's run down, we run 'em up. We got carpenters, brick masons, electricians, we got everything we need in the black community to rebuild the black community."[323] The Nation of Islam provides an example for the entire Blackamerican population and by extension for all op-pressed nations in the world. "We are at the bottom," Farrakhan explains, "said to be hopeless, wicked, past, irredeemable, irreformable and impos-sible to deal with." To these, the deadest of dead at the bottom of the cemetery, came Master Farad Muhammad and raised Elijah Muhammad who raised Louis Farrakhan who is "reforming them. Bringing them back. Putting the woman in decent garment. Cleaning us up from the old life we used to live." The accomplishment enables Farrakhan to say proudly to the world: "Look! If we can do this there is hope for everyone."[324]

As much as the notion of white supremacy is an obstacle to a just soci-ety, its correlative notion of black inferiority has to be overcome. To this end, the thesis of black supremacy negates the thesis of white supremacy. It is a case of "an eye for an eye and a lie for a lie."[325] The black-man-is-God thesis of the Nation functions as a psychological lever, aiming to break the mental chain of inferiority by which the African American is said to be stuck at the bottom ladder of society. In this respect, it is an extreme version of positive thinking, a therapy that evidently is func-tional, as a significant number of individuals prove capable of trans-forming their lives against all odds by holding on to a new self-esteem: I-Self-Lord-Am-Master.

Using black supremacy as a shield against white supremacy does in-volve questionable sentiments, however, that nonblacks might justifiably feel uneasy about. Objections to reverse racism are common among ob-servers, while the movement's apologists strongly deny that they are ra-cist at all. So, is this racism? The NOI's theory of the genetically given divinity of the black man and the genetically given evilness of the white man cannot be termed other than racist, if racism is defined as a theory proposing that the different races, by nature, have distinct mental as well as physical qualities. Is it therefore reverse racism, comparable with the racist doctrine of white supremacy? Those who agree that it is overlook a component that when merged with a racist doctrine makes it truly dan-gerous: power. An imagined superiority for members of a specific race turns into an ideology of domination only if combined with a dispropor-tionate concentration of political and economical resources in the hands of members of the specific race in question. As such it is an instrument of oppression. This differs from the imagined superiority of members of a specific race who are disproportionally deprived of economic and politi-cal resources. As such, it can be an instrument of liberation, a means toward empowerment. Only when the distribution of wealth and power tends to be equal can the racist theories proposed by individuals of different races be equated. Concerning the racist religious doctrine of the Nation of Islam, the oppressive potential is still dormant as it is not combined with substantial power. Should, however, social conditions fundamentally be altered and the black community come to power under the leadership of the Nation of Islam, their ideology could possibly be transformed into an instrument of domination. This is, however, far from reality and as much as the hypothetical differs from the factual, so does the NOI's doctrine of black supremacy differ from the doctrine of white supremacy.

Those who unequivocally condemn Minister Farrakhan and the Nation of Islam should pause to reflect on what they actually are attacking. Farrakhan is not so much a problem as he is a *symptom* of the problems presently tearing apart American society. Should Farrakhan disappear, he would be replaced by another voice produced by the same conditions that produced Farrakhan. The Nation is a consequence of the black experience, it is a *social product* stamped with a "Made in the U.S.A." Irrespective of one's opinion of Minister Louis Farrakhan, his presence on the contemporary American scene points to issues that are impossible to avoid, as they are of key importance for the future of the American project. Perhaps it all boils down to one central question that needs to be addressed: Which way America?

Notes

===

Introduction

1   Juergensmeyer 1993:2.
2   Ahmed 1992:102f.
3   Ibid., 99.
4   For an illuminative presentation of the fear of the foreign West, see Mernissi 1993:13ff.
5   Haddad 1991:217.
6   Stone 1991:27f.; Johnson, S. A. 1991:111, 123 n. 1; Barboza 1994:9 n. 4; "Muslims in America," 1993; Gardell 1994.
7   For studies of the Islamic communities in the United States, see the anthologies, Waugh, Abu-Laban, and Quereshi 1983; Haddad 1991; Haddad and Smith 1994.
8   FBI file 105-24822-101, 2/13/62.
9   Farrakhan 1992a.
10 Most of these studies deal with the NOI during the earthly leadership of the Honorable Elijah Muhammad. The black sociologist of religion, C. Eric Lincoln, published an excellent thesis entitled *The Black Muslims of America* in 1961, with a revised edition published in 1973. The Nigerian political scientist E. U. Essien-Udom published his grassroots-oriented study *Black Nationalism* in 1962. In 1963, Louis E. Lomax published *When the Word is Given* from a reporter's perspective. Malu Halasa published her biography, *Elijah Muhammad,* written for young adults, in 1990. Clifton E. Marsh focuses on the transformation of the NOI under the leadership of Imam Warithuddin Muhammad in his *From Black Muslims to Muslims.* Martha F. Lee carried out a study of the NOI in terms of theories on millenarianism in her 1988 study, *The Nation of Islam: An American Millenarian Movement.* Although she includes valuable information, Lee overlooks the religious rationale of the NOI and leaves the messiology unnoticed. Useful information is found in Steven S. Barboza's *American Jihad,* a compilation of interviews with American Muslims, including a section on the NOI under the leadership of Minister Louis Farrakhan, published in 1994. None of the studies mentioned above deal with the Second Resurrection of the NOI in the way this study does, which is why it hopefully will fill a void in the field research on black Islamic nationalism.
11 Hobsbawn 1990:3.

12   Juergensmeyer 1993:6. For discussions on alternative definitions of nation and nationalism, see Hobsbawn 1990; Kellas 1991; Gellner 1983.

1   Restoration of Dignity: The Rise of
Black Nationalism

1   Moses 1978:6.
2   Ibid., 7.
3   Gregor Johann Mendel (1822–84) published his *Versuche mit Pflanzenhybriden* in 1865, but it was not acknowledged until the year 1900.
4   See Goodrick-Clarke 1992.
5   Du Bois 1988:76.
6   For an excellent introduction to evolutionism, see Morris 1987:91ff.
7   Lincoln 1986:6. For the de-Africanization process, see Bernal 1987.
8   Bastide 1967:317.
9   Stanton, W. 1982 (1960):7; Bastide 1969:314; Washington, J. R. 1984. The theory of blackness as a curse was popular but was not received with universal acceptance by white theologians.
10   Washington, J. R. 1984:470.
11   Bastide 1969:315.
12   Washington, J. R. 1984:19.
13   Cited in Lindqvist 1992:96.
14   Cited in Moses 1978:241.
15   Cited in Redkey 1969:36.
16   Washington, B. T. 1956 [1900]:11.
17   Ibid., 89.
18   Ibid., 105–9.
19   Washington, B. T. 1968 [1895]:196–99.
20   Du Bois 1961 [1903]:48.
21   Du Bois 1940:70.
22   Ibid., 47. See also Moses 1978:133.
23   Du Bois 1988 [1897]:73–85.
24   Du Bois 1940:321.
25   Ibid., 402–3.
26   Cited in Moses 1978:67.
27   Cited in ibid., 73.
28   Cited in ibid., 49.
29   Cited in ibid., 78.
30   For the history, politics, and operations of the ACS, see Redkey 1969:73–149.
31   Cited in Moses 1978:21.
32   Lynch 1967:60–63.
33   Cited in Lynch 1967:117.
34   Redkey 1969:4f.
35   Cited in Redkey 1969:171.
36   Cited in ibid., 41f.
37   Cited in ibid., 37.
38   Cited in Moses 1978:201.
39   For the history of the International Migration Society, see Redkey 1969:195–251.

40   Cited in Austin 1984:66.
41   Clarke, P. B. 1986:28; Redkey 1969:11.
42   Halliday and Molyneux 1981:52.
43   Cited in Moses 1978:158.
44   Garvey 1986 [1923]:5.
45   Ibid., 96.
46   The biographical account is based on the autobiographical material published in
      Garvey 1986 [1923] and [1925]; Garvey 1987. Besides Garvey's own sometimes
      inconsistent memories, see Cronon 1969 and the anthology edited by Clarke, J. H.
      1974.
47   Garvey 1986 [1925]:126.
48   Ibid., 126.
49   Garvey 1987:37.
50   Cronon 1969:205.
51   Garvey 1986 [1925]:120.
52   Among those who opposed the draft were Franklin E. Frazier, A. Philip Randolph,
      Chandler Owen, and Ida B. Wells.
53   Cited in Mullen 1973:45.
54   Cited in ibid., 45.
55   Cited in ibid., 46.
56   Cited in ibid., 247.
57   Garvey 1986 [1923]:77.
58   Garvey 1987:269.
59   Garvey 1986 [1923]:13.
60   Ibid., 52.
61   Hill and Bair 1987:xxxix–xliv.
62   Garvey 1987:29–32.
63   Cronon 1969:198.
64   Cited in Cronon 1969:162.
65   Garvey 1987:7ff.
66   Garvey 1986 [1923]:44.
67   Burkett 1989.
68   Ibid., 66, 70.
69   Cited in Cronon 1969:52. The Black Star Line was a strictly commercial venture
      and not intended to transport all African Americans back to Africa, as is some-
      times said.
70   Cited in Cronon, 1969:60.
71   Garvey 1986 [1923]:10.
72   Garvey 1987:39.
73   Ibid., 43–53.
74   Clarke, J. H. 1974b:100f.
75   Hill and Bair 1987:lxiv.
76   Powers 1987:128.
77   Cronon 1969:98–99.
78   Churchill and Wall 1988:27; Cronon 1969:100.
79   Cronon 1969:114f.
80   Cited in Cronon 1969:127.
81   Garvey 1986 [1925]:239.

2   The Crescent of the Occident: Islam in Black America prior to 1930

1   Winters 1975:428.
2   Van Sertima 1995 [1992]:29–81.
3   Wangara 1995 [1992]:169ff.
4   Winters 1975; Wangara 1995 [1992]:169–214.
5   TT-AFP 1992.
6   Lincoln 1984:28; Winters 1975:428.
7   Austin 1984:29–36.
8   Austin 1984:121–240.
9   Cited in Austin 1984:268.
10   Austin 1984:265–307.
11   Ibid., 445–523.
12   Winters 1975:431.
13   Cited in Austin 1984:298.
14   Cited in ibid., 295.
15   Cited in ibid., 391.
16   Cited in Raboteau 1978:47.
17   Cited in ibid., 47.
18   al Mahdi 1989:330.
19   Redkey 1969:44.
20   Blyden 1967 [1887]:231.
21   Quran 31:12–19. Compare the translations and commentaries of Maulana Muhammad Ali and Yusuf Ali; Redkey 1969:49f.
22   Cited in Lynch 1967:74.
23   Muhammad, A-R. 1977.
24   Muhammad, E. 1965:80.
25   Ibid., 221. Parenthesis his.
26   Ali, N. D., "Koran Questions."
27   Marsh 1984:41; Al-Ahari Bektashi, ms., 1994:22ff.
28   Ali, N. D., "Divine Constitution."
29   Ibid., Act 6.
30   Ali, N. D., *Holy Koran* (HK):46:2–7.
31   Ali, N. D., HK:47:6; "Koran Questions," q. 54.
32   Ali, N. D., HK:47:7.
33   Ibid., 16–17.
34   Ali, N. D., "Koran Questions," q. 66.
35   Ali, N. D., HK:2:18–25.
36   Ali, N. D., "Koran Questions" q. 79–85.
37   "The Cause and the Cure."
38   Ali, N. D., HK:48:1.
39   Ali, N. D., HK:I.
40   Ibid.
41   Dowling, L. H. 1987 [1907].
42   Dowling, E. S. 1987:9f.
43   Cited in Dowling, E. S. 1987:9. For the teachings of the cosmic ages, see pp. 1–4.
44   Dowling, L. H. 1987 [1907]:15:31. For the education of Mary and Elizabeth, see chs. 7–12.

45 Ibid., chs. 21–55.
46 Whyte 1964:384.
47 Ali, N. D., HK, p. 4.
48 Dowling, L. H. 1987 [1907]:20:5.
49 Ali, N. D., HK:5:5.
50 The nineteenth copied part is identical to parts of the Akashic Record Man, published as an introduction to the Aquarian Gospel.
51 Ali, N. D., HK:6:1–11; Dowling, L. H. 1987 [1907]:21:1–11.
52 Ali, N. D., HK:5:12–21; Dowling, L. H. 1987 [1907]:20:12–21.
53 Dowling, L. H. 1987 [1907]:48–55; for the legendary accounts, see Al-Ahari Bektashi (ms.) 1994:22ff.
54 Ali, N. D., HK:48:3.
55 Ibid., 6–7.
56 Ali, N. D., "Koran Questions," q. 19–21; Al-Ahari Bektashi (ms.) 1994:26.
57 Fauset 1971 [1944]:42f.
58 Ali, N. D., "Supreme Words"; FBI file 62-25889-118.
59 Ali, N. D., "The Additional Law," Act 4.
60 Ali, N. D., HK:28:2–3.
61 "The Cause and the Cure."
62 FBI file 62-25889-1.
63 FBI file 62-25889-6.
64 Ibid.
65 FBI file 62-25889-79.
66 Lincoln 1973:55; Essien-Udom 1962:35; Fauset 1971 [1944]:43.
67 "Claude Green Shot," 1929.
68 Jones, D. R. 1932.
69 "Cult Leader Dies," 1929; Jones, D. R. 1932.
70 "Most Noble," 1929.
71 FBI file 62-25889-79; Marsh 1984:49.
72 Al-Aharai Bektashi (ms.) 1994:9, 50.
73 FBI files 62-25889-70 and 62-25889-79.
74 Al-Ahari Bektashi (ms.) 1994:9, 49.
75 These Moorish divisions include: the United Moorish Republic, the Moorish Orthodox Church, the Circle Seven Brotherhood, the Moorish Institute, the National Council of Sheiks of the Moorish Divine, the Moorish Holy Temple of Science, the Moorish Divine and National Movement, the Moorish Circle of Fulfillment, the Moorish Great Seal, the One Nation Moorish Science Mosque, and the Moroccan Tribe.
76 Al-Ahari Bektashi (ms.) 1994:9.

3   The Genesis of the Nation of Islam

1 Halasa 1990:17. For the life of Southern sharecroppers, see Lemann 1992.
2 Halasa 1990:18–22.
3 Elijah Muhammad would have nineteen children, eight with Clara.
4 For an excellent study of the Great Migration, see Lemann 1992. Shelby Brown recalls her naive vision of Chicago, formed by the stories friends told about the city: "People told me that money was even growing on trees there. I went and got me two sacks to carry with me for that money tree in Chicago" (cited in Ferris 1984:6).

5   Lemann 1992:16.
6   Lincoln 1969:456.
7   Lincoln and Mamiya 1990:95.
8   Ferris 1984:28; Howlin' Wolf, "Highway 49."
9   B. B. King, "Why I Sing the Blues," 1987.
10   Cited in Ferris 1984:111, 135, 191n. 6.
11   Perkins 1987:20f.; Drake and Cayton, 1962:65–73.
12   MacLean 1994:184.
13   Halasa 1990:41.
14   Elijah Poole worked for a number of companies, among others the American Nut Co. (1923), the American Copper and Brass Co. (1923–25), and the Chevrolet Axle Co. (1925).
15   Muhammad, Wali Farad, as told in Barboza 1994:272.
16   In fact, the Prophet was known by many names. In addition to the more common names cited in the main text, he was called Wali Farad, Professor Ford, and F. Muhammad Ali.
17   Muhammad University of Islam 1973:24ff.
18   The earliest scholarly account of the NOI is found in Benon 1938. Compare with Lincoln 1973:12ff.
19   Bontemps and Conroy 1945:177; Essien-Udom 1962:35f.; Marsh 1984:49.
20   Essien-Udom 1962:35.
21   These were Abdul Muhammad and Othman Ali (Lee 1988:34n. 26).
22   See Lincoln 1973:57.
23   Brotz 1964:11f.
24   Hill and Bair 1987b:383.
25   Ehrman 1971.
26   Brotz 1964:12.
27   Ibid., 57.
28   Ehrman 1971:106.
29   Hill and Bair 1987b:383. Compare with Ehrman 1971.
30   FBI file 105-63642-22, 2/3/58.
31   FBI file 100-43165-15; LA FBI file 105-4805.
32   In November 17, 1918, a café owner named Wallie D. Ford was arrested by the Los Angeles police for assault with a deadly weapon and was released. The following year, he met a young woman named Hazel Brown who moved into his apartment above the café on 347 S. Flower Street. On September 1, 1920, she gave birth to a son, Wallace Dodd Ford. In 1921 or 1922, Hazel moved out from her fiancé, taking the child with her. On January 20, 1926, Ford was arrested for bootlegging and received a short sentence. Less than a month later, on February 15, Ford and his associate Edward Donaldsen were trapped in a drug sting. Halfway through a petty deal in narcotics, they discovered that the buyers were undercover agents and, without success, tried to withdraw. The police searched Ford's restaurant and found narcotics worth a few hundred dollars. This time the law showed no mercy. Ford was sentenced to prison for six months to six years on May 28 and started serving his term in San Quentin on June 12, 1926. After three years behind bars, Ford was released on May 27, 1929 (FBI files 100-43165-15; 100-43165-1; 100-43165; 105-63642).
33   FBI file 100-43165.

34 Interviewed by the police, Hazel recalled Ford to be reluctant to talk about his background. He never mentioned his place or date of birth, nor anything about parents or relatives. He did, however, mention that he had been married in Oregon and had fathered a boy in 1914 or 1915. The separation had been bitter, and he had been unable to receive a divorce, which is why Hazel and Ford could not get legally married. Hazel claimed that she once had found an old letter in her fiancé's belongings. It was addressed to a Fred Dodd in Salem, Oregon. Reading the letter, she became convinced that Fred Dodd was identical with Wallace Ford. She further recalled that a waitress working for Ford had helped him write letters to his parents in New Zealand. This is congruent with the birth certificate of their son, on which Ford stated that he was born in New Zealand on February 26, 1891. Summarizing this line of evidence, the FBI suggest as one possibility that Ford was born Wallace Dodd in New Zealand. His father was British and his mother Polynesian. Somewhere prior to 1914, he migrated to the United States and settled in Portland, Oregon. He married, possibly Pearl Allen, who married a Fred Dodd from Salem, Oregon, on May 9, 1914, but soon tried to obtain a divorce. His wife refused, and he bitterly decided to abandon her and their son. To escape legal difficulties, he moved to Los Angeles under a new identity and opened a restaurant (FBI files 105-63642; 105-63642-3; 105-63642-22; 100-43165-15; 105-4805).

35 Montgomery 1963.

36 FBI file 100-43165-15.

37 Cushmeer 1971:70.

38 As, for instance, in 1968, when the special agent in charge in Boston is "authorized to furnish derogatory information about the Nation of Islam (NOI) to [BUREAU DELETION] Radio Station WEAN, Providence, Rhode Island. . . . Emphasize to him that the NOI predilection for violence, preaching of race hatred and hypocrisy, should be exposed. . . . WEAN covers Rhode Island and Southern Massachusetts, an area with a Negro population of 20,000. A program exposing the NOI should be particularly valuable on this station" (FBI file 100-448006-10, 2/27/68).

39 The NOI belief that God came to the United States on July 4 is not unambiguous. In contradiction with this belief, which was and is standard in the NOI teachings, Elijah Muhammad said at times that God had studied in California prior to his appearance in Detroit. In 1970, Elijah Muhammad stated that "He (Master Farad Muhammad) told me that for 20 years, He came in and out without anyone knowing who He really was. And He went to school with the white people in their University, right out here in California. Born to deliver you and me. But He must know how to do the job, so He goes and He looks like one of them" (Muhammad, E. 1970a).

40 Beynon 1938:896.

41 Lincoln 1973:15f.

42 Compare with the practice of the Moorish Science Temple.

43 Beynon 1938:902.

44 Cowans 1932.

45 FBI file 105-63642.

46 Lomax 1963:52.

47 Elijah Muhammad, cited in Lee, M. F. 1988:34.

48 Cowans 1932.
49 Beynon 1938; Cowans 1932; Jones, D. R. 1932.
50 Cowans 1932. The story carries the thrilling additional headline: "Social Work-
    ers 'Marked for Death' by Voodoo Killer."
51 Jones, D. R. 1932.
52 Cowans 1932.
53 Ibid.
54 "Voodoo Cult Killer," 1932.
55 Allah 1974a.
56 Muhammad, M. F., Lesson #1.
57 Barboza 1994:115f.
58 "Voodoo Cult Killer," 1932.
59 Muhammad University of Islam, 1973.
60 Allah 1973.
61 FBI file 100-63165; 100-63642-15; Chicago FBI file 100-12899.
62 In 619, the situation for the modest Muslim congregation in Mecca deteriorated
    rapidly. Muhammad Ibn Abdullah lost his first wife, Khadidja, and his benefac-
    tor, clan leader Abu Talib, died. The unbelievers' increased repression made
    Muhammad accept an offer to move to Yathrib, later known as "the City," Medi-
    nah. Between July and September 622, the community of believers discreetly
    migrated (hijra), with the prophet Muhammad leaving in September. Tradition
    says that he learned of a lethal conspiracy. Ali Ibn Abu Talib volunteered to sleep
    in the Prophet's bed to trick the assassins, while Muhammad and Abu Bakr
    escaped in the night. Ali remained in Mecca and settled the Prophet's business
    before joining the Medinah congregation (Rodinson 1981:116; Momen 1985:12).
63 FBI file 105-63642-28.
64 Ayman Muhammad as interviewed in Barboza 1994:269.
65 X, C. D. 1974.
66 One persistent rumor, noted by Lomax (1963:53) and still circulating in the black
    community, is that Master Farad Muhammad was sacrificed and thus trans-
    formed into a saviour. Although some of Muhammad's critics may "hint darkly at
    the coincidence of Fard's disappearance at the moment of Muhammad's rise to
    power" (Lincoln 1973:17), this is as yet unsupported speculation. For the author,
    the explanation for Master Farad's elevation is found in the blackosophic gnosis
    at the core of the NOI creed, as will be described in chapters 6 and 7.
67 In the earliest NOI statements, Farad is said to have gone up to the mountains to
    escape the "cavies," that is, the whites (Barboza 1994:269), to Mecca (Goldman
    1979:37), and to Mexico (Lee, M. F. 1988:35). Later, his final destination is spec-
    ified to be another place, which will be revealed later in this study.
68 Muhammad University of Islam, 1973.
69 Ayman Muhammad, as cited in Barboza 1994:269; Elijah Muhammad as cited in
    Lee, M. F. 1988:36; Evanzz 1992:30. Kallatt Muhammad was murdered in 1935.
70 Muhammad University of Islam, 1973; Muhammad, D., interview, 1989. Two of
    Muhammad's earliest followers in Washington, D.C., were Benjamin and Clara
    Muhammad, interviewed in Barboza 1994:79ff.
71 See Introduction, note 10. In The History of the Nation of Islam, a compilation of
    old interviews with Messenger Muhammad published by Nasir Makr Hakim in
    1993, is found the Messenger's comments of these studies as well as other inter-
    esting material for the uninitiated scholar of the movement.

72   Muhammad, E. 1965:174ff., 200ff.
73   Alexander 1989:55–71; Khasif and 4X, 1974; 4X, G 1974; Rassoul 1974; Khasif 1974.
74   Lincoln 1973:97.
75   Muhammad, E. 1973a:97.
76   FBI file 105-24822.
77   Lincoln 1973:132.
78   Khasif and 4X, 1974.
79   For a study of the NOI educational system, see Vontress 1965. Vontress was unable to find any significant difference in the knowledge between NOI students and other black students, although some facilities were found inadequate and some teachers unqualified. Essien-Udom (1962:231–49) includes a discussion on the NOI schools. In 1959–60, the curriculum was as follows: reading and spelling, penmanship, languages and general civilization, arithmetic and simple metric system, advanced arithmetic, algebra, advanced algebra, general geometry and trigonometry, astronomy, chronological history from 13,000 B.C., solar system, spook being displayed for 6,000 years, chronology, English (reading, writing, composition, literature), science (general science, biology, chemistry, hygiene), languages (Arabic), social studies (American history, world history, geography, sociology, civics), art (typing, shorthand, home economics), and religion (Islam).
80   Benz is among those who have misunderstood the NOI prohibition against interracial marriage. Benz believes the rule to be a "biologisk absurditet" (biological absurdity) that will exclude the large majority of the black American population as only 3 percent are of unmixed African descent. Contrary to the pseudoscientific race biological inquiries practiced in Nazi Germany, the NOI generously includes all nonwhites among the black race. Elijah Muhammad did not apply the rule of endogamy retrospectively to condemn the results of previous interracial unions. The spectrum of colors was seen as a consequence of white rapists who had taken advantage of black female slaves. The ones to blame were not the offspring but the offenders. Elijah Muhammad spoke in terms of the future and sought to break the white monopoly of defining beauty.
81   Muhammad, E. 1967:60.
82   Muhammad, E. 1972:46f.
83   "Poison drinks along with a mixture of good and poison food have shortened our lives, on the average of about 63.5 years at the present time," wrote the Messenger. "This is a long way from the 600-800-900 years of our fathers." God taught him that the people on Mars "lived an average life of the equivalent of 1200 years of our earth calendar" (Muhammad, E. 1972:7). By eating proper food once a day, the life expectancy could be extended to 140 years. By eating only once every second day, almost all sickness would be avoided. By eating once every seventy-two hours, one would never be sick and would live for 1,000 years (Muhammad, E. 1967:53).
84   Muhammad, E. 1972:135.
85   Ibid., 96, 105–24.
86   Ibid., 128.
87   Ibid., 77f.
88   Muhammad, E. 1967:4–8, 63.
89   Ibid., 7, 12, 65.

90   Ibid., 7, 92, 109; Muhammad, E. 1972:89.

91   Muhammad, E. 1972:50f.

92   Ibid., 48, 55.

93   Khasif and 4X 1974; Rassoull 1974; Muhammad A. Nasser, NOI Minister in Bar-
      bados, personal information, May 1989; Imam Warithuddin Muhammad, as told
      in Marsh 1984:108.

94   Lincoln 1973:111.

95   Ibid., 136.

96   Ibid., 140. John Woodford (1990:92) claimed a circulation of 650,000 during his
      time as editor in chief, and Abass Rassoull claimed a circulation of 850,000
      (Rassoull 1974). Louis Lomax gathered news and C. E. Lincoln corrected galley
      proofs for the first issue, while they were both working on their respective stud-
      ies of the NOI (Evanzz 1992:93). *Muhammad Speaks* was to become the most
      successful NOI paper. In addition, a number of less successful publications were
      launched: *The Final Call of Islam* (1934), a tabloid paper, *The Islamic News*
      (1959), a magazine, *The Messenger* (1959–60) a journal, and the journal *Salaam*
      (1961).

97   Woodford 1990.

98   Muhammad University of Islam 1973.

99   Lemann 1991:64.

100   Ibid., 1991:70.

101   Essien-Udom 1962:70; Muhammad, D., interview, 1989.

102   Earl Little was a UNIA organizer and Louis Little was a secretary/journalist on the
      Negro World.

103   Earl Little was found dying on the trolley tracks, severely battered, his body
      almost cut in half. The police said he had "fallen" on the tracks and been run
      over. Later investigation exposed many of the policemen, including some trolley
      car policemen, among the members of a Ku Klux Klan splinter group called the
      Black Shirts (Evanzz 1992:7).

104   According to Malcolm's sister Yvonne and brothers Bob, Wilfred, and Philbert,
      the part of the *Autobiography* describing Malcolm's criminal life was exagger-
      ated to make the postconversion change greater (Lee, S. 1992:44ff). This is a
      common phenomenon among born-again ex-criminals or addicts, increasing the
      appeal as the cured curer. On the other hand, Malcolm's family may want to play
      down the mean side of their late brother.

105   Evanzz 1992:66.

106   See Wiley 1992; Gardell 1993a.

107   Muhammad Ali, Abdul Rahaman, and Jeremiah Shabazz as interviewed in
      Hauser 1991:89–95.

108   Malcolm X's presence made Clay's advisors warn him to cease to associate with
      the Muslims as he had "promised to stay away from politics and religion"
      (Tucker 1964).

109   X, M. 1973 [1965]:306f.

110   Grimsley 1964.

111   Cited in Hauser 1991:101. The announcement stunned mainstream observers,
      some of whom refused to believe it. Pat Putnam reported that Clay was "less than
      happy with Muhammad's unveiling" and that he angrily refused to comment the
      Messenger's claim (Putnam 1964).

112 See, for instance, "Negro Leaders Blast Cassius," 1964.

113 Cited in Hauser 1991:139.

114 Hauser 1991:171–81.

115 Cited in Hauser 1991:167.

116 Hauser 1991:172–81.

117 Jeremiah Shabazz as interviewed in Hauser 1991:135.

118 Hauser 1991:193ff.

119 Ali received numerous sport awards and was invited by President Gerald Ford to visit the White House (Hauser 1991:280ff.).

4   Forces of Evil

1   FBI file 105-63642-15, 1/15/58.

2   Beynon 1938:904.

3   This, of course, was an impression developed by the skilled Japanese propaganda machine. It was, for example, a widespread sentiment among South East Asians that the Japanese fought on their side, to liberate the Asians from European colonialism. This impression changed when the Philippine and Indonesian populations experienced Japanese imperialism.

4   FBI file 100-6582-[?], 6/19/42.

5   Orro 1942.

6   "Cultist 'Guilty,'" 1942; "25 Found Guilty," 1942.

7   FBI file 105-63642-[?], 2/21/57.

8   FBI file 105-63642-[?], 2/21/57.

9   Elijah Muhammad was sentenced to five years in prison for violation of the Selective Service Act. He became eligible for parole on December 17, 1943, but was not given a conditional release until August 24, 1946. His full term expired on December 17, 1947 (FBI file 105-24822-25, 8/9/57).

10 Garrow 1981; Churchill and Wall 1988; Blackstock 1988; O'Reilly 1989; Glick 1989; Carson 1991; Evanzz 1992; Friedly and Gallen 1993.

11 The studies made on the FBI's targeting of Malcolm X—Carson 1991 and Evanzz 1992—though not focusing specifically on the NOI, include material from the FBI files in regard to the Nation.

12 O'Reilly 1989:275.

13 Garrow 1981:11.

14 FBI file 105-24822-13, 12/31/56.

15 FBI file 105-248822-56X, 10/30/59.

16 On May 27, 1960, authorization was obtained for additional taps in "a secret hide-a-way" on 8205 S. Vermon, after the secret telephone number had been provided by a highly placed informant in NOI inner circles (FBI file 105-24822-80, 5/17/60). On September 25, 1961, technical and microphone surveillance was installed in Muhammad's residence at 2118 E. Violet Drive, Phoenix, Arizona (FBI file 105-24822-[?], 5/28/63).

17 FBI file 105-248822-56X, 10/30/59.

18 FBI file 100-448006-[?], Chicago FBI file 100-35635-Sub B, 4/22/68.

19 Cushmeer 1971:39f.

20 FBI file 105-24822-[?], 4/26/62.

21 Essien-Udom 1962:70.

22 FBI file 100-448006-[?], 4/22/68; Chicago FBI file 100-35635-Sub B, 4/22/68.

23 FBI file 105-24822-[?], 4/26/62.

24 FBI file 100-448006-[?]; Chicago FBI file 100-35635-Sub B, 4/22/68.

25 Lincoln, C. Eric, in discussion with the author at Duke University, N.C., May 23, 1989.

26 See, for instance, the lyrical presentation of the NOI jet (Khasif 1974). Hundreds of onlookers came out to see it at different airports when it toured the United States, as the Messenger wanted for people to "see for themselves, the great things in store for them under the guidance of Allah and His Apostle." In Newark, Minister James Ibn Shabazz boarded it "before He [the Honorable Elijah Muhammad] Himself has been aboard. What other Leader and Teacher has ever loved his people so much?" Minister Charles X from Wilmington said that "seeing the plane has inspired me and the Muslims from Temple No. 35 to do even more to help the Honorable Elijah Muhammad."

27 FBI file 105-24822-[?], date unreadable, 1960.

28 FBI file 105-24822-[?], 4/26/62.

29 Ibid.

30 Ibid.

31 Ibid.

32 Cited in Garrow 1981:159.

33 Sullivan in an anonymous letter to Martin Luther King Jr. Cited in Garrow 1981:124.

34 FBI files 105-24822-142 and 105-24822-202. Sister Evelyn Lorene Williams eventually filed a paternity suit against Elijah Muhammad.

35 FBI file 105-24822-[?], 7/25/62.

36 FBI file 100-448006-[?]; Chicago FBI file 100-35635-Sub B, 4/22/68.

37 FBI file 100-448006-[?]; Chicago FBI file 100-35635-Sub B, 4/22/68.

38 See, for instance, Hannerz 1969:78ff.

39 The sources differ in regard to the legal status of the Prophet's relation with the Jewish woman Raihana Bint Zaid. Some state that they were married and some state that they were lovers but not formally married. For the Prophet's view on women, sexuality, and his marital relationships, see Mernissi 1985; Mernissi 1991; Morsi 1990.

40 X, M. 1973 [1965]:299.

41 Goldman 1979.

42 Breitman 1986 [1976]:48.

43 Evanzz 1992.

44 Lee, S. 1992:66.

45 See, for instance, FBI file 105-24822-80, 5/17/60.

46 X. M. 1973 [1965]:290.

47 FBI file 105-24822-[?], 4/26/62.

48 FBI file 105-24822-[?], 7/25/62.

49 X, M. 1973 [1965]:294–97.

50 Ibid., 295.

51 Yusuf Shah (Captain Joseph) as told to Lee, S. 1992:61; Farrakhan, L. interview, 1989b; compare with Lee, S. 1992:52.

52 FBI file 105-24822-[?], 5/28/63.

53 X, M. 1965:301. The Messenger had ordered his followers to not comment on the

assassination. Malcolm's remark was given in reply to a journalist after a December 3, 1963, speech "God's Judgement of White America" (X, M. 1971). X, M. 1965:301.

54 FBI file 105-24822-[?], 1/27/64.

55 FBI file 105-24822-133, 2/7/64.

56 X, M. 1970:2. In a March 19 interview with A. B. Spellman, Malcolm declared the move to be practically motivated only and not signifying a change in orientation. "I am a follower of the Honorable Elijah Muhammad," he said. "The only reason I am in the Muslim Mosque Inc. is because I feel I can better expedite his program by being free of the restraint and the other obstacles that I encountered in the Nation" (X, M. 1970:5).

57 Evanzz 1992:214.

58 X, M. 1973 [1965]:340.

59 Sharieff 1971.

60 Cleaver 1968:74; Goldman 1979:210.

61 Breitman 1967:77–78; Appendix A. OAAU was patterned after the Organization of African Unity that had been established in 1963.

62 FBI file 105-24822-142, 10/9/64; Carson 1991:321f.

63 Goldman 1979:134.

64 These words became a powerful slogan in the Malcolm X cult that developed after his death. They appear for the first time in an interview in December 1964. When asked where he was headed, Malcolm answers: "I have no idea. I can capsulize how I feel—I'm for the freedom of the 22 million Afro-Americans by any means necessary. By any means necessary. I'm for a society in which our people are recognized and respected as human beings, and I believe that we have the right to resort to any means necessary to bring that about. So when you ask me where I'm headed, what can I say? I'm headed in any direction that will bring about some immediate results" (Goldman 1979:222).

65 X, M. 1989a:135. For the contacts between the NOI and the extreme right, see chapter 9.

66 X, M. 1989b:111–34.

67 X, M. 1989a:147.

68 X, M. 1989b:125.

69 Goldman 1979:409.

70 Ibid., 411; Marsh 1984:85; "Claims Malcolm," 1977.

71 Breitman 1976:16.

72 Barboza 1994:150n. 34. In December 1993, Abd al-Aziz was greeted as an innocent man at a NOI rally in New York (X and Muhammad 1994).

73 Murad Muhammad recalls, "You could not fault Elijah [Muhammad]. Elijah was the man and either you joined him or you left him the hell alone. And if you messed with him, I don't care whether you be black or Caucasian, you had to deal with us! And that's how Malcolm lost his life" (as told to Barboza 1994:150).

74 FBI file 105-24822-[?], 3/23/64.

75 Cited in Goldman 1979:247–48.

76 Cited in FBI file 105-24822-[?], 2/27/65.

77 Evanzz 1994:281.

78 Lee, S. 1992:63.

79 FBI file 105-24822-[?], 3/12/64.

80 Evanzz 1992:289ff.

81 Lee, S. 1992:63.

82 Goldman 1979:416f.

83 Lee, S. 1992:64. The author refrains from mentioning their names in respect for the fact that they are innocent until proven guilty.

84 FBI file 105-24822-[?], 8/7/64.

85 Evanzz 1992:198. When Ali later confronted Lomax about the alleged connection, Lomax replied that he had the information from reliable sources (Evanzz 1992:207). Evanzz notes that Lomax's source was possibly found inside the Seattle FBI Office.

86 Evanzz 1992:197–208.

87 Marsh 1984:74.

88 Evanzz 1992:294.

89 Goldman 1979:259f., 285n, 295n; Churchill and Wall 1988:396n. 59.

90 Evanzz 1992:xivf.

91 William O'Neal infiltrated the Chicago Black Panther Party (BPP) and proved useful to the bureau. He rose rapidly in the BPP to become chief of security and Fred Hampton's personal bodyguard. O'Neal instigated the first armed clash between the Panthers and the Black P Stone Nation at a time when it seemed as if the street gang would be politicized and eventually merge with the BPP. A number of covert actions were planned to disrupt the black coalition (the BPP would have doubled in number had the street gang become affiliated). That goal accomplished, O'Neal continued his efforts to destroy from within. Besides routine activities, such as channeling BPP material and plans to the bureau, O'Neal suggested that party members engage in armed robberies, he spread false rumors and accusations about members, he opted to construct an electric chair to deal with informers (rejected), he initiated weapons training and stockpiled arms later "discovered" in a FBI raid. In October 1969, Hampton and his fiancée Deborah Johnson rented a four-room apartment on Chicago's West Side, for personal and political use. In November, O'Neal engaged in the murder plot staged under the pretext of an illegal weapons raid on the Hampton apartment. O'Neal provided the police with a detailed floor plan, including information on Hampton's sleeping habits. On December 4, O'Neal prepared a late dinner (or a last supper) for the Panthers staying in the apartment. After he left, the heavily armed raiders took action. Two subteams forced their way in, using O'Neal's floor map to locate the targets. Gloves Davis shot the dozing Mark Clark and put a bullet in Brenda Harris, a teenager sleeping in a front-room bed. Davis and others sprayed automatic fire with submachine guns through the walls, aiming at Hampton's bed. The raiders found him hit but alive and added two more shots point-blank in Hampton's head. Mission accomplished, the raiders aimed at the remaining Panthers, who were hiding in the other bedrooms. Doc Satchell was hit four times, Blair Anderson twice, and a second teenager, Verlina Brewer, was also shot twice. The surviving Panthers were dragged onto the street where they were arrested on charges of attempted murder and aggravated assault. O'Neal received a cash bonus as it was his information that ensured the raid's success. Due to an unrelated murder case, O'Neal's identity as infiltrator was exposed in 1973 (Churchill and Wall, 1988:64–77).

92 John X Ali's attitude does not necessarily mean that he is identical with the top

informant. He had reportedly a grudge against Malcolm since the late 1950s when Ali was under Malcolm's command in Temple #7 (see Evanzz 1992:202ff.), a dislike that possibly evolved into hatred upon observing Malcolm's "treason."

93   FBI file 100-448006-[626?], 1/22/69.

94   Farrakhan, L., interview, 1989b.

95   FBI file 100-448006-[?], 3/13/69.

96   FBI file 100-448006-1381, 8/29/69.

97   O'Reilly 1989:229–38.

98   Cited in O'Reilly 1989:242f.

99   The FBI used strategically placed individuals, such as owners or employees of liquor stores, taverns, drugstores, pawnshops, candy stores, barbers, and taxi drivers (O'Reilly 1989:267f.).

100   O'Reilly 1989:264–77.

101   FBI file 100-448006-[?], 8/25/67.

102   FBI file 100-448006-17, 3/4/68.

103   FBI file 100-448006-[?], 3/4/68.

104   FBI file 100-448006-47, 4/1/68.

105   FBI file 100-448006-80, 4/5/68.

106   FBI file 100-448006-[?], 4/5/68.

107   FBI file 100-448006-[?], 2/27/68. The FBI deleted the names of the three top officials targeted. Louis Farrakhan was at that time minister of Mosque #7, New York.

108   FBI file 100-448006-[?], 2/27/68.

109   FBI file 100-448006-[?], 4/8/68.

110   FBI file 100-448006-179, 6/26/68.

111   Ibid.

112   FBI file 100-448006-[?], 8/28/68.

113   FBI file 100-448006-[?], 11/29/68.

114   The SAC in Tampa wrote Elijah Muhammad the following letter, signed "Sister X" (FBI file 100-448006-124, 5/17/18):

> Dear Saviour Allah Our Deliverer:
> I believe you better check on the money [BUREAU DELETION] is sending in. He is messing around with the money and I don't think he is turning it all in.

115   FBI files 100-448006-[?], 9/6/68; 100-448006-[?], 9/13/68; and 100-448006-[?], 9/25/68.

116   Norfolk agents suggested that a bogus letter be sent to Elijah Muhammad from "devoted brothers and sisters" who are afraid to give him their names, as "Captain Sam has threatened to harm anyone who would write directly to the Messenger" (FBI file 100-448006-[?], 10/23/68). In the letter, the fictitious members said that their minister, being a "hypocrite and unbeliever" and father of an illegitimate child, should be "disciplined" accordingly. The bureau approved the suggested action, hoping that it would "cause the NOI to investigate the local minister and perhaps remove him," adding that "the removal and replacement of an NOI minister usually results in a loss of membership in the local group" (FBI file 100-448006-[?], 11/7/68).

117   FBI file 100-448006-[?], 9/27/69.

118   FBI file 100-448006-[?], 9/27/68.

119   In FBI file 100-448006-681, 2/19/69, the SAC in Miami reports on internal strife

amongst the leadership in Mosque #29, a situation that, together with the local minister's alleged extramarital affairs, should be used to undermine the minister's position by mailing an anonymous letter to Elijah Muhammad. This time their request was authorized by the bureau (FBI file 100-448006-750), which previously had denied similar requests from Miami, in order to avoid jeopardizing the effect of anonymous letters from the SAC in Norfolk, by arousing the Messenger's suspicions (FBI file 100-448006-384, 11/8/68). Later, the SAC in Miami reported that the targeted leader had been removed and concluded that "the counterintelligence letter submitted by the Miami Office may very well have some effect in the removal of [BUREAU DELETION] of the Miami mosque" (FBI file 100-448006-[?], 4/7/69).

120   For Birmingham, see FBI file 100-448006-441, 11/29/68, and for Miami, see FBI file 100-448006-[?], 4/7/69.

121   FBI file 100-448006-[?], 6/1/68. In addition the SAC in Houston reports that the NOI treasurer had been ousted, accused of stealing funds, a fact that gave their informants the possibility of accusing additional NOI laborers.

122   FBI file 100-448006-[?], 11/18/68.

123   See, for instance, Churchill and Wall 1988:42f. Ron Karenga's organization was called Simba Wachuka (Swahili for "young lions") but was popularly known as the United Slaves organization.

124   FBI file 100-448006-[?], 5/3/68.

125   See FBI files 100-448006-[?], 6/26/70; 100-448006-[?], 11/13/70; 100-448006-2150, 12/31/70; 100-448006-[?], 1/14/71; 100-448006-2123, 12/10/70; 100-448006-2147, 12/21/70; and 100-448006-2254, 2/22/71.

126   FBI file 100-448006-[?], 6/26/70.

127   SAC in Richmond wrote to the director of the FBI that Panthers and Muslims sold their newspapers in the same downtown area, which is why the following letter ought to be addressed from "NOI" to BPP:

Dear Brother [BUREAU DELETION]

As-Salaam Alaikum:

You boys is sellin panthre papers on Broad Street and there cuttin in to our territory and hurtin our selin papers. Them black panthres got the rong ideas any way. You should no better. You cant deel with this devil.

"The above letter," continues the local agent, "could obviously be the basis for future counterintelligence letters attributed to [BUREAU DELETION] and the NCCF group, directed to the MM#24 and vice versa" (FBI file 100-448006-[?], 11/13/70).

The director turned down the Richmond suggestion on the grounds that it could be disclosed as a "hoax," and ordered them to direct "a letter to NOI headquarters . . . either anonymously or with a fictitious name, complaining that the BP newspaper is sold in conjunction with the NOI newspaper. . . . the [fictitious] writer [should] object to the take-over of the NOI of the Panthers" (FBI file 100-448006-[?], 11/25/70).

The following letter from the SAC in Richmond to the Messenger of Allah (FBI file 100-448006-2150, 12/31/70) is the result:

Dear Honorable Elijah Muhammad,

As-Salaam Alaikum

I don't want to say who i is but i do want you to no somthin you should no and need to no because it is bringin desgrase on you Mosque in Richmond, Va. For a long time the brothers has been sellin the paper on Broad St., now a few weeks ago them panthers start to sell there paper and some of the brothers has been seen jiven with them panthers. Last week more panthers was sellin there paper then the brothers and people is sayin some of the brothers has join the panthers and other brothers is afraid to sell the paper when the panthers is sellin there. Them panthers is no good for the so called american negro and i think them panthers is goin to take over your Mosque in Richmond.

128 FBI file 100-448006-2254, 2/22/71.
129 FBI file 100-448006-2147, 12/21/70. The SAC in New York suggested that the following letter be sent to the Black Panthers:

Brother Huey Newton:
Let this be a warning to you and your followers:
We will not tolerate the actions [BUREAU DELETION] or [BUREAU DELETION] any longer. We know that both of these men who claim to be Black Panthers and your followers have been active in the area of our Mosque and have been bothering our women and children.
We know for a fact that [BUREAU DELETION] got one of our Muslim girls drunk and then he raped her at the Black Panther Headquarters in the Bronx, NY.
We know for a fact that [BUREAU DELETION] is drunk most of the time and also has attempted to attack our women.
Brother Newton, we members of the Fruit of Islam has no argument with you but if you cannot make your followers [BUREAU DELETION] and [BUREAU DELETION] behave, then we will have to discipline them in our own way.
Lionel 3X
Fruit of Islam
Mosque 7c
New York

The director rejected the request "in its current format at this time" (FBI file 100-448006-2147, 1/6/71).
130 FBI file 100-448006-[?], 3/27/68. A less serious but still fanciful suggestion was put forward by the division of St. Louis. To create animosity between the Nation and other black nationalist organizations, the local agent suggested a move based on Elijah Muhammad's views on bearded men. In a *Muhammad Speaks* article of July 4, 1969, the Messenger wrote that the beard is an unsanitary germ catcher. The SAC in St. Louis proposed that all local divisions should send the names and addresses of "all bearded extremists" in their territories. Reprints of the *Muhammad Speaks* article would then be mailed "anonymously to all bearded Black Militants in the United States." St. Louis thought this action would "increase irritation between NOI and all other Black militant groups" and "injure" their future cooperation (FBI file 100-448006-[?], 7/16/69).
131 FBI file 100-448006-569, 12/24/68.
132 FBI file 100-448006-569, 1/6/69; 100-448006-[?], 1/27/69.
133 Muhammad, E. 1969.
134 FBI file 100-448006-624, 1/22/69.
135 FBI file 100-448006-624, 2/5/69. The agents were ordered to make sure that Withcome understood the strictly confidential basis of the cooperation. It was important that the operation did not cause any embarrassment for the bureau and that no hints of the FBI's interest in this matter surfaced.

136   FBI file 100-448006-1381, 10/21/69; 100-448006-1367, 10/23/69. The bureau was pleased to learn that "the station received more favorable phone calls than the switchboard could handle . . . three civic organizations have asked to show the film to their members as a public service, and the Broward County Sheriff's Office plans to show the film to its officers and in connection with its community service program."

137   Muhammad, E. 1969b.

138   O'Reilly 1989:346.

139   FBI file 100-448006-1519, 4/27/71; see also 100-448006-1518, 4/28/71.

140   FBI file 100-448006-[?], 8/7/72.

141   Glick 1989:7f.; O'Reilly 1989:350f.

142   Garrow 1981:221ff.

143   As, for example, Blackstock 1988.

144   O'Reilly 1989.

145   As, for example, against the American Indian Movement (see Churchill and Wall, 1988) and the Puerto Rican and Chicano Movements, Ben Chavis, and others (Glick 1989:20–33).

146   Garrow 1981:208f.

147   Lincoln 1984:131f. For a debate on "civil religion," see Rouner 1986.

148   Bellah 1967. Compare with Rouner 1986.

149   Ortner 1979:95.

150   Moltmann 1986:55.

151   Wilson, J. F. 1986:115.

152   Public Enemy, "I Ain't Mad at All," 1994.

153   See, for instance, Final Call, 2/12/90. The original poem runs: "Give us your tired, your poor, your wretched refuse, yearning to breathe free; the huddled masses of your teeming shores. Send these, the homeless tempest tossed, to me. I lift my lamp beside the golden door."

154   Farrakhan 1983:9.

155   Muhammad, K. A., speech, 1993.

156   Muhammad, E. 1965:237ff.

157   Muhammad, E. 1973:68.

158   Public Enemy, "Hitler Day," 1994.

159   Muhammad, K.A., speech, 1989.

160   For the cultural homogeneity of the bureau, see Garrow 1981:225f.

161   See, for instance, FBI files 100-448006-[?], 4/5/68 and 105-248822-56X, 10/30/59.

162   There seems to be a rather irrational and highly emotional popular limitation for the First Amendment. One has the right to state, express, and believe anything, as long as one does not sacrilege the pillars of American civil religion. This was highlighted in the 1989–90 nationwide and extremely emotional debate on whether or not an American had the right to desecrate the Stars and Stripes. The bill to criminalize flag-burning and other acts of contempt for the national symbol was defeated in Congress as it would have implied a limitation on the First Amendment. The bureau never did put their actions to test with public opinion or the congressional vote. But their reaction to the NOI is analogous with the 1989–90 rage over the black artist who exhibited a desecrated Star-Spangled Banner at a Museum of Modern Art.

163   FBI file 100-448006; Chicago FBI file 157-2209, 4/22/68.

164 Farrakhan, L. 1992b [1973].
165 Muhammad, E. 1965:216–17; "Muslim's Riot," 1962; Pace 1972; Farrakhan 1972; Craft 1972; 5X 1974.
166 Some of the FBI informers reconverted while infiltrating the Nation of Islam and turned around as counterspies (Farrakhan, interview, 1989b; X, M. 1973 [1965]:258).
167 See for instance, Farrakhan, speech, 1989; Farrakhan, speech, 1988.
168 See, for instance, X, G. 1974.
169 Farrakhan, 1992b:73.
170 Muhammad, E. 1973:200.
171 Public Enemy, "Party for Your Right to Fight," 1988.

5   The Fall of the Nation

1   Shah 1973.
2   Shah 1974.
3   Farrakhan 1992c [1974]:63.
4   67X 1974.
5   Karriem 1974.
6   FBI file 100-448006-571, 1/7/69.
7   FBI file 100-448006-[?], 1968. From George Moore, chief of racial intelligence, to William C. Sullivan, head of the Domestic Intelligence Division. FBI file 100-448006-121, 5/15/68, suggests "Herbert Muhammad be targeted to remove him as a possible successor to his father. . . . Neutralization of Herbert Muhammad would help our high-level NOI informants to exercise more control over the NOI."
8   FBI file 100-448006-[?]; Chicago FBI file 100-35635-Sub B, 4/22/68. In FBI file 100-448006-626, 1/22/69, the bureau again emphasized that Wallace Muhammad was their choice, the only one who "could give proper guidance to the organization."
9   State of Illinois Medical Certificate of Death #605408 dated February 25, 1975: "The cause of death was congestive heart failure and arteriosclerotic disease."
10 Rassoull 1992:xxxiii.
11 Kashif 1975.
12 Muhammad, A., speech, 1986.
13 Rasheed, interview, 1987.
14 Muhammad, H. 1975.
15 He was released on parole on January 10, 1963. Muhammad, H. 1975.
16 Mamiya 1982:143.
17 Muhammad, E., speech, 1964.
18 FBI file 105-24822-202.
19 W. D. Muhammad as told to Gans and Lowe 1980.
20 Cited in Muhammad, H. 1975.
21 Muhammad, W. D. 1975a.
22 Muhammad, W. D. 1975b.
23 Muhammad, W. D. 1975c.
24 Muhammad, W. D. 1975d.
25 Muhammad, W. D. 1975e.
26 Muhammad, W. D. 1975f.

27   Muhammad, W. D. 1975g.
28   Muhammad, W. D. 1975h. Compare with Muhammad, W. D. 1975b.
29   Muhammad, W. D. 1975i.
30   Sharieff 1975.
31   Muhammad, W. D. 1975j.
32   Muhammad, W. D. 1975c; Muhammad, W. D. 1975k; Muhammad, W. D. 1975h.
33   Muhammad, W. D. 1975c.
34   Muhammad, W. D. 1975l.
35   Muhammad, W. D. 1975h.
36   Akbar 1975.
37   Muhammad, W. D. 1975k.
38   See, for instance, Muhammad, W. D. 1986.
39   Muhammad, M. F., *The NOI Student Enrollment Lesson.*
40   Muhammad, W. D. 1975f.
41   The NOI creed will be discussed in chapter 7.
42   Muhammad, W. D. 1975f.
43   This became standard in the *Muhammad Speaks* as well as in Minister Muhammad's lectures from the Muslim paper from August 1975.
44   Muhammad, W. D. 1976a.
45   Muhammad, W. D. 1976b. Compare with Muhammad, E. 1974a:36.
46   Muhammad, W. D. 1976b.
47   Ibid.
48   Sharif 1985:95.
49   Ibid., 71.
50   Muhammad, W. D. 1975m.
51   Ibid.
52   Muhammad, W. D. 1985:151. In January 1976, the *Jumah* prayer (Congregational Friday prayer) was instituted.
53   In November 1977, Wallace D. Muhammad led a delegation of 200 members on *hajj.*
54   Willoughby 1976.
55   Seifullah 1977.
56   Lincoln 1989b:354.
57   Mustafa 1988:91ff.
58   Muhammad, W. D. 5n; Muhammad, W. D. 1985:150.
59   Muhammad, James, 1975.
60   Muhammad, W. D. 1975n.
61   Lincoln 1973:226.
62   Cited in Goldman 1979:433.
63   Muhammad, W. D. 1976c.
64   Ibid.
65   Ibid.
66   Cited in Muwakkil 1977. Still, the imam promised prosperity to members who adhered to the true Islamic doctrine, and in the early 1990s, the community circulated a directory with more than 1,500 Muslim-owned companies (Barboza 1994:118).
67   Muhammad, W. D. 1976c.
68   Muhammad, W. D. 1985:152.

69 For the reader wishing to keep track on paper, the list of name changes is as follows: From *Mr. Muhammad Speaks* to: *Bilalin News,* November 14, 1975; *World Muslim News,* November 6, 1981; *American Muslim News,* May 14, 1982; *American Muslim Journal,* May 21, 1982; and finally (?) *Muslim Journal,* May 10, 1985.

70 Muhammad, W. D. 1985:151ff.

71 Muhammad, W. D. 1976d.

72 Muhammad, W. D. 1975o. The statement thus preceded the Bilalian declaration and is representative for the first transitional moves taken by Minister Muhammad.

73 Um'rani and Nurrudin 1977.

74 Muhammad, W. D. 1985:152. It was called the Committee for the Removal of All Images that Attempt to Portray the Divine (CRAID).

75 Muhammad, W. D. 1986:16.

76 Ibid., 5.

77 Kareem, interview, 1987.

78 Muhammad, W. D. 1986:18.

79 Ibid., 20.

80 Sharif 1985:123.

81 Ibid., 121ff.

82 The project failed, according to Brother Abdullah of the New York AMM, because a legal suit was initiated by heirs of Elijah Muhammad, claiming the property. The court placed the land in fallow awaiting the coming legal decision and was later taken by the probate court (Brother Abdullah, interview August 28, 1987: Imam Muhammad as cited in Mustafa 1988:59ff.).

83 Brothers Luqman Kareem and Abdul, interview, 1987. There already exists an all-Muslim village in the United States. The multiracial commune called Dar al-Islam is located on 8,500 acres of desert in Abiquiu, New Mexico (Barboza 1994:43).

84 Muhammad, W. D. 1976e. As with former innovations, this move was described as a fulfillment of Elijah Muhammad's vision.

85 Muhammad, W. D. 1977.

86 Smothers 1977.

87 Muhammad, W. D. 1977b.

88 Muhammad, W. D. 1977c.

89 Marable 1985:267. Compare with Jones, C-V. 1984.

90 Cited in Mustafa 1988:83.

91 Cited in ibid., 49. As early as 1979, the WCIW won a $22,000,000 contract to produce precooked combat rations for the United States Army (Marsh 1984:97).

92 Muhammad, W. D. 1986:22.

93 "Muhammad at White," 1977.

94 Barboza 1994:98. In June 1991, Siraj Wahhaj become the first Muslim to offer morning prayers for the United States House of Representatives.

95 Bilail 1977.

96 Sharif 1985:118.

97 Mustafa 1988:82f., 91f. Brother Rasoull, conversation, May 10, 1989.

98 Mustafa 1988:92.

99 Cited in ibid., 82.

100 Whitehurst 1980:229.
101 Mamiya 1982:138–52.
102 Weber 1976.
103 Mamiya 1983:245.
104 X, M. 1973 [1965]:159f.

6   The Resurrection of the Nation of Islam

1   The biographical sketch of Minister Farrakhan is based on tape-recorded inter-
     views in May 1989. Compare with Daniel 1993; "Farrakhan, Louis," 1992; "Fiery
     Leader," 1994.
2   Farrakhan, interview, 1989a.
3   Pace 1972; Farrakhan 1972; Craft 1972.
4   Walker 1974.
5   Adkins 1975.
6   Muhammad, W. D. 1975n.
7   Farrakhan, interview, 1989b.
8   Lemann 1991:81f.
9   Rassoull 1992:xvii–xxi.
10 Farrakhan, interview, 1989b.
11 See, for instance, Khasif 1975b; 4X, A. 1975a; 4X, A. 1975b; Muwakkil 1975.
12 Russell 1978; Madhubuti 1978.
13 "Muslims dedicate," 1989.
14 Muhammad, J. 1985:207.
15 Muhammad, L. 1977; Muhammad, J. 1985:207.
16 Muhammad, J. 1993.
17 Farrakhan, interview, 1989b. Compare with Farrakhan, speech, 1990a.
18 Muhammad, E., speech, 1972. Abass Rassoul (1992:xvi) confirmed that Muham-
     mad uttered those words. On July 16, 1972, the Messenger again called Farrakhan
     before the congregation saying that this is a man who is "full of the fire of the
     Holy Spirit of Allah" (Muhammad, E., speech, 1972b).
19 Farrakhan, interview, 1989a.
20   Muhammad, J. 1993b.
21 Farrakhan, interview, 1989a.
22 Farrakhan, interview, 1989b.
23 Louis and Khadidja Farrakhan (then Betsy) married on September 12, 1953. In
     1989, they had nine children and twenty-one grandchildren.
24 67X 1975; X, M. E. 1975.
25 "Wedding bells," 1990.
26 Farrakhan, speech, 1991.
27 Muhammad, J. 1985:14. Compare with Muhammad, J. 1984:81 and with Rassoull
     1992:xv.
28 Muhammad, J. 1984:80.
29 Muhammad, J. 1985:32.
30 The Holy Qur'an 20:29–32, in the translation of A. Yusuf Ali.
31 The Holy Qur'an 7:142, translated by A. Yusuf Ali.
32 The Holy Qur'an 20:90–97, translated by Yusuf Ali; commentary 2619.
33 "Message sent," 1975.
34 Muhammad, T. 1986:84.

35 Rassoull 1992:xxi.
36 Muhammad, J. 1984:80.
37 Farrakhan, interview, 1989a.
38 Farrakhan, interview, 1989a. Compare with Muhammad, J. 1991.
39 Farrakhan, interview, 1989a.
40 Muhammad, J. 1985:59.
41 The Holy Qur'an, 23:50, in the translation of A. Yusuf Ali.
42 Farrakhan, speech, 1989b.
43 Farrakhan, dinner conversation, May 21, 1989.
44 Farrakhan, 1992b [1973]:78.
45 Farrakhan, speech, 1989b.
46 Muhammad, J. 1984:84; X, E. 1990:30.
47 Muhammad, J. 1985:203.
48 Ibid., 2.
49 Ibid., 4.
50 Farrakhan, interview, 1989a.
51 Farrakhan, interview, 1989b.
52 Muhammad, J. 1985:164.
53 What is described is a summary of a story, told by Minister Farrakhan on May 18,
    1989, and recorded by the author.
54 Farrakhan, 1989:3.
55 Farrakhan, interview, 1989a.
56 See Psalms 82:6; John 10:34.
57 Muhammad, T. 1991. Farrakhan was lifted up into the heavens and entered a
    craft that docked with the Mother Ship where he heard the voice of Elijah Mu-
    hammad from a speaker, a course of events likened to Revelation 4, where John
    describes his vision: "After this I looked and, behold, a door was opened in
    heaven: and the first voice which I heard was as it were of a trumpet talking with
    me; which said, Come up hither, and I will show thee things which must be
    hereafter."
58 Muhammad, J. 1984:62.
59 Farrakhan, interview, 1989a.
60 Muhammad, J. 1985:229.
61 Farrakhan, interview, 1989b; Muhammad, A. A., speech, n.d.
62 Farrakhan, unrecorded dinner conversation, May 21, 1989. Jabril Muhammad
    wrote that "these two Messiahs are the Honorable Elijah Muhammad, and the
    Honorable Louis Farrakhan" (Muhammad, J. 1991b).
63 Farrakhan, speech, n.d.; Muhammad, J. 1991c.
64 Muhammad, J. 1991c.
65 Farrakhan, speech, 1988a.
66 Farrakhan, interview, 1989b.
67 "Emam Wallace," 1978.
68 Ibid.
69 Russell 1978.
70 Lee, S. 1992:55.
71 Lee, M. F. 1988:105.
72 Muhammad, D., interview, 1989.
73 Muhammad, W. D. 1986:4.
74 Jones, C-V. 1984.

75 Muhammad, W. D. 1986:4.
76 El-Amin, M. 1991.
77 Sharif 1985:97.
78 Muhammad, J. 1984:74 (originally written in May 1983).
79 Lincoln, C. Eric, conversation with author, May 23, 1989; Muhammad, Jabril, 1985:195.
80 Muhammad, Jabril, 1990a; Muhammad, Jabril, 1990b.
81 Muhammad, Jabril, 1990c.
82 Barboza 1994:135f., 143. Abass Rassoull, who believes that Elijah Muhammad has entrusted him to keep the NOI united and exactly as it was before 1975, argues that Imam Muhammad and Minister Farrakhan must "renounce the feud of vanity" and restore the past organization: "Minister Louis Farrakhan and Imam Warith D. Muhammad must bury their egos and personal animosity, and come together in a United Nation of Islam" (Rassoull 1992:xxxvii). This hope is hardly likely to be fulfilled, however.
83 Mount 1986; Re:Estate of Elijah Muhammad, Appellate Court of Illinois; Re:Estate of Elijah Muhammad, Appeal from the Circuit Court of Cook County. In this case, Marie Muhammad Farrakhan was one of the petitioners.
84 The Palace was sold for $500,000 (Barboza 1994:133).
85 "N.O.I.," 1988.
86 See, for instance, "National Center," 1988.
87 Muhammad, W. 1988.
88 Farrakhan, speech, 1989a.
89 "Muslims dedicate," 1989.
90 "19" is the mathematical code of the Qur'an (see chapter 7); "7" is a number laden with meaning as earlier described and Allah is the center 24 hours a day.
91 Farrakhan, record, 1984.
92 This is to be discussed in chapter 10, as is the way the NOI spread its ideas by the power of example through practical community improvement measures.
93 "See and Hear," 1995.
94 Lee, M. F. 1988:105f.
95 Muhammad, J. 1985:7.
96 Muhammad, R. 1992.
97 Farrakhan, 1994a.
98 *The Muhammad Mosque Provisional Constitution,* ratified 1986, p. 19.
99 Muhammad, D., interview, 1989: "FCN Progress!" 1994.
100 Farrakhan, 1983b.
101 Ibid., 1.
102 Ibid., 19.
103 Salaam 1994; Blumenthal 1994; X Curry 1994a.
104 See, for instance, "N.O.I. official," 1988; "African Liberation," 1989.
105 Addy 1994; X Curry 1992a; "Nation's Ghana," 1992; Jabir 1993; "Boston mosque," 1993. 2X Williams 1994.
106 Muhammad, James 1994e.

7 A Nation of Gods: The Creed of Black Islam

1 Muhammad, A., speech, 1986; Muhammad, A., 1993; Farrakhan, 1993; Muhammad, E. 1992:97f., 105.

2   Farrakhan, speech, 1990b.

3   Muhammad, A., speech, 1986. Concerning life on the other planets of the solar system, the earthly humans have most in common with the population on Mars. The original people keep pictures of the Martians and understand "how to communicate with them in their own language" (Muhammad, E. 1969c).

4   Muhammad, E. 1970b; Muhammad, E. 1992a:86, 117f.

5   Muhammad, Jabril 1985:25.

6   Muhammad, A., speech, 1986; Muhammad, Jabril 1985:224.

7   Farrakhan, 1991a. Here I must add that the NOI sources vary. Sometimes there are twenty-four imams plus the Supreme One; more often it is as described above: twenty-three imams plus the Supreme One.

8   Muhammad, J. 1993c.

9   Muhammad, E. 1974a:96f.

10 Ibid., 42.

11 Muhammad, E. 1974b:9f.; Farrakhan, 1991a.

12 Farrakhan, speech, 1991; Muhammad, E. 1974a:98, 119.

13 Muhammad, E. 1974a:98; compare with Muhammad, E. 1971.

14 Here the sources vary, sometimes stating the number composing the circle to be twenty-four and otherwise twelve. The reason is that only the inner circle of twelve greater imams were in the exact knowledge in full details, while the outer circle of lesser imams had the knowledge of God, but were not filled in absolutely perfectly (Muhammad, Jabril 1988).

15 Muhammad, E. 1974a:61; Farrakhan, speech, 1991.

16 Farrakhan, 1987.

17 Muhammad, E., speech, 1972c.

18 Muhammad, E., speech, 1972c; Muhammad, E. 1965:31.

19 Muhammad, Jabril 1985:24.

20 Muhammad, Jabril 1984:24f.

21 Muhammad, Jabril 1985:25, 224.

22 Ibid., 226.

23 Ibid., 25.

24 As is written in Daniel 12:4, "shut up the words, and seal the book, even to the time of the end."

25 Muhammad, E. 1965:110f.; Muhammad, E., speech, 1972d.

26 Muhammad, E., speech, 1972d; Farrakhan, speech, 1989c.

27 Farrakhan, speech, 1989c. The dialogue is (as the reader familiar with Islam undoubtedly will have noticed) a paraphrase of Qur'an 2:30.

28 Farrakhan, speech, 1989c.

29 Muhammad, E. 1965:113.

30 Farrakhan, speech, 1989c; Farrakhan, 1994b; Muhammad, E. 1992a:199ff.

31 Farrakhan, speech, 1989c.

32 Muhammad, K. A., speech, 1989.

33 Farrakhan, 1989a.

34 Farrakhan, speech, 1990c.

35 Schmidt 1980:128; Haywood 1944; Baigent and Leigh 1989:260f.

36 Robinson, J. J. 1989:223; MacNulty 1991:88.

37 Farrakhan, speech, 1990b.

38 Farrakhan, 1990d; cf. Muhammad, T. 1995:21ff.

39 The coming description is, if not otherwise noted, based on an interview with

Minister Farrakhan, May 18, 1989; Farrakhan, speech, 1989c; Farrakhan, speech, 1989d; Farrakhan, 1994c; Farrakhan, 1994b.

40   The Holy Qur'an 3:110, translated by Yusuf Ali.

41   Farrakhan, 1991b.

42   Farrakhan, speech, 1989c. Compare with Farrakhan, speech, 1988a.

43   Farrakhan, 1989 [1987]:84.

44   Muhammad, D., interview, 1989.

45   Jabril Muhammad wrote that "whites who accept Minister Farrakhan will be saved" (Muhammad, Jabril 1991b).

46   Farrakhan, interview, 1989a.

47   Farrakhan, speech, 1992; Muhammad, E. 1965:117f. Compare with Genesis 3:24.

48   Farrakhan, speech, 1989c; Farrakhan, speech, 1992. Compare with Robinson, J. J. 1989:204f.

49   Farrakhan, speech, 1989c.

50   Farrakhan, speech, 1989c.

51   Muhammad, E. 1965:121; Farrakhan, speech, 1989c.

52   Genesis 1:28.

53   Farrakhan, speech, 1990b.

54   Farrakhan, speech, 1992.

55   Farrakhan, speech, 1990b.

56   Elijah Muhammad (1965:107) wrote: "The Indian part of the name [Red Indians] must refer to the name of the country from which they came, India. The all-wise Allah said that they came here 16,000 years ago and that they were exiled from India for breaking the law of Islam." The Native Americans are thus part of the original people, and Columbus, who as Master Farad Muhammad was half-original, prefigured what was to come when he encountered the Red Lost and Found Nation of Islam in the Wilderness of North America (Muhammad, T. 1992).

57   Farrakhan, speech, 1990e.

58   Muhammad, Jabril 1993d. John Hawkins is infamous as one of the first slave traffickers between Africa and the West Indies. Already Marcus Garvey focused on him as a symbol for the slave trade (Garvey 1974 [1913]:79).

59   See, for instance, Muhammad, E. 1966a.

60   Farrakhan, speech, 1989c.

61   Esposito 1988:93.

62   Farrakhan, speech, 1989a.

63   Farrakhan, speech, 1990c.

64   Farrakhan, speech, 1989a.

65   Muhammad, A., speech, 1986.

66   Muhammad, T. 1986:122.

67   Muhammad, A., speech, 1986.

68   Farrakhan, 1991c.

69   Minister Ava Muhammad (speech 1986) said that Farad's mother was a Muslim descendant of the few female whites left behind in Mecca when the whites were exiled to Caucasus. Elijah Muhammad (speech 1973) said that Alphonse Muhammad took his wife from "the hills" in order to produce a saviour. His first child was a girl, and a female could not fill the role of a saviour. Alphonse then produced another one and this time it was a son, and he named him Farad. Minister Farrakhan (speech 1991) stated that the mother of Master Farad was "a

woman from the Caucasus mountains," which perhaps also is the idea indicated by Elijah Muhammad's "hills."

70 Farrakhan, speech, 1991.
71 I Thessalonians 5:2; II Peter 3:10; Muhammad E., speech, 1973.
72 Muhammad, A., speech, 1986.
73 Isaiah 9:2 (Revised Standard Version).
74 Muhammad, E. 1973:69.
75 Farrakhan, speech, 1989b.
76 Muhammad, A., speech, 1986.
77 Italics included in the interpretation by Yusuf Ali.
78 Farrakhan, speech, 1990d.
79 Farrakhan, speech, 1990f.
80 Muhammad, E., speech, 1972c.
81 The Glorious Qur'an 3:86, from the translation by Muhammad Marmaduke Pick-thall.
82 Muhammad, Jabril 1985:17f.
83 Farrakhan, speech, 1990f.
84 Farrakhan, speech, 1989b.
85 Ezekiel 1 and 10.
86 Muhammad, E. 1965:291.
87 Muhammad, E. 1973:240f.
88 Muhammad, E., speech, 1972e.
89 Muhammad, E. 1969d.
90 Muhammad, E., speech, 1972e.
91 Mostly the number is said to be 1,500 as in Muhammad, E. 1965:291, but at least once they are said to be 15,000 (Muhammad, E., speech, 1972e).
92 Muhammad, E., speech, 1972e.
93 Muhammad, E. 1966b.
94 This is discussed in Muhammad, T. 1986:64.
95 Muhammad, E. 1965:294.
96 This is to be discussed further in chapter 10.
97 See, for example, "State of emergency," 1991.
98 Muhammad, E. 1965:270.
99 The words "expectations and disappointments" should not be understood as though the members necessarily looked forward to the final battle with joy. A serious belief in a cataclysm of this form would, if reflected upon, probably lead to mixed feelings of a kind expressed by Sister Mildred when interviewed by Essien-Udom (1962:142): "I guess I would be glad provided I was living a completely righteous life. But then it would be a dreadful day. I would be sad to leave my parents and close relatives behind to be destroyed. It would be a dreadful day for me and I would say, give them one more chance. I would search myself to see if I am ready. Maybe I would need another day, a week or a month."
100 Festinger, Riecken, and Schachter 1964:216.
101 Ibid., 139.
102 Ibid., 169.
103 This argument is partly built on Geels and Wickström 1989:303–20.
104 The Second Coming of Christ was, according to the followers of William Miller in New England, to be expected sometime between March 21, 1843, and March 21, 1844. When these dates passed without Christ reappearing, the movement ac-

cepted with renewed enthusiasm a prediction by Samuel S. Snow, that the date of the Second Coming would be October 22, 1844. Businessmen closed down their shops; on one of them a sign read, "This shop is closed in honor of the King of Kings who will appear about the 20th of October" (Ljungdahl 1969:128). The Millerite movement collapsed when nothing happened, but was renewed in different sects, one of them being the Seventh Day Adventists, which taught the prophecy to have been correct although misunderstood. The Coming of Christ, his Judgment and Cleansing had occurred, but in heaven. He has now entered a sacred realm in heaven to fulfill his duties and will, after completion of these duties, return to Earth to judge the wicked and save the faithful. The Seventh Day Adventists have been largely successful in preaching this gospel (Wilson, B. 1970; Festinger and Schachter 1964).

105   The Jehovah's Witnesses proclaim, like the NOI, the year 1914 as fateful for the world. For Russell, leader of the movement which at that time still was known as the Watchtower Bible and Tract Society (the name Jehovah's Witness was revealed first in 1931), it was the year marking the beginning of the Millennium. When nothing happened, a rationalization was adopted claiming that the Kingdom of Christ was established in heaven that year. Though a temporary numerical setback occurred, the failure led in the long run to renewed proselytizing, and the small movement is today global with members numbered in the millions.

106   Hjärpe 1994:91.

107   de Lama and Moseley 1991; Muwakkil 1991.

108   Farrakhan, L., speech, January 14, 1991, cited in "So, you think," 1991.

109   "So, you think," 1991.

110   This is partly derived from Revelation 8:10–11, Matthew 24:29, and Imamiyya eschatology (Momen 1985:169).

111   Muhammad, T. 1991b.

112   Matthew 24:7.

113   Matthew 25:31–33.

114   Matthew 25:41.

115   Farrakhan, speech, 1990f.

116   Essien-Udom 1962:139.

117   Public Enemy, "Countdown to Armageddon," 1988.

118   Farrakhan, interview, 1989b. Compare with Mark 13:26.

119   Muhammad, T. 1986:90.

120   Muhammad, E. 1974a:126f.

121   Ibid., 110.

122   Revelation 21:1–5.

123   Muhammad, E. 1974a:99. Emphasis his.

124   Muhammad, E. 1965:120.

125   Ibid., 133.

126   Muhammad, K. A., speech, 1989.

127   Muhammad, E. 1965:121.

128   Compare with Genesis 3:24.

129   Farrakhan, speech, 1992. Farrakhan elaborated, "You say, a righteous God would never make the devil. Why not? He created us and everything about us is atoms. In the atom is positive and negative charges. God created opposites. He started in darkness and created light. He fought against darkness until He pushed darkness

back. Can God decree that the devil should have a season and then allow a devil to work for Him? If God gave evil a season, He had to bring forth a vessel that would facilitate evil. 'I am going to place a ruler in the earth,' God said. [The angels/originals asked], 'What will you place in it, except that which will create mischief and cause the shedding of blood?' White people had a Divine job to do for God. What was their job? It was to turn the earth into a veritable hell and begin to burn humanity with a certain kind of fire and would purify the human being and get the human family ready for the Kingdom of God."

130 Farrakhan, speech, 1990b. The Qur'anic verse referred to is 15:28, which is central indeed for most black Islamic groups. The different Qur'an translations pose a problem here, as not all of them actually specify the color of the mud or clay used. Yusuf Ali has God "to create man, from sounding clay. From mud moulded into shape," and is thus never used in this context. Pickthall's version reads, "I am creating a mortal out of potter's clay of dark mud altered." Imam Isa's translation reads, "I will create a mortal being (Adam) from black mud (clay) shaped and fashioned."

131 Farrakhan, speech, 1990b.

132 Farrakhan, speech, 1990e; Farrakhan, interview, 1989a.

133 Farrakhan, interview, 1989a.

134 Holy Qur'an 7:12, as translated by Yusuf Ali.

135 Farrakhan 1990b. Compare with Farrakhan 1988a.

136 Muhammad, E. 1965:123f.

137 For the non-anthropologically educated reader: "emic" means briefly "from the actor's perspective" and "etic" means "from the observer's perspective"; the former is the actor's own models, ideas and his/hers understanding of his/her own behavior and the latter is the understanding a researcher will form on the basis of collected and analyzed data, such as observed behavior.

138 Muhammad, E. 1965:112.

139 Farrakhan, speech, 1992.

140 So far, I have only once heard a rationalization effort of this kind, in the speech referred to above.

141 Muhammad, E. 1965:73f.

142 Muhammad, E. 1974a:97.

143 Before the present era, the closed circle of divine scientists had a considerably longer life span than those living in the era of evil. During the past 6000 years, the average was "about 500 years" (Muhammad, Jabril 1993c).

144 His power and wisdom is, according to Elijah Muhammad (1974a:97), envisioned in the Holy Scriptures: "The Bible and the Holy Qur'an both verify . . . that one day a Wiser God than Them all will exist in a new Universe."

145 Muhammad, E. 1965:4.

146 Ibid., 8.

147 Ibid., 5.

148 Ibid., 6.

149 Muhammad, A., speech, 1986.

150 Muhammad, E. 1965:6.

151 Ibid., 7; emphasis his.

152 Ibid., 72; emphasis mine.

153 See, for instance, Muhammad, E. 1965:1–4, 9–13.

154   Muhammad, Jabril 1985:25.
155   Farrakhan 1990d.
156   Farrakhan, speech, 1991.
157   Farrakhan, speech, 1990d.
158   Muhammad, E. 1974a:56.
159   See, for example, Farrakhan 1991d.
160   Muhammad, Jabril 1988b. Jabril Muhammad, elaborating on "the fall" and the opening of the door to the path of Resurrection, admits that "we did not receive detailed information about just what led to that which occurred 66 trillion years ago."
161   Farrakhan, speech, 1986a.
162   Farrakhan 1987.
163   Muhammad, Jabril 1988b.
164   Farrakhan 1991e. "Does God die?" Farrakhan continues. "Just the physical. But when the physical goes another one will stand and the wisdom comes right through that one, and he is deputized to carry out the wisdom of the Originator."
165   Compare Muhammad, Jabril 1988a with Muhammad, Jabril 1988b and Farrakhan, speech, 1991.
166   Muhammad, E. 1974a:57; emphasis his.
167   Farrakhan, interview, 1989a.
168   Farrakhan 1991d.
169   Prince Akeem Muhammad, interviewed in Spady and Eure 1991:299.
170   See, for example the reasoning in Farrakhan, speech, 1980; and Muhammad, Jabril 1988c.
171   Compare Muhammad, Jabril 1993e with Muhammad, Jabril 1988a and 1988c.
172   Farrakhan, speech, 1991.
173   Muhammad, E. 1992a:118.
174   Nathaniel 1972; Muhammad, E. 1974a:49; Muhammad, E. 1992a:71.
175   As for example in Farrakhan, speech, 1990g.
176   Farrakhan, speech, 1989a; Farrakhan, speech, 1989b.
177   See, for example, Muhammad, Ava 1993.
178   Boyer 1992:307–11. This is an interesting development in itself. In the sixteenth to the eighteenth centuries, prophecy speculation and research attracted some of the most prominent intellectuals of their time, e.g., Milton, Newton, Leibniz, Napier, and the leaders of New England and powerful heads of theological seminars and universities such as Harvard, Yale, and Princeton. In the nineteenth and early twentieth centuries, prophecy ceased to attract most intellectuals, but could still engage officially prominent individuals. By contrast, the late twentieth century premilleniarian speculation attraction ceased almost entirely to become a concern for nonintellectuals and laypersons.
179   Boyer 1992:310.
180   Farrakhan, speech, 1990b.
181   Muhammad, D. 1993a.
182   Muhammad, Ava 1993.
183   Farrakhan, interview, 1989a.
184   Farrakhan, speech, 1990b. Compare with Farrakhan, speech, 1989c and Farrakhan, speech, 1988a.
185   Farrakhan, speech, 1990d.

186 The first publication of this department, *The Secret Relationship between Blacks and Jews,* is discussed in chapter 9.

187 Farrakhan, conversation with author, May 19, 1989.

188 Muhammad, T. 1986:81.

189 Ibid., 16. Rashad Khalifa himself claims that he discovered that "19" is the Qur'anic code and God's stamp on his Creation in January 1974. The year is important as 19 prefixes 74, which points to Surah 74 where God hid the code in verse 30. In the Islamic calender, the year of discovery was 1393. As Muhammad Ibn Abdullah began to receive the Revelation in 13 B. H., this makes 1393 + 13 = 1406, or 19×74, again displaying the Code and the year of discovery (Khalifa 1989:615).

190 Muhammad, T. 1993a.

191 Muhammad, T. 1986:17.

192 Haddad and Smith 1993:139f. Masjid Tucson, headquarters of the "United Submitters International," is situated on 739 E. 6th Street, Tucson, AZ, 85719. The USI publishes a monthly bulletin first called *Muslim Perspective,* then *Submission Perspective,* and then *Submitters Perspective,* and the Masjid Tucson publishes a monthly named *Muslim Perspective.*

193 Khalifa 1981a:86, commentary to the translation of the Qur'anic verse 6:21–24. In Appendix 16 (1981a:507) to his Qur'an translation Khalifa wrote, "The computerized study of the Quran's numerical code generated physical, indisputable proof, showing the following":

1. That the Quran is complete, perfect, and shall be the sole source of religious statutes and commandments;

2. that Hadith, Sunna, and regulations made up by various "imams" are all false doctrines sponsored by Satan, though in accordance with God's will; and

3. that these false doctrines are permitted by God as a necessary test to distinguish the true believers from the false believers; the true believers will uphold Quran, the whole Quran, and nothing but the Quran.

194 Khalifa 1981a:471.

195 Ibid., 476.

196 Khalifa published his initial findings in 1976 in the *Miracle of the Quran: Significance of the Mysterious Alphabets.* With *The Computer Speaks,* Khalifa reached a wider audience.

197 Quran: The Final Scripture, 1981. The translation has been revised twice, in 1989 and 1992, the latter published after Khalifa's death.

198 Khalifa 1982.

199 Translation by Muhammad Marmaduke Pickthall; emphasis mine. In Khalifa's own translation it reads, "This was sent down by the One who knows the SECRETS in the heavens and the earth."

200 Khalifa 1981a:471. Khalifa lists a number of facts to prove his theory, divided into "Simple Facts" and "Intricate Facts." As a service to the interested reader, I will quote the list of nineteen "simple facts" from Khalifa 1981b:199f.:

1, The opening statement of Qur'an consists of 19 Arabic alphabets; 2, The famous words that constituted the first Quranic revelation were 19 words; 3, The last Quranic revelation was 19 words; 4, The Quran consists of 114 chapters, i.e., 19 × 6; 5, First Chapter in the order of revelation is placed in position number 19 from the end of the Quran; 6, First chapter in the order of revelation (Chapter 96) consists of 19 verses; 7, The first Quranic revelation (the famous 19 words) is made up of 76 letters, and $76 = 19 \times 4$; 8, The first chapter in the order of revelation consists of 285 letters, i.e., 19×15; 9, The first word in the Quran's opening statement occurs in the whole Quran exactly 19 times; 10, The second word of the opening statement (Allah) occurs in the whole Quran 2698 times, or 19×142; 11, The third word of the opening statement (al-Rahmaan) occurs in Quran 57 times, or 19×3; 12, The fourth word of the opening statement (al-Raheem) is found in the Quran 114 times, or 19×6; 13, The opening statement is missing from chapter 9, but this deficiency is compensated in chapter 27, verse 30. This makes the frequency of the opening statement 114, or 19×6; 14, The distance between the missing "Bismillah" of chapter 9 and the extra 'Bismillah' of chapter 27 is exactly 19 chapters; 15, The second Quranic revelation consisted of 38 words, or 19×2; 16, The third Quranic revelation consisted of 57 words, which is three multiples of 19; 17, The fourth Quranic revelation brought the number 19 itself, and declared that anyone who claims that Quran is 'man-made' will be proven wrong by means of the number 19; 18, The fifth revelation brought the first complete chapter, (The Opener—al-Fatihah) and this revelation positioned the opening statement (which is the foundation of this code) directly following the number 19 of the 4th revelation; 19, Why the number 19? Because this number declares, loud and clear, the Qurans theme. The Qurans theme is "God is One." As it turns out, the number 19 equals "one." The Arabic word for "one" is "waahhid," and the numerical value of this word is 19.

201   Khalifa 1989a:640. Khalifa lists a number of Qur'anic instances said to prove his claim. The root word of the name Rashad, Rashada, is mentioned 19 times; the word Rashad occurs in 40:29 and 38:26; the word Khalifa "vicegerent" is a well-known Qur'anic concept; adding the sum of all surahs and verse numbers where all Rashada and Khalifa occur, add up to 1493 (19×77); the total of all surahs and verses where only "Rashada" occur is 1369 ($19 \times 72 + 1$) and for the word "Khalifa" 94 ($19 \times 5 - 1$)—a fact that, still according to Rashad Khalifa, demonstrates that they have to be seen together, as Rashad Khalifa and not just any Rashad or any Khalifa.

202   Khalifa 1989a:639. This event, according to Khalifa, occurred in Zul-Hijjah 3, 1391/December 21, 1971. His soul was taken to a place in the universe, where he was placed sitting. God had all previous prophets show themselves as they had appeared when on their earthly mission, dressed in their respective mode. Khalifa was introduced as the Messenger of the Covenant and all prophets greeted him in an atmosphere of mutual respect and joy. He was struck by the strong resemblance between the prophet Abraham and his own family, indicating a direct descendancy. The date of this most unique experience reveal God's stamp, as the month (12), day (3), and year (1391) add up to $1406 = 19 \times 74 =$ the number of years from the revelation of the Qur'an to the revelation of the code.

The opening verse of Surah 17, "Glory to (God) who did take His Servant for a Journey by night from the Sacred Mosque to the Farthest Mosque," is the point of departure for numerous legends describing prophet Muhammad's soul journey to Jerusalem and the Seven Heavens, where he was introduced to the previous prophets (for an early account, see Ibn Ishaq 1967 [1956]:181–87).

203 Haddad and Smith 1993:150.

204 Khalifa 1989a:v, 639f., 642.

205 Cited in Haddad and Smith 1993:151. Khalifa (1989b) intended to summon all believers: Muslims, Jews, Christians, Buddhists, Hindus, and Sikhs. To reach a universal brotherhood of religionists, one must concentrate on the common link, Khalifa argued, identifying this as the belief in the Creator alone. A Muslim is one who submits to the will of God which is why "one can be a Muslim Jew, a Muslim Christian, a Muslim Buddhist, a Muslim Hindu or a Muslim Muslim."

206 These three were President Numieri of Sudan, President Mahmoud Ali of South Yemen, and President Bourguiba of Tunisia. In August 1988, Khalifa sent a message to "presidents and kings" in the Islamic world, announcing the glad news that he was sent as a messenger to save the Muslims (Haddad and Smith 1993:151–57).

207 Khalifa (1989c) wrote: "After I die millions of believers will know that I represent the Messiah the Jews have been waiting for, the Christ Christians have been expecting, the Mehdi the Muslims have been praying for . . . I am the Messenger of the Covenant."

208 Inserted "Preface" to Khalifa 1992:xi; Haddad and Smith, 1993:137. In February 1993, the police arrested seven members of the militant black Muslim organization Fuqra and charged D. Williams and E. Flinton for masterminding the plot to kill Khalifa. Fuqra had since four years been under FBI surveillance. Colorado police already prior to the deed found evidence for Fuqra's preparations to take Khalifa's life, including surveillance notes of the mosque and police patrolling in the area, different murder methods and photos of Khalifa with followers. Further evidence is said to have been disclosed when in October 1989, police raided a 101-acre compound of the Fuqra used as a military training camp and confiscated a huge arsenal, including AK-47s, M-16s, and M-14s. The police reportedly warned Khalifa of the plans against his life. Whether the arrested were the actual assailants or not is, to my knowledge, still an open question (Durte 1993).

209 Khalifa 1981a:207. This year, 2280, is, of course, a multiple of 19 (19×120).

210 Muhammad, T. 1990a and 1990b. This was also the opinion of Minister Farrakhan who, in a recorded interview of May 11, 1989, suggested the year 2001 as the year of Armageddon.

211 Muhammad, T. 1986:72.

212 Ibid., 80. See also Muhammad T. 1994 [1981]:9.

213 Muhammad, T. 1986:70.

214 Ibid., 87.

215 Nor is it a coincidence that the name of the author, Mattias Gardell, contains fourteen letters.

216 Muhammad, T. 1986:102. The name Muhammad was also added to Minister Farrakhan's.

217 Khalifa 1982:243. Wahid spelled Waw (=6), Alif (=1), Ha (=8) and Dal (=4), which equals 19 (6+1+8+4).

218 Muhammad, T. 1986:118. The methods implied differ as Wahid is 19 digits when the letters are reduced to their number value and then resolved individually, while Master Fard Muhammad contains 19 letters (and, as the observant reader undoubtedly will have noticed, Tynetta Muhammad does not call him Farad in this context). If one examines "Mahdi," we find the word "ahd," meaning "one" in the middle. Take the letter "M," turn it upside down and get a "W." Reverse the

two last letters and you get "id" instead of "di." Then spell the word given after these changes are made and Mahdi turns to Wahid, with the numerical value 19, and the cover title for God's coming in the latter days is revealed.

219   Muhammad, T. 1988.

220   This should, of course, not be understood as a direct equation between the theories of Isaac Luria Ashkenazi (1534–72) and those of the Nation of Islam. Isaac Luria was in many respects an innovative Kabbalistic thinker, developing the basic theological and cosmogonical speculations of the earlier Kabbalah. In the Lurianic Kabbalah, the Infinite En-Sof extended without end and he could only manifest after he had first withdrawn, or contracted (*zimzum*) into himself, thus abandoning a region from himself to emptiness, leaving room for the subsequent worlds he created. Into the empty vacuum, named *tehiru*, the worlds were created by a repetitive dualistic process involving the two principles act and react; retraction and emanation; inhale and exhale. The supreme manifestation of the first ray of divine light penetrating primordial space is termed "the Primordial Man," Adam Qadmon. When this divine vessel in the form of a human broke, elements of the divine "fell" into *qellipah,* the sphere of evil. By *tiqqun,* a process of restoration or reintegration, the ideal order is restored by the help of man. When Adam, the first earthly man was created the restoration process of the supernal-cosmic Anthropos was near completion. But Adam, the earthly anthropos, repeated the primordial catastrophe and "fell" with the result that the divine sparks sank even deeper into *qellipah,* and the restoration process had to begin all over again (Scholem 1973; Scholem 1974).

221   Cited in Momen 1985:148. Compare with the following statement by Tynetta Muhammad (1994 [1982b]:ii): "The Likeness of His Light is a Messenger that He makes from Himself in His Own Image to Reflect His Divine Light and Power, Force and Will. . . . The Messenger becomes, then, the Second Self of God."

222   Momen 1985:149.

223   Haddad and Smith 1991.

224   Corbin 1983:42; Daftary 1990:139f. In this context it can be interesting to note that Tynetta Muhammad (1993a) has come "to recognize a pattern" in the intervals of years between significant events: a turn is taken every seventh year, which leads her to conclude: "The Nation of Islam stands today at a most critical turning point in our history from its beginning in 1930. If we continue tracing back in time in intervals of 7 from the year 2000 and 2001 A.D. to 1930, we have exactly 10 cycles equaling 70 years."

225   Corbin 1983:43–47.

226   Ibid., 43–46, 69ff., 82ff.

227   Ibid., 50.

228   Ibid., 45f.

229   Baldwick 1989:84f.; see also Momen 1985:208f.; Schoun 1976:102f.

230   Goodrick-Clarke 1992:18ff.

231   For the ideas and developments of Rastafari, see Barret 1988; Campell 1987; Cashmore 1983 [1979]; Jacob 1985. The first is a comprehensive academic study of the movement in Jamaica, the second a study by a black Jamaican political activist and teacher, the third an academic study of the movement in England, and the fourth a book written from the believer's perspective.

232   Lanternari 1965 [1963]:111. In Smohalla's vision, God created the Native Ameri-

cans. From them came, successively, the French, then the priests, much later the Americans, then King George's men (i.e., the English), and finally the blacks.

233   Steinmetz 1953:135.

234   For a study of black Masons, see Muraskin 1975.

235   Essien-Udom 1962:140n. 45. This theme is, of course, not restricted to black Masons and the Nation of Islam, but is recurrent in most black nationalist religions.

236   Boyer 1992.

237   Barker 1989:148.

238   Man's ability to tune in the thoughts of others will be discussed in chapter 8.

8   The Sun of Islam Will Rise in the West

1   Esposito 1988:68. For a problematization of this distinction, see the discussion in Hedin 1996.

2   Esposito 1988:69.

3   The Alawiyya began after the Imamate of Ali al-Hadi, the tenth imam of the Shi'i Imamiyya branch, through the teachings of Muhammad ibn Nusayr an-Namiri. He has been accused of elevating Ali al-Hadi (and by some of elevating Ali ibn Abu Talib) to be God, although others rebut these charges, saying he only proclaimed himself as the *Bab* (Gate) to Ali al-Hadi while his son Muhammad was regarded as the Mahdi. Later writers relate the claims of Mahdiship to the son of Hasan al-Askari, thereby accommodating the Alawiyya to the common Imamiyya line of acknowledged imams. During the Hamdanid dynasty, the Alawiyya grew through the work of Husayn ibn Hamdan al-Khasibi and established strongholds in what is presently Syria and Turkey. The sect has recurrently suffered severe repression by different rulers, from the Crusaders to the Ottomans. An aborted attempt was made by the French occupants to establish a separate Alawi state in western Syria after World War I, but the sect soon grew to political prominence in Syria and is presently powerful through the regime of the Alawi President Hafiz Al-Assad.

4   Lincoln 1973:183.

5   Curtis 1994:56.

6   Statement published in the *Pittsburgh Courier,* January 10, 1959; cited in Essien-Udom 1962:312.

7   On several occasions, feuds between the Nation of Islam and black mainstream Muslim organizations and members became violent. People who were perceived as attacking or defaming the Messenger of Allah were brutalized by more or less freelancing FOI soldiers, competing mosques in the black community were burned to the ground, and people feared for their lives. See, for instance the stories of Murad Muhammad and Sulaiman Abdul-Haqq published in Barboza 1994:150f., 153f.

8   Mamiya, Lawrence, unpublished manuscript, 1987; Marable 1986 [1984]:178. According to Khaalis, he joined the NOI in 1951 and served as national secretary in 1956 and broke with the NOI in 1958. The NOI stated that his highest position was as head of the University of Islam in Chicago, while FBI files confirm his position as national secretary under Malcolm X (Brandon 1973; Evanzz 1992:202).

9   Abdul-Rauf, prominent spokesman for the American Muslims and director of the

Islamic Center in Washington, D.C., defended the NOI, assuring "that the whole Muslims world which includes 700 million is behind you [Elijah Muhammad]." In reaction to this, the mainstream paper *Al-Islam* called for his ouster because of his support for the "heretical Black Muslims" (Wheeler 1972).

10   Marable 1986 [1984]:178.

11   Ali, J. 1973.

12   Hazziez 1973. Compare with Shah 1973b.

13   Wedad 1973; Holy Qur'an 16:116.

14   Lewis and Robinson, 1973; Reed 1991.

15   Kashif 1974b; Marable 1986 [1984]:178.

16   Muwakkil, interview, 1994. According to Muwakkil, the group was based in Philadelphia and had affiliations in Mosque #25, Newark, New Jersey (see also chapter 4). In 1973, members of the group became convinced that its minister, James Shabazz, stood in the way of the "New World of Islam," in which the Honorable Elijah Muhammad would be fully deified and revered as Allah. After they had shot Minister Shabazz to death, an internal war broke out. Police found two decapitated bodies in a lot close to the home of the late minister. The New World of Islam group, nicknamed the Death Angels, reportedly conspired to take control of the mosque but the plot was uncovered by the police (Barboza 1994: 115). According to Muwakkil, the group is still around and has been responsible for the slaying of a few other defamers of Elijah Muhammad.

17   Hamaas Abdul Khaalis argued that Allah had taken command through his soldiers, demanding that those guilty of the 1973 massacre be delivered to the Hanafis. In addition they wanted to stop the showing of a newly released movie, *Mohammad, Messenger of God,* to find Malcolm X's assassin, and to summon all the Arab ambassadors. After meeting the ambassadors from Egypt, Iran, and Pakistan, who sat down and discussed the Qur'an with him, Hamaas surrendered (Greider and Harwood 1977a and 1977b; Barboza 1994:215).

18   "Notice," 1975.

19   Lincoln 1984:163.

20   Prominent American *ulama,* such as Muhammad Abdul-Rauf, praised the evolution of the reformation process (Willoughby 1977). Former opposers, such as the Pakistani Ahmadiyya, sent condolences upon the death of the Messenger, which was described as "a loss of dynamic leadership," after Pakistani dailies had carried the news of his death (Ahmed 1975).

21   Farrakhan, speech, 1990g.

22   Farrakhan, speech, 1984a.

23   Farrakhan, interview, 1989b.

24   Farrakhan, speech, 1984a.

25   Farrakhan states that Elijah Muhammad's reasons for choosing December as the month for his followers to fast were justified and wise, at a time when the NOI needed to distance itself from the disgraceful and disrespectful pagan worship of a righteous servant of God as God. "Now," Farrakhan wrote, "the followers of Elijah Muhammad, having matured in our understanding, are now fasting with the entire Islamic world" (Farrakhan 1988a).

26   Farrakhan, speech, 1973.

27   Farrakhan, speech, 1980.

28   Only to clarify: this does not change the NOI creed. The NOI still believes that

Allah came in the person of Master Farad Muhammad, whose Last Messenger is Elijah Muhammad, the exalted Messiah. Such an open declaration of faith can still be heard, although less frequently than before.

29   Farrakhan, speech, 1990h. This is not to say that other ministers adopt the same approach. Minister A. A. Muhammad said in 1993: "In the name of Allah, the Beneficent the Most Merciful Who came to us in the Person of Master Farad Muhammad and in the name of the Messiah the Exalted Christ, the Most Honorable Elijah Muhammad as your brother and helper to their Representative, Minister Louis Farrakhan in the Last Cause, I greet you with the spirit of the greetings of peace and paradise, *as-Salaam Alaikum*."

30   Farrakhan, interview, 1989b.

31   Farrakhan, speech, 1990g.

32   Farrakhan, speech, 1984a.

33   Farrakhan, speech, 1990g.

34   Ibid.

35   Muhammad, E. 1974a:89.

36   "What is Islam?" 1967.

37   Muhammad, E. 1974a:89.

38   10X 1972.

39   Farrakhan, personal information, May 19, 1989.

40   Farrakhan, interview, 1989a. This recalls the doctrines of "the hidden Imam" of shi'i Islam, especially of its Imamiyya variety, but the use and definition of the concept differ considerably. According to Imamiyya doctrine, the twelfth imam, passing through the stage of "the lesser occultation," reached the present stage, "the greater occultation," in the year 329/941. From then on, Muhammad Ibn Hasan, identified as al-Mahdi, lives incognito in the community of believers, probably in the body of a scholar. His life has been extended by God and his followers await his remanifestation at the end of time when evil shall be overcome and the earth be filled with justice and equality.

The NOI and the Imamiyya doctrines both believe that al-Mahdi is hidden due to the hostility of his enemies and their plotting against his life. The NOI and the Imamiyya further share the idea of al-Mahdi as "a living reality and a particular person living among us in flesh and blood," participating in the suffering and hope of the believers (as-Sadr 1980:21), and they both eagerly await his return. But they differ in one essential respect, making the NOI more similar to Imamiyya during the "lesser occultation" period than in its present phase. Imamiyya of today do not know exactly where al-Mahdi is or under what name he lives hidden, and can therefore not communicate with him. The NOI knows exactly where he is, on the Mother Ship, and Farrakhan can confer with him and act as an intermediary agent, a role similar to the one of the four *abwab* "gates" or *Sufara*, "ambassadors" of the hidden imam in the era of the lesser occultation (255/868–329/941). (See Momen 1985:161–83; as-Sadr 1980; Hussain 1982.)

41   Farrakhan, interview, 1989b.

42   Esposito 1988:129, 169f., 178; Esposito 1992:55f.; Enayat 1982:76, 101.

43   Farrakhan, speech, 1990g.

44   Farrakhan, speech, 1990c and 1990f.

45   Farrakhan, speech, 1990f.

46   Ibid.

47   Farrakhan, speech, 1990g.
48   Farrakhan, speech, 1990f.
49   Baghdadi 1993.
50   Farrakhan, interview, 1989a.
51   Farrakhan, 1990i.
52   Farrakhan, speech, 1990g.
53   For a study of this subject, see Lewis 1990.
54   Farrakhan, speech, 1990c.
55   Farrakhan, interview, 1989a.
56   The following account is based on Davis 1987; Ayoub 1987; Bearman 1986; Gardell 1992b.
57   Bearman 1986:2.
58   Muhammad Ali ibn al-Sanusi (1787–1859) was born in Algeria in a family claiming descent from Ali Ibn Abu Talib and Fatima, daughter of the prophet Muhammad. He studied Islamic jurisprudence in Cairo and Mecca. In the holy city, he became a disciple of the Sufi reformer Ahmad ibn Idris who called for the purification of Sufism and a return to the pristine Islam, purged from the distortions of conservative mainstream *ulama*. Upon the death of his teacher, al-Sanusi moved to present-day Libya, where he founded the Sanusiyya. The militant activist brotherhood created a network of desert settlements, or Sufi lodges, across the Sahel region and became involved in the resistance against French colonialism in North and West Africa.
59   Davis, J. 1987:29.
60   In 1954 the largest export industry was iron waste from the World War II desert armies.
61   His father Mohammed Abdul Salem Ben Hamid Ben Mohammed, known as Abu Meniar, and his mother, Aisha, were both nomads from the Berber tribe Qadhdhafa. Brought up as a Bedouin, Mu'ammar was sent to primary school at Sirte. He slept in the mosque as his father could not afford lodging expenses. As one of only four Berber Bedouin pupils in school, Mu'ammar was the victim of prevalent prejudice. In 1956 his family moved to Sabha, the main town of the Fezzan district, to give Mu'ammar the possibility of receiving a secondary education.
   In Fezzan, Mu'ammar Qadhdhafi got involved in politics. Together with friends of a similar background, notably Abdessalam Jalloud, who presently ranks second in the Libyan political hierarchy, he formed a pro-Nasserite study group. His involvement in radical political actions advocating anticolonialist nationalism led to his expulsion from school.
   In 1961, Qadhdhafi moved to Misrata near Tripoli where he completed his secondary education and formed an underground movement of some importance. It was a civilian movement, independent of party politics, and had as its goal the creation of a Pan-Arabian union and social justice. In Misrata, Qadhdhafi became convinced that only a militant revolution (i.e., ousting by force the corrupted royal rulers) had any viable prospects of transforming Libyan society in the desired direction, and he, therefore, enrolled in the Benghazi Military Academy.
62   Ayoub 1987:23.
63   Cited in Bearman 1986:63.
64   Ayoub 1987:24.
65   Davis, J. 1987:249.

66 Cited in Ayoub 1987:24.
67 The Libyan revolution may, Ayoub argues (1987:31ff.), be divided into three
    phases: (1) the formative phase, from September 1, 1969, to April 15, 1973; (2) the
    transitory phase, from April 15, 1973, to March 2, 1977; and (3) the post–*Green
    Book* or the Jamaihriyan phase, from March 2, 1977, still unfolding.
        Some of the features of the first, formative, phase have already been noted
    above: the nationalization of the petroleum industry, the ousting of foreign mili-
    tary forces, and the repatriation of Italian nationals. The Arabization extended to
    reform the educational system from its previous Western model, Arabic became
    the official language, the precedence of the Arabic alphabet was reinstated, signs
    were painted over in Arabic, and Italian street and place names were changed to
    Arabic.
        Revenues from the nationalized oil industry financed development programs
    in education (where impressive progress was made in levels of literacy and
    primary education), ambitious housing construction (by 1974, Libya's construc-
    tion rates exceeded those of all Western states except Sweden and Denmark),
    medical and health care (in ten years, between 1968 and 1978, the number of
    hospitals had risen by 50 percent and the number of beds by close to 200 per-
    cent), transportation nets and the green or agrarian revolution.
        The achievements noted above were accomplished through heavy state inter-
    vention, and thus ran counter to the romanticized Bedouin ideal of precapitalist
    statelessness. Traditional centers of power gave rise to other frustrating prob-
    lems. This power was mainly vested in the hands of conservative tribal chiefs
    who seemed to hamper a genuine decentralization, discriminate against less
    mighty tribes, and counteract the revolution's unfolding.
        The establishment of the Arab Socialist Union (ASU) in 1971 was an unsuccess-
    ful effort to mobilize the masses. The traditional elite used this apparatus to
    enhance its position, frequently in collusion with the ascending commercial and
    capitalist class tied together through knots of kinship. Frustrated with this clique
    which interposed itself between the young leadership and the people, Qadhdhafi
    called in 1973 for a populistic "cultural revolution," with certain points of re-
    semblance with its contemporary Chinese counterpart. Different authoritarian
    institutions and politico-religious movements such as traditional *ulama,* Isla-
    mists, Marxists, Monarchists, and Baathists were targeted. The cultural revolu-
    tion drove a wedge between Qadhdhafi and some of his more bureaucracy-
    inclined RCC compatriots, but merged the former with a section of dedicated
    youths forming a revolutionary cadre. Beginning in 1975, the ASU was gradually
    dismantled and substituted with a more decentralized power structure of locally
    based popular congresses.
68 The Revolutionary Command Council initially adopted a Nasserite strategy of
    state-controlled capitalist economic development. From the cultural revolution
    onwards, Qadhdhafi formed a more libertarian socialist model which distanced
    him from his more Nasserite-oriented RCC compatriots. Omar al-Meheshi, plan-
    ning minister and RCC member, became the leading proponent for state interven-
    tion in the economy and began to gather support from capitalists, *ulama,* and
    tribal leaders. Mehesi, probably backed by Anwar Sadat, organized underground
    cells of dissidents within the armed forces and the state apparatus, with the aim
    of ousting Qadhdhafi. His plans eventually reached Qadhdhafi's attention and in

1975 Meheshi fled to Tunisia and was later granted asylum in Egypt (Bearman 1986:145ff.).

69   *The Green Book* consists of three parts, written and originally published separately in the years of 1976, 1979, and 1980, and was supplemented by two commentaries, in 1984 and 1987, respectively. Islam, Bedouin traditions, and Pan-Arabian ideologies are together with Greek philosophy the main sources of inspiration for Qadhdhafi's thoughts, meaning that Qadhdhafi leaned less on contemporary Western models than did other Islamic modernists.

70   Qathafi 1980:9.

71   Ibid., 15f.

72   Ibid., 23–26, 29f.

73   Ibid., 33.

74   Ibid., 57ff.

75   Ibid., 67.

76   Ibid., 65.

77   Ibid., 89.

78   Ibid., 98.

79   Qathafi 1982a:91. Qadhdhafi asserts that nationalism is to mankind as instinct is to animals and gravity to celestial bodies (1980:76).

80   Qathafi 1982a:77. Compare with Ayoub 1987:51: "The sound principle is that every people must have their own religion . . . to every people their religion." This idea is incompatible with Islam's universal claim and other parts of Qadhdhafi's doctrines. The inconsistency is, however, merely theoretical. The Libyan *dawa* organization, the World Islamic Call Society carries out an ambitious missionary program the world over, from China to Chicago.

81   What these are supposed to mean are never clarified.

82   Qathafi, M. 1982a:107.

83   Ibid., 108.

84   Ibid.

85   Ayoub 1987:75.

86   Muhammad Geleidi informed the author that "even though the Brother-Leader of the Revolution did the very act of writing he was not the actual author. He was guided by divine inspiration to formulate the eternal Truths generations upon generations throughout the world have experienced and sought to express in their different ways" (conversation, Tripoli, Libya, January 9, 1989).

87   Qadhdhafi 1982b.

88   Qadafi 1986:21. In 1982b, Qadhdhafi states that "Chapter One of the Green Book is in fact a clarification and correct interpretation" of verse 42:38.

89   Qadhdhafi 1983; Ayoub 1987:76.

90   Qadhdhafi 1982c.

91   Ibid.

92   Qadhdhafi 1982b.

93   What must be done, first, is to reconsider the foundation for *Sharia,* second, to separate the eternal (principle) from the temporal (implementation), and third, to transfer the principle of consensus to those concerned (i.e., to the Popular Conference). The people are mandated to interpret *Sharia* and to make supplementary laws as long as they protect "human rights and dignity" (Ayoub 1987:64).

94   Ayoub 1987:84.

95   "Axioms in the Islamic Fiqh," 1988.

96   Ayoub 1987:95.

97   Bearman 1986:163. Compare with Davis, J. 1987 and Ayoub 1987:92.

98   Mortimer 1982:280f.

99   Qadafi 1986:27ff.

100   al-Khalot 1982.

101   For the activities of the World Islamic Call Society, see the following reports: *Activities,* 1983; *Final Declaration,* 1982; *The World Islamic Call Society,* 1986; *The World Islamic Call Council,* 1395 D.P. [Death of Prophet].

102   Qadhdhafi 1986b.

103   *The World Mathaba,* 1988; for the international's aim, methods, and organization, see *The World Mathaba for Resistance,* 1986; *New World,* 1987; *Why We Support,* 1987.

104   "The First," 1988.

105   Qadhdhafi 1986c.

106   Politically, both movements represent a "Third Position" beyond capitalism and communism. Both view nations and nationalism as of fundamental importance, believe that the blacks will be future world rulers, and speak up for minority people's right to self-determination. Economically, both regard the present North-South division as a global crime, believe in common ownership of the means of production, and envision a future classless, corporate society. Socially, both preach a similar moral based on clean-living family units, and religiously they share an understanding of the reasons for Islam's present decline, the need to return to the roots, and both adopt a modernist style of scriptural interpretation.

107   Muhammad, E. 1992a:78. Compare with Muhammad, E. 1970c. Richard Helms, CIA director, got word of "the danger" from an informant who claimed that "Nasser has contacted Elijah Muhammad to come to Egypt and wants to cause trouble (through) Elijah Muhammad (in the United States)" (see [letter 109-12-376-172 (14)] and FBI file 105-24822-202, 11/1/68). In 1960, the NOI sent a delegation to greet Nasser at the airport when he arrived to the U.S. (Evanzz 1992:85). Elijah's sons Akbar and Wallace both studied at Al Ahzar in Cairo and reportedly developed personal friendships with Nasser (Evanzz 1992:219).

108   Muhammad, E. 1970c.

109   al-Sharif, interview, 1989.

110   FBI file 105-24822-221. In 1973, the FBI worried about Libyan-NOI negotiations for possible oil business, reporting that Libya eventually would give the NOI oil tankers to transport oil to the United States, a deal that never was implemented (FBI file 105-24822-[?], 6/15/73).

111   Walker, Joe 1972. Compare with Bearman 1986:107.

112   Rassoull 1992:xxxviii.

113   Muhammad, E. 1972b; "Big Libyan," 1972.

114   10X 1972b. The Libyans agreed to extend the payments over a period of nine years, with a possible termination of the payments as early as June 1973.

115   al-Sharif, interview, 1989.

116   Baesho, interview, 1989.

117   As for example, Muftah Abouisha of the World Islamic Call Society (conversation with author, Tripoli, February 1, 1989) and Ibrahim Said, head of the World Center for Researches and Studies of the Green Book (conversation with author,

Tripoli, January 14, 1989). This, of course, is hardly surprising given the Gulf-Arabian and pro-American orientation of Imam Warithuddin Muhammad.

118   Farrakhan, interview, 1989b.

119   This refers to the NOI POWER program, which is described in chapter 10.

120   Rashadeen 1984:108, 114.

121   "Farrakhan Introduces," 1985.

122   Qathafi 1985.

123   See, for example, Williams, J. 1985.

124   "U.S. blast," 1985.

125   Farrakhan, speech, 1985a.

126   Farrakhan, interview, 1989b.

127   O'Reilly 1989:270.

128   Locke 1987a.

129   Jeff Fort, head of the El Rukn (then known as the Blackstone Rangers), had as early as the 1960s been talking about turning his gang toward community-building activities and adopting a black nationalist ideology.

   In 1967, the Blackstone Rangers received government funding of $927,000 together with their archrival, the Gangster Disciples, in a program administered by The Woodlawn Organization (TWO) as part of President Johnson's War on Poverty campaign. TWO was to put the Rangers and the Disciples to work, the gang fighting was to cease, and the youths' restless energy directed in a constructive manner. It turned out to be a complete failure. The deadly war between the Rangers and the Disciples continued with a number of deaths; Fort and the number-two man in the Rangers, Eugene Hairstone, were arrested on separate murder charges and three other Ranger activists in a Fort-run training center were arrested for rape. In May 1968, the program was shut down.

   The Rangers continued their dual existence. They received funding from the Ford Foundation, two members were invited to participate in one of President Nixon's inaugural balls in 1969, and the gang, renamed Black P (for "power") Stone Nation, initiated several plans for improving the black ghettos.

   In 1968, Fred Hampton of the Black Panther Party (BPP) was reported by FBI infiltrator William O'Neal to be seeking a merger between the Chicago-BPP and the Black P Stone Nation. As Fort's street gang was several thousand soldiers strong, the BPP, which was small at that time, would have multiplied its membership if Hampton were to succeed. O'Neal was ordered to instigate animosity between Hampton and Fort. The skilled provocateur, who had risen up to the position as BPP chief of security and who was to be responsible for the subsequent murder of Hampton, accomplished his task, resulting in armed clashes between the BPP and the Black P Stone Nation.

   In 1972, Fort was convicted of defrauding the TWO program mentioned above. In prison, Fort converted to Islam, changed his name to Malik and renamed the gang a second time, now to El Rukn. They bought an old theater that they remodeled into a mosque and headquarters for Imam Malik and his El Rukns. Meantime, Black P Stone Nation reemerged among those who opted not to follow Imam Malik (see Lemann 1992:245–49; Churchill and Wall, 1988:65ff.).

130   Muwakkil, interview, 1994.

131   Locke 1987b; "Mystery," 1987.

132   The two charged with going to Libya to negotiate agreement were Rieco Cran-

shaw and Leon McAnderson; Imam Malik (Jeff Fort) was accused of having orchestrated the plot from a Texas prison where he was serving time for a narcotics conviction (Locke 1987b; Locke 1987c; "El Rukns," 1987).

133   Farrakhan, interview, 1989b; Farrakhan, 1988b.

134   Farrakhan, interview, 1989b. Even though some readers might feel this to be an unlikely federal move for the post-COINTELPRO era, a later case may be illuminating. In a 1991 trial, the government used former El Rukn general Harry Evans as a key witness. He testified that he had delivered cocaine to the NOI South Side headquarters on several occasions, and that the El Rukn and the NOI were working on a deal "in which Farrakhan would receive cocaine from the gang in exchange for a warehouse full of fish" to be sold in fast-food fish restaurants to be established (O'Connor 1991). Evans's testimony, which smeared Farrakhan's reputation but failed to indict him, led to the conviction of three El Rukn generals. However, in 1993, the court ruled for renewed trials as government misconduct was revealed. The prosecution had given Evans and another cooperative gang members favors, such as receiving clothing and money, have conjugal visits with their wives and were allowed to obtain cocaine in jail. The U.S. Attorney further suppressed the fact that the witnesses had tested positive for drug use (see O'Connor 1993; "The El Rukn Embarrassment," 1993).

135   The prosecution built their case on the testimony of a former El Rukn "general," Tramell Davis, who was given a lighter sentence for his cooperation. He interpreted taped telephone conversations in the prosecution's favor, told of a video where some fifty El Rukn members pledged loyalty to Qadhdhafi, and exposed the content of the Qadhdhafi "terrorist deal." The defense argued that the El Rukn delegation went to Libya seeking money for rebuilding their mosque, described them as a peaceful youth religious group and indicated the arsenal to be planted, as no fingerprints from the defendants were found on the weapons.

136   Jeff Fort received eighty years in prison ("El Rukns Guilty," 1987; Locke 1988).

137   Farrakhan, speech, 1986b. In his introduction, Farrakhan said that Elijah Muhammad taught "that whenever there is a need in the nation, out of that need men will be born to satisfy the need. So, a collective need produces a leader who is the servant of the collective. . . . Every time a people are oppressed, everytime a people are enslaved, everytime a people are deprived of liberty and justice, a need is created, a longing is created and out of that longing and that need a leader is born . . . and . . . whenever the oppressor recognizes that that anointed leader has arrived on the scene, then the . . . schemes begin to deprive the people of that leader. . . . You and I have seen many of those leaders snuffed out. We have buried those leaders with tears but, as long as the need persists, another leader will come. Such a leader was Patrice Lumumba. Such a leader was Gamel Abdel Nasser; such a leader was Kwame Nkrumah. Such a leader was Amilcar Cabral. Such a leader was . . . Muritala Muhammad. Such a leader was . . . Mao Tse Tung. Such a leader is Fidel Castro; such a leader is Imam Khomeini and such a leader is Muammar Qadhafi."

138   Qadhdhafi 1986b.

139   Farrakhan, speech, 1986c. Published in Muhammad, T. 1986:39–43.

140   Farrakhan, speech, 1986c; Muhammad, T. 1986:39. Compare with Farrakhan 1989a.

141   Farrakhan, speech, 1986c; Muhammad, T. 1986:40f.

142 Farrakhan 1986e.

143 Bearman 1986:xi.

144 Ayoub 1987:138.

145 Bearman 1986:288–90.

146 Ronald Reagan, governor at that time, at a 1971 political dinner in Sacramento, cited in Boyer 1992:142.

147 Bearman 1986:291f. The document does cite one piece of evidence, the 1979 closing of the U.S. Embassy in Tripoli in a mass protest against Carter's policy toward Iran. This could, however, hardly be taken as proof of state-sponsored terrorism, should the concept be used in any standard meaning.

148 Bearman 1987:287. Libya was later indirectly cleared for the Berlin bombing, as American intelligence claimed that Syria and the PFLP-GC were the actual conspirators.

149 Bearman 1987:287f.

150 The other two children were the three-year-old Saef al-Islam and four-year-old Khamees. The bombed-out Qadhdhafi home has become a symbol of Libya as a victim of unfair United States aggression. The house has not been repaired but is left on display, and foreign delegations are routinely taken there on guided tours. Magazines with photo-essays, posters and postcards showing the ruin and Qadhdhafi playing with a smiling baby Hana are widely distributed as are invitations to anniversaries commemorating the event (Bearman 1986:287ff.; Muhammad Gelaidi, conversation with author, Tripoli, January 12, 1989).

151 Farrakhan, speech, 1990d.

152 Muhammad, T. 1986:22f.

153 Farrakhan's tour included England, where he was refused entrance by the immigration officials who escorted him back to the plane leaving for Nigeria. In Lagos, Nigeria, Farrakhan was scheduled to speak at the National Theater, but found the theater surrounded by soldiers and police who were turning away the arriving crowd with tear gas. In Senegal, a representative from the NOI delegation was arrested on arrival. These events stand in sharp contrast to the support shown by the Libyan and Ghanan authorities. President Rawlings met personally with Farrakhan and gave him the unusual honor of speaking to the Armed Forces. Farrakhan's tour also included Saudi Arabia, where he met with distinguished *ulama,* as mentioned above.

154 Muhammad, A. W. 1986.

155 The suit was filed in Federal District Court on June 25, 1986 (Payne 1986).

156 Farrakhan 1986.

157 Meyers, L. 1988. The Nation of Islam continued to defy the presidential decree banning travel to Libya and was represented by *Final Call* editor Abdul Wali Muhammad at the 1987 and 1988 anniversaries of the April bombings. In 1987, Abdul Wali Muhammad traveled together with a 250 men strong U.S. delegation, comprised of African and Native Americans, Chicanos and Inuits, including the American Indian Movement representative Wabun-Inini, a.k.a. Vernon Bellecourt, from the White Earth Chippewa Nation in Minnesota, and Bob Brown from the All African Revolutionary Party. Bellecourt, who spoke at a Nation of Islam organized rally in August 1988, in support of Libya, was imprisoned in September together with Brown for refusing to testify before the grand jury investigating the activities of "the Libyan 8," a ring of alleged Libyan agents.

On July 21, 1988, eight Arab students were arrested by the FBI in conjunction with the investigation of a pro-Libyan plot to assassinate high government officials, including Oliver North, and for allegedly organizing travel to Libya in defiance of the presidential decree. Bob Brown of the AARP and Akbar Muhammad of the NOI were subpoenaed for violation of the presidential decree and associated and implicated in the alleged plot (Jamison 1988; Muhammad, James, 1987; "Black journalists," 1988; Bratt 1987; COINTELPRO, 1988; "Freedom Day," 1988; "Brown, Bellecourt," 1988).

158   Meyers, L. 1988.

159   As, for example, the assassination of Anwar Sadat in October 1981; the kidnapping of American administrator David Dodge in Beirut in July 1982, which was the first of a series of kidnappings in Lebanon of American and Western nationals; the suicide attacks carried out by Hizbullah/Islamic Jihad against Israeli, United States, and French contingents in Lebanon in 1983, the most spectacular of which was the October 23, 1983, suicide truck bomber killing 241 U.S. marines, leading to U.S. withdrawal from Lebanon; the Shi'i bombings in Kuwait in December 1983; the hijacking of TWA flight 847 to Beirut, when twenty-nine Americans were held hostage for seventeen days in June 1985; the Palestine Liberation Front boarding of the Italian cruiser Achille Lauro in October 1985; the hijacking of an Egyptian flight to Malta on November 24, 1985; and the Abu Nidal-led Palestinian Revolutionary Brigades on December 27, 1985, carrying out simultaneous attacks on El Al passengers in Rome and Vienna, leaving fifteen people (four attackers included) dead. (For an interesting study of Hizbullah's and Islamic Jihad's militant actions in Lebanon, see Kramer 1990.)

160   Amiri Baraka is a renowned poet, essayist, and dramatist who has written numerous works. For the interested, the most comprehensive collection so far is Baraka 1991.

161   In the late 1960s, Hubert Rap Brown (who says rap music was named after him, Barboza 1994:49) was chairman of the Student Nonviolent Coordinating Committee and minister of justice of the Black Panther Party. He made his declaration of faith while imprisoned at Riker's Island in 1971. Jamil Al-Amin won parole in 1976 and organized an Atlanta-based Sunni Muslim congregation, the Community Mosque. His religio-political thoughts as a Muslim revolutionary are found in Al-Amin 1993.

162   Dhoruba Bin Wahad was one of the defendants in the New York Panther 21 conspiracy case of April 1969. He was released in 1990 on his own recognizance after his conviction was vacated. The reversal is, however, to be appealed by the Manhattan District Attorney. See Still Black, 1987.

163   Curtis 1994:51–73.

164   Muwakkil 1989. For the increasing Islamic presence in the African American community see Barboza 1994; Goldman 1989; Bernstein 1993; Terry 1993; "Muslims in America," 1993; Hirsley 1994; Muwakkil 1989b.

165   Muhammad, K., interview, 1989.

166   Kuss 1990 and 1991.

167   Muhammad, S. 1990b (1977). See also Muhammad, S. 1990c (1989).

168   John X Ali of Chicago was national secretary, Jeremiah Shabazz was minister in Philadelphia, Wali Bahar was personal captain to Elijah Muhammad, and John Muhammad of Detroit is one of the Messenger's brothers. They are all members of

the board of directors, called the Council of Elders, which also includes: Minister John Muhammad of Chicago, Minister Theodor Hamzah of Cleveland, Minister Jeremiah Shabazz of New York, John Ali of Chicago, and Silis Muhammad, who is chief executive officer (C.E.O.). The New York–based national representative, Kuba Abu Kuss, is not a member of the Council of Elders.

169 Muhammad, Amira 1992. The LFNOI had by 1992 not set up any University of Islam or other educational institutions, but plans have been made for a day-care center in Atlanta. The twenty-one mosques established by 1992 and their chief officers are:
1. New Orleans, LA: Acting Minister Karim Rahim, 1713 Oretha Haley Blvd., New Orleans, LA 70113; 2. Atlanta, GA: Minister Malik Al-Akram, 3040 Campbellton Rd. S.W., Atlanta, GA 30311; 3. San Antonio, TX: Bro. Joshua Abdul Shakir, 319 S. Pine, San Antonio, TX; 4. Philadelphia, PA: Min. Haleem Asadi, 2314 Cecil B. Moore Ave., Philadelphia, PA 19121; 5. Richmond, VA: Min. Adib Siraj Nabawal, 1001 N. 27th St., Richmond, VA 23223; 6. Southern New England: Acting Min. Intisar Rasulallah, 1535 Central Ave., Ste. 314, Bridgeport, CT 06610; 7. Memphis, TN: Min. Ishmael Shabazz, 552 East Trigg Ave., Memphis, TN 38106; 8. Oklahoma City, OK: Min. Taqiyy Saleem, 737 NW 23 St., Oklahoma City, OK 73106; 9. Nashville, TN: Min. Yusuf Ayatullah, 319 Bellshire Terrace Court, Nashville, TN 37207; 10. Newark, NJ: Min. Wazir Abu Hussein, 466 Conover Terrace, Orange, NJ 07050; 11. Asheville, NC: Bro. Dawud Al Karriem, 5 N. Crescent St., Asheville, NC 28801; 12. Washington, D.C.: Min. Najee Mustafa, Carlyle Suite Hotel, 1731 New Hampshire Ave., NW, Washington, D.C. 20009; 13. Austin, TX: Bro. Abu Bakr Mustafa et Bro. Ansar Mustafa, 7100 N.E. Dr. No. 210 St., Austin, TX 78723; 14. Los Angeles, CA: Min. Taji Ali, 1713 W 108th St., Los Angeles, CA 90020; 15. Houston, TX: Min. Omar Hassan, 2401 Francis St., Houston, TX 77004; 16. Jackson, MI: Min. Al-Malik Al-Jihad, 617 W Capitol, Jackson, MI 39202; 17. Chicago, IL: Min. Malik Mawalin, P.O. Box 378303, Chicago, IL 60637; 18. Tallahassee, FL: Min. Ajani Mukarram, no address; 19. Cleveland, OH: Min. Hakeem Rashad, 572 E. 104th St., Cleveland, OH 44110; 20. Phoenix, AZ: Acting Min. 161. Faheerah Fedayeen, 2235 W. Avalon Drive, Phoenix, AZ 85015; 21. New York, NY: Min. Kuba Abu Kuss, Mail:P.O. Box 210461, Bushwick Retail Station, Brooklyn, NY 11221-0620.

170 X, E. 1990:31.

171 The LFNOI denounces as deceitful and contradictory to the teachings of Elijah Muhammad the following aspects of the NOI Messiology: the identification of Elijah Muhammad with the awaited Messiah, the denial of Elijah Muhammad's death, the presentation of his departure to the Mother Wheel where he was hailed by the four and twenty elders as the Lamb, the expectations of his imminent return to judge the wicked, and Farrakhan's position as the living Messiah's chief representative to the world community (Muhammad, S. 1990).

172 Kuss 1991.

173 Mahdi 1991.

174 Kuss 1991.

175 Muhammad, S., speech, 1989a.

176 Al-Akram 1991a.

177 Al-Akram 1991b.

178 Al-Akram 1992.

179   Muhammad, S. 1991a.
180   Cited in Al-Akram 1991a. Hakim adds: "My testimony is not a foolish belief. I am
      not a foolish woman, falling in love with a Black man and saying anything I can
      to please him."
          In 1991, Ida Hakim wrote, "You, the Gods and Godesses of the Lost Found
      Nation of Islam, are the answer to my prayer. . . . I am grateful and thankful for the
      resurrection of every one of you, most especially for your leader, Mr. Silis Mu-
      hammad, and for my own husband and teacher, the God who woke me up to the
      reality of Islam. How much I believe in him and in all of you. . . . With my own
      mind I envision the Kingdom of God. How beautiful it will be. How excellent is
      your potential as Creators. I believe it is your stature as Gods that most greatly
      concerns the American Caucasian devil" (Hakim 1991a).
181   Saleem 1991a. Ida Hakim likewise acknowledges Silis Muhammad "as my God. I
      pray my prayers to him" and "it is my prayer to be worthy of His Divine Mercy as
      long as I live" (Hakim 1991a).
182   Saleem 1991a.
183   See Copeland 1988; Goldberg 1992.
184   Harriet Abu Bakr is ex-daughter-in-law of Elijah Muhammad. She married Silis
      Muhammad in 1965 and was active in the old Nation. Harriet was chief organizer
      for the Mr. Muhammad Speaks distribution for the West Coast. In 1977, she began
      her studies at UCLA School of Law and completed her Juris Doctor in 1980. She is
      now chief attorney and treasurer for the LFNOI.
185   Al-Akram, 1992.
186   Mahdi 1991a.
187   Muhammad, S. 1991b.
188   Muhammad, S. 1991c.
189   Muhammad, S. 1991a.
190   Muhammad, S., speech, 1990.
191   Kuss 1991.
192   Muhammad, S., speech, 1989b.
193   In the NOI "Lost Found Lesson #2," dating from the early 1930s, earthquakes were
      said to be "caused by the Son of Man by experimenting [with] high explosion."
194   Muhammad, S., speech, 1989b.
195   Ibid.
196   Muhammad, S. 1991a.
197   Muhammad, S. 1990a; Muhammad, S. 1991a; "World Saviour," *Muhammad
      Speaks* 7, no. 2 (1991):17; Muhammad, S., speech, 1989a.
198   Muhammad, S. 1991b; Muhammad, S., speech, 1990.
199   Muhammad, S. 1991a.
200   Muhammad, S. 1991a and 1991b.
201   Muhammad, S. 1991b.
202   Ibid.
203   Muhammad, S. 1991a.
204   Muhammad, S. 1991b.
205   Saleem 1991b; Hakim 1991b.
206   "Lawyer Focuses," 1992.
207   Tariq 1992.
208   Kuss 1990. Compare with Muhammad, S. 1990a.

209 Muhammad, S. 1991a. Compare with Muhammad, S., speech, 1989a.

210 Muhammad, S. 1990a.

211 Muhammad, S. 1990a; Muhammad, S. 1991d.

212 For those interested in this theological dispute, see letters published in Muhammad, S. 1990b and 1990c.

213 Kuss 1990; Asidi 1990.

214 Muhammad, S. 1992.

215 Farrakhan, L. 1994d.

216 Muhammad, James 1994a.

217 The LFNOI has even reversed the trend toward reconciliation initiated by Elijah Muhammad.

> Ramadan is back in December and the members are not even required to fast: "We are not Fasting (in December), we are just abstaining from taking part in false worship," i.e. Christmas celebration ("Ramadan," 1991).
>
> Rather than encourage Muslim holidays the LFNOI celebrates its own holidays, thereby marking its nonalignment with mainstream Islam:
>
> 1. Saviour's Day, February 26, commemorates the birth of Allah in the Person of Master Farad Muhammad.
>
> 2. April 1 is a National Holiday to remember the forefathers whose lives were lost during the "holocaust" in America (see Mukkaram 1991).
>
> 3. Mother's Day, October 7, celebrates the birth of Our Holy Mother, Elijah Muhammad, who became impregnated by God and gave birth to the Body Christ. On this day it is appropriate to honor one's biological mother, too, with cards and gifts.
>
> 4. Ramadan, December, antidevil worship holiday.

218 Mahdi 1991b.

219 The Honorable Silis Muhammad Presents What The Muslims Believe, point 3.

> During the leadership of Messenger Muhammad, the NOI published ten points under the caption "What the Muslims Want" (A) and twelve under "What the Muslims Believe" (B). While Farrakhan and the NOI have retained these points, the LFNOI has adopted an alternative version. Gone for example is the old call for a prohibition against inter-marriage (A10) (thus Ida Hakim). The LFNOI puts more emphasis on Exodus with the demands for land and transportation and citizenship in Egypt or elsewhere in Africa (New A6), and there is no longer a request for territory in America (formerly point A4). New B3 speaks of the New World conditions and a New Revelation and the new B11 identifies Elijah Muhammad as Moses.

220 Cited in Saleem 1991a.

221 This section is largely based on an excellent article by Nuruddin 1994.

222 FBI file 157-3376-[5?], 9/17/65.

223 FBI file 157-3376-6.

224 X Walker 1993.

225 Adherence to a standard dress code has always been a feature of the cult, although recommended dress has changed over time. In 1967, "black nationalist" outfits were the rule: they wore black and green and carried the symbols of the six-pointed star and upright crescent along with the ankh. In 1968 they metamorphosed to "African" attire: Akbarders and the Hausa head covering called *fuwm*. The "Africanization" continued from 1969, with male members wearing

black tarbush and having a bone in the left ear and a nose ring. In 1973, they changed to a more "Sudanese" outfit, wearing a shorter white garment and a white turban, which was substituted in 1978 with the dress described in the main text.

226   The address is 719 Bushwick Avenue, Brooklyn, New York.

227   This is based on the perceived practice established by Abraham, the Messiah Jesus, who is said to have been part of the Essene commune—and the *hijra* of the prophet Muhammad (al Mahdi 1989:81f.).

228   al Mahdi 1989:62.

229   The word "cult" used to describe the Ansaaru Allah Community is the one preferred by Isa al Mahdi because "the word cult is simply the root of the word culture or cultivate, and that's exactly what I am trying to do. I'm cultivating my people, teaching them about their true culture and way of life: Al Islaam" (al Mahdi 1989:51).

230   al Mahdi 1989:53–56. Bilial Philips, a Jamaican-born Muslim critic of the Ansaar, now living in Riyadh, Saudi Arabia, claims that Isa was born in the United States as Dwight York in 1935. He allegedly changed his birth date to fit the pattern of the famous hadith that stipulates a reformer (*mujeddid*) to be sent every 100 years.

   G. M. Ahmed (1991:21) states that Isa did not change his name to include al Hadi, until the death of Al Hadi Abdur Rahman al Mahdi during an Aba Island rebellion in 1969. Ahmed holds that Isa's first version was that al Hadi had married his mother in America, made her pregnant, and then returned to the Sudan. Ahmed further asserts that Isa's "fake claims of genealogy" have been recurrently criticized by both Sudanese Americans and orthodox Muslims.

231   al Mahdi 1989:57–60. Bilial Philips claims that Isa was raised in Brooklyn and never visited the Sudan prior to 1973. He states that the young York was a gang member, involved in crimes and drugs. After a number of run-ins with the police, he was sentenced to jail in the early sixties where he met followers of Elijah Muhammad. Should Isa's account be correct, he enrolled in the State Street Mosque at the age of 12, in 1957.

232   al Mahdi 1989:81.

233   Ibid., 135.

234   al Mahdi 1986a:94.

235   al Mahdi 1989:70, 73.

236   Ibid., 81. Isa al Mahdi wrote (1986a:79) that he started in 1967, but "opened the seal in 1970 as prophesied. I founded this Community exactly One-Hundered years after the foundation of the Ansaaru ALLAH Community . . . in Sudan by Muhammad Ahmad Al Mahdi (AS), my great grandfather. This is no co-incidence!!!"

237   al Mahdi 1989:319f. Isa interprets Revelation 8:1, "And when he (the Lamb) opened the seventh seal, there were silence in heaven about the space of half an hour," as meaning that all judgment would be held up for thirty years. Thereby, the AAC as does the NOI, holds the 1990s as the final decade of the present world order.

238   Ibid., 134. Isa says that although qualified, he abdicated this position in favor of his uncle, As Sayyid Ahmad Abdur Rahman Al Mahdi of Sudan, who thus is the khalifa of the Ansaars, while Isa is a khalifa.

239   Ibid., 168. This Sufi order was established in 1984.

240   Ibid., 169f. This is not to be understood that Isa claims to be Allah. For the AAC, Allah is not "a god" and cannot incarnate into any individual man. Isa is said to be a divine being as he has an extra portion of divinity in addition to the supremacy every black man can evolve into. When a black submits to Allah, he becomes a supreme being, controlled by God who works through him.

241   al Mahdi 1986a:79.

242   al Mahdi 1986b:155.

243   al Mahdi 1989:161. Observe: a Messiah, not the Messiah. The Ansaar teach that the foretold return of Jesus Christ, the Messiah (Isa al Masih), will be in the spirit of all devout believers or Ansaars, "helpers of God." The AAC thereby adopt the idea of the Body Christ, a notion also featuring in the theological teachings of Imam Warithuddin and Silis X Muhammad. Isa's claim that Isa al Masih will return as the Mujeddid, however, indicates that he himself has an additional Messianic spark, making him a Messiah, head of the Body Christ.

244   Ibid., 206.

245   al Mahdi 1986c:65. These twenty-four Elders originally lived in Salaam City in the Land of Mu before the explosion that separated Arabia from Africa and created the Red Sea. They fled on an aircraft called the Mothership or the Wheel of Ezekiel, on which they now reside (compare with the NOI creed).

246   al Mahdi 1989:206.

247   Ibid., 60.

248   al Mahdi 1986a:76. Isa claims that Elijah Muhammad knew that Master Farad Muhammad was not God in Person but used this image as a tactical approach as the Christian African Americans were used to worshiping God in flesh. What Elijah Muhammad never became aware of, however, was the scheme orchestrated by global communism and nazism, whose agents killed Master Farad Muhammad and replaced him with their German undercover man, Wallace D. Fard. The plot failed, however, as Elijah Muhammad succeeded to build the NOI on the original teachings of Master Farad, published in the Supreme Wisdom (al Mahdi 1989:131–35).

249   al Mahdi, Isa, speech, n.d.

250   al Mahdi 1989:189–225.

251   Ibid., 293f.

252   Ibid., 189f.

253   Ibid., 189f., 195–203, 220f.

254   Ibid., 214–25. Isa teaches that the white man is the physical offspring of the 200 Fallen Angels, headed by Azaazil. When God sent the Flood to get rid of the community of evil Angels, they escaped to Saturn. After the flood, they returned and set up the cities of Sodom and Gomorrah and their modern equivalents, New York and Riyadh. Allah cursed the descendants of Canaan with leprosy, which explains the white skin of the devils' seed (al Mahdi 1989:259ff.; 1986a; 1986b).

255   al Mahdi 1989:50.

256   Ibid., 68.

257   al Mahdi 1986a and 1986c.

258   al Mahdi 1989:247. "CT" means "Curse Them" and "CH" means "Curse Him."

259   Ibid., 25.

260   Ibid., 35.

261 al Mahdi 1986b. In his pamphlets, Isa frequently publishes revealed pictures of the black prophets, from Adam to Muhammad.

262 In his early pamphlets, Isa frequently used and referred to the corpus of Ahadith, but soon joined the "Protestant" camp, denying the Traditions as a divine source of Law. The man-made post-Prophet text collections—Talmud in Judaism, the New Testament (except the Injil) in Christendom, and the hadith in Islam—are held responsible for the deviations from the straight path revealed through the prophets (al Mahdi 1989:95). As does Qadhdhafi, Isa stresses the distinction between hadith and sunna, and holds it as obligatory to follow the latter. Isa states that living communally, wearing a white dress, having a beard and either shaving all hair or leaving it untrimmed is the sunna of the prophet Muhammad and thus compulsory to emulate.

263 al Mahdi 1989:49.

264 Ibid., 308.

265 Ibid., 322–73.

266 Ibid., 374f. As Suhuf is mentioned in 98:2 and Al Hikmah in 3:48 of the Holy Qur'an. "The Book of Life" was revealed in 3126 B.C. to the prophet Adam; "The Book of Sin" was revealed in 3776 B.C. to the prophet Seth; "The Book of Time" was revealed in 3284 B.C. to the prophet Enoch; "The Book of Generation" was revealed in 1958 B.C. to the prophet Abraham; and Al Hikmah was revealed in 1671 B.C. to the prophet Luqman.

267 See, for instance, al Mahdi 1986a and 1986c.

268 al Mahdi 1989:368–73, 378ff. Followers of Rashad Khalifa deny that Isa al Mahdi discovered the code. According to them, Isa was one of the first who studied Khalifa's teachings, but a schism between the two Muslim leaders soon developed (interview with anonymous Submitters).

269 Translation by Isa al Mahdi, published in 1989:257f. Compare with the translations of Yusuf Ali and Muhammad M. Pickthall, respectively:

> Likewise did We make for every Messenger an enemy,—evil ones among men and Jinns, inspiring each other with flowery discourses by the way of deception. If thy Lord had so planned, they would not have done it: so leave them and their inventions alone.

> Thus have We appointed unto every Prophet an adversary—devils of humankind and jinn who inspire in one another plausible discourse through guile. If thy Lord willed, they would not do so; so leave them alone with their devising.

270 al Mahdi 1987:9. Hasan al-Askari counts as number ten for the AAC and as number eleven for Imamiyya, due to the fact that the AAC numbers the imams after Ali and the latter after Muhammad.

271 Ibid., 1. As the AAC does not recognize the alleged son of Hasan al-Askari, Abul Qasim Muhammad, as the Mahdi, they depart here from the Imamiyya and close the first cycle of imams with al-Askari. The second cycle comprises nine imams: Muhammad Al Muntadhar; Adul Kaber; Uthman; Yuwnus; Muhammad; Abdullah; Fahl; Sayyid; and finally Muhammad Ahmad as number 19 and the Seal of Imams.

272 Ibid., 9f. Compare with al Mahdi 1986b:42f.

273 al Mahdi 1987:26; compare with the Mahdiyya, "and Muhammad al Mahdi is the

successor to the Apostle of Allah." According to Isa al Mahdi, the full text of the Shahada, correctly translated, reads: "Nothing would exist if Allah did not create it. Muhammad is the one sent from Allah and the Mahdi Muhammad is the successor to the one sent."

274   Ibid., 10.
275   al Mahdi 1989:428.
276   Ibid., 447, 450.
277   Ibid., 453–62. Kissing of Kaba's black stone is said to be idolatrous stone worship and as offensive as visiting the tomb of Muhammad.
278   Ibid., 464ff. Concerning the use of alcohol, Isa makes a distinction between legitimate use (for medical and social purposes) and forbidden misuse (to get drunk). Isa bases his argument mainly on the Old Testament, even though Luke (10:34) and the Qur'an (4:43, 46; 47:15) also are referred to (al Mahdi 1989:475). Isa said (speech, n.d.): "The Quran does not say you cannot drink, the Quran says do not become drunk. But it does tell you you can't smoke and you can't use hashish or cigarettes because those are intoxicants, poison. Wine is not an intoxicant."
279   al Mahdi 1989:195f.
280   Isa al Mahdi visited the Sudan in 1973, 1982, and 1983.
281   Ahmed, G. M. 1991:21.
282   Sadiq al Mahdi visited on several occasions, 1978, 1979, and 1981.
283   al Mahdi 1989:123; Ahmed, G. M. 1991:21.
284   This refers mainly to matters of orthopraxy and outward appearance (such as dress code) and not that much to the creed. The Sudanese objections to Isa's frequent use of the Bible were, for example, ignored.

9   Strained Seeds of Abraham: Is the NOI an Anti-Christian, Anti-Semitic Nazi Cult?

1   Esposito 1992:26f.
2   Muhammad, E. 1973:169.
3   Muhammad, E. 1974a:172.
4   Muhammad, E. 1965:94.
5   Ibid., 168.
6   See, for example, Muhammad, E. 1957:25; Muhammad, E. 1965:303f.
7   Muhammad, E. 1974a:165.
8   Ibid., 174–81.
9   Muhammad, E. 1992b.
10   Messenger Muhammad wrote: "Over at home (Asia) we have camel stations (The camel station is where camels are for hire). They are called mail camels. The camel is a very sensitive and fast runner. The mail camels go from forty to fifty miles per hour and it was one of the mail camels they hired. From Jerusalem to Cairo, Egypt, is about six hundred miles. The camel knew the route well. He travels it daily. Nothing is necessary except to tell the camel where you want him to go and he will go right direct to the place" (1992b:6; parentheses his).
11   Farrakhan, speech, 1990j.
12   Farrakhan, speech, 1989b; John 8:32.
13   Public Enemy, "Welcome to the Terrordome," Fear of a Black Planet, CBS Records, 1990.

14   Farrakhan, speech, 1990c.
15   Farrakhan, speech, 1990j.
16   Farrakhan, speech, 1986a.
17   Ibid.
18   Muhammad, E. 1974a:162.
19   Lincoln and Mamiya 1990:10ff.
20   Wilmore 1986:x.
21   Lincoln and Mamiya 1990:10ff.
22   The first independent black churches were Baptist; the African Baptist "Blue-stone" Church was established in 1758, and the Silver Bluff Baptist Church was established in 1773–75, according to the historical records, or 1750, according to an inscription on the cornerstone. For an account of the first black churches and their history, see Raboteau 1978; Wilmore 1986; Frazier 1974 [1964]; Lincoln 1974; and Lincoln and Mamiya 1990.
23   Wilmore 1986:74–134; Frazier 1974 [1964]:35ff.
24   Wilmore 1986:140–2.
25   X, M. 1973 [1965]:247.
26   Lincoln and Mamiya 1990:212.
27   Wilmore 1979:67.
28   For Cleage's view on Malcolm X, see Cleage 1969:189–200. Albert J. Cleage founded his Shrine of the Black Madonna in Detroit in 1953 and is attributed with having used the term Black Theology as early as during the Detroit uprising in 1967 (Wilmore 1979:67f.).
29   Cone 1970:23.
30   Ibid., 113.
31   Cone 1993:296.
32   Cone 1989:182.
33   Lincoln and Mamiya 1990:169, 179f. The pastors of 1,531 urban churches of the seven major denominations were asked in a questionnaire, "Have you been influ-enced by any of the authors and thinkers of black liberation theology (e.g., James Cone, Gayraud Wilmore, DeOtis Roberts, Major Jones, William Jones, etc.)?"
34   Ibid., 180f.
35   Ibid., 224–26.
36   Marable 1985:272.
37   See, for instance, Chavis 1984.
38   Lincoln and Mamiya 1990:338, 388f.
39   Cited in Muhammad, A. W. 1990.
40   Cited in ibid.
41   Farrakhan, speech, 1990c.
42   Lincoln and Mamiya 1990:160.
43   "Farrakhan Speaks," 1993.
44   Muhammad, Akbar 1992.
45   Cited in Muhammad, A. W. 1990.
46   Muhammad, A. W. 1990.
47   Walker, M. 1989.
48   Muhammad, James 1993a.
49   Muhammad, James 1993b. The historic pledge for unity will be further discussed later in this and the following chapter.

50   Farrakhan, speech, 1985a.
51   Muhammad, Jabril 1992. Compare with Muhammad, Jabril 1993f.
52   Farrakhan, speech, 1985a.
53   Farrakhan 1993b.
54   Farrakhan 1993c.
55   Farrakhan 1993a.
56   Zipperer 1993.
57   Farrakhan 1993d.
58   Here Farrakhan assumes that Tao and Shinto were historical "teachers" or "enlightened ones." The reader should not let this incorrect assumption obscure the meaning of his message.
59   Farrakhan 1993d.
60   "Farrakhan Speaks," 1993.
61   *Louis Farrakhan, Special Edition,* 1987.
62   Kaufman 1988:19–22.
63   Between 1881 and 1914, close to two million East European Jews migrated to the United States (Howe 1976:58; on Jewish socialism, see pp. 287–324; see also Levin 1978:65–196).
64   Howe 1976:411f.; Zenner 1991:136.
65   Chalmers 1981:71; Kaufman 1988:23–28. The slur "kikes" was actually first employed by the German-Jewish community as a derogatory description of Eastern European Jews, but became adopted by racist Americans. The lynched Jew was Leo Frank, who was accused of raping and murdering a young female employee, and a Georgian court in an unprecedented move allowed a black man to testify against a white. He was not the first Jew to be lynched, however. By the early 1870s the Klan began attacking white Methodists and Shakers, and in Tennessee, Klan members lynched a Jewish storekeeper who tried in vain to protect his black employee (Katz 1986:44f., 108).
66   Meier and Rudwick 1973:225, 293, 335f.; Garrow 1981:27ff.; Garrow 1993 [1986]; Carson 1989:113–30. For the Klan bombings, see a list of targets from 1956 to 1963, in Chalmers 1981:356–65.
67   Glazer 1983:34; Glazer 1989:108; Zenner 1991:131; Wistrich 1994:123. Koreans have increasingly replaced Jews as shopkeepers in the black ghettos, and anti-Korean sentiments are on the rise (Cho 1993:196–211).
68   Lemann 1991:82.
69   Wistrich 1994:120.
70   For an account of the affirmative action debate, see Glazer 1983:159ff. and Mills 1994.
71   Wistrich 1994:114.
72   Kaufman 1988:274–75. The term "The media elite" refers to people working for the *New York Times,* the *Washington Post,* the *Wall Street Journal, Time, Newsweek, U.S. News & World Report,* the news divisions of NBC, CBS, and ABC, and public television. At one time or another in the 1980s, Kaufmann states, the deans of the law schools at Harvard, Yale, Stanford, and Columbia were all Jews, as were the presidents of Princeton, Dartmouth, and Columbia.
73   Kaufman 1988:274.
74   Just to mention one, significant example, as an illustration: When the first African American United Nations Ambassador Andrew Young was forced to resign

in 1972 after a fifteen-minute meeting with the PLO's United Nations observer, 200 major black leaders, among them Jesse Jackson, signed a declaration described as a "watershed" in black-Jewish relations, or as a black declaration of independence. The resolution condemned the American double standard and Israel's ties to South Africa, called for a meeting between Joseph Lowery, head of the SCLC and the UN PLO observer, and stated that while Jews earlier had supported black causes when in their own best interest, this was a new age in which Jews should consult black leadership before taking action against the best interests of the African American community (see Kaufmann 1988:245f.; Sklar 1989:132ff.).

75   Collins 1986:221.

76   Strausberg and Locke 1984; Strasser, Monroe, Cooper, and P. King 1984; Kaufman 1988:254f. By February 1984, ten people had been arrested and charged with plotting to assassinate Jesse Jackson.

77   Farrakhan, speech, 1983; Muhammad, A. A. 1984.

78   Farrakhan, speech, 1984b.

79   Farrakhan, speech, 1983.

80   Farrakhan 1989e [1984]:73.

81   Farrakhan, speech, 1983.

82   Farrakhan, L. 1989e [1984]:76.

83   Farrakhan, speech, 1984c; Strausberg 1984; Morganthau, Colton, Greenberg, Warner, and DeFrank 1984.

84   Atkinson 1984a; Kaufman 1988:256.

85   Atkinson 1984a and 1984b.

86   Cited in Kaufman 1988:258; compare with Collins 1986:222.

87   See Collins 1986:223.

88   Farrakhan, speech, 1984d. Parts of the lecture are published verbatim in "Farrakhan on Race," 1984.

89   Matlick and Lathem 1984; "Nation of Islam's," 1984. Despite this, Jackson did well in New York. He received 87 to 89 percent of the black vote statewide and 92 percent of the vote of African Americans between the ages of 18 and 29. He received the support of two-thirds of all first-time voters and 34 percent of all ballots in New York City (Marable 1985:273f.).

90   As for example in, Randolph 1984; Shapiro and Broder 1984.

91   Farrakhan said to Coleman in a taped phone call, "There have never been threats, none now and never will be threats to your life, brother, or your family. That will go on the record" (Atkinson 1984c).

92   See for example, Johnson, H. 1984; Morganthau, Monroe, Weathers, Maier, and V. Smith 1984.

93   Randolph and Atkinson 1984.

94   See, for example, Collins 1986:225.

95   "Jesse's Pal," 1984; Lathem and Peritz 1984; Shapiro 1984.

96   Farrakhan 1989f [1984]:120. Speaking to Jews in the audience at Northwestern University, Farrakhan said, "Hitler hated Jews. Hitler hated blacks with a passion. Why should I praise Hitler?" (Farrakhan, speech, 1988a).

97   See Lindqvist 1992.

98   Farrakhan 1989e [1984]:118.

99   Marable 1985:287.

100 "Speakes Lauds," 1984. See also Marable 1985:288.
101 "Reagan Aides," 1984. Reagan later disavowed his Klan backers ("Reagan Spurs," 1984). While the Jackson-Farrakhan connection regularly appeared on the front pages, the ties between the Klan and Reagan never received widespread coverage.
102 Pianin 1984.
103 See, "Don't Lock Out," 1984; Straussberg 1984b.
104 "Jackson, Invoking," 1984. For some black critical voices, see Locke 1984a; Jones, C-V. 1984; Marable 1985:267.
105 Locke 1984b and 1984c.
106 Strausberg 1984c.
107 "Farrakhan Aides," 1984.
108 Skelton 1984.
109 Martz 1988.
110 Reed 1989.
111 Farrakhan, speech, 1989e.
112 Farrakhan, speech, 1989e.
113 Farrakhan 1989h [1987]:242f.
114 Farrakhan, speech, 1989e.
115 Farrakhan, speech, 1990c.
116 Farrakhan, speech, 1985b.
117 Farrakhan, speech, 1986a.
118 Farrakhan, speech, 1989a.
119 Malachi 4:1 reads: "Behold, for the day cometh, that shall burn as an oven; and all the proud, yea, and all that do wickedly, shall be stubble: and the day that cometh shall burn them up."
120 Farrakhan, speech, 1989e.
121 As, for example, Farrakhan's effort to explain that he did not criticize "Judaism" but "the state of Israel and Zionism . . . and that's not anti-Semitism" (Farrakhan 1989e [1984]:122), or his assurance that "we are not against Jews . . . we are condemning exploitation, we are condemning racism, we are condemning Zionism" (Hardy and Pleasant 1987:45).
122 Farrakhan, speech, 1985c.
123 Ibid.
124 Farrakhan, speech, 1988a.
125 Farrakhan, interview, 1989b. The NOI demands for reparations are discussed further in chapter 10.
126 Farrakhan, speech, 1990k.
127 Farrakhan, speech, 1990c.
128 Farrakhan, speech, 1990j. The original East German statement read, "We ask the Jews of the world to forgive us. We ask the people of Israel to forgive us for the hypocrisy and hostility of official East German policy towards Israel, and for the persecution and the degradation of Jewish citizens also after 1945 in our country. We declare our willingness to contribute as much as possible to the healing of mental and physical suffering of survivors, and to provide just compensation for material loss."
129 Farrakhan, speech, 1985c.
130 Farrakhan, speech, 1989b.

131 Farrakhan 1989e [1984]:59.

132 Farrakhan, speech, 1985c.

133 Gams, interview, 1994.

134 The ADL continues to circulate reports to Minister Farrakhan and the NOI, such as *Louis Farrakhan: In His Own Words*, n.d.; *Louis Farrakhan. An Update*, 1985; *The Louis Farrakhan: Continuing the Message of Hate*, 1988; *Louis Farrakhan: The Campaign to Manipulate Public Opinion*, 1990; *The Anti-Semitism of Black Demagogues and Extremists*, 1992; *Special Report. Louis Farrakhan: In His Own Words—1993*, 1993.

135 Farrakhan 1989e [1984]:53.

136 Farrakhan, speech, 1985c.

137 Farrakhan 1989f [1984]:139f.

138 Farrakhan, speech, 1990h.

139 Farrakhan, speech, 1985c. The Jewish pattern of solidarity and cooperation is described in Zenner 1991:140ff.

140 Suall, interview, 1994. Suall goes on to state that "we're in the realm of psychopathology here, but that's where it belongs, and Farrakhan is a perfect example of it. [In *The Age of Totalitarism*, the author says that] Hitler in many ways charged the Jews with aspirations that were actually his own aspirations. Almost invariably, when you find anti-Semites discussing the qualities of the Jews that they find so horrible, the qualities are in many ways a projection of their own, whether it's conscious, semiconscious, or unconscious wishes. And I think that's absolutely true of Farrakhan as well."

141 Farrakhan, speech, 1990f.

142 Farrakhan, speech, 1989b.

143 Farrakhan, speech, 1989c.

144 Farrakhan argues that Jews put money in black organizations and back black candidates in order to manipulate the direction of the organizations and leaders and to check the movements so they do not deviate from what is considered to be appropriate (Hardy and Pleasant 1987:36).

145 Farrakhan, speech, 1985a.

146 *The Secret Relationship*, 1991.

147 Cited in *Jew-Hatred*, 1993:ii.

148 *The Secret Relationship*, 1991:ii, 196.

149 Abdul Allah Muhammad (1991) is one example, writing that "those who want a 'Black-Jewish relationship' should not forget that the vast majority of the slave ships were owned by Jewish slave traders." The same goes, of course, for others who use the study. When Tony Martin, professor of black history for the past twenty years at Wellesley College near Boston, included *The Secret Relationship* among the books assigned to his students, he was charged with using his position to cover the spread of anti-Semitic propaganda (Muwakkil 1993).

150 Quoted from the back cover of Farrakhan 1993i.

151 Holland 1993.

152 Johnson, A. 1993.

153 Farrakhan has over the years reached out to the Jewish community, offering dialogue and reconciliation. See for example Farrakhan, speech, 1988a; Muhammad, R. 1992b; and Tatum 1994. Although welcomed by some more liberal or leftist Jews, the Jewish mainstream has almost automatically dismissed such

offers (see, for example, McCall 1990; "Farrakhan's Proposal," 1990). In the fall of 1993, Farrakhan actually met with Jewish leaders Rabbi Marks and Rabbi Shalman during a meeting arranged by Dick Gregory, George O'Hare, and *Chicago Sun-Times* editor, Irv Kupcinet. Farrakhan relates how Rabbi Marks gave him a list, stating that Farrakhan could clean up his act if he proved that he had changed direction. As he had frightened Jews with his statements, he would have to say a lot of good things and do good deeds over a protracted period of time. They also demanded that Farrakhan should disavow *The Secret Relationship between Blacks and Jews*. Farrakhan said that he wanted to be their friend, which is why he participated in the meeting, but that he would not compromise with the truth. He would only disavow the book if the Jews disavowed the Jewish scholars it is based on, and as there is more history of evil done by Jews to blacks, he needed a promise of good words and deeds as well. "When I said that and walked out of the house," Farrakhan related, "I knew that the die was set. But God wants a showdown anyway" (Farrakhan 1993e).

154   Johnson, A. 1993. Kotzin, who is the director of an umbrella body of forty Jewish organizations in the Chicago area, said, "I do not think there is a sincere effort of that sort, or a meaningful effort of that sort. . . . My conclusion [is that this is] a public relations attempt to make it look to the general public as though [Farrakhan] is the peacemaker, he's the guy reaching out."

155   Suall, interview, 1994. It should be added that the Farrakhan call for dialogue is not always dismissed by Jewish spokespersons. When the NOI held a Saviour's Day rally in Atlanta in October 1992, an October 16 editorial in the Atlanta *Jewish Times* read, "The road to a healing between Black Muslims and American Jews must start now. Jewish organizations, on some level, should talk to the Nation of Islam. And the Nation of Islam, at the highest level, as Jewish groups repeatedly do when it comes to racism, should repudiate anti-Semitism."

156   See, for example, Muwakkil 1993. See also Tynetta Muhammad's (1993b) denouncement of internal critics and Jabril Muhammad's (1993g) rebuttal, where he states that "those who claim that [Farrakhan] has sold out to the Jews are telling lies."

157   Farrakhan, speech, 1993a. Compare with Farrakhan 1993e.

158   Saperstein, letter, 1993: "Confidential and Personal" letter to Mrs. Coretta Scott King, Rev. Walter Fauntroy, Bill Lucy, Rev. Jesse Jackson, William Gibson, Rev. Ben Chavis, and Lane Kirkland. Saperstein is at the Religious Action Center of Reform Judaism.

159   Strausberg 1993.

160   Muhammad, Jabril 1993h.

161   Farrakhan 1993f.

162   Duke 1993.

163   Page 1993.

164   Gilliam 1993.

165   Suall, interview, 1994.

166   Muhammad, K. A., speech, 1993.

167   "Minister Louis Farrakhan," 1994.

168   Muhammad, K. A., speech, 1993.

169   Ibid.

170   "You are not from the original people," Khallid charges. "You are a European

strain of people who crawled around on all fours in the caves and heels of Europe, eatin' Juniper roots and eatin' each other." Arabs are semites and Jews fighting Arabs and dispossessing Palestinians become the true anti-Semites. But, Khallid adds, "You say I'm anti-Semitic? If you are a Semite, I'm goddamit, whatever, I'm against whatever you are. Whatever you are, I'm anti" (ibid.).

171   Ibid.

172   Khallid like Farrakhan argues that the Holocaust was a white-on-white crime, but unlike Farrakhan he expresses, if not sympathy for Hitler, at least understanding. Said Khallid Abdul Muhammad in the same speech, "Everybody always talks about Hitler exterminating six million Jews. But don't nobody ever ask what did they do to them folks? They went in there, in Germany, the way they do everywhere they go, and they supplanted, they usurped, they turned around a German, in his own country, would almost had to go to a Jew to get money. They had undermined the very fabric of society. Now, he was an arrogant no-good devil bastard, Hitler, no question about it. He was wickedly great. Yes, he was. He used his greatness for evil and wickedness. But they [the Jews] are wickedly great too."

173   Khallid claimed that the Pope was a deceiving liar, who pretends to represent the Christ but who knows that he does not, a fact manifested when he was shot. He should have felt comfortable facing death if he expected paradise to be his destiny. But he seemed not to, calling on all medical expertise to save his life and praying, not before a white image of Jesus but in front of a black Mary and a black Jesus. "Go to the Vatican in Rome," Khallid said, "the old, no-good Pope, you know that cracker. Somebody needs to raise that dress up and see what's really under there."

174   Muhammad, K. A., speech, 1993.

175   Ibid.

176   Baghdadi 1994. In his article, Baghdadi charged that the majority of those who condemned Khallid's speech were remarkably silent about the February 24 massacre of more than fifty praying Muslims in the Ibrahim Mosque at the hands of the Brooklyn-born Jewish fundamentalist Baruch Goldstein, with possible backers.

177   "Jackson Says," 1994. Kwesi Mfume is a Maryland Democrat and head of the Congressional Black Caucus. Wyatt Tee Walker is senior pastor of Canaan Baptist Church in Harlem, N.Y., and Rev. Al Sharpton is a dedicated and controversial black nationalist agitator.

178   Farrakhan, speech, 1994.

179   Ibid. Farrakhan also appeared to rebuke the caucus: "What happened to our agreement? That if we had any criticism of one another, we would call each other, and go behind the door and speak frankly and candidly to one another. Why could not I have been spoken to and a meeting arranged with me to discuss this issue and how we should handle it, so that this issue would not be allowed to fracture our budding relationship, nor destroy the hope in the black community that was created by our budding but fragile unity."

180   Foxman, speech, 1994.

181   Milk 1994.

182   Farrakhan, speech, 1994; Talbott 1994. Farrakhan told an anecdote, saying he used to wonder why Khallid Abdul Muhammad always clung so close to his

Bible, until he saw it fall open one day: Khallid had cut open the Bible and kept his gun there to provide security for Farrakhan ("Minister Farrakhan," 1994).

183   Johnson, M. A. 1994.

184   Muhammad, D. 1994a.

185   "Muslim Shooting," 1994; "Suspect," 1994; Mydans 1994; Murr, Gordon, Smith, and McCormick 1994.

186   Wade 1994; "Khallid Resumes," 1995.

187   In Farrakhan's speeches delivered during the regime of the Honorable Elijah Muhammad, Jews are rarely mentioned. If spoken of unfavorably, it is in a specific, non anti-Semitic, context. Thus, Farrakhan disliked Jewish pre–Black Power participation in the major black civil rights organizations and linked black leaders' denouncement of the Messenger to that fact, and he condemned the pro-Israeli, anti-Arab lobby (Farrakhan 1992c [1973]:44, 62). When discussing the killings of Jesus of Nazareth and of the previous prophets, no references to Jews are made (Farrakhan 1992d [1972/73]:67–93). He discussed Baptist, Methodist, and Episcopalian slave owners, but not Jewish (Farrakhan 1992e [1970]:114).

188   As, for example, the Jewish-owned Lerner Newspapers in Chicago, which printed the *Muhammad Speaks* during its early years when Malcolm X was editor in chief (Woodford 1990:95). The white Jew Bob Arum was one of five in the Main Bout, Inc., a promotional firm marketing ancillary rights to Muhammad Ali's fights, and thus worked closely with John X Ali and Herbert Muhammad (Hauser 1991:150f.).

189   It is noteworthy that Essien-Udom, who published his *Black Nationalism* in 1962, did not feel it necessary to discuss anti-Semitism separately. C. Eric Lincoln included a section on the tensions with the Jewish community in his 1973 updated edition of *The Black Muslims in America* (1973:175–82). He notes that a minority of the NOI members considered Jews not as white but as Semites, and thereby included among the original people. This attitude holds Jews to be traitors who conceal their true identity, trying to pass off as whites themselves. The majority position was that Jews were whites, who cling to their white identity despite their experience of being oppressed by other whites. Jews differed from other whites in that they were more intelligent, and because of their visibility as business owners in the black ghettos. Their ghetto businesses were criticized as exploitation and Lincoln notes that "the negative image of the Jewish merchant is likely to be exaggerated" (1973:177). The creation of Israel on Muslim land was condemned and Jews were accused of controlling the mass media to support the Zionist cause as well as for trying to control black organizations. Lincoln concludes that "none of the beliefs are more virulent than those held by the Muslims about the white man in general. The Jews have not been singled out, so far, as a special target of a concentrated attack" (1973:178).

190   Brackman 1994.

191   Cited in Tatum 1994.

192   Farrakhan wrote, "I am not now, nor have I ever been, anti-Semitic. I denounce anti-Semitism in all forms and manifestations" (Farrakhan 1994e; compare with Walker, J. H. 1988).

193   Cited in Hardy and Pleasant 1987:44f.

194   Farrakhan makes frequent references to the Torah and Jabril Muhammad (1994) claims that "the Torah they [the Jews] have backs the Minister up 100 percent."

195 In 1992, *Behold a Pale Horse* by ex-Naval Intelligence agent William Cooper became "recommended reading by Minister Farrakhan" and was sold by *The Final Call*. It is a rather odd compilation of "hidden information," from UFO reports over the assassination of John F. Kennedy to anti-Semitic forgeries like *Protocols of the Wise Men of Zion*. Cooper adds an author's note, stating that the *Protocols* has been written to deceive people, and that "for clear understanding . . . any reference to 'Jews' should be replaced with the word 'Illuminati,' " showing that Cooper believes in the old conspiracy theory predating "the international Jew" theory that ascribes all the evils in modern world history to conspiracy by the secret society called Illuminati (see the *Final Call*, April 20, 1992, 8; Cooper 1991).

196 Erwin Suall, Tomas Harper, and Gail Gams of the Anti-Defamation League. Interview, January 20, 1994.

197 This will be further discussed in chapter 10.

198 Farrakhan, speech, 1989b. The NOI clearly view the ADL as antiblack, seeking to promote division in the black community and hamper the empowerment and embetterment of the African American community (Muhammad, James 1994b).

199 Lee, M. F. 1988:115.

200 Muwakkil 1993.

201 Farrakhan, speech, 1990d.

202 Farrakhan, speech, 1993a.

203 Farrakhan, speech, 1990d.

204 Farrakhan, speech, 1989b.

205 Farrakhan, speech, 1990a.

206 Farrakhan, speech, 1989b. As the reader hopefully will understand, the Bible and the Qur'an do not charge the entire Jewish people with any such crime.

207 Farrakhan, speech, 1990d.

208 Henry 1994.

209 See "Farrakhan and His," 1986; "Playing," 1987; "The New Axis," 1987; "The Political Soldiers," 1988; "Horst," 1988; "Political Soldiers Ride Out," 1988.

210 "The State of Britain's," 1988.

211 *Louis Farrakhan*, 1990:29.

212 Berlet 1991; Muwakkil 1991.

213 Lindeborg 1991. Compare with Fogelqvist 1989; Gable 1991:257f. Gerry Gable even believes Farrakhan is under the control of "masters in Iran and Libya."

214 Garvey 1986a [1923]:37.

215 Garvey 1986b [1925]:70f.

216 Ibid., 71.

217 X, M. 1971:137.

218 X, M. 1989a:135.

219 X, M. 1989b:122–26.

220 Chalmers 1981:375. For the reader unfamiliar with Klan terms and titles (quoted from Ridgeway 1990:70):

> *Empire.* The national Ku Klux Klan organization.
> *Realm.* The Klan in a particular state.
> *Dominion.* Five or more counties of a Realm.
> *Province.* One to three counties in a Dominion.
> *Klanton* or *Den.* Local chapter.

Klavern. Local meeting place.
Imperial Wizard. Head of a national Ku Klux Klan.
Grand Dragon. Head of a Realm.
Grand Titan. Head of a Dominion.
Giant. Head of a Province.
Exalted Cyclop. Head of a Klanton.
Klaliff. Vice President to Exalted Cyclops.
Kladd. Assistant Exalted Cyclop.
Kleagle. An organizer.
Kludd. Chaplain.
Klokard. National lecturer.

221 FBI files 105-8999 and 100-399321, cited in Carson 1991:203. As Malcolm said the meeting took place in December 1960, this means that either Malcolm's memory lapsed or that he had actually taken part in more than one meeting with the Ku Klux Klan.

222 Evanzz 1992:206, 285.

223 Ibid., 205f. Evanzz claims that the deal was worked out in November 1960.

224 Lincoln 1973:193.

225 Rockwell later became commander of the World Union of National Socialists (WUNS), an umbrella organization of different Nazi groups of the world, founded by British Nazi Colin Jordan in 1962. Although small, WUNS became instrumental in coordinating the Nazi activities in different countries (Lodenius and Larsson 1991:213).

226 Evanzz 1992:206; Carson 1991:359; King, W. 1985.

227 Halasa, M. 1990:86; King, W. 1985.

228 Lodenius and Larsson 1991:149.

229 Some of the leading neo-Strasserites were Nick Griffin, law student and son of a Tory politician, Derek Holland, student of history and instrumental in the NF support campaign for the NOI, Ian Anderson, student at Oxford, Pat Harrington, student of philosophy and NF candidate in an immigrant-dense London suburb, Michael Walker, student at Harrow College and editor of *Scorpion* (formerly *National Democrat*), the Irish Steve Brady and Joe Pearce, ex-convict leader for NF's youth organization and editor of *Nationalism Today* (Lodenius and Larsson 1991:147f., 154f.; Gable 1991:259).

230 "Thomas Sankara," n.d.

231 "Ghana," 1989.

232 "G.K.C. and Qathafi," n.d.; "Libya," 1989; "NF Chiefs," 1988.

233 "Iran," 1989.

234 "Garvey's Vision," n.d.

235 "Black Propaganda," n.d. The NF supported Jackson as a "Black Power candidate" on the ground that his campaign, "apart from creating a welcome White backlash," also has "upset America's rich and powerful Jewish community."

236 In 1984, the NF staff were still ignorant of basic facts about Farrakhan. He was hailed for calling Michael Jackson a sissy, for his stand against the Jewish community, and for calling Hitler a great German, but also for occupying the headquarters of the B'nai B'rith (termed "the American Jewish equivalent of the Gestapo"), an occupation that the reader will recall was carried out by Hanafi opponents to the NOI ("Black Propaganda," n.d.).

237   In "Let My People Go," 1985, the author(s) argue that a separate black state is "a small price to pay for the survival of our own people"; Griffin 1985. "Men and Women of Every Race," 1987. In "Louis Farrakhan," 1986, Farrakhan is portrayed and an address for those who wish to make contact with the NOI is included.

238   "Garvey's Vision," n.d.

239   Muhammad, A. W. n.d.

240   "The New Alliance," 1988.

241   "American Impressions," 1988. Malone (a.k.a. Mat Unger) is the editor of *Third Way* and was in 1987 second in charge in the American National Democratic Front, headed by Gary Gallo. Hoy has made contacts with separatists in the Republic of New Africa, the Black Hebrews, the American Indian Movement, and the Nation of Islam. FOM has participated in a series of conferences on separation (see, for example, "Living Alternative," 1988).

242   "American Impressions," 1988; "Multi-Racists on the Run." The NOI dopebusters will be discussed in the next chapter.

243   The leaflets carried one picture of Louis Farrakhan and one of an NF march and a little white girl, and the words: "Louis Farrakhan. He Speaks for His People. We Speak for Ours. National Front," and phone number ("Racial Realities" and "Get to Work," *National Front News*, no. 94).

244   "Farrakhan Aid."

245   "A Message for MI5."

246   The letter ("Rantings") ended with "in that context, I have [now] found allegiance with the British Nationalist Party."

247   "A Common Cause."

248   "Race."

249   The Manchester chapter of NF, for instance, notified the NFN editorial board that they "are not prepared to distribute issue number 99 of *National Front News*. The reason for this decision is because of the slogan 'Fight Racism' which encircles a clenched black fist upon the front page" (letter published in *From Ballots to Bombs*, n.d.).

250   "NF Send Vauxhall Voters the Message." The black persons backing Harrington were U.S. resident Robert Brock of the Self-Determination Committee and Osiris Akkebala of the Pan-African Inter-National. The NF received fewer votes than minor fringe groups like the Maoist supporters of Peruvian Senduro Luminoso, the RCP ("The Lessons of Vauxhall").

251   Lodenius and Larsson 1991:163.

252   Arthur Butz denies that gas chambers ever existed in Auschwitz and argues that the Holocaust is a gigantic hoax orchestrated by an international Jewish conspiracy. Butz is part of the revisionist network organized in the Institute of Historical Review and part of the editorial board for the IHR *Journal of Historical Review* (Lodenius and Larsson 1991:256ff.).

253   Grand Dragon is the second highest rank in the Ku Klux Klan; see Klan lexicon in note 220. Metzger has a long history of far-right activism. He joined the John Birch Society in the early 1960s, but left the organization as he found them soft on Jews. In 1975 he joined the Louisiana-based Knights of the Ku Klux Klan (KKKK) headed by David Duke and also became minister in the Identity group New Christian Crusade Church, led by James K. Warner. In 1979, Metzger moved to California and formed a vigilante border patrol of armed Klansmen that hunted

down illegal Mexican immigrants. In 1980, Metzger left the KKKK and formed the California Knights of the Ku Klux Klan. The same fall, he won a California Democratic Party primary and ran an unsuccessful race against Republican Clair Burgner (he was defeated, receiving 35,107 votes to Burgner's 253,946 in California's 45th Congressional District). Following his defeat, Metzger formed the White American Political Association to promote white candidates, and later the White Student Union, which was headed by his son John Metzger. In 1983, WAR and in 1987, its affiliate the Aryan Youth Movement, again with the Metzgers as heads, were founded and they began a series of overtures to neo-Nazi skinheads (i.e., "boneheads"). The WAR was initially successful, but a case linking the Metzgers with a group of Portland East Side White Pride Skins who murdered Ethiopian guest student Mulugeta Serew in 1988, won in 1990 by Morris Dees and associates from the Southern Poverty Law Center, will mean at least a temporary setback, as the defendants were forced to pay $12,500,000 in punitive damages. In 1987, Dees linked the United Klans of America with the lynching of a black female student in Alabama and bankrupted this once powerful Klan by winning a $7,000,000 verdict (*Extremism on the Right,* 1988:64, 128f.; Ridgeway 1990: 169–76; Dees and Fiffer 1993).

254   Bleifuss 1985; "Brothers in Bigotry," 1985; Rosenblatt 1985. P.O.W.E.R. (an acronym for People Organized and Working for Economical Rebirth) was launched by Farrakhan in 1985 as an economic plan for the NOI and the black community, to be discussed in the next chapter.

255   The October 1985 meeting was held near Flint, Michigan, on the Cohocta farm owned by Robert Miles, Klan leader and minister for a Christian Identity-related Mountain Church. Miles's farm housed annual extremist summits during the 1980s as part of Miles's efforts to unite the different organizations on the far right. At the 1985 meeting, some 200 leaders and their supporters from various groups were present. Besides Metzger, Arthur Jones from the neo-Nazi America First Committee and one-time candidate for the National Socialist White People's Party, hailed Farrakhan, saying that the enemy of his enemy was his friend, and that he saluted Louis Farrakhan and anyone else who stands up against the Jews (King, W. 1985; Ridgeway 1988:110).

256   Ridgeway 1990:175; Barkun 1994:236.

257   Gallo 1990. Gallo, a Maryland lawyer, founded the NDF in 1985 as a revolutionary movement based on Romanian National-Christian socialism, Italian fascism, and German National Socialism. Gallo was clearly inspired by the NF Third Positionist leadership. He lived with the NF during 1984, officially to help them finance the organization through sales of T-shirts, badges, books, tapes, etc. Mat Unger, alias Mat Malone, was second in command in the NDF when he traveled to Britain to confer with the NF. According to NF writers, the relationship with Gallo later ran sour and Mat Unger established the FOM.

The idea of dividing the United States into different areas populated by different ethnic groups is not unique to the NDF or Metzger, but is shared among other white racialist organizations, for example, by the Aryan Nations and David Duke's NAAWP (the National Association for the Advancement of White People—an organization created in 1980). In many plans, the Northwestern states (Washington, Oregon, Montana, Wyoming, and Idaho) would be the homeland for white racists; the Southwest (except Navaho territories, which would become all

Native Indian) turned Hispanic; New Africa would be set up in parts of Georgia, Alabama, and Mississippi; Long Island and Manhattan would become West Israel, with the remainder of New York City becoming home for various minorities; Dade County with Miami would become New Cuba, and the Hawaiian Islands would become the home for East Asians (*Extremism on the Right*, 1988:42; "American Impressions," 1988; Gable 1991:253, 259; Ridgeway 1990:148–51).

258 "Islam Nation," 1990.

259 LaRouche was born to right-wing Quakers and became a member of the Trotskyist Socialist Workers Party in 1948 and was expelled in 1966. In the early 1970s LaRouche began his shift toward the far right, developing friendships with key individuals such as Willis Carto, founder of Liberty Lobby, and he ran as the candidate for America's right-wing extremists in the 1980 presidential campaign. LaRouche uses cultish strategies in recruiting new members and controls the cadre through depersonalizing psychological methods. Aiming to create a perfect world populated by a biological master race, "the golden souls," LaRouche intends to shoulder the burden of global dictatorship and purge the earth of the influence from Jews, leftists, environmentalists, and other inferior minds who are manipulated by the British Zionist oligarchical forces of evil. Dennis King has shown that LaRouche, twisting the concepts in an Orwellian fashion, argues that those who call themselves Jews are the real Nazis, that Hitler was put in power by Rothschild and other British Jews-who-are-not-really-Jews, that Menachim Begin is a Nazi, and Elizabeth a Queen of the Jews. The German Nazis who opposed the Jews-who-in-reality-are-the-true-Nazis thus are the real anti-Nazis, as are their successors in the modern neo-Nazi movement. (For an account on LaRouche, see King, D. 1989. See also, *Extremism on the Right*, 1988:114f.; Berlet 1993a; 1993b; 1993c.)

260 Berlet 1991b.

261 Bierre 1990.

262 Berlet 1991b. The Chicago Conference attracted some 350 participants and was entitled "Development is the New Name for Peace," but proved to be the annual LaRouchie Food for Peace conference. During the meeting a videotaped message from the Iraqi cultural attaché in the United States, Mayser Al Mallah, was shown and LaRouchies Mel Klenetsky and Nancy Spannaus acted as moderators.

263 Muhammad, A. W. 1991a. This was not the first time *Final Call* staff used material from the EIR. In 1990, an essay on Panama, Bush, and Noriega was reprinted from the *Executive Intelligence Review* (Wesley 1990).

264 Muhammad, James 1994a. It seems as if the LaRouchies are more eager to connect with the NOI than vice versa. A strange incidence occurred in Stockholm, Sweden, on September 20, 1995. The author was invited by a student organization at Stockholm University to give yet another open lecture about the Nation of Islam. Halfway through the lecture, an angry voice cut across the jam packed lecture hall. "I strongly object to your misrepresentation of Minister Farrakhan," a black man, standing in the back, shouted. "I represent the Nation of Islam, and this man is misrepresenting the Minister." I responded that I don't misrepresent Minister Farrakhan and that I in fact did not represent him at all. I told him that I was not a member but a researcher, who was only trying to explain what the NOI was all about. Then I realized that the angry black man did not speak Swedish and had not been able to understand anything of what I had been saying. Trying

416 Notes to Chapter Nine

to be fair, I asked the man to let me finish my lecture and offered him a possibility to address the audience after the question-and-answer session. This he did. To my surprise, he presented himself as "Gardell X" and began to talk. On the back of his blue jacket was three yellow block letters, "EAP," in the famous "FBI" fashion. EAP is the Swedish branch of the LaRouchie organization, and during his aggressive speech he surely exposed himself as a LaRouchie. He spoke far more about LaRouche than Minister Farrakhan, mainly arguing that LaRouche and the Nation had built a strong coalition. Claiming that LaRouche sponsored the upcoming Million Man March, he devoted most of his time trying to clear LaRouche of all "misunderstandings" surrounding his leader. Later, I checked his claims, finding no trace of LaRouchie organizations in the list of official sponsors of the Million Man March. Moreover, I found out that his claimed name, Gardell X, was a fake and probably adopted to cause confusion. According to informants who for a long time have been following the LaRouchie sect's undertakings in Sweden and abroad, he used a conventional LaRouchie strategy to get attention.

265   Lindeborg 1991.

266   Lodenius and Larsen are more in tune with the white extreme far-right organizations and leaders than with the NOI and Farrakhan. Besides numerous errors in their account of the NOI history and an underestimation of Farrakhan's influence in the African American community, the authors argue that white racists and blacks have an established "cooperation." The authors allege that "the connections between the Nation of Islam and the British NF roughly followed the same pattern as in the United States" and thereby indicate that American white extremist nationalists have promoted the growth of the Nation, the way they describe the NF doing in England. Lodenius and Larsen further claim that unidentified and undefined "serious black activists" take exception with Farrakhan (do they mean that only those who distance themselves from Farrakhan are serious activists?) but that his ideas "aroused great enthusiasm among traditional white racists who for years have propagated exactly the same form of apartheid and anti-Semitism." The last unfounded statement only reveals the authors' ignorance of the NOI creed, as does the assertion that the NOI is a "fundamentalist church." (Lodenius and Larsen 1991:157f. Translation mine.)

267   Farrakhan, interview, 1989b.

268   Ibid.

269   Ibid.

270   Qur'an 30:14, as translated by Maulana Muhammad Ali.

271   Farrakhan, interview, 1989b.

272   "Official," 1990.

273   See, for example, "Klan shooting," 1990.

274   X Massop 1993.

275   The reader should note that far from all skinheads are neo-Nazis or racists. The skinhead movement started as an outgrowth of the mods and rude boys in Britain and was heavily influenced by Caribbean immigrants, as is obvious in their Ska music. Most skins were working class and if politically interested, frequently oriented toward workers' power ideologies, such as authoritarian socialism (social democracy or communism) or libertarian socialism (anarchism and/or revolutionary syndicalism). Many American skin individuals and gangs belong to the SHARP and RASH federations (Skin Heads Against Racial Prejudice and Red and

Anarchist Skin Heads). Fascist, neo-Nazi, and racist skinheads are known as boneheads. For Metzger's influence on West Coast boneheads, see Dees and Fiffer 1993.

276 Besides Minister Farrakhan, the death list included Rev. Cecil Murray of the First AME Church, Rodney King (who was almost murdered by the LAPD in 1991), Rev. Al Sharpton, Easy E (a renowned rapper), and Danny Bakewell (a community activist). See, Dellios 1993; Muhammad and Moore 1993; Muhammad, Rosalind 1993. Metzger, of course, denied any association with the Fourth Reich Skinheads. Federal officials said that besides WAR, the FRS also had ties to the Florida-based white supremacist Church of the Creator.

277 British Israelism originated with Richard Brothers (1757–1824), a visionary who argued that he was a direct descendant of King David and therefore the rightful King of England. Brothers, who was sent to an asylum, found no support for his thesis until after his death, when John Wilson published his restatement in a series of five volumes called *Lectures on Our Israelitish Origin,* published between 1840 and 1876 (the last volume published posthumously). In 1871, Edward Hine published the one time best-seller *Identification of the British Nation with Lost Israel* in which Germans were purged from the Lost Tribes and identified with the "lost" Assyrians. This locked the British and the Germans in a battle commenced in biblical times, articulated in Hine's time in the conflict between the British Empire and the reunited Germany. Early exponents in the United States were M. M. Eshelman, minister in the Church of Bretheren and author of *Two Sticks or the Lost Tribes of Israel Discovered* (1887), and J. J. Allen, whose *Judah's Sceptre and Joseph's Birthright* (1902) became a best-seller, spreading British-Israelism in Adventist and Bible study circles. Early independent Identity churches were the Worldwide Church of God, founded by Church of God (Seventh Day) minister Herbert W. Armstrong and the Anglo-Saxon Federation of America, founded by Howard B. Rand, former editor of *Dearborn Independent,* the Henry Ford paper that was instrumental in spreading anti-Semitism and the *Protocols* in the United States. After World War II, Gerald K. Smith's *Christian Nationalist Crusade* inspired many of the prominent Identity churches in modern time. British-Israelism in the United States transformed into Christian Identity. Adherers generally believe that America was settled by the thirteenth tribe, the Manasseh. Their number had a bearing on early American history: there were thirteen original colonies, thirteen stars and stripes on the first flag, on the official seal there are thirteen stars in the glory cloud, thirteen arrows in the eagle's claws, thirteen bars on the escutcheon borne on its breast, and thirteen letters in the motto *E pluribus unum.* Although Christian Identity in the United States is composed of different, sometimes warring factions, they unite on a higher ideological level to form one movement based on the convictions that they are the chosen people of the Sacred Covenant and that Jews and, to a varying extent, the nonwhite mud races, are descendants of the Devil, thus representing forces of good and evil locked in an eternal battle for global hegemony. This opposition is accentuated by Bob Miles, minister of the Mountain Kirk, who founded "the Dualist religion," based on the belief that God and Satan represent primal forces that use the earth as a battle stage to which they have sent down armies of look-alike races, soldiers of light versus mud, in their quest for universal dominion. This dualism echoes the racist dualist Theosophy known as Theozoology of Jörg

Lanz von Liebenfels, which in turn influenced Himmler and the S.S. (Barkun 1994; Melton 1992:68ff.; Ridgeway 1990:53ff.; Goodrick-Clarke 1992:92).

278   Law enforcement agencies estimated that some 1,700 different organizations were scattered around the country in the 1970s and 1980s. Most were fairly small and remained unknown by the majority of United States citizens, but the total membership exceeded more than 100,000 members (Corcoran 1990:36).

279   Posse Comitatus was founded in Portland, Oregon, in 1969 by Henry L. Beach, who in the 1930s had been an officer in the American Nazi Silver Legion (known as Silver Shirts), organized on the model of the contemporary Nazi German S.A. by William Dudley Pelley (who believed a number of "demon souls" were reincarnated in the Jews, Stalin, and other enemies of his).

Posse Comitatus differs from the bulk of neo-Nazi groups in the United States with their masquerade-like obsession with World War II Nazi paraphernalia. Posse talks less of Hitler than of the American dream of the pioneer farmers, appealing to the genuinely American myths of the lone ranger and the hardworking, law-abiding, and God-fearing family man who creates his own fortune despite difficult odds. Posse is one of the largest far-right organizations, numbering between 12,000 and 50,000 (although Beach claimed a membership of 100,000).

Posse Comitatus is Latin for "power of the county," the highest legitimate form of government according to Posse doctrine. The county sheriff is the highest law enforcement authority, and if he were to do his duty he properly would enroll the assistance of vigilante white citizens, a posse, as Western sheriffs did in the good old days, and apply righteous old-fashioned justice, such as hanging criminals by the rope.

Posse further believes that the original Constitution was derived directly from the Bible and given by God himself to the Founding Fathers of the promised land. All amendments after the Bill of Rights are believed to be unconstitutional and part of a conspiracy led by the breed of Satan, Jews, and the mud races.

The year 1913 is thought to be when the conspirators gained the upper hand, as it was the year when the laws allowing the federal government to tax personal incomes and the Federal Reserve Act were ratified. The evil continued with the money notes substituting gold and silver coins, the creation of the United Nations, desegregation, civil rights for minorities, and today usury-crazed Jewish bankers try to take away the farmers' land through the scheme called loan-with-interest.

Christian Identity Posse preachers such as William Gale of the Ministry of Christ Church and the paramilitary California Rangers, and James Wickstrom of the Life Science Church and National Director of Counter-Insurgency, provided religious confirmation and guerrilla training compounds, as Posse believed each white man's duty was to engage in armed resistance. Said Wickstrom, "These fools [the federal government] think we are a political organization, not realizing that we have declared a Holy War against them" (cited in Corcoran 1990:29f.; see also Ridgeway 1990:109–29).

280   The Aryan Nations was founded by Rev. Richard Butler who built his headquarters at Hayden Lake, Idaho. Butler became head of the Church of Jesus Christ, Christian, when its founder, Wesley Swift, died in 1970. Butler moved the Church's headquarters to the capital of the Aryan Nations, which became a

Mecca for American white religious racists. In 1982, Butler organized the first International Congress of the Aryan Nations, which gathered the most important ideologists of white supremacists. Butler advocates the separatist "ten percent solution" in which the Northwestern states Washington, Oregon, Montana, Wyoming, and Idaho, would secede from the United States and form an independent monoethnical state, the white bastion of the Aryan Nations (see Flynn and Gerhart 1989; Ridgeway 1990:89f.).

281   The Covenant, Sword and Arm of the Lord (CSA) was founded in 1971 by James Ellison. The CSA is a paramilitary Christian Identity "survivalist" organization that prepares its members for the onslaught of Armageddon, in which they will serve God as his Soldier-Saints. During the final battle, the CSA forces will clean the earth of all mud races of the anti-Christ, whereupon God will elevate his soldiers into true sonship and establish his eternal white kingdom on earth. Military training was provided in CSA school, the Endtime Overcomer Survivalist Training School, located at CSA's 224-acre Missouri commune, Zarepath-Horeh, on the shores of Bull Shoals Lake, close to the Arkansas border. It was sold following a raid by the Bureau of Alcohol, Tobacco and Firearms in 1985. Ellison was sentenced to twenty years in prison on charges of manufacturing automatic weapons and acts of bombing and arson (Barkun 1994:216; Corcoran 1990:34f.; *Extremism on the Right,* 1988:14f.).

282   The Christian Defense League was founded in 1977 by James K. Warner as the armed wing of the New Christian Crusade Church of which Warner is minister. Warner has a long record of far-right activism, ranging from having been officer in the American Nazi Party to membership in David Duke's Knights of the Ku Klux Klan in Louisiana.

283   The Order or the Silent Brotherhood was founded by Robert Mathews and modeled on the Order, a white resistance group in *The Turner Diaries,* a best-selling novel by National Alliance founder William Pierce. The *Diaries* is a work of futuristic fiction in which a dedicated group of Aryan warriors initiates the Battle of Armageddon, wipes out all nonwhites, homosexuals, communists, race traitors, and ZOG agents and establishes their hegemony in an all-white ideal state. Mathews, who belonged to the Aryan Nations Identity Church but also held Odinist beliefs, formed an armed group that operated according to an insurrection agenda, involving counterfeit activities and armed robberies to add to the war chest, the assassination of key enemies, and actual guerrilla warfare. Matthews was implicated in the 1984 assassination of Alan Berg, a Jewish talk show host in Denver, and was killed in a shoot-out with FBI agents in December the same year (Flynn and Gerhart 1989).

284   The Ku Klux Klan is far from what it was in its most powerful period in the mid-1920s, when the Klan had a membership of three to four million. On the decline since the late 1920s, the Klan of today is split into a number of warring Klans with national aspirations. The most important Klans are the United Klans of America; the Invisible Empire, Knights of the Ku Klux Klan; Knights of the Ku Klux Klan; and Christian Knights of the Ku Klux Klan. The total membership of all the Klans in 1991 was estimated by the ADL at approximately 4,000. Some, but not all, of the Klans adhere to the Christian Identity movement (*The KKK Today,* 1991; Chalmers 1987; Katz 1986).

285   Klassen was born in the Ukraine and migrated with his family to Mexico and

Canada before settling in the United States. In 1958, Klassen moved to Florida and was in 1966 elected to the lower house of the Florida State Legislature after a campaign against busing. In the late 1960s, Klassen was active in the John Birch Society and was the Florida chairman of George Wallace's American Independent Party.

286   Klassen 1987:124ff.

287   Ibid., 228. "You might think that I would be the last person in the world with whom God would have an in-depth, heart-to-heart talk, or even a tête-à-tête," Klassen wrote. "But not so. There is every reason why he should, and the fact is, he did. The time was October 25, 1986, and we spent a cozy six hours, from 2:00 PM to 8:00 PM of that day, reviewing and discussing the overwhelming propblems of the world" (1987:226). Although God "has been around since time immemorial," he looked like a strong Aryan warrior about thirty-five years of age (1987:228). Then Klassen asked God if he was in favor of racial segregation, and God smashed his powerful fist onto the table, thundering that he in no way intended the bastardization of his beautiful people through race mixing with "monkeys, gorillas, niggers and other inferior sub-species." "Then you don't consider the niggers and mud races as part of the human race?" Klassen ventured to ask, and God reacted: "The color was rapidly rising in his florid cheeks and I could see the wrath of God erupting like a vulcano before my eyes. 'Do I look like a goddam stinking Hottentot? Do I look like a filthy New Guinea headhunter?' he thundered back at me with fire in his eyes. The whole room was beginning to vibrate and I shook in my cowboy boots for having asked such a stupid question. 'No,' I admitted meekly, 'you sure don't and I retract the question. But what about the Mexicans?' 'I loathe and detest the Mexicans [God answered]. I hate all mongrels . . . [and] the Jews are the excrement of humanity—doomed for ever to be miserable parasites' " (1987:230). God then made a binding covenant with the white race, stating that if they rose up and fought not only for their survival but also for their expansion and advancement, he "would bless them to become super-beings, a true human race, in fact, demi-gods, faithfully created in my image" (1987:234). For further information on Klassen's religious views, see Klassen 1981.

288   The white far-right groups are clearly influenced by the Black Power movement, adopting terms such as White Pride and White Power, and organizational names such as NAAWP, the National Association for the Advancement of White People.

289   Goodrick-Clarke 1992; Gasman 1971; Barkun 1994; Melton 1992.

290   FBI file 100-399321, 5/17/61, reports that "Malcolm X expressed himself as a great admirer of Nicloai [sic] Lenin and Joseph Stalin and stated that they were actually non-white men. He explained that Lenin was of the yellow race descending from the Mongols and Stalin descending from Semitic-Arabs and a Muslim mixture with dark skin."

10   A Divine Nation in a Decaying World

1   Henderson 1994:12, 17.

2   Farrakhan, speech, 1989e.

3   Farrakhan, speech, 1990d.

4   The use of the term "youth" here should not obscure the fact that the nations' leaders are adults.

5   Katz 1991; Stolberg 1992.

6   Stolberg 1992.

7   Ford 1992.

8   "Gangbanging" in black English is to be an active gang member.

9   Muwakkil 1993b. The rival federations Crips and Bloods are composed of a number of loosely affiliated gang sets. Not only is the feud between the Crips and Bloods deadly, but so are the conflicts between some of the different sets in each federation. For an account of Los Angeles gang life from the members' perspective, see Bing 1991.

10 Muwakkil 1993b; Perkins 1987.

11 Farrakhan, speech, 1990k.

12 Farrakhan, speech, 1990e.

13 Farrakhan, speech, 1990k.

14 Farrakhan, speech, 1990d.

15 Cited in Muwakkil 1993b.

16 Farrakhan, speech, 1987.

17 Farrakhan, speech, 1990e.

18 Farrakhan, speech, 1989b. For NOI reactions to the reallocation of FBI agents to target black street gangs, see Muhammad and Muhammad 1992; Farrakhan 1992f.

19 Farrakhan 1989b; "Assault on gangs," 1989.

20 Farrakhan, speech, 1990e.

21 Moore 1992; Strausberg 1992; Gardell 1992a; "Marines," 1992; "Rebuild," 1992; Oliver, Johnson, and Farrell 1993:117–20; Ditz, unpublished, 1992. Several of those killed seem to have been shot by police and white civilian snipers in a manner similar to the Central American death squadrons (Mandel 1993:157f.).

22 "King verdict," 1992; Baker 1993:42; Gardell 1992a.

23 Baker 1993:43.

24 Cited in "King verdict," 1992.

25 Gross and Blum 1992. On April 17, 1993, Stacey Koon and Laurence Powell were convicted in Federal Court of violating King's civil rights and sentenced to 30 months in prison. Timothy Wind and Theodore Briseno were acquitted. The notion of flagrant injustice was strengthened by an almost identical but racially reversed event during the following rebellion. White trucker Reginald Dennis was dragged from his vehicle by a number of black men and severely beaten. The LAPD had an easy task in rounding up the suspects as the assault was videotaped. The subsequent trial resulted in Damian Williams being sentenced to ten years in prison, while codefendant Henry Watson arrived at a plea bargain and was sentenced to serve three years probation and 320 hours of community service ("Police Arrest 3 Men," 1992; X Moore, Rosalind 1993a and 1993b; Muhammad, Rosalind 1993b and 1993c).

26 "The Price of Injustice," 1992.

27 Farrakhan 1992a.

28 Cited in Patterson 1993:174f. Bush's analysis is on par with Hoover's understanding of the uprisings in the 1960s (see chapter 4), indicating that not much has been learned in the past twenty-five years.

29 Said by Bong, interviewed in "We Gotta Do Shit," Wildcat TV.

30 The Los Angeles uprising was multiethnic, involving mostly blacks, Hispanics, and illegal immigrants. The population of South Central Los Angeles is today

nearly 50 percent Hispanic, with a substantial influx of Korean businessmen who have replaced the Jewish shopkeepers. Blacks and Hispanics share poverty rates but differ in that the former in general are unemployed poor and the latter working poor in low-income jobs in nonunionized shops. According to police records, 42 percent of the participants were African American, 44 percent were Hispanic, 9 percent were white, and 2 percent other (Simmons 1993:142; Oliver, Johnson, and Farrell 1993; Williams, R. 1993).

31 Farrakhan 1992a.

32 X Moore, Rosalind 1992a; Gardell 1992a; Davis, M. 1993:147; Ditz, unpublished, 1992.

33 Davis, M. 1993:146f.; Davis, M. 1992.

34 See, for instance, Jonsson 1993:92; Davis, M. 1993:146f.

35 X Moore, Rosalind 1992a.

36 "Bloods/Crips," 1993:274–82. The Bloods/Crips' proposal calls for the city to purchase all burned and abandoned structures and build community service or recreation areas on the sites. All pavement and sidewalks must be repaired, lighting increased in the streets and alleys, and trees planted in the neighborhoods. The "Educational Proposal" calls for improvement of educational standards in low-income areas, including repairing school buildings, purchasing books, computers and supplies, raising teacher salaries, and implementing a number of student and foreign-exchange programs. The "Human Welfare Proposal" calls for three new hospitals and forty new health care centers, day care centers for single parents, a facelift of parks and twenty-four-hour security, and replacement of welfare with state-financed work. The "Economic Development Proposal" calls for low-interest loans to small business owners and firms that hire 90 percent of the employees from the community. The "Law Enforcement Proposal" calls for commanding police officers to be residents of the community. In addition, former gang members should go through police training to be uniformed, but unarmed "patrol buddies" of the LAPD. The final section of the Bloods/Crips' proposals read: "In return for these demands the Bloods/Crips Organization will: 1. Request the drug lords of Los Angeles take their moneys and invest them in business and property of Los Angeles. 2. Encourage these drug lords to stop drug trafficking and get them to use the money constructively. We will match the funds of the state government appropriations and build building for building. 3. Additionally, we will match funds for an AIDS research and awareness center in South Central and Long Beach that will only hire minority researchers and physicians to assist in the AIDS epidemic."

37 In Chicago it is called Unity in Peace.

38 Lee 1993.

39 Muhammad, Richard 1993a.

40 "Gang Summit," 1993.

41 Younger 1993.

42 Muhammad, Richard 1993b; "Gang Summit," 1993.

43 Farrakhan 1993g.

44 Younger 1993.

45 Muhammad, Richard 1993c.

46 Boland 1992.

47 For the efforts to reform gangs in the 1960s, see note 129 in chapter 8.

48 Muhammad, Richard 1993c.

49 Younger 1993.

50 Cited in Muwakkil 1993b. One of those jailed leaders influential in the peace effort is Larry Hoover, legendary leader for the Gangster Disciples (GD). Believing he would do more good if released, some prominent black leaders, including Farrakhan, requested that he be given parole. Jack Hynes of the state attorney's gang prosecution unit rejected the bid, claiming that Hoover still controlled the GD's drug, murder, and other criminal enterprises from the inside. Hoover, who was convicted of murder in 1973, was denied parole by the Chicago state board on August 12, 1993 (Muhammad, Richard 1993d; "State Denies Parole," 1993).

51 Boland 1992.

52 See Muwakkil 1993b.

53 Farrakhan 1993h.

54 For an eminent description of the hip-hop movement, see Rose 1994.

55 Muhammad, D. 1993b; X Curry 1993a; Daniels 1993.

56 Quoted in Spady and Eure 1991:202. Message rap can be said to continue the black liberation music tradition of John Coltrane, James Brown, the Last Poets, and others.

57 Afrika Bambaataa 1991. Afrika Bambaataa, founder of the Zulu Nation, here pumps up a song originally performed by James Brown. The "King of Soul," Brown represents a break with the previous blues tradition and like Aretha Franklin and other soul singers articulates more outspoken black pride and resistance against what is perceived as an injust system.

58 Dyson 1993:16.

59 Public Enemy 1990.

60 Cited in Spady and Eure 1991:203.

61 Zulu King Shabazz of the Defiant Giants, interviewed in Muhammad, D. 1991a.

62 K-Solo 1990.

63 Shockin' Shawn, interviewed in Spady and Eure 1991:129.

64 Brand Nubian 1990. The same goes for a number of songs on their *In God We Trust* album (1992) like "Allahu Akbar," "Ain't No Mystery," "Meaning of the 5%," and "Allah and Justice."

65 Professor Griff, "Crucified," 1991; The Undaground Soldier and Thayod 1994; KAM 1995.

66 Muhammad, D. 1988. As NOI members, Kool-Aid is Bro. Brian X and Rapp-Operaman is Bro. Robert 3X.

67 Spady and Eure 1991:265ff.; Toop 1991; Muhammad, James 1991; Muhammad, D. 1991b; Prince Akeem 1991.

68 NWA, "F*** Tha Police," 1988. The message was similar on the albums *100 Miles and Running* (1990) and *Efil4zaggin* (1991). The latter name should be read backward.

69 Da Lench Mob 1992.

70 Bernard 1992. As member of Mosque #27, L.A., he is Bro. Jerome 3X ("Mob Control," 1993).

71 Ice Cube 1990; Ice Cube 1991; Ice Cube 1993. Also the first of these reflects NOI teachings, as does Da Lench Mob's *Guerillas in tha Mist* (Muhammad, D. 1991c; "Mob Control," 1993).

72 McDaniel 1994.

73 Coker 1994.

74 The first album, *Yo! Bum Rush the Show,* includes Malcolm X samplings and other sources of black Islam, but is less heavily NOI inspired. Fernando (1994: 136ff.) includes a section on the Public Enemy–NOI connection.

75 Chuck D., interview, 1990 (partly published in Gardell 1990).

76 Ibid. Professor Griff, who by 1990 had established his own group, the Last Asiatic Disciples, similarly performed flanked by the Asiatic Ghetto Soldiers (see *Pawns In The Game,* 1990).

77 Dyson 1993:17.

78 Public Enemy 1990; 1991; 1992; 1994.

79 "Overwhelming Event," 1988; Muhammad, A. W. 1988a; Muhammad, D. 1988; Muhammad, D. 1989; Muhammad, D. 1991d; Muhammad, D. 1991e; "Rappin' in the Hood," 1991; "Saviour's Day," 1991; Muhammad, James 1992; X Curry and Muhammad 1994; X Curry 1994b.

80 See "Where Ya At?" 1995; "Famous Faces," 1995; George 1990; "Drugs Challenged," 1988, Muhammad, Richard 1989a; Muhammad, D. 1990; Muhammad, D. 1991a; Muhammad, D. 1991e; Muhammad, D. 1992; Muhammad, D. 1994b.

81 Farrakhan, speech, 1989c.

82 Adler, Foote, and Sawhill 1990.

83 The song "Cop Killer" was dedicated to the LAPD and Police Chief Daryl Gates. The anger Ice-T expresses against brutal police officers invading the black areas is explicit indeed:

> COP KILLER, It's better you than me.
> COP KILLER, fuck police brutality!
> COP KILLER, I know your family's grievin' Fuck them!
> COP KILLER, but tonight we get even.

The song is clearly directed against police brutality, "Fuck the police, for Rodney King. Fuck the police, for my dead homies." In 1991, three policemen were killed in the entire state of California. The same year, eighty-one people in Los Angeles alone were killed by police in proven police-misconduct cases. "Cop Killer" communicates a message of "enough is enough, we will not take this any more." As such, it is of course more an act of catharsis, channeling frustrations and desperation, than a song that will cause a series of actual police killings. After a police officer in Houston, Texas, discovered the song, he established a group known as the Fraternal Organization of Cops. The police group organized a boycott of Warner Brothers and the controversy became well publicized. Fatal threats poured in to Warner Brothers and two bombs were sent to them. Ice-T decided to pull the record, but does not retract the above lyrics. "The only concession I'll make," Ice writes, "is to the honest cops who misunderstood the record and took it as a blatant attack on all police officers, which it is not. It's directed at your criminal partner, who you have to deal with. It's his record" (Ice-T 1994:180; Ice-T, "Cop Killer," 1992).

84 Cederskog 1990; Public Enemy 1989.

85 *The Anti-Semitism of Black Demagogues and Extremists,* 1992:31ff.

86 X Moore, Rosalind 1991a.

87 Leland 1992; West 1993:123.

88 Defiant Giants, cited in Spady and Eure 1991:203f.

89 Pistol Pete 1992.

90   Barboza 1994:135. Fifty-nine thousand Americans died in Vietnam. Approx-
      imately 20,000 of these casualties were blacks. With a black death toll of 10,000 a
      year, the killing streets in the West would take out nearly five times as many lives
      as in Vietnam. In 1994, AIDS passed homicide as the number-one killer of black
      men between the ages twenty-five to forty-four; see AIDS section below.
91   Leland 1992.
92   Coker 1994.
93   In the words of X-Clan, Island Records, 1990.
94   Jungle Brothers 1989.
95   Farrakhan, speech, 1989a.
96   Cited in Spady and Eure 1991:289.
97   Simmons 1993:152.
98   DeParle 1990.
99   Chomsky 1991:343; McCoy 1991:47ff.
100   McCoy 1991:19, 288f., 318.
101   Lee and Shlain 1992:262.
102   Scott and Marshall 1991:187; McCoy 1991:441ff.
103   Scott and Marshall 1991:186.
104   Farrakhan 1993i:17.
105   Muhammad, D., interview, 1989.
106   Muhammad, James 1988a.
107   *Time Magazine,* May 9, 1988.
108   3X Bryant 1988.
109   Muhammad, James 1988a.
110   "Community Outraged," 1988; Muhammad, Richard 1989b.
111   According to *Final Call* reports, drug dealers clashed a few times with the FOI
      soldiers. Charles X Johnson and Napoleon and Daryl Muhammad were arrested
      in July 1989, for "assault with a deadly weapon" after an incident at Mayfair
      Mansion. When the dopebusters intervened against a drug deal in a parking lot,
      the dealers tried to run them down but wrecked their car and eventually man-
      aged to escape. Later the Muslim patrols had an argument with an intoxicated
      "associate of the drug dealers" whose arm was broken. The FOI men, in a classic
      explanation, alleged that the man fell and broke his arm when trying to escape
      (Muhammad, Richard 1989b). In 1991, two shooting incidents occurred. In the
      first, Tyrone X was injured by a gunman firing six shots into the Muslim security
      guard booth. In the second, Rodney Muhammad was hospitalized after an attack
      by armed men in a car chase. Shots shattered the car windows and some sixteen
      bullets were found in Muhammad's vehicle. Muhammad managed to escape but
      was hit three times and left with a bullet in his neck ("Back on Track," 1991). In
      1993, "a mob" of people attacked the Muslim guards with pipes, bats, and guns,
      but the FOI managed to contain the group. When police arrived at the scene,
      arguments broke out again, resulting in a few injuries on both sides, now the
      police officers versus NOI Security men (2X McKeiver 1993).
112   Muhammad, Richard 1990a.
113   Farrakhan 1990a.
114   X Curry 1992b; Tabor 1992; Foxman and Boland 1992; X Curry 1993b; Ihejirika
      1994; Holmes 1994.
115   Holmes 1994.

116 Tabor 1992.

117 Doherty 1991.

118 Samad 1992; Doherty 1991.

119 X Moore, R. 1992b.

120 Ellingwood 1992.

121 Foxman and Boland 1992.

122 Ellingwood 1992.

123 Muhammad, Rosalind 1994.

124 Muhammad and X Moore 1993; Muhammad, Rosalind 1994.

125 X Curry 1992c.

126 The comments were made at a February 3 press conference, summoned due to demands that the NOI contract should be terminated. These demands were voiced after the Kean College speech by Khallid Muhammad was brought to the public's attention. Mayor Schmoke said that he was "in no way supporting the comments of Khallid Muhammad," but that he did "believe that this local security organization has done an effective job and made a contribution to the citizens of Baltimore" (X Grandison 1994; X Curry 1993b; Holmes 1994).

127 CHA Chairman Vincent interviewed in Ihejirika 1994b. Richard Hirschaut, director of the Greater Chicago Region of the Anti-Defamation League, commented: "It strikes us as inappropriate at the least, and bordering on outrageous. We will weigh in with a very fierce and strong objection." Lake said that it was not about religion but about who could get the job done, asking how he could reject somebody simply because he was Muslim when many contracts are made with Protestants and Jews.

128 Ihejirika 1994a.

129 See, for example, Lincoln 1973:84; Lomax 1962:147–48.

130 Muhammad, D., interview, 1989.

131 Christie 1993:119f. Compare with Robinson, C. J. 1993:77.

132 McSwine 1993:253.

133 Farrakhan, speech, 1986a; X Moore, G. 1994; Muhammad, D., interview, 1989.

134 Elias Sengor, for instance, relates how he in the late 1960s was treated for being an NOI official in the Green Haven Correctional Facility in Stromville, New York. Guards could storm his cell, throw the Qur'an on the floor, rip the Messenger's teachings, and punish him with the isolation cell or the strip cell where inmates sit completely naked. He says that going through the abuse of prison and watching people be brutalized for being Muslim was "the best thing that could have happened to me. . . . Because I seen the white men as he really is" (cited in Barboza 1994:178).

135 Moore 1991.

136 This was made in *Fulwood v. Clemmer, Brown v. McGinnes,* and *SaMarion v. McGinnes,* all cases in New York State (Ibid., 141).

137 Cited in Moore 1991:143.

138 Moore 1991:145.

139 Ibid., 148.

140 Ibid., 144.

141 Farrakhan 1993i:115.

142 Farrakhan, interview, 1989b.

143 Farrakhan, speech, 1989c.

144   Farrakhan 1993i:120.
145   Ibid., 116.
146   Ibid., 122.
147   Marable 1986 [1984]:4f.; Du Bois 1961:35f.; Goldston 1968:140ff.; Karenga 1987 [1982]:106.
148   Farrakhan 1990b.
149   Farrakhan, speech, 1988b.
150   Farrakhan 1989c.
151   Farrakhan 1992g.
152   Aiyetoro 1989.
153   Wilcox 1990; "Detroit," 1989.
154   HR 3745, introduced in 1989, and HR 1684, introduced in 1991.
155   "Campaign," 1993.
156   "Minister Farrakhan Supports," 1993.
157   Farrakhan 1993i:89.
158   Farrakhan, speech, 1990i.
159   Muhammad, E. 1965:172f.
160   "Jackson Given Support," 1984.
161   Strausberg 1984d.
162   Farrakhan 1989i [1987]:214f.
163   Farrakhan 1989d.
164   Farrakhan, speech, 1989b.
165   Farrakhan 1989f [1984]:126.
166   Farrakhan 1990c.
167   Farrakhan 1990a.
168   Muhammad, Richard 1990b.
169   George X Cure got 1,376 votes, or 1 percent of the votes. Shawn X finished fourth in a race among eleven candidates, receiving 10,276 votes, or 8 percent ("Election 1990," 1990).
170   Norris 1990a.
171   Norris 1990b.
172   Muhammad, A. W. 1991b.
173   "The New Politics of Race," 1992.
174   Farrakhan 1993i:3.
175   Ibid., 38.
176   Ibid., 37.
177   Ibid., 159f.
178   Ibid., 157.
179   Ibid., 51.
180   Henry 1994.
181   See, for instance, Farrakhan 1993i:69.
182   Farrakhan, speech, 1990h; Farrakhan 1995.
183   Farrakhan 1989i [1987]:201ff.
184   Henderson 1994:20.
185   Jones and Harrison 1994:217.
186   Henderson 1994:19.
187   Williams, R. 1993:85.
188   Farrakhan, speech, 1985c.

189   Farrakhan, speech, 1990i.
190   *NOI POWER Proclamation,* 1985.
191   Farrakhan, speech, 1985c.
192   The Clean 'N' Fresh products are shampoo, hair conditioner, hair pomade, skin lotion, liquid soap, and deodorant.
193   Muhammad and Muhammad, 1991.
194   Muhammad, E. 1965:192–97.
195   Farrakhan 1991f. As is the case for the Sharia abiding Islamic banks, a number of fees substitute the interest. The advantage is still considerable, however, as the practical interest tends to be much less than in a commercial non-Islamic modern bank.
196   "Three Year Economic Program," 1994.
197   Farrakhan 1993i:84ff. In *A Torchlight,* Farrakhan discusses the American economy in general and what should be done to reverse the negative trend. Raising taxes for the rich and the corporations and on alcohol, tobacco, and luxury items to meet the federal debt and the budget deficit is suggested. The government should be prohibited from spending more than it collects in taxes, and the citizens should be able to direct 15 percent of their tax payments to earmarked projects. The military receives $300 billion, one-fifth of the budget, and should have its expenditures reduced by one-third or more.

   Finding the situation with ten million Americans unemployed totally unacceptable, Farrakhan suggests a right-to-work policy and gives priority to retraining programs. The United States, less than any other industrialized country, spends only 0.05 percent of its GNP on retraining. When businesses and whites abandoned the inner cities, they sunk into decay with homelessness, unemployment, violence, drugs, and gangs. Here, the Nation of Islam can be of service, Farrakhan suggests. No business will be established in a crime-ridden area, but the NOI is capable of reducing crime and restoring peace, as its record shows. Farrakhan further proposes a social pact between business, government, law enforcement, and the gangs. Let the inner cities become garment manufacturing centers instead of exporting the jobs to Asia.

   Echoing Qadhdhafi, Farrakhan argues that America should encourage its people to work better by making them partners, not wage slaves. Combined with the NOI lifestyle, which rejects drugs, tobacco, criminality, and immorality, people could work more at lower salaries, which is why the NOI should be entrusted to educate its people (all non-WASPs). Welfare should be substituted with retraining, jobs, and, for the former slaves, reparations.
198   Farrakhan, speech, 1988a.
199   Farrakhan, speech, 1980.
200   Farrakhan, speech, 1990k.
201   Farrakhan, speech, 1984e.
202   Farrakhan, speech, 1990a.
203   Muhammad, K., interview, 1989.
204   Farrakhan 1993i:47.
205   3X Bryant 1989.
206   2X McKeiver 1993b.
207   See, for instance, X Robinson 1991.
208   Farrakhan, speech, 1990j.

209 Farrakhan 1993i:48f.

210 Ibid., 57f.

211 Prince Akeem, interviewed in Spady and Eure 1991:266f.

212 Farrakhan 1993i:63.

213 Morganthau, Marby, Washington, Smith, Yoffe, and Beachy 1992.

214 Muhammad and 2X McKeiver 1994. The article is based on a national health report released in mid-June 1994.

215 Farrakhan, speech, 1990j.

216 "Muslim Minister/Physician," 1988.

217 Lee and Shlain 1992:24f.

218 Ibid., 42f.

219 Ibid., 36.

220 SIPRI 1973:194, 203–5, 288.

221 "Hearings before a Subcommittee of the Committee of Appropriations, U.S. House of Representatives, 87th Congress, 2nd session, Washington, March, 1962." Cited in Anderson, unpublished essay, 1989:3.

222 Anderson, unpublished, 1989:5.

223 Cited in SIPRI 1973:314.

224 SIPRI 1973:319.

225 Ash 1992.

226 Cary 1992.

227 Farrakhan, speech, 1990d.

228 DeParle 1990.

229 See, for instance, Gadlin 1991; Muhammad and Justice 1991.

230 Muhammad, A. W. 1991c and 1991d. Abdul Alim Muhammad suggested that racism was behind the absence of media coverage concerning the new drugs. "If Dr. Davy Koech was a different complexion by now he'd be known all over the world and probably have a Nobel Prize in Medicine" ("AIDS Activists," 1991).

231 Muhammad, Richard 1992c.

232 "NOI Gets Exclusive," 1992.

233 The full name of the coalition is the Sankofa Community Coalition for HIV/AIDS Services. See 2X McKeiver 1993c; Cohen 1993; X Booker 1993; Goldstein 1993.

234 Goldstein 1993; X Booker 1993.

235 See "NIH Tries," 1994.

236 The report is entitled "Health United States 1990." The figures are from 1988, and the life expectancy rate for black males is down from 65.2 years in 1987. For the first time in this century, life expectancy is thus on the decline.

237 Henderson 1994:17f.

238 Farrakhan 1993i:141.

239 Farrakhan 1991g.

240 Farrakhan 1991h.

241 Muhammad and Muhammad 1991.

242 Farrakhan 1993i:138f.

243 Muhammad, Ava 1991.

244 See, for instance, Muhammad, H. 1975b.

245 Farrakhan, speech, 1992.

246 Farrakhan, speech, 1990i.

247 Farrakhan, speech, 1987. See also Farrakhan 1994f.

248   Farrakhan 1990h.
249   Farrakhan, speech, 1990b.
250   Farrakhan, speech, 1990c.
251   Farrakhan, speech, 1985a.
252   Farrakhan, speech, 1990c.
253   Farrakhan, speech, 1985a.
254   Farrakhan, speech, 1990b.
255   Jones and Harrison 1994:232.
256   Henderson 1994:17f.
257   Farrakhan, speech, 1990b.
258   X, M. 1973 [1965]:227.
259   Muhammad, Richard 1994.
260   Muhammad, James 1994c.
261   2X, D. 1970.
262   Farrakhan, speech, 1984f. In clear contradiction to this interpretation of Genesis, Sister Minister Tynetta Muhammad writes: "After God made the man in His Own Image, from a Single Being or Soul, then He made the woman to give comfort and to be a Help-mate" (Muhammad, T. 1994 [1982]:10).
263   Farrakhan, speech, 1985c.
264   Farrakhan, speech, 1988a.
265   Farrakhan 1993i:58.
266   X, A. 1990.
267   Farrakhan 1989g [1987]:102.
268   Farrakhan 1989f [1984]:131.
269   Farrakhan 1989g [1987]:96.
270   Ibid., 97, 103, 108f.
271   Farrakhan, speech, 1989f.
272   Farrakhan, speech, 1990c.
273   Farrakhan 1989g [1987]:102.
274   Farrakhan 1993i:109.
275   Ibid., 111.
276   X Moore, R. 1991b.
277   Farrakhan, interview, 1989b; Farrakhan, speech, 19901; Farrakhan, speech, 1990b.
278   Farrakhan 1993i:156f.
279   Farrakhan, speech, 1993b.
280   Farrakhan 1990b.
281   Farrakhan 1989f [1984]:131.
282   Farrakhan 1993i:105.
283   Farrakhan, speech, 1990h.
284   Farrakhan, speech, 1990m.
285   Ibid.
286   Farrakhan, speech, 1990h.
287   Ibid.
288   Muhammad, D., interview, 1989.
289   Enayat 1982:89f.
290   See, Muhammad, James 1988b; Muhammad, A. W. 1988b; Muhammad, James 1988c; Muhammad, James 1988d; Leid 1988; "A Visit by Maryam," 1990. For another perspective, see Taibbi and Sims-Phillips 1989.

291   Farrakhan 1990b.
292   "Another Ugly Mob," 1990; Pleasant 1990.
293   Muhammad, K., interview, 1989.
294   See, for instance, Muwakkil 1989c.
295   Farrakhan, speech, 1990a; Farrakhan, speech, 1989a; Farrakhan 1989b.
296   Farrakhan 1993i:40.
297   Muhammad, James 1993c; Farrakhan 1993j. The Conference was held in Washington on August 27, 1993.
298   Muhammad, James 1993d.
299   Muhammad, James 1993b.
300   Chavis 1994.
301   Among these were Rev. Ben Chavis, William Gibson, Ben Andrews, Rupert Richardson (NAACP), Jesse Jackson (Operation PUSH), Rep. Kwesi Mfume (D-Md. and the Congressional Black Caucus), Minister Louis Farrakhan, Leonard Muhammad and Mustapha Farrakhan (the Nation of Islam), Conrad Worill (National Black United Front), Rev. Al Sharpton, Dr. Cornell West, Dr. John Henrik Clarke, Dr. Betty Shabazz, Mayor Kurt Schmoke, Ron Daniels, Jylla Foster (Zeta Phi Beta Sorority), Howard Woods (Prince Hall Masons), Dr. Leonora Fulani (New Alliance Party).
302   Muhammad, James 1994d; X Grandison 1994b; Worill 1994; Terry 1994a; Terry 1994b; Terry 1994c; Rosenthal 1994.
303   Farrakhan 1994g.
304   Terry 1994d; Meyers 1994; Holmes 1994b; Newman 1994.
305   Farrakhan 1994h.
306   Farrakhan, speech, 1990c.
307   See Farrakhan 1995a.
308   Farrakhan 1995b; Farrakhan, speech, 1995a.
309   Farrakhan, speech, 1995b.
310   Cf., for example, Booth 1995; Dewey 1995; Jones, R. I. 1995; Janovsky 1995; Marriott 1995; Pulley 1995; Fletcher and Harris 1995; and Freeberg 1995.
311   "Million Men March Poll," 1995.
312   Farrakhan, speech, 1995b.
313   Farrakhan, speech, 1995b. See also Gardell 1995b and 1995c.
314   Farrakhan, speech, 1984f.
315   Farrakhan 1993i:63.
316   Farrakhan, speech, 1984f.
317   Farrakhan, interview, 1989a.
318   Farrakhan, speech, 1990h.
319   Farrakhan, speech, 1987.
320   X, S. 1974.
321   Farrakhan 1993i:145–49.
322   Farrakhan, speech, 1984f.
323   Ibid.
324   Farrakhan, interview, 1989a.
325   In the words of Public Enemy in "Whole Lotta Love Goin On in the Middle of Hell," 1994.

Bibliography

═══

Unpublished sources

Interviews

Baesho, Bashir Ali. 1989. Interview by author. Tripoli, Lebanon, January 23.
Chuck D. 1990. Interview by author. Stockholm, Sweden, March 31.
Farrakhan, Louis. 1989a. Interview by author. Tape recording. Chicago, Ill., May 11.
Farrakhan, Louis. 1989b. Interview by author. Tape recording. Chicago, Ill., May 18.
Gams, Gail. 1994. Interview by author. Tape recording. New York, N. Y., January 20.
Muhammad, Don. 1989. Interview by author. Tape recording. Boston, Mass., June 8.
Muhammad, Khadir. 1989. Interview by author. Tape recording. Newark, N. J., June 14.
Muwakkil, Salim. 1994. Interview by author. Tape recording. Chicago, Ill., February 11.
Kareem, Luqman. 1987. Interview by author. Harlem, N. Y., August 28.
Rasheed, Imam Ali. 1987. Interview by author. Harlem, N. Y., August 23.
al-Sharif, Muhammad Ahmad. 1989. Interview by author. Tripoli, Lebanon, February 1.
Suall, Erwin. 1994. Director of the Fact-Finding Department of the ADI. Interview by author. Tape recording. January 20.

Speeches

Farrakhan, Louis. n.d. "The Voice of One Crying in the Wilderness." Video recording from the *Final Call* Building, Chicago, Ill.
——. 1973. "Introduction of Elijah Muhammad." Saviour's Day, February.
——. 1980. "True and Proper Education: The Making of Gods." June 22.
——. 1983. "Founder's Day Speech Operation Push." December 3.
——. 1984a. "The Arab Press Conference." Howard Inn, Washington, D.C., August 17.
——. 1984b. "Saviour's Day Address."
——. 1984c. "Report on Syria." Speech delivered at Operation Push meeting in Chicago, January.
——. 1984d. Broadcast on Chicago radio station WBEE, March 11.
——. 1984e. "Education is the Key." Speech delivered at the Book Cadillac Hotel, Detroit, May 12.
——. 1984f. "Your Hand Must Produce God's Kingdom." Radio broadcast, *Final Call* Building, November 18.

——. 1985a. "True Christian Love." Speech delivered at the Life Center Church, Chicago, March 21.

——. 1985b. Farrakhan Speaks in Madison Square Garden, October 7.

——. 1985c. "Power at Last . . . Forever!" Speech delivered at the John F. Kennedy Center, Washington, D.C., July 22.

——. 1986a. "Self Improvement: The Basis for Community Development." Speech delivered at Symphony Hall, Phoenix, Ariz., October 21.

——. 1986b. "Introduction of Muammar Al Qadhafi." Tripoli, Libya, March 15.

——. 1986c. "Address to the World Conference Against Racism—Zionism—Imperialism." Tripoli, Libya, March 16.

——. 1986d. "Warning to President Reagan." Washington, D.C. press conference, February 5.

——. 1987. "How to Give Birth to a God." Chicago, July 26.

——. 1988a. "Black/Jewish Relationship!" Speech delivered at Northwestern University, Evanston, Ill., May 30.

——. 1988b. "The Black Agenda." Speech delivered to the 1988 Democratic and Republican National Conventions, Wheat Street Baptist Church.

——. 1989a. "The Dedication of the Great Mosque: The Fulfillment of Scripture." Speech delivered at the Palladium II in Baltimore, Maryland, January 28.

——. 1989b. "The Crucifixion of Jesus: The Destruction of Black Leadership." Speech delivered at Mosque Maryam, Chicago, March 26.

——. 1989c. "The Origin of the White Race: The Making of the Devil." Speech delivered at Mosque Maryam, Chicago, April 23.

——. 1989d. "The Dawn—A New Beginning." February 26.

——. 1989e. "A Time of Danger: The Signs of the Fall of America." Speech delivered at the University of Maryland, March 29.

——. 1989f. "A Celebration of Mother." Mothers Day Address, Mosque Maryam, Chicago, May 31.

——. 1990a. "The Murder of Malcolm X: The Effects on Black America 25 Years Later." Speech delivered at Malcolm X College, Chicago, February 21.

——. 1990b. "The Re-Unification of the Black Family." Speech delivered at the Temple Theater, Tacoma, Wash., January 26.

——. 1990c. "A Time of Danger for the Black Man in America: Decision, Deliverance or Doom." Speech delivered at the Syria Mosque, Pittsburgh, April 13.

——. 1990d. "By the Time Surely Man is at Loss." Speech delivered at Michigan State University, February 18.

——. 1990e. "Stop the Killing II." Los Angeles, February 2.

——. 1990f. "When the Sun Rises in the West—Saviour's Day 1990." Speech delivered at Mosque Maryam, Chicago, February 25.

——. 1990g. "The Three Rules that Prove There Is No God but Allah and Muhammad Is His Messenger." Speech delivered at Mosque Maryam, Chicago, January 14.

——. 1990h. "The Law of Redemption." Speech delivered at Mosque Maryam, Chicago, May 6.

——. 1990i. "The Sickness of Envy." Speech delivered at Muhammad University, Chicago, March 7.

——. 1990j. "Passover, Easter and Ramadan: How They Relate to the Black Struggle in America." Speech delivered at Southern University, Baton Rouge, La., April 18.

——. 1990k. "Stop the Killing." Speech delivered at the Omni Center, Atlanta, April 28.

——. 1990l. "The Sick Doctrine of White Supremacy and Black Inferiority." Speech delivered at State University of New York at Oswego, February 23.

——. 1990m. "The Nature of the Black Man." Speech delivered at the Muhammad University of Islam, Chicago, June 20.

——. 1991. "Who Is God?" Speech delivered at Christ Universal Temple, Chicago, February 24.

——. 1992. "Black and White: A Solution to the Race Problem." Speech delivered at Christ Universal Temple, Chicago, February 23.

——. 1993a. "Has Farrakhan Changed Direction?" Speech delivered at Mosque Maryam, Chicago, July 11.

——. 1993b. "The Problem of Suicide and the Causes of Homosexuality." Speech delivered at the Muhammad University of Islam, April 7.

——. 1994. "Washington Press Conference." NRP radio station, February 3.

——. 1995a. "Jesus Saves! Who Will Save the Black Man? The Million Man March and Why." Saviours' Day Address, Chicago.

——. 1995b. "Million Man March Address." Washington, D.C., October 16.

Foxman, Abraham. 1994. Interview on NRP radio station, February 3.

al Mahdi, Isa, n.d. "The True Light Tapes: Message to the Blackman."

Muhammad, Adul Allah. n.d. "Introduction to Louis Farrakhan: 'The Voice of One Crying in the Wilderness.' " Video recording from the Final Call Building, Chicago.

——. 1993. Speech at Mosque Maryam, July 11.

Muhammad, Ava. 1986. "The Power of Master Fard Muhammad." Recorded radio speech, WBEE 1570, February 23.

Muhammad, Elijah. 1964. "Warning to the Hypocrites." Tape recorded.

——. 1972a. "The Theology of Time." Tape recorded.

——. 1972b. "The Theology of Time." July 16.

——. 1972c. "The Theology of Time." June 4.

——. 1972d. "The Theology of Time." June 25.

——. 1972e. "The Theology of Time." July 2.

——. 1973. "Saviour's Day Address." Video recorded.

Muhammad, Khallid Abdul. 1989. "666—The Mark of the Beast—Babylon and America." Speech delivered at Mosque Maryam, Chicago, December 3.

——. 1993. "The Secret Relationship between Blacks and Jews." Speech delivered at Kean College, N.J., November 29.

Muhammad, Silis. 1989a. "Moses Raises the Serpent." October 7.

——. 1989b. "The Resurrection of Jesus." Speech delivered in Georgia, August 21.

——. 1990. "Blacks in America—The Chosen People of God." Saviour's Day Address, February 26.

Songs and Records

Afrika Bambaataa. "Say It Loud (I'm Black, I'm Proud)," *The Decade of Darkness*, EMI Records, 1991.

B. B. King. "Why I Sing the Blues," *The Best of B. B. King*, MCA Records, 1987 [1973].

Brand Nubian. "Wake up (stimulated dummies mix)," *One For All*, Elektra Entertainment, 1990.

——. *In God We Trust*, Elektra Entertainment, 1992.

Da Lenchmob. *Guerillas In Tha Mist*, Atlantic Recording, 1992.

Farrakhan, Louis. *Let Us Unite*, A.V.C. Music, 1984.

Howlin' Wolf, [Big Joe Williams]. "Highway 49," *Blues Legends: the Best of Howlin' Wolf*, PMF, 1990.

Ice Cube. *Amerikkka's Most Wanted*, Priority Records, 1990.

Ice Cube. *Death Certificate*, Priority Records, 1991.

——. *Lethal Injection*, Priority Records, 1993.

Ice T. "Cop Killer," *Body Count*, Time Warner, 1992.

Jungle Brothers. "In Dayz '2' Come," *Done by the Forces of Nature*, Warner Bros. Records, 1989.

KAM. *Made in America*, Atlantic Recording, 1995.

K-Solo. "The Messenger," *Tell the World My Name*, Atlantic Recording, 1990.

NWA. "F*** Tha Police," *Straight Outta Compton*, Priority Records, 1988.

——. *100 Miles And Running*, Priority Records, 1990.

——. *Efil4zaggin*, Priority Records, 1991.

Prince Akeem. *Coming Down Like Babylon*, Hollywood Records, 1991.

Professor Griff. *Pawns in the Game*, Skywalker Records, 1990.

——. "Crucified," *Kao's II Wiz*7*Dome*, Luke Records, 1991.

Public Enemy. *Yo! Bum Rush the Show*, CBS, 1987.

——. "Countdown to Armageddon," *It Take a Nation of Millions to Hold Us Back*, Def Jam, 1988.

——. "Party for Your Right to Fight," *It Takes A Millions To Hold Us Back*, Def Jam, 1988.

——. *Welcome to the Terrordome*, Def Jam/CBS, 1989.

——. "Fight the Power," *Fear of a Black Planet*, Def Jam/CBS, 1990.

——. *Apocalypse 91 . . . The Enemy Strikes Black*, Def Jam/Sony Music Entertainment, 1991.

——. *Greatest Misses*, Def Jam/Sony Music Entertainment, 1992.

——. "I Ain't Mad at All," *Muse Sick-N-Hour Mess Age*, Def Jam, 1994.

——. "Hitler Day," *Muse Sick-N-Hour Mess Age*, Def Jam, 1994.

——. "Whole Lotta Love Goin On in the Middle of Hell," *Muse Sick-N-Hour Mess Age*, Def Jam, 1994.

Reed, Lou. "Good Evening Mr. Waldheim," *New York, New York*, Sire Records, 1989.

The Undaground Soldier & Thayod. "Honor and Respect, featuring Minister Farrakhan," *State of Emergency, Society in Crisis (Vol. 1)*, Mad Sound Records, 1994.

X-Clan. *To the East, Blackwards*, Island Records, 1990.

FBI files

FBI file 62-25889-1.

FBI file 62-65889-6.

FBI file 62-25889-70.

FBI file 62-25889-79.

FBI file 62-25889-118.

FBI file 100-399321, 5/17/61.

FBI file 100-43165.

FBI file 100-43165-1.

FBI file 100-43165-15.

FBI file 100-448006-[?].

FBI file 100-448006-[?], 1968. From George Moore, chief of racial intelligence, to William C. Sullivan head of the Domestic Intelligence Division.

FBI file 100-448006-[?], 8/25/67.

FBI file 100-448006-[?], 2/27/68.

FBI file 100-448006-[?], 3/4/68.

FBI file 100-448006-[?], 3/27/68.

FBI file 100-448006-[?], 4/5/68.

FBI file 100-448006-[?], 4/8/68.

FBI file 100-448006-[?], 5/3/68.

FBI file 100-448006-[?], 6/1/68.

FBI file 100-448006-[?], 8/28/68.

FBI file 100-448006-[?], 9/6/68.

FBI file 100-448006-[?], 9/13/68.

FBI file 100-448006-[?], 9/25/68.

FBI file 100-448006-[?], 9/27/68.

FBI file 100-448006-[?], 10/23/68.

FBI file 100-448006-[?], 11/7/68.

FBI file 100-448006-[?], 11/18/68.

FBI file 100-448006-[?], 11/29/68.

FBI file 100-448006-[?], 1/27/69.

FBI file 100-448006-[?], 3/13/69.

FBI file 100-448006-[?], 4/7/69.

FBI file 100-448006-[?], 7/16/69.

FBI file 100-448006-[?], 9/27/69.

FBI file 100-448006-[?], 6/26/70.

FBI file 100-448006-[?], 11/13/70.

FBI file 100-448006-[?], 11/25/70.

FBI file 100-448006-[?], 1/14/71.

FBI file 100-448006-[?], 8/7/72.

FBI file 100-448006-10, 2/27/68.

FBI file 100-448006-17, 3/4/68.

FBI file 100-448006-47, 4/1/68.

FBI file 100-448006-80, 4/5/68.

FBI file 100-448006-121, 5/15/68.

FBI file 100-448006-124, 5/17/68.

FBI file 100-448006-179, 6/26/68.

FBI file 100-448006-384, 11/8/68.

FBI file 100-448006-441, 11/29/68.

FBI file 100-448006-569, 12/24/68.

FBI file 100-448006-569, 1/6/69.

FBI file 100-448006-571, 1/7/69.

FBI file 100-448006-624, 1/22/69.

FBI file 100-448006-624, 2/5/69.

FBI file 100-448006-626, 1/22/69.

FBI file 100-448006-681, 2/19/69.

FBI file 100-448006-750.

FBI file 100-448006-1367, 10/23/69.

FBI file 100-448006-1381, 8/29/69.

FBI file 100-448006-1381, 10/21/69.

FBI file 100-448006-1518, 4/28/71.

FBI file 100-448006-1519, 4/27/71.

FBI file 100-448006-2123, 12/10/70.

FBI file 100-448006-2147, 12/21/70.

FBI file 100-448006-2147, 1/6/71.

FBI file 100-448006-2150, 12/31/70.

FBI file 100-448006-2254, 2/22/71.

FBI file 100-63165.

FBI file 100-63642-15.

FBI file 100-6582-[?], 6/19/42.

FBI file 105-24822.

FBI file 105-24822-[?], date unreadable, 1960.

FBI file 105-24822-[?], 4/26/62.

FBI file 105-24822-[?], 7/25/62.

FBI file 105-24822-[?], 5/28/63.

FBI file 105-24822-[?], 1/27/64.

FBI file 105-24822-[?], 3/12/64.

FBI file 105-24822-[?], 3/23/64.

FBI file 105-24822-[?], 8/7/64.

FBI file 105-24822-[?], 2/27/65.

FBI file 105-24822-[?], 6/15/73.

FBI file 105-24822-13, 12/31/56.

FBI file 105-24822-25, 8/9/57.

FBI file 105-24822-56X, 10/30/59.

FBI file 105-24822-80, 5/17/60.

FBI file 105-24822-101, 2/13/62.

FBI file 105-24822-133, 2/7/64.

FBI file 105-24822-142, 10/9/64.

FBI file 105-24822-202.

FBI file 105-24822-202, 11/1/68.

FBI file 105-24822-221.

FBI file 105-4805.

FBI file 105-63642.

FBI file 105-63642-[?], 2/21/57.

FBI file 105-63642-3.

FBI file 105-63642-15, 1/15/58.

FBI file 105-63642-22.

FBI file 105-63642-22, From SAC [Special Agent in Charge], Chicago to Director, FBI, February 3, 1958.

FBI file 105-63642-28.

FBI file 157-3376-[5?], 9/17/65.

FBI file 157-3376-6.

Chicago FBI file 100-12899.

Chicago FBI file 100-35635-Sub B, 4/22/68.

Chicago FBI file 157-2209, 4/22/68.

Los Angeles FBI file 105-4805.

Other:

Al-Ahari Bektashi, Muhammad Abdullah. 1994. End of Time and Fulfillment of Prophecies: The Story of American Islamic Nationalism. Unpublished monograph.

Anderson, Roj. 1983. "The Scientist and Our Time." Unpublished essay.

Berlet, Chip. 1993a. "Populist Party, LaRouchian and Other Neo-Fascist Overtures To Progressives." Public Eye Network, November 22.

——. 1993b. "Fascists as Information Sources." Public Eye Network, November 22.

——. 1993c. "Progressive Researchers and Fascist Sources." Public Eye Network, November 22.

"The Cause and the Cure." Unsigned Moorish pamphlet.

Ditz, Jeff. 1992a. "No Justice No Peace: General Strike Shuts Down L.A." Unpublished essay.

——. 1992b. "Truce on the Streets." Unpublished essay.

Mamiya, Lawrence. 1987. "The Black Muslims as a New Religious Movement." Contribution to the International Symposium on Conflict and Cooperation between Contemporary Religious Groups, Tokyo, Japan.

Re:Estate of Elijah Muhammad, Appellate Court of Illinois.

Re:Estate of Elijah Muhammad, Appeal from the Circuit Court of Cook County.

Saperstein, Rabbi David. 1993, August 13. "Confidential and Personal," letter to Mrs. Coretta Scott King, Rev. Walter Fauntroy, Bill Lucy, Rev. Jesse Jackson, William Gibson, Rev. Ben Chavis, and Lane Kirkland.

"We Gotta Do Shit. Collage on the Uprising in L.A., 1992." Berlin: Wildcat TV.

Holy Scriptures

Holy Bible. 1982. Authorized King James Version. Nashville: Holman Bible Publishers.

Holy Bible. 1982. Revised Standard Version. Nashville: Holman Bible Publishers.

The Glorious Qur'an. Text and explanatory translation by Muhammad Marmaduke Pickthall. Tripoli: Islamic Call Society.

The Holy Qur'an. 1946. Translation and commentary by A. Yusuf Ali. Islamic Propagation Centre International.

Holy Quran. 1991. English translation and commentary by Maulana Muhammad Ali. Columbus, Ohio: Ahmadiyya Anjuman Isha'at Islam Lahore, U.S.A.

Quran: The Final Scripture. 1981. Translation and commentary by Rashad Khalifa. Tucson, Ariz.: Islamic Productions.

Quran: The Final Testament. 1989. Translation and commentary by Rashad Khalifa. Tucson, Ariz.: Islamic Productions.

Quran: The Final Testament. 1992. Revised edition, translated by Rashad Khalifa. Fremont, Ca.: Universal Unity.

Published books, magazines, and newspapers

"A Common Cause." *National Front News,* no. 93, editorial.

"A Message for MI5 and Special Branch: We Fight On!" *Nationalism Today,* no. 39, editorial.

"A Visit by Maryam." 1990. *Final Call,* March 21.

Activities of the Association of the Islamic Convocation. 1983. Tripoli, Libya: The Islamic Convocation.

Addy, James D. 1994. "Drugs Are Tool of Colonizer: Akbar Warns." *Final Call,* June 17.

Adkins, J. I. Jr. 1975. "Muslims Hail New Chief." *Chicago Defender,* February 27.

Adler, Jerry, Jennifer Foote, and Ray Sawhill. 1990. "The Rap Attitude." *Newsweek,* March 19.

"African Liberation Day in Caribbean." 1989. *Final Call,* June 11.

Ahmed, Akbar S. 1992. *Postmodernism and Islam.* London and New York: Routledge.

Ahmed, Gutbi Mahdi 1991. "Muslim Organizations in the United States." In *The Muslims of America,* edited by Yvonne Haddad. New York and Oxford: Oxford University Press.

Ahmed, Nasir. 1975. "Letter of Condolences." *Muhammad Speaks,* April 11.

"AIDS Activists Briefed on Treatment from Africa." 1991. *Final Call,* October 28.

Aiyetoro, Adjoa. 1989. "Reparations Now! Coalition Forges United Effort to Get Justice." *Final Call,* July 31.

Akbar, Na'im. 1975. "Whites in the Nation." *Muhammad Speaks,* August 1.

Al-Akram, Malik. 1991a. "White Bible Scholars Reject Jesus' Teachings: Why?" *Muhammad Speaks* 7, no. 3.

——. 1991b. "The Honorable Elijah Muhammad's Birthday—MOTHERS DAY 1991." *Muhammad Speaks* 7, no. 7.

——. 1991c. "Caucasian Bears Witness." *Muhammad Speaks* 7, no. 2.

——. 1992. "Cheap Shot by the *Atlanta Journal-Constitution.*" *Muhammad Speaks* 8, no. 5.

Al-Amin, Jamil. 1993. *Revolution by the Book (The Rap is Live).* Beltsville, Md.: Writers' Inc. International.

Alexander, Curtis E. 1989. *Elijah Muhammad on African American Education.* New York: ECA Associates.

Ali, John (X). 1973. "Traitors, Deserters Seek to Stop Spread of Islam to Blacks in the U.S." *Muhammad Speaks,* January 19.

Ali, Noble Drew. n.d. *The Holy Koran.*

——. n.d. "Koran Questions for Moorish Children."

——. n.d. "The Divine Constitution and By-Laws."

——. n.d. "The Additional Law."

——. n.d. "Supreme Words of the Prophet Noble Drew Ali."

Allah, Karriem. 1973. "The Early Days of the Messengers Mission." *Mr. Muhammad Speaks,* August 10.

——. 1974. "The Early Days." *Muhammad Speaks,* June 21.

"American Impressions." 1988. *Nationalism Today,* no. 44 (January).

"Another Ugly Mob Taunts Bensonhurst Protestors." 1990. *Final Call,* June 22.

The Anti-Semitism of Black Demagogues and Extremists. 1992. New York: Anti-Defamation League.

Ash, Vernon. 1992. "AIDS Man-Made?" *Final Call,* April 20.

Asidi, Haleem. 1990. "It Begins with a Feeling." *Muhammad Speaks* 6, no. 3.

"Assault on Gangs, Drugs: Guise to Cover-Up Holocaust on Youth." 1989. *Final Call,* July 31.

Atkinson, Rick. 1984a. "Peace with American Jews Eludes Jackson." *Washington Post,* February 13.

——. 1984b. "Jackson Denounces 'Hounding' from Jewish Community." *Washington Post,* February 22.

———. 1984c. "Muslim Denies Threat on Life." *Washington Post*, April 6.

Austin, Allan D. 1984. *African Muslims in Antebellum America*. New York and London: Garland Publishing.

"Axioms in the Islamic Fiqh." 1988. *Risalat al-Jihad*, Cultural Islamic Monthly published by the Islamic Call Society, July.

Ayoub, Mahmoud Mustafa. 1987. *Islam and the Third Universal Theory: The Religious Thought of Mu'ammar al-Qadhdhafi*. London: KPI Ltd.

"Back on track: Injured Muslim Healed, Rededicated." 1991. *Final Call*, October 7.

Baghdadi, Ali. 1993. "Muslims Cannot Agree on Eid (Holiday) Celebrations." *Final Call*, June 30.

Baghdadi, Ali. 1994. "Silence is Goldstein: Where is the Outcry for the Hebron Killings." *Final Call*, March 30.

Baigent, Michael, and Richard Leigh. 1989. *The Temple and the Lodge*. New York: Arcade Publishing.

Baker, Houston A. 1993. "Scene . . . Not Heard." In *Reading Rodney King/Reading Urban Uprising*, edited by Robert Gooding-Williams. New York and London: Routledge.

Baldwick, Julian. 1989. *Mystical Islam*. London: I. B. Tauris.

Baraka, Amiri. 1991. *The LeRoi Jones/Amiri Baraka Reader*. Edited by William J. Harris. New York: Thunder's Mouth Press.

Barboza, Steven. 1994. *American Jihad: Islam after Malcolm X*. New York: Doubleday.

Barker, Eileen. 1989. *New Religious Movements*. London: Her Majesty's Stationery Office.

Barkun, Michael. 1994. *Religion and the Racist Right: The Origins of the Christian Identity Movement*. Chapel Hill and London: University of North Carolina Press.

Barret, Leonard E. 1988. *The Rastafarians*. Revised and updated edition. Boston: Beacon Press.

Bastide, Roger. 1967. "Color, Racism and Christianity." *Daedalus: The Journal of the American Academy of Arts and Science* 96, no. 2 (spring).

Bearman, Jonathan. 1986. *Qadhafi's Libya*. London and New Jersey: Zed Books.

Bellah, Robert N. 1967. "Civil Religion in America." *Daedalus* 96, no. 1 (winter).

Benz, Ernst. 1973. "Black Muslims. Svart islam i USA." In *Nya Religioner*. Stockholm: Natur och Kultur.

Berlet, Chip. 1991. "Strange alliances . . . LaRouche Quietly Invades Anti-War Movement." *In These Times*, January 30–February 5.

Bernal, Martin. 1987. *Black Athena: The Afroasiatic Roots of Classical Civilization*. Vol. I. *The Fabrication of Ancient Greece 1785–1985*. London: Free Association Books.

Bernard, James. 1992. "Steady Lenching." *The Source*, December.

Bernstein, Richard. 1993. "A Growing Islamic Presence: Balancing Sacred and Secular." *New York Times*, May 2.

Beynon, Erdmann D. 1938. "The Voodoo Cult among Negro Migrants in Detroit." *The American Journal of Sociology* 43, no. 6 (May).

Bierre, Christine. 1990. "Internationell mobilisering i Paris: USA måste frige LaRouche!" *Ny Solidaritet*, December 19.

"Big Libyan Loan for Muslims Here." 1972. *Chicago Sun-Times*, May 8.

Bilail, Samuel Ayyub. 1977. "Emam's Gary Address Stresses Natural Human Growth." *Bilalian News*, July 22.

Bing, LÇon. 1991. *Do or Die*. New York: HarperPerennial.

"Black Journalists Visit Libya." 1988. *Final Call*, May 9.

"Black Propaganda." n.d. *Nationalism Today*, no. 22.

Blackstock, Nelson. 1988. *COINTELPRO: The FBI's Secret War on Political Freedom*. New York: Anchor Foundation.

Bleifuss, Joel. 1985. "In the Shadows." *In These Times*, October 9–15.

"Bloods/Crips Proposal for LA's Facelift." 1993. In *Why L.A. Happened*, by Haki R. Madhubuti. Chicago: Third World Press.

Blumenthal, Ralph. 1994. "After Arrest, Police Seek 2 Others in Mosque Clash." *New York Times*, January 21.

Blyden, Edward W. [1887] 1967. *Christianity, Islam and the Negro Race*. Edinburgh: Aldine Publisher.

Boland, Mira L. 1992. "Wishful Thinking Spurs Efforts to Co-Opt Gangs." *Wall Street Journal*, October 6.

Bontemps, Arna, and Jack Conroy. 1945. *They Seek a City*. Garden City, N. Y.: Doubleday.

Booth, William. 1995. "As Many Meanings as Marchers." *Washington Post*, October 14.

"Boston Mosque Supports the N.O.I. Ghana Mission." 1993. *Final Call*, November 10.

Boyer, Paul. 1992. *When Time Shall Be No More: Prophecy Belief in Modern American Culture*. Cambridge: Harvard University Press.

Brackman, Harold. 1994. *Ministry of Lies: The Truth behind The Nation of Islam's "The Secret Relationship between Blacks and Jews."* New York and London: Four Walls Eight Windows.

Brandon, Ivan C. 1973. "Hanafi Moslem Chief Quit Key Muslim Post." *Washington Post*, February 2.

Bratt, Peter. 1987. "Ett år efter USA-bombningen. Indianer till Khadaffi." *Dagens Nyheter*, April 16.

Breitman, George. 1967. *The Last Year of Malcolm X*. New York: Pathfinder.

——. [1976] 1986. "Malcolm X, the Man and His Ideas." In *The Assassination of Malcolm X*, edited by G. Breitman, Herman Porter, and Baxter Smith. New York: Pathfinder.

"Brothers in Bigotry." 1985. *Time*, October 14.

Brotz, Howard. 1964. *The Black Jews of Harlem*. London: Macmillan.

"Brown, Bellecourt: Victims of 'Witch Hunt.'" 1988. *Final Call*, November 4.

Burkett, Randall K. 1989. "Religious Ethos of the UNIA." In *African American Religious Studies*, edited by G. S. Wilmore. Durham and London: Duke University Press.

"Campaign Continues Struggle for Reparations for Blacks." 1993. *Final Call*, July 14.

Campell, Horace. 1987. *Rasta and Resistance*. Trenton, N.J.: African World Press.

Carson, Claybourne, Jr. 1989. "Blacks and Jews in the Civil Rights Movement." In *Jews in Black Perspective*, edited by J. R. Washington. Lanham: University Press of America.

——. 1991. *Malcolm X: The FBI File*. New York: Carroll and Graf.

Cary, Lorene. 1992. "Why It's Not Just Paranoia." *Newsweek*, April 6.

Cashmore, Ernest. 1983 [1979]. *Rastaman*. London: Allen and Unwin.

Cederskog, Georg. 1990. "Det vita USA startar krig mot rap-musik." *Dagens Nyheter*, March 15.

Chalmers, David M. 1981. *Hooded Americanism: The History of the Ku Klux Klan*. 3d ed. Durham: Duke University Press.

Chavis, Benjamin F., Jr. 1984. "Theology Under the Rainbow," *The Witness*, no. 5, May.
——. 1994. "The Farrakhan Sideshow." *New York Times*, July 12.
Cho, Sumi K. 1993. "Korean Americans vs. African Americans: Conflict and Construction." In *Reading Rodney King/Reading Urban Uprising*, edited by Robert Gooding-Williams. New York and London: Routledge.
Chomsky, Noam. 1991. *Deterring Democracy*. London: Vintage Books.
Christie, Nils. 1993. *Crime Control as Industry*. London and New York: Routledge.
Churchill, Ward, and Jim Vander Wall. 1988. *Agents of Repression*. Boston: South End Press.
"Claims Malcolm Killers Innocent." 1977. *Chicago Defender*, December 8.
Clarke, John Henrik, ed. 1974a. *Marcus Garvey and the Vision of Africa*. New York: Vintage Books.
Clarke, John Henrik. 1974b. "Comments." In *Marcus Garvey and the Vision of Africa*, edited by J. H. Clarke. New York: Vintage Books.
Clarke, Peter B. 1986. *Black Paradise: The Rastafarian Movement*. Wellingnorough, Northampshire: Aquarian Press.
"Claude Green Shot to Death in Unity Hall." 1929. *Chicago Defender*, March 16.
Cleage, Albert B., Jr. 1969. *The Black Messiah*. New York: A Search Book.
Cleaver, Eldridge. 1968. *Fråga inte ditt land [Soul on Ice]*. Prisma.
Cohen, Richard. 1993. "Federal Money for Racists." *Washington Post*, July 29.
"COINTELPRO Hinted in Libyan Students' Arrest." 1988. *Final Call*, September 16.
Coker, Cheo H. 1994. "Down for Whatever." *The Source*, February.
Collins, Sheila D. 1986. *The Rainbow Challenge: The Jackson Campaign and the Future of U. S. Politics*. New York: Monthly Review Press.
"Community Outraged. D. C. Police Assault 'Dopebusters.'" 1988. *Final Call*, October 3.
Cone, James H. 1970. *A Black Theology of Liberation*. Philadelphia and New York: J. B. Lippincott.
——. 1989. "Black Theology as Liberation Theology." In *African American Religious Studies*, edited by G. S. Wilmore. Durham and London: Duke University Press.
——. 1993. *Martin & Malcolm & America: A Dream or a Nightmare*. London: Fount Paperbacks.
Cooper, William. 1991. *Behold a Pale Horse*. Sedona, Ariz.: Light Technology Publishing.
Copeland, Larry. 1988. "Charitable Collections . . . Or a Cult's Scam?" *Atlanta Journal and Constitution*, October 30.
Corbin, Henry. 1983. *Cyclical Time and Ismaili Gnosis*. London: Kegan Paul.
Corcoran, James. 1990. *Bitter Harvest. Gordon Kahl and the Posse Comitatus: Murder in the Heartland*. New York: Penguin.
Cowans, Russell J. 1932. "Death List Found in Voodoo Cult." *Chicago Defender*, December 3.
Craft, Mona. 1972. "Eyewitnesses Describe Police Attack on New York Temple." *Muhammad Speaks*, April 28.
Cronon, E. David. 1969. *Black Moses: The Story of Marcus Garvey*. Madison: University of Wisconsin Press.
"Cult Leader Dies: Was in Murder Case." 1929. *Chicago Defender*, July 27.
"Cultist 'Guilty'; 32 Given Jail Sentences." 1942. *Chicago Defender*, October 10.
Curtis, R. M. Mukhtar. 1994. "Urban Muslims: The Formation of the Dar ul-Islam

Movement." In *Muslim Communities in North America,* edited by Y. Y. Haddad and J. Smith. New York: State University of New York Press.

Cushmeer, Bernard. 1971. *This Is the One. Messenger Elijah Muhammad. We Need Not Look for Another.* Phoenix, Ariz.: Truth Publications.

Daftary, Farhad. 1990. *The Ismailis.* Cambridge: Cambridge University Press.

Daniel, Frances. 1993. "A Look at Minister Louis Farrakhan: America's Other Son." *N'Digo,* no. 48 (November).

Daniels, Ron. 1993. "Rap, Black Music and the Revolution." *Final Call,* September 8.

Davis, John. 1987. *Libyan Politics. Tribe and Revolution.* London: I. B. Tauris.

Davis, Mike. 1992. "L.A.: The Fire This Time." *Covert Action,* no. 41 (summer).

——. 1993. "Uprising and Repression in L.A." In *Reading Rodney King/Reading Urban Uprising,* edited by Robert Gooding-Williams. New York and London: Routledge.

Dees, Morris, and Steve Fiffer. 1993. *Hate on Trial: The Case against America's Most Dangerous Neo-Nazi.* New York: Villard Books.

Dellios, Hugh. 1993. "Young Plotters in L.A. Linked to Older Hate Groups." *Chicago Tribune,* July 19.

DeParle, Jason. 1990. "Talk of Government Being Out to Get Blacks Fall on More Attentive Ears." *New York Times,* October 29.

"Detroit Council Votes: Reparations Bill Approved." 1989. *Final Call,* May 11.

Dewey, Jeanne. 1995. "March Leaders Shift Focus off Farrakhan." *Washington Times,* October 14.

Doherty, Shawn. 1991. "Nation of Islam Offers to Patrol Housing." *Los Angeles Times,* December 22.

"Don't Lock Out Jackson, Muslim Tells Democrats." 1984. *Washington Post,* April 23.

Dowling, Ewa S. 1987. Introduction to *The Aquarian Gospel of Jesus the Christ,* by Levi, H.D. Marina del Rey, Calif.: DeVorss.

Dowling, Levi H. 1987 [1907]. *The Aquarian Gospel of Jesus the Christ.* Marina del Rey, Calif.: DeVorss.

Drake, St. Clair, and Horace R. Cayton. 1962. *Black Metropolis.* New York: Harper.

"Drugs Challenged." 1988. *Final Call,* November 30.

Du Bois, W. E. B. 1988. [1897]. "The Conservation of Races." In *W. E. B. Du Bois Speaks: Speeches and Addresses 1890–1910,* edited by Philip S. Foner. New York: Pathfinder.

——. 1961 [1903]. *The Souls of Black Folk.* Greenwich, Conn.: Fawcett Publications.

——. 1940. *Dusk of Dawn.* New York: Harcourt.

Duke, Lynne. 1993. "Congressional Black Caucus and Nation of Islam Agree on Alliance." *Washington Post,* September 17.

Durte, Carmen. 1993. "7 Charged in Conspiracy to Murder Tucson Islamic Leader." *Arizona Daily Star,* April 11.

Dyson, Michael E. 1993. *Reflecting Black: African American Cultural Criticism.* Minneapolis: University of Minnesota Press.

Ehrman, Albert. 1971. "Explorations and Responses: Black Judaism in New York." *Journal of Ecumenical Studies* 8 (winter).

El-Amin, Mustafa. 1991. *The Religion of Islam and the Nation of Islam: What is the Difference?* Newark, N.J.: El-Amin Productions.

"Election 1990: D.C., Virginia and Maryland Results." *Washington Post,* September 12.

Ellingwood, Ken. 1992. "Nation of Islam Security Patrol Hearing Set Sept. 15." *Los Angeles Times,* September 6.

"The El Rukn Embarrassment." 1993. *Chicago Tribune,* June 11, editorial.

"El Rukns Guilty." 1987. *Chicago Defender*, November 25.

"Emam Wallace D. Muhammad's Appeal to Minister Farrakhan." 1978. *Bilalian News*, April 28.

Enayat, Hamid. 1982. *Modern Islamic Political Thought*. Austin: University of Texas Press.

Esposito, John L. 1988. *Islam: The Straight Path*. New York: Oxford University Press.

——. 1992. *The Islamic Threat: Myth or Reality?* New York and Oxford: Oxford University Press.

Essien-Udom, E. U. 1962. *Black Nationalism*. Chicago: University of Chicago Press.

Evanzz, Karl. 1992. *The Judas Factor: The Plot to Kill Malcolm X*. New York: Thunder's Mouth Press.

Extremism on the Right: A Handbook. 1988. New York: Anti-Defamation League.

"Famous Faces and the Million Man March." 1995. *Final Call*, October 16.

Farrakhan, Louis. 1972. "Police Assault Fails to Crush Muslims." *Muhammad Speaks*, April 28.

——. 1983a. *Warning to the Government of America*. Chicago: Hon. Elijah Muhammad Educational Foundation.

——. 1983b. *The Meaning of the F.O.I.* Chicago: Hon. Elijah Muhammad Educational Foundation.

——. 1986. "America: Are You Any Better Than Your Fathers?" *Final Call*, undated special edition, vol. 5, no. 13.

——. 1987. "Look Toward Leader Within." *Final Call*, June 10.

——. 1988a. "Fasting Strengthens Discipline." *Final Call*, May 27.

——. 1988b. "Warning! A Message to the Believers." *Final Call*, June 30.

——. 1989a. *The Announcement: A Final Warning to the U. S. Government*. Chicago: Final Call.

——. 1989b. "Black Youth Marked for Death by U.S. Government." *Final Call*, July 31.

——. 1989c. "Time Must Dictate Our Agenda." *Final Call*, May 11.

——. 1989d. "Your Agreement with Hell Will Not Stand!" *Final Call*, December 31.

——. 1989e [1984]. "What Is the Need For Black History?" In *Back Where We Belong: Selected Speeches by Minister Louis Farrakhan*, edited by Joseph D. Eure and Richard M. Jerome. Philadelphia: PC International Press.

——. 1989f [1984]. "Speech at Morgan State University." In *Back Where We Belong: Selected Speeches by Minister Louis Farrakhan*, edited by Joseph D. Eure and Richard M. Jerome. Philadelphia: PC International Press.

——. 1989g [1987]. "How to Give Birth to a God." In *Back Where We Belong: Selected Speeches by Minister Louis Farrakhan*, edited by Joseph D. Eure and Richard M. Jerome. Philadelphia: PC International Press.

——. 1989h [1987]. "Are Black People the Future World Rulers?" In *Back Where We Belong: Selected Speeches by Minister Louis Farrakhan*, edited by Joseph D. Eure and Richard M. Jerome. Philadelphia: PC International Press.

——. 1989i [1987]. "Politics without Economics is Symbol without Substance." In *Back Where We Belong: Selected Speeches by Minister Louis Farrakhan*, edited by Joseph D. Eure and Richard M. Jerome. Philadelphia: PC International Press.

——. 1990a. "Muslims Ready to Serve Community." *Final Call*, May 31.

——. 1990b. "Add It Up!" *Final Call*, June 22.

——. 1990c. "The Danger of 'Cross-over' Politicians." *Final Call*, May 3.

——. 1991a. "Who Is God? Part Three." *Final Call*, April 22.

——. 1991b. "Who Is God?" *Final Call*, May 29.

——. 1991c. "Who Is God? Part Five." *Final Call*, May 20.

——. 1991d. "Clash of the Worlds." *Final Call*, June 17.

——. 1991e. "Why Did God Make Devil?" *Final Call*, May 20.

——. 1991f. "The Black Man Must Do for Self or Suffer the Consequences!" *Final Call*, October 28.

——. 1991g. "Declare War on Obesity (Fat)!" *Final Call*, July 22.

——. 1991h. "Exercise to Stay Alive." *Final Call*, August 19.

——. 1992a. "The Worst is Yet to Come." *Final Call*, June 5.

——. 1992b. "Woe to the Hypocrites" (speech delivered in 1973), reprinted in *7 Speeches by Minister Louis Farrakhan*, WKU and Final Call Inc.

——. 1992c. [1974]. "Minister Farrakhan interviewed by Joe Walker, New York Editor of Muhammad Speaks." In *7 Speeches by Minister Louis Farrakhan*, edited by Ministry Class of Muhammad's Temple No. 7. WKU and the Final Call, Inc.

——. 1992d [1972/73]. "Woe to the Hypocrites." In *7 Speeches by Minister Louis Farrakhan*, edited by Ministry Class of Muhammad's Temple No. 7. WKU and the Final Call, Inc.

——. 1992e [1970]. "Black Solidarity Day Address." In *7 Speeches by Minister Louis Farrakhan*, edited by Ministry Class of Muhammad's Temple No. 7. WKU and the Final Call, Inc.

——. 1992f. "Black Youth: Marked for Death." *Final Call*, February 10.

——. 1992g. "America's Debt. Reparations are Owed to the Black Man and Woman." Speech delivered at the 20th Annual Congressional Black Caucus Legislative Weekend, September 27, 1990, Washington, D.C. Excerpt printed in *Final Call*, April 6.

——. 1993a. "We Are the Overcomers." *Final Call*, June 30.

——. 1993b. "The Coming of the Messiah." *Final Call*, November 10.

——. 1993c. "Giving New Meaning to Race." *Final Call*, October 13.

——. 1993d. "Principles of Religion." Speech delivered at the Parliament of the World's Religions, Chicago, September 2. Published in the *Final Call*, December 22.

——. 1993e. "I Will Never Bow Down." *Final Call*, September 8.

——. 1993f. "Minister Farrakhan to Jewish leaders: Let My People Go!" *Final Call*, September 22.

——. 1993g. "Our Young People: The Most Powerful Generation We've Produced Since Slavery." Speech delivered in St. Paul, Minnesota, July 17. Excerpt published in *Final Call*, October 11.

——. 1993h. "Address to the Gang Summit, Part Two: Let Us Make Man." Speech delivered in St. Paul, Minnesota, July 17. Published in *Final Call*, August 25.

——. 1993i. *A Torchlight for America*. Chicago: FCN Publishing.

——. 1993j. "The Honorable Louis Farrakhan Speaks on the Cities." *Final Call*, November 24.

——. 1994a. "To the F.O.I." *Final Call*, July 6.

——. 1994b. "Let Us Make Man." *Final Call*, March 30.

——. 1994c. "The Wobble in Human Nature." *Final Call*, January 19.

——. 1994d. "An Open Letter to Brother Silis Muhammad." *Final Call*, March 2.

——. 1994e. "Farrakhan on Anti-Semitism." *Final Call*, February 16.

——. 1994f. "Domestic Violence." *Final Call*, August 17.

——. 1994g. "The Burden of Change is on Us." *Final Call*, July 6.

———. 1994h. "Are Black Leaders and Organizations Really Ours?" *Final Call*, September 14.

———. 1995a. "A Holy Day of Atonement and Reconciliation." *Final Call*, August 30.

———. 1995b. "Why a Million Man March?" *Final Call*, August 30.

"Farrakhan Aid." Editorial, *Nationalism Today*, no. 39.

"Farrakhan Aides Detain Reporters." 1984. *Chicago Defender*, July 9.

"Farrakhan and His Fellow Travellers." 1986. *Searchlight*, December.

"Farrakhan Introduces the Leader of the First of September Revolution Moammar El Qathafi to Blacks Annual Conference." 1985. *The World Center: The Contribution of leader Moammar El Qathafi to U.S. Blacks Conference*. Libya: Mathaba.

"Farrakhan on Race, Politics and the News Media." 1984. *New York Times*, April 17.

"Farrakhan's Proposal Described as 'Phoney.' " 1990. *Chicago Defender*, March 7.

"Farrakhan Speaks, Jews Leave." 1993. *Christianity Today*, October 4.

"Farrakhan, Louis." 1992. *Current Biography*, April.

Fauset, Arthur Huff. 1971 [1944]. *Black Gods of the Metropolis: Negro Religious Cults in the Urban North*. Philadelphia: University of Pennsylvania Press.

"FCN Progress!" 1994. *Final Call*, July 6.

Ferris, William. 1984. *Blues from the Delta*. New York: Da Capo Press.

Fernando, S.H., Jr. 1994. *The New Beats: Exploring the Music, Culture, and Attitude of Hip-Hop*. New York and London: Doubleday.

Festinger, Leon, Henry W. Riecken, and Stanley Schachter. 1964. *When Prophecy Fails*. New York: Harper Torchbooks.

"Fiery Leader and Loyal Follower in the Nation of Islam: Louis Farrakhan." 1994. *New York Times*, March 3.

Final Declaration of the Second Islamic Call Conference. 1982. Tripoli, SPLAJ, August 14–19.

"The First International Conference for the Liberation of Indian Peoples of The Americas." 1988. *The World Mathaba*, June.

Fletcher, Michael A., and Hamil R. Harris. 1995. "Rift between Farrakhan, Jewish Leaders Reemerges." *Washington Post*, October 14.

Flynn, Kevin, and Gary Gerhart. 1989. *The Silent Brotherhood: Inside America's Racist Underground*. New York: Free Press.

Fogelqvist, Jonas. 1989. "Khadafis nya vänner. De nya 'radikala' fascisterna." *Arbetaren*, May 5.

Ford, Andrea. 1992. "Doubts Cast on Data in Gang Report." *Los Angeles Times*, May 29.

Foxman, Abraham, and Mira Boland. 1992. "Fruit of Islam on U.S. Tab?" *Washington Times*, August 19.

Frazier, Franklin E. 1974 [1964]. *The Negro Church in America*. New York: Schocken Books.

Freedberg, Louis. 1995. "Farrakhan Swipes Again at Jews, Saying They Were 'Bloodsuckers.' " *San Francisco Chronicle*, October 14.

" 'Freedom Day' set for Houston in August." 1988. *Final Call*, July 20.

Friedly, Michel, and David Gallen. 1993. *Martin Luther King Jr.: The FBI File*. New York: Carroll and Graf Publishers.

From Ballots to Bombs: The Inside Story of the National Front's Political Soldiers. London: Searchlight Publishing.

Gable, Gerry. 1991. "The Far Right in Contemporary Britain." In *Neo-Fascism in Eu-*

rope, edited by Luciano Cheles, Ronnie Ferguson, and Michalina Vaughan. London and New York: Longman Group U.K.

Gadlin, Satephanie. 1991. "AIDS: The Black Plague." *Final Call*, July 22.

Gallo, Gary. 1990. "What Do 'White' Nationalists Believe?" *Final Call*, March 21.

"Gang Summit Claim Progress." 1993. *Chicago Tribune*, July 19.

Gans, Bruce M., and Walter L. Lowe. 1980. "The Islam Connection." Playboy, May.

Gardell, Mattias. 1995a. "Farrakhan talar sanning: de svartas problem i USA är lika mycket de vitas problem." *Dagens Nyheter*, October 21.

———. 1995b. "Vita Husets svarta dag." *Arbetaren*, October 27–November 2.

———. 1990. "Brand möter Public Enemy." *Brand*, no. 2 (April).

———. 1992a. "Änglarnas uppror: No Justice–No Peace." *Brand*, no. 4 (September).

———. 1992b. "Muammar al-Khaddafi och den Libyska revolutionen." *Anarkistisk Tidskrift*, nos. 6–7.

———. 1993a. "Malcolm X och den svarta revolutionen." *Arbetaren*, March 12–18.

———. 1994a. "Halvmånen och stjärnbanéret. Islam i nordamerikansk historia och nutid." In *Majoritetens Islam*, edited by Ingvar Svanberg and David Westerlund. Stockholm: Arena.

———. 1994b. "The Sun of Islam Will Rise in the West." In *Muslim Communities in North America*, edited by Y.Y. Haddad and J. Smith. New York: State University of New York Press.

———. 1996. "Behold, I Make All Things New." In *Questioning the Secular State: The Worldwide Resurgence of Religion in Politics*. London: C. Hurst; & New York: St. Martin's.

Garrow, David J., 1981. *The FBI and Martin Luther King, Jr.* New York: Penguin.

———. 1993. [1986]. *Bearing the Cross: Martin Luther King Jr., and the Southern Christian Leadership Conference*. London: Vintage Books.

Garvey, Marcus. 1986a [1923]. *The Philosophy and Opinions of Marcus Garvey*. Vol. I. Edited by Amy J. Garvey. Dover, Mass.: Majority Press.

———. 1986b [1925]. *The Philosophy and Opinions of Marcus Garvey*. Vol. II. Edited by Amy J. Garvey. Dover, Mass.: Majority Press.

———. 1987. *Marcus Garvey: Life and Lessons*. Edited by Robert A. Hill and Barbara Bair. Berkeley: University of California Press.

———. 1974 [1913]. "The British West Indies in the Mirror of Civilization." In *Marcus Garvey and the Vision of Africa*, edited by J. H. Clarke. New York: Vintage Books.

"Garvey's Vision." n.d. *Nationalism Today*, no. 42.

Gasman, Daniel. 1971. *The Scientific Origins of National Socialism*. London: Macdonald.

Geels, Antoon, and Owe Wickström. 1989. *Den religiösa människan*. Löberöd: Plus Ultra.

Gellner, Ernest. 1983. *Nations and Nationalism*. Oxford: Blackwell.

George, Nelson. 1990. *Stop the Violence: Overcoming Self-Destruction*. New York: Pantheon Books.

"Get to Work." 1987. *National Front News*, no. 94.

"Ghana: A Study in the Third Position." 1989. *Nationalism Today*, no. 45 (April).

Gilliam, Dorothy. 1993. "A Peace Pact toward True Black Power." *Washington Post*, September 18.

"G.K.C. & Qathafi." n.d. *Nationalism Today*, no. 42.

Glazer, Nathan. 1983. *Ethnic Dilemmas 1964–1982*. Cambridge: Harvard University Press.

——. 1989. "What Happened to the Grand Alliance?" In *Jews in Black Perspective,* edited by J. R. Washington. Lanham: University Press of America.

Glick, Brian. 1989. *War at Home.* Boston: South End Press.

Goldberg, David. 1992. "Let the Giver Beware. Officials: Sect Solicits for Non-Existent Charities." *Atlanta Journal and Constitution,* June 16.

Goldman, Ari L. 1989. "Mainstream Islam Rapidly Embraced by Black Americans." *New York Times International,* February 21.

Goldman, Peter. 1979. *The Death and Life of Malcolm X.* Chicago: University of Illinois Press.

Goldstein, Amy. 1993. "Black Gays in New D.C. Coalition Wary About Muslim Doctor's Role." *Washington Post,* September 29.

Goldston, Robert. 1968. *Den svarta revolutionen.* Pelarbok/SAGA.

Goodrick-Clarke, Nicholas. 1992. *The Occult Roots of Nazism: Secret Aryan Cults and Their Influence on Nazi Ideology.* London and New York: I. B. Tauris.

Greider, William, and Richard Harwood. 1977a. "Hanafi Muslim Bands Seize Hostages at 3 Sites; 1 Slain, Others Wounded." *Washington Post,* March 10.

——. 1977b. "Tell Them Payday Is Here . . . No More Games." *Washington Post,* March 10.

Griffin, Nick. 1985. "The Riots: An Open Letter to Blacks in Britain." *Nationalism Today,* no. 35 (November/December).

Grimsley, Will. 1964. "Cassius 'A Proud Muslim.' " *Miami Herald,* February 28.

Gross, Larry, and Justin Blum. 1993. "4 Cops Found Not Guilty in Rodney King Beating." *Chicago Defender,* April 30.

Haddad, Yvonne Y. 1991. "American Foreign Policy in the Middle East and Its Impact on the Identity of Arab Muslims in the United States." In *The Muslims of America,* edited by Y. Y. Haddad. New York: Oxford University Press.

Haddad, Yvonne Y., ed. *The Muslims of America.* 1991. New York: Oxford University Press.

Haddad, Yvonne Y., and Jane Smith. 1991. "The Druze in North America." *The Muslim World,* 81 (April).

——. 1993. *Mission to America.* Gainesville: University Press of Florida.

Haddad, Yvonne Y., and Jane Smith, eds. 1994. *Muslim Communities in North America.* New York: State University of New York Press.

Hakim, Ida. 1991a. "Let's Talk Justice." *Muhammad Speaks* 7, no. 1.

——. 1991b. "Caucasian Calling on White Support for Reparations to Black People." *Muhammad Speaks* 7, no. 6.

Halasa, Malu. 1990. *Elijah Muhammad.* New York and Philadelphia: Chelsea House Publishers.

Halliday, Fred, and Maxine Molyneux. 1981. *The Ethiopian Revolution.* London: Verso.

Hannerz, Ulf. 1969. *Soul Side: Inquiries into Ghetto Culture and Community.* New York and London: Columbia University Press.

Hardy, Michael, and William Pleasant. 1987. *The Honorable Louis Farrakhan: A Minister for Progress.* New York: New Alliance Publications.

Hauser, Thomas. 1991. *Muhammad Ali: His Life and Times.* London: Robson Books.

Haywood, H. L. 1944. *Famous Masons.* Chicago: Masonic History Co.

Hazziez, Shirley. 1973. "All Blacks are Muslims, Believe It or Not." *Muhammad Speaks,* February 2.

Hedin, Christer. 1996. "Ortodoxi och ortopraxi." *Svensk religionshistorisk årskrift.* Forthcoming.

Henderson, Lenneal J. 1994. "African Americans in the Urban Milieu: Conditions, Trends, and Development Needs." *The State of Black America 1994.* Edited by Billy J. Tidwell. New York: National Urban League.

Henry, William A., III. 1994. "Pride and Prejudice." *Time Magazine,* February 28.

Hill, Robert A., and Barbara Bair. 1987a. "Introduction." In *Garvey, Marcus, Life and Lessons,* edited by Robert A. Hill and Barbara Bair. Berkeley: University of California Press.

Hill, Robert A., and Barbara Bair. 1987b. "Glossary of Names and Terms." *Garvey, Marcus, Life and Lessons,* edited by Robert A. Hill and Barbara Bair. Berkeley: University of California Press.

Hirsley, Michael. 1994. "U.S. Muslims Search for Understanding." *Chicago Tribune,* February 11.

Hjärpe, Jan. 1994. *Araber och arabism.* Rabén Prisma.

Hobsbawn, Eric J. 1990. *Nations and Nationalism since 1780.* Cambridge: Cambridge University Press.

Holland, Bernard. 1993. "Sending a Message, Louis Farrakhan Plays Mendelssohn." *New York Times,* April 19.

Holmes, Steven A. 1994a. "As Farrakhan Group Land Jobs from Government, Debate Grows." *New York Times,* March 4.

——. 1994b. "N.A.A.C.P. Board Dismisses Group's Executive Director." *New York Times,* August 21.

"Horst with No Name." 1988. *Searchlight,* April.

Howe, Irving. 1976. *The Immigrant Jews of New York.* London and Boston: Routledge and Kegan Paul.

Hussain, Jassim M. 1982. *The Occultation of the Twelfth Imam.* London: The Muhammad Trust.

Ice-T. 1994. *The Ice Opinion: Who Gives a Fuck. As Told to Heidi Sigmund.* London: Pan Books.

Ihejirika, Maudlyne. 1994a. "New Life's Weapon: Respect." *Chicago Sun-Times,* February 13.

——. 1994b. "Muslim Gets CHA Deal. Farrakhan Aide's Firm to Patrol Rockwell." *Chicago Sun-Times,* February 13.

"Iran: An Assessment." 1989. *Nationalism Today,* no. 45.

ibn Ishao [Sirat Rasul Allah]. 1967. *The Life of Muhammad.* Translated by A. Guillaume. Karachi: Oxford University Press.

"Islam Nation Leader Says Blacks Must Gain Equality Separately. Farrakhan Calls for Separate Black and White Development." 1990. *Spotlight,* July 23.

Jabir, Taqir. 1993. "American Blacks Focus on Ghana." *Final Call,* September 22.

"Jackson Given Support from Chicago Blacks." 1984. *Washington Post,* February 11.

"Jackson, Invoking 'Integrity' Repeals Farrakhan Defense." 1984. *New York Times,* May 6.

"Jackson Says Farrakhan Aide Gave Racist Speech at a College." 1994. *New York Times,* January 23.

Jacob, Virginia Lee. 1985. *Roots of Rastafari.* San Diego, Calif.: Avant Books.

Jamison, Harold. 1988. "Activists Arrest stir Cointelpro fear." *Amsterdam News,* July 30.

Janovsky, Michael. 1995. "Wary of Divisions, Leaders of Million Man March Play Down Farrakhan Role." *New York Times,* October 13.

"Jesse's Pal Says 'Hitler was a very great man.' " 1984. *New York Post*, April 11.

Jew-Hatred as History: An Analysis of the Nations of Islam's "The Secret Relationship between Blacks and Jews." 1993. New York: Anti-Defamation League.

Johnson, Allan. 1993. "Farrakhan Making Overtures. Amid Scepticism, Controversial Leader Beckons Jews." *Chicago Tribune*, May 19.

Johnson, Haynes. 1984. "The Hot Fires of a Moral Crisis Endanger Jackson's Promise." *Washington Post*, April 8.

Johnson, Mary A., 1994. "Firing Goes Flak from Both Sides. Fans, Critics Hit Mixed Message." *Chicago Sun-Times*, February 4.

Johnson, Steven A. 1991. "Political Activity of Muslims in America." In *The Muslims of America*, edited by Y. Y. Haddad. New York: Oxford University Press.

Jones, Cynthia-Val. 1984. "Imam Muhammad on Farrakhan's mission." *Chicago Defender*, April 21.

Jones, Dewey R. 1932. "Voodoo Rites of the Jungles in Odd Contrasts with Background of City." *Chicago Defender*, December 10.

Jones, Dionne J., and Greg Harrison. 1994. "Fast Facts: Comparative Views of African-American Status and Progress." In *The State of Black America 1994*, edited by Billy J. Tidwell. New York: National Urban League.

Jones, Rachel L. 1995. "Controversy and a Scramble Before Million Man March." *Philadelphia Inquirer*, October 14.

Jonsson, Stefan. 1993. *De Andra: Amerikanska kulturkrig och europeisk rasism.* Stockholm: Norstedts.

Juergensmeyer, Mark. 1993. *The New Cold War: Religious Nationalism Confronts the Secular State.* Berkeley and Los Angeles: University of California Press.

Karenga, Maulana. 1987. *Introduction to Black Studies.* Los Angeles: Kawaida Publications.

Karriem, Stanley. 1974. "For Our Transgressions." *Muhammad Speaks*, November 28.

Kashif, Lonnie, 1974a. "Muslim Jet Attracts Huge Crowds." *Muhammad Speaks*, August 23.

——. 1974b. " 'Hanafi' Trial Ends, Nation of Islam Absolved." *Muhammad Speaks*, March 31.

——. 1975a. "Muslim Ministers Declare Support for New Leadership." *Muhammad Speaks*, March 14.

——. 1975b. "Muhammad's Message Crowns Jamaican Events." *Muhammad Speaks*, June 27.

Kashif, Lonnie, and Alonzo 4X. 1974. "Progressive Strides of Messenger Muhammad's Chicago Labor Revealed." *Muhammad Speaks*, March 8.

Katz, Jesse. 1991. "Gang Killings in L.A. County Top a Record 700." *Los Angeles Times*, December 8.

Katz, William. 1986. *The Invisible Empire: The Ku Klux Klan Impact on History.* Washington, D.C.: Open Hand Publishing.

Kaufman, Jonathan. 1988. *Broken Alliance: The Turbulent Times between Blacks and Jews in America.* New York: Charles Scribner's Sons.

Kellas, James G. 1991. *The Politics of Nationalism and Ethnicity.* Houndmills and London: Macmillan.

Khalifa, Rashad. 1981a. "Appendix 1–19." In *Qur'an: The Final Scripture.* Tucson, Ariz.: Islamic Productions.

——. 1981b. *The Computer Speaks: God's Message to the World.* Tucson, Ariz.: Renaissance Productions.

——. 1982. *Quran: Visual Presentation of the Miracle.* Tucson, Ariz.: Islamic Productions.

——. 1989a. "Appendix 1–38." *Quran: The Final Testament.* Tucson, Ariz.: Islamic Productions.

——. 1989b. "New Era in Human History: Divine Call to All Believers in God." *Muslim Perspective,* July.

——. 1989c. "After I Die Millions of Believers Will Know." *Submission Perspective,* September.

"Khallid Muhammad Resumes Post." 1995. *Final Call,* July 19.

al-Khalot, Abdel Aziz. 1982. *Islam: A Continuous Revolution.* Libyan Jamahiriya.

King, Dennis. 1989. *Lyndon LaRouche and the New American Fascism.* New York: Doubleday.

"King Verdict, Rioting Were Wrong." 1992. *Chicago Defender,* May 2.

King, Wayne. 1985. "White Supremacists Voice Support of Farrakhan," *New York Times,* October 12.

The KKK Today: A 1991 Status Report. 1991. New York: Anti-Defamation League.

"Klan Shooting Heightens Tensions in Ohio Town." 1990. *Final Call,* February 22.

Klassen, Ben. 1981. *The White Man's Bible.* Otto, N.C.: Church of the Creator.

——. 1987. *Rahowa! This Planet Is All Ours.* Otto, N.C.: Church of the Creator.

Kramer, Martin. 1990. "The Moral Logic of Hizballah." In *Origins of Terrorism,* edited by Walter Reich. New York: Cambridge University Press.

Kuss, Kuba Abu. 1990. "Qur'an versus Hadith: Is Hearsay Superior to Revelation?" *Muhammad Speaks* 6, no. 3.

——. 1991. "Saviour's Day Retrospect. 'Unspeakable Joy.' " *Muhammad Speaks* 7, no. 2.

de Lama, George, and Ray Moseley. 1991. "UN Chief to Propose Kuwait Peace Force." *Chicago Tribune,* January 12.

Lanternari, Vittorio. 1965 [1963]. *The Religions of the Oppressed.* Chicago: Mentor Books.

Lathem, Niles, and Jack Peritz. 1984. "Furor Grows Over Jesse Pal's Hitler Remarks." *New York Post,* April 12.

"Lawyer Focusses on Reparations Battle." 1992. *Muhammad Speaks* 8, no. 4.

Lee, Gary, 1993. "Organizers Call Street-Gang Summit a Success." *Washington Post,* May 3.

Lee, Martha F. 1988. *The Nation of Islam, An American Millenarian Movement.* Lewiston, N.Y.: Edwin Mellen Press.

Lee, Martin A., and Bruce Shlain. 1992. *Acid Dreams. The Complete Social History of LSD: The CIA, the Sixties and Beyond.* New York: Grove Weidenfeld.

Lee, Spike. 1992. *By Any Means Necessary: The Trials and Tribulations of the Making of Malcolm X . . . (while ten million mutherfuckers are fucking with you!).* New York: Hyperion.

Leid, Utrice C. 1988. "Suspect!" *Final Call,* November 30.

Leland, John. 1992. "Rap Race." *Newsweek,* June 29.

Lemann, Nicholas. 1992. *The Promised Land: The Great Black Migration and How It Changed America.* London: Papermac.

"The Lessons of Vauxhall." *National Front News,* no. 120.

"Let My People Go." 1985. *Nationalism Today,* no. 29 (May).

Levin, Nora. 1978. *Jewish Socialist Movements, 1871–1917: While Messiah Tarried.* London and Henley: Routledge & Kegan Paul.

Lewis, Alfred E., and Timothy S. Robinson. 1973. "Seven 'Executed' in District's Biggest Mass Murder." *Washington Post,* January 19.

Lewis, Bernard. 1990. *Race and Slavery in the Middle East.* New York and Oxford: Oxford University Press.

"Libya: A Study of the Third Position in Practice." 1989. *Nationalism Today,* no. 44 (January).

Lincoln, C. Eric. 1969. "The Black Muslims as a Protest Movement." In *Black History: A Reappraisal,* edited by Melvin Drimmer. New York: Anchor Books.

———. 1973. *The Black Muslims in America.* Boston: Beacon Press.

———. 1984. *Race, Religion and the Continuing American Dilemma.* New York: Hill and Wang.

———. 1989a. "The Development of Black Religion in America." In *African American Religious Studies,* edited by Gayraud S. Wilmore. Durham and London: Duke University Press.

———. 1989b. "The Muslim Mission in the Context of American Social History." In *African American Religious Studies,* edited by G. S. Wilmore. Durham and London: Duke University Press.

Lincoln, C. Eric, and Lawrence H. Mamiya. 1990. *The Black Church in the African American Experience.* Durham: Duke University Press.

Lindeborg, Lisbeth. 1991. "Antisemiter på frammarsch. Om sambandet mellan nynazism och islamisk fundamentalism." *Dagens Nyheter,* February 2.

Lindqvist, Sven. 1992. *Utrota varenda jävel.* Stockholm: Albert Bonniers förlag.

"Living Alternative." 1988. *National Front News,* no. 104 (April).

Ljungdahl, Axel. 1969. *Profetrörelser, deras orsaker, innebörder och förutsättningar.* Stockholm: Almqvist & Wiksell.

Locke, Henry. 1984a. "Black Journalists Blast Farrakhan." *Chicago Defender,* April 9.

———. 1984b. "Jewish Leaders Denounce the JDL." *Chicago Defender,* May 29.

———. 1984c. "Muslims, JDL Swap Barbs." *Chicago Defender,* May 30.

———. 1987a. "Closing Arguments Due in El Rukn Trial." *Chicago Defender,* November 18.

———. 1987b. "Gang's Arsenal at Trial." *Chicago Defender,* November 19.

———. 1987c. "Mystery Surrounds El Rukn Trial Figures." *Chicago Defender,* November 24.

———. 1988. "El Rukns Sentenced for Bibbs Killing." *Chicago Defender,* November 15.

Lodenius, Anna-Lena, and Stieg Larsson. 1991. *Extremhögern.* Stockholm: Tidens Förlag.

Lomax, Louis E. 1963. *When the Word is Given. . . .* Cleveland and New York: World Publishing Company.

Louis Farrakhan: An Update. 1985. New York: ADL, Spring.

Louis Farrakhan: The Campaign to Manipulate Public Opinion. 1990. New York: Anti-Defamation League.

The Louis Farrakhan: Continuing the Message of Hate. 1988. New York: ADL, June.

Louis Farrakhan: In His Own Words. n.d. New York: Anti-Defamation League.

"Louis Farrakhan—Pointing the Way for Black America." 1987. *Nationalism Today,* no. 37 (March).

Louis Farrakhan. Special Edition. 1987. Anti-Defamation League of B'nai B'rith-Civil Rights Division, October.

Lynch, Hollis. 1967. *Edward Wilmot Blyden: Pan-Negro Patriot.* London: Oxford University Press.

MacLean, Nancy. 1994. *Behind the Mask of Chivalry: The Making of the Second Ku Klux Klan.* New York: Oxford University Press.

MacNulty, W. Kirk, 1991. *Freemasonry.* London: Thames and Hudson.

Madhubuti, M. 1978. "BBB Interviews Minister Abdul Farrakhan." *Black Books Bulletin,* vol. 6.

al Mahdi, As Sayyid Isa Al Haadi. 1986a. *The True Story of Noah [PBUH].* Part 2. Brooklyn, N.Y.: Nubian Islaamic Hebrews, Ansaaru ALLAH Community.

———. 1986b. *Racism in Islam.* Brooklyn, N.Y.: Nubian Islaamic Hebrews, Ansaaru ALLAH Community.

———. 1986c. *The True Story of Noah [PBUH].* Part 1. Brooklyn, N.Y.: Nubian Islaamic Hebrews, Ansaaru ALLAH Community.

———. 1987. *The Call of the Mahdi in America.* Brooklyn, N.Y.: Ansaaru ALLAH Community.

———. 1989. *The Ansar Cult: The Truth about the Ansarullah Community in America. Truth is Truth. Rebuttal to the Slanderers.* Brooklyn, N.Y.: Original Tents of Kedar.

Mahdi, Joshua. 1991a. "The New World of Truth." *Muhammad Speaks* 7, no. 3.

———. 1991b. "The New World of Truth, Part III." *Muhammad Speaks* 7, no. 6.

Mamiya, Lawrence H. 1982. "From Black Muslim to Bilalian. The Evolution of a Movement." *Journal for the Scientific Study of Religion* 2, no. 6 (June).

———. 1983. "Minister Louis Farrakhan and the Final Call: Schism in the Muslim Movement." *The Muslim Community in North America,* edited by Abu-Laban Waugh and Quereshi. Edmonton: University of Alberta Press.

Mandel, William L. 1993. "What Los Angeles Means: 'Negroes Are Lynched in America.'" *Why L.A. Happened,* edited by Haki R. Madhubuti. Chicago: Third World Press.

Marable, Manning. 1985. *Black American Politics.* London: Verso.

———. 1986 [1984]. *Race, Reform and Rebellion: The Second Reconstruction in America, 1945–1982.* Jackson: University Press of Mississippi.

"Marines, Army Soldiers Pull Out of Riot-Torn L.A." 1992. *Chicago Defender,* May 11.

Marriott, Michel. 1995. "Black Women Speak of Anger and Elation on Men's March." *New York Times,* October 13.

Marsh, Clifton E. 1984. *From Black Muslims to Muslims: The Transition from Separatism to Islam, 1930–1980.* Metuchen, N.J., and London: Scarecrow Press.

Martz, Larry. 1988. "The Power Broker." *Newsweek,* March 21.

Matlick, Marylin, and Niles Lathem. 1984. "Jackson Backer Threatens 'Slur' Reporter." *New York Post,* April 3.

McCall, Nathan. 1990. "Jewish Leaders Doubt Farrakhan Plea for Peace." *Washington Post,* March 3.

McCoy, Alfred W. 1991. *The Politics of Heroin: CIA Complicity in the Drug Trade.* Revised and expanded edition. New York: Lawrence Hill Books.

McDaniel, Matthew. 1994. "Bad for Your Health: Ice Cube's Lethal Injection Gets Under Amerikkka's Skin." *Rap Pages,* March.

McSwine, Bartley. 1993. "L.A. 1992: Race, Class and Spiritual Poverty in the American

Empire." In *Why L.A. Happened*, edited by Haki R. Madhubuti. Chicago: Third World Press.

Meier, August, and Elliot Rudwick. 1973. *CORE: A Study in the Civil Rights Movement.* New York: Oxford University Press.

Melton, Gordon J. 1992. *Encyclopedic Handbooks of Cults in America.* Revised and updated edition. New York: Garland Publishing.

"Men and Women of Every Race Understand that Race-Mixing Destroys Our People." 1987. *National Front News*, no. 93 (August).

Mernissi, Fatima. 1985. *Beyond the Veil: Male-Female Dynamics in Muslim Society.* London: Al Saqi Books.

——. 1991. *Women and Islam: An Historical and Theological Enquiry.* Oxford: Basil Blackwell.

——. 1993. *Islam and Democracy: Fear of a Modern World.* London: Virago Press.

"Message Sent Muslims: City in Tribute to Muhammad; Mass for Muhammad." 1975. *Chicago Defender*, February 26.

Meyers, Lewis, Jr. 1988. "Terrorist Task Force: Cointelpro 80's style. Part II." *Final Call*, November 30.

Meyers, Michael. 1994. "The Fight to Save the N.A.A.C.P." *New York Times*, August 3.

Milk, Jeremy L. 1994. "Inspiration or Hate-Monger? Aide to Minister Farrakhan Draws Praise and Condemnation for His Campus Speeches." *The Chronicle of Higher Education*, January 19.

"Million Men March Poll." 1995. *Washington Post*, October 17.

Mills, Nicolaus, ed. 1994. *Debating Affirmative Action.* New York: Dell Publishing.

"Minister Farrakhan Meets the Press." 1994. *Final Call*, March 2.

"Minister Farrakhan Supports Congressman in Reparations Effort." 1993. *Final Call*, October 13.

"Minister Louis Farrakhan and the Nation of Islam Claim They are Moving Toward Moderation and Increased Tolerance. You Decide." ad, 1994. *New York Times*, January 16.

"Mob Control: Rapper Shorty of Da Lench Mob Vows to Continue to Rap Only the Raw Truth." 1993. *Final Call*, September 22.

Moltmann, JÅrgen. 1986. "Christian Theology and Political Religion." In *Civil Religion and Political Theology*, edited by L. S. Rouner. Notre Dame, Indiana: University of Notre Dame Press.

Momen, Moojan. 1985. *An Introduction to Shi'i Islam.* New Haven and London: Yale University Press.

Montgomery, Ed. 1963. "Black Muslim Founder Exposed As a White." *Los Angeles Evening Herald Examiner*, July 28.

Moore, Marian. 1992. "L.A. Residents Watch as Riots Set City Ablaze." *Chicago Defender*, May 2.

Moore, Kathleen. 1991. "Muslims in Prison: Claims to Constitutional Protection of Religious Liberty." In *The Muslims in America*, edited by Y. Haddad and J. Smith. New York and Oxford: Oxford University Press.

Morganthau, Tom, Elizabeth O. Colton, Nikkiefinke Greenberg, Margaret Warner, and Thomas M. DeFrank. 1984. "Jesse Wins a 'Syria Primary.'" *Newsweek*, January 16.

Morganthau, Tom, Sylvester Monroe, Diane Weathers, Frank Maier, and Verne Smith. 1984. "Jackson's Albatross? A Supporter's Remarks Make News—and Trouble." *Newsweek*, April 23.

Morganthau, Tom, Marcus Marby, Frank Washington, Vern E. Smith, Emily Yoffe, and Lucille Beachy. 1992. "Losing Ground." *Newsweek*, April 6.

Morris, Brian. 1987. *Anthropological Studies of Religion*. Cambridge: Cambridge University Press.

Morsi, Magali. 1990. *Profetens hustrur [org. Les Femmes du Prophäte]*. Lund: Alhambra.

Mortimer, Edward. 1982. *Faith and Power: The Politics of Islam*. London: Faber and Faber.

Moses, Wilson Jeremiah. 1978. *The Golden Age of Black Nationalism, 1850–1925*. New York and Oxford: Oxford University Press.

"Most Noble Drew Ali Is Laid to Rest." 1929. *Chicago Defender*, August 3.

Mount, Charles. 1986. "Muhammad's Heirs to Share in the Fortune." *Chicago Tribune*, July 11.

Muhammad, Abdul Akbar. 1984. "To Serve His Own." *Our Time Has Come*. FC Records Inc.

Muhammad, Abdul Alim, and Barbara Justice. 1991. "Recommendations to the Black Nation concerning AIDS." *Final Call*, October 7.

Muhammad, Abdul Allah. 1991. "Black/Jewish Relationship False." *Final Call*, July 1.

Muhammad, Abdul-Rauf. 1977. *Bilal Ibn Rabah: A Leading Companion of the Prophet Muhammad*. American Trust Publications.

Muhammad, Abdul Wali. n.d. "Nation of Islam." *Nationalism Today*, no. 39.

——. 1986. "Welcome Home!" *Final Call*, undated special edition, vol. 5, no. 13.

——. 1988a. "Minister Farrakhan Welcomes 12,000 to National Convention. Crescent and Star Rises over Saviour's Day '88." *Final Call*, November 4.

——. 1988b. "Glenda Brawley Continues Fight for Justice." *Final Call*, June 30.

——. 1990. "Muslim/Christian Relationships: One Faith, One Religion." *Final Call*, March 21.

——. 1991a. "Mr. Bush, New Dictator." *Final Call*, April 22.

——. 1991b. "Exclusive Interview with the Honorable Minister Louis Farrakhan." *Final Call*, December 21.

——. 1991c. " 'Miracle' Drugs Relieve AIDS Symptoms." *Final Call*, October 7.

——. 1991d. "Controversy Surrounds Kemron Development." *Final Call*, October 7.

Muhammad, Akbar. 1992. "Colonial Masters behind Muslim/Christian Clashes." *Final Call*, January 6.

Muhammad, Amira. 1992. "The Contemporary Muslim Woman." *Muhammad Speaks* 8, no. 5.

Muhammad, Ava. 1991. "Control Reality! Minister's Message Gives Us the Power." *Final Call*, July 22.

——. 1993. "Bones of Contention. Scientific Fantasy Vs. Divine Reality." *Final Call*, July 28.

Muhammad, Donald. 1988. "Saviors' Day Musical Extravaganza: Black Music Giants Perform under Big Top." *Final Call*, November 4.

——. 1989. " 'Righteous' Rap Ignites a 'Party' under the Big Top." *Final Call*, April 6.

——. 1990. "Fitzgerald Honored: Rap to Define the 1990s." *Final Call*, January 29.

——. 1991a. "Defiant Giant down to the Liberation Struggle." *Final Call*, May 20.

——. 1991b. "Coming down like Babylon: Prince Akeem Crushing Falsehood with Righteous Rap." *Final Call*, October 28.

——. 1991c. "Ice Cube Delivers Hot Lyrics. Dr. Khallid Muhammad Fires up 'Death Certificate.' " *Final Call*, December 21.

——. 1991d. "Godfather of Hip Hop: Afrika Bambatta [*sic*]." *Final Call*, April 22.

——. 1991e. "Doug E.'s Rap Still (Clean and) Fresh." *Final Call*, June 17.

——. 1992. "1991: A Year of Conscious Black Music in Review." *Final Call*, January 27.

——. 1993a. "Jurassic Parc. Tall Tales About Tall Tails." *Final Call*, July 14.

——. 1993b. "The Truth on Violence and Rap." *Final Call*, December 22.

——. 1994a. "Dr. Muhammad Spoils ADL Plot to Split N.O.I. Leadership." *Final Call*, March 2.

——. 1994b. "1993: The Year in Music." *Final Call*, February 2.

——. 1994a. *History of the Nation of Islam*, edited by Nasir Makr Hakim. Cleveland, Ohio: Secretarius Publications.

——. 1994b. *The Time and the Judgment*, edited by Nasir Makr Hakim. Cleveland, Ohio: Secretarius Publications.

Muhammad, Elijah. n.d. *The Supreme Wisdom*. Vol. 2. Newport, Va.: United Brothers Communications System.

——. 1957. *The Supreme Wisdom: Solution to the so-called NEGROE's Problem*. Newport, Va.: National Newport News and Commentator.

——. 1965. *Message to the Blackman*. Philadelphia: Hakim's Publications.

——. 1966a. "The Gods at War." *Muhammad Speaks*, December 30.

——. 1966b. "Battle in the Sky." *Muhammad Speaks*, January 7.

——. 1967. *How to Eat to Live*. Chicago: Muhammad's Temple of Islam No. 2.

——. 1969a. "Open Letter to the Chicago Tribune." *Muhammad Speaks*, February 7.

——. 1969b. "The TV Broadcast of Richard Whitcomb." *Muhammad Speaks*, December 12.

——. 1969c. "The Teachings of the Holy QUR-AN." *Muhammad Speaks*, July 4.

——. 1969d. "The Mother Plane." *Muhammad Speaks*, August 29.

——. 1970a. "A Great and Terrible Day." *Muhammad Speaks*, March 13.

——. 1970b. "Man Is Not Created without Aims and Purpose." *Muhammad Speaks*, June 12.

——. 1970c. "The Sudden Death of President Nasser of Egypt." *Muhammad Speaks*, October 9.

——. 1971. "Old World Going Out with Great Noise." *Muhammad Speaks*, November 26.

——. 1972a. *How to Eat to Live, Book Two*. Chicago: Muhammad's Temple of Islam No. 2.

——. 1972b. "The Great Gift of Our Libyan Brothers." *Muhammad Speaks*, May 19.

——. 1973. *The Fall of America*. Chicago: Muhammad's Temple of Islam No. 2.

——. 1974a. *Our Saviour Has Arrived*. Chicago: Muhammad's Temple of Islam No. 2.

——. 1974b. *The Flag of Islam*. Chicago: n.p.

——. 1992a. *The Theology of Time*. Edited by Abass Rassoull. Hampton, Va.: U.B. and U.S. Communications Systems.

——. 1992b. *The True History of Jesus as Taught by The Honorable Elijah Muhammad*. Compiled by CROE. Chicago: Coalition for the Remembrance of Elijah (CROE).

Muhammad, Herbert. 1975a. "First Official Interview with the Supreme Minister of the Nation of Islam, Wallace D. Muhammad." *Muhammad Speaks*, March 21.

——. 1975b. "On Family Relations." *Muhammad Speaks*, April 11.

Muhammad, Jabril [Cushmeer, Bernard]. 1971. *This Is the One. Messenger Elijah Muhammad. We Need Not Look for Another*. Phoenix: Truth Publishing.

——. 1984. *A Special Spokesman*. Phoenix: Phoenix and Co.

——. 1985. *Farrakhan, the Traveler*. Phoenix: Phoenix and Co.

——. 1988a. "Allah's Nature in Original Man." *Final Call*, November 4.

——. 1988b. "Path to God Revealed to Blacks." *Final Call*, October 3.

——. 1988c. "I Will Bring the Blind a Way That They Know Not." *Final Call*, June 16.

——. 1990a. "Envy." *Final Call*, January 29.

——. 1990b. "Reason Govern Way Muslim Resolve Doctrinal Differences." *Final Call*, February 5.

——. 1990c. "Farrakhan and the Judgement." *Final Call*, March 21.

——. 1991a. "Minister's Special Combination of Qualities." *Final Call*, December 2.

——. 1991b. "Minister Arose on Basis of Faith." *Final Call*, October 28.

——. 1991c. "Farrakhan's 'Great Commission.'" *Final Call*, September 9.

——. 1992. "Who Represents Christ? Minister's Message Unmasks Impostors." *Final Call*, May 4.

——. 1993a. "Clear Guidance from God's True Servant." *Final Call*, September 22.

——. 1993b. "His Own Received Him Not." *Final Call*, October 13.

——. 1993c. "The Hidden Reality of God Is Now Being Made Manifest." *Final Call*, August 11.

——. 1993d. "The Bible: A True Testament to the Divine Mission of the Honorable Elijah Muhammad." *Final Call*, July 14.

——. 1993e. "Pain and Suffering: The Ingredients in the Making of Divine Men." *Final Call*, June 30.

——. 1993f. "Is the Pope the True Representative of Jesus?" *Final Call*, September 8.

——. 1993g. "Allah's (God's) Secret Wisdom Revealed to One Chosen from among Black People." *Final Call*, July 28.

——. 1993h. "'An Act of Cowardice!' Negro Leaders Bow Down to Jewish Pressure: Ban Min. Farrakhan from March on Washington." *Final Call*, September 22.

——. 1994. "Torah Exposes Jewish Lies on Farrakhan." *Final Call*, January 25.

Muhammad, Jamillah. 1975. "Divided among Ourselves." *Muhammad Speaks*, August 1.

Muhammad, James. 1987. "Education, Islam: Source of Libya's Revolutionary Spirit." *Final Call*, June 10.

——. 1988a. "Community Welcomes Muslim 'Dope Busters.'" *Final Call*, May 27.

——. 1988b. "Brawley Family Challenges Court System." *Final Call*, June 16.

——. 1988c. "Cover-up Confirmed in Brawley Rape." *Final Call*, July 20.

——. 1988d. "Tawana Guest at Saviors' Day." *Final Call*, November 4.

——. 1991. "Rapping for Farrakhan: Prince Akeem Takes Hip-Hop to New Level." *Final Call*, June 17.

——. 1992. "World Series vs. World Serious: Farrakhan Speech Outdraws Baseball Game in Atlanta." *Final Call*, November 16.

——. 1993a. "Muslim-Christian Unity at Mosque Maryam." *Final Call*, June 30.

——. 1993b. "Farrakhan, Chavis Unite: Fulfilling a Unity Pledge, NAACP Leader Is Guest at Mosque Maryam." *Final Call*, November 10.

——. 1993c. "Ignorance, Misplaced Priorities Plague Cities, Farrakhan Warns." *Final Call*, September 22.

——. 1993d. "Our Unity Is the Key. Black Leaders Pledge to Work Together During International Telecast." *Final Call*, October 13.

——. 1994a. "Farrakhan Gives Guidance, Rebuke at Saviours' Day." *Final Call*, March 16.

——. 1994b. "Is the ADL Anti-Black?" *Final Call*, February 16.

——. 1994c. "12,000 Strong! Black Men Join Farrakhan at 'Men Only' Rally." *Final Call*, February 16.

——. 1994d. "Black Leaders Stand Together." *Final Call*, July 6.

——. 1994e. "Saviours' Day Seals Pan African Vision." *Final Call*, November 2.

Muhammad, James, and Rosalind X Moore. 1993. "Death Plot or F.B.I. Scheme? Minister Farrakhan on Skinhead 'Hit List.' " *Final Call*, August 11.

Muhammad, James, and Richard Muhammad. 1991. "Blacks Must Do for Self . . . Or Else. Min. Farrakhan Launches 3-Year Economic Savings Plan During Tribute to Muhammad." *Final Call*, October 28.

——. 1992. "FBI Target: Crime or Black Youth?" *Final Call*, February 10.

Muhammad, Lawrence. 1977. "New Farrakhan Thrust. Opposes Muslim Ideology, Still in Skin Game." *Chicago Defender*, December 3, weekend edition.

Muhammad, Master Farad. n.d. Lesson #1.

Muhammad, Master Farad. n.d. Lost Found Lesson #2.

Muhammad, Master Farad. n.d. *The NOI Student Enrollment Lesson.*

The Muhammad Mosque Provisional Constitution. Ratified 1986.

Muhammad, Richard. 1989a. "Public Enemy, Big Daddy Kane Highlight Anti-Drug Concert in D.C." *Final Call*, July 31.

——. 1989b. "Police Arrest 3 Dopebusters at Urging of Drug Dealers; Harassment Suspected." *Final Call*, July 31.

——. 1990a. "Drug-Free Community Celebrates Arrival of Muslims." *Final Call*, May 31.

——. 1990b. "Dopebusters Enter Political Arena." *Final Call*, May 31.

——. 1992a. "Nation Pays Tribute to *Final Call* editor Abdul Wali Muhammad." *Final Call*, January 27.

——. 1992b. "Mayoral Welcome Stirs Controversy in Atlanta." *Final Call*, November 16.

——. 1992c. "Muslim Doctor: African AIDS Drug Effective, Needs FDA Approval." *Final Call*, February 10.

——. 1993a. "Peace in the 'Hood.' " *Final Call*, June 30.

——. 1993b. "Peace . . . There It Is." *Final Call*, October 11.

——. 1993c. "Stand with Gang Truce Movement. Chicago Peace Summit Brings Peace Movement to World's Attention." *Final Call*, November 10.

——. 1993d. "Killer or Peacemaker? Black Community Debates Parole for Legendary 'Gang' Leader." *Final Call*, August 25.

——. 1994. "Farrakhan Home! 10,000 Black Men Stand with Farrakhan." *Final Call*, January 5.

Muhammad, Richard, and Rosalind X Moore. 1993. "Efforts to Undermine N.O.I. Security Continue." *Final Call*, October 13.

——. Muhammad, Richard, and Tyrone 2X McKeiver. 1994. "The True Face of AIDS." *Final Call*, August 3.

Muhammad, Rosalind. 1993a. "Skinhead Pleads Guilty to Plotting a Race War." *Final Call*, November 10.

——. 1993b. "L.A.-4 Defendant Remains Jailed; Mom Warns Cops of Death Threats." *Final Call*, November 24.

——. 1993c. "Damian Williams Sentenced 10 Years." *Final Call*, December 22.

——. 1994. "Residents Cry Out for Return of N.O.I. Security." *Final Call*, March 16.

Muhammad, Silis. 1989. "Moses Raises the Serpent." Speech delivered on October 7.

——. 1990b [1977]. "Letter Delivered to Imam Wallace D. Muhammad." In *Letter and Articles Package of Correspondence Between Minister Louis Farrakhan, Four of His Officers and I, Silis Muhammad.* Chicago: Shabazz Publication.

——. 1990c [1989]. "Letter to Minister Abdul Muhammad." In *Letter and Articles Pack-*

age of Correspondence Between Minister Louis Farrakhan, Four of His Officers and I, Silis Muhammad. Chicago: Shabazz Publication.

——. 1990a. "Farrakhan Fulfills Prophecies. In Sheep's Clothing—Beast II." *Muhammad Speaks* 6, no. 3.

——. 1991a. "A World Saviour Is Born." *Muhammad Speaks* 7, no. 2.

——. 1991b. "You Are the Uncle and He Is the Nephew." *Muhammad Speaks* 7, no. 5.

——. 1991c. "Should Blacks Be Required to Pay Taxes?" *Muhammad Speaks* 7, no. 3.

——. 1991d. "The Symbolic Beast, 'Mopping Up.'" *Muhammad Speaks* 7, no. 2.

——. 1992. "Nation of Islam Joined in Its Defense Against Atlanta *Journal-Constitution.*" *Muhammad Speaks* 8, no. 5.

Muhammad, Tynetta. 1995. *Million Man March.* Chicago: FCN Publishing and The Honorable Elijah Muhammad Educational Foundation.

——. 1994 [1982]. *The Woman in Islam Educational Series.* Part One. Chicago: The Final Call Inc.

——. 1994 [1981]. *The Woman in Islam Educational Series.* Part Two. Chicago: The Final Call Inc.

——. 1994 [1982b]. *The Woman in Islam Educational Series.* Part Three: *The Divine Light.* Chicago: The Final Call Inc.

——. 1986. *The Comer by Night.* Chicago: Honorable Elijah Muhammad Educational Foundation.

——. 1988. "Oneness of God and Man." *Final Call,* May 9.

——. 1990a. "Unveiling the Number 19, 1990: The Final Decade." *Final Call,* March 21.

——. 1990b. "Parable of 19: Satan's Time Is Up!" *Final Call,* May 31.

——. 1991a. "Minister's Vision like Revelator's." *Final Call,* May 6.

——. 1991b. "Physical Signs of Armageddon." *Final Call,* May 29.

——. 1992. "Islam Is Mathematics." *Final Call,* November 16.

——. 1993a. "Minister Farrakhan Establishes Friendships in All Walks of Life." *Final Call,* June 30.

——. 1993b. "The Great Separation." *Final Call,* September 8.

Muhammad University of Islam. 1973. *"History," Year Book No. 2.*

Muhammad, Wali. 1988. "Minister Farrakhan Welcomes over 12,000 to National Convention: Crescent and Star Rises over Saviors' Day '88." *Final Call,* November 4.

——. 1990. "Slained Muslim Honored by 17,000 in Los Angeles." *Final Call,* February 12.

Muhammad, Wallace D. 1975a. "The Second Resurrection, Part 1, The Light behind the Veil." *Muhammad Speaks,* April 11.

——. 1975b. "The Plane of the Prophets." *Muhammad Speaks,* August 15.

——. 1975c. "Remake the World, Part 1." *Muhammad Speaks,* May 16.

——. 1975d. "Jesus: A Sign." *Muhammad Speaks,* August 8.

——. 1975e. "All Eyes Shall See Him." *Muhammad Speaks,* May 9.

——. 1975f. "Who Is the Original Man?" *Muhammad Speaks,* August 22.

——. 1975g. "The Destruction of the Devil." *Muhammad Speaks,* July 11.

——. 1975h. "Justice Is Come: The Death of White Supremacy." *Muhammad Speaks,* July 18.

——. 1975i. "Remake the World, Part 2." *Muhammad Speaks,* May 23.

——. 1975j. "Invisible White Divinity by Visible Whitened God." *Muhammad Speaks,* April 4.

——. 1975k. "Crown of Creation." *Muhammad Speaks,* June 20.

——. 1975l. "Artificial Humanism." *Muhammad Speaks*, August 1.

——. 1975m. "Ramadan." *Muhammad Speaks*, August 29.

——. 1975n. "Nation of Islam: The Alternative Cure for America." Interview with W.D. Muhammad for CBS-TV by Randy Daniels. Excerpt printed in *Muhammad Speaks*, July 25.

——. 1975o. "World Saviour." *Muhammad Speaks*, May 2.

——. 1976a. "Self-Redemption." *Bilalian News*, February 6.

——. 1976b. "Self-Government in the New World." *Bilalian News*, March 19.

——. 1976c. "State of the Nation Report." *Bilalian News*, March 19.

——. 1976d. "New Names for Bilalians." *Bilalian News*, February 13.

——. 1976e. "New Flag for the Nation of Islam." *Bilalian News*, March 12.

——. 1977. "World Community of Islam in the West: Purpose, Aim and Goal." *Bilalian News*, April 3.

——. 1977b. "New World Patriotism Day." *Bilalian News*, June 24.

——. 1977c. "New World Patriotism Day Address." *Bilalian News*, July 22.

——. 1985. *Challenges That Face Man Today.* Chicago: W. D. Muhammad Publications.

——. 1986. *An African American Genesis.* Chicago: Progressions Publishing Company.

"Muhammad at White House Set." 1977. *Chicago Defender*, December 21.

Mukkaram, Ajani K. 1991. "Lest We Forget." *Muhammad Speaks* 7, no. 8.

Mullen, Robert W. 1973. *Blacks in America's Wars.* New York: Pathfinder.

"Multi-Racists on the Run." *National Front News*, no. 109.

Muraskin, William Alan. 1975. *Middle Class Blacks in a White Society: Prince Hall Freemasonry in America.* Berkeley: University of California Press.

Murr, Andrew, Jeanne Gordon, Vern E. Smith, and John McCormick. 1994. "A Shooting Stirs Tension in the Nation." *Newsweek*, June 13.

"Muslim Minister/Physician Speaks to Black Students about Peril of AIDS. Mosque No. 4 Minister's Visit Stirs U. of Md. Campus." 1988. *Final Call*, May 9.

"Muslim Shooting Suspect Killed His Brother in 1970's, Reports Say." 1994. *New York Times*, June 1.

"Muslims Dedicate Mosque to 'Wisdom of Allah.'" *Final Call*, April 6.

"Muslims in America." 1993. *CQ Researcher*, April 30.

"Muslim's Riot. Cultist Killed; Policeman Shot." 1962. *Los Angeles Times*, April 28.

Mustafa, Ayesha K., ed. 1988. *Focus of Al-Islam: A Series of Interviews with Imam W. Deen Mohammed.* Chicago: Zakat Publications.

Muwakkil, Salim. 1975. "Uganda Muslim Leader Applauds Nation of Islam as 'True Muslim.'" *Muhammad Speaks*, September 12.

——. 1977. "Emam Muhammad. We've Forgotten What's Important." *Bilalian News*, August 5.

——. 1989a. "NIA: Bringing the Believers Together." *In These Times*, April 5–11.

——. 1989b. "For More Blacks, Islam Is the Old-Time Religion." *In These Times*, April 5–11.

——. 1989c. "The Black Summit Tackles Some of the Big Uneasies." *In These Times*, May 3–9.

——. 1991. "Peaceful Desires Unite Religious Blacks." *In These Times*, February 6–12.

——. 1993a. "Disharmony. While Farrakhan Fiddles, Black-Jewish Relations Burn." *In These Times*, June 14.

——. 1993b. "Ganging Together." *In These Times*, April 5.

Mydans, Seth. 1994. "Suspect Linked to Muslim Fringe Group." *New York Times,* May 31.

Nathaniel, Brother. 1972. "Muhammad Clarifies Truth! Condemn Liars." *Muhammad Speaks,* October 27.

"Nation of Islam's Leader Threatens Post Reporter." 1984. *Washington Post,* April 3.

"Nation's Ghana Mission in Action." 1992. *Final Call,* February 10.

"National Center Renovation: Flurry of Activity." 1988. *Final Call,* September 9.

"Negro Leaders Blast Cassius for 'Naivete.'" 1964. *Miami Herald,* February 29.

"The New Alliance." 1988. *National Front News,* no. 103 (March).

"The New Axis." 1987. *Searchlight,* September.

"The New Politics of Race." 1992. *Newsweek,* May 6.

New World Movement. 1987. Tripoli: n.p.

Newman, Maria. 1994. "N.A.A.C.P. Will Remain Strong, Supporters Say." *New York Times,* August 22.

"NF Chiefs Visit Libya." 1988. *National Front News,* no. 111.

"NF Send Vauxhall Voters the Message. Black Separatists Back Front Candidate." *National Front News,* no. 120.

"NH Tries to Kill Kemron Trials." 1994. *Final Call,* March 16.

"NOI Gets Exclusive Rights to Immunex." 1992. *Final Call,* March 23.

"N.O.I. 'going home.'" 1988. *Final Call,* July 20.

"N.O.I. Official Harassed in New Zealand." 1988. *Final Call,* October 3.

NOI POWER Proclamation. 1985. n.p.

Norris, Michele L. 1990a. "Blacks Flex Political Muscle in Pr. George's." *Washington Post,* September 10.

———. 1990b. "Glending, Hoyer Sail to Victory." *Washington Post,* September 12.

"Notice to Muslims." 1975. *Muhammad Speaks,* October 3.

Nuruddin, Yusuf. 1994. "The Five Percenters: A Teenage Nation of Gods and Earths." In *Muslim Communities in North America,* edited by Y. Y. Haddad and J. Smith. New York: State University of New York.

O'Connor, Matt. 1991. "Rukn Chieftain Says He Gave Cocaine to Aides of Farrakhan." *Chicago Tribune,* June 7.

———. 1993. "Ruling Threatens Rukn Convictions." *Chicago Tribune,* June 5.

O'Reilly, Kenneth. 1989. *"Racial Matters": The FBI's Secret File on Black America, 1960–1972.* New York: Free Press.

"Official Chastised for Farrakhan Statement." 1990. *Final Call,* April 12.

Oliver, Melvin L., James H. Johnson Jr., and Walter C. Farrell Jr. 1993. "Anatomy of a Rebellion: A Political-Economic Analysis." In *Reading Rodney King/Reading Urban Uprising,* edited by Robert Gooding-Williams. New York and London: Routledge.

Orro, David H. 1942. "Sedition: Race Hate Used by Tokio to Lure 85 Nabbed by FBI." *Chicago Defender,* September 26.

Ortner, Sherry B. 1979. "On Key Symbols." In *Reader in Comparative Religion,* edited by William A. Lessa and Evon Z. Vogt. New York: Harper and Row.

"'Overwhelming Event' Approaches." 1988. *Final Call,* October 3.

Pace, Eric. 1972. "5 Policemen Hurt in Harlem Melee." *New York Times,* April 15.

Page, Clarence. 1993. "Bringing Farrakhan into the Fold." *Chicago Tribune,* September 19.

Patterson, Tiffany. 1993. "Postscript to the Los Angeles Riot: Atlanta and the Crisis of

Black Leadership." In *Why L.A. Happened*, edited by Haki R. Madhubuti. Chicago: Third World Press.

Payne, Ethel L. 1986. "Fight for Rights." *Final Call*, undated special edition.

Perkins, Useni Eugene. 1987. *Explosion of Chicago's Black Street Gangs, 1900 to Present*. Chicago: Third World Press.

Pianin, Eric. 1984. "Media Trying to Discredit Jackson's Campaign, Farrakhan Says." *Washington Post*, April 20.

Pistol, Pete. 1992. "Souljah Bares All." *The Source*, no. 39.

"Playing with Fire." 1987. *Searchlight*, September.

Pleasant, William. 1990. "Introduction." In *Independent Black Leadership in America*. New York: Castillo International Publications.

"Police Arrest 3 Men in Televised Beating." 1992. *Chicago Defender*, May 13.

"The Political Soldiers." 1988. *Searchlight*, January.

"Political Soldiers Ride Out." 1988. *Searchlight*, July.

Powers, Richard Gid. 1987. *Secrecy and Power: The Life of J. Edgar Hoover*. New York: Free Press.

"The Price of Injustice." 1992. *Chicago Defender*, May 4.

Pulley, Brett. 1995. "Thousands in New York Prepare for Black Men's March." *New York Times*, October 13.

Putnam, Pat. 1964. "Muslim Claims Cassius; Champ Angry, Silent." *Miami Herald*, February 27.

Qathafi [Qadhdhafi], Muammar Al. 1980. *The Green Book*. 10th ed. Benghazi: World Center for Studies and Research of the Green Book.

——. 1982a. *The Green Book*. New ed. Tripoli: Public Establishment for Publishing, Advertising, and Distribution.

——. 1982b. "Speech at the Second Conference of the Islamic Call." *The World Islamic Call Society*. From the Second to the Third Conference. Report on Activities and Programs between 1/9/1982–1/9/1986.

——. 1982c. Speech at the Second Conference of the Islamic Call, August 18, partly reprinted in *The World Islamic Call Council: From a Thought to Reality*. Tripoli: 1395 D.P. (Death of Prophet).

——. 1983. "Resuming the Jihad Role of Islam." *Activities of the Association of the Islamic Convocation*. Tripoli.

——. "The Contribution of Leader Moammar El Qathafi." The World Center: The Contribution of leader Moammar El Qathafi to U.S. Blacks Conference.

——. 1986a. *Islamic World Exposed to a New Invasion*. The Islamic Call World Society.

——. "Inaugural Address by the Leader of the Revolution." *The World Mathaba* for Resistance against Imperialism, Zionism, Racism, Reaction and Fascism. Second Mondial Congress, Tripoli.

——. 1986c. "To the African Progressive Forces." Speech delivered at Syrte, Tripoli: World Mathaba.

Raboteau, Albert J. 1978. *Slave Religion*. New York: Oxford University Press.

"Race: The New Reality." *National Front News*, no. 84.

"Ramadan in December: Why and How." 1991. *Muhammad Speaks* 7, no. 6.

Randolph, Eleanor. 1984. "Meeting Urged with Reporter. Jackson Calls Farrakhan Threat 'Wrong.' " *Washington Post*, April 4.

Randolph, Eleanor, and Rick Atkinson. 1984. "Second Farrakhan Controversy Caused by Calling Hitler 'Great.' " *Washington Post*, April 12.

"Rantings from the Bunker." *Nationalism Today*, no. 39.

"Rappin' in the Hood." 1991. *Final Call*, August 19.

Rashadeen, Maleek. 1984. "The Blacks Will Prevail in the World." *Social Issues*. Tripoli: World Center for Researches and Studies in the Green Book.

Rassoul, Abass. 1974. "National Secretary Catalogues Accomplishments." *Muhammad Speaks*, August 23.

——. 1992. "Introduction." In *Muhammad, Elijah, The Theology of Time*, edited by A. Rassoull. Hampton, Va.: U.B. and U.S. Communications Systems.

"Reagan Aides Silent about Klan Backing." 1984. *Washington Post*, April 17.

"Reagan Spurs Klan Support." 1984. *New York Times*, May 2.

" 'Rebuild LA' Underway." 1992. *Chicago Defender*, May 7.

Redkey, Edwin S. 1969. *Black Exodus, Black Nationalist and Back-to-Africa Movements, 1890–1910*. New Haven and London: Yale University Press.

Reed, Adolph, Jr. 1991. "False Prophet I—The Rise of Louis Farrakhan." *Nation*, January 21.

Ridgeway, James. 1990. *Blood in the Face: The Ku Klux Klan, Aryan Nations, Nazi Skinheads, and the Rise of a New White Culture*. New York: Mouth Press.

Robinson, Cedrick J. 1993. "Race, Capitalism and the Antidemocracy." In *Reading Rodney King/Reading Urban Uprising*, edited by Robert Gooding-Williams. New York and London: Routledge.

Robinson, John J. 1989. *Born in Blood: The Lost Secrets of Freemasonry*. New York: M. Evans and Company.

Rodinson, Maxime. 1981. *Muhammad*. Stockholm: Gidlunds.

Rose, Tricia. 1994. *Black Noise: Rap Music and Black Culture in Contemporary America*. Hanover and London: Weslyan University Press.

Rosenblatt, Roger. 1985. "The Demagogue in the Crowd." *Time*, October 21.

Rosenthal, A.M. 1994. "On My Mind; Supping with the Bigott." *New York Times*, June 14.

Rouner, Leroy S. 1986. "To Be at Home: Civil Religion as Common Bond." In *Civil Religion and Political Theology*, edited by L. S. Rouner. Notre Dame, Ind.: University of Notre Dame Press.

Russell, Carlos. 1978. "An Interview with Abdul Farrakhan." *Chicago Defender*, February 11, weekend edition.

as-Sadr, Muhammad Baqir. 1980. *An Inquiry Concerning al-Mahdi*. Teheran: World Organization for Islamic Services.

Salaam, Yusuf. 1994. "Lesson #1: Muslims Do Not Play. Protecting Their Mosque, Muslims Injure Four Cops." *Amsterdam News* (New York), January 15.

Saleem, Mustafa Nasir. 1991. "Our Saviour Has Arrived." *Muhammad Speaks* 7, no. 5.

——. 1991b. "Support the War Chest." *Muhammad Speaks* 7, no. 5.

Samad, Abdullah. 1992. "JDL and ADL: The 'Hate Groups' of Black Housing." *Final Call*, January 27.

"Saviours' Day: A Fitting Tribute." 1991. *Final Call*, October 28.

Schmidt, Alvin J. 1980. *Fraternal Organizations*. Westport and London: Greenwood Press.

Scholem, Gershom. 1973. *Sabbatai Sevi: The Mystical Messiah*. Princeton: Princeton University Press.

——. 1974. *Kabbalah*. Jerusalem: Keter Publishing House.

Schoun, Frithjof. 1976. *Understanding Islam*. London: Unwin.

Scott, Peter Dale, and Jonathan Marshall. 1991. *Cocaine Politics: Drugs, Armies and the CIA in Central America.* Berkeley and Los Angeles: University of California Press.

The Secret Relationship between Blacks and Jews. 1991. Chicago: NOI Research Department.

"See and Hear Minister Louis Farrakhan." 1994. *Final Call*, August 17.

"See and Hear Minister Louis Farrakhan." 1995. *Final Call*, September 27.

Seifullah, Abdul. 1977. "Islamic Leaders, Ambassador Laud Emam's Work." *Bilalian News*, May 20.

Shah, Yusuf. 1973a. "Messenger Muhammad's Health." *Muhammad Speaks*, December 28.

——. 1973b. "Haters of Muhammad." *Muhammad Speaks*, February 2.

——. 1974. "Messenger Muhammad's Health. Part II." *Muhammad Speaks*, January 4.

Shapiro, Margaret. 1984. "Jackson Again on Defensive over Farrakhan." *Washington Post*, April 13.

Shapiro, Margaret, and David S. Broder. 1984. "Jackson Disavows Statement but Candidate Refuses to Repudiate Farrakhan." *Washington Post*, April 9.

Sharieff, Raymond. 1971. "The Devil Uses Malcolm." *Muhammad Speaks*, June 4.

——. 1975. "Supreme Minister to Update Lessons." *Muhammad Speaks*, July 11.

Sharif, Sidney R. 1985. *The African-American (Bilalian) Image in Crisis.* Jersey City, N.J.: New Mind Productions.

Simmons, Charles E. 1993. "The Los Angeles Rebellion: Class, Race and Misinformation." In *Why L.A. Happened*, edited by Haki R. Madhubuti. Chicago: Third World Press.

SIPRI [Stockholm International Peace Research Institute]. 1973. *The Problem of Chemical and Biological Warfare.* Vol. 2, *CB Weapons Today.* Stockholm: Almqvist and Wiksell.

Skelton, George. 1984. "Jackson Delegates Favor Farrakhan, Survey Finds." *Los Angeles Times*, July 16.

Sklar, Richard L. 1989. "Africa and the Middle East: What Blacks and Jews Owe to Each Other." In *Jews in Black Perspective*, edited by J. R. Washington. Lanham: University Press of America.

Smothers, David. 1977. "Changes Reflect Real [unreadable] of Nation of Islam Founder." *Bilalian News*, May 27.

"So, You Think the War Is Over?" 1991. *Final Call*, March 11, editorial.

Spady, James G., and Joseph D. Eure. 1991. *The Hip Hop Vision.* New York: PC International Press.

"Speakes Lauds Bush's Remark to Jews." 1984. *Washington Post*, April 11.

Special Report. Louis Farrakhan: In His Own Words—1993. 1993. New York: Anti-Defamation League.

Stanton, William. 1982 [1960]. *The Leopard's Spots: Scientific Attitudes toward Race in America 1815–59.* Chicago: University of Chicago Press.

"State Denies Parole to 'Reformed' Gang Leader." 1993. *Final Call*, September 8.

"The State of Britain's Right. 12 January 1988." *Searchlight*, January 1988.

"State of Emergency: Bush." 1991. *Final Call*, December 2, editorial.

State of Illinois Medical Certificate of Death #605408, February 25, 1975.

Steinmetz, George H. 1953. *The Lost Word and Its Hidden Meaning.* New York: Macoy Publishing and Masonic Supply Company.

Still Black, Still Strong. Survivors of the U.S. War against Black Revolutionaries. 1993.

Edited by Jim Fletcher, Tanquil Jones, and Sylvère Lotringer. New York: Semio-text(e).

Stolberg, Cheryl. 1992. "150,000 Are in Gangs, Report by D.A. Claims." *Los Angeles Times,* May 22.

Stone, Carol L. 1991. "Estimate of Muslims Living in America." In *The Muslims of America,* edited by Y. Y. Haddad. New York: Oxford University Press.

Strasser, Steven, Sylvester Monroe, Nancy Cooper, and Patricia King. 1984. "Jesse Jackson and the Jews." *Newsweek,* March 5.

Strausberg, Chinta. 1984a. " 'All the Signs are Hopeful': Exclusive Comments from Jesse Jackson in Syria." *Chicago Defender,* January 3.

———. 1984b. " 'Don't Lock Blacks Out': Min. Farrakhan Stresses Political Trust." *Chicago Defender,* April 23.

———. 1984c. "Jesse Rebukes Min. Farrakhan." *Chicago Defender,* June 30.

———. 1984d. "Muslims Get into Politics; Hundreds Register to Vote." *Chicago Defender,* February 11.

———. 1992. "Bush, Jesse, Seek End to Violence." *Chicago Defender,* May 2.

———. 1993. "Farrakhan Banned from March." *Chicago Defender,* August 30.

Strausberg, Chinta, and Henry Locke. 1984. "Muslim Faithful Honor Jackson." *Chicago Defender,* February 27.

"Suspect Is Arraigned in Shooting of Speaker from Nation of Islam." 1994. *New York Times,* June 2.

Tabor, Mary W. 1992. "Muslim Guards: Security Unit Maintaining Pride." *New York Times,* January 6.

Taibbi, Mike, and Anna Sims-Phillips. 1989. *Unholy Alliances: Working the Tawana Brawley Story.* San Diego: Harcourt Brace Jovanovich.

Talbott, Basil. 1994. "Aide Praised as a 'Warrior.' " *Chicago Sun-Times,* February 4.

Tariq, Khadira A. 1992. "Project Exodus Manifested." *Muhammad Speaks* 8, no. 1.

Tatum, Wilbert A. 1994. "Farrakhan: An Exclusive Interview. An Invitation to the Jews; an Appeal to Us All to Stop the Killing." *Amsterdam News* (New York), January 8.

Terry, Don. 1993. "Black Muslims Enter Islamic Mainstream." *New York Times,* May 3.

———. 1994a. "U.S. Blacks Gathered to Chart a Path." *New York Times,* June 11.

———. 1994b. "N.A.A.C.P. Shows Split as Leaders Hold Meeting." *New York Times,* June 13.

———. 1994c. "Blacks Say Unity Seems a Bit Closer." *New York Times,* June 15.

———. 1994d. "Director of N.A.A.C.P. is Fighting for Survival." *New York Times,* August 17.

"Thomas Sankara. In Memoriam." n.d. *Nationalism Today,* no. 42.

"Three Year Economic Program: Progress Report." 1994. *Final Call,* March 30.

Toop, David. 1984. *The Rap Attack: African Jive to New York Hip Hop.* Boston: South End Press.

———. 1991. "Louis Farrakhan and Muslim Rap." *The Face,* October.

TT-AFP. 1992. "Världen enligt Khaddafi." *Dagens Nyheter,* November 20.

Tucker, William. 1964. " 'X' Marks the Champ." *Miami News,* February 19.

"25 Found Guilty of Draft Law Evasion." 1942. *Chicago Defender,* October 24.

Um'rani, Munir, and Aquil Nurrudin. 1977. "Destroy All Racial Images of God." *Bilalian News,* June 7.

"U.S. Blast Khadafy's Cry for Black Revolt." 1985. *Washington Post,* February 26.

Van Sertima, Ivan. 1995a [1992]. "Address to the Smithsonian." In *African Presence in*

Early America, edited by Ivan Van Sertima. New Brunswick and London: Transaction Publishers.

Van Sertima, Ivan. 1995b [1992]. "Egypto-Nubian Presences in Ancient Mexico." In *African Presence in Early America,* edited by Ivan Van Sertima. New Brunswick and London: Transaction Publishers.

Vontress, Clemmont E. 1965. "The Black Muslim Schools." *Phi Delta Kappan* 47, no. 2 (October).

"Voodoo Cult Killer is Declared to Be Insane." 1932. *Chicago Defender,* December 17.

Wade, Greg. 1994. "Muslim Unity Belies Media Schism Claims." *Final Call,* October 17.

Walker, Jesse H. 1988. "Farrakhan Denies Anti-Semitic Charges." *Amsterdam News* (New York), September 24.

Walker, Joe. 1972. "Police, City Maintain Unjust Charges against Temple No. 7 Muslims." *Muhammad Speaks,* May 5.

———. 1974. "Massive N.Y. Muslim Rally: 70,000 Attend!" *Muhammad Speaks,* June 14.

Walker, Maxine. 1989. "A Voice Crying in the Wilderness: 'Let My People Go.' " *The Platform Magazine,* May/June.

Wangara, Kofi. 1995 [1992]. "Mandinga Voyages across the Atlantic." In *African Presence in Early America,* edited by Ivan Van Sertima. New Brunswick and London: Transaction Publishers.

Washington, Booker T. [1900] 1956. *Up from Slavery.* New York: Bantam Books.

Washington, Booker T. [1895] 1968. "The Atlanta Exposition Address." In *Black Protest: History, Documents and Analyses, 1916 to the Present,* edited by Joanne Grant. New York: Fawcett Premier.

Washington, Joseph R. 1984. *Anti-Blackness in English Religion 1500–1800.* New York and Toronto: Edwin Mellen Press.

Waugh, Earle H., Baha Abu-Laban, and Regula B. Quereshi, eds. 1993. *The Muslim Community in North America.* Edmonton: University of Alberta Press.

Weber, Max. 1976. *The Protestant Ethic and the Spirit of Capitalism.* 2d ed. London: Allen and Unwin.

Wedad, Dorothy. 1973. "Opposers of Muhammad." *Muhammad Speaks,* February 2.

"Wedding Bells Ring for Farrakhan, Muhammad." 1990. *Final Call,* February 12.

Wesley, Carlos. 1990. "Holocaust Still Active in the U.S." *Final Call,* May 31.

West, Stan. 1993. "How the L.A. Uprising Will Affect the '92 Election." In *Why L.A. Happened,* edited by Haki R. Madhubuti. Chicago: Third World Press.

"What Is Islam?" 1967. *Muhammad Speaks,* February 3.

Wheeler, Constantine. 1972. "A Rebuttal to Charges by So-Called Muslims." *Muhammad Speaks,* December 12.

"Where Ya At?" 1995. *Final Call,* October 20.

Whitehurst, James Emerson. 1980. "The Mainstreaming of the Black Muslims: Healing the Hate." *The Christian Century,* February.

Why We Support Liberation Movements. 1987. Tripoli: n.p.

Whyte, Abbie. 1964. "Christian Elements in Negro American Muslim Religious Beliefs." *Phylon: The Atlanta University Review of Race and Culture* 25, no. 4 (winter).

Wilcox, Preston. 1990. "Reparations, Not a Hand-Out." *Final Call,* February 12.

Wiley, Ralph. 1992. "Great 'X'pectations." *Premiere* 6, no. 3 (November).

Williams, Juan. 1985. "Desert Military, Blacks Urged. Qaddafi Speaks to Meeting of Muslims in Chicago." *Washington Post,* February 25.

Williams, Rhonda. 1993. "Accumulation as Evisceration: Urban Rebellion and the New Growth Dynamics." In *Reading Rodney King/Reading Urban Uprising,* edited by Robert Gooding-Williams. New York and London: Routledge.

Willoughby, William F. 1976. "Islamic Scholar Urges Muslims to Accept Each Other." *Bilalian News,* February 11.

Wilmore, Gayraud S. 1979. "Introduction to 'The Attack on White Religion.'" In *Black Theology: A Documentary History, 1966–1979,* edited by Gayraud S. Wilmore and James H. Cone. Maryknoll, N.Y.: Orbis Books.

——. 1986. *Black Religion and Black Radicalism: An Interpretation of the Religious History of Afro-American People.* 2d ed. Maryknoll, N.Y.: Orbis Books.

Wilson, Bryan, 1970. *Religiösa sekter.* Aldusuniversitetet.

Wilson, John F. 1986. "Common Religion in American Society." In *Civil Religion and Political Theology,* edited by L. S. Rouner. Notre Dame, Ind.: University of Notre Dame Press.

Winters, Clyde. 1975. "A Survey of Islam and the African Diaspora." *Pan-African Journal* 13, no. 4.

Wistrich, Robert S. 1994. *Antisemitism: The Longest Hatred.* New York: Schocken Books.

Woodford, John. 1990. "Messaging the Blackman." *Voices From the Underground.*

Worill, Conrad. 1994. "Attacks on the Great Summit." *Final Call,* July 20.

The World Islamic Call Council: From a Thought to Reality. 1395 D.P. (Death of Prophet). Tripoli: n.p.

The World Islamic Call Society. 1986. From the Second to the Third Conference. Report on Activities and Programs between 1/9/1982–1/9/1986.

The World Mathaba, 1988. First Year, Zero Issue, June.

The World Mathaba for Resistance against Imperialism, Zionism, Racism, Reaction and Fascism. 1986. Tripoli: Second Mondial Congress.

X, April. 1990. "Min. Ava Muhammad, Featured Speaker at Women's Conference." *Final Call,* June 22.

X Booker, Simon III. 1993. "Attempts to Stop AIDS Treatment." *Final Call,* July 14.

X, Charles D. 1974. "Witnesses." *Mr. Muhammad Speaks,* June 28.

X Curry, Lamont. 1992a. "N.O.I.'s Ghana Mission a Continual Success," *Final Call,* November 16.

——. 1992b. "NOI Security Inc.: Making a Difference in the Community. Muslims Aid Elderly." *Final Call,* April 20.

——. 1992c. "Muslims Aid Elderly." *Final Call,* April 20.

——. 1993a. "N.Y. Preacher Protest Lyrics in Rap Music." *Final Call,* July 14.

——. 1993b. "Muslims Bring Peace to Another Housing Project." *Final Call,* August 25.

——. 1994a. "Cops Storm New York Mosque." *Final Call,* February 2.

——. 1994b. "Rappers welcome Farrakhan to New York," *Final Call,* January 5.

X Curry, Lamont, and James Muhammad. 1994. "21,000 Welcome Farrakhan Home." *Final Call,* January 5.

X, Eddie. 1990. "Letter to Silis Muhammad." In *Letters and Articles Package of Correspondence between Minister Louis Farrakhan, Four of His Officers and I, Silis Muhammad.* Chicago: Shabazz Publications.

X, George. 1974. "Reveal FBI Plan to Prevent Black 'Messiah.'" *Muhammad Speaks,* April 19.

X Grandison, Lyle. 1994a. "Mayor Lauds N.O.I. Security Success in Baltimore." *Final Call*, March 2.

——. 1994b. "Over 1,000 Commemorate Black Summit." *Final Call*, July 6.

X, Malcolm. [1965] 1973. *The Autobiography of Malcolm X, As Told to Alex Haley.* New York: Ballantine Books.

——. 1970. *By Any Means Necessary.* Edited by George Breitman. New York: Pathfinder.

——. 1971. "God's Judgement of White America." In *The End of White World Supremacy*, edited by Benjamin Karim. New York: Seaver Books.

——. 1989a. "Question from the Press." In *Malcolm X: The Last Speeches*, edited by Bruce Perry. New York: Pathfinder.

——. 1989b. "There Is a World Wide Revolution Going On." In *Malcolm X: The Last Speeches*, edited by Bruce Perry. New York: Pathfinder.

X, Mary Eloise. 1975. "Two Great Families Unite." *Muhammad Speaks*, February 14.

X Massop, Marceeah. 1993. "Blacks in United Kingdom Join Forces against Racist Attacks." *Final Call*, November 24.

X Moore, Gregory. 1994. "Self-Improvement Program Penetrates Prison Walls." *Final Call*, March 30.

X Moore, Rosalind. 1991a. "Jewish Group Boycotts Rap Album." *Final Call*, December 2.

——. 1991b. "Preserve Family, 7,000 Told in San Francisco." *Final Call*, July 22.

——. 1992a. "Truce Called by L.A. Gangs." *Final Call*, June 5.

——. 1992b. "HUD Puts Muslims on Hold." *Final Call*, April 20.

——. 1993a. "Frustration Clouds L.A. 4 Trial." *Final Call*, August 25.

——. 1993b. "L.A.'s Scapegoats or Killers? L.A. 4 Trial Opens with Contrasting Picture of Defendants." *Final Call*, September 8.

X Robinson, Latonja. 1991. "Dallas Mosque Awards Graduates." *Final Call*, August 5.

X, Sharolyn. 1974. "Who Are the Civilized?" *Muhammad Speaks*, June 21.

X Walker, Vernon. 1993. "Interview with Brand Nubian." *Final Call*, August 25.

2X, Denise. 1970. "Truth of Muhammad's Teachings Gives Dignity to Muslim Woman." *Muhammad Speaks*, September 25.

2X McKeiver, Tyrone. 1993a. "N.O.I. Security Official Demands City Probe Police 'Attack' on Anti-Crime Patrol." *Final Call*, November 10.

——. 1993b. "M.U.I. Opens in Washington. Discipline Is Hallmark of Muslim School." *Final Call*, July 14.

——. 1993c. "Blacks, Latinos Unite Against AIDS." *Final Call*, September 22.

2X Williams, Brian. 1994. "Nation of Islam and Ghana Unite." *Final Call*, January 19.

3X Bryant, Richard. 1988. " 'Dopebusters.' Muslim Anti-Drug Patrols Bring Calm in D.C." *Final Call*, June 16.

——. 1989. "U. of Islam Dedicated; Opens in April." *Final Call*, April 6.

4X, Alonzo. 1975a. "Muslims Get State Welcome." *Muhammad Speaks*, August 29.

——. 1975b. "Muslims from U.S. Headline Uganda T.V. Special." *Muhammad Speaks*, August 29.

4X, George. 1974. "Muslims Trade with Peru." *Muhammad Speaks*, March 15.

5X, Larry. 1974. "8-Hour Siege of Unarmed Muslim Temple: 5 Arrested." *Muhammad Speaks*, May 10.

10X, Nathaniel. 1972a. "Muslim Nation of Abu Dabhi Unites to Help Nation of Islam." *Muhammad Speaks*, October 20.

——. 1972b. "Loan to Nation of Islam Reduced by Libyan Brother." *Muhammad Speaks,* October 20.

67X, Charles. 1974. "On Messenger Muhammad's Health." *Muhammad Speaks,* September 27, editorial.

——. 1975. "Two Great Families." *Muhammad Speaks,* February 14.

Younger, Lucille W. 1993. " 'We're Building a Black Army.' Summit Draws Hundreds." *Chicago Defender,* October 23.

Zenner, Walter P. 1991. *Minorities in the Middle.* Albany: State University of New York Press.

Zipperer, John. 1993. "The Elusive Quest for Religious Harmony." *Christianity Today,* October 4.

Index

Mattias Gardell is Professor of Theology at Uppsala
University, Sweden. He is currently a visiting scholar
in the Department of Political Science at Syracuse
University.

Library of Congress Cataloging-in-Publication Data
Gardell, Mattias.
In the name of Elijah Muhammad : Louis Farrakhan and
the Nation of Islam / Mattias Gardell.
p.   cm.— (Black religion and culture)
Includes bibliographical references (p.   ) and index.
ISBN 0-8223-1852-0 (cloth : alk. paper). —
ISBN 0-8223-1845-8 (pbk. : alk. paper)
1. Black Muslims.   I. Title.   II. Series.
297'.87—dc20   96-22666 CIP